ENCYCLOPAEDIC DICTIONARY OF INFORMATION TECHNOLOGY AND SYSTEMS

ENCYCLOPAEDIC DICTIONARY OF INFORMATION TECHNOLOGY AND SYSTEMS

A.E. CAWKELL

London • Melbourne • Munich • New Jersey

British Library Cataloguing in Publication Data
A catalogue record for this book is available from the British Library

Library of Congress Cataloguing in Publication Data
Cawkell, A. E.
  Encyclopaedic dictionary of information technology and systems/
Tony Cawkell.
    p.   cm.
  ISBN 1-85739-036-9
    1. Information technology–Dictionaries.   2. Computers–
Dictionaries.   I. Title.
T58.5.C39 1993   93-25291
004'.03–dc20   CIP

Published by Bowker-Saur
60 Grosvenor Street, London W1X 9DA
Tel: +44(0)71 493 5841 Fax: +44(0)71 580 4089

Bowker-Saur is a division of REED REFERENCE PUBLISHING

ISBN 1857390369

Cover design by John Cole
Phototypesetting by Tradespools Ltd, Frome, Somerset
Printed on acid-free paper
Printed and bound in Great Britain by Bookcraft, Bath

PREFACE AND ARRANGEMENT OF THE ENCYCLOPAEDIC DICTIONARY

Electronic communication will jumble experience and creatively juxtapose ideas, forms, and experiences previously disseminated in different and isolated ways. In turn this will create new patterns of knowledge and awareness.

J.W. Carey

In the above quotation Carey was commenting on the views of Marshall McLuhan as set out in McLuhan's book *Understanding Media*. His words could well be applied to new kinds of information made available through developments in information technology.

In this Encyclopaedic Dictionary a fairly broad view of IT is taken and the entries cover people, organizations, and technology. Judging by the range of activities which it seemed appropriate to include, McLuhan's prophesies seem to be well founded.

A major problem is making the book up to date. I have endeavoured to include the variety of terms which existed as at April 1993. For example you will find entries for BLOB, FRACTAL, VIRTUAL REALITY and ULTIMEDIA. The field is so broad that you will probably have no difficulty in not finding some items which you think should be there, but I hope there will not be too many.

The capitalized words within entries are a form of cross reference indicating that those words are covered in separate entries. Acronyms are followed by the words which they signify, but if those words are capitalized a full entry follows in its alphabetical order, thus:-

ACM
Association for Computing Machinery
AI
ARTIFICIAL INTELLEGENCE

. . . indicates that ARTIFICIAL INTELLIGENCE appears as a full entry in its alphabetical order elsewhere, but ACM does not. Additionally, many entries are followed by "See" references.

Narrative describing wide areas such as IMAGE, NETWORKS, SEMI-CONDUCTORS, etc., have been split up under separate headings such as NETWORKS – BROADBAND ISDN, NETWORKS – INTELLIGENT, NETWORKS – INTERNET, etc., so try more than one section as necessary.

I would like to acknowledge with thanks Aslib's permission to include some entries and figures which were previously published in *Critique*. Acknowledgements for other items are included in the place where they appear. Above all I must thank my wife Kathleen for her unstinting help and restraint when I was "otherwise engaged" in working on this publication.

Tony Cawkell
Iver Heath, May 1993.

A

A/D CONVERTER
ANALOGUE TO DIGITAL CONVERTER.

ABINGDON CROSS BENCHMARK
A test image consisting of a thick cross in a noisy background used for comparing the processing performance of imaging systems. The tests consist of removing the noise, and then performing morphologic operations on the cross in order to thin it so that its intersecting portions are 1 pixel wide. The benchmark is a measure of the system's effectiveness in carrying out these operations and the time taken to do it.

ABIOS
Advanced Basic Input Output System. See under BIOS.

ACCENT
Aston Campus Communications for Europe and Ninety-Two.

ACM
Association for Computing Machinery.

ACOUSTIC COUPLER
A MODEM incorporating receptacles for a telephone handset. When the handset is in place the earphone can receive tones representing incoming data, and the microphone can transmit outgoing tones. The acoustic coupler plugs into a telephone line socket.

ACRL
Association of College and Research Libraries.

ACROBAT
A software product first announced by ADOBE in November 1992. It is expected to produce a considerable impact in 1993. Acrobat is said to be able to provide a portable document which can be run on any computer, operating system, or application – in other words it is an attempt to introduce a universal document communication language for viewing or printing.
It embodies a Postscript-like format called

the Portable Document Format (PDF). A PDF file can describe documents containing any combination of text, graphics and images of any complexity, which is also resolution independent.
The Acrobat Distiller, which is a part of the system, is a software program which translates Postscript files into Portable Document Format (PDF). The Acrobat PDF Writer is a printer driver which converts PDF files from applications.
The PDF file can be created from any application program which supports Postscript, and which starts as a word processing file, illustration, work sheet, or graph from a spreadsheet program. The JPEG COMPRESSION system will be used for compressing colour and greyscale images with ratios varying between 2:1 and 8:1. Adobe claims that PDF is the first universal alternative to ASCII. It is claimed to work equally well on Macintosh, Windows, Unix, DOS and other operating systems.

ACS
American Chemical Society.

ADAPTIVE EQUALIZATION
A technique which establishes a standard model for the decoding of transmitted bits and continually modifies this model during transmission to avoid distortion. It is normally used for switched networks because the routing is likely to change between successive calls.

ADAPTIVE PREDICTIVE CODING
Speech coding method which uses LPC for the vocal tract model excited by an adaptive predictive voice source.

ADOBE
Adobe Systems Inc., of Mountain View CA, United States, was founded in 1982 by Charles Geschke and John Warnock after they left the Xerox PARC Team in the late nineteen seventies. They started working on an electronic publishing system and later moved on to software for the Apple LaserWriter. This work

1

turned into the well-known POSTSCRIPT product and continued with ILLUSTRATOR. Postscript was improved with another product called TYPE MANAGER for Apple Computers.

In November 1992 Adobe announced a new product called ACROBAT.

ADONIS
AUTOMATIC DOCUMENT ONLINE INFORMATION SYSTEM.

A system in which a number of major publishers have arranged to provide articles from selected journals on CD-ROM to co-operating libraries and other organizations.

ADONIS became operational on January 1st 1991. It has been demonstrated that cost savings can be made compared with conventional photocopying, and that the ADONIS identifier, a number allocated at the time of indexing, is superior to other methods of uniquely identifying an article.

The service is primarily for medical subjects, but other fields including Agriculture, Biology, Chemistry, Engineering, Pharmacology, Physics, Public Health and Veterinary Medicine may be included.

Initially 437 journal titles were covered by agreement with their publishers with the subject distribution (Ulrich definition) Medicine (47%), Biology (19%), Pharmacology 16%, Chemistry 11%, Physics 2%, Veterinary Medicine 1%, and General Science 1%.

Software is supplied and discs delivered to libraries two weeks after receipt of printed journals for "a modest annual subscription fee and royalties depending on whether the library subscribes to the printed version of the journal".

Tests have shown that retrieval and printing from an ADONIS CD-ROM and workstation can produce cost savings of up to 50% compared with the costs associated with conventional photocopying. There may be other significant savings such as shelving economies, binding costs, etc.

Several improvements have been made in optimizing printing speed. A US-based support facility is being considered, networking and jukebox support is being developed, and support for other operating systems may soon be introduced. A list of the large number of journals covered is available on CD-ROM. It is re-issued weekly.

It was hoped that compression would enable 15,000 pages to be included per CD but at the compression ratio needed, laser print quality was unsatisfactory. At 10,000 pages per CD, print quality is said to be excellent.

Among the findings at a presentation in the US to drug companies, it was said that:- "the royalty payments to Copyright Clearance Centre and ADONIS are perceived to be a threshold for the US pharmaceutical industry to commit themselves ... networking the library is perceived to be crucial for information management".

Following the conclusion of its trial service, the ADONIS commercial service offered more than the maximum 7000 pages per CD-ROM disc achieved in the trial and started with 1991 journals. Indexing is done by Excerpta Medica in the Netherlands, scanning by Satz Rechen Zentrum, Berlin, disc production by Nimbus at Monmouth, UK, and software development by Lasec, Berlin.

In December 1992 Adonis announced that it is assessing the best approach and the economic viability of adding chemistry titles and possibly titles of other disciplines in demand. An experimental database of Adonis articles has been set up on a Dec VAX machine enabling users to search using title words, authors names, and contents pages from specific journal issues.

By February 1993 there were nearly 100 subscribers in 27 different countries. Adonis now covers 450 Life Science journals.

ADP
Automated Data Processing.

ADPCM
Adaptive Differential Pulse Code Modulation.

ADTV
Advanced Definition Television.

ADVANCED NETWORKED SYSTEMS ARCHITECTURE (ANSA)
A project which was originated in the UK under the Alvey Information Program, later extended into a consortium project under the European ESPRIT program. Members of ANSA include many of the major European electronics companies. Its main applications are expected to be for office systems.

AFIPS
American Federation of Information Processing Societies.

AI
ARTIFICIAL INTELLIGENCE.

ALA
1. Associate of the Library Association.
2. American Library Association.

ALEXANDRIA, LIBRARY OF
A very large library planned by Ptolemy I, but actually created by Ptolemy II in the period 308 to 246 BC. The aim was to collect the whole of the existing literature in the best available copies. The library contained velum or papyrus scrolls numbering some hundreds of thousands. It was based on Aristotle's library.

ALGORITHM
A set of step-by-step rules in software for solving a problem.

ALIASING
1. Interference produced by frequencies outside the pass-band of interest produced by sampling action when converting an analogue into a digital signal. If the sampling frequency is high enough there should be little or no aliasing. Any aliasing present may be removed by the insertion of a filter.
2. An error caused by processing an image in a system where the resolution is inadequate to display its fine detail. For example because an insufficient number of picture elements are displayed a jagged appearance is imparted to curves or diagonals on a CRT screen. The data was originally sampled at too low a frequency. "Anti-aliasing" can be provided by passing the signals through a low pass filter to smooth fast transitions, or by automatically adjusting the brightness level of pixels in the vicinity of an edge.

ALLOPHONE
A PHONEME variation formed by the co-articulation effects of the phonemes which precede and follow one particular phoneme, as, for example, the "k" sounds in "allocate" and "evoke". The stress, pitch, and duration characteristics of the allophone may be expressed as data for application to a speech synthesizer.

ALOHA
Additive Links On-line Hawaii Area System.

ALPHA-GEOMETRIC CODING
See VIDEOTEX.

ALPHA-MOSAIC CODING
See VIDEOTEX.

ALPHA-PHOTOGRAPHIC CODING
See VIDEOTEX.

ALU
Arithmetic Logic Unit.

AM
AMPLITUDE MODULATION.

AMPLITUDE MODULATION
A method of transmitting data on a carrier waveform by varying its signal strength (amplitude) in proportion to the data impressed upon it.

ANALOGUE SIGNAL
A voltage or current varying in proportion to a change in a physical quantity – as produced, for example, by a microphone.

ANALOGUE TRANSMISSION
A method of electrical communication in which the signal level varies in proportion to the level of the voice or other message.

ANALOGUE TO DIGITAL CONVERTOR
An electronic circuit used to convert, at discrete intervals, the levels of a varying continuous waveform into a set of corresponding numerical values.

ANISOTROPIC
See ISOTROPIC.

ANSA
ADVANCED NETWORKED SYSTEMS ARCHITECTURE.

ANSI
American National Standards Institute.

ANSWERBACK
A reply message from a receiving terminal to

verify to the transmitting terminal that it is operational.

ANTI-ALIASING
A method adopted on some computers for reducing ALIASING effects. "Anti-aliasing" can be provided by passing the signals through a a lowpass filter to smooth fast transitions, or by automatically adjusting the brightness level of pixels in the vicinity of an edge.

ANTIOPE
See VIDEOTEX.

API
Application Programming Interface.

APL
A Programming Language.

APOLLO
Article Delivery Over Network System.

APPC
Advanced Program to Program Communication. See LU 6.2.

APPLE
Apple Inc., is a computer company well known for its adoption of the WYSIWYG idea – What You See Is What You Get.

Apple was founded by Steve Wozniak who designed the Apple II machine, and Steve Jobs, responsible for the Macintosh. The company started the Lisa project in 1979 the same year that the Motorola 68000 processor, with its 24 bit internal and 16 bit external busses, became available. Apple developed a unique memory management system for re-locating large blocks of codes controllable by the 68000.

When Lisa was launched it was not successful partly because of its high price and partly because its potential was not recognized. The Macintosh announced in 1984 together with the development of the Laser Printer, page formatting software etc., gave rise to the desktop publishing idea. The Mac was steadily improved with a larger memory, Appletalk network software, the incorporation of a 32 bit 68030 microprocessor, etc.

In 1984 the Macintosh, as it then was, was found to be unsatisfactory for office use and it failed to be adopted in businesses. In May 1985 Steve Jobs was replaced by John Sculley from the Pepsi Cola Company. Sculley promoted Lewis Gassee, head of Apple's French operations, to head of R&D. Shortly afterwards Apple and the Aldus Company developed software to run the Apple laser printer, and Apple rode on the success of desktop publishing systems. In 1986 the Mac+ was produced which worked with Microsoft's Excel spreadsheet package, and the Mac SE which could accommodate boards made by other vendors. In 1986 the sales of Mac machines went up to 575,000 units worth over $1 Billion.

In September 1990 the company announced a low priced machine – the Classic – and by 1992 it had re-organized its range to consist of the Classic, Powerbook, the powerful Quadro, and Macintosh II models. At the top of the range is the Quadro 900 which runs on a 25 MHz MC68040 chip. It includes SCSI and Nubus ports, an Ethernet adaptor, and a video system incorporating a VRAM. It uses dedicated I/O processors and provides mono and stereo output. It includes 4 Mbyte RAM expandable up to 64 Mbytes, and a 160 Mbyte hard disk drive,

In 1992 Apple deleted a number of their older models, including their portable, but retained the 3 Powerbook models. Powerbooks are notebook computers using the 68000 processor operating at 15.66 MHz. Powerbooks use a 640 x 400 pixel display using a super twisted nematic LCD, backlit with a cold cathode tube.

Pen-based computers do not seem to have achieved their expected popularity. However Apple launched their Newton pen-based machine in mid-1992. The machine measures only 4" x 7" and there is no keyboard – just a screen with a pen-like stylus on which you write. Your writing is converted to digital form. The machine uses a Flash Memory card and communicates with a host computer for off loading stored data via an infrared beam, later expected to become a radio communication channel.

See also OPERATING SYSTEMS – APPLE SYSTEM 7.0, QUICKTIME, MULTIMEDIA, and DESKTOP PUBLISHING.

ARCHITECTURE
The design and philosophy of both the hard-

ware and software of a computer system.

ARIST
Annual Review of Information Science and Technology.

ARPA
Advance Research Projects Agency.

ARQ
AUTOMATIC REQUEST FOR REPEAT.

ARRAY PROCESSOR
A parallel processor with a matrix-like structured organization for the extremely fast processing of large volumes of data. See also COMPUTERS – SUPER COMPUTERS.

ARTIFICIAL INTELLIGENCE (AI)
Artificial Intelligence is regarded by serious researchers as the use of computers controlled by programs which learn from their experience. A trend noticeable in the literature is the retention of the term "artificial intelligence" for machines which apparently possess real "intelligence" – for example those able to "understand" language or "see" images. The machine solves problems in these areas by referring to a body of stored knowledge.

ARTIFICIAL INTELLIGENCE – EXPERT SYSTEMS
An Expert System is a program for problem solving associated with a database of knowledge, often known as a Knowledge Base, usually for the use of non-experts in that branch of knowledge. Knowledge-based System is a synonym for Expert System.

Decision Support Systems sometimes encroach into AI although the connection is tenuous. More usually this phrase is used by suppliers to describe integrated tools and services to assist management decisions.

The term "Expert System" seems to be displacing "Artificial Intelligence" in computer applications where modelling of the brain's activities are not involved – the word "Intelligence" is perhaps then considered to be unacceptably pretentious. For example a set of rules could be devised for a relatively simple expert system automatically to connect an online searcher to the one database most likely to contain the answer to his question. The words or phrases in the question would

be matched against a vocabulary of words each of which had been previously labelled with a code representing the database most likely to cover the subject. Thus the words "Coherent Radiation" might cause the user to be logged on to the INSPEC database as first choice.

However, unambiguously clear usage of the terminology does not seem to have progressed very far. The phrase "Knowledge-based System" seems better than "Expert System" for the obvious reason mentioned in the next paragraph. One way of identifying knowledge-based systems is to be clear how they differ from conventional software.

Another trend is to up-rate conventional software by re-naming it as an expert system to increase its appeal in the market.

In 1984 Microsoft announced a version of LISP for running on microcomputers with the MS-DOS operating system such as Act Sirius, IBM PC, etc. The software, called mu-LISP-82, is an Artificial Intelligence Development System of limited performance, probably most useful for research work.

Texas Instruments developed a product called Personal Consultant costing about £700 in 1984 to run on its Professional micros. It is a LISP-based shell capable of generating a complete Expert System using the development system also provided.

GoldWorks from Gold Hill Computers, Cambridge, MA, runs on an IBM PC/AT and requires 512 Kbytes of memory, 5 Mbytes of extended memory and 10 Mbytes of disc. It comes on 31 diskettes with 5 manuals and cost $7500. Its Knowledge Base representation techniques include frames for structuring data, forward and backward chaining, and object programming for associating Lisp functions with frame objects.

A whole series of GoldWorks-like (but mainly simpler) products – that is shell software for handling inputted knowledge, rule development and execution, chaining, etc., several based on Hypercard, and costing from $150 to $5000 – have been described. All run on Apple Mac machines, and graphics feature in several of them, as might be expected.

A number of large expert systems were in use by mid-1992. ICL's Decisionpower is used by Cathay Pacific Airways to control aircraft schedules and Grand Metropolitan uses a system for market analysis. Swiss Bank uses a system called ART-IM embodying rules which help to assist in making loan decisions.

ARTIFICIAL INTELLIGENCE – HISTORY

In 1936 Alan Turing wrote an article in the Proceedings of the London Mathematical Society which showed that it was not possible to devise a system which would determine any given outcome from a position in a game by evaluating all possible positions and outcomes.

In 1950 his celebrated article "Can a machine think?" appeared in *Mind*. He suggested a game which would demonstrate the existence of machine intelligence. A human was required to interrogate a machine and another human by posing a series of questions to both of them. If the machine could fool its human interrogator into believing it to be human by participating in a wide range of possible conversations, then it could be concluded that the machine was, indeed, "Passing the Turing Test".

Although nothing much happened for some years following Turing's 1950 paper, his interest and reputation directed attention to the subject. In 1956 a meeting was held at Dartmouth College in the US to discuss the subject and this meeting is considered to be a milestone since it inspired the early work. One ambitious early system was called General Problem Solver, capable of solving theorems and puzzles, but it did little to demonstrate machine intelligence.

The first demonstration of the real possibilities was the DENDRAL system developed at Stanford University by Lederberg, Feigenbaum, and Djerassi in 1966. DENDRAL used a computer language for describing the structures of organic compounds and was able to generate structures and postulate tests compiled from data about a compound for comparison with the structure and test results known from the actual compound.

ARTIFICIAL INTELLIGENCE – INFERENCE

Quillian's (University of Sydney) semantic network representation scheme, later embodied in an algorithm called ID3, and Winograd's NL system, were other milestones. Quillian's scheme consist of a tree-like data structure of nodes and links and an inference program which operated on this data to find a

solution – a part of the system often called the Inference Engine.

A major feature of the data structure is the "is a" link connecting the nodes which represent concepts – for example a node "mammal" connecting to node "whale" by an "is a" link. Inference can be drawn from the information contained in the network.

ARTIFICIAL INTELLIGENCE – INFORMATION RETRIEVAL APPLICATIONS

Front End Processors with a Natural Language Interface for Knowledge Based Information Retrieval (IR) are receiving particular attention. This simply means asking a system in plain English for documents containing wanted information and hoping to obtain what you asked for.

In most systems today, in order to avoid taking courses on probabilistic information systems, an enquirer usually asks via an intermediary who converts the enquiry into a form suitable for a computer. The enquirer rarely gets exactly what was requested – only more or less what was requested.

The system will intervene if syntactical errors are made and will provide the user with information about the nature of the error. To do this a software module called a Parser is used. Syntax is a set of rules about the grammatical arrangement of words, while parsing is the resolving of a sentence into its component parts. Parsing software must therefore have access to information about grammar – in this case in the query language.

O'Neill suggests that "Expert system technology is being taken up in almost all financial institutions and large national and international organizations, covering such diverse area as audit control, loan arrangements, computer configuration, cement manufacture, fault diagnosis, tax and personnel advice, etc". And "Considerable research is already under-way on ES to aid in traditional library tasks of cataloguing, indexing, online searching ... etc".

According to Thorngate:- "The success of schemes depends greatly on at least three factors:

1. The extent to which keywords faithfully encode information.

2. The extent to which keywords distinguish the information which they encode.

3. The extent to which the keywords that encode information are the ones we use to retrieve it.

Thorngate goes on to discuss system misconceptions and proposes an online thesaurus with an "intelligent user model component" to alleviate them. "The output of the component could be used to ... suggest what search options to use and how ... the output could also be fed into a terms translation process which would require knowledge about the subject area integrated with the classification scheme into an "online thesaurus" based on the frame-based semantic network knowledge representation scheme we have proposed".

ARTIFICIAL INTELLIGENCE – KNOWLEDGE BASES

Most of the early experimental work involved continuous close "hand-made" attention by the expert who was attempting to move his knowledge into the system in a useable form. During the development of a system called MYCIN by Duda and Shortliffe in the 1970s at Stanford, David, a co-worker, developed some software, called TEIRESIAS, for debugging purposes.

It separated the software concerned with the expert's knowledge – the Knowledge Base – from the part concerned with problem-solving (inference), and turned out to be the first important step in decoupling the human expert from the system. It then became possible for a wider range of knowledge to be added, not necessarily by the same expert.

The knowledge base and the way it is imparted to the machine by the human expert, is still receiving much attention. In domain-specific systems a Parser (syntax analyser) may be associated with a Synonym Dictionary or Lexicon, covering a limited vocabulary.

The knowledge base may also hold stored knowledge about Categories to be slotted into Frames. For example the PLEXUS system was set up for Gardening questions using Objects (e.g. insects), Operations (e.g. action on an insect), Environment (e.g. a lawn). Time (of the year), etc., are expected in questions. A frame containing slots for class number, synonyms, and expected associated concepts is started for each word found in the dictionary.

The system then juggles with the contents of frames according to a set of rules – for instance "IF frame A is type OPER3 AND there is another, B, of type OBJECT 8, THEN transfer the term name of B to the slot OBJECT in A AND transfer the term name of A to the slot ACTION in B". It proceeds on this basis through a network of frames, asking the user for more information when it cannot fill slots, and then forms a search statement by scanning the frames.

In January 1990 Ovum published a report on knowledge Based Systems. The report suggests that they went through a crisis in 1987-1988, but are now recovering with more multi-user applications, a better choice of tools and a stronger industry. Sales in the US should increase to over $1 billion in 1992, with Europe increasing to more than $700M.

ARTIFICIAL INTELLIGENCE – NATURAL LANGUAGE

One of the most important roles of AI/Expert Systems is the easing of communication between man and machine. Eventually Natural Language (NL) schemes will make computer systems available to a wide public using the English language instead of only to those who understand formalized computer language.

Natural language systems do fairly well if the machine controls the dialogue in order to obtain expected categories of answers in a narrow subject domain. MYCIN, a very well known early system for medical diagnosis, worked like this, with questions of the kind:-

Q: How old are you?
A: 28
Q: Are you male or female?
A: Male
A: Have you attended this clinic before?
And so on.

This type of "natural language" is as far removed from a machine which "understands" any kind of typed statement, as is a trained-to-one-voice word recognition machine removed from one which recognizes continuous speech from any speaker.

ARTIFICIAL INTELLIGENCE – SHELLS AND CHAINING

By 1985 attempts were being made to devise domain-independent inference systems or "shells". If this was feasible a subject expert could be presented with ready to use rule-making software enabling him to insert his own knowledge base, do some tests to check that the rules worked, and complete the design of an expert system in far less time than previously with less attention to "housekeeping procedures".

Some combination of "forward and backward chaining" is often used in the inference engine. Forward chaining uses various rules, particularly those based on "if then. . ." statements, to move to a conclusion. If the conclusion is known but the sequence to arrive at it is not, then backward chaining can be used to deduce the set of conditions needed to arrive at the conclusion.

ARTIFICIAL INTELLIGENCE – SOFTWARE AND HARDWARE TRENDS

The software used in a shell inference engine is likely to be written in LISP or PROLOG. This software is used to search a knowledge database and enables retrieved data to be used in conjunction with decision making rules according to the requirements of the programmer.

There was some US-European rivalry in the adoption of these languages – LISP, supposedly better for practical applications but requiring efficient programming, having been developed at MIT in the 50s, and PROLOG, supposedly better for research work and easier to use, developed later in Europe. PROLOG is being adopted by the Japanese in their fifth generation systems, and attempts are being made to provide software combining the best features of both.

Fox (1990) distinguishes between AI myths, legends, and facts and concludes by stating that "Currently about 3000 systems are estimated to be in daily use round the world for example Ace (Bell Labs cable maintenance advisory system), XCON (Carnegie Mellon's design for DEC's computer ordering system), and Dispatcher (also used by DEC for assemblies)." A number of other examples are listed mainly in US industries.

ARTIFICIAL INTELLIGENCE – VISION SYSTEMS

A system which attempts to model visual images is an example of an intelligent Machine system. Information is contained in a TV-like representation of an image fed into the machine via its camera-eye. A set of stored rules will have been worked out in order to display an image reconstructed from informa-

tion received by the machine's eye. At the present state of development the rules enable it to "know" something about just one type of scheme – for instance the interior of a living room.

The machine examines edges contained in the electrical image -it might test for vertical edges consisting of a sequence of more than n elements followed by an abrupt change of contrast. When found it might be labelled "wall boundary". The machine might then explore long, not necessarily continuous, edges which join the wall boundary in order to construct the outline of the complete wall.

ASCII

American Standard Code for Information Interchange – a code widely used for the transmission of text in communications and computers. It is a 7 bit (plus 1 parity bit) code providing for 128 alpha-numeric and other symbols.

ASIC

Application-Specific Integrated Circuit. It may be fabricated by a specialist company, or by a customer with automated tools provided by the manufacturer.

ASIS

American Society for Information Science.

ASLIB

Association of Special Libraries & Information Bureaux (new title is The Association for Information Management).

ASSASSIN

A System for Storage and Subsequent Selection of Information.

ASSASSIN is a database software package developed at ICI. Following a management buy-out it has been further developed and is now sold by AKS Ltd., Stockton, UK.

ASSEMBLER

A utility program that translates symbolic assembly language instructions into machine instructions or data on a one-to-one basis.

ASSEMBLY LANGUAGE

A computer language using symbols, often mnemonics, which are translated by the assembler conversion program into machine code. It enables a programmer to work in a language more like English instead of having to work with the bit patterns of machine code.

For example if the assembly symbol for register C is "C" and the symbol for the ASCII code for K is "K", then the assembly language statement "MV C, K" would mean "Move the ASCII code for K to register C. In micro-computers each proprietary CPU has its own assembly language according to the nature of its architecture.

Assembly language may appear to be "of higher level" than machine language and so qualify as a high level language, but it is not so regarded because it does not have all the features of higher languages; a single instruction in a high level language often translates into a series of sub-routine and/or machine code instructions.

A Cross-Assembler is a program which translates an assembly language program written for one type of microcomputer into a machine code for another computer.

ASYNCHRONOUS TRANSFER MODE (ATM)
ATM is a protocol to be used for transporting all data over the B-ISDN in the same format. The format bears some resemblance to the format used for packet switching. See also NET-WORKS.

AT&T
Automatic Telephone & Telegraph Co.

ATHENA
A computer system installed at MIT in the United States by the joint effort of MIT, IBM, and DEC. By mid-1991 there were about 11,000 users mainly using workstations based on Berkeley UNIX. Interconnection is over a fibreoptic FDDI network running at 100 Mbps.

ATM
1. Automatic Teller Machine.
2. ASYNCHRONOUS TRANSFER MODE.

ATTENUATION
The decrease in amplitude of a signal, usually measured in decibels.

AU
A unit for the measurement of very small distances. 1 Angstrom Unit = 10^{-10} metres.

AUTODIALLER
A device for automatically dialling telephone numbers under software control, for instance by pressing one key. Often many different numbers may be typed in by the user for permanent storage to be recalled by the software for single key "dialling".

AUTOEXEC.BAT
A file which runs automatically when a PC is turned on. It contains a number of instructions inserted by the user to set up various DOS operating requirements.

AUTOMATIC FALLBACK
An automatic decrease in the speed of transmission of a signal if the transmission channel is unable to sustain the existing speed.

AUTOMATIC INDEXING AND RETRIEVAL SYSTEMS
See INDEXING – AUTOMATIC.

AUTOMATIC REQUEST FOR REPEAT (ARQ)
A method of error correction in which each block of data – a block is some fixed number of data elements – is checked at the receiver and if an error is detected a request for a repeat is automatically sent to the transmitter.

AUTOMATIC SHIFT-DOWN
See AUTOMATIC FALLBACK.

AVI
Audio Video Interleaved.

B

B-ISDN
Broadband Integrated Services Digital Network. See also NETWORKS.

BABBAGE, CHARLES
1792-1871. English mathematician often credited as the person who established the basic principles of modern computers. Babbage built a mechanical machine capable of handling quadratic functions and proposed a much more elaborate "Difference Engine" to compute tables. It was far ahead of its time and was never built. His machines inspired LADY LOVELACE to write what were effectively the first computer programs. See also COMPUTERS – HISTORY, and LOVELACE, LADY.

BACKBONE
The main cable interconnecting several systems or networks.

BACKGROUND PROCESSING
Processing which once initiated continues without user intervention, while FOREGROUND PROCESSING is continuing.

BACKUP
To make a copy of stored data in case the original data is lost because of a computer malfunction.
The backing up of data to be stored separately from the machine, enables operations to continue in the event of a fault or loss of data. For example, data may be periodically copied from a fixed disc to a removable or floppy disc.

BALLOTS
Bibliographic Automation of Large Library Operations using a Time Sharing System.

BAND-PASS FILTER
A filter used to retain signals in a particular band of frequencies, removing frequency components outside the pass-band.

BANDWIDTH
The range of signalling frequencies which can be conveyed by a communications device or channel with some defined small amount of attenuation and distortion.

BANKING
See HOME BANKING.

BARDEEN, JOHN
Born in 1908, Bardeen was a co-inventor of the point contact transistor with Brattain and Shockley, with whom he shared the Nobel prize for Physics in 1956. Bardeen received a second Nobel prize for his work on the theory of superconductors in 1973.

BARREL SHIFTER
A circuit which performs extremely fast shift operations in a single cycle; it can shift as many bit locations as it has bits. For example, a 32-bit barrel shifter can shift a 32-bit word up to 32-bit locations in a single cycle. It also enables a field of pixels to be rotated.

BASEBAND
The transmission of a digital signal without the use of a carrier, i.e. without modulation.

BASIC
BEGINNERS ALL-PURPOSE SYMBOLIC INSTRUCTION CODE. See also COMPUTERS – LANGUAGES.

BASIC RATE INTERFACE (BRI)
An ISDN interface consisting of two 64 Kbps (B channel) circuits and one 16 Kbps signalling circuit (D channel), operating over a 2-wire twisted-pair line. See also NETWORKS.

BATCH MODE
Computer processing of data in one operation from start to finish.

BAUD
The unit of signalling speed. 1 baud = 1 signalling element per second.

BAUDOT
A 5-bit data code commonly used for low speed transmission over telegraph and telex circuits. The International Telegraph Alphabet Number 2 (ITA2).

BBC
British Broadcasting Corporation.

BCD
BINARY CODED DECIMAL.

BCPL
Basic Combined Programming Language.

BDLC
Burroughs Data Link Control.

BDOS
Basic Disk Operating System.

BEGINNERS ALL-PURPOSE SYMBOLIC INSTRUCTION CODE (BASIC)
A high level language developed by Kemeny and Kurtz at Dartmouth College, USA in 1964. It was the first language to become very widely used in microcomputers and still is widely used.

BELCOS
Bell Companies. The Bell operating companies formed after the splitting of AT&T in 1982 following an anti-trust suit.

BELL, DANIEL
Professor of Sociology at Harvard University. His book *The Coming of the Post-Industrial Society* written in 1973, has had a considerable influence. Bell developed the idea that advanced industrialized countries were moving into a new era of service/information economies.

BELL, ALEXANDER GRAHAM
Born in 1847 and died in 1922. Bell invented the telephone and various aids for assisting the deaf. He also founded one of the two most prestigious scientific journals – *Science*. (The other is *Nature*.)

BENCHMARK
A performance rating for a computer calculated from the results of running a number of standard test programs.

BELLCORE
Bell Communication Research Inc.

BERNAL, J. D.
Bernal was a physicist specializing in crystallography. He worked with Sir William Bragg at the Royal Institution in the twenties and later became interested in the sociology of science. Bernal was born in 1901 and died in 1971. His communist sympathies led him to defend T. D. Lysenko, the discredited Russian genetic scientist.

Bernal's influential book *The Social Function of Science* is a sufficient reason for his inclusion in this encyclopaedia. In the book, published in 1967, Bernal suggested that an organization called The Scientific Information Institute should be formed. It would be concerned with the indexing, selection, and distribution of scientific information.

BIBLIOGRAPHIC COUPLING
A phenomenon first observed by Kessler in 1963. Kessler awarded 1 bibliographic coupling unit to two documents each containing 1 identical reference, 2 if they contained two identical references, and so on.

Cleverdon proposed that the measure should also take account of the percentage of the total number of references which are common to both; thus two articles containing, say, 5 references in common out of a combined total of 25 are more closely coupled than two with 5 in common out of a total of, say, 100 references.

The closer the coupling between articles the more likely is it that they will be about similar subject areas.

BIBLIOMETRICS
The study of bibliographies in scientific articles and books leading to conclusions about scientific literature and its authors, and about the sociology of science. The arrival of the Science Citation Index in the early nineteen sixties enable such studies to be carried out systematically.

See also BIBLIOGRAPHIC COUPLING, SCIENTOMETRICS, and SCIENCE CITATION INDEX.

BIBLIOTHEQUE NATIONALE.
An important library in Paris known as the

BILDSCHIRMTEXT

Bibliotheque Roi before the revolution. It was founded by Charles V. It includes the Direction de Bibliotheque which overseas all the libraries in France.

BILDSCHIRMTEXT
See VIDEOTEX.

BILEVEL
An image whose elements have two intensity values – black or white, 1 or 0.

BINARY CODED DECIMAL (BCD)
A code which represents decimal numbers in binary form.

This system is used when fixed length binary codes are needed. Each decimal digit in a number is coded as a four bit binary number. Thus, since the binary codes for the digits in the number 709 are 0111, 000, and 1001, BCD for 709 is simply 0111 0000 1001.

BINARY NOTATION
A numbering system to the base 2. In the binary notation the characters are either a 0 or a 1. "Bit" is the commonly used abbreviation for binary digit, the basic unit of data with which the computer works. A bit can take the form of a magnetized spot, an electronic impulse, a positively charged magnetic core, etc. A group of bits forming a code are used to represent a character in a computer. See also BIT, BYTE and HEXADECIMAL.

The decimal number 135 is composed as follows :-

$$5 \times 10^0 = 5 \times 1 \quad = \quad 5$$
$$3 \times 10^1 = 3 \times 10 \quad = \quad 30$$
$$1 \times 10^2 = 1 \times 100 = \underline{100}$$
$$135$$

The same number in the binary notation, 10000111, is composed as:-

$$1 \times 2^0 = 1 \times 1 \quad = \quad 1$$
$$1 \times 2^1 = 1 \times 2 \quad = \quad 2$$
$$1 \times 2^2 = 1 \times 4 \quad = \quad 4$$
$$0 \times 2^3 = 0 \times 8 \quad = \quad 0$$
$$0 \times 2^4 = 0 \times 16 \quad = \quad 0$$
$$0 \times 2^5 = 0 \times 32 \quad = \quad 0$$
$$0 \times 2^6 = 0 \times 64 \quad = \quad 0$$
$$1 \times 2^7 = 1 \times 128 = \underline{128}$$
$$135$$

Thus we could store binary numbers up to 255 (11111111) if we had eight circuits, each capable of being switched to the "on" or "off" state. (256 is 100000000). Because of the great difference in the "on" or "off" output voltages held in associated storage circuits, the digits can be "read" without errors at a later time.

BIOS
Basic Input Output System. A *de facto* software standard designed by IBM for its PC and stored in ROM. The original BIOS was designed to make it difficult for competitors to design "clones". Later, IBM introduced ABIOS for its PS/2 machines using 80286, 80386, etc., processors.

It was not long before the system was understood and BIOS "improvements" were introduced making compatibility doubtful. A company called Phoenix wrote a BIOS program in such a way that IBM could not sue them for infringement. This version of BIOS is still quite widely used and will result in machine inter-compatibility.

BIOS data is stored in the high end of the 640 KByte memory used for DOS programs and consists of the basic input output system, extensions and peripheral data, and memory-map screen data such as EGA, VGA etc. A BIOS instruction is invoked by one of a number of interrupt signals which control video instructions, machine configuration, memory size, disc and serial operations, keyboard control, printer and timing. BIOS software also performs test functions when a machine is booted. See also DISPLAYING COLOUR AND GRAPHICS.

BIOSIS
Bio-Sciences Information Service.

BIPOLAR
Until comparatively recently there were two major planar (layer by layer fabrication) technology productions – Bipolar and MOS (Metal Oxide Silicon). The elements of Bipolar transistors function rather like the original junction transistors. In the MOS an aluminium "Gate" electrode controls the conductivity of the silicon between two p-type regions.

The basic MOS is often called The MOS "field effect transistor" (FET) because it is the field created near the gate which changes the conductivity of the silicon locally between the "source" and "drain" regions. There are several variations of both types – for instance

MOS devices may be called PMOS or NMOS according to the type of silicon used near the gate.

Bipolar Emitter Coupled Logic (ECL) circuits are among the fastest working devices. ECL is a two-transistor circuit specifically arranged to reduce delays in current switching to the absolute minimum. In spite of that, integrated circuits used in computers are now predominantly MOS devices because they are easier to manufacture and consume less power.

The first microprocessor used P-MOS; the pioneering Intel 8080, still in widespread use, uses N-MOS; N-MOS is widely used in today's microprocessors such as the Intel 8086 and 80286. See also SEMICONDUCTORS.

BISTABLE MULTIVIBRATOR
A multivibrator in which one transistor is on and the other off until the states are changed over by a triggering pulse.

BIT
Abbreviation for a unit in the BINARY SYSTEM. In data transmission, if one signalling element contains one unit of data, one bit per second equals one baud. In multi-level signalling, more than one unit of data may be sent per baud. For example if 8 level signalling is used, 8 bits are sent per baud, and the signalling rate is $\log 2^8 = 3$ bits per second. See also BINARY NOTATION.

BIT MAP
A method of organizing a CRT display where (in a black-and-white display) each pixel in a particular position on the screen is controlled by a 0 or 1 bit in a particular position in a memory. In colour and halftone displays each screen pixel is controlled by a number of bits in memory. The term is also applied to an image which has been digitized and is represented by rows of bits, derived from rows of picture elements.

BMP
Bit Mapped. A format for image files

BIT PLANES
Separate parallel memories which store the component digits of a pixel in order to speed up changes in a CRT display. For instance, a four-bit code could alter a pixel to be dis-

played at any one out of 16 grey levels on a CRT. If the four digits were delivered simultaneously, one from each of four bit planes, they would be delivered four times faster than serial delivery from a single store.

Each plane or store contains as many stored elements as there are pixels displayed on the screen; a plane is a map of the screen. There are as many planes as there are bits per pixel – say four. Thus the 4 bits for the 7th pixel in row 180 on the screen are held in, say, position 187 in each of the stores. (See Figure).

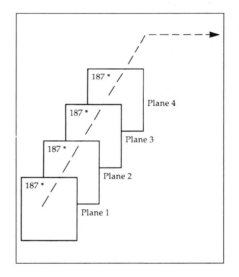

Each time the CRT beams arrive at the position corresponding to pixel 187 all four bits are simultaneously delivered to the tube from the four stores. The total bit rate is therefore one quarter of the rate it would be if the bits were delivered in series from a single store. As many bit planes as may be needed are used in systems with a very large choice of colours.

BIT RATES AND PRESENTATION
State of the Art developments in microcomputers enable the bits from fast sources to be processed and stored, but speed constraints in the input boards, in the busses, and at the display end of the micro, restrict the essential requirement of transporting a sufficient number of bits to reproduce an image with the required quality on to the screen in the available time.

BIT RATES AND PRESENTATION

The table shows the stage that image data-handling volumes and rates have reached and the constraints to be overcome for future developments. While large volumes of data can be moved quickly from the input to the output of the microcomputer, the data then has to be converted back to analogue form for presentation to a human.

The top four rows in the table show the number of bits which require to be displayed on a CRT for an image of given "quality". The fourth of these four rows is in fact what is now achievable with a good 19" (diagonally across the tube) monitor capable of displaying 100 pixels/inch.

The third column is included to bring a sense of scale to the figures. It shows the number of pixels which would form the vertical part of a 1.4 mm (4 point) character at the given resolution. At 100 dots/inch there would be an insufficient number of pixels to clearly define such a character clearly.

The fourth column shows the number of pixels across the useable dimensions of a 19" tube (about 15.6" x 11.7 inches), and the last three columns the total number of pixels on the screen for a one-bit per pixel (black and white) image, an 8-bit image (256 half-tones or colours), and a 24-bit image (about 16 million colours).

For example in the case of a 19" tube with a 100 x 100 pixels/inch image, the last row shows the total number of Mbits on the screen for 1-bit, 8-bit, and 24-bit per pixel images – 1.8, 14.4, and 43.2 Mbits respectively. The extra bits are supplied as changes in CRT beam intensity levels.

The rate at which bits must be supplied to a tube when the screen is "refreshed" 60 times per second, for example in the 100 x 100 case for 1-bit, 8-bit, and 24-bit pixels, is shown along the bottom row of the next set of columns – 108, 864, and 2592 Mbits/sec respectively. 864 Mbits (108 mbytes/sec) is currently feasible using bit sources in parallel, and higher speeds will, no doubt, be available in due course.

Finally the bottom 4 columns in the table show the storage requirements for 1 minute of 25 frame/sec motion-video in Gbytes. Considering, for example, the 100 pixels/inch 1 bit case and assuming a displayed video image of the same size, the amount of storage needed is 1.8 x (25 x 60) = 2700 Mbits = 2700/8 = about 337 Mbytes = 337/1000 = 0.337 Gbytes.

For higher quality images the numbers become very large. A 300 pixels/inch CRT with 24-bit colour might be feasible within 5 years. This would provide almost perfect reproduction. The bit rate then required would be 23,640 Mbits/sec.

Unfortunately the enormous bandwidth or

Pixels/in	Pixels/mm	Pix./ Char.*	Pix./19"CRT‡ Hor. × Ver.	1-bit	Total Mbits for 19"CRT‡ 8-bit	24-bit
400 × 400	15.75 × 15.75	22	6240 × 4680	29	232	696
300 × 300	11.8 × 11.8	17	4680 × 3510	14.4	131	394
200 × 200	7.87 × 7.87	11	3120 × 2340	7.3	58	175
100 × 100	3.94 × 3.94		1560 × 1170	1.8	14.4	43.2
		Screen fill bit rate		1740	13920	41740
		at 60Hz (Mbits/sec.)		984	7872	23616
		corresponding to last		438	3504	10500
		three columns above		108	864	2592
		Storage required (Gbytes)		5.437	43.5	130.5
		for 1 minute motion-video		3.075	24.6	73.9
		corresponding to same		1.37	10.9	32.8
		three columns		.337	2.7	8.1

* Number of pixels in 1.4mm high (4 point) character.
‡ 19" CRT display area is assumed to be 15.6" horiz. & 11.7" vert.

Displayed bits and bit rates for given conditions

the design of buffering arrangements needed to deliver bits at this rate are unlikely to be developed in the foreseeable future. Perhaps semiconductor colour displays which do not require to be refreshed will by then have been developed for high quality pictures.

BIT STUFFING
See under NETWORKS – SYNCHRONOUS DIGITAL HIERARCHY.

BIX
BYTE Information Exchange. A word used in the ELECTRONIC MAIL address of *Byte* magazine.

BL
BRITISH LIBRARY.

BLAISE
British Library Automated Information Service.

BLCMP
Birmingham Libraries Co-operative Mechanisation Project.

BLDSC
BRITISH LIBRARY DOCUMENT SUPPLY CENTRE. See also BRITISH LIBRARY.

BLEND
Birmingham and Loughborough Electronic Network Development. See also ELECTRONIC JOURNAL.

BLISS, HENRY E.
A librarian who published a system of Bibliographic Classification in 1935.

BLLD
British Library Lending Division.

BLOB
Binary Large Object. A description of an object which may be of any type, including images, occupying a field in a database, particularly in relational database management systems. BLOBs are indexed with words and for retrieval and storage purposes are managed like any other record although they may be very large records.

BLOCK
A continuous sequence of BITS or BYTES.

BLOCK DIAGRAM
A drawing in which circuit functions are represented as blocks of various geometries.

BLOT
A region of an image bounded by connected pixels.

BLUMLEIN, A. D.
Alan Blumlein was born in 1903 and killed in 1942 when the Halifax bomber in which he was testing H_2S equipment caught fire.

Blumlein first worked at Standard Telephones and moved to Columbia Records which subsequently became a part of EMI, where he worked under Isaac Shoenberg, Director of Research. Blumlein was granted 128 patents many of them basic to today's electronics. He patented a number of devices to do with measurement in telephone systems, a moving coil stylus for cutting gramophone records and an improved moving coil microphone.

He filed wide-ranging patents on stereophonic recording and reproduction. Subsequently Blumlein worked on the world's first public television system designed at Marconi EMI for the BBC and took out numerous patents. During the war one basic patent was for a device called the Miller Integrator, one of the most commonly used devices in wartime electronics. He also developed the Airborne Interception (AI) radar which was instrumental in the destruction of 102 enemy aircraft at night during May 1941. Blumlein was the key engineer in the development of H_2S.

BMA
British Medical Association.

BNB
British National Bibliography.

BOOT
To start up a computer with a program which is automatically initiated when the computer is switched on ("powered up"). It checks the system and loads up the operating system.

Bpi
Bits per inch.

BPO
British Post Office.

Bps
Bits per second or sometimes Bytes per second.

BRADFORD, SAMUEL C.

"Bradford's Law" was first formulated by Bradford in 1934 in the journal *Engineering* and later in Bradford's book *Documentation* published in 1948. With reference to scientific publications Bradford's Law states that "the numbers of periodicals in the nucleus and succeeding zones will be as 1, n, n^2 ...". Some important conclusions followed from this.

For example quite a small well chosen selection of core journals covering a particular subject contain a relatively high proportion of significant articles published in all of the journals in which articles about that subject appear.

This has important consequences, particularly for libraries; although it may be necessary to subscribe to, say, 1000 journals to cover a field comprehensively, 200 would provide quite a high proportion of the total number of articles published. See also ZIPF.

BRATTAIN, WILLIAM H.

Born 1902. Co-inventor of the point contact transistor with Bardeen and Shockley, sharing the Nobel prize for Physics in 1956.

BRI

BASIC RATE INTERFACE.

BRIDGE

A bridge interconnects two LANs. It reads all packets on LAN A, and retransmits on LAN B, which uses the same protocol, all packets addressed to a host on B. It also performs the reverse B to A function. See also ROUTER and GATEWAY.

BRITISH LIBRARY (BL)

The BL, which became 18 years old in 1992, employs a staff of 2,400 and supports the Document Supply Services at Boston Spa, Patent Delivery and Information from the old patent office library, BLAISE an online service, and a considerable research and publishing programme.

The UK has no national information policy.

The British Library is answerable to government and dependent on it for funding but it has not been able to look to governments for leadership.

The importance and financial requirements of the custodian of the country's intellectual inheritance is hard to assess. Its role has been discussed by Orna who talks about the government's lamentable role in supporting the British Library. Seeking to bring government to appreciate the facts is a vital aspect of the Library's policy.

Government support for the BL is being steadily withdrawn. Government attitudes were made quite clear when they sold a site in London and the Treasury pocketed £9 million of the proceeds. It is said that the whole of it was promised for the new building in St. Pancras.

While the government's attitude should be deplored there does not appear to be a determined campaign mounted by the British Library to arouse national interest, particularly in regard to its highly effective service at Boston Spa which is unknown to the general public.

At the end of 1990, BL had to stop buying some foreign translations and cancelled subscriptions to over 200 periodicals because of shortages in government funding.

The BL earns over £10 million out of its total annual cost of £44 million from its activities at Boston Spa usually known at the British Library Document Supply Centre (BLDSC). The centre handles loans or photocopies via the UK inter-library loan network, or by direct request.

The BLDSC's staff of 750 handled 3 million requests in 1980 of which one sixth came from abroad. The Division supplies material mainly in the science and technology area, to over 120 countries. It is probably the largest facility in the world dedicated to the supply of material on loan. It recovers its direct costs by appropriate charges.

In 1986, BL planned a centralization of its diverse services in a new building at St. Pancras, London. The building would have a gross floor area of over 100,000 sq. metres on 13 floors and would cost over £400 million. It was scheduled to be completed in two phases ending in 1993 and 1996, but progress with the building is badly behind schedule for various reasons.

In September 1992, the British Library's Research & Development Department was re-organized into four divisions to cope with a number of new tasks. It now comprises four sections – development, research grants, information policy research, and an international office and consultancy section.

BRITISH LIBRARY DOCUMENT SUPPLY CENTRE (BLDSC)
A division of the British Library situated at Boston Spa, Yorkshire, for supplying documents, in particular photocopies of journal articles, to approved users for a fee. See BRITISH LIBRARY.

BRITISH MUSEUM LIBRARY
The library was founded in 1753 by the acceptance of a bequest from Sir Hans Sloane, physician to King George II and President of the Royal Society. Two other important collections from Sir Robert Cotton and Robert Harley were added soon afterwards. George II's Royal Library was added in 1757. The Library, which became part of the British Library, has the right to the legal deposit of every book published in the British Isles.

BROADBAND
Of wide bandwidth. Implying the ability to transport data at high speed, that is at a transmission rate of about 2 Mbps or more.

BROADBAND ISDN
See under NETWORKS.

BROADBAND SERVICES
The kind of services (for a proportion of users and not just for the "top 100 "organizations), to be expected when eventually the costs and the availability of a general purpose wideband data network/highway make them feasible. They could be carried over a channel providing about 600 Mbps of bandwidth available in up to four channels of 150 Mbps each. Utilization might be 64 Kbps for voice, 1 Mbps for data, and 45 Mbps upwards for motion video depending on resolution, colour fidelity, etc.

The throughput of a switch (of which there may be a number at the exchange) capable of handling a large number of subscriber lines carrying data at this rate, will need to be of the order of 1 Terabit per second (1 Tbps = 10^{-12}

seconds).

The fastest switching speeds currently achievable are around a few Gbps but much faster speeds will soon be developed. Fibreoptic cables will be essential; present designs involve various electrical to optical conversions which take time and introduce losses. It seems likely that future wideband networks will require optical control and switching systems which are still in their infancy. Such systems must get to the production stage, and must be installed and tested in the field, before becoming used by subscribers.

A system of this kind will be preceded by various evolutionary systems. The first tentative step in this direction is the INTEGRATED SERVICES DIGITAL NETWORK (ISDN) – See under NETWORKS.

BS
British Standard.

BSC
Binary Synchronous Communication.

BSI
British Standards Institute.

BT
British Telecom. See also DEREGULATION.

BTLZ
See LEMPEL-ZIV.

BUCKET
A numbered sub-division of a file in which data is located having been placed there by using a hashing technique. See HASHING.

BUFFER
A storage unit organized to act as a reservoir for data being moved between a source and a destination which operate at different data rates.

BUG
A program error.

BULLETIN BOARD
The electronic equivalent of a public notice board, on which announcements, message exchanges etc., may be "posted" by any user who has access to the board via the network used to service the board.

BUS

A set of electrically conducting lines between data source and destination.

BUSH, VANNEVAR

Bush was born in 1890, and died in 1974. He held a number of important posts during World War II, including Chairmanship of The Research & Development Board. He organized a corps of over 30,000 engineers and scientists who developed radar, the proximity fuse, and other devices.

In 1942, Bush supervized the development and building of the differential analyser, a machine for solving differential equations, and the mechanical pre-cursor of electronic computers. Bush wrote an article which is often cited – "As we may think" (*The Atlantic Monthly*, July 1945 pp 101-109), in which he envisaged a machine called "Memex" – a device "in which an individual stores all his books, records and communications ... for consultation with exceeding speed and flexibility".

Memex would use a kind of associated index allowing trails to be formed through the system to pick up different aspects of a subject in anticipation of a future technology which could make it feasible. Some of these ideas have been implemented but an effective "Memex" has yet to be invented.

BYTE

A group of 8 bits, which may include a parity bit, forming a code to represent data. See also BIT.

C

See COMPUTERS – LANGUAGES.

CAB
Commonwealth Agricultural Bureau.

CABLE
1. The word "Cable" is commonly used to describe a system that delivers entertainment television by wire (cable) to a subscriber's TV receiver, often by a number of selectable channels.

Some cable systems can carry other services such as data transmission and the telephone.

A cable "main line" must pass fairly close to an office or house in order for an economically viable connection to be made. Until now, a cable conveying a number of separate channels, selectable from the users receiver, has been used as an alternative way of conveying entertainment television. Experiments have been carried out with two-way cables capable of supporting interactive information systems. So far capital costs have inhibited their introduction. Cheaper fibreoptic cables could make such services viable.

2. A system comprising copper cables, or CO-AXIAL or FIBREOPTIC cables, with terminating equipment, for long distance voice or data communication overland or under the sea. Repeaters (a kind of amplifier) may be incorporated.

CABLE – FIBREOPTIC
See FIBREOPTIC CABLE.

CABLES – GENERAL
Electrical energy is attenuated as it passes along a cable. The longer the cable and the wider the bandwidth and bit rate, the greater the attenuation.

Twisted pairs of copper wire can carry voice frequencies for many miles, but must be shortened for data transmission at fast bit rates.

For medium speed LANs quite short lengths can be used. For Ethernet LANs coaxial cable is preferred but twisted-pair is often used although the result is noisier and error rates are higher unless the distances are very short. Shielded twisted pair (the shield reduces interference) became acceptable in 1990 with the arrival of a Standard covering its use called 10BASE-T.

Coaxial cables consist of two conductors – a central copper wire separated from an outer copper tube by insulating material. Coax can carry high speed data over long distances, or may carry a number of "multiplexed" channels.

CABLE TELEVISION INSTALLATIONS
The authors from the American ATC Company (See under CABLE TELEVISION SYSTEMS) talk about the long term benefits of fibre as a "non-switched delivery system which puts no additional boxes on top of the subscriber's TV or VCR".

The importance of this last comment becomes evident should you subscribe to the services of the Windsor Cable Company. Only one black box, receiving signals from the cable and outputting them to the TV's aerial (antenna) socket, appears on top of the TV. Unfortunately no information of any kind is provided except verbally by the installation engineer. Expert engineers are not expert in human communication.

But you are now confronted with three portable keypads for controlling the black box, the TV set, and the VCR – provided, of course, that one of them is not lurking under a cushion or the cat.

The cable entering the house includes a telephone line routed from the local BT telephone exchange. That route was enabled firstly because British Telecom was forced to agree to inter-connect with Mercury under new deregulatory rulings, and Windsor was the first cable company to do a deal with Mercury. This arrangement is an additional inducement to subscribe to cable because Windsor charges considerably less than BT for telephone service.

The same codes are dialled on the Windsor/Mercury telephone as are dialled on the

BT system. The monthly cable subscription will be more or less financed by the reduced cost of using it for all outgoing calls.

Surprisingly, Windsor Cable's telephone line is an ordinary twisted pair accompanying the wideband cable. As the system stands there is no wideband two-way link for home services. Presumably a frequency band could be made available on the cable for such services, but that must be backed by wideband switching at the exchange. This would mean that the wideband cable channel to homes backed by wideband switching would be duplicating the channels and wideband switching planned for a later version of the ISDN – the Broadband ISDN – by the telephone companies, an illogical but politically possible eventuality.

In April 1991 the Cable Television Association objected to the charges to be paid to BT and Mercury Communications. The charges are an access-deficit fee to compensate BT for costs not met by quarterly rentals. OFTEL has suggested that cable companies may have to pay 0.3p per minute for local calls, 1.8p for national calls, and 11.6p for international calls in addition to charges for use of the network.

Full reciprocity does not exist between the UK and the liberalized telecommunications regime in the US – the rhetoric of free and fair competition has not been backed with reality. Major US telephone companies such as PacTel and US West are now major shareholders in the UK Cable-TV industry. They are to be allowed to offer telecommunications services in competition with BT, yet BT is not allowed to carry TV pictures for at least seven and possibly ten years in its own country, let alone in the United States.

CABLE TELEVISION SYSTEMS

Cable provides two-way communication for homes today in some parts of the UK, thanks to deregulation. In the US it is illegal for cable companies to provide telephone service – hence the considerable investment of US telephone companies in UK cable. They see it as a way of breaking into UK communications generally and into the PSTN in particular.

UK Cable systems have had a chequered career; in 1982 the Hunt report was released by the government recommending a franchise scheme for wideband cable television services. By 1983 11 franchises had been granted.

By 1985 disillusionment had set in due to high costs and low demand.

By mid-1990 over 100 franchises had been awarded but relatively few homes had been connected out of a possible half million or more passed by a cable. If all the franchisees laid cable in their areas following the conclusion of the franchise allocations, nearly 15 million homes would be passed.

That was in spite of a considerable government initiative in 1981 when it was expected that Cable would provide an entertainment-led route into wideband information services.

However cable is showing some signs of revival. A number of American companies have invested in UK Cable, particularly telephone companies who believe that it will eventually lead them to participation in UK general telecoms. In 1990, 26 new franchises were offered by the government, and the ban on foreign ownership was lifted. There were at least 300,000 subscribers by 1990.

The latest figures from the Independent Television Commission showed a net increase of 40,000 in the number of cabled homes during the first quarter of 1992. By the end of the year there was a total of 461,455 homes connected by cable systems – 172,000 of them connected to modern multi-channel networks.

So far telephone service is available in six areas and 30,000 telephone lines have been provided. The Cable Television Association expected the number to increase to 100,000 by the end of 1992.

The number of cable subscribers has risen by 48% over the past year with the overall penetration rate rising from 19 to 22.4%. The gradual regulatory thaw has encouraged UK Cable operators to try out quite different kinds of service. Thus in 1987, Windsor Cable arranged for a connection to Mercury and started a pilot telephone service aimed at local businesses. The Bell company US West has a substantial shareholding in Windsor Cable.

Cable installations started with short runs of twisted pair wires which could carry a few TV channels, but most now use co-axial cable, capable of carrying many more. Coax will be replaced by fibreoptic cables in due course providing sufficient bandwidth for numerous channels, two way services, and HDTV.

Deregulation measures include permission for foreign-owned cable franchises, and operators are permitted to offer telecom services.

The belief that the "last mile" problem for telecom services – that is how to connect cables to homes – may be solved, presumably by an arrangement with BT or Mercury, has been strong enough to encourage US investment on a scale out of all proportion to the TV potential. US West now been joined by Nynex, Pacific Telesis and United Artists who all have a stake in UK franchises.

The capabilities of Cable systems also depends on layouts. With "tree and branch" the main supply line splits off to cables for delivery to households, where a desired channel is selected. With "star" networks – an arrangement amenable to interactive two-way services – cables radiate out to local distribution boxes from which channels are switched into the cable for each household as controlled by the cable operator according to the customer's subscription schedule. However Cable in the UK will need to become much more successful. It connects a few percent of homes compared to 60% in the US. People in the UK will not tolerate above-ground wires, and digging up streets is expensive – three times the US installation costs.

Engineers with American Television & Communications Corporation (ATC) – interested in the realities of operating a cable company with four million subscribers – have provided some information about US cable technology, particularly in regard to the feasibility of wiring homes with fibre. Their remarks provide a guide as to what may be expected with a media which some people think may be the first to provide two-way wideband communications to homes.

ATC are running fibreoptic cable from the head-end at the cable control centre along the existing coaxial cable ducts to distant network nodes, the coax having been disconnected. The existing coax from nodes to`subscribers completes the network. Consequently the noise generated by, and the power supply and maintenance required by the amplifiers at intervals along the disconnected coax are no longer a matter of concern.

ATC consider this evolutionary "fiber backbone" approach and the introduction of other necessarily gradual pay-as-you-go measures to be appropriate because "the enormous investment in completely new plant necessitated by a radical change to new architecture would be highly imprudent unless set-off by huge new revenue streams". The implication is that all-fibre systems are going to be slow in arriving in the US and even slower in other countries. Implementation in the UK may well be ten years away.

CACHE MEMORY
A relatively small fast storage buffer unit organized to handle data called from disk on a "probability of need" basis which can be transferred into main memory faster than from disk into main memory. A cache memory is programmed temporarily to store that information which is most likely to be wanted first. The art of programming it is to design algorithms which guess what data to fetch from main memory, when to bring it into the cache, and when to replace it.

When a computer executes instructions, particularly looped cache instructions, it tends to repeatedly access the same memory locations. One idea is to design a fully associative cache where the n locations in the cache always store the last n memory locations accessed by the CPU.

The criteria of performance is the "hit ratio" – that is the percentage of cache memory cycles versus the percentage of main memory cycles. For example the net memory cycle time with cache memory in the Texas 99000 is claimed to be 190 ns with a 9:1 hit ratio compared to 330 ns without the cache.

CAD
Computer Aided Design.

CAE
Computer Aided Engineering.

CAFS
Content Addressable File Store.

CAI
Computer-Aided Instruction.

CAIRS
Computer-Assistant Information Retrieval System.

CALS
Computer Aided acquisition and Logistical Support system.

CAM
Computer Aided Manufacturing.

CANDELA (Cd)
The SI unit of luminous intensity equivalent to the luminous intensity of a black body normal to the surface at specified conditions of temperature and pressure.

CAPTAINS
CHARACTER AND PATTERN TELEPHONE ACCESS INFORMATION SYSTEM. See under VIDEOTEX.

CARRIER SENSE MULTIPLE ACCESS/ COLLISION DETECTION (CSMA/CD)
A data link control protocol for networks in which all stations can receive all messages. A station can detect the presence of a transmitted message by sensing the transmission carrier. When a station wishes to send a message it first waits until no other station is transmitting. When two or more stations try to send messages concurrently, collisions may occur since a station will not receive another station's signal until after it has begun transmitting. A collision detection (CD) mechanism detects the collision, causing the stations to terminate their current transmissions, and they try again later.

CARTRIDGE
A container for housing removable facilities. For example an optical disc cartridge is a plastic case containing an optical disc which may be inserted into an optical drive.

CAS
Chemical Abstracts Service.

CASE
Computer-aided Software Engineering – the use of general-purpose computers and special application software to speed and control software development.

CATHODE RAY TUBE (CRT)
An enclosed glass tube with a flat screen upon whose surface is deposited a fluorescing layer. An electron beam, modulated by data to be displayed and deflected to provide a zig-zag trace on the screen called a Raster, causes the screen to glow at the point of impact. The beam produces the impression of a steady full-screen image because the raster is rapidly repeated. CRT's are likely to hold their own for some years against competitive display devices. See also COLOUR – ELECTRONIC DISPLAY.

CATV
Cable Television.

CAV
Constant Angular Velocity.

CB
Citizen's Band.

CBR
Constant Bit Rate.

CCD
CHARGED COUPLED DEVICE.

CCIR
Center for Communication and Information Research.

CCITT
COMITE CONSULTATIF INTERNATIONALE DE TELEGRAPHIE ET TELEPHONE.

CCTA
Central Computer and Telecommunications Agency.

CD
COMPACT DISC.

Cd
Candela. The SI unit of luminous intensity.

CD-I
COMPACT DISC INTERACTIVE.

CD/MA
Collision Detector/Multiple Access. See also CSMA/CD.

CD-ROM
COMPACT DISK READ ONLY MEMORY.

CD-ROM XA
COMPACT DISC READ ONLY MEMORY EXTENDED ARCHITECTURE.

CD-TV
COMPACT DISC – TELEVISION. See MULTIMEDIA HARDWARE.

CD-V
COMPACT DISK VIDEO. See DIGITAL VIDEO INTERACTIVE.

CEBUS
CONSUMER'S ELECTRONIC BUS STANDARD. See HOME.

CEC
Commission of the European Community.

CEEFAX
A teletext service offered by the British Broadcasting Corporation via its television channels. Data is broadcast during an interval within each frame unoccupied by "conventional" TV signal data. See also VIDEOTEX – TELETEXT.

CELLULAR RADIO
A mobile radio telephone system comprising a large number of short range base stations linked to the PSTN, controlling a small area or "cell". As a vehicle moves from one cell to the next it is transferred automatically to the new cell's base station.

CELP
CODEBOOK EXCITED LINEAR PREDICTIVE CODING.

CENTRAL PROCESSING UNIT (CPU)
A set of computer circuits, usually at least an Arithmetic and Logic Unit (ALU), and a Control Unit, which interpret and execute instruction. See also MICROCOMPUTERS.

CENTREX
Central Terminal Exchange. Remote PABX facilities provided by a telecoms authority which appear to the subscriber as if there is a PABX exchange on his premises.

CEPT
Conference Europeene des Administrations des Postes et des Telecommunications.

CETIS
Centre Europeene pour le Traitement de l'Information Scientifique.

CGA
Colour Graphics Adapter. A printed circuit board installed in an IBM-compatible PC for colour display. See also DISPLAYING COLOUR AND GRAPHICS.

CGM
Computer Graphics Metafile.

CGROM
Character Generator Read Only Memory.

CHANNEL
See under TELECOMMUNICATIONS.

CHARGED COUPLED DEVICE (CCD)
A semi-conductor element in which data is stored as an electrical charge which may be transferred to an adjacent element by a control pulse. In a CCD image sensor, a charge is generated when light is focused upon it. Sensors may be arranged in the form of a strip of CCD elements associated with an electronic transport system. After a given light exposure time, the charges are shifted by the transport system along to an output terminal where they represent a bit-by-bit serial representation of the light reflected from a strip of the image.

Such an Image Sensor is manufactured using techniques similar to those used for other integrated circuits. The strip may consist, for instance, of 1728 elements spaced at 0.127 mm, with about 8 elements per mm or about 200 per inch. The output from such a strip represents a strip of the image 0.127 mm wide and about 21.9 mm long (0.005 x 8.6 inches).

CHARGED COUPLED DEVICE (CCD) CAMERA
A camera embodying a CCD array for detecting an image instead of a film or plate. CCD camera elements can be made small enough for photographing images for high resolution reproduction. A camera introduced by JVC in 1993 produces an output resolution in multiples of 736 x 576 pixels up to 4416 x 3456 at a colour depth of up to 32 bits per pixel.

The camera moves the image relative to the CCD area by an optical system in extremely small steps. A computer is able to accumulate a number of separate images which are assembled to produce one very high resolution image.

CHIP
See SEMICONDUCTORS – INTEGRATED CIRCUIT.

CHIP MARKETS
The size of the market for chips is now so large that it has become feasible to modify manufacturing policy from the processor, through the processor plus co-processor stage, to the "embedded" processor. Sales of a sufficient number of machines for a particular application must be expected in order to justify a pur- pose-designed chip "embedded" to handle just that one application.

The Japanese dominance in chip manufacture was effected by a remarkable coup according to Anderla and Dunning.

In 1987 the Americans had a comfortable world lead in the supply of chips including RAM chips, mainly up to 64K capacity. The rapidly falling curve describing price reduction versus time must eventually flatten out as production volumes and methods stabilize; manufacturers then recover their investment and move into profit.

The curve for 64K RAMs had flattened out and the chips were profitable. The price per Kbyte for 32K RAMs was 5.5 cents, 64K 3.1 cents, and 128K 1.4 cents. Moving along this progression, a further reduction in the price per Kbyte might be expected for chips of still higher capacities.

Anticipating this trend the Japanese eschewed the 64K market and started producing 256K RAMs, charging 1 cent per Kbyte, no doubt accepting initial losses. The Americans were not ready and surrendered the leadership in the face of this draconian price cutting.

However at the 1990 International Solid State Circuits Conference (ISSCC) in San Francisco – the major forum for research announcements – the ratio of US to Japanese papers was 4:3. It was concluded that the US still lead in other semiconductor fields, notably in microprocessors.

CHROMA
Synonym for SATURATION.

CHROMINANCE
The HUE and SATURATION of an image which define its colour.

CHUNK
See CODING – HUMAN.

CICS
Customer Information Control System.

CIDST
Centre d'Information et de la Documenta Scientifique et Technique.

CIM
Computer Input Microfilm.

CIMTECH
National Centre for Information Media Technology.

CIO
Chief Information Officer.

CIRCUIT
1. A set of interconnected electr components.
2. A connection between telecommun ing devices.

CIRCUIT SWITCHING
A technique of switching in a data netv whereby a physical route or a fixed data is dedicated to the two interconnected dev for the duration of the connection. Someti called line switching.

CISC
Complex Instruction Set Computer.

CITATION INDEX
See SCIENCE CITATION INDEX.

CIX
Commercial INTERNET Exchange.

CLASSIFICATION
The placement of items in different categc according to their similarity.

Aristotle (384-322 BC) sub-divided the mal kingdom into birds, fish, insects, et system later developed by Linnaeus into Phylum, Class ... Genus, Species, clas cation system. Sokal says in his classic w about the subject:- "Classification is the or ing or arrangement of objects into group sets on the basis of their relationships". also INDEXING.

CLEVERDON, CYRIL
See INDEXING-SYSTEM PERFORMANCE.

CLOCK
A master timing device to provide timing pulses for synchronizing the operation of a system.

CLOSED USER GROUP (CUG)
A group formed to give designated users exclusive access to part of a system – for instance a data base.

CLUT
COLOUR LOOKUP TABLE.

CLV
Constant Linear Velocity.

C-MAC
C(Sound)-Multiple Analogue Component. A method of transmission used in satellite communications.

CMOS
COMPLIMENTARY METAL OXIDE SILICONE.

CNA
Chemical Notation Association.

CNRS
Centre Nationale de la Recherche Scientifique.

CO-PROCESSOR
A second processor that takes over some of the tasks which would otherwise be performed by the CPU.

COAX
CO-AXIAL CABLE.

CO-AXIAL CABLE
The name of a type of cable consisting of a central core of signal wire, contained within an outer metallic tube but separated from it by a low loss insulating material. This form of construction provides a wideband telecommunications channel.

COBOL
Common Business Oriented Language.

CODASYL
Conference on Data Systems Languages.

CODATA
Committee on Data for Science and Technology.

CODE -S -ING
A code is a system of symbols representing data. Thus a "7 bit binary code" could represent up to 128 data elements. Sometimes coded data may be recoded. For instance in facsimile systems, re-coding is used to transform data derived from scanning the image into a suitable form for transmission.

According to E.C. Cherry, the encoding of messages is a process of organization – converting or transforming messages from one sign representation to another, possibly more suited to the type of communication channel employed. The constraints of the channel determine a preferred statistical structure for the transmitted signals.

The problem of statistical matching is to find a suitable code for the source such that the ensemble of transmitted signals is given a statistical structure which maximizes the rate of transmission of information through the noisy channel.

One of the earliest effective codes was devised by Samuel Morse who noted the frequency of use of type at the local printers. He arranged that the most frequently used letter should have the shortest code – "e" is signalled by ".", but "q" by "- - . -".

Another early – and most effective – "post Shannon" code was devised by HUFFMAN. A minimum redundancy code yields the lowest possible average message length for a given number of coding digits.

An ingenious code due to Ziv, entirely based on Shannon considerations, has been developed by British Telecom and adopted by the CCITT in the V42bis recommendation for error-correcting and data-compressing modems. The idea has become feasible in fast real-time processing thanks to current developments in technology. The encoder does not know the characteristics of the source initially but observes it for a period and accumulates high-frequency strings in its store. Upon the next occurrence of a stored string it outputs a short codeword in substitution. See also ENCRYPTION, HUMAN ENCODING and

INFORMATION THEORY.

CODE -S -ING DIVISION MULTIPLE ACCESS (CDMA)

A method of communication in which all users share the same frequency but each signal carries a unique code called the spreading code which transmits the signal piecemeal on a number of different set frequencies.

CODE -S -ING – HUFFMAN

A form of run length one dimensional code, named after its inventor in 1952. Huffman arranged the letters of the alphabet in order of probability of occurrence, highest probability first, and allocated variable length codewords to them arranged in order of length, shortest first.

For example E is 101 and Q is 0111001101. The net effect is that the total number of bits used to represent a passage of text will be much less would be the case if a fixed length code was used.

Letter	Code	$-\log_2 p_i$
Space	000	2.4
E	101	2.9
T	0010	3.7
A	0100	4.0
P	011110	6.0
Q	0111001101	10.4
Z	0111001111	11.0

Huffman Code

Huffman also designed the code for the lowest possible H (See INFORMATION THEORY) by a suitable choice of code groups to make the code "uniquely decipherable" or "comma free", meaning that it does not need spaces between letters (as in the Morse code) – the digits used for one letter never appear as the leading digits of a different letter.

A modification of the Huffman code is recommended by CCITT for data reduction in group 3 facsimile machines.

CODE -S -ING – HUMAN

A typical human subject can only remember 9 binary digits after reading them once, but can remember 8 decimal digits (25 bits), 7 English letters (33 bits) or 5 monosyllabic words (50 bits).

Experiments on sight reading at the piano, typing, tapping targets, marking squares, reading word lists etc., have been conducted in attempts to obtain high signalling rates and realize the full capacity of the human communications channel. The best rates obtained were about 40 to 50 bits per second.

G.A. Miller and Herbert Simon have considered this topic. The contrasts of the terms *bit* and *chunk* serves to highlight the fact that we are not very definite about what constitutes a chunk of information. We are dealing here with a process of organizing or grouping the input into familiar units or chunks, and a great deal of learning has gone into the information of these familiar units.

Humans are extremely good at *recoding* information. Experiments with grand-masters of chess and ordinary players showed that after a ten second inspection of 24 randomly arranged pieces both were able to place only about 6 pieces correctly. From these and reviews of numerous other experiments, Simon concludes that "a chunk of any kind of stimulus material is the quantity that short-term memory will hold five of".

CODE -S -ING – TEXT

Files for use in DTP pages may contain "own-keyboard-created" (OKC) text, or "OCR-created" text. The OCR function is often available in software supplied with a scanner. Existing printed text is scanned as already described, the software isolates the succession of dot-structures representing characters, and then each is compared for best match with a set of stored characters.

Characters in OKC and OCR text files are usually stored as 8-bit ASCII code. Most Word Processing (WP) software automatically generates ASCII coded characters from OKC text. With OCR, a code normally ASCII, is generated when a match is found. The data in ASCII code describes only the character and case – when decided the information A, a, B, b, etc., becomes available. The code does not provide information like "print this text in 10 point Prestige Elite".

In ordinary WP systems the codes sent to the printer will reproduce characters in the FONT dictated by the printing head in use. In DTP systems, font choice and other instructions are available as a facility provided with the DTP page formatting software.

The big advantage of ASCII coded OKC or OCR text is that the number of bits required to code, say, the 80 characters in a line, is only 8 x 80 = 640. If a line 6" long containing 80, 0.14" high, 10 point characters is scanned from a page at 300 pixels per inch, the number of bits generated in this scanned area is (0.14 x 300) x (6 x 300) = 75,600.

This method, fine for reproducing all the fine detail on the page such as image data, results in very large numbers of bits – an inefficient way of conveying information compared with the much simpler method of conveying just sufficient coded data to represent a character set. Obviously, if the requirement is simply to reproduce text in a single font, ASCII coded text is the preferred choice.

CODEBOOK EXCITED LINEAR PREDICTIVE CODING (CELP)

See under PULSE CODE MODULATION.

CODEC

Coder-Decoder. The H.261 Codec was developed under an EEC programme and has been ratified under CCITT aegis. Its purpose is to provide compression in videoconferencing schemes. It compresses a 352 x 288 line image in what is known as the Common Intermediate Format (CIF) running at 30 frames/sec, into a bit rate of 64 Kbps for transmission, for instance, via the ISDN.

COLOSSUS

An electronic computer built at the Post Office Research Station in Dollis Hill, London, during 1943. Subsequently it was taken to Bletchley Park and used for the analysis of encrypted messages coded on the German Enigma machine. Later a number of more reliable Mark II machines were built. No details were released about the machine until 1977. Until that time it had been assumed that ENIAC was the first electronic computer.

Although opinions may differ about exactly what constitutes a computer, it appears that COLOSSUS was the first although it was not a general purpose machine like ENIAC. The COLOSSUS Mark II machine broke the codes used by a machine known by the British as Tunny, manufactured by the German company K. Lorenz. COLOSSUS was able to read characters at 25,000 per second – a remarkable

achievement considering the available technology.

See also COMPUTERS – HISTORY.

COLOUR – DEFINITION OF

Colour is specified in terms of *hue* which is determined by the frequency of the radiated energy, *saturation* (purity) – the amount of white light present in addition to the hue, and *luminosity* (brightness). The sensation of a particular hue may be invoked either by the radiation of a particular wavelength (specified these days in nanometres, abbreviated to nm, $1nm = 10^{-9}$ metres) or by a mixture of other colours.

For measurement purposes a given colour may be specified by matching against a colour composed of measured proportions of the primary colours red, green, and blue. Special instruments called Colorimeters are available for the purpose. Equal proportions – .33 of red + .33 of green + .33 of blue = 1 = white. Any other colour may be reproduced by variations of these proportions. The coefficients (proportions) are called *trichromatic units*. The tristimulus theory of colour was advanced by Clerk-Maxwell in 1856 and has stood the test of time; it is supposed that the retina of the eye is composed of three types of receptors sensitive to the proportions of primary colours present.

Substance was given to these ideas by the Commission International de l'Eclairage back in the nineteen twenties who put forward the CIE *Chromaticity Diagram* shown in the figure (see over). This has assumed particular importance for measuring and specifying colour as produced by Cathode Ray Tubes (CRTs) for colour television. The y and x axes represent the proportions of green and red (and in consequence blue since pR + pG + pB = 1) to produce the range of colours shown.

The wavelength of hues is shown round the edge of the diagram.

The typical range of colours provided by a colour CRT could be shown on this diagram as a triangle with its apices some way inside the corners of the diagram (e.g. one apex at "TV red" as shown), not providing a complete colour range, but a range considered to be good enough for most purposes.

The above remarks apply to colour produced by radiated light. The sensation of colour generated from coloured, painted or

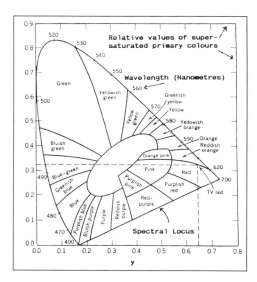

CIE Chromaticity diagram

printed surfaces is produced by selective absorption of the component colours of white (ideally) light. What we see are the components which are reflected. If the surface is viewed by reflection from a source which is not pure white the reflected components will of course be different.

Colour data is usually conveyed as Red Blue Green (RGB), Hue Saturation Intensity (HSI), or YUV (in television) signals. Each representation may be electronically converted into the other. HSI corresponds fairly closely to the way the eye perceives colour, and changes in computer HSI colour representation can be directly adjusted. YUV consists of Y, a luminance signal, and U and V are colour difference signals R-Y and B-Y respectively.

YUV is an economical way of transmitting colour data, devised for TV purposes, in order to reduce the transmission bandwidth occupied and to simplify the design of receivers. The YUV components may be digitized by sampling and the data reduced by using fewer samples. Since TV signals are widely captured and digitized, digitized YUV signals, amenable to data reduction and compression, are sometimet used in computer video boards. For example "YUV 4.2.2" means "8-bit colour signals sampled as Y 4

bits, U 2 bits, and V 2 bits.

COLOUR – ELECTRONIC DISPLAY
In colour CRTs each beam of electrons from three electron guns passes through a small hole in a mask which aligns the beam with the same dot in every three-dot "triad" pixel deposited on the screen. As a dot is struck by the beam from its gun it glows with a characteristic colour. One gun always produces a Red glow, a second Blue, and the third gun, Green (RBG).

The eye perceives a colour produced by the combined effect of the dots in each triad. Colour signals applied to each gun control the contribution of each dot. The triad pitch is about 0.3mm in good colour tubes. With some overlapping this represents a density of up to about 200 triads or pixels per inch.

The current in a gun is infinitely variable so if each is controlled by an *analogue* signal which varies according to the proportions of red, green, and blue in each pixel, colour reproduction should be excellent. This is the way it is done in television systems; the colour is as good as the whole system allows – from the TV camera, through the transmission channel and the circuits in the TV receiver to the tube.

Digital computers work in "bits" – signals which are either on or off. If the beam in a single gun CRT is switched on by one impulse or data bit for a few microseconds during its traverse across the screen it will produce one dot or pixel. A pattern of such "on" or "off" pixels, rapidly repeated, can be made to represent a "bilevel" ("black and white") image.

Colour electronics in digital systems is handled in various ways. The earliest and the simplest is quite adequate for the reproduction of text in a number of different colours. An on-off arrangement with three guns instead of one is used. A 4-bit control signal is applied giving 16 colours from 16 possible combinations of R, G, B, and one different overall intensity level. This arrangement has been extended to a 6-bit system providing 64 colours with R,r, G,g, and B,b, where RGB represents full intensity, and rgb represents (say) half intensity.

The controlling electronics called "TTL" (Transistor-transistor-logic) involves straight forward switching and is quite simple. However the principle becomes less attractive for a larger number of colours requiring more wires in a cable and wider bandwidth to deal with faster data.

To provide a much wider range of colour more conveniently, data is transmitted, stored, and processed in *digital* form and three sets of digital signals, specifying multiple levels of red, green, and blue intensity in bits, feed three digital-to-*analogue* converters (DACs) which translate the digital signals into voltage levels. The DACs connect to the three guns in the tube to control the current intensities.

The three guns project electrons at three dots on the screen which glow Red, Blue, and Green comprising a triad pixel. The perceived combination-colour depends on the relative intensity of each dot. If each gun is controlled by, say 8 bits, or 256 levels, then the combined effect of these variations provides the possibility of 256 x 256 x 256 = 16.7 million colours.

The vendor will probably call this "24 bit colour" (2^{24} = 16.7M). The system is slow unless associated with considerable computing power because of the huge number of bits which have to be shifted each time the screen is "refreshed" at the frame repetition rate. To overcome the speed problem the alternative "COLOUR LOOKUP TABLE" (CLUT) system is used.

The performance of the system depends on its "bits in – bits out" capacity, where the number of bits input (2^{ni}) represents the number of colours displayable at one time and the number of bits out ($2^{3 \times no}$) the number of available colour combinations produced by the three guns. Thus an 8 bits in/8 bits out system would provide 4096 colours at one time, out of a possible $2^{3 \times 8}$ = 24 bits = 16.7M colours.

Each triad in the CRT's "picture frame", typically totalling 640 x 480 = 307,200 elements, must be refreshed 50 times a second or more to provide a flicker-free image so the total *bit rate* becomes 307,200 x 50 = 15.4 Megabits per second (Mbps). The amount of additional data required to provide multi-level analogue control as well raises the total to a much larger number than in the simpler methods already described.

If the colour signals applied to the guns each specify, say, 16 levels (4 bits per primary colour, 12 bits in total) the bit rate must then be 15.4 x 12 = 185 Mbps.

See also DISPLAYING COLOUR AND GRAPHICS.

COLOUR GRAPHICS ADAPTOR
See under DISPLAYING COLOUR AND GRAPHICS.

COLOUR LOOKUP TABLES (CLUT)
In a microcomputer with good colour there is likely to be a 24 bit system with 8 bits for each gun providing 2^8 or 256 colours at one time on the screen. A *"palette"* is also provided, from which these colours are selected, enabling any combination of the 256 levels of each gun to be chosen. This provides any 265 colours out of 16.78M colours (256 x 256 x 256 = $2^{3(8)}$ = 2^{24} = 16.78M)

A change in the combination is performed by a memory called a "Colour Lookup Table" (CLUT) situated just before the DACs. The colour bits forming the word describing the colour of a pixel is input to the CLUT as an address. At that address resides another word which has been programmed into the CLUT representing a different colour. It may be slightly different or considerably different from the input word. This word is output to the DACs. All pixels passing through the CLUT are input in the same way in order to output the "switched colour" to the DACs.

COLOUR PRINTING
Printed colour is produced by laying down the "subtractive" colours cyan (turquoise), magenta (bright pink), yellow, and black (as opposed to RGB radiation which is additive). Some colour printers use "process" ribbons having lengthwise bands in these colours. Combinations produce other colours e.g yellow + magenta = red, cyan + magenta = blue.

A great deal of data has to be managed when storing, processing, or communicating images in colour. An "image" in this context means a "bit-mapped image" – that is the representation of an image by an array of very small picture elements usually called pixels. Good quality requires that there be a sufficient number of pixels to define the fine structure of an image("high resolution"), that tonal qualities are realistically presented, and that an good range of colours are displayed.

Colour printed material is still expensive. In the UK a full page in colour in one of the high-circulation tabloid newspapers costs up to £42,000. Colour, economics, and state-of-art colour technology are tightly coupled in this area. Huge advertising expenditure based on the cost per thousands of consumers reached may be shifted from TV to print media or vice versa. Advertisers think that the effectiveness of certain items – for instance succulent food advertisements – considerably depend upon good colour.

In the Desktop Publishing (DTP) world the rule of thumb is that colour costs "six to ten times more".

The heart of the matter lies in the response to the question "How good must colour quality be to be acceptable when used in publication x?". Professionals in the colour printing business would say that current technology plus craft is essential, the second ingredient being the more important.

At the bottom end of the scale a 24 bit colour scanner, a Mac II, a paintjet printer, and appropriate software may be purchased. Short runs of pages in colour from the printer will be acceptable for many purposes.

For "quite good colour" COLOUR SEPARATIONS (see next section) will be required – a significant step in terms of equipment, the necessary expertise and the cost of page printing in colour.

Considerable work has been done in recent years to improve colour matching between displayed and printed colour and colour generated by various kinds of equipment.

The Pantone matching system is made up from 1000 inks of different colours. Pantone also provide their process colour system with 3000 combinations of the colours cyan, magenta, yellow and black (CMYK -the k meaning key or black). To use the system for printing a specific colour, the printed colour must be matched to a specified Pantone colour. See also DISPLAYING COLOUR AND GRAPHICS.

COLOUR – PRINTING WITH SEPARATIONS

Software is available said to provide prints from 24-bit data on Macintosh machines with 256 colours out of a 16M palette good enough for "colour proofing" – that is checking what an image will ultimately look like when printed from separations. To this end it provides for "gamma correction" – "gamma" being the relationship between input data and output results. As with Cathode Ray Tubes, gamma correction is necessary in printers for the best results in order to correct for non-linearity between input and output.

Professional human-printers would disagree with the idea that a colour proof of this kind is good enough for approving material to be reproduced later in print. The present method is to have a "cromalin" (patented by Du Pont) proof sent back from the printing house, with colours closely resembling those to be finally printed.

Principal (Haslingden, Lancs., UK) supply the Spectrum/24 card for an Apple Macintosh II machine using Apple's recently introduced 32-bit Quickdraw software. Principal can also supply the Supermac 19" monitor which uses a Trinitron tube displaying 1024 x 768 pixels – about 72 pixels/inch on this screen.

At present there appears to be a gap between "low end" colour printing and professional colour printing. Low end means colour prints from printers of the kind just mentioned, or (for higher volumes) from software claimed to be able to produce separate files containing colour data or colour separation transparencies printed on a printer, destined for plate making.

Software is available for a Mac (the Apple Macintosh nearly always seems to be the starting point) enabling transparencies or discs to be created in house and sent to a bureau for plate-making. Some would say that this in definitely not "low end colour reproduction".

A bureau in Oxford, UK, called Typo-Graphics will provide film for printing, created from customer's material, at about £115 per page according to content. They do it with a Mac II, Truvel colour scanner, and a Linotronic 300. Software called PhotoMac is used to produce colour separation files. They claim that this is a "stepping stone to high quality colour".

These methods seem to be good enough for some but not for others. Good colour printing still needs up-market equipment and expertise. Good-looking material in colour may be provided by pasting-in colour items on to DTP-produced pages and sending them away for printing.

A high quality relatively inexpensive route is the "Apple Mac – Quark XPress – Scitex Visionary" route. The minimum equipment needed is a Mac II machine with Visionary Software. Visionary is a modified version of the Quark XPress DTP software which produces files of Scitex formatted data. Alternatively it will convert any POSTSCRIPT file into Scitex. The image source will probably be a photograph scanned in colour by a colour scanner.

The Visionary software generates special files for use by a bureau with Scitex equipment in particular a "Page Geometry file" which, among other things, specifies the CMYK value of each pixel in an image. The Scitex equipment (a Scitex workstation costs £200,000) then takes over to produce the transparencies for printing. Superb results can be obtained.

COM
Computer Output Microfilm.

COMITE CONSULTATIF INTERNATIONALE DE TELEGRAPHIE ET TELEPHONE (CCITT)
The realization of the need for Standards in public national and international telecommunication networks was appreciated back in 1865 when the International Telegraph Union was formed. It changed its name to the International Telecommunication Union (ITU) in 1932 and since 1947 has been a United Nations Agency. Its membership, mainly PTTs, is drawn from over 160 countries. Its major sections are the International Telegraph and Telephone Consultative Committee (CCITT) and the International Frequency Registration Board (CCIR).

The CCITT considers the recommendations of a large number of "Study Groups" at its Plenary Assemblies which take place every four years. Following each Assembly it publishes a "Blue Book", "White Book", "Green Book" etc., whose colour is associated with a particular Quadrennial Assembly. These books are divided into sections in which "The CCITT unanimously declares the view...." that item XYZ should be provided, adopted, arranged etc., often providing highly detailed specifications.

For example if the complete details for handshaking and signalling with flow diagrams between Group 3 facsimile machines are wanted they will be found in the 50 pages, or thereabouts, of "Recommendation T.30 in Volume 7.2 of the "Yellow Book" covering the 7th Assembly of the CCITT in 1980.

It has been expected that the ITU/CCITT would make changes, recognizing that four year assemblies are hardly adequate to deal with the requirements of its members who are much prodded and are gradually waking up.

From the beginning of 1992, CCITT recommendations will not only appear in the blue books published after each 4 year plenary assembly but they will also be issued as separate documents as soon as they are approved.

COMMON CHANNEL SIGNALLING SYSTEM NO. 7
A system for controlling data networks.

The interconnection of switching nodes in a data transmission system from origin to destination requires that information be conveyed to the switches. This information is referred to as signalling. It includes the selection of appropriate nodes/lines with appropriate resources, supervision, and charging functions. The system is particularly important for controlling ISDN and INTELLIGENT NETWORKS.

COMMUNICATION, HUMAN
See under CODING, HUMAN.

COMMUNICATIONS SCIENCE
The science of Human Communications.

J.R. Beniger from the Annenberg School of Communications, remarked "American communications seems to be the one field – ironically enough – that remains largely oblivious to the growing convergence of interest on theories of information structures and processing, communication, and control in virtually every other discipline".

Beniger shows by citation analysis that in many other fields, there is a keen interest in aspects of information – structures, processing, communication, and control – as indicated by citations from those fields to such authors as Chomsky, Wittgenstein and Levi-Strauss.

Using Burger and Chaffee's *Handbook of Communication Science* as a reference source Beniger noted that Communication Science seeks to understand the production, processing, and effects of symbol and signal systems in interpersonal, organizational, mass, political, instructional, or other contexts, by developing testable theories. But he was

COMPACT DISC (CD)

1. Chomsky (1965)
2. Levi-Strauss (1958/1963)
3. Chomsky (1957)
4. Saussure (1915/1959)
5. Wittgenstein (1922/1961)
6. Wittgenstein (1953/1968)
7. Austin (1962)
8. Jakobson and Halle (1956)
9. Searle (1969)
10. Propp (1966/1968)

The most-cited Communication Science works

unable to find any mention by Berger and Chaffee of key authors from the central focus of this new convergence.

The closeness of Communication Science to Information Science can more easily be appreciated when information transfer in the business/office system field is considered. Kulnan suggests that communication is needed for one or more of the following four reasons, but without ever mentioning Communication Science:-

1. For the acquisition of factual or technical data.
2. For the exchange of information between people relating to duties and responsibilities, particularly for control purposes.
3. For the exchange of information between people, to realize objectives, to elicit co-operation, etc.
4. For the exchange of information between people for emotional reasons – for instance to establish credibility or to express feelings.

COMPACT DISC (CD)

A disc system originally developed for sound recording to a Philips/Sony specification. When recording, marks are made on the disc corresponding to the digits of digitized sound. They are read back by a low-power laser. Elaborate error correcting arrangements are included in the system.

The first player – the Sony CDP-101 – appeared in 1984. Players connect to amplifiers or hi-fi equipment. CDs are now one of the dominant forms of sound recording, having displaced vinyl records. Certain aspects of CD technology have become the forerunners for a number of variations described in the next few entries in this book.

It seems not to be widely known that Compact Disc players do not necessarily reproduce the potentially excellent sound quality available from a CD. To digitize sound for recording purposes, 8-bit samples are generated by sampling the analogue waveform at 44 KHz. However the process results in the acquisition of harmonic data which sounds unpleasant.

To get rid of it a technique called "oversampling and filtering" is used in CD and CD-ROM players. The scientific basis for it is doubtful, but the improvement is undoubted. Bit rates are increased and if the discerning purchaser knows how to ask the right questions and the vendor knows the answers (which he may not), he will hear about "8 x 2", "16 x 4" etc players. The first figure denotes the number of bits per sample, and the second the pseudo-sampling ("oversampling") rate.

The best CD players, such as the Cambridge Audio CD3, embody "16 x 16" which means "16 bits with 16 times oversampling". Oversampling is also used in the Amiga CDTV.

In January 1993 Nimbus announced that they could play 2 hours of video from a special disc run on a compact disc player. An ordinary CD player can be used for full motion video because the laser track used by Nimbus is only 1.2 microns wide and track read speed is reduced. The net result is a doubling of the data density.

A black box developed by Nimbus and C-Cube connected between the output of the player and a TV receiver contains a C-Cube chip which decodes the MPEG algorithms as they come off the disc. A double density 12 centimetre CD can contain over 2 hours of full colour motion digital video with sound.

COMPACT DISC INTERACTIVE (CD-I)

CD-I was developed from Compact Disc Digital Audio – CD-DA, the CD you buy in your record shop described in the previous entry. Sales of CD-DA's, launched in 1982, are now OVER 700 million, with add-on CD players costing less than £100 in the UK.

A CD delivers data at 170.2 Kbytes/second and has a total capacity of 650 Mbytes. Such a disc could store about 650 PAL colour TV frames, each containing 1 Mbyte of data. If the whole of the disc was used for motion video there would be 650M/86.4K = 7523 frames of it. If played back at TV rates it would provide a programme lasting about 30 seconds, but at the CD rate of 170.2 Kbytes/second the programme would be in slow motion and would last a bit longer. (See also the previous entry).

A US NTSC television frame is often digitized at 512 x 480 pixels but for CD-I, because the eye is relatively insensitive to colour variations, a reduced-rate alternate line coding scheme is used for colour component signals (CHROMINANCE) called DYUV producing 360 x 240 pixels – one third of NTSC, i.e. a 3:1 compression ratio. With 8-bit colour, a frame then consists of 360 x 240 x 8 = 691 Kbits = 86,400 Kbytes.

In a CD-I system the CRT is refreshed 15 times per second (half the TV rate), and the CD playback bit-rate is 170 Kbytes/sec. Therefore there are only 170/15 = 11,330 bytes available 15 times per second for the screen. A full screen requires 86,400 bytes 15 times per second but what it gets is 11,330 bytes so only 86,400/11,330 = 13% of its pixels can be updated each second.

CD-I players will play discs in CD format but the discs may include motion video so special players are needed. A CD could store about 600 PAL 625 line colour TV frames. To play the data at TV frame-repetition rates, data delivery would need to be at a rate of at least 25 Mbytes per second and the disc would play for 24 seconds or less.

However CD-I is organized to process data in a different way – quite different from the usual method of delivering data in a linear fashion, line by line and frame by frame.

Since a CD-I actually delivers data at 170 Kbytes per second, special measures must be taken for displaying it. A store in the player holds 1 frame of data which is scanned at TV rates, but new data is fed into it only when there is a *change* of information – quite unlike normal TV practice where the system always runs at the equivalent of about 25 Mbytes per second whether there is a change of information or not. In CD-I a number of other coding and display techniques are used to overcome the data rate problem.

The data stored permanently on the CD is likely to be audio, graphics, text, motion-video, etc., which is loaded in and out of the hard disc as needed. The picture on the screen usually consists of overlaid separately-controlled areas with *part* of each one sometimes

containing motion video, all parts controlled by the software which also selects which data to shift from the hard disc. Applications include interactive games, interaction with encyclopaedias, interactive learning systems, etc.

The organization of CD-I includes various facilities to enable a variety of programmes to be presented without the "refill rate" – far slower than the bit rate in conventional TV – from affecting the picture including:-

* Reduction of the colour data in images by a special coding scheme.
* Provision for the coding of text and graphic images using a COLOUR lookup table and run length coding.
* Provision of the means for up-dating small areas of the screen at a rate acceptable to the eye – normally at 10 to 15 frames per second.
* Provision of 4 separate stores ("image planes") with a total capacity of 1 Mbyte capable of storing four sets of data which may be scanned out in parallel to present four sets of data on the screen.
* Provision for using the planes as overlaid "matte" images. A "front" image may be partially transparent allowing parts of a "back" image to be displayed, or a solid small front image may have a transparent surround to reveal a background image.
* Provision for moving one image over another to provide full screen animation requiring far less data than is required for a full-motion picture.

The associated software provides the necessary control such as that required for "interactive play" routines. Thus a user with a control device such as a "joystick" may operate the figure of a golfer to play a shot towards what appears to be, say, the 18th hole at St. Andrews, or possibly towards any hole on that course or on any other course of his choice.

CD-I was lanched in the US at the end of 1991 with 100 disc titles, and players with interactive control software. One title is "a guide to photography" where a user adjusts his camera settings to photograph a subject, take the shot, and then looks at a "print" to check the results. Another title displays "pages from a colouring book" and a child can fill in the colours.

CD-I should include full-screen motion

video in due course. Most players contain a slot for a motion-video decoder scheduled for late 1992. There were about 50 titles at the start. Combined sales estimates for CDTV and CD-I of about 400,000 units have been forecast for 1994.

The biggest question is over the home market, says one observer. Can CD-I achieve all that Philips hopes for it or have they missed the boat as some critics believe? Rumours of a DVI unit targetted at the home cannot be dismissed, although software for it will be a crucial issue, and what impact will CDTV have ...? Corporate communications, depending as they do on networking, will move with systems which support this need.

COMPACT DISC – PHOTO
See under PHOTO-CD.

COMPACT DISC – READ ONLY MEMORY (CD-ROM)
A CD-ROM is a CLV 4.7" disc containing data recorded in a similar digital format to CD. Evidently the coded content of the signal does not demand "oversampling" to improve results so there are no "superior quality oversampling CD-ROM players". A CD ROM drive comes in a separate box for connection to a microcomputer or as a unit which will slide into the drive aperture provided on the front of a microcomputer. There is a trend to connect a CD-ROM to the controlling micro through the SMALL COMPUTER STANDARD INTERFACE (SCSI).

Standardization and drive problems are quite different from CDs where disc format was standardized from the start and compatible players followed thanks to the domination of two manufacturers, Philips and Sony, and their specifications in the "Yellow Book".

CD-ROM software formats must include uniform ways of describing and locating on a disc information about a single Volume (a CD-ROM disc), a Volume Set or collection of discs, and a file. A file is any named collection of data.

Each set of several sets of files could be a self-contained information product and a user could be allowed access to one or more products on the same disc. Alternatively the product might be so large that the file set for that product occupied a Volume Set comprising

several volumes. There are other aspects of importance such as automatic error correction and file directory arrangements. Because CD-ROMs are read-only discs, there is scope for an optimum directory arrangements (achieved, perhaps, by a HASHING algorithm) to minimize seek time which is inherently slow.

In the event, software formats were initiated by the High Sierra (HS) group – formed from a number of manufacturers in the US and including Philips and Sony. Successive attempts at finalization before the end of 1986 were unsuccessful, but agreement was eventually reached and HS became a *de facto* standard with the intention of getting it through as an ISO standard to add universality and respectability.

This idea was fine in principle and it enabled the industry to develop. The process was remarkably quick since it had been pushed by a relatively small number of organizations. It duly became the basis for ISO 9660, independent of machines/operating systems, approved, again remarkably quickly, by late 1987.

The "standard standards" problem then began – how to develop and implement bug-free software conforming to ISO 9660. HS was not widely replaced by ISO 9660 because it had been adopted and it worked. Suppliers either would not wait for the ISO software or would not use it because their customers did not have version 2.0 of MS-DOS extended memory called for by ISO. Although ISO 9660 is being slowly adopted a special plea on behalf of users who want hassle-free choices which work on any system has been made for its adoption.

Although "making CD-ROM discs/players work" is relatively easy for the user, "relatively" means compared with the other frightful hassles accompanying your average IT system. This means that many people will not find that installation is easy. The difficulties to be expected have been discussed. They are sufficient to call for articles telling you how to get out of them. One particular problem was "easily" tackled by Pournelle but Pournelle is a computer buff with very wide experience. Just how easy is it may be assessed from the following extract:-

"Of course the solution was obvious, Access to CD-ROM drives requires two actions.

First you have to load the CD-ROM driver with CONFIG.SYS. Then you have to execute the MSCDEX.EXE program which loads Microsoft DOS extensions that allow DOS to recognize disc drives larger than 33 Mbytes. Then use LOADH1 to install the Amtek Laserdek driver with CONFIG.SYS and when I wanted to access the CD-ROM drive open a window and execute MSCDEX.EXE command inside the window". Easy for a computer buff, but for others?

Although CD-ROMs have not been as successful as was expected by the ebullient forecasters, they have been successful enough to have become well established in the "information world", competing mainly against online searching. The capacity of a CD-ROM at around 550 Mbytes, is sufficient to store quite a large textual database. No telecommunication charges, delays, or problems, are incurred when using one.

The fact that colour, graphics, illustrations, etc., can also be stored is an added bonus, although such additions eat up storage space. One of the highly effective methods of data compression could be introduced to deal with CD-ROM products requiring graphics, or higher capacity discs could be introduced. The problem is that it would be difficult, if not impossible, to introduce such improvements without making existing players obsolete.

Unlike online systems, CD-ROMs cannot be easily and cheaply up-dated, so the greater the need for frequent up-dates, the less suitable is a CD-ROM for the application. However this price/up-date frequency difficulty does not disqualify CD-ROMs from being suitable for many different kinds of application.

A number of organizations will undertake to prepare a master disc from a customer's database and produce copies from it. A special tape must be prepared together with the directory structure, ready for making the "pre-mastering" tape which will include synchronization bits, headers, error correction etc., to the "Yellow Book" standard. From this a master disc is prepared to produce copies – the CD-ROMs for customers. A specialized software house will prepare the pre-mastering tape and the price for preparing a master disc from that tape will average about £2000, with the price of copies ranging from about £50 each for a small quantity, reducing to £3 each for large numbers (Philips prices).

CD-ROMs may now be produced at a price appropriate to non-professional producers. The Philips CDD521 drive is sold with an Adaptek 1542 SCSI-2 adaptor, Advanced SCSI Programming Interface (ASPI) driver, software MSCDEX.EXE, and DOS utilities called CD-Write.

The system can be used for publishing because the CD can be written on – it carries a groove covered by a layer of organic die and a reflected layer. The laser fuses the die to the substrate to create pits which can be read by normal CD-ROM readers.

CD recording depends on an uninterrupted stream of data particularly when the drive runs at twice normal CD speed which requires a sustained transfer rate of at least 300 Kbps. An associated hard disc is used for assembling material which is to be written to CD. CD-Write converts data on the fly from the hard disc's DOS file system to the CD's ISO 9660 file system.

With regard to "transportability", most CD-ROM discs are readable using different microcomputers controlled by different operating systems. The micro is loaded with a driver program provided that all discs have a standardized logical file structure. If that structure is known to the programmer who writes the driver, this will enable files to be opened and data to be interpreted.

Not only that, only if the arrangement of data in the files is standardized will the user's application program be able to search the files and obtain results meaningful to the user each time he places a disc from a different information provider on his drive.

A new type of drive called "multispin" drives are now being developed and the first to appear on the market is the NEC InterSect CDR-74 – available in both Macintosh and PC versions. The drive speed is doubled and transfer times and search times are speeded up. The speeds of current CD-ROM drives are set to make CD audio play at the right speed for audio reproduction. Manufacturers have solved this problem in the new drives by adding controllers that play back the audio tracks correctly.

COMPACT DISC READ ONLY MEMORY – EXTENDED ARCHITECTURE (CD-ROM XA)

CD-ROM XA, announced by Philips, Sony, and Microsoft in September 1988, is software providing some of the functions available on CD-I without departing much from established CD-ROM techniques. It conforms to the ISO 9660 standard.

The main advance towards multimedia with XA is a new standard text/graphics format for microcomputers independent of operating systems, and a coding system for sound as specified for CD-I, but with discs playable on both CD-ROM and CD-I players.

A fully compatible XA drive incorporates Adaptive Differential Pulse Code Modulation (ADPCM) decoding and decompression for separating interleaved audio channels. One objective in using CD-ROM XA is that Kodak photo CD discs may be run on it. A CD-ROM XA drive should also be able to cope with multi-session photo CD discs where the disc contains several different batches of pictures.

COMPACT DISC – READ ONLY MEMORY PRODUCTS

Semi-standardized CD-ROM players are now reaching the critical mass needed to encourage the supply of a wide range of products for similar applications – for instance for bibliographic database distribution.

From about 1985 onwards, CD-ROM versions of well known databases such as ERIC, MEDLINE, SCIENCE CITATION INDEX, etc., have become a viable complement, if not a replacement, for printed or online-searchable versions. At least two other major applications are of interest – selected data distribution (for example the supply of census data to be selectively transferred to hard disc for specialized use), and "Smart Discs" (where included software enables retrieved information to be further processed).

CD-ROMs have expanded into areas beyond bibliographic databases. In Armstrong's 1990 directory, 19 titles are selected for comprehensive evaluation. Of these 10 are bibliographic databases, 6 are directories, dictionaries, or encyclopaedias, 1 includes full text abstracts, and 1 is a numeric database. Libraries probably still form the main market, but business applications are now showing the fastest growth.

As early as 1987 the financial CD-ROM Lotus One Source, sold 19,000 copies, followed by Microsofts's Bookshelf with 10,000.

CD-ROM drives cost between £550 and £850 in the UK and are available as internal units for a micro or in external separate boxes. NEC, Hitachi, and Panasonic are the major manufacturers. Storage capacities are either 630 or 560 Mbytes.

Next Technology, Cambridge, England have developed a jukebox to hold 270 CD-ROM discs – a storage capacity totalling 175 Gbytes (1400 Gbits). It contains 8 drives, so more than one CD-ROM is accessible at one time. The jukebox is controlled by a PC and it takes 5 seconds to transport a disc on to a drive. The cost is £22,000.

The Perform 600 can be bought with a fast internal CD drive, the AppleCD 300i. The 300i provides a serious price and performance improvement over Apple's external CD-ROM drive, the Apple CD 150. It also has full-blown support for Kodak's PhotoCD system, and there is a direct sound connection from the drive to the Perform's internal speaker.

A recording system is available from Philips. Philips bundles a drive with an Adaptec 1542 SCSI-2 adapter and ASPI (advanced SCSI programming interface) driver, SCSI cable, MSCDEX.EXE, and a set of DOS utilites called CD-Write. CD recording depends critically on an uninterrupted stream of data, particularly when – as with the CDD521 – the drive runs at twice the normal CD play speed, requiring a sustained transfer rate of better than 300 KBps.

The work space where you assemble the material written to the CD is a hard disk. CD-Write converts on the fly from the hard disk's DOS file system to the CD's ISO 9660 file system. It can also redirect the ISO 9660 images that it creates to a hard disk and can write such a preformatted image to the CD.

An increasing number of CD-ROM disks which are now coming onto the market specify that they are designed to run on multimedia PCs. A multimedia PC is an ordinary 386/486 PC with a high resolution colour display, a CD-ROM drive, a sound board and a sufficiently large amount of RAM and hard disk memory. Some computer manufacturers are already selling so called multimedia systems, though in many cases the appellation of "multimedia" is more a matter of sales hype than reality. What is a reality is, however, is that any existing PC AT may be expanded into a multimedia system.

The first necessary addition is a sound card. There are quite a few different types on the market today, but the most widely used, compatible with most CD-ROM multimedia disks, is the Sound Blaster from Creative Labs. This card will allow the system to generate high quality music and sound effects, as well as offering a digitized voice channel and a text to speech synthesizer. Output is of FM quality with up to 11 voices. Output power of 4 watts per channel is sufficient to directly run loudspeakers.

The next requirement in a multimedia system is a suitable user interface programme. Here the choice is simple since there is only one suitable product on the market, Windows 3.1. This version is a considerable advance on version 3.0 and includes support for both CD-ROM drives, and sound cards. It is also an interface which is compatible with a lot of the products from CD-ROM disc publishers. A good example of a multimedia PC composed of all the necessary units, together with Windows 3.1, is the Multimedia Beethoven disk produced by Microsoft.

Included in the mission of First Cities is the creation of a significant marketplace for networked multimedia information and entertainment products and services by accelerating developments of a national infrastructure for entertainment, distance learning, health care, and electronic commerce. According to Craig Fields, MCC chair and CEO, "Our ultimate goal is the creation of a seamless environment for the spontaneous use of integrated interactive multimedia services in the home, the community, or on the move". MCC will provide:-

* Software that will enable individuals to connect their homes to the interactive multimedia services networks.
* Software to enable communication delivery organizations to provide a gateway through which customers can connect.
* Applications servers that will enable distribution of a wide range of services through the gateway and into individual homes.

The companies joining MCC in the initial phase of a national multimedia testbed are Apple Computer, Bell Communications

Research (Bellcore) Bieber-Taki Associates, Corning, Eastman Kodak, Kaleida Labs, North American Philips, South-Western Bell Technology Resources, Sutter Bay Associates, Tandem Computers, and US West. Discussions are under way with additional companies whose services include cable television, satellite, telephony, entertainment programming and publishing.

As with other areas of IT, predictions about CD-ROM growth have been wide of the mark. In a forecast as late as 1988, Wall forecast 1000 titles by the beginning of 1989. However Armstrong (1990) lists 508 products in his directory and 409 are listed in the Cuadra/Elsevier 1990 directory.

Knowledge Research estimated that about 25,000 drives had been installed in Europe by 1988, and would increase to over 47,000 in 1989. Link estimated that the CD-ROM market will be worth nearly $1 billion per year by 1991, of which less than one tenth will be in Europe.

The business market for multimedia software and systems in the US and Europe will grow from £500 million in 1991 to £9 billion in 1997, according to *Multimedia; strategies for the business market*, a report produced by Ovum.

Ovum points out that in 1991 there were only two significant uses for multimedia in business – interactive computer-based training systems and point-of-information/point-of-sale kiosks.

But by 1994 its survey – based on detailed case studies of 25 systems suppliers, software developers and users – reckons that there will be four main products operating system extensions that support multimedia, multimedia enhancements to spreadsheets and wp packages; business presentation packages, and information access packages that include publications, databases and tools.

By 1997 it adds, two new categories will extend the market still further – multimedia-enhanced electronic mail packages and groupware, including videoconferencing facilities.

COMPACT DISC – TELEVISION (CDTV)
See MULTIMEDIA – HARDWARE.

COMPANDING
A non-linear Analogue/Digital or Digital/Analogue technique used in telecommunica-

tions applications to increase the resolution of low amplitude signals at the expense of the resolution of high amplitude signals.

COMPARATOR
A circuit which compares the value of two input signals and outputs a signal when they are equal.

COMPATIBILITY
A word used to indicate that one device can exchange "information" with another.

COMPENDEX
Computerized Engineering Index.

COMPILER
A program which translates a program in a high level language into a low-level one (usually in machine language). See also COMPUTERS – LANGUAGES.

COMPLIMENTARY METAL OXIDE SILICON (CMOS)
In 1974 RCA manufactured the Complimentary Metal Oxide Silicon (CMOS) 1802 microprocessor and this technology was introduced by others as improved manufacturing techniques enabled CMOS to be re-considered. Until then, CMOS technology, invented in 1962, was thought to be too complex and expensive to make. One driving force was the need for low power in small portable applications like digital watches.

In CMOS a current of less than 0.1 microamperes is drawn when one of the two complimentary transistors in an MOS circuit is "on". No current is needed periodically to maintain this condition. Appreciable current flows only for the brief period when the two transistors are switched from "on-off" to "off-on".

The voltages in a memory bank of CMOS transistors representing either 1's or 0's, do not gradually decay. Data remains stored so long as power is applied, unlike memories using earlier transistors which required "refreshing" every few milliseconds by a charging current. CMOS transistors consume little power when used in portable battery-operated equipment. The equipment can be switched off leaving only the memory connected to the battery without losing stored data.

See also SEMICONDUCTORS.

Fractal compression. Upper picture 768 Kbytes, lower 20 Kbytes (About 39:1). (By courtesy of Iterated Systems Ltd)

COMPRESSION – FRACTAL
Fractal compression has been described by Beaumont in some detail using a number of illustrations to show effects in working systems.

He describes a scheme which compresses an 8-bit per pixel halftone picture into a picture requiring only 0.8 bits per pixel – that is a 10:1 compression – "without introducing artefacts obvious to the untrained eye". Compression down to 0.5 (16:1) produces visible artefacts but the picture quality is still reasonable".

A fractal compression system has been introduced by co-inventors Dr. Michael Barnsley from the UK and Dr. Alan Sloan for the US, both mathematicians, who have set up a company, Iterated Systems Ltd., in the UK.

Computer algorithms act on portions of complex images and perform transformation operations on them called Iterated Function Systems (IFS) – from which a set of points may be plotted providing a coarse image of salient features called Fractal Transform (FT) codes. An example (the example on this and on the following page are by courtesy of Iterated Systems Ltd.) is shown in the above figure.

The needed information about the spatial relationship between points is preserved in the codes, enabling the original image to be reconstructed by an iterative scaling-up process.

The reduction process amounts to the elimination of redundant geometric information. The compression ratio between the original and the reduced image and the time taken to generate the latter depends on the complexity of the shapes present in the original. Some parts may exhibit great redundancy, in others there may be none at all.

Barnsley claims very large compression ratios. A high quality compression board for plugging in to a 386 MSDOS micro-computer with 640K memory and hard disk is sold by the company for £6000 with software for around £2000. It will accept 24-bit colour input files in various formats.

A system user could compress a file, to, say, 10 Kbytes and send it on disk or transmit it very cheaply to another location and load it into any suitable micro which contains the decompression software – for instance a 286 or higher machine with 640K and a VGA display. The resident decompression software is licensed at £95 per user for up to 100 users, reducing for larger numbers. No special hardware is necessary for decompression.

The second example shown here from an Iterated Systems' brochure lacks their original colour and probably suffers a little from being re-reproduced. The method provides resolution independence and mathematical zoom-in. In conventional zoom-in both the size of the image and the size of the pixels change.

A zoom-in at a resolution of 1280 x 600 pixels is shown – it is only one quarter of a 1280 x 600 image originally scanned into the system. It was printed after decompression from a 10 Kbyte compressed file. Another image, also printed from a 10 Kbyte compressed file, is zoomed-in to provide a picture of 5120 x 3200.

The printer used is a Mitsubishi 600 dots/inch printer. An effective compression ratio of nearly 5000:1 is claimed. The picture quality does not seem to have suffered much from this enormous ratio.

The time taken to compress and decompress presumably depend to some extent on the power of the machines being used. It could be 10 minutes for compression but only a few seconds for decompression.

Using this system a very large database containing high quality pre-compressed pictures could be stored in megabyte instead of gigabyte storage capacity. A few seconds for the decompression of a retrieved picture would be acceptable.

There is some controversy about this method. A research user says that the obtainable compression ratios and quality as obtained on a range of images are no better than those obtained with alternative proprietary systems and they will not be using it; the appearance of compressed pictures depends very much on their content. But a commercial

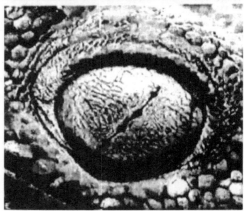

Another example of fractal compression

user is pleased with the system and reports that for his purposes it performs satisfactorily.

COMPRESSION – JPEG

The Joint Photographic Experts Group (JPEG) have developed a standard for the compression of still images.

Numerous devices now incorporate chip-implemented compression schemes to this standard which provides for "lossless" 2:1 compression – that is the compressed picture is virtually perfect. When the compression ratio reaches about 30:1 degradation starts to become noticeable. A set of pictures provided to demonstrate the results show just acceptable 32:1 compression; at 300:1 the picture is hardly recognizable; fine detail is lost and edges are very ragged.

In the version of DTC incorporated in the Joint Photographic Experts Group (JPEG) standard – worked out by ISO and CCITT groups – a digitized image is coded by processing blocks of 8 x 8 pixels in sequence from the top to the bottom of the picture.

Each block is scanned in order to generate information about the rate of change between the pixels present. A checker-board pattern in a block would produce a stream of high frequency data elements; an all-white or all-black block would represent a low frequency change. The "information" in the block is confined to the high frequency elements which are Huffman (See under CODE – HUFFMAN) encoded – a highly economic code. Decompression goes through the same processes in reverse.

The Inmos A121 chip was developed during 1989 to handle this type of operation. It runs at 320M operations/second, taking 3.2 microseconds to carry out an 8 x 8 transform process and taking 15 ms to handle a 625 x 625 pixel image.

In April 1990 the 27 MHz C-Cube Microsystem CL550 chip, designed to perform according to the JPEG standard, was announced. It will compress an 8 Mbit video frame by 10 times in 0.033 seconds for use with 30 frames per second video. Alternatively it will compress a 200 Mbit high resolution full colour still picture to 8 Mbits in 1 second.

Instead of ratios, compressions are often expressed as "bits per pixel". In a recent subjective assessment of JPEG compression ratios from original 16-bit per pixel pictures, the following subjective assessments were made:-

8	bits/pixel	(2:1) compression		"Lossless".
1.5	..	(11:1)	..	"Indistinguishable from original".
0.75	..	(22:1)	..	"Excellent quality".
0.25	..	(64:1)	..	"Useful image".
0.10	..	(160:1)	..	"Recognizable image".

COMPRESSION – MOTION VIDEO

For motion video, the delivered bits, after decompression, must run at the designed rate for the application. For example for 30 US television frames per second to be delivered to a US television receiver or computer screen and to provide normal-looking pictures, the data rate is about 28 Mbytes or 224 Mbits per second. Applications of motion video compression are discussed in the MULTIMEDIA entries.

A variation of JPEG called Motion-JPEG is JPEG speeded up to enable motion video to be compressed and decompressed in real time. However attention is now moving on to the Moving Picture Experts Group (MPEG) Standard where bit rates become particularly important. A major objective is to compress TV bit rates down to 1 to 1.5 Mbps or lower.

In 1992 C-Cube Microsystems introduced a decoder type CL450. Its purpose is to handle full motion colour video compression and decompression, particularly with respect to CD-I systems. It will handle NTSC or PAL video at 30 frames per second.

COMPRESSION – PRINCIPLES OF

Considerable compression development work followed the adoption of digitization – implemented because the handling of data in digital form provides substantial advantages over analogue. This advantage is partially offset by the greater bandwidth occupancy of the digital form. Digitization of analogue audio or video signals requires that the varying level of the analogue waveform be "sampled". The value of levels are transmitted as a code.

Accordingly speech compression work has often revolved round PULSE CODE MODULATION (PCM) methods – the basic method of waveform quantization and the transmission of digitized coded levels.

Speech compression is the art of ingenious methods of bit reduction. The PCM coded transmission of a smooth waveform, normally containing several digits of code, must be carried out once per cycle (Hz) for complete reconstruction of the waveform at the receiving end. In the case of a complex waveform containing many components of different frequencies, numerous samples are required. When represented as a continuous graph the quantized waveform assumes a step-like appearance.

A crude method of compression, which results in a steady reduction in quality and the introduction of quantization noise, is simply to reduce the number of samples taken from the speech waveform.

To reduce redundancy (See under COMPRESSION – REDUNDANCY) the general characteristics of the data must be known and predictable. One principle that is often used in practice for images is "run length coding" -the replacement of long runs of unchanging data by the shortest possible code.

For example if the "grey levels" of an image are quantized into 16 levels in order to be digitized, the level "off-white" will always be quantized as, say, "level 2". A strip of the image consisting, when scanned, of, say, 289 off-white elements, may then be represented as a long string of twos amenable to compression as a code which says, in effect, "289 twos, signifying off-white, follow".

As another example – to be expected when we have digital television during the next decade – uniformly blue sky occupying one third of a frame normally requiring around 2 Mbits of data, could instead be transmitted as a short code meaning "the next two million bits will be blue". Decoding takes place just before display at the receiving end and blue pixels would be reproduced in the sky area.

Much work has been done on compressing FACSIMILE data to enable detailed images to be transmitted quickly. Stand-alone scanning-machines have inherited the RUN LENGTH CODING software used – it is a good working compromise providing effective compression with reasonable compression and decompression processing times.

The time taken to compress and decompress, and the compression ratio achieved, vary according to page contents, the compression algorithms (rules) used, the power of the processor, and whether or not special chips are used for the purpose.

The processing may take under a second or more than a minute. For a short business letter consisting of lines of text with much white space the compression ratio will be 20 to 40, while for a page consisting of halftone illustrations there may be no compression at all.

Compression has become increasingly important with the increase in demand for high quality images in order to reduce the enormous number of bits which must be transmitted and stored. The images are compressed as early as possible in the system, and de-compressed as late as possible in order to provide the maximum benefit.

The mathematical process known as the Discrete Cosine Transform (DCT) is a classic example of the elegant use of the compact processing power currently available to perform the elaborate operations in real time needed to substantially compress data "on the fly". See COMPRESSION – JPEG.

Another area where compression is widely used is in Compact Disc (CD) systems where the disc can only deliver data at a certain rate, but the human requirements call for a much faster rate. (See under headings for different CD systems).

JPEG compression (See under COMPRESSION – JPEG) works by compressing the halftone or colour bits which are applied to the beam or beams as voltages to change the intensity level of a displayed pixel. Because of the importance of the maximum bit rates that can be delivered by different media – for example CD-ROMs, Video Recorders, etc., an important objective is to compress pictures to the bit rate which a particular media can deliver. The delivered data is converted to real time data by the de-compression software running on the associated machine.

COMPRESSION – REDUNDANCY

Redundant information in a stream of meaningful data may be excluded without affecting the meaning. However elements are commonly included in a message to improve the likelihood of correct reception.

For example much redundant information is present in human languages; if all the vowels are removed from a message in English the meaning of the message may still be understood. Another example is the addition of codes to each code group before transmission to enable devices at a receiver to perform checking, and in some cases auto-

---

56   THE BELL SYSTEM TECHNICAL JOURNAL, JANUARY 1951

first line is the original text and the numbers in the second line indicate the guess at which the correct letter was obtained.

```
(1) T HERE  I S    NO  R EV ERSE  ON  A  MOTORCYCLE  A
(2) 1 1 15 11 21  1 21 1 15 11 71 11 21 32 1 22 7 1 1 1 14 1 1 1 1 31
(1) FRI END  OF  MI NE  FOUND  THIS  OUT
(2) 8 6 13 1 11 1 11 1 1 1 11 6 21 1 11 1 12 11 1 1 11
(1) RATHER  D RAMATI C ALLY  THE  OTHER  DAY
(2) 4 1 1 1 11 1 115 11 1 11 11 11 11 6 111 1 11 1 11 1 11 1        (9)
```

Out of 102 symbols the subject guessed right on the first guess 79 times, on the second guess 8 times, on the third guess 3 times, the fourth and fifth guesses 2 each and only eight times required more than five guesses. Results of this order are typical of prediction by a good subject with ordinary literary English. Newspaper writing, scientific work and poetry generally lead to somewhat poorer scores.

Shannon's measurements of redundancy in language

matically to correct an erroneous code group. An increase in the probability of correctness has been achieved at the expense of an increase in redundancy.

Redundancy in human speech for example depends upon both the development of a language by long-term experience and a human's advance knowledge of a particular subject. C.E.SHANNON conducted a redundancy experiment in which subjects were shown a passage of text and and then asked to guess the next letter. The results obtained are shown in the above figure.

COMPRESSION – RUN LENGTH CODING

A code in which a sequence of identical data elements, each of which would normally be individually coded, are collectively coded. The net effect is a considerable reduction in the number of codes required.

See under COMPRESSION – PRINCIPLES OF.

COMPUTER

A device able to store data and a program for processing the data. An Analogue computer works on continuously variable data such as voltage. A Digital computer operates on BINARY digits which form a coded represen-

tation of the item being measured.
See also MICROCOMPUTER.

COMPUTER CONFERENCING AND TELECONFERENCING

Computer conferencing is of two kinds classifiable as serious and light-hearted. Goldmark tried out serious computer conferencing as a means of reducing travelling, accommodation etc., but the best known early work was done by Turoff and Hiltz as part of their Electronic Information Exchange System (EIES) at the New Jersey Institute of Technology, starting around 1972. Similar work followed at Loughborough as part of the Blend project in the eighties.

Some reasons why success has been hard to achieve have been given by Short who anticipated "the coffee and biscuits" syndrome with videoconferencing using a TV link; similar considerations apply for computer conferencing. "We had arranged for coffee and tea to be served and he didn't have any. We sat there drinking our coffee and passing the biscuits around while he looked increasingly glum".

Other reasons suggested are that "the omission of social chat may have deleterious consequences ... the busy executive ... may feel it advantageous to put in an appearance ..

IBM Person to Person/2 teleconferencing system

chatting with subordinates". Some would say that this function, plus the handing out of praise and occasional brickbats, is an essential function of the busy executive.

With regard to the supposed benefit of saving travelling time:- "In the case of very large conferences it is not uncommon for a company to pay the expenses of its employees to travel and stay at a hotel to be wined and dined and generally to mix business with pleasure".

The above photograph (by courtesy of IBM) shows a single-user conferencing system in use. The second, more light-hearted type of computer conferencing is a less formal and more widespread activity of a rather different kind which is outside the "business system" area.

It consists of special interest groups running mailbox-type operations such as "Car & Drive", "Bulletin Boards" etc., for the exchange of information between computer enthusiasts, and general purpose information services such as "The Source", "PRODIGY" and others. Prodigy, a teleshopping system, is charged at $10 per month for unlimited access. It is financed by intrusive advertising.

COMPUTERS – FOURTH GENERATION

The term given to computers which succeeded the current generation, for which designs are supposed to have stopped around 1970. The new generation works effectively on the current range of high level languages and is easier to program. The hardware consists mainly of integrated circuits and the machines have fast, large, memories. Fourth generation machines are followed by the fifth generation, currently under development, and characterized by possessing some degree of "intelligence".

COMPUTERS – GROWTH RATE

The history of computers is the history of faster more complex processing. In 1960, scientific and business computer sales totalled about $700 million, each type taking about half of this total. By 1977 the situation looked quite different. The major computer types were general purpose mainframes, earning about $10 billion, and Minicomputers earning nearly $6 billion. Personal Computers and Supercomputers were each earning less than $100 million.

In 1982, mainframe and minicomputer sales

were $19 billion and $16 billion respectively, while personal computers had increased to $7 billion. Supercomputers were earning over $200 million and Workstations $35 million.

By 1987 personal computer sales had increased to $35 billion, followed by minis at $32 billion, and mainframes at $25 billion. Supercomputers stood at about $900 million and Workstations at $2 billion. A new category christened "minisupercomputers" had emerged which earned about $250 million in 1987.

COMPUTERS – HISTORY

The little console within which a German, William Schikard, built his mechanical calculator in 1592 has the look of a computer about it. It includes a row of knobs and dials on the front of it and could perform addition and subtraction using rods, gears, and an automatic carrying mechanism.

However the machines made by a Frenchman, Blaise Pascal, in the 1640s are often considered to be the ancestors of digital computing. In one example each gearwheel in an array of coupled gearwheels registering units, tens, hundreds etc., could be rotated by inserting a peg. To carry tens a weighted ratchet was gradually raised as a wheel was rotated from 0 to 9; then the ratchet dropped on to the next wheel to advance it by one unit. Some years later Leibnitz developed the idea using complex gearwheels in a machine capable of addition, subtraction, and multiplication.

Charles Babbage's nineteenth century machines do not look much like computers, but the available functions or the functions planned by Babbage and Ada, Countess of Lovelace, only child of the poet Byron included several of the major functions performed by today's computers. Professor of Mathematics at Cambridge University, Babbage was fascinated by the new technology like many other Victorians. He was involved with Post Office systems, printing, pin-making and railway trains but soon became absorbed with calculating machines.

In 1822, having constructed his three-register Difference Engine (A register is a device for storing digits) which could handle quadratic functions, he obtained a grant for something much more elaborate in order to compute tables to twenty places of decimals.

Support was withdrawn after considerable expenditure and Babbage turned to something yet more ambitious – his Analytical Engine – which was intended to carry out more complex calculations – a tremendous advance on the special-purpose Difference Engine. Columns of wheels, gears, and linkages would be used with control rods operated by the holes in punched cards as were used in Jacquard looms, invented some years previously. Results would be output as moulds from which print could be cast. The machine was far ahead of its time and was never built.

Ideas for programming the machine were developed by Ada Lovelace. Babbage's machine and Lovelace's programs were to embody the essential functions of today's computers by having the sections –
* A control unit to actuate a sequence of operations
* An input mechanism for feeding in instructions and data
* An output mechanism for delivering results
* A Mill (Babbage's word for the Arithmetic Unit) for performing operations on numbers
* Stores for retaining data and ongoing results.

Ada Lovelace described in her programming notes ideas which were not realized until a century later. They included the notion of repeating a set of instructions again and again and, at some point, jumping to alternative instructions.

Every country has its own version of history; by checking literature from both sides of the Atlantic we can take note of several major advances in more recent years. There were a number of active pioneers in the US in the nineteenth century. A machine which used a keyboard very much like those in use today was invented by Dorr Felt and the name he chose stuck – the Comptometer – forerunner of modern calculating machines. William Burroughs invented a similar type of machine.

Herman Hollerith made something of a breakthrough with his punched card tabulating and sorting machines, used in the 1890 US census. His company – The Tabulating Machine Company – eventually became a division of a US company which is quite well known today; IBM.

National pride being what it is, claims to the invention of the first electronic computer are numerous. Quite a few hinge on the definition of a computer. Babbage's projected machine of the 1830s – being reconstructed at the Science Museum, London, mainly out of turned brass parts to see if it could have worked – was a kind of computer. Babbage's collaborator, Ada Lovelace has been called "the world's first programmer".

The best claims to the title of the world's first electronic computer seem to lie with ENIAC or COLOSSUS. ENIAC, built at Princeton University in 1945 is often claimed to be the first. COLOSSUS was started in February 1943 at the Post Office Research Station, Dollis Hill, London, and completed the following January. Subsequently it was moved to Bletchley Park and several were made for deciphering messages encyphered by German ENIGMA machines. Since, to this day, it is clothed with obsessive British secrecy, its claims to fame are overdue.

COLOSSUS contained 2000 valves and used a loop of 5-hole punched paper tape as input. The construction team was led by Tommy Flowers and included Max Newman, "Doc" Coombs and Sydney Broadhurst.

The machine was smaller than Eniac; several versions were built by a team led by Professor Flowers at the old Dollis Hill Research Laboratories of the Post Office. It contained all the basic sections found in modern machines except that it did not run on a stored programme – the programme had to be keyed in.

The first machine to enter regular commercial service with a microprogramming system was probably LEO, started in 1949 by J. Lyons & Co., in West London. It was used for payroll work and has been described by J.M.M. Pinkerton. It was based on a machine called EDSAC built at Cambridge.

It used a paper tape reader. Pinkerton was an expert in ultrasonic wave propagation in liquids – a necessary qualification because LEO's memory was made out of mercury-filled delay lines capable of storing 2048 17-bit words. 150 LEO 3s, an improved version which used transistors and magnetic core storage, were built.

A major problem with early models was the reliability of the 5000 valves (tubes) which LEO contained. All kinds of precautions were taken like regular testing of each valve, slow warm-up of the heaters before applying the HT voltage and special pre-operational testing which lasted up to one hour. The result was a mean time between failures of around 10 hours.

Much of the work done as a part of the enormous R&D effort in valve (vacuum tube) electronics mounted during the second world war found its way into the early computers. Many of the circuits and devices for waveform generation and processing required in radar, and later in computers, were developed by A.D. Blumlein who worked at EMI and at TRE, a research establishment at Malvern, England.

Having made stereo recordings in 1934, Blumlein went on to invent the television combined picture and synchronization waveform used in the television service launched by the BBC in 1936. In 1940 he designed the Air Interception (AI) radar system and by 1942 he had designed the H_2S ground mapping radar with a plan-position indicator (PPI) CRT display. Blumlein was killed when the aircraft in which he was flying on an H_2S test crashed in 1942.

At about the time that Blumlein completed his television work in 1936, an extraordinary paper was read to the London Mathematical Society describing a stored programme computer – "The Universal Machine" – by Alan TURING. Turing may have disussed this idea later with Von Neumann, who is usually credited with it.

Turing went on to work on decoding messages encoded by the German Enigma machine at Bletchley Park, worked on the Colossus computer in 1944, and proposed a design for the ACE computer later built at the National Physical Laboratory.

Colossus may have been the first electronic computer, but because of British obsession with secrecy, its existence was not even admitted until 30 years later. In 1944 a universal calculating machine – the Automatic Sequence Controlled Calculator – was completed by IBM to the designs of Aiden of Harvard University. This electro-mechanical machine used registers made out of sets of wheels, received data on punched cards, and read out data on cards or on a teletypewriter.

Very soon afterwards Eckert and Mauchley built an all electronic machine, ENIAC, at the Moore School of Engineering, University of Pennsylvania, Philadelphia, which contained

18,000 valves and consumed 150 Kilowatts, most of which had to be ducted away as heat. Based on ideas by Von Neumann, it was first used in 1946, mainly for calculating shell trajectories.

The domination of the world's computer industry was settled with the first of a series – the IBM 701 to be followed by the highly successful 1401.

IBM consolidated with other computers and a series of devices, including a 5 Mbyte disc storage system in 1955 with one second random access, removable disc packs, chain printers etc. The System 360 computer family arrived in 1965. IBM introduced floppy discs in 1970 and Winchester discs in 1973. The company went on to dominate the industry.

COMPUTERS – HOME
See HOME COMPUTERS.

COMPUTERS – LANGUAGES
Computer programs used to be written in machine code, that is in binary digits – an extremely time consuming and error-prone process. Later a kind of building block method called Assembly Language was introduced where the programmer could use symbols (Mnemonics) like SUB for Subtract and LD for Load. Every time a Source Code like this is used, the computer automatically translates it into binary digit Object Code for direct use by the machine using a program called an Assembler.

Assembly Language is an enormous improvement but program design and writing is still very laborious. An Assembly program consists of a series of single machine instructions, address assignments, and housekeeping details. However a Listing File, which is a line by line record of how the Assembler handles the program, may be printed, and Assembly Language overcomes the need for a laborious re-write if a change is required; instructions can be deleted or added rather easily.

An Assembly Language is peculiar to the particular processor for which it was written and is the means of putting together the Instruction Codes to form a program. A program consists of lines of code each typically consisting of several fields. For example the first field may be a Label which is simply a name by which the code line is identified, the

second an Opcode – that is an instruction from the instruction set – and the third an Operand – that is a quantity or function upon which the operation is to be performed.

High level machine-independent languages are easier to recognize by any programmer than the processor-specific instructions in Assembly Language. In such languages English-like statements are automatically translated into a large number of machine instructions so that where, say, ten lines of code would be needed in Assembly, one suffices in High Level. Thus although programmes will be much faster to write, they will also be more restrictive since direct access to all the features of the machine, as is provided by an Assembly Language, is denied.

Interpreters and Compilers are software packages used to translate the High Level language into the language of the machine in question. Although the actual language used in a High Level language may be machine independent, the means by which it is translated for use is not – each type of machine requires its own translation program.

Basic, an acronym for Beginners All purpose Symbolic Instruction Code, was developed for the purpose described by its title by Kemeny and Kurtz at Dartmouth College in the USA in 1964. Microsoft provided a version in 1975 for the 8080 CPU. Later MBASIC, like various other versions, became far more widely used than just as a beginners software. By 1980 it was being used in over 300,000 microcomputers of 55 different makes with several different operating systems.

C is a programming language derived from BCPL which was implemented on many machines. C is one of the most popular languages for use on Unix systems. It is a modern high-level language able to address hardware in a manner resembling assembly language. C is also quite widely used on microcomputers.

As the use of Unix has grown so has the use of C which has several derivatives such as Numeric C, Objective C, C+ and C++. C and its derivatives include the means for implementing OBJECT oriented techniques. A standard for C was ratified in 1989.

Fortran (FORmula TRANslation) is a language which has endured for many years and is still widely used. It was first introduced by IBM in 1956 to be followed by several versions, in particular Fortran IV, standardized by ANSI as Fortran 66. Fortran uses algebra-like schemes well suited for scientists to specify their computations. Later Fortran 90 was adopted as an OSI standard confirming its popularity. In 1993 Fortran 90 compilers started to appear, considerably simplifying programming operations.

PASCAL, named after the French mathematician Blaise Pascal was developed by Nicholas Wirth in 1970 but did not start to be used in microcomputers until about 1978 when compilers were introduced by the University of California (San Diego). Pascal has displaced Basic as the "serious programmers" language because having the advantage of a well defined standard it is reliable and maintainable and is considered to have a better structure than Basic.

Another advantage of Pascal is the provision for the creation of data types with listings of variables. For example Sunday, Monday ... Saturday, could be a list under the Type "Day" with the variables today, yesterday, tomorrow, enabling program statements like "If yesterday = Monday then tomorrow = Wednesday".

COMPUTERS – LIBRARIES, IN
See LIBRARIES – COMPUTERS IN.

COMPUTERS – NEURAL NETWORKS
Neural Networks consist of large numbers of "neurons" which are small computing units whose outputs are the result of input signals modified by weights and threshold levels which can be changed. Neurons are multiply interconnected by links called "synapses" providing a system somewhat resembling the human brain. Problems like the "travelling salesman (shortest tour) problem" or problems in fields like pattern recognition and artificial intelligence are solved by the movement of, and operations on, fed-back or fed-forward data.

Neural Networks are said to "learn by example". Weights are changed by small amounts by "error feedback" during operations on mathematical functions.

A neural network will perform computations which are extremely difficult to specify formally in a conventional program. Pattern recognition problems – as required in speech or character recognition – in which the network "learns" from its mistakes – are its forte.

It will teach itself how to recognise a range of patterns instead of recognizing only those for which it is programmed.

Neural networks are related to but more advanced than a class of computers known as array processors. An array processor contains a number of processors, each with its own memory. Instructions are executed simultaneously and the array forms part of a host machine. However it has no "learning" capacity.

A processor's operation is controlled by a "transfer function" which determines its output signal according to the input signals modified by "adaptive coefficients" stored in its memory. An adaptive coefficient is a weight, and it is the combined effect of the weighted input signals which control the value of the output. The topology – the pattern of interconnections which determines what data each processor receives – also affects the performance of the system.

A neural network is trained by supplying it with input data which will provide known answers after appropriate computation. In a training session the neural network performs a feedback run in order to modify weights after comparing its answers to the correct answers – a "learning" process. Several feedback iterations are performed until it is decided that the output error is small enough for whatever purpose it will subsequently be used.

When the network is used for a real task, the computations it performs can be either controlled by fixing the weights at the values reached during the training session, or by varying them according to data applied from a source associated with the task – for instance from sensors in a robot.

COMPUTERS – OPTICAL
Optical computers are the second recent development. Optical computers are likely to be based on bistable switches where a control light beam determines whether or not a switching device will reflect or appear to be transparent to an input beam. The active material is a substance such as lithium niobate whose refractive index will switch when the intensity of the controlling optical beam exceeds a particular level.

Optical computing is much faster than electronic computing but it will be some years before practical systems appear. However a research team at Glasgow University has succeeded in developing an optical switch operating at a speed of 10 femtoseconds (10^{-14} seconds).

Meanwhile the considerable problem of how to feed data into such a system at a rate compatible with its processing ability is receiving attention.

At the end of 1992 several companies and universities in the United States headed by Conductus Inc., announced their intention of developing a proto-type machine to be suitable eventually for desktop use.

The properties of photochromic glass (used in sunglasses) are altered by exposure to light. Other sensitive materials such as lithium niobate exhibit similar properties. A photodiode made from layers of gallium aluminium arsenide can trap photons under the control of an applied potential. The device, called an S-SEED (Symmetric Self Electro-optic Effect Device) acts as an optical switch.

Optical amplifiers have been constructed at BT's Martlesham Laboratories out of erbium-doped glass and a pump laser which will amplify light pulses without applied potentials. They have worked with pulse rates of nearly 40 Gbps.

Magnetic discs can deliver data at around 3 Mbytes/second. Optical discs with multiple tracks read out in parallel should be able to deliver at hundreds of Megabytes per second. A new type of memory called a Page Oriented Holographic Memory (POHM) may provide appropriate storage densities and speeds. An area one millimetre square has a capacity of about 1 Mbit. Readout rates of over 1000 Mbytes/second should be possible.

COMPUTERS – PEN

Pen Computers were introduced in 1992 but large sales were not forthcoming. The Momenta Corporation filed for bankrupcy in 1992 having used up its $40 million capital. Its Pen Computer was too large and failed to recognize the handwriting of some users. The IBM Thinkpad 700T sold a few hundred units and Dataquest a forecasting company reduced its 1992 sales forecast from 300,000 to 77,000. The task of recognizing any persons script writing is not an easy one.

In spite of the lack of demand a new machine was introduced by Amstrad in March 1993 which is about the size of a small book. Data entry is by a pen and it has no keyboard. The machine sells for £299.

COMPUTERS – SUPER-COMPUTERS

A 1987 personal computer was more powerful than a scientific or business computer of 1960. Workstations are powerful multi-facility personal computers for modelling, design purposes, and image processing. The increased power of minisuper-computers, and supercomputers was enabled by the introduction of vector and parallel processing designed to solve complex scientific and engineering problems.

A vector in this context is simply an array of numbers processible en masse at high speed by appropriate algorithms. An algorithm is a prescribed set of rules. In a vector processing machine, each register in an array or matrix of registers stores a number. Vector processing speeds up executing mathematical calculations on long strings of numbers with a single instruction reducing overheads and time. A "pipelining" technique is used whereby several instructions are in various stages of execution at the same time.

For example the Titan minisupercomputer, introduced by Ardent (Sunnyvale CA.) early in 1988, uses 256 32-bit registers. Words are 64 bits wide. It moves data about at 256 Mbytes/second. Such a machine is much less powerful than a supercomputer but will work at up to 10 megaflops at a low price of $13,000 per megaflop (a Cray X-MP supercomputer moves data at over 3 Gbytes/second).

Vector processing with pipelining is a form of synchronous parallel processing. But in 1990 the word "parallel" seems to be mainly associated with Single Instruction Multiple Datastream (SIMD) schemes where a central unit controls multiple interconnected processors. The next stage of development is likely to be the provision of autonomous processors.

Massively Parallel Processor (MPP) is a computer architecture based on thousands of microprocessors instead of the more usual arrangement of up to 16 processors. The results are likely to produce processing power at least 100 times greater than at present. In late 1992 the Japanese NEC SX-3 computer using gallium arsenide chips operated at 20 Gigaflops. MPP also appears to be the policy adopted by

United States manufacturers who are confident of getting their MPPs to run at teraflop speeds.

See also COMPUTERS – NEURAL NETWORKS, and COMPUTERS – OPTICAL.

COMSAT
Communications Satellite Corporation.

CONCENTRATOR
Generic name for devices which organize the transport of data in two or more circuits within a single telecommunications channel without mutual interference.

CONCURRENT
Software which can perform two or more tasks simultaneously.

CONFIG.SYS
A file that runs automatically when a PC is turned on. It contains details of the configuration of the system, as inserted by the user.

CONFIGURATION
A particular grouping of hardware/software elements designed to meet a particular requirement.

CONSTANT BIT RATE (CBR)
Data, such as audio and video data, which must be transmitted at a constant rate through a data transmission system, because its nature demands a constant rate of reception for proper interpretation.

CONSUMER'S ELECTRONIC BUS STANDARD (CEBUS)
See under HOMES – BUSSES.

CONTENTION
A condition on a communication channel or in a peripheral device when two or more stations try to transmit at the same time, or when access to a resource is simultaneously required by two or more users.

COORDINATE INDEXING
See INDEXING – COORDINATE INDEXING.

COPYRIGHT
Copyright protection goes back to Queen Anne's Statute to protect the rights of book authors in England, introduced following pressure from the Stationer's Company in 1710. Similar laws were enacted in many countries according to the local background – whether based on Roman or Anglo-Saxon tradition. International agreement came with the Berne Convention of 1886.

Since then there have been many changes, notably at the Universal Copyright Convention, Geneva, 1952, and the Paris 1971 revisions taking special account of the needs of developing countries.

A copyright subsists in an "original work of authorship fixed in any tangible medium of expression" (US Copyright Act 1976), extending for the life of the author, usually plus 50 years, the same term as in the UK.

Items subject to copyright include:-

Text	Exclusive rights
Graphics	Copyright when fixed in a medium
Software	Source and object code usually covered by program's copyright
Music	Composer, publisher, recording Company, and musician have rights over a recorded program
Film	Every frame copyright.

Areas of abuse for a number of products include:-

Books	Photocopying, translating, reprinting
Journals	Photocopying
Computer programs	Copying, cloning, translating
Machine readable data	Copying of Citation records, abstracts, full text articles, CD-ROM data & software copying
Cassettes	Duplication for sale
Trademarks/patents	Counterfeiting, copying.

Copyright protection in the US extends to collective works – that is where a number of independent works are assembled into a collective whole. This is thought to cover full text databases such as Lexis even although this database is a compilation of public domain material. If this kind of information is, in fact, protected, databases containing the full text of articles not in the public domain contributed by separate authors, would also seem likely to be covered.

Two documents proposing reforms were published in the UK – the Whitford Report (Anon, 1977) and the 1981 "Green Paper" (Anon, 1981). Whitford was in favour of blanket licensing for photocopying whereby an organization like the US Copyright Clearance Centre (CCC) would collect royalties and distribute the proceeds to publishers with no exceptions as are now provided for research purposes. But the Green Paper proposed that the exceptions should be retained "with some tightening to control abuse". Neither the British Library nor the Publishers were happy with the Green Paper, the publishers considering that the approach to photocopying was inconclusive.

The UK Copyright, Designs, and Patent Act 1988, became law on August 1st 1989, replacing the out-dated 1956 Act.

The 1972 Williams & Wilkins v. United States case is a copyright landmark. The US Court of Claims commissioner recommended that a publisher, Williams & Wilkins, was entitled to compensation for the photocopying of its journal articles by the National Library of Medicine (NLM). In 1970, NLM handled 120,000 photocopying requests. 18 months later, in a 4 to 3 decision, the Court rejected the commissioner's recommendation, finding no evidence of economic harm to Williams & Wilkins. This decision was upheld by an equally divided Supreme Court in 1975.

One consequence of this decision was a re-defined and formalizing of the manner and extent of photocopying in libraries, introduced in the US 1976 Copyright Act. In 1978 the Copyright Clearance Centre (CCC) was set up to handle royalties accruing from library photocopying in excess of the permitted quantity. Journals print the royalty due on the title page of each article. The CCC soon ran into difficulties because the royalties collected did not cover the processing costs. However things improved in 1980 when royalty collection increased to $300,000 compared with £57,000 in 1978.

COPYRIGHT – FAIR USE

In many countries provision is made for taking a copy of a journal article for "research or private study" which is considered to be "fair use". Section 7 of the UK 1956 Copyright Act, for example, says this may be done provided that the person taking the copy signs a declaration that the copy is for this purpose only.

The UK Society of Authors and Publishers suggest that re-publishing of an extract, or multiple extracts of a work not exceeding 10% of the length of the work, might not infringe copyright. If this be so then the re-publishing of short abstracts or bibliographic references certainly would not infringe.

Fair use continues under the 1988 Act with a tightening up of certain aspects of photocopying in libraries such as "one copy of the same article per person" and "allowing photocopying of no more than a reasonable portion of a book". In view of the difficulty of policing self-service photocopying machines to be found in all libraries these points seem unrealistic. Fair use in electronic media is discussed under COPYRIGHT – "OTHER MEDIA".

In a 1992 copyright case a scientist within Texaco had been routinely photocopying articles from a particular journal (Journal of Catalysis, published by Academic Press) for personal retention and use as part of his duties as a research scientist. A question was raised as to whether R&D scientists can, in general, routinely photocopy articles of interest to them and keep them in a personal file if they work in a commercial company.

The Court concluded that such photocopying was not "fair use" and that Texaco was guilty of copyright infringement. The reasoning centred largely on two arguments, namely that;-

(1) Texaco was a company which is making profits, and therefore that this weakened the "fair use" doctrine, which is strongest when the copying is intended for research and private study in the not-for-profit sector.

(2) there were clear alternative ways in which Texaco could have provided the extra copies to its scientists, such as ordering more copies of the original journal, or ordering phototocopies from a Copyright Clearance Centre registered organization, which would charge higher sums but which would pass on a portion of those sums to the copyright owner.

The case will go to an appeals court.

COPYRIGHT – "OTHER MEDIA"

The advent of technology enabling text and images to be electronically created, easily reproduced, and then copied with a quality quite closely approaching the original, introduces many new copyright problems.

Emerging problems became evident in the seventies. Warnings were officially promulgated when the list of exclusive rights was extended in a 1980 amendment to the US 1976 Copyright Act. Following a description of "derivative works" the following phrase was added "...or any other form in which a work may be recast, transformed, or adapted".

This is intended to extend protection from the print-on-paper medium to any form of media – notably current and future media enabled by new technology. There have been a number of image-related examples illustrating the point.

For example *the Sporting News* wanted to purchase the rights to the cards showing football players owned by the Topps Company. They wanted to publish a CD-ROM about football. This would involve negotiations with up to 1000 player's lawyers so the idea was abandoned; project viability required a royalty not exceeding 0.15%. At a recent Multimedia and CD-ROM conference exhibitors claimed they were put on notice by the American Society of Composers, Authors, and Publishers (ASCAP) that "spotters" would be at the show listening for copyrighted music in multimedia presentations.

In June 1990 a judge found in favour of Lotus against the *VP Paperback Planner* because of similarity between a Paperback and the *Lotus 1-2-3* spreadsheet interface.

In 1-2-3 the choice, structure, and presentation on the screen were found to be original and non-obvious and therefore copyrightable. VP-Planner had been deliberately copied from 1-2-3.

In March 1991 there was some further support for the idea that "look and feel" could be copyrightable in the well publicized case of Apple versus Microsoft and Hewlett-Packard. These companies claimed that Apple's iconic interface infringed Xerox's copyright covering, for instance, features in the Star machine which caused a sensation in the late seventies.

A judge gave Apple permission to pursue its copyright suit, considering that there was no evidence of Apple's infringement of Xerox's "look and feel" copyright. In regard to Apple's claim that Microsoft and Hewlett Packard were infringing Apple's own look and feel copyright, the judge obviously thought that this was too wide a concept. His permission to allow Apple to proceed was based on the point that there could be specific features of the two company's software which infringed.

In June 1991 there was a case of copyright infringement which was so evidently blatant that arrests in the United States followed an investigation. Those arrested were employed by a number of Taiwanese companies making or using copies of Nintendo's chips for computer games.

There is a quite a different aspect which affects the earnings of museums and art galleries. How can museums and art galleries earn revenue by selling reproduction rights for multimedia products containing thousands of images without hampering the market? They currently earn up to $500 per picture for allowing reproduction in commercial publications. These kinds of prices per image applied to multimedia would encourage infringement.

In 1991 an informal meeting between several major museums was held and a "Model Agreement" was proposed to cover conditions of use and royalty payments for multimedia usage.

A CEC draft directive concerning database copyright was issued in 1992. It defines a database as a literary work which raises questions about whether DOWNLOADING is an infringement or fair dealing. It appears that the downloading of "insubstantial parts" (whatever that is) for commercial or private use will not be an infringement.

The draft was issued partly to resolve ambiguities about the definition and to take care of pirating possibilities. The definition of a database used by the EC makes it clear that databases will be copyrightable just as Literary Works are copyrightable. Ambiguities embodying a number of definitions which suggested that a database might be a cable program, for instance, have now been removed. Other items in the draft proposal have not satisfied the information community, with whom, it is suggested, there were inadequate consultations.

COUNTER

A circuit which generates a pulse after receiving n input pulses. Thus a counter can also be an exact time Divider – if a decade counter is triggered once per second it will emit an output pulse once every ten seconds. Counters are used in digital watches and other timers to divide down from some accurate master oscillator, sometimes crystal controlled to ensure stability. The sub-divided impulses are equally accurate. A counter often consists of a string of flip-flops each of which must be triggered successively before the last generates an output pulse.

CP/M

Control Program Monitor, the most widely used microcomputer early operating system. It was developed by Gary Kidall of Digital Research in 1975. A large number of versions of it have been written. CP/M 80 1.4 was well used for 8 bit microcomputers but was then outdated by other versions including CP/M 86 for 16 bit machines (which was somewhat less successful), and a multi-user version called MP/M.

CP/NET

Control Programme for Networks.

Cps

Characters per second.

CPU

Central Processing Unit.

CR

Carriage Return.

CRASH

A serious computer malfunction such as a disc failure, which may result in the loss of programs and/or data.

CRC

1. Communication Research Centre.
2. CYCLIC REDUNDANCY CHECK.

CROSS ASSEMBLER

A Cross-Assembler is a program which translates an assembly language program written for one type of microcomputer into a machine code for another computer.

CROSS-BAR SWITCH

A device which can select and transfer data from multiple sources to multiple destinations. For example the 74AS8840 can switch from 4 up to 64-bits of data in a single cycle.

CRT

Cathode Ray Tube.

CS

1. Circuit Switched.
2. Chip Select.

CSMA/CD

CARRIER SENSE MULTIPLE ACCESS/COLLISION DETECTION.

A method of packet transmission used in LANs where a station checks the channel before sending. If it is in use it tries again after a delay. Every station checks passing packets, only capturing those addressed to it. In the event of a collision, both stations re-transmit after a delay.

CUG

Closed User Group.

C&W

Cable & Wireless.

CYCLIC REDUNDANCY CHECK (CRC)

A method of error correction consisting of extra numbers added at the end of a block. It provides additional information about the numbers within the block so that errors may be detected.

CYMK

The "primary" colours – Cyan, Yellow, Magenta and Key (Black) – used in colour printing.

D

D/AC
Digital/Analogue Convertor.

DAISY WHEEL PRINTER
A type of impact printer printing-head comprising a rotating spoked wheel with an embossed character at the end of each spoke. When printing, the required spoke is positioned over the paper and pressed against it through an ink ribbon.

DARC
Description, Acquisition, Retrieval, Conception.

DAT
Digital Audio Tape.

DATA
Plural of Datum.
1. Symbols assigned a meaning in order to convey "information".
2. Data in a message which may be used to form images, electronic mail, facsimile messages, etc.

DATA BASE
See under DATABASE.

DATA BROADCASTING
Data broadcasting is the sending of data to many points simultaneously where return transmission is not required. Its great advantage is that an unlimited number of receiving stations can be set up without any increase in transmission costs per station. Data broadcasting may be carried out by using a subcarrier on a radio broadcasting station's system, by using spare lines for sending bursts of data on broadcast television TELETEXT channels, or over a SATELLITE link.

When television is used, messages may be delivered via a teletext system. Data is sent on TV frame lines which are not occupied by TV signals – as in teletext services such as (in the UK) Ceefax and Oracle, the US Viewtron, the French Antiope/Didon, the German Bildschirmtext, and the Japanese Captains (See also VIDEOTEX). The receiver is inexpensive

– a box which is, in effect, a modified TV receiver. A standard teletext TV receiver costs somewhat more than a standard TV receiver. See also VIDEOTEX – TELETEXT.

DATA BROADCASTING – SATELLITE
A geostationary satellite picks up broadcast signals from an earth station and then retransmits them back to earth. The signal is powerful enough for it to be received direct (by the consumer) by means of a domestic dish aerial fixed to the roof (or in the garden) measuring as little as 90cm in diameter.

British Aerospace, one of the six holders of a Special Service Satellite Operator's licence issued under the UK 1988 deregulatory rules, offer a data service with receiving equipment operating at 64 Kbps, or at 2 Mbps.

The cost of a complete service at the 64 Kbps rate, assuming 50 receiving stations and 300 Mbits of data daily, would be £1650 a year per station. This works out at about 24p per 200 Kbit page. At the 2Mbps rate the cost would be about 57p per page. However for 10 times as much data the cost becomes 4.7p and 5.8p per page respectively. This is in sight of the costs of sending information by post.

Aircall Teletext, operating as a data service-supplier using spare lines on IBA TV channels, will be offering a new service via satellite which may well bring page prices down to postal levels for a more reasonable volume of data. The method will be similar to the British Aerospace system just described, but will use simpler receivers providing the same error rates as in the BA system.

The maximum data rate theoretically possible over the PSTN is about 30 Kbps. During the last few years rates have gone up from the usual 2400 bps to 9600 bps which seemed to be about the maximum possible. In the last year or two this been increased to around 20 Kbps. At this speed the PSTN could form a land-link to the transmitter in a data broadcasting system.

DATA BROADCASTING – TELETEXT
Data Broadcasting self-evidently means a "point-to-multipoint" data delivery service

with no return path from recipient to originator. One of the parts of the UK 1984 Cable & Broadcasting Act authorised the BBC and the IBA (commercial TV) to provide "subscriber to group teletext".

Teletext became widely established during the eighties in the UK when the add-on cost of the teletext components in a TV receiver dropped with the falling cost of chip-based electronics, and because there were no out-of-pocket costs to the viewer for the service.

The BBC have been offering their "Datacast" service for some time by transmitting client's data sent to their TV centre by land-line, over a TV channel. The data transmission rate of teletext signals is about 7 Mbps – but transmission occurs in a series of bursts when the spare lines unoccupied by TV signals recur in every frame.

Some of the spare lines are occupied by teletext data. Rows of teletext characters on the screen are controlled by these data bursts. Because each 7 Mbps burst only lasts for a fraction of a second, the total number of bits per second is much lower – less than 20 Kbps in fact. Teletext rows 30 and 31, unoccupied by either TV or teletext signals, are available for data broadcasting.

The duration of a TV 625 line signal, the number of lines which are available in each frame, and the method used for encoding bits into a TV line is such that a maximum of 19.2 Kbits may be sent each second.

Datacast runs at 12 Kbps at a charge of 3.8p per Kbit, so the BBC's charge for a list containing 500 words (say 3000 8-bit characters) would be about £1. However if that cost was recovered from 100 users each would pay only 1p. A bit-mapped page of data containing text and graphics compressed to 200 Kbits (a fairly typical figure) would cost about £7.60. For larger volumes of data transmitted at night – say 300 Mbits per night (about 4.4 hours of transmission time at 19.2 Kbps) – when special rates apply, the cost would fall to about one tenth of this – 76p.

Datacast is used in the UK among other purposes for transmitting racing data to 800 betting shops by Coral Racing, for sending data to Post Offices for display on TV sets presented to a general public languishing in queues for PO services, by the Financial Times services for the display of financial data at a number of places, and by the Stock Exchange

("Market Eye" service).

Another variation is offered by Data Broadcast Services who are marketing a "Faxcast" service over a system provided by Aircall Teletex using spare lines in ITV channel 3, "Oracle style", at up to 1200 bits per second.

In the BBC's Datacast service, client's data is usually received via a modem and leased line and is appropriately added to the broadcast video signal. Reception is on receivers with special decoders.

It is expected that when the UK TV Channel 5 is introduced more sophisticated use of the allocated spectrum will include a much greater data broadcasting capacity for teletext data.

DATA CAPTURE
The collection of data, usually with a view to storage and "information" access.

DATA COMMUNICATION EQUIPMENT (DCE)
The data network side of a telecoms interface, usually a modem. See also DATA TERMINAL EQUIPMENT.

DATA COMPRESSION
See COMPRESSION.

DATA PROTECTION ACT
See PRIVACY.

DATA REDUCTION
See COMPRESSION.

DATA TERMINAL EQUIPMENT (DTE)
The user's side of a data network interface such as a computer terminal, teleprinter, or office workstation. See also DATA COMMUNICATION EQUIPMENT.

DATA TRANSMISSION
The transmission of data along a telecommunications channel.

For the first hundred years or so of electrical communication systems, speech was conveyed along wires as an *analogue* signal – as a voltage from a microphone varying in proportion to the applied sound pressure level.

Analogue signals which fluctuate in proportion to the information which they carry become distorted and weaker during transmission. The amplifiers used generate "noise" heard as a hiss. If several amplifiers (called "repeaters"), have to be used on a long cable, the hiss may become louder than the signals.

Analogue signals may be digitized by deriving groups of on-off impulses from the fluctuations to form a Code. These impulses are unaffected by distortion and they can be regenerated by an electronic circuit when they become weak without the addition of much noise. Moreover digital signals can be stored in, or processed by, computers or other digital equipment.

A bandwidth penalty is paid for digitization (which does not, however, offset the benefits). This is a second reason for operating towards the upper part of the frequency spectrum – the pulses in the code replacing the analogue information contain high frequency components. The channel needed for their proper reproduction requires a much wider bandwidth than is required for analogue signals.

In 1937 Alec Reeves invented Pulse Code Modulation (PCM). In British Patent 535960 (A.H. Reeves, 1939) he specified a method of digitizing analogue waveforms in great detail.

A smooth analogue waveform is sampled by an electronic device at fixed intervals to determine its height. This "quantization" process changes it into a "staircase" appearance, each step representing a value to be transmitted. There must be at least two samples of the highest frequency component in one cycle of the waveform. In this new waveform, the numerical value of each step is transmitted as a code of binary impulses. If there are, say 8 levels, each may be represented by a 4-bit code, so if the waveform is sampled 10 times per second, 40 bits per second will be transmitted.

The greater the number of levels the larger the number of bits per second transmitted. 256 levels (8 bits) is sufficient to make the "staircase" waveform resemble the original waveform well enough for almost perfect reproduction.

If an on-off signalling element (Binary Signalling) is transmitted once per second the signalling rate is said to be one *baud*. Since one baud carries one bit of data, a rate of, say, 2400 Bauds corresponds to a bit rate of 2400 bits per second (bps). However data may be added to

a signalling element – for example by arranging for it to be transmitted as any one of four different known voltages which could represent four different symbols.

This added data amounts to $\log_2 x\ 4 = 2$ bits so if the signalling rate remains at 1 Baud, the bit rate is now two 2 bps – in other words the Data Rate has been doubled.

In practice a variety of methods which are much more ingenious than this simple example are used to increase the bit rate without increasing the signalling rate but they all come against the problem of Noise – present in all electrical circuits.

A receiver called upon to read added detail in the presence of noise faces a harder task than when called upon simply to distinguish between an "on" pulse and an "off" pulse. The Signal to Noise Ratio plays a crucial role in SHANNON's work. The lower the ratio the higher the probability of errors. There is a limit to the amount by which the signal power can be increased and the noise level decreased.

Once in digital format, the data can be handled like any other data transmitted or processed by a computer. This enormous advantage is partially offset by the far lesser but still considerable disadvantage that the bandwidth required satisfactorily to "transport" the binary data impulses, now representing the data from the analogue waveform, is about ten times wider than before.

DATA TRANSMISSION – ASYNCHRONOUS
A method of transmitting data suited to sending characters spaced at unknown intervals – e.g. when a human is sending direct from a keyboard. Each fixed length byte, normally of 8 bits, is preceded by a single bit going high (e.g. forming a positive pulse) to warn the receiver that an 8 bit byte follows. The receiver clock then counts in 8 data bits. The transmitter concludes with a stop bit going low so that the receiver will know that the next bit going high is a start bit.

DATA TRANSMISSION – SYNCHRONOUS
A method of transmitting and receiving data using synchronized sequences of characters without the need for start and stop bits to define each character. A clock runs continu-

ously at the receiver at a rate close to the speed of a clock at the transmitter and is pulled into synchronism by clock-controlled transmitted signal transitions.

If a fixed, known, period of time exists between groups of bits forming characters, for example for an eight bit code, provided transmitter and receiver are synchronized, every ninth bit must be a space.

Since each character is of fixed duration the receiver is able to separate characters by timing circuits. An advantage of synchronous transmission is that larger (variable) data blocks can be used without a framing overhead.

DATABASE

A database is a collection of rapidly accessible structured data.

A database may be used to provide information about a particular subject and may be publicly available and searchable ONLINE – for example via a database bureau. Alternatively a data-base may be self-contained, run on a MICROCOMPUTER, and operated by, or on behalf of, a single person or a small group.

Databases often work as a computerized filing system. In FILES based on paper, information is ordered by a single attribute – thus to find Bloggs in a card file a user thumbs through the ordered "B" cards. However if the user wants to find out how many employees in the company are under 21 in that file, he or she must look at all the cards. A database search will co-ordinate indexed records and respond to multi-aspect questions, assuming the appropriate data is available, such as "what are the names and addresses of the people who are members of the Institute of Information Scientists and live in London?"

Four kinds of computerized systems are in use known as File Management Systems (FMS), Hierarchical Filing Systems (HFS), Relational Database Systems (RDS), and, comparatively recently, Object Oriented Databases (OOD).

FMSs such as the Lotus 1-2-3 add-on Data Manager, or Scimate, are well suited to office use. Scimate enables fast searches to be made of text in records, each describing numbered shelved documents – reports, cuttings, books, etc. The Displayed "hit" records provide enough information to decide whether to get the document from the shelf.

For branching "family-tree-like" applications, HFS or RDS is preferred. For example the paint stored in warehouse bays could be supplied by different Manufacturers who make paint of different Types in a range of Colours. The connections in an HFS enable a response to be obtained from questions like "Which bin contains Dulux high-gloss primrose paint? But for the system to respond to questions like "Which bins contain high-gloss paint made in the UK?", additional "many to many" multiple links and pointers must be added "across the family tree".

An RDS system performs like a hierarchical "many to many" linked file but does it in a more elegant and simpler way. It is arranged as a series of SPREAD-SHEET-like grids with attributes in the cells. This enables logical operations to be performed, the most important of which is perhaps "join" – meaning "joint tables together to form a new table". The rules and operations for relational databases were formulated by Ted Codd in a classic paper.

Later a language called the Structured English Query Language (SQl or "Sequel") was developed at IBM. There is some argument about whether the claims made by some suppliers that their database software is "relational" are true.

Following the management system in Lotus 1-2-3 a number of database software packages suitable for office use appeared. The Ashton Tate db series are probably the best known. Little is known about how widely they are used in offices. This will depend on the paper-to-computer changeover organizing effort and transition time, ease of use, and whether individuals or specialized staff (for instance the information/library staff) do the groundwork.

Object-oriented databases are a considerable step forward in complexity and performance. They allow objects to be manipulated in response to requests concerning their attributes. For example in an OOD a class of objects grouped together might be called "Ships" having the same attributes, each being listed with its various values.

For example data associated with a ship might consist of its destination port, its speed, its position and so on. A message can be sent to a ship object containing a question such as "calculate the time of arrival at the next port from the known position, heading and speed". The means of performing this calculation and a whole range of similar calculations is provided by a special program.

This description of a very basic OOD operation shows that the database can deal with complex relationships between objects and provide answers derived from active data unlike the previous databases described which are simply a deposit of passive data. See also BLOB.

DATABASES – FULL TEXT SEARCHING

Developments in technology have enabled database suppliers and host computer bureaux to offer full text searching of articles, books, newspaper reports etc. In many cases every word is searchable, so the text is self-indexed.

In cases where the text is structured, some organizations, such as the American Chemical Society and the International Research Communications (IRCS) System, divide it into individually searchable fields -for example "Introduction", "Materials and Methods", and "Results". This helps to reduce the retrieval of irrelevant parts ("false drops") of the text. WESTLAW, a US legal full text database, adds indexing terms in the form of separately searchable keywords and summary notes.

The full text of every article has been "indexed" to some degree by its author, and to some degree by database creators when they select articles for inclusion according to their coverage definition e.g. "Chemistry" "Tropical Medicine" or "Ornithology". Thus a person searching in a full text online database covering Business Journals using the words ECONOMIC INDICATOR/ is much more likely to find a number of articles which have some relevance than he would find in, say, the IRCS medical article database.

However it seems unlikely that the principles of information retrieval appertaining to the searching of article indexing terms can be readily applied when searching the full text of an article.

The retrieval performance of full text databases has been reviewed by Tenopir who quotes from an investigator who sums up the full-text searching situation:- "all the problems of lack of vocabulary control and bulk which might be anticipated are encountered with the obvious advantage of speed and completeness as tradeoffs".

It would be expensive for full-text database suppliers to introduce some form of comprehensive indexing in order to reduce user's expenditure on expensive computer time, and suppliers emphasize the need to adopt practices which are different from those applied to indexed material. Proximity indicators are an important aid. In many systems searchers can specify that search words should be spaced apart by n or not more than n words.

For example the phrases "banks have decided to increase their interest rates", "the government has decided that bank interest rates...", "Barclays Bank, unlike other banks, has decided to maintain its interest rate at 12.5%" occurring in articles, would be retrieved by the question BANK/ (8) RATE/ meaning "find all articles in which the words BANK/ and RATE/ occur separated by up to 8 words". The third phrase would not be retrieved.

Other necessary precautions are to anticipate the synonym problem in full text and restrict the search to specific fields when they are available.

Tenopir concludes that full-text searching is potentially a good answer to document retrieval problems. There is a market for full text databases with numbers of satisfied users prepared to accept the disadvantages. A major disadvantage at present, as with many other methods, is the absence of retrieval of the graphics which come with the original text.

DATABASES – TERM SEARCHING

The results of a search for information contained in one or more data items somewhere within a collection of such items, depends on the contents of the collection, on the indexing and search facilities that are provided, and on the way the searcher uses the system. An "item" may be a letter, a product data sheet, a journal article, an electronically stored report, etc., or a SURROGATE for any of these items.

The searcher can exercise some control over the results by posing a "broad", or "narrow" question, or a question somewhere between these extremes. Most of the relatively small number of items retrieved from a narrow question will be of interest but a number of interesting items within the collection outside the range of the question will be missed. On the other hand nearly all the items of interest in the collection will be retrieved by a broad question but they will be accompanied by many of marginal or zero interest ("noise").

This is just another way of expressing the RECALL/PRECISION relationship – even more important for computer-based information systems because of the huge amount of information which can be searched, the tendency in some systems to include everything in case somebody might want it, and the potentially huge amount of unwanted information ("noise") which may be communicated to the user.

When the searcher ends up with a number of information-containing items she/he will be able to rank-order them (in some cases the system itself may do this) by "importance", "relevance" or useful "interest" to her/him. First will come the item containing the "best" information, and last will be an item containing very little or perhaps no useful information.

When assessing the results of a broad-question search, the searcher will have to decide on a point of cut-off below which he believes that time spent in reading will be unrewarding.

In personal systems the same principle applies, but the problem is usually less severe because of the small size of the database, the user's intimate knowledge of it, and the fact that if he is both indexer and user the effects of the HUMPTY DUMPTY SYNDROME will be much less severe.

Searching a computer database can be done by batching, or interactively online. Batching means collecting together all the queries from a number of subscribers and putting them on to disc or tape. These data are matched against the data records in a database by a computer "pass". When a match occurs, the matching record or "hit" is stored separately, and hit data records are sorted and printed or run on to floppy discs at the end of the operation and sent to subscribers.

If a question is badly formulated a user will have to change it, have it re-inputted, and await the results from the next occasion the database is passed through the computer to observe the effectiveness of the change.

In interactive online searching, a user sits at a terminal connected to a computer on which a database is mounted, usually on discs. He types queries and the matching process is rapidly carried out, hits being displayed or printed at the terminal. If the results are unsatisfactory the query may be re-formulated, perhaps more narrowly, the user tries again, and so on until he or she gets it right. Matching usually involves comparing "strings".

A string is a sequence of characters and spaces. Thus COMPUT is a string, and if that term is used as a question all records containing COMPUT (e.g. COMPUTING, COMPUTER, COMPUTERS, etc., will be hits). ELECTRONIC MAIL SYSTEM is another string.

It seems unlikely that batch searching will be used much in an office system. Most people will want to get at "paperwork" quickly and expect an almost immediate response in the form of a display of text. The rate of that response will depend upon many factors, but the ones with which we are here concerned are the ways in which the files are organized for ease of searching and the way in which they are indexed. Armstrong and Large's book (1988) is recommended for further reading.

Most computers are still based on Von Neumann architecture. They are designed for arithmetical computation with relatively small amounts of stored data. Applications in text searching require character string comparisons on large amounts of stored data. Most software is still written for Von Neumann machines.

One way of searching files – collections of textual data – is to arrange for the computer system to search serially through the records for strings matching the query string. Hits, in the form of complete records will be transferred to the user's terminal for viewing, or to his printer if he wants a permanent copy. This involves searching through the complete text of records so very high speeds are essential.

In a database of records containing details about information in documents, documents will usually be represented as surrogates – that is as short summaries or abstracts – so the search will obviously be completed more quickly.

A surrogate must contain the essence of the document. The document may be of a simple kind e.g. a letter for which addressee details may be considered sufficient, or it may be a report whose essence may have to be a brief description of the subject – its title, keywords or an abstract. The document will have been indexed.

If the title only is used then that is the index – an index which won't work unless its originator has given some thought to it or it has been supplemented by an indexer. Thus the words "The wiring of Britain" would be unhelpful in a title-based retrieval system for a searcher looking for information about cable television.

A "hit", in the case of searching surrogates, will be a display of the hit surrogate so that the viewer can decide whether to get the whole document. Obviously an arrangement must be made for each record in the searchable surrogate collection to "point" to the associated complete document containing the wanted information. The "pointer" might be to a location in computer storage, or it might be a code indicating the location of a paper document.

Until quite recently, serial searching of full text online has been unacceptably slow, and searching of suitably arranged surrogate records has usually been used. The inverted file and the multilist or threaded-list file arethe most widely used out of several schemes for directory searching which have been developed for medium to large databases.

The INVERTED FILE seems to have gained widest acceptance. It is a directory to the keys used in records. A key is simply a search term such as a word, an author's name, a chemical formula etc. This idea has been mentioned before – peek-a-boo cards are an invertèd file system.

For example a database might comprise a series of records describing company reports. Each record might be a surrogate with report titles and added keywords, author, data, and a shelf number indicating whether the print-on-paper report itself is kept.

In an inverted file system it is the smaller directory of keys which is searched by the computer, not the relatively large totality of surrogate text in records (or the full text in systems where each record contains the complete document). Inverted files are often searched using Boolean expressions – for instance in "Find records containing ELECTRONIC MAIL and MICROCOMPUTER" the machine has to identify the addresses of records containing both keys in a keyword list in order to locate hit records.

The keys will be selected according to certain rules – for example there may be a "stop list" of trivial words ("the", "of", etc.,) which are not used as keys.

The number of hits resulting from this directory search can be displayed without the need for the records themselves being retrieved so that the user can quickly re-formulate his question if necessary. The records can, of course, be retrieved as needed because their disc addresses remain stored in computer memory as a result of the search.

Penalties are paid for the convenience and operational speed of an inverted file system in the form of software complexity and storage space. When a new record is added to the record file, information may also be added to the separate key/records address directory (the inverted file). Even if a key is already in the directory, the address of a new record must be added. When that key is used as a search term, the address of the old and the new records will then be identified.

The key directories occupy considerable storage space. Depending on the diversity of the file this space can approach in size that needed for the records themselves. In a batch system, a collection of new records are added periodically and the necessary re-organization process for that collection is carried out at some convenient time. Until that time, use of the new records is denied to users.

If the system is simultaneously useable for information retrieval and record up-dating the software and power of the system must be capable of coping with both without much degradation of performance.

DATAGRAM
A self-contained package of data sent independently of other packages.

dB
DECIBEL.

DBMS
Data Base Management System.

DBS
DIRECT BROADCASTING SATELLITE.

DCE
Data Communications Equipment.

DCT

DCT
DISCRETE COSINE TRANSFORM.
  See COMPRESSION.

DDCMP
Digital Data Communications Message Protocol.

DEA
Data Encryption Algorithm.

DEBUGGING
The detection and correction of program faults.

DEC
DIGITAL EQUIPMENT CORPORATION.

DECIBEL (dB)
A measure of relative magnitude (of power, current, voltage, etc.). The number of decibels equals 10 times the log (to the base 10) of the ratio of the measured power to the reference power level, or 20 times the log of the ratio of the voltage or current to the reference voltage or current level.

DECISION SUPPORT SYSTEMS
See INFORMATION TECHNOLOGY – IN MARKETING.

DECT
DIGITAL EUROPEAN CORDLESS TELE-COMMUNICATION.

DEDICATED LINE
A communications line permanently assigned for specific requirements and not part of a switched network. Also called a private line.

DEFAULT VALUE
A value which is assigned in a program, assumed unless a different specific value is indicated. For example, if the number of lines on a page are not set by an operator using a word processor program, the number of lines will be set to the default value.

DEREGULATION
The general economic benefits which follow from good communications are well known and until recently many governments have considered it appropriate to run the telephone service as a public monopoly.

"Universal Telecommunications" may mean the opportunity for anyone who wants a telephone to be able to have one so long as they can pay the market price for it, or it may mean the opportunity for anyone who wants or needs a telephone to have one with part of the cost paid for by somebody else. Alternatively it may mean that an area, a country, or a continent, has a telecoms system in place able to transport rapidly large volumes of data of any kind to anyone else at the market price, or at an assisted price. It means, in other words, that "a fast broadband data highway" is universally available.

When the telephone system is operated by a monopoly, pricing based on "welfare economics" e.g. some kind of marginal cost pricing is sometimes used; revenues from business lines may be used to subsidize rural lines. One problem has always been who is to decide on the degree of assistance, to whom it shall be given, and what is the reference "market price".

A company which runs a competitive business has to make a profit to survive and normally charges "the market price". The people who pay the price get the product or service; the people who need it but "cannot afford it" do not.

"Compunications" means the functions performed jointly by merged computer and transmission technologies. It was this merging which was a major reason for deregulation in the United States – a trend now being followed in other countries.

AT&T, a monolithic organization, was required to operate, maintain, and improve the US telephone network, a rather leisurely activity (which it did rather well). It was not organized to introduce an appropriate range of computerized fleet-of-foot operations based on state of the art hardware with a life of a few years needed to meet the demands of a rapidly changing market.

Some countries are following the trend relatively quickly, some more slowly, and others hardly at all. The slow movers have a telephone system which provides some kind of a service and are unwilling to rock the boat by provoking powerful vested interests such as telecom suppliers, trade unions, and political opponents who will say that the consequence will be benefits for business but price increases for ordinary telephone users.

The situation we now have in the UK, and to some degree in other European countries, is that conventional terrestrial circuits based on an enormous investment, of necessity requiring much more investment and laboriously introduced changes, are not the only contenders for an improved public telecoms system.

Specialized satellite communications have been introduced quite widely, and television entertainment distributed into homes by Direct Broadcast Satellites has taken off. In the UK at least one million homes are now receiving these services. The cost of two way satellite communications using Very Small Aperture Terminals (VSATs) is falling steadily.

The general economic benefits which follow from good communications are well known. Controversy about achieving them by running telecommunications services as a state-controlled monopoly or as a collection of private competitors with some degree of regulation, has also been well aired.

One author considers that on the whole, privatization has benefitted only a small group of users. It has had little effect on a market with a vast potential; whatever impact that has come about is at the equipment end. OFTEL (the UK regulating agency) is ineffective.

Another attributes the effectiveness of competition in benefitting users, the telecommunications industry, and the economy as a whole in the UK, to OFTEL, providing as examples the range and variety of equipment available, a wide selection of competitive VANs and data services, growing competition from Mercury and cable, and greater benefits from telecom services.

The effect of UK deregulation on the average consumer is hard to assess, partly because whingeing at public services is a national pastime. Opinions of BT reached an all time low in 1987, since when there has been a steady improvement. BT retains at least 95% of the telecoms market.

DEREGULATION – CEC

The CEC uses diplomatic language to describe what it is trying to do – break what it considers to be the restrictive practices stranglehold of the PTTs. Its 1989 Green Paper was "a programme of regulatory change to meet the twin challenges of 1992 and technological development" The CEC's interest is understandable since it estimates that about half the present global value of the "Information business" – about £500 Billion – is in telecoms.

The CEC's major timed targets were an open market for all services, particularly VANs, except voice, telex, and datacoms by end of 1989, and free competition for terminals by end of 1990. Untimed proposals included tariffs to follow costs trends; separation of regulatory and operational activities; definition of "Open provisions" for leased lines, data networks, and ISDN; establishment of a Standards Institute (ETSI); guidelines for competition and a fair market; open PTT procurement.

The Open Network Provision (ONP) concerns the standardization of interfaces so that value added service providers will be able to offer compatible services throughout the Community.

The CEC is having a hard time. It obtained a compromise agreement on VANs in 1992. "Open provisions" have been put off. PTTs can get an extension of their leased line monopoly to 1996 if they can show that their packet-switched network is inadequate.

Exasperated by slow action in freeing terminals, the CEC invoked Article 90 of the Treaty of Rome to force compliance, but an advocate to the European Court of Justice advised that the use of Article 90 should not be allowed. But Article 90, which supposedly allows the Commission to issue directives directly without the laborious process of Community ministerial consultations, does not, in fact, ensure compliance.

France took the Commission to the European Court over an earlier ruling about allowing competition for the supply of PTT terminals. In February 1990, the Advocate General to the Court, whose advice is usually taken, advised it to over-rule the Commission.

This meant that the Commission's attempt to achieve the compliance of all PTTs over terminal competition in one operation would have to be replaced by country-by-country negotiations. It could result in non-uniform policies and substantial delays in implementation.

The CEC had more success following the threat of legal action against a proposal by the CEPT (a PTT club), considered to be anticompetitive, to provide a managed data network. It was abandoned. The CEPT was also forced to abandon a cartel-like plan for fixing leased line tariffs.

A July 1990 press release from Brussels says that its two new directives for open networks and competitive new services "herald the dawn of a new era". The commissioners sounded optimistic, as they always have done, in spite of the great difficulty they have had with the PTTs in trying to get an efficient European network in place if not by 1992, then perhaps by 1995. They say that their new measures will "open up unlimited opportunities for the telecommunications industry, for business users and for the individual consumer".

The new Services Directive has required the force of Article 90 of the Treaty of Rome behind it to ensure action. It had postponed bringing it into effect until agreement had been reached over open networks provision. It requires the PTTs to allow competitive value added telecoms services over their networks throughout the Community. From January 1st 1993 competitors will be able to resell leased line capacity.

The above Services Directive contains various "escape clauses" which will enable reluctant PTT's to drag their feet. For instance countries who claim that their packet-switched data services are insufficiently developed may get an extension so that capacity resale need not be allowed until January 1996.

As already mentioned the EC was dissuaded by a court advocate from invoking Article 90 of the Treaty of Rome to support its directive to the European PTT's to purchase terminals on the open market. The ruling had been opposed by France. The usual procedure was to buy from the home market. Although the matter has been overtaken by events – terminal liberalization has, in fact, taken place – the European Court of Justice has belatedly found in favour of the EC action. The importance of this ruling lies in the establishment of a precedent which the EC will probably use to force through other measures leading to improved European-wide communications which are being slowed up by recalcitrant PTTs.

Uniquely in Europe, the UK has usually been ahead of the CEC in its deregulatory ideas so the effects of CEC activities on UK telecoms are small. The CEC's most recent endeavours are aimed at Satellite Communications.

Although progress has been made since the EC published a Green Paper on telecommunication services in 1987, a number of bottlenecks remain. The commission now envisages four possible options for dealing with the matter.

* Freezing the liberalization process to maintain the status quo.
* Introducing the regulation of tariffs and investments to remove the bottlenecks.
* Liberalizing all voice telephony.
* Opening up voice telephony competitively between states.

The fourth option would probably provide a solution to the most serious bottlenecks.

DEREGULATION – SATELLITES

In the US a new-entrant transatlantic satellite company has to convince the government that its satellite will be in the national interest, must get FCC approval and the approval of INTELSAT (the organization with which it will be competing), must do a deal with a foreign PTT (or in the UK with Mercury), and must show that it has the finance to launch and operate the system.

PanAmSat was launched on Ariane 4, a new generation of launcher, in August 1988. It had to overcome numerous political obstacles before becoming operational as did Orion Network Systems, another contender.

But the UK has altered its stance on satellite regulations which are steadily becoming more liberal. In 1988 it considered applications for specialized satellite licences for point to multipoint services – that is for up-linking data to a satellite without a return path via satellite. Until then only BT, Mercury, and Hull telephone were allowed to operate satellite services. Licences were duly awarded to six Special Service Satellite Operators (SSSOs) – British Aerospace, Electronic Data Systems, Maxwell Satellite Communications, British Satellite Broadcasting, Satellite Information Services, and Uplink.

In November 1989 the UK Department of Trade and Industry (DTI), removed the restrictions on within border operations, allowing SSSOs to broadcast throughout Europe. See also SATELLITES – VERY SMALL APERTURE TERMINALS.

The EC 1990 Green Paper on satellite communications is aimed at deregulation mainly in order to increase demand so that European suppliers can achieve the necessary economies of scale to compete. It points out that such economies can reduce satellite manufacturing costs by up to 40% The US manufacturer Hughes has sold more than 30 standardized satellites, charging up to 33% less than its competitors.

The EC's paper proposed liberalization of the earth segment – that is freedom to operate private terminals in Europe, freedom for users to buy satellite transponders, and freedom for space segment providers to sell or lease capacity. In effect, this removes the PTT's monopoly on satellite communication services.

However in February 1992 John Milman, General Manager of a satellite service company called Brightstar Communications was highly critical of the situation at that time. France Telecom imposes financial penalties on any company wishing to use transportable facilities, Italy and Belgium will not allow them to be used. Austria allows them to be used but charges £600, and Deutsche Bundespost charges 4000 Marks for a licence, and then the client must use a German transponder.

The Paper of November 1990 entitled "Toward Europe-wide systems and services – Green Paper on a common approach in the field of satellite communications in the community" suggested four major requirements:-
* Full liberalization of the earth segment
* Unrestricted access to space segment capacity
* Commercial freedom for space segment providers
* Harmonization to ease the provision of Europe wide services.

The Council of Telecommunication Ministers agreed in November 1991 on the framework to implement these measures. It started preparations leading to draft legal measures expected to be approved in 1993, to be incorporated in national legislation in 1994. Such is the pace of change in this area.

DEREGULATION – UK, UP TO 1990

In the UK, British Telecom was first liberalized and then privatized because, like AT&T, it was over-cumbersome, because it ran the telephone system for its own rather than for its customer's benefit, and because privatization was the political philosophy of the Conservative administration.

The Telecommunications Bill, privatizing British Telecom, became law in 1984. Kenneth Baker, Minister for Industry and Information Technology, addressing the committee considering the Bill in November 1983 said:- "we do not intend to license operators other than BT and Mercury Communications to provide the basic communications service over fixed links during the seven years following this statement".

This arrangement continued for the prescribed seven years so there was plenty of time to consider its effectiveness. Telephone users must connect to BT's or Mercury's public networks and larger subscribers must use lines leased from them for site inter-connection.

Various deficiencies in the arrangements have prompted numerous suggestions for changes. It was concluded that large users should not be allowed by the government to set up their own networks – for instance using microwave communications.

It was suggested that the resale of excess lease line capacity should be licensed, that restrictions on the provision of voice telephone by cable networks and their interconnection with other networks should be removed, that additional public networks should be licensed, and that resale of international private circuits should be permitted.

However these suggestions suffered the embarrassment of dismissing as unfeasible things that the government implemented without waiting for the review at the end of the prescribed seven years. Resale was permitted by OFTEL and three UK personal communication network operators were licensed.

In 1988 the UK's cabinet's Advisory Council on Science and Technology (ACOST) proposed that a very large investment should be made in a National Wideband Fibreoptic network. Next, the White Paper "Broadcasting in the 90s: competition, choice and quality", appeared (November 1988) after two years of deliberation.

It proposed abolishing the Cable Authority which promoted cable, placing Cable under a new Independent Television Commission (ITC), and encouraging TV microwave distribution for television, thus providing a cheaper solution than cable for the "last mile".

Incidentally this type of microwave distribution can be used for interactive information services only with a provision for two-way use.

In December 1988 the "McDonald Report" about the regulatory future was provided by the Department of Trade and Industry (DTI). The DTI was influenced by a report which it had commissioned from PA Consulting and Telecommunications. McDonald rejected the National Fibreoptic Network, estimated to cost £20 billion, for various reasons, but in particular that:- "technology continues to advance very rapidly. The UK might end up locking itself into a sub-optimal technical infrastructure".

Agreeing with the White Paper which encouraged competitive technologies including microwave delivery, McDonald hoped that cable franchise holders would subsequently compete with BT in providing two way services, and believed that BT would install fibre in the local loop anyway whether it was permitted to deliver entertainment TV or not.

In 1988 a report from a House of Commons committee headed by Kenneth Warren, received unanimous support from its members and heavily criticised McDonald. Warren said that the government's refusal to support the fibreoptic network was a golden opportunity missed – a conclusion which appeared to be at odds with its other non-interventionist noises.

DEREGULATION – UK AFTER 1990

What happens when it becomes possible to present a telephone subscriber with alternative services for his or her choice? For most people reliability and cost are the prime requirements. For business and high volume users a careful assessment of the offerings could be well worth while.

Competitive services have undoubtedly been introduced – Mercury competes with BT, there are numerous mobile radio and data network operators, six satellite service providers, and many cable-TV and VAN competitors. But BT retains at least 95% of the telecoms market with little further reduction in sight in the near future.

If connection choices to and from your actual telephone are to become available, not just only long distance choices via whatever local loop exists (which normally means BT),

it seems most unlikely that they will be provided by digging up the road yet again to enable different lines to enter your premises.

More likely alternatives are Cable, if it passes your door, or a microwave link to the nearest point of distribution owned by a competing telephone company. Such a link involves a very small dish with a line-of-sight path to the distribution point. Such a link could carry a number of channels.

There is one place in the UK where subscribers have a choice of long distance calls (reports suggest that the local service would be hard to better), and that is in Hull. Hull is unique in somehow escaping the clutches of the Post Office earlier in this century. A subscriber who starts by dialling a 12 for out-of-Hull calls connects via BT, a 13 via Mercury. They get one bill from Hull.

However the idea of multiple choices both for local connection and long distance could introduce some severe practical problems. Among them are people's inertia if it is difficult to make a change, billing, and telephone numbers. For example what happens to your telephone number, your directory entry, and the ease with which others can be informed of your number should you change to a different local network?

The "7-year review" – a Green Paper (for discussion) – was published in November 1990. Conclusions were published in April 1991. (See previous section). Most of these proposals were adopted in the April 1991 White Paper ("decisions") but there were some notable exceptions. BT's price arrangements were altered, but there was no international pricecap.

The Green and White Papers take a line which confirms unfolding events. A network capable of transporting voice, text, graphics, halftone and colour pictures etc., is laboriously evolving, with the accent on voice communication. The industry obviously believes that voice has plenty of mileage to come – Mobile Cellular Radio has been a huge success.

Cellular Radio is an example of a winner in the network business. It overcame the severe "critical mass" problem which inhibits the widespread adoption by the market at which the network is aimed – business users. These users are the information-conscious section of the public at large.

A new network somehow has to get itself into a "take-off" situation – a situation which has long since been surpassed by the existing telephone system where potential subscribers know that they will be able to talk to a significant fraction of the world's population when they are connected.

The complexity of political, financial, and technical interaction between Cable, Direct Broadcast Satellites, Terrestrial Television, Fibreoptic Networks, Mobile Cellular, Telepoint, Personal Communication Networks, the ISDN etc., is such that it is bound to take years for winners to emerge. So far as voice is concerned, and in spite of the enthusiasm of the industry, it is not at all clear whether new forays into voice will be as successful as Mobile Cellular.

The two major changes were in line with expectations – more alternative telephone services with equal access, and construction of own networks with resale of spare capacity.

Following the White Paper, OFTEL decreed that the cost of access by competitors to BT lines should be calculated on data supplied by BT. In 1990 30% of the revenues of Mercury and Racal was paid to BT as interconnection charges. It was considered that these payments were excessive because they include a component representing BT's historic inefficiency.

In July 1991 OFTEL changed its mind and proposed that BT should not charge its competitors for using its local network until its market share fell below 85% or until one of BT's competitors gets more than 10% of the market. The charges were particularly important at the time because the government was about to sell off its remaining shareholding in BT and connection charges could alter the revenue to be obtained from the sale.

DEREGULATION – UK, ALTERNATIVE SERVICES

There are other possible alternatives – ISDN or its equivalent, or satellite. Assuming you have an average existing local line to an exchange already, then that same line's bandwidth will be adequate for more than one service via the ISDN. The basic ISDN service uses the line for two data (of which one will usually be telephone voice data) and one signalling channel. BT's basic ISDN service, intended for voice and data, is run by BT, so BT would be

required to provide access to a competitor for access to the competitor's services to be possible. (See also ISDN).

Telephone via satellite, requiring of course a two-way link, seems a more distant prospect. A satellite infrastructure to handle a large number of users would first be needed to get the economics right – the typical "chicken or the egg" problem, unless the phone service could ride on an existing DBS entertainment channel which is currently one-way – an unlikely alternative.

Several contenders have emerged who would be well placed to provide alternative services. National utilities such as the Post Office, British Rail, and British Gas possess their own comprehensive telecom networks, or national-wide networks of strips-of-land, or both. Mercury already uses British Rail land for carrying a large portion of its fibreoptic network.

British Rail is a contender for alternative services. British Rail Telecom, a new subsidiary formed in 1990, already possesses a 17,000 KM network of which 2500 KM is optical. It is prepared to spend a further £400 million if it is allowed to provide public services. It enjoys the considerable advantage of enjoying a nationwide network of streets which do not have to be dug up – the railway network with cables alongside. But would it be any better at running telecoms than in running the railways?

The Cable companies find themselves in a more ready-made situation. Cable companies wishing to offer telephone services to non-Cable customers must connect via BT or Mercury at present. Presumably they will be able in future to use their networks, interconnected with the networks of other franchise holders, and complete the "last mile" with a microwave link instead of laying local cable. That is assuming, of course, that they decide to provide two-way service.

Foreign companies now can invest and have invested strongly, BT says that it is disappointing that the government plans to allow free entry to the UK market to foreign monopolies, meaning the Baby Bells, for instance, and that it has no apparent intention of using access to the UK markets as a lever to secure equivalent access to overseas markets for UK companies.

BT has a point – once the ban on foreign

investment was lifted, foreign companies saw the possibilities of entry into the UK telephone market via the cable networks and invested heavily. They now own 90% of the franchises.

If BT is prevented from setting retail prices which reflect efficient use of economies of scale, customers will pay inflated prices for the alleged benefit of market entry by overpriced competitors.

In spite of the government's endorsement of genuine, effective, competition, it is in fact contemplating further and more extensive so-called "managed" competition which is another way of saying that it intends to continue the existing, and introduce new, restrictions and handicaps on BT. With regard to these last remarks BT does not have a point. It should expect some restraints in view of its enormous head-start.

OFTEL's aim should be to create conditions in which efficient new competitors can come into the market. But as things stand, it may be erring in BT's favour. Not only will competitors have to pay BT for using its network, they will also have to pay an access charge to contribute to the losses BT incurs in running its network.

BT faces a deficit in running its local networks. Political pressure is responsible for BT keeping its line rental charges at below costs, so it seems reasonable that competitors should pay a fair share of the deficit. But the procedure by which OFTEL is proposing to calculate this deficit – taking BT's line rental and connection revenue and subtracting its costs – looks doubtful. The costs may be inflated because OFTEL is relying on BT's own methods for allocating costs between its different services.

The resale of excess network capacity and the purchase of it by an entrepreneurial company to form its own network to provide its subscribers with an "automatic best choice" is another idea. Connections would be made via an automatically selected lowest price route and the company would provide a single bill. Problems of calculating the break-even point and the time to achieve it in order to justify the initial investment suggest that such a venture should not be undertaken by the faint-hearted.

In one respect BT's life may be eased – other telecom companies may be required to shoulder a part of its social burden. If the profits of BT's business services are appreciably reduced by the requirement that it must provide rural services at a loss, then competitors should be required to take on part of that burden or BT should be compensated in some other way. BT will not be allowed to put up local prices in order to reduce its tariffs for long distance.

Mercury has had a hard time versus BT, and it appears as if the path of new entrants may be easier. It has been suggested that a new entrant is most likely to attack the same market – in other words attempt to cream off the most lucrative business telecoms.

Two new companies are poised to enter the newly-deregulated UK telecommunications market to challenge British Telecom and Mercury Communications, the existing long-distance operators.

British Waterways, the public utility which runs the UK canal system, has linked up with privately-owned US Sprint, the third-largest US long-distance telecoms carrier, with a view to providing an alternative long-distance network in the UK.

The newly privatized electricity supply industry is also considering entering both the long-distance and local telecoms markets. Recently, the chairmen of the twelve regional electricity companies and the National Grid Company discussed forming a joint-venture to apply for licences.

Both moves were prompted by the government White Paper which opened the £10 billion-a-year telecommunications market to competition and paved the way for any company to apply for licences to supply telecommunications services.

Ionica, a private UK group, and US-based Millicom want to put telephone aerials on the roofs of homes and use radio signals rather than copper wire to transmit phone calls to and from exchanges. They believe this will be cheaper and faster than digging up the roads to lay cables.

British Aerospace Communications and Alpha Lyracom, a private US group, have been awarded international satellite licences. They plan to provide businesses with private networks by installing dishes on office roofs and bouncing the signal off satellites.

BAe has been granted satellite licences in France and Germany and is part of a multinational consortium that plans to build the $500 million Orion satellite system in 1995. Alpha Lyracom owns the Pan American satellite and has licences in the US, France and Germany.

Mercury, Hong Kong's Hutchison Telecom and Unitel, a consortium including US West – have been licensed to form personal communications networks, a rival type of service. Both Vodafone and Unitel have asked the government for licences to provide fixed services to customers.

DEREGULATION – UNITED STATES

Competitive telecoms has been in place longer in the United States than anywhere else. A number of regional "Baby Bell" regional telephone companies were formed out of AT&T. According to Judge Greene, who conducted the anti-trust trial, with regard to price, innovation, quality, and broadening of the industry's base – divestiture is fulfilling its promise. The cost of both local and long distance service is down. Hundreds of new businesses have sprung up. MCI, US Sprint, and others, have not gone under.

But Greene has also been quoted as saying that the Baby Bell's behaviour does not inspire confidence and that, should they be permitted to enter other lines of business, they would treat competitors in an even-handed manner. Indeed one might ask "why should they?"

The Consumer Federation of America translates Greene's remarks into "a complete slam-dunk of the regional holding companies which have done everything errant monopolies would do. Five years after divestiture have the goals been attained? On balance the answer seems to be "yes" notwithstanding a few twists and turns on the way".

However workers in the industry take a poor view of the situation. They argue that the policy has led to increases in rates for individual consumers and small businesses and a poorer quality of service. When asked who benefitted first from the change in a random sampling of 1062 people from the Canadian telephone industry workforce, 1% said themselves, 82% the company, 14% business customers, and 4% individual customers.

Another observer is rather disillusioned about the whole business. The traditional model of public service monopoly has never worked very well in any country. On the other hand the competition that has been permitted in the United States to date is extremely limited and far from sufficient to seriously entertain the possibility of justifying deregulation in reality. The era of so-called competitive "deregulation" in the United States has involved more detailed regulation than ever was applied in the period of regulated monopoly.

One outcome of deregulation is to highlight an activity called "Slamming" where subscribers are switched to a particular service without their consent. In that country subscribers can tell the local telephone company which long distance telephone company they want to use. There is supposed to be no local loop choice since that is provided by the local phone company monopoly. However local loop "Bypassing" – for instance by microwave links – seems to be a national activity.

Some attempts are made to counteract the "little old lady in the Shetlands losing her telephone argument" with "reassurances by recounting the American experience". Since the breakup of the huge AT&T network into Baby Bells, it has been claimed that many consumers have enthusiastically embraced the freedom to shop around for a carrier. Prices for long distance calls – a market led by AT&T (65%), MCI (16%), and Sprint (10%) – have fallen.

In July 1991 Judge Harold Greene, who supervised the break up of AT&T, allowed Bellcos to enter the US information services industry. However Greene said that this might result in an undue concentration of information sources and he stopped the ruling coming into effect until it had been reviewed by an appeal court.

In 1992, the Senate ended three days of debate by voting 71-24 in favour of lifting the manufacturing restrictions on the Bellcos, decided upon at the time of the AT&T divestiture. The bill was introduced in January by Sen. Ernest Hollings, who proposed to let the Bells design, develop and manufacture telecommunications equipment.

This is as far as any such legislation has got in numerous attempts to reduce the long distance, information-content and manufacturing restrictions on the Bells.

DES

Data Encryption Standard. A transformation adopted by the US Government for the protection of data.

DESCRIPTOR
Synonym for TERM.

DESKTOP PUBLISHING
A system for preparing pages ready for publishing on inexpensive equipment.

As for many other microcomputer-based enterprises, the ancestor of desktop publishing systems was the Xerox Star machine with its Smalltalk software – demonstrated at the Palo Alto Research Centre (PARC) in 1978 with page printing on a laser printer.

Many of the ideas from the Star were incorporated into the Apple Lisa machine which was offered for sale in January 1983 at $12,000. However desktop publishing did not advance until the laser printer became commercially available when Apple introduced the Macintosh with its Desktop Manager, WYSIWYG interface, and laser printer.

The idea of using the Mac for desktop publishing seems to have been started by an article by Terry Ulick in 1985 in *Professional and Corporate Publishing*. Ulick suggested the

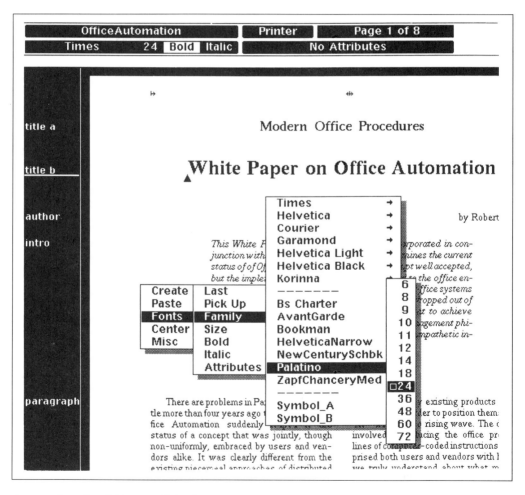

*A screen from Quark Express DTP software
(by courtesy of Surrey County Council)*

cost of typesetting sales literature could be greatly reduced if pages were produced instead in-house using a Macintosh. Ulick then launched a publication called *Personal Publishing* whose pages were prepared on the Mac, covering desktop publishing ideas. It rapidly achieved a circulation of 10,000.

Since then a number of comprehensive page-preparation software systems have been introduced, most of them being constantly up-dated. The user is presented with an area on the screen representing a page into which may be run files of text, graphics, etc.

A range of paste-up and scaling facilities and a choice of fonts are provided to allow pages to be individually styled. The major Page Formatting Systems (PFS) are Interleaf, Ventura, Pagemaker and Quark Express.

Pages may be created whose format, contents, and quality approach those created by professional publishing houses. A desktop publishing outfit usually consists of a CCD scanner for inputting images, a microcomputer with a keyboard for creating text, software for page preparation, a MONITOR for displaying a representation of a page to be printed, and a laser PRINTER.

With this equipment pages may be printed locally in small quantities for in-house publications. Alternatively they may be sent directly, or as data on a disk, to be reproduced in quantity on a typesetting machine.

Page Formatting Software (PFS) – the heart of a DTP system – presents an area on a screen representing a blank page into which the page ingredients such as stored files of text, graphics, created-as-you-go material etc., may be fitted by using the various command facilities provided.

The appearance of a page created on a DTP system is shown in the figure on the next page together with an explanation of some of the terms used to describe its features.

A range of electronic paste-up and scaling facilities with choice of fonts are provided to allow pages to be individually styled. The display is controlled by the machine's operating system in association with the PFS.

PFS is used to prepare pages with better and more varied typography than would be possible by using WP software although the difference between the two is becoming blurred. Line drawings such as pie charts and boxed diagrams, or illustrations and graphics

suitably sized may be included. They may be captioned in fonts chosen from a large range and embedded in wrap-around text appropriately columnized. The leading PFS software suppliers are mentioned above.

Text may have been prepared by keying into the resident word processing (WP) software or it may have been imported via disk or telecoms, or by scanning pages of text using a scanner operating in "OCR mode". In the case of pages containing both text and line graphics it may have been scanned from printed material in "image scanning" mode.

In recent years desktop publishing systems have been adopted by the professional printing world. For example the London *Evening Standard* runs its editorial department using 75 Macs with 8 file servers, 6 scanners, and other equipment. The *European* newspaper, before its closure, used Scitex/Visionary and Quark Express software on Macintosh machines, and its reporters used Mac SE20s.

KEY TO THE FIGURE (OVER)

1. Line lengths adjusted by equal-width inter-word spacing, not inter-character spacing.
2. Space between baselines ("leading") is made to equal the point size plus two points.
3. The baseline is a line along the base of non-descending letters.
4. Automatically justified lines are hyphenated at optimum break-points.
5. No aliasing (false contours or "jaggies").
6. Different fonts on the same page.
7. Font of a particular weight (Bold).
8. Style of font (italics).
9. No Orphans or Widows.
10. Multiple columns.
11. Auto-kerning.
12. Proportional spacing.
13. Ascender.
14. Descender.
15. Glyph.

The first figure which follows shows how text can be made to follow the contours of an illustration automatically.

The second demonstrates how the car image on the left hand side may be blown up so that a written caption may be placed upon it – in this case rather crudely by using the cursor controls of the machine, since an electronic pencil" was not available.

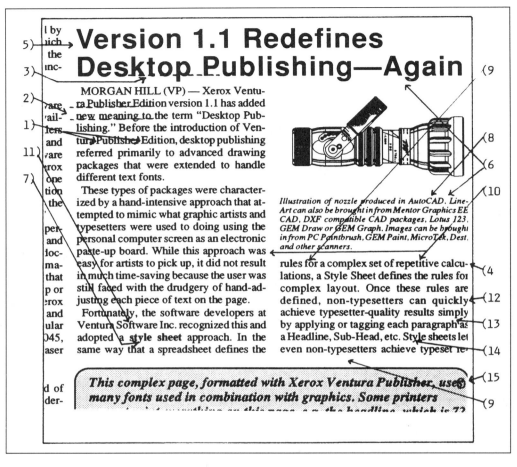

Inside the figure (text):

5) l by
   uich → the
3) inc-

2) are
   ail-
1) ters
   and
11) vare
   rox
7) one
   tion
   the
   '
   per
   and
   loc-
   ma-
   that
   p or
   erox
   and
   ular
   045,
   aser

d of
der-

Version 1.1 Redefines
Desktop Publishing—Again

MORGAN HILL (VP) — Xerox Ventu-ra Publisher Edition version 1.1 has added new meaning to the term "Desktop Publishing." Before the introduction of Ventura Publisher Edition, desktop publishing referred primarily to advanced drawing packages that were extended to handle different text fonts.

These types of packages were characterized by a hand-intensive approach that attempted to mimic what graphic artists and typesetters were used to doing using the personal computer screen as an electronic paste-up board. While this approach was easy for artists to pick up, it did not result in much time-saving because the user was still faced with the drudgery of hand-adjusting each piece of text on the page.

Fortunately, the software developers at Ventura Software Inc. recognized this and adopted a style sheet approach. In the same way that a spreadsheet defines the

Illustration of nozzle produced in AutoCAD. Line-Art can also be brought in from Mentor Graphics EE CAD, DXF compatible CAD packages, Lotus 123, GEM Draw or GEM Graph. Images can be brought in from PC Paintbrush, GEM Paint, MicroTek, Dest, and other scanners.

rules for a complex set of repetitive calculations, a Style Sheet defines the rules for complex layout. Once these rules are defined, non-typesetters can quickly achieve typesetter-quality results simply by applying or tagging each paragraph as a Headline, Sub-Head, etc. Style sheets let even non-typesetters achieve typeset re-

This complex page, formatted with Xerox Ventura Publisher, uses many fonts used in combination with graphics. Some printers

(9
(8
(6
(10
(4
(12
(13
(14
(15
(9

Part of a page formatted by Ventura software

When the image is reduced and positioned on the page the effect is as shown on the right of the figure.

The next figure (opposite) shows a printing

Run-around text can help to eliminate unwanted white space and integrate text with graphics. Use run-arounds to fill the white space around irregularly shaped artwork. Run-around text can help to eliminate unwanted white space and integrate text with graphics. Use run-arounds to fill the white space around irregularly shaped artwork. Run-around text can help to eliminate unwanted white space and integrate text with graphics. Use run-arounds to fill the white space around irregularly shaped artwork. Run-around text can help to eliminate unwanted white space and integrate text with graphics. Use run-arounds to fill the white space around irregularly shaped artwork.

Flowing text round graphics

artefact not shown in the preceding figure – an example of a "ligature" – a kind of composite glyph. This is followed by a diagram (opposite) showing type sizes in points.

DEWEY, MELVIL

Dewey was born in 1851, he worked at the New York State Library, and founded the American Library Association. He developed the Universal Decimal Classification (UDC) System details of which were published in 1876. He died in 1939.

The UDC uses decimals as notation symbols dividing subject classes hierarchically from major subjects down to specific topics.

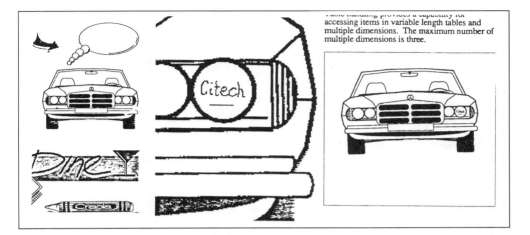

Zooming in and out

The fusion of class numbers to represent more complicated concepts is denoted by a colon which indicates a relationship between the coupled subjects.

DIANE
Direct Information Access Network for Europe.

DIDON
French teletext system similar to British teletext but using a different code and character repertoire requiring a degree of extra complexity. See also VIDEOTEX.

DIGITAL
Data represented as a series of coded pulses having only two possible states "on" or "off", "1" or "0", etc. Digital signals can be more easily stored, processed, regenerated, and transmitted than ANALOGUE data.

DIGITAL/ANALOGUE CONVERTER
A device which converts a digital code representing an analogue value into a continuous value of voltage or current.

With the exception of certain areas such as process control systems, electrical information systems are being changed from analogue to digital the world over, but since most of them were originally analogue, many are still a mixture – for example television and computer systems, the telephone system, etc.

Digital television is on the way, but television is still mainly analogue; some types of TV cameras produce digital output (but not for public TV). Digital computers are mainly digital except at the display end. The data is usually digital almost up to the CRT connection where it must be converted back to an

---

abcdefghijklmnopqrstuvwxyzABC*abcdefghjklmnopq*

abcdefghijklmnopqrstuvwxyzABC*abcdef*

BRITAIN is to expand unoffi-

E1	**Ea**	**Ea1**	**Ea1**	**Ea1**	**Ea1**	**Ea1**	**Ea1**
48	36	20	16	12	10	8	6

Fonts, ligatures, and type faces

analogue value to be visually acceptable when displayed.

Consequently Analogue/Digital and Digital/Analogue converters are a hardware feature in many systems.

Say a grey scale for the representation of tones from white through shades of grey to black is generated by an image sensor as voltages in the range 0 to 256. If 197 volts is generated when the sensor is exposed to a particular shade and is applied to a digital computer, it would be digitized by an A/D converter to change it to an 8-bit number -11000101 (197) before processing or storage.

After being stored in the machine and just before being applied to the CRT it must be converted back to 197 volts by a D/A converter so that a pixel is displayed at an appropriate intensity to produce the sensation of a particular shade of grey corresponding to the original in the human who is looking at it. (The numbers do not represent operational values; they have been chosen for convenience in the example).

Colour systems require three D/A converters in order to convert digital levels representing values of Red, Green, and Blue, to the analogue values needed to produce the sensation of a particular colour when the CRT's RGB beams strike a triad element on the screen.

DIGITAL AUDIO
The storage and processing of audio signals in the digital domain. It may require at least 16-bits of linear coding to represent each digital sample for processing and subsequent faithful reproduction of the original sound. See also MULTIMEDIA.

DIGITAL EQUIPMENT CORPORATION (DEC)
DEC is an American computer company which once made "mini computers". The company was founded on the machine called the PDP 11. At least 600,000 of these machines are believed to have been sold. 20 years after it was launched, the PDP 11/93 was put on the market following a great deal of pressure exerted by earlier PDP users.

In 1977 the company announced the first of its Vax computers which were later expanded into a wide range. The range extends from the Microvax systems through the VAX models 4000, 6000 and 9000. The VAX design allows clusters of systems to operate together to form a powerful system. The company is a strong supporter of its version of UNIX called ULTRIX. In 1982 it introduced its well-known general purpose office software called "All-in-1".

The company's profits after tax dropped to £41 million in the year ending June 1990 compared with profits of over $1 billion the previous year. It plans to bring about further substantial reductions in its work force during 1993 having already incurred a $400 million restructuring charge in 1990.

DIGITAL EUROPEAN CORDLESS TELECOMMUNICATION (DECT) STANDARD
A Standard which specifies the system to be used for DECT based on Time Division Multiple Access (TDMA). TDMA, as used for DECT, is an arrangement in which the available bandwidth is split into 10 carrier channels and each of these is split in the time domain. This enables 24 time slots to be provided within each carrier providing 12 channels, one for receiving and one for transmitting.

DIGITAL FILTER
A device which removes unwanted information or noise from a signal (which is represented in a digital sequence) to retain only the significant information within the signal.

DIGITAL SIGNAL PROCESS -ING -OR
The processing of digital signals by performing some type of algorithmic or numerical computation.

A DSP is a microprocessor to which analogue data is input and which outputs high speed arithmetic so that the processor can perform floating point multiplication with no accumulation overhead. A typical DSP is the Texas Instruments TMS320C40 which has 32 bit address and data busses and several internal busses. It also includes six communication ports which run at 20 Mbytes per second.

The capabilities of current DSPs are well exemplified in the Thunder II jointly developed by Supermac Technology, Eastman Kodak and Storm Technology. The DSP and other components are mounted on a card which includes 24 bit colour graphics, image processing acceleration, and 1920 x 1080 HDTV-style display resolution.

It is said to increase the speed of image manipulations, photo retouching, enhancement etc., by up to 26 times the rate of earlier devices.

Texas introduced a new Digital Signal Processor in 1992, type TMS320M500. The processor is a 16 bit 17 Mips device which supports audio and video software and is for use with IBM PC busses. It can support multiple tasks – for instance it will decompress colour images in the JPEG compression format, decode audio, and control a 2400 baud modem at the same time.

DIGITAL TRANSMISSION

A method of signalling by coded impulses. Its advantages are that impulses which become weak may be regenerated without adding noise (as is added in amplifiers for analogue signals); signals may be stored, processed etc., by cheap mass produced semiconductor circuits; forms of coding, and error correction may be used in a much more convenient way than with ANALOGUE TRANSMISSION.

See also DATA TRANSMISSION.

DIGITAL VIDEO INTERACTIVE (DVI)

A system developed by General Electric/ RCA to enable data for one hour's motion video playing time to be stored on a Digital Video Interactive (DVI) disk – the same size as a CD-ROM disk.

Having started in 1983 at RCA's David Sarnoff research centre, DVI work continues there under the control of GE who took it over in 1985, and from 1988 when it was acquired by Intel.

To produce the disk the data is compressed using a mainframe computer. In a DVI player decompression will be carried out by two Very Large Scale Integration (VLSI) chips. One runs the decompression algorithm at 12.5 million instructions per second (mips) and the other deals with the display format.

A VLSI chip contains 100,000 or more translators. The DVI VLSI chips were developed at the Sarnoff Research Centre, but Intel has acquired the technology and expects to manufacture them.

The compression of a rapid succession of slightly different images enables different data between successive images to be coded and signalled. When a succession of very similar images are handled in this manner huge compression ratios may result.

A current DVI disc can provide up to 72 minutes of full screen motion video at 30 frames per second. Alternatively it can provide up to 40,000 still pictures, 40 hours of audio, 650,000 pages of text or some pro rata combination.

Intel have announced several products – a plug in board for PC AT computers for capturing and storing data in local storage, and a playback and decompression board at a total price of about £4000. A complete DVI playback PC with monitor and CD-ROM drive is expected to sell for £7000. IBM is expected to announce a DVI workstation.

Intel introduced a Digital Video Interactive (DVI) development system for CD media called Pro750 ADP in 1989, followed by a product called ActionMedia using a DVI CD-ROM in 1990.

The major difference between CD-I and DV-I is that DV-I incorporates MPEG compression using inter-frame content comparisons so that only new data is supplied to a frame. No data flows into unchanged parts. The net data rate reduction enables one hour of full-screen motion video to be stored and delivered from a CD-ROM, should that be needed.

DV-I is not in the "CD hierarchy" – it is currently an Intel product. However it builds on CD disc technology – a DV-I disc is basically a high capacity CD-ROM disc running on a CD drive. Until recently, motion video had to be recorded on a DV-I disc via a mainframe computer to compress it to 5 Kbytes per frame. When decompressed the disc will then play 72 minutes of full-screen colour motion digital video (VCR quality 256 x 240 pixels).

Astonishing advances in compression techniques enabled Intel to announce in November 1990 the availability of plug-in boards for microcomputers with 80386 processors, containing chips with on-chip proprietary microcode capable of "mainframe" online compression rates. The microcode can be replaced so that DV-I compression/decompression algorithms can be made to comply with expected standards in due course.

One consequence of this development is that with an Intel TV-rate frame-grabber board installed in a micro, motion video from a camera or a broadcast TV signal can be compressed and captured on a removable hard disc in real time, the disc removed and transferred to another machine and the TV programme played back on it.

Current floppies have insufficient capacity so the most convenient removable "disc" could be the removable cartridge on an external Bernouilli drive.

It has been reported that the IBM/Intel ActionMedia II supports high quality full-motion video at 30 frames per second, VGA and XGA images, and digital audio. It conforms to a series of de facto MULTIMEDIA standards that ensure inter-operability. Instead of the usual still images, IBM and Intel use full-motion footage. More important, ActionMedia II stores the video images and digital sound on a standard Netware file server hard drive instead of on a slower CD-ROM drive.

With regard to another product, "Curtain Call", a reviewer says:- "Imagine how powerful your presentation would be at the next meeting if you could mix your slides with photographs and recorded sound. Imagine presentation text and drawings other than the usual Times Roman, Helvetica, and black line art that you usually see... full-motion animation and video will be coming shortly".

The cost of the authoring experience, preparational time, artistic design ability, source material acquisition, synchronization, continuity editing etc., required for such a presentation is not discussed.

DIGITIZATION
See DATA TRANSMISSION.

DIN
Deutsches Institut fur Normung. Standards issued from this Institute are quite widely used in the IT, photographic, and other industries.

DIP
1. DOCUMENT IMAGE PROCESSING. See IMAGES – DOCUMENT IMAGE PROCESSING.
2. DUAL INLINE PACKAGE SWITCH.

DIRECT BROADCASTING SATELLITE (DBS)
See under DATA BROADCASTING.

DIRECT MEMORY ACCESS (DMA)
A method by which data can be exchanged between a computer memory, and any device on the bus, as a continuous stream while the processor engages in other operations.

DISC ARRAYS
An arrangement of discs on a single controller, known as a host adapter, where the discs are written or read in parallel providing a very high transfer rate.

In a system which consists of several host adaptors each with its own disc array, data may be distributed across the drives so that, for instance, if each of four drives has an 8 bit SCSI connection which can transfer data at 2Mbps, by striping the data across the drives in 32 bit chunks, the total transfer rate becomes 8Mbps.

To improve reliability two of the discs in the system may contain the same data so if one fails a duplicate becomes available. Other RAID (Redundant Array of Inexpensive Discs) arrangements in the series RAID 0 to RAID 5 provide alternative arrangements for storing check data to assist in data recovery from other discs.

DISC – BERNOUILLI
(or BERNOULLI). Bernouilli 8″ or 5.25″ discs are removable hard discs housed in an external box supplied with a board which plugs in to the associated PC, PS/2, or Macintosh microcomputer. The box is connected to the micro with a cable.

The demountable feature means that alternative discs of up to 44 Mbytes may be used and that discs may be removed to secure storage. The manufacturers, Iomega, provide a software package which allow the discs to become PC/PS2/Mac file-exchange systems.

DISC – FLOPTICAL
See OPTICAL DISC.

DISC – OPTICAL
See OPTICAL DISC.

DISC STORAGE SYSTEMS
A Disc Storage System consists of a plastic disc coated with aferromagnetic material, a drive for rotating the disc, and a read/write head which is moved across the rapidly rotating disc by a stepper motor to a given pos-

ition. When the current through wire coils in the head is switched on, a small area of the disc immediately beneath the head becomes magnetized. Because the disc is revolving, a track is formed consisting of small magnetized or un-magnetized areas storing bits of data.

Data cannot be instantly written on to, or read from the head. It takes time ("seek" time) to move the head to a required track, and more time ("latency") for the disc to rotate until the required point on the surface of the disc comes round beneath the head.

Data is transferred to a computer via the disc control circuits. The first discs were called "hard" discs and were provided in units for mainframe computers consisting of one or more discs fixed concentrically on a rotatable spindle, each with its own movable head (see also DISC – WINCHESTER). In the early nineteen seventies floppy discs, or "diskettes", were introduced of a smaller size and much simpler construction.

In a floppy system the disc rotates within a plastic envelope containing a radial cut-out slot to provide access to the head. The trend has been for discs to be decreased in size and increased in capacity. Floppy discs were replaced by 3.5 inch diameter discs spinning inside a plastic container. Part of the container is cut away to allow head access, protected by a metal shutter which slides back when the disc is inserted into the drive.

See also OPTICAL DISCS and COMPACT DISCS.

DISC – WINCHESTER
A disc for magnetic storage introduced by IBM in the late nineteen sixties. In a Winchester disc system, the read/write head embodies two rail-projections which trap a small volume of air, the head element being situated between the rails. When the disc rotates, aerodynamic forces cause the head to hover less than a millionth of a metre above the surface, and in consequence there is no wear upon it.

DISCRETE COSINE TRANSFORM (DCT)
See COMPRESSION – JPEG.

DISK
See DISC.

DISPLAYING
Entries follow DISPLAY entries.

DISPLAYS
A display is the means of delivering the result of computer, television, or other operations in a clearly visible properly designed form.

People engaged in image processing activities will require an effective display with adequate, perhaps the best, resolution and probably good colour, almost certainly using a Cathode Ray Tube.

Colour has reached a degree of perfection, first because of the CRT R&D work undertaken to produce colour TV tubes, and second because of R&D undertaken in connection with computer colour software resulting in 24-bit systems permitting a display of up to 16 million different colours. The correlation between what you see on the tube and what you get when it's printed on paper remains a black art.

There is some confusion about resolution so it's as well to understand the basics. The important factors are the resolving power of the eye and the CRT spot size.

In the 19th century Lord Rayleigh discovered that under specified conditions the eye can resolve 2 points subtended by about 1 minute of arc at its surface. These days, 2 minutes is usually the figure used.

Two minutes of arc at a normal viewing distance seems to correspond to viewing the finest detail on 19" (diagonal) monochrome tubes with an 11" vertical display area, providing a total of about 2500 lines (227 lines per inch). It is generally agreed that any further increase produces no perceptible improvement. Suitable tubes (which are not generally available) require a spot no larger than about 0.1 mm and a bandwidth for incoming signals of over 800 MHz. See also BIT RATES AND PRESENTATION.

The best generally available colour tubes have a spot size of about 0.28 mm providing about 100 dpi. Therefore we are not yet at the stage where tube resolution is better than the eye's ability to make use of it.

Within limits, the closer the viewer is to the tube the higher the perceived resolution. For instance if some fine detail is indistinct at a viewing distance of 1 metre, it will become clearer at 0.6 metres – not too close for focusing the eye. These matters are discussed here because it is often asked whether it is worth buying an expensive large-screen external monitor for probably the most popular general purpose imaging machines – Apple Macs which incorporate only a small 72 dpi screens.

The points to watch are whether such monitors provide just increased size or higher resolution as well. For instance a Hitachi Colour Mac monitor provides up to 24-bit colour but still has the same resolution as a Mac. The main advantage is that 72 dpi is provided over a full-page area instead of a half-page. Alternatively a Hitachi Multiscan monitor will provide substantially better resolution at 1600 x 1200 dpi.

A phrase such as "virtual resolution 4000 x 4000 pixels" sometimes appears. This means that the area actually displayed of say, 1000 x 700 pixels acts as a window on to a larger area – i.e any 1000 x 700 pixels part of, say, a 4000 x 4000 area may be viewed at one time.

See also other adjacent DISPLAY entries.

DISPLAYS, LARGE

Whatever the outcome of existing controversies and differing proposals for Standards, some company will successfully develop and manufacture a flat panel display which measures at least 40" diagonally and produces a picture as bright as a conventional TV picture. It is very likely that the company will be Japanese.

In October 1988, MITI and 12 Japanese companies asked for $40 million to help fund the development of a liquid crystal display with an area of one square metre. The Ministry of Posts and Telecoms together with four other companies has asked the Japan Key Technology Centre for $30 million for a similar project. Plasma panel displays, which work by switching rows of very small elements which glow when energized, have been developed up to a 20" size but they are not yet bright enough. NHK hope to produce a 50" plasma panel for HDTV by 1993.

By 1989 MITI and the 12 company consortium had increased their commitment to $400 million for the large liquid crystal display. Meanwhile improved large displays have been produced using three projection cathode ray tubes with 6" screens, one for each colour. A picture up to 5 ft. wide can be provided.

Hawashima and others have described a receiver with a 50" rear projection display and another receiver with a 180" projection display for use in theatres. Receivers using back projection on to a 40" screen are expected to sell for $3000 in the 1990s – about the same price as consumers paid for a colour television receiver in the United States in the 1950s.

DISPLAYS – LIQUID CRYSTAL DISPLAY (LCD)

Liquid crystal displays first appeared for forming figures on the faces of digital watches; cheap small screen LCD monochrome TV sets were manufactured in the early 80s, the screen consisting of a rather low resolution array of LCD elements.

An LCD element consists of two closely-spaced light-polarizing glass plates separated by about 10 microns (millionth of a meter) and containing a liquid crystal compound. The action of this cell is controlled by potentials applied to transparent electrodes. The glass plates are arranged with their polarizing planes at right angles and the intervening molecules within the cell impart a twist to the light passing through it according to the applied potential.

If the light is twisted it can pass in and out of the cell, but if it is not twisted it can enter one side but will not emerge from the other. Such a cell is called a "twisted nematic" LCD. The improved "super-twisted" LCD provides better viewing angles, contrast ratios, and a faster response.

Each LCD element is extremely small and forms part of a large panel. Originally LCD panels controlled reflected light. More recently the brightness has been improved by incorporating a light source at the back.

During the last year or two there has been a further improvement with the adoption of a ferroelectric molecular material in which the polarization of the light can be changed by simply applying a pulse, rather than a fixed potential.

Another new technique has been adopted called "active-addressing" or "acting-matrix screen". In this case thin film transistors are bonded to the screen which control the switching which is much faster than the slower passive-matrix technology.

In a colour LCD panel, light from a fluorescent lamp passes through individual cells each being controlled by its own thin film transistor and colour filter.

For example the Toshiba T4400SXC notebook computer, introduced in mid-1992, incorporates an active-matrix LCD screen. The display provides a SUPER VGA display of 640 x 480 pixels with 256 colours from a large palette and very good brightness and colour without the need for any adjustment. The screen contains nearly 1 million thin film transistors. See DISPLAYING COLOUR AND GRAPHICS.

The chemicals used in LCDs were once a European monopoly, although manufacture of the screens took place mainly in the United States and Japan. In the late eighties the Japanese took over production and many American companies closed or were sold.

In 1990 the US accused the Japanese of trying to shut down all American competition by exporting and dumping LCD panels. About three-quarters of all panels used in portable computers are made from LCDs, the balance of the screens being PLASMA or ELECTRO-LUMINESCENT. These three technologies all provide a thin robust flat screen but LCDs are currently by far the most successful.

In 1992 the cathode ray tube driven Liquid Crystal Light Valve panel through which a separate light source projects an image on to the viewing screen, was described. The LCLV may come into use for large screen displays in theatres or cinemas.

DISPLAYS – MONITORS

A monitor is a visual display unit (VDU), housed outside a computer.

The displays normally supplied within microcomputers are much better than they used to be and are quite adequate for working with text. For looking at a clearly legible complete page or at good quality illustrations in colour, something better is needed.

The display requirements for text or diagrams in colour, and for illustrations in colour – or for that matter for text or diagrams in black and white and halftone illustrations – are rather different. In text and diagrams resolution may be of prime importance. In illustrations, particularly "pictures" – that is artistic works – it is the colours or halftones, and their gradations and range which are usually of greater importance.

If what you are looking at is going to be printed then ideally you would like to see a good representation on the screen of what will ultimately be seen on paper. In DESKTOP PUBLISHING a full size representation of a whole page under preparation is a consider-able advantage. Resolution and colour will still fall well short of what can be achieved with print on paper unless a very costly monitor is used. Know-how, experience, and additional facilities are needed to relate CRT colour to printed colour.

Details about high quality colour monitors are given on the next page with one monochrome example for comparison. A major reason for the superiority of the Exact 8000 is the size of the single-beam spot compared with the size necessary to provide a tri-beam triad spot in colour tubes. The resolution of the Exact approaches 300 pixels/inch.

High quality colour is not yet available on the variety of display devices which are gradually being introduced in competition with CRTs.

DISPLAYS – RESOLUTION

The maximum number of discernible elements.

Vertical resolution is usually specified in lines per inch or lines per millimetre, horizontal in pixels or lines per inch or millimetre. In FACSIMILE systems when manufacturers specify resolution details, the time taken to transmit an average document on A4 paper may also be specified because of the interchangeability of time and resolution.

DISPLAYS – VISUAL (VDU)

A device for displaying textual or graphical information. When used with a keyboard, as is usually the case, "VDU" is virtually synonymous with "terminal".

DISPLAYING COLOUR AND GRAPHICS

Substantial advances in the handling of colour and graphics in microcomputers have been made because it has become feasible to handle the required processing power by installing a computer within a computer. The CPU still exercises overall control but a graphics/colour processor, video section, or "adaptor board" handles the Graphics User Interface (GUI).

1. IBM PCs.

Since the early eighties when the PC was launched, IBM have introduced a series of "adaptor" boards providing for improvements in colour and graphics.

When text is used in conjunction with graphics, text data is stored as two bytes per

Supplier and type	Screen size inches	Resolution	Bandwidth MHz	Scan f.(KHz)	Video inputs	Price
Flanders Exact 8000 (**Mono**)	11.0 x 8.5	2560 x 3300	750	205	–	$3000
Chugai CPD-2040	14.2 x 10.3	1280 x 1024	120	58–70	Analogue	$3495
NEC Multisync XL	13.8 x 10.2	1024 x 768	65	21–50	Anal. TTL	$3200
Taxan Ultravision 1150	14.0 x 10.3	1280 x 1024	?	30–72	Analogue	£2800
Hitachi HIscan 20	14.0 x 10.6	1280 x 1024	?	30–64	Analogue	£2175

Representative high resolution colour monitors (with one mono)

character, the first for the ASCII code and the second for the appearance and/or colour of the character. In different systems the number of pixels available for storing a character may differ – for example in MDA the pixel array is 9 x 14, and in the CGA array 8 x 8.

The first adaptor provided by IBM was the Monochrome Display Adaptor (MDA) providing for the construction of boxes, tables etc. This was followed by the Colour Graphics Adaptor (CGA) which provided a display of 640 x 200 pixels with a choice of 16 colours, and Enhanced Graphics Adaptor (EGA) with improved resolution.

These schemes used "TTL" logic (switching), but when IBM went in for colour seriously with the Video Graphics Adaptor (VGA), they adopted a digital/analogue converter system for changing digital values of colour held in a table into analogue voltages for driving the cathode ray tube. With this arrangement the resolution was improved to 640 x 480 pixels with a choice of 16 colours displayed at one time out of a choice of over 260,000 different colours.

In 1990 the Video Electronics Standards Association (VESA) exploited the hardware used in VGA to provide SUPER VGA performance. This involves using the VGA bit architecture in which several memories in parallel are connected to the CRT, each memory holding 1 bit of a pixel's colour description. VESA provides for a resolution of up to 1280 x 1024 pixels, with a choice of 256 colours. These improvements are enabled by increasing memory up to 0.5 Mbytes, and adding instruction lines into BIOS to accept additional interrupts which then control the improved performance.

2. APPLE MICROCOMPUTERS.

APPLE Computer started with a different concept of computer design to IBM – descended from the Xerox Star machine and its revolutionary GRAPHICS USER INTERFACE (GUI).

Apple really invented the GUI with its WIMP – windows, icons, mouse and pop up menus. Instead of having to type in coded messages, the user was able to point and select pictures – hence the descriptive phrase "GRAPHICS USER INTERFACE".

The Apple design consists of a Tool Box which forms parts of a proprietary operating system which allocates hardware resources including Quickdraw for image and text creation, Font Manager for font creation routines, Event Manager which is the mouse keyboard interface, and a Windows Manager.

Quickdraw creates everything that appears on the screen and provides fast interactive service.

When the Mac II became available at the end of 1987 it came with a video card providing only 16 shades of grey. However if you added a Multiscan Monitor and plugged in an expanded video card, the machine would display 256 colours on the screen at one time.

In 1989 Apple released a 32 bit version of Quickdraw providing for 24 bit colour. When used with a Radius colour board monitor, 256 colours appear on a 1152 x 882 pixel screen drawn from a palette of 16.7 million colours. In late 1990 Apple introduced its new software, System 7.0, which includes provision for multitasking and a re-designed toolbox with new communications architecture.

In 1991/1992 Apple revised its range deleting a number of machines and adding some less expensive machines, for example the Classic, and some more powerful, for example the Quadra.

See also COLOUR.

DISPLAYING HALFTONES
See HALFTONES.

DISTRIBUTED COMPUTING
A computing system with computing power distributed over a system of interconnected WORKSTATIONS and other units as opposed to concentrating the power in one MAINFRAME.

DISTRIBUTED SYSTEMS
A computer complex made up of separate networked co-operating computers at different locations as opposed to a centralized system.

DITHERING
A method of halftone printing with a laser printer by sub-dividing a bit-mapped area into small blocks of pixels – say 4 x 4 blocks – and filling them with from 0 to 16 pixels in some pre-arranged pattern corresponding to the average brightness detected in corresponding areas of the original image. See also HALFTONES.

DMA
DIRECT MEMORY ACCESS.

DMS
Data Management System.

DNA
Digital Network Architecture.

DOCUMENT CONTENT ARCHITECTURE
A standardized and rather complex method for specifying document layouts in terms of the contents of page areas – that is parts occupied by text, diagrams, illustrations etc.

DOCUMENT DELIVERY
Documents which may contain illustrations and "figures" on pages can be delivered by printing many copies (example: journals), by sending a photocopy, or, since about 1980, by sending a facsimile. Photocopies or fax do nor handle halftones very well; special types of these machines can be used for sending rather expensive and not very good images in colour.

The scale of production operations for a journal publisher may well justify electronic composition methods where pages, including pages containing images, may exist in digitized form at some stage of its production.

Ultimately the printed page may become obsolete (by the year 2100?). Meanwhile "document delivery services" usually means the delivery of pages in electronic form converted to that form from the printed version published earlier.

The constraints against composing and distributing pages in digitized form in the first place (already overcome, at least for composition, in very large scale operations such as newspaper publishing) have been the inadequate quality of digitized images, storing a very large volume of data until needed, telecommunicating it at an acceptable speed and cost, and storing and reproducing it at the receiving end.

One way of doing it is via CD-ROM, as with the ADONIS system. The discs have the capacity to accept a large number of articles including images. When the chips referred to in the COMPRESSION entry are incorporated into players the improved capacity of CD-ROMs should further strengthen their market.

Storage and telecommunications have made enormous strides but still constrain document-with-images delivery systems. With one of the latest 18 Kbit/second error-correcting modems operating at a realistic 16 Kbits/second, and a currently achievable 5:1 compression ratio it takes about 30 seconds to send a printed page including a quarter-page half-tone illustration (4.8 Mbits or 0.6 Mbytes) over the PSTN. About 67 pages would fill a 40 Mbyte disc in 33 minutes.

When the Integrated Services Digital Network and compression devices providing ratios of 25:1 become widely available, perhaps in 5 to 10 years time, it will become feasible and cheap to send the same page in about 1.5 seconds. 40 Mbytes would hold about 335 pages.

The amount of data from pages with illustrations can be greatly reduced by appropriate coding. Text is encoded (as is done when using any WP system) by generating ASCII or a similar code, and only illustrations and

DOCUMENT IMAGE PROCESSING

figures are encoded at, say, the 300 x 300 dots per inch needed to provide adequate resolution. The wasteful alternative is to code the whole page at 300 dots/inch which is actually needed only for that part of it containing an illustration.

There are three different cases of digitizing pages with illustrations – author composition of the page, digitization of an already composed page, and digitization of an already printed page.

If the author is prepared to learn the codes and nuances of standardized SGML or ODA, he or she can designate parts of the document for appropriate coding. Systems are commercially available, such as Interlink's Active Document Systems, for tagging page components, usually called Object Linking and Embedding (OLE).

If pages are already composed and available in machine-readable form – say on the disc of a WP system or on CD-ROM – then each page may be presented on a screen so that an operator can frame and designate areas for appropriate coding.

Nagy has described a system for automatically identifying blocks of information such as title, abstract, footnote, text segment, illustration etc., in a family of journals with standardized formats (in this case IEEE journals) on CD-ROM. When viewing a retrieved article, labelled page blocks, e.g. "abstract" may be selected, expanded, and read.

If pages with illustrations are only available as already-printed pages then they have to be converted to machine-readable form, prior to re-coding.

DOCUMENT IMAGE PROCESSING
See IMAGES.

DOD
Department of Defense.

DOI
Department of Industry.

DONGLE
A sealed electronic circuit, plugged into a PC, which prevents illegal copying.

DOS
Disc Operating System.
See OPERATING SYSTEMS.

DOWNLOADING
Moving data from a source to a destination computer, usually through a telecommunications link.

DOWNSIZING
The trend to move down the scale of computer sizes towards the microcomputer. A 1992 survey in Japan showed that less than half of mainframe users intended to replace them with another mainframe. Instead they intended to shift to network-based distributed data processing using smaller computers.

DP
1. Data Protection.
2. Data Processing.

DPNSS
Digital Private Network Signalling System. A system used by most UK PABX suppliers to provide for setting up dialled subscriber to subscriber circuits between PABXs, and for other control purposes.

DRAGGING
Holding down a button on a mouse while moving the mouse in order to shift the position of a designated object while observing this activity on a cathode ray tube screen.

DRAM
Dynamic Random Access Memory.
See SEMICONDUCTORS – MEMORY CHIPS.

DRAW
Direct Read After Write.

DRCS
DYNAMICALLY REDEFINABLE CHARACTER SET.

DRIVER
A small program of routines controlling a PERIPHERAL device.

DSE
Data Storage Equipment.

DSP
DIGITAL SIGNAL PROCESSING.

DSS
Decision Support System.

DTE
Data Terminal Equipment.

DTI
Department of Trade and Industry.

DTL
Diode Transistor Logic.

DTP
DESKTOP PUBLISHING.

DUAL INLINE PACKAGE (DIP) SWITCH
An arrangement of miniature switches used, for example, to set up certain operating conditions in a microcomputer.

DUOBINARY SIGNALLING
A method of signalling in which two level impulses, 0, 1, are encoded into three levels 0, +1, and -1.

DUPLEX TRANSMISSION
Data transmission in both directions at once. A receiver can interrupt a transmitter without waiting for the conclusion of transmission.

DVI
DIGITAL VIDEO INTERACTIVE.

DYNAMIC RANDOM ACCESS MEMORY (DRAM)
A memory formed from a number of transistors associated with a capacitor capable of storing "1 bit". A DRAM requires periodically "refreshing" in order to maintain the capacitor charge.

DYNAMICALLY REDEFINABLE CHARACTER SET (DRCS)
See under VIDEOTEX.

E

EBCDIC
Expanded Binary-Coded Decimal Interchange Code.

EC
European Commission.

ECCLES-JORDAN CIRCUIT
A bistable multivibrator.

ECL
EMITTER COUPLED LOGIC.

ECM
Extended Core Memory.

ECMA
European Computer Manufacturers Association.

ECOM
Electronic Computer Originated Mail.

ECS
European Communications Satellite.

Ecu
European Currency Unit.

EDDY CURRENT
A current induced in a conducting material by a magnetic field. Eddy currents are used to provide the levitation in vehicles with a suspension system consisting of electromagnets on the vehicle, and the track on which the vehicle runs. The idea was first tried out on the Birmingham Airport system in 1974.

Another application is in nondestructive testing where currents in an object being inspected are measured to indicate conductivity, permeability, homogeneity, coating thickness etc. Eddy currents can also produce undesirable effects, for example in transformers where they produce losses in the iron core. Such cores are usually made from layers of thin sheet insulated from one another to reduce the effect.

The effects of eddy currents are important in VDUs and MONITORS.

EDGE NOTCHED CARDS
A pre-computer method of sorting indexing cards.

Long needles were pushed through selected coded holes and notches in a suspended stack of edge-notched cards. The numbered holes which had been notched to correspond to coded subject terms covering the contents of an item on a card fell out of the stack (See Figure).

The stack was vibrated via a suspension system actuated by a loudspeaker armature.

As an information system it worked but was unsuccessful because the arrangements for indexing, coding, and notching each card according to its contents were too laborious.

See INDEXING.

Edge-notched card

EDI
ELECTRONIC DATA INTERCHANGE.

EDIFACT
ELECTRONIC DATA INTERCHANGE FOR ADMINISTRATION COMMERCE AND TRANSPORT.

See also ELECTRONIC DATA INTERCHANGE.

EDISON, THOMAS ALVA

Edison, born in 1847, died in 1931, was a prolific inventor. He took out over 1000 patents. His patents covered the phonograph, incandescent bulbs, a form of motion pictures, telegraph repeaters, the carbon telephone transmitter and the telephone microphone, alkaline storage batteries and many others. He started as a newsboy and later founded the General Electric Co., following a merger between Edison Electric Co., and Thomson-Houston.

EDSAC

Electronic Delayed Storage Automatic Computer.

EDTV

Extended Definition Television.
   See TELEVISION – HIGH DEFINITION.

EEC

European Economic Community

EEPROM

Electrically Erasable Programmable Read Only Memory.
   See also SEMICONDUCTORS – MEMORY CHIPS.

EEROM

Electrically Erasable Read-Only Memory.

EFT

Electronic Funds Transfer.

EFTPOS

Electronic Funds Transfer from Point Of Sale.

EGA

Enhanced Graphics Adaptor. See also DISPLAY COLOUR AND GRAPHICS.

EIA

Electronic Industry Association.

EIES

ELECTRONIC INFORMATION EXCHANGE SYSTEM

EIRP

Equivalent Isotropically Radiated Power.

EIS

EXECUTIVE INFORMATION SYSTEM.

EISA

EXTENDED INDUSTRY STANDARD ARCHTECTURE.

EL

Electroluminescent.

ELECTRO-ETCH RECORDING

A now obsolete recording method in which the stylus in a receiving printer scans the surface of sensitive paper in synchronism with the transmitter's scanner. Contact is made when a "black" signal element is received, and a current passes across the contact point producing a mark on the paper.

ELECTROLUMINESCENT DISPLAY PANEL

A possible replacement for a CRT display consisting of a flat panel display composed of a large number of small elements each consisting of a sandwich of a phosphor layer and electrodes. The phospher glows when a high voltage is applied to the electrodes. The system requires a rather elaborate high-voltage driving circuit arrangement. EL panels have been used in portable micro-computers. Large screens up to 18″ in width have been manufactured.

ELECTRONIC BOOKS

According to a recent article, soon you won't have to worry about running out of space on your bookshelves and you will not have to carry those heavy boxes of books from one house to another when you move. Electronic books are fast coming into being. The term was coined by Andries van Damm over 25 year ago.
   The same article also dwells at length, but gets off the point, on the virtues of the US Department of Defence's Computer Aided Acquisition and Logistic Support System (CALS), and on the virtues of the Standard Generalized Markup Language (SGML) for

publications.

Kay and Goldberg, working at Xerox's remarkable ideas factory at Palo Alto usually known as PARC, must have had something like the Electronic Book in the illustration at the beginning of this article in mind when they introduced the "Dynabook" in 1977.

This idea was a landmark. Kay said in an interview:- "I started designing the machine in the late 1960s. I went to Xerox Palo Alto Research Centre with the explicit purpose to make the machine. As it turned out Xerox sort of punked out midway in the thing. All we did was to invent workstations and Macintoshes and stuff like that".

Kay suggested that "future computers will let you move beyond McLuhan's individual". (MCLUHAN had suggested in the *Gutenberg Galaxy* (1962) that new media determines the nature of the social organization). Kay waxed lyrical:- "The retrieval systems of the future are not going to retrieve facts but points of view. The weakness of databases is that they let you retrieve facts, while the strength of our culture over the last seven hundred years has been our ability to take on multiple points of view".

"The true significance of the Dynabook (will be)... the effect that intimate computing will have on our culture... five or ten years from now we'll judge our AI systems not on how smart they are but how well they are able to explain themselves to us".

The Dynabook was intended to be a "notebook with a million pixel screen, eight processors, and both wireless and cable networking". Kay's estimation of what might become technically possible was not far wrong although his time forecast was incorrect.

An electronic book proposed, was based on VLSI (Very Large Scale Integrated) circuits. It would be book-size with a flat screen display, the words being encoded as 12 bit numbers stored, together with coarse graphics, in a memory of about 14 Mbytes.

The method of compression would enable the text of a novel to be stored. "Books" would come in small plug-in memories, and an on-board microprocessor would handle decoding and presentation. The device would include a keyboard and STRING-searching capabilities for "publications" requiring that facility. It is suggested that the electronic book would "alter the nature of libraries, increase the efficiency of the scientific, legal, and medical professions, minimize information access time in industry, and modify the operation of the educational system".

In 1987 two Australian companies announced the two-part "Smartbook" comprising credit-card like objects housing a micro-chip on which the text is stored, costing about $50 each, and an electronic reader which displays and manipulates the text and should retail for around $250.

The front of the reader has a small flat-screen display which is lit from behind. Below the screen the six keys which control a variety of search options form a menu line. The reader can mark several points within a book or even use the built-in concordance to present all the phrases in a text which feature a selected word.

"At the moment the Bible is the only title available for Smartbook. But agreements have been signed with major publishers for the right to publish their reference titles in the Smartbook format (said the New Scientist, September 3rd, 1987). By the time the device reaches full-scale production there should be a reasonable library of reference works". Nothing has been heard of it since.

Some years ago a device called the Izon micrographics reader was developed, supposedly to sell for about $100. It used an optical compression system with a form of Fresnel lense housed in a book-size box, with the expectation of breaking the portability barrier imposed by normal microfiche readers. Like the Smartbook it disappeared without a trace. The market will decide what kind of electronic books we will have.

With reference to today's notebook computers, it is said in a much more recent article that for a PC to qualify as a notebook it has to meet certain criteria. It must be about the size of an A4 notepad, not more than two inches thick so it can easily fit into a standard briefcase, weigh under 3 Kgms, be able to run under battery power for a least two hours, and perform most of the functions of a desktop machine. About 20 machines which fall within this specification are listed.

We recognize printed pages bound between covers as a book, but contents, arrangement, and purpose are often so different that these attributes are the only things they have in common. Novels, dictionaries, telephone books, textbooks, anthologies, instruction manuals, proceedings of meetings, directories – you could go on and on – are as different as chalk and cheese.

A recent article about "Reading and writing the electronic book" is actually about "electronic document systems". As you read further it turns out to be about "multimedia electronic document systems". Finally it turns out to be about a "hypertext document system". A report entitled "Further developments of the electronic book" turns out to be about "publishers of chip-based electronic books" and concludes:-

"Whatever the medium of delivery, the move towards multimedia currently evident throughout all forms of electronic information delivery looks equally irresistible in electronic book development.

Sony's palmtop CD-I player looks like being the forerunner of the ultimate form of electronic book, offering sound, text, images – including full-screen, full motion video – together with intuitive user interfaces and screen resolutions easily matching the traditional quality of the printed page. Perhaps we are moving towards the concept of a single, personal, palmtop information centre, part electronic book, part computer, part global communications centre".

The "Death of Print" has been forecast for many years and today the forecasters are as busy as ever. The idea is phrased in dramatic terms:- "The 500-year era of print is drawing to its close" says Dr. Frank Lukey, future product manager of Silver Platter, CD-ROM supplier. "In only 5-10 years a range of electronic books will be available of which the most common will be the portable book which will really sell the idea".

A small hand-held personal organizer was introduced in the UK in 1993. The product is called Financial Alert and it represents a step twoards a genuine electronic book. It combines a personal organizer and a radio pager enabling a user to receive and display City information, stock market prices, company news etc. Prices are constantly up-dated and there is a gap of up to 30 seconds between a price change in the market and the recording of the change in the unit. It consists of an LCD display, a touch keypad, computer, and rechargeable battery. It can work almost anywhere in the UK.

ELECTRONIC BOOKS – FUTURES

Information 2000, a multi-authored compilation, carries the imprimatur of the British Library. It says about electronic books:- "In order to become acceptable to consumers, the electronic book must have features which bring additional benefit over and above the experience of reading continuous text from a printed book... It is likely to be most effective as a reference work. This is borne out by early electronic books – they are dictionaries."

Other reference material might include "airline and train schedules, telephone directories, tourist guides, service and product directories and almanacs... electronic books will occupy a niche in reference publishing where their particular combination of characteristics will differentiate them from printed material and from computer-stored databases".

But while laptop and notebook computers now represent the fastest growing segment of the computer industry, "the ultimate easy-to-use hand-held computer has somehow failed to materialize. Companies such as Sharp, Psion, Agenda and Casio all have pocket-sized machines, but none of them successfully merges the advantages of a desktop PC with the convenience and flexibility of pen and paper" said Prochak in 1992.

Sevonius, in a side-swipe at Kay and Lancaster says:- "A romantic quality characterizes the writing of many who depict the potential of the new technology for future information systems. A recurring theme is that of paperless information systems, whose most eloquent visionary is Lancaster. He epitomizes the paperless society in terms of an intelligent terminal located in one's home through which one can access, in interactive mode, books and periodicals, factual information such as airline schedules and football scores, and the information in one's personal files. Through the same terminal one can also shop, bank, receive and send mail, and participate in conferences".

Goodrum et al believe that "The Electronic Book being talked about can either be one of the brief-case-sized computer screens that are increasingly seen on people's laps in airplanes, or the flat screens seen on designer's work benches... The Book of the Month Club

85

can send its volumes around in envelopes instead of the complicated cardboard packages it now uses; disks or chips or plastic cards all offer cheaper postage, less damage in transit.

Fred Croxton of the Library of Congress, Ithiel de Sola Pool of M.I.T. and Tom Surprenant of Queens College, City University of New York express concern about the effect of the on-demand book on libraries. All three express the belief that this innovation will come in the working lifetime of present library administrators and should be anticipated by present supervisors.

ELECTRONIC BOOKS – READING

In research on reading text-on-paper versus reading text on a screen, the variability of the results discouraged continuation with the work, although research hardly seems necessary to discover that academics prefer reading "hard copy" to CRT-displayed text. It seems very unlikely that many people would prefer to use a screen for any kind of lengthy reading, or for browsing or scanning text, provided that the text is readily accessible in print.

Although numerous tests through to the late eighties nearly always showed that reading from a screen was slower than reading from print, it is now reported that experiments demonstrate that reading from computer screens that are readily available can be equivalent in speed and comprehension to reading from a book. Approximately 30% of the activity of skilled readers can be characterized as skimming. Skimming speed was markedly different for the two media. Skimming in the book condition was 41% faster than skimming in the CRT condition.

ELECTRONIC BOOKS – REFERENCE

Publishing companies see electronic books as a way to save production costs and to improve accuracy and timeliness. The particular books in question are engineering maintenance and operations manuals.

In 1984 it was forecast that in the library of the future, videodiscs containing the digital text of reference books would be received from publishers. They would be consulted using interactive color monitors "permitting modes of access that are not possible today".

These modes of access have arrived and at least one type of electronic book – the electronic encyclopaedia – is here. Several have appeared resembling Weyer's (1985) extraordinary seven year old model. He suggested that a future electronic encyclopaedia "should be as comprehensive and detailed as the best current encyclopaedias, but full advantage should be taken of not just text and static pictures but also video sequences, animation, simulations, music and voice... what the user sees would be custom-generated and based on the encyclopaedia's system model of the user's interests, vocabulary, knowledge of specific subjects and previous interactions with the system".

He provided an example of his intentions by showing a Hypercard-like access to an entry with interactive learning facilities. "After specifying a load on a bridge we see the effect of forces transmitted to various truss members (See Figure on the next page).

The bridge article might "lead us to the collapse of the Tacoma Narrows bridge from movie footage available on videodisc".

McGraw-Hill's 1992 *Multimedia Encyclopaedia of Mammalian Biology* is published on CD-ROM and runs on a CD-ROM drive compatible with Microsoft Multimedia Extensions to Windows 3.0. A DVI board is desirable for the full effect. It provides for text, sound, data, pictures, and motion video, with interactive software. The disc includes 300 motion video clips associated with selected text entries each of which will provide about 15 seconds of full-screen motion video.

Weyer-like interaction is provided. Data display options are offered, and that data may be plotted graphically as demanded by the user. The encyclopaedia includes 3500 still colour illustrations as well as the motion clips.

A major difference between this and alphabetically ordered encyclopaedias is that searches can be carried out using concept-based retrieval incorporating the BBC's TELCLASS classification system.

ELECTRONIC BOOKS – VERSUS PRINTED BOOKS

Compared with a variety of objects labelled as "electronic books" today, ordinary books possess overwhelming advantages. There are a few, as yet unproven, specialized applica-

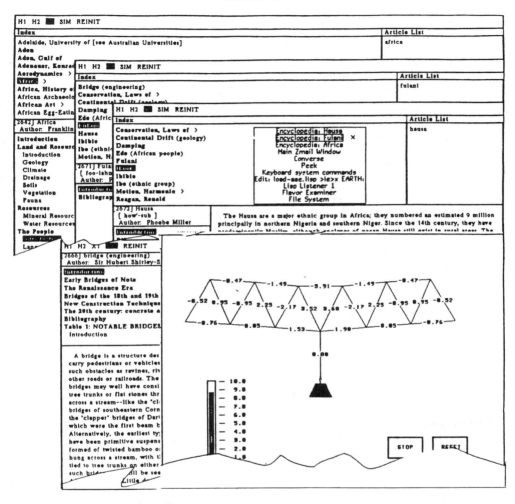

Weyer's Electronic Encyclopaedia

tions for Electronic Books which have any potential – for example Encyclopaedias and Instruction Manuals.

Information in print will endure for many years because inefficient as the paper book or journal may be, the fact is that at the presentation interface the print-human match is far better than the machine-human match, both in terms of information transfer and of human behaviour. For general browsing, reading, annotating, scanning news items, appreciating pictures or drawings, and being generally entertained, print on paper is superior.

A screen still cannot compete with printed pages in terms of ease of annotation, portability, convenience, quality, colour, aesthetics, immediate availability of large chunks, and, at least as important, the ease and speed with which large chunks may be ignored.

Print can be written on, carried about, and digested in aeroplanes, on trains, or in the bath. It looks nice on shelves, and makes a very acceptable gift. In newspaper form it continues to be used, even when all its information functions are over, as a heat retaining fish and chips container.

As one author says "there is simply no experience in life that matches silent reading...

readers make everything happen just the way they want it to. The actions, scenes, and voices in a book come to life entirely in the reader's mind... Sometimes when I can't go to sleep I see the family of the future. Dressed in three-tone shorts and shirts of disposable papersilk they sit before the television wall of their apartment; only their eyes are moving. After I've looked for a while I always see – otherwise I'd die – a pigheaded soul in the corner with a book; only his eyes are moving but in them there is a different look''.

ELECTRONIC DATA INTERCHANGE (EDI)

EDI is a form of electronic mail for business transactions with the exchange of invoices, orders and other transactional documentation in a standardized manner carried out between the computers of trading companies.

The system elements are a Data Dictionary defining the contents of message elements, Message Standards defining the format and content of messages for different business areas, and a Message Syntax defining message structures. A major objective, by standardizing and simplifying, is the shortening of the time between ordering and delivery. In "just-in-time" manufacturing, this time shortening is the key to success.

As with electronic mail a number of organizations can offer EDI services. They include Transpac in France, AT&T and IBM, Istel (a joint venture between GEIS and ICL), British Telecom as from late 1991, and others.

EDI requires a paperwork re-organization on an extensive scale and a number of larger companies have adopted it. For example Marks & Spencer operates an EDI scheme for its clothing suppliers. Motor manufacturers and traders use UK exchange transactions via the Istel service. In Singapore a system called TRADENET has been established with 1600 users who exchange transactions with government buying agencies.

In the United States the Department of Defence is a major operator, running EDI with many of its suppliers. Its major procurement centre operates this way with over 5000 contractors.

The main standards in use appear to be ANSI X12 in the United States, ODETTE in the motor industry, and the Article Number Association's (ANA) standard who developed it for trading in the UK.

There are probably over 30,000 EDI-using companies in the world. More than half are in the United States, and in Europe the UK with 5000 users has more than the rest of Europe put together. The income derived from EDI carriers according to one source amounted to $150 million in 1990, and to another source to $86 million in that year.

EDI is expected to expand in Europe in consequence of market unification although the vast majority of European companies are probably too small to be able to use it with advantage. The EC is trying to show that it can in fact benefit small businesses through a number of cross-border pilot projects.

ELECTRONIC DATA INTERCHANGE FOR ADMINISTRATION COMMERCE AND TRANSPORT (EDIFACT)

In an attempt to introduce international standardization an organization called The Electronic Data Interchange for Administration Commerce and Transport (EDIFACT) held its first meeting in Brussels in June 1988. EDIFACT has continued to develop and message parameters are continously being added to it.

Edifact is intended to provide a generic national and international EDI syntax and message set able to accommodate many current standards. EDI standards were developed within the UN/ECE WP4 committee, to form an International Standard – ISO 9735, with a Data Directory (ISO 7372). US EDI are based on X12, and European on a numerical system. X400 is the recommendation for standardizing and interconnecting message systems.

X12 and EDIFACT are expected to be integrated during 1994 but widespread adoption of the system is not expected until the late 1990s.

ELECTRONIC FUNDS TRANSFER AT POINT OF SALE (EFTPOS)

Automatic transfer of funds from a purchaser's account to a retailer's in consequence of a message sent to the purchaser's bank from a point of sale terminal.

ELECTRONIC INFORMATION EXCHANGE SYSTEM (EIES)
See under ELECTRONIC JOURNAL.

ELECTRONIC JOURNALS
"It seems likely that the electronic journal will not soon replace the traditional journal format, which has served us so well for these many decades", says Freeman (1987). "Rather, more likely it will carve out its own niche by providing those kind of services unique to the electronic medium, services which emphasize interactive capabilities with databases and other colleagues, the communication of brief and highly current information, as well as the handling of large blocks of statistical information so valuable to the scientific community".

Journals, usually scientific in nature, compiled edited and "published" using a computer, and disseminated via computer terminals have been much discussed. At least two large experiments have been carried out, the first at The New Jersey Institute of Technology called The Electronic Information Exchange System (EIES); two actual journals were published called *Chimo* and *The Mental Workload*.

The second was a scheme carried out at the Universities of Loughborough and Birmingham sponsored by the British Library called the BLEND experiment. Journals called *Computer Human Factors and References* and *Abstracts and Annotations Journal* were published.

A number of other projects are in progress but none seems to be making much progress partly because of technical problems, but more particularly because of administrative problems such as copyright and refereeing.

The book *Information 2000* says that "in some areas printed (scientific and technical) journals may disappear because the major product of the system is data, and the deposit of data in a databank may be accepted as the equivalent of a journal article... The "publish or perish" syndrome may change... publication on CD-ROM with the end users paying for each contribution printed down or downloaded may also lead to the effective demise of the journal structure".

It may sound reasonable that technically-oriented scientists and technologists will take to electronic media, which presumably includes reading from an electronic display of some kind. The book devotes seven pages to the electronic journal but manages to avoid saying that all attempts at publishing several different variations of it have ended in failure – assuming that success is judged by the desire of a sufficient number of people to contribute to, and read them.

Humans are conservative and don't like to see a serious disturbance of well-established customs which more or less ensure that ability is rewarded. The sociology of science has been well documented – it hinges on established publication practices.

There are several electronic journals running on the Bitnet and Usenet networks in the US and they will be joined by *Current Clinical Trials* published by the AAAS.

Eugene Garfield considers that "the definition of peer reviewing undergoes a metamorphosis" in networked electronic publication. But "while some scientists such as Nobel laureate Joshua Lederberg believe that the peer review process is the glue that holds the scientific establishment together, others are now questioning what would be lost by the disappearance of refereeing. In the latter instance readers would have to decide the merits of a paper for themselves, which, some argue, is already necessary because of ineffectual refereeing".

ELECTRONIC MAIL (E-MAIL)
A system for the delivery of messages from networked computer terminals to storage at addressee's terminals for retrieval on demand. A basic electronic mail system consists of a store and forward computer, and the appropriate software. A network interconnects users with terminals.

An electronic mail system may be operated as a national or international public service, or it may be owned by a particular organization using its own system and telecommunications.

In 1980 the SG VII discussion group was formed at the CCITT to deal with message handling. In 1984 it produced recommendation X400 Message Handling Standards. The standard consists of rules enabling users to compose or send messages to others across various systems and links (See separate entry). It is "OSI model" compatible.

Other kinds of systems are sometimes called electronic mail systems. They include facsimile, telex, and other schemes for conveying messages in a less formal style than X400-based electronic mail systems.

A message sent under X400 consists basically of an "envelope", carrying the address including the name of the originator and recipient ("an O/R address"). The body of a message can contain any kind of file composed of ASCII code, spread sheets, images, etc. The system is made up of one or more "user agents" (UA), for example a user and his PC, and one or more "Message Transfer Agents" (MTA).

When a user sends a message to another remote user it is handled by the "local" MTA which communicates with the remote user's MTA, and hence to that user.

An electronic mail system can consist of a single user with the necessary equipment and software directly connected to a network – for example PSS in the United Kingdom – or it may consist of a group of users on a LAN with certain common equipment, connected via a network to external subscribers.

The same basic elements of an EM system are present in association with a single or multiple user system although with the latter there may be single elements working on behalf of all users.

A typical arrangement might consist of a number of PCs connected via a LAN to a "gateway PC" which acts as an MTA on behalf of the whole group. The gateway PC contains an X25 card which connects it via a modem to the network.

For a group subscriber to a system such as BT's Mail Box service there are three software elements which come on a disc and are loaded into each PC – the basic electronic mail system software, X400 software, and software associated with the modem connecting the group to an external network eabling it to transfer message files.

If the system is for use between LAN PCs and does not include a service operator such as BT, alternatives to X400 are available.

X400 becomes competitive on a per-user basis when there are many users of the same system. Competing "X400-like" software is available from other companies such as Action Technology with their Message Handling Service (MHS) software, which acts in the same way but is more limited. X400 is one of the earliest properly worked out applications which fits into the OSI top applications layer. The advantage of using it is that it should work satisfactorily with any other remote system also using X400.

A service may provide various additional facilities. For example the British Telecom Mailbox Service includes a message management package, enables telexes to be sent and received within the same system, and provides for messages to be sent to Group 3 fax machines.

Apart from systems devised by electronic mail carriers such as BT, there are a large number of competing E-mail packages for private use, for instance, for people in the same organization who are widely dispersed but are all on a large LAN. Unless each user on any EM system uses the same gateway arrangements, conversion software will be needed to accommodate other gateways. Many packages include options for alternative gateways and will work with a number of them such as X400 or MHS.

A major problem with electronic mail has been the inadequate number of subscribers and the absence of subscriber directories. One of the attractions of any mail system is to know that there is a critical mass of users – the chances that anybody with whom you wish to communicate on the system is high. At present the chances of communication within your own country are far greater than the communication possibilities with subscribers in other countries. Interconnection of X400 electronic mail services between countries is proceeding rather slowly.

The introduction of directory services has also been slow; an associated CCITT recommmendation called X500 is being gradually introduced. X500 will consist of a directory on a geographically distributed but inter-connected database compatible with the OSI layer structure. The directory will be arranged as a tree with a root – countries, states, towns etc., with increasing detail as you go up the tree to the address of the person to whom you wish to address a message. So far as is known no such database is yet in existence.

Electronic mail has been subjected to a great deal of publicity but does not seem to be making the progress that was originally forecast. This may be partly due to the inroads of facsimile systems for which there is a critical mass of users and for which there is no need to become familiar with the workings of a computer system in order to send a message. Forecast for EM's progress are so different that they are not worth quoting.

E-mail is used by some major libraries as part of an online ordering system. The most successful use in the library world appears to be over ALANET which has over 2000 mailboxes and is used by members of the American Library Association, having been launched in the early 1980s. A number of online databases and newsletters are available on it. LANET, launched by the UK Library Association in 1989, and merged with an electronic mail system between librarians in polytechnics and universities, is based on BT's X400 system.

The cost of an electronic mail system depends on the method of costing it. For a large private system it has been calculated that the relative costs per message are $1.66 for fax, $0.51 for a letter, and $0.22 for electronic mail.

ELECTRONIC NUMERICAL INTEGRATOR AND AUTOMATIC CALCULATOR (ENIAC)
A computer containing 18,000 vacuum tubes (valves) widely regarded, perhaps incorrectly, as the world's first real electronic computer controlled by a stored program. It was built by J W MAUCHLY and J P ECKERT and used at the Moore School of the University of Pennsylvania, in the period 1946 – 1950.

See also COMPUTERS – HISTORY.

ELECTRONIC PUBLISHING
A phrase covering a multitude of activities in which electronics is used at some stage of publication.

The idea of "On-Demand Publishing" – that nothing is published until you order it – was discussed in the early seventies.

"Technical advances have led system planners to think about a time when published texts-books, journals, and the like – would not reach the public via printing on a press, physical transport to distributors, and, finally, sales through bookstores. This traditional route has become costly and cumbersome. In the new scheme, books would not be printed on a press at all, but would enter the home via the direct expedient of the home communications set (HCS)", said one writer.

Manuscripts formatted by computer into electronic pages that when printed out would look like pages of a traditional book, would be entered digitally (that is, broken down into a coded stream of electronic bits) into a computer. The "book" would be stored in the computer's memory until it was called up by someone who wanted to purchase it at home. The facsimile printer on the purchaser's home communciations set would then print it out and the system would bill him on his quarterly statement.

Or the subscriber might "borrow" the book, perhaps in a form restricted to page-by-page reading on the screen. (Authors could be compensated each time their books were borrowed – a practice already common in Swedish libraries).

The borrowing possibility led enthusiasts of two-way systems to envision central libraries – perhaps only one in a state or province in North America or a whole country in Europe – where all computerized books would be stored, ending the need for multiple "hard" copies in a series of local libraries.

Books stored digitally in computers would never be "out" of the library when you came to borrow them. Older books would not have to be discarded to make room for new ones on the shelves.

Something like this will happen for certain kinds of books according to *Information 2000* :-

"Publishers of text monographs will increasingly keep infinite backlists in electronic form for on-demand laser printing and to target smaller markets – to a certain extent this is happening already. One consequence of this will be an ever greater reliance on catalogues; if taken to its extreme, academic bookshops will look more like Argos catalogue stores".

The book also envisages a much more adventurous future for on-demand publishing:-

"The technology for the electronic book combined with the concept of on-demand publishing makes the production of one-off, on-demand, academic monographs or novels a real possibility. More interesting from the point of view of the entity 'published' is the possibility of customers going to bookshops to have their computer card/cartridge loaded with data from different sources that they themselves select.

Likewise subsets of textbooks could be downloaded at different times for different courses, and customers will be able to download from online databases for local storage and manipulation. Appropriate charging mechanisms will need to be devised".

ELECTRONIC SHOPPING
See HOME SHOPPING.

ELECTROSTATIC RECORDING
A recording method in which a "writing" element charges a point on the surface of nonconductive paper or intermediate drum, corresponding to a "black signal" element. A liquid or particle "toner" then adheres to charged points and is fixed permanently by heat.

ELHILL
Lister Hill National Center for Biomedical Communication.

EM
1. The width of the GLYPH "m" in a font, used for reference purposes since it is the widest lower case letter, nominally the same size as the POINT size. Other Glyph widths are not directly related to Point size.

2. ELECTRONIC MAIL.

EMBASE
Excerpta Medica Data Base.

EMITTER COUPLED LOGIC (ECL)
A 2-transistor circuit arranged to reduce delays in current switching to the absolute minimum.

EMS
Expanded Memory Specification.

EMULAT- ION -OR
The use of programming techniques and special machine features to permit a computing system to execute programs written for another system. A particular example is where a microcomputer with the addition of special hardware and/or software can be made to act as a terminal compatible with a mainframe computer.

EPS
Encapsulated POSTSCRIPT. A format for file printing.

ENCRYPTION
A code is the substitution of codewords for plain language, while the two major types of cypher – transposition and substitution – are operations on individual characters. Cyphers and cryptography (from the Greek kryptos, hidden, and graphein, to write) are used to prepare secret messages.

The two major encryption methods in use today are the DES or Data Encryption Standard and the PKA or Public Key Algorithm. They provide protection against the theft of tapes or disks, or against the interception of data in the course of transmission.

The DES specifies an enciphering algorithm for the high speed processing of data by computer hardware. A 56 bit key is used for multiple permutations of blocks of plain text composed of 65 bits inclusive of 8 error-detection bits. To decipher, it is only necessary to apply the same algorithm to an enciphered block using the same key. Everyone knows the algorithm but only the sender and receiver know the selected key.

There are 72 quadrillion possible keys and there has been some controversy about the effort and cost needed to produce a computer capable of breaking the algorithm, with charges of collusion between the US National Security Agency and IBM who developed it. There may or may not be any foundation in these charges.

The PKA, however, embodies an additional factor to nullify the possible effect of the security risk inherent in the DES; with DES, information about keys could be intercepted en route to perhaps many correspondents. PKA uses two separate keys – a public enciphering key and a different secret deciphering key. The inverse of the enciphering functions cannot be derived even if the enciphering functions are known.

The distribution of information about keys to the message recipient is not necessary because of the "trap-door" method of using one way enciphering and inverse functions. The PKA also embodies a signature to authenticate the sender as actually being the person he is purporting to be.

A computerized encryption scheme somewhat resembling a one-time pad, widely used during the last war, seems to be emerging as a new contender.

The key in the "one-time pad", invented by G. Vernam in 1917, is a sequence of randomly generated bits, held by both message sender and recipient. The message to be sent, coded into bits, is "XORed" with the key. The recipient XORs his received message with the same key to decypher the message.

An Xor (Exclusive or) logic device has two input terminals, X and Y, and one output terminal. Its operation can be expressed as "X or Y but not both" – i.e. identical inputs produce a 1 output, non-identical a 0.

Thus:- 0,0,= 1 0,1,= 0 1,0,= 0 1,1,= 1.

As used in World War II, the one-time pad "key" was contained in a pad of numbered pages containing lines of columnized randomly generated decimal numbers held by message sender and recipient. The letters of a message to be sent were first encoded into numbers using a simple substitution code. The sender subtracted each number, without borrowing, from a one time pad number, starting at a particular column and line on a particular page, and the result was transmitted. The message contained a group at the beginning telling the addressee where to start on his pad.

The recipient, starting at the place indicated by the sender on his copy of the same one-time pad, subtracted each received number from his one-time pad number without borrowing thereby de-ciphering the message, and then changed the numbers back to the original letters using the same substitution code as used by the sender. Provided each new message was enciphered using a part of the pad never used previously, the method was perfectly secure.

The new version is more like Vernam's, and was invented recently by Robert Mathews, also the science correspondent of the Daily Telegraph. It overcomes the inconvenience of distributing keys to intended message recipients in advance. It includes a device which always generates the same set of random numbers when triggering a number which generates a new set of random numbers.

Actually the system as just described could not work because a truly random number list cannot be repeated. The numbers are "pseudo-random", generated by electronic circuits capable of generating the same set of pseudo-random numbers when triggered by the same triggering number, but sufficiently different from any other set of pseudo-random numbers generated by different triggering numbers to make cipher-breaking almost impossible.

The design background to such systems is discussed by Zeng et al (1991). The only way to determine the randomness, and hence the undecipherability of a message using a particular system design, is to subject messages to "merciless attacks" using the armoury of known cipher-breaking techniques to see if the system can resist them.

A different solution is needed for the case when a large computer, connected to a communication network, contains files of different security classifications, and it is desired to make the installation available to a number of people who themselves are within different security categories.

Machines can embody a security "kernel" or interface between the operating system – that is specialized software controlling computer functions – and the hardware. The function of the kernel is to check the access rights of each user to any information-containing system element. It may, of course, be necessary to encrypt data flowing through the network as well.

See also CODES, HACKERS, PRIVACY & FREEDOM, TRANSBORDER DATA FLOW, VIRUSES & WORMS.

ENHANCED GRAPHICS ADAPTOR
See under DISPLAY COLOUR AND GRAPHICS.

ENIAC
ELECTRONIC NUMERICAL INTEGRATOR AND AUTOMATIC CALCULATOR.

EPC
EDITORIAL PROCESSING CENTRE.

EPLD
Electrically Programmed Logic Device.

EPOS
Electronic Point of Sale.

EPROM
Erasable Programmable Read Only Memory.
  See also SEMICONDUCTORS – MEMORY CHIPS.

EQUALIZING
A method of compensating for distortion introduced in a communications channel by adjusting circuit elements externally connected to it. Usually this means, in effect, increasing the channel response to higher frequencies to compensate for the greater line attenuation at those frequencies.

ERIC
Educational Research Information Center.

ERLANG
A unit used for defining the volume of telephone traffic, measured as the connection rate of calls multiplied by their mean holding time.

ESA
European Space Agency.

ESA-IRS
ESA Information Retrieval Service.

ESPRIT
ESPRIT – the European Strategic Programme for Research and Development in Information Technology – was launched in 1984. It supports companies with up to 50% of the costs of approved research projects, and universities and research centres with up to 100%.

In 1989, 292 large companies, 386 small and medium-sized (up to 500 employees) companies, 184 universities and 109 research and other institutes were involved in Esprit. The priority areas for RACE II and Telematic Systems are:-
  Integrated Broadband Communications (IBC).
  Intelligent networks; communications resource management.
  Mobile and personal communications.
  Image and data communications.
  Integrated services technology.
  Information security technologies.
  Advanced communication experiments.
  Infrastructures and interworking supporting other areas.
  Trans-European network administration.
  Road transport telematics.
  Health care telematics.
  Flexible and distance learning.
  Library services.
  Linguistics.
  Rural areas.
  These areas are part of two related schemes – RACE II (Research and Technological Development Programme in the field of Communication Technologies) covering the period 1990-1994, supported with 484 million Ecu (10 Ecus = £7 = $11.5 approx) and "Research and Technological Development Programme in the field of Telematic Systems of General Interest" supported with 376 million Ecu.

ESRIN
European Space Research Institute.

ESRO
European Space Research Organization.

ETAM
Entry Telecommunication Access Method.

ETHERNET
A widely used Local Area Network conforming to the provisions of the OPEN SYSTEMS INTERCONNECTION (OSI) seven layer model.
  See also NETWORKS – LANS.

ETSI
European Telecommunication Standard Institute.

EURIPA
European Information Providers Association.

EURONET
European Network for Scientific and Technical Information.

EUSIDIC
European Association of Scientific Information Dissemination Centres.

EUTELSAT
European Telecommunications Satellite Organization.

EXECUTIVE INFORMATION SYSTEMS (EIS)
A computer-based database and information system characterized by ease of use and explicit graphics designed for executives to assist them to manage the company. The title for this type of system may have been introduced because of the poor reputation of many Management Information Systems and Decision Support Systems.

One authority considered that:- "To some extent the difficulties which so many organizations have been having with computer-based management information systems can be attributed to gaps in our understanding of the decision-making process itself".

The title "Executive Information Systems" may indicate that some new ideas have emerged – it is said that by 1990 over one thousand EISs were in use in the united States.

A number of companies supply such systems, the leader probably being Comshare with its Commander system. EIS usually require a degree of customizing to suit the company for which they are intended in order to supply and up-date the kind of information that executives require.

Today's EIS have moved in a rather different direction, and have been able to do so because of developments in computer power, business software, and graphic displays. Current trends seem to be as follows:-
1. Providing special software for the selective retrieval of data available from an organization's mainframe computer, and/or from external information sources.
2. Arranging for the software to provide access in critical data sources via an interface directly useable by executives, rather than by information specialists, with "key indicator" information displayed in well designed colour graphic form.
3. Exploiting financial modelling usually of the multiple spreadsheet type, and the provision of calculations controlled by rules which may be switched by the user.
4. Providing exception reporting – i.e. providing information about key data when it varies by more than some pre- determined amount.

The choice of the regularly up-dated information to be presented on the screens of an EIS is a key factor for its success. EIS's first costs are likely to be at least £50,000 and preparational and running costs will be substantial. It was found in a survey that organizations took 12 weeks on average to provide a first attempt "at a cost of many weekends and late-night sessions to meet delivery".

Most EISs pursue an evolutionary course because "senior executive's work is largely unstructured and subject to constantly changing pressures and fresh priorities. As a result prospective users are rarely certain about what they want to see". According to Richard Munton, ICI's EIS manager "stop developing and you've had it".

Negotiating with departments to include their data in the system raises some of the biggest problems. It is important to develop an EIS for groups of executives as opposed to an individual thereby making the survival of the system less dependent on any key user.

EXHAUSTIVITY
See INDEXING SYSTEM PERFORMANCE – EXHAUSTIVITY AND SPECIFICITY.

EXPANDED MEMORY
See MEMORY.

EXPANSION SLOTS
Slots provided in a computer for receiving boards, or cards, enabling the machine to carry out additional operations.

EXPERT SYSTEM
See ARTIFICIAL INTELLIGENCE.

EXPONENT
The power to which the number base is raised e.g. in 10^3 and 2^8, 3 and 8 are the exponents.

EXTENDED INDUSTRY STANDARD ARCHITECTURE (EISA)

A bus architecture agreed by a consortium of manufacturers including AST Research, Compaq, Epson, Hewlett-Packard, NEC, Olivetti, Tandy, Wyse and Zenith. The incentive for the bus was provided by the licensing fees charged by IBM for its PS/2 MICRO-CHANNEL ARCHITECTURE (MCA).

EXTENDED MEMORY

See MEMORY.

F

FACSIMILE ("FAX")
A system for transmitting a copy of an image on a piece of paper from one fax machine to another via a communication channel, usually the PSTN.

A facsimile machine converts an image, uually text or graphics printed on paper, into electrical impulses for transmission. The impulses are converted back to a virtually identical image by a remote machine of a similar kind. Each machine works either as a transmitter or as a receiver.

The transmitted impulse speed is set to run within the limits of the telephone line's bandwidth. There is a "tradeoff" situation; in images without fine detail and so requiring fewer transmitted bits, the scanning speed can be increased to enable the entire page to be transmitted in, say, 2 minutes. But if fine detail is present, the speed must be decreased for, say, a 6 minute transmission time. This enables three times the number of elements to be transmitted without generating high frequency components outside the passband of the line.

Estimates of the number of machines in use are up to about 250,000 in the UK and up to about 3.5 million worldwide.

The reproduction of halftones in illustrations between proprietary machines is improving and although colour facsimile has been demonstrated it is unlikely to be widely used for some years because of equipment and transmission costs.

Other recent developments include a steady reduction in the price of machines in a market totally dominated by the Japanese, and the addition of numerous "bells and whistles". Some of these may be sales gloss added for an intensely competitive market, others useful additions, depending on the user's requirements. In 1988 machines became available in the UK for less than £1000.

In "Group 3" (the present generation) and "Group 4" (the next generation) machines, each of a series of tiny photosensitive elements in a row wide enough to span the paper, generates a voltage proportional to the intensity of light reflected from the small area beneath it. All these voltages are transmitted as a series of digital impulses, the paper is moved a fraction of an inch by rollers, the elements sense another horizontal strip, and the process is repeated until the entire image is scanned. At the remote receiver, voltages are applied to a strip of printing elements and a line of marks appears on the special printing paper in synchronism with the scanner.

Current developments are concentrated on the means of sending the maximum number of bits in the shortest possible time to reduce telephone costs and inconvenience. When wider bandwidth telecommunications become available it will be possible to send fax images much more quickly.

Plug-in circuit boards have appeared to convert Personal Computers into fax machines. Although the cost is around £1000, the features included make the PC perform like a higher priced fax machine.

By 1993 a large number of facsimile servers for networks have also become available. A network client passes his service request to the faxserver. There are several ways of arranging fax-on-a-network. In a peer-to-peer arrangement the fax server at a user's workstation communicates directly via a network protocol. In another arrangement the file server is used to handle directory problems. In another system faxes are conveyed round the network using E-mail transport.

All the systems provide image conversion, and facsimile transmission and reception. One quite severe problem remains – and that is sending a fax to a specific user who is on a fax network, because there is no standard way of addressing such a user. It usually requires an intermediary at the receiving end to route the fax to the appropriate person.

FACSIMILE – FACILITIES
Most of the "new developments" are not really new – "PC-fax" is one of the few fairly new trends. Rather is it that different functions are being introduced by combining known features in different ways. These functions are being included with some machines

at a lower price.

Additional facilities are now often available including:-

* Short code dialling; allows a number to be auto-dialled by depressing one key or two keys.
* Automatic re-try.
* Delayed send: set the machine to send the document loaded into it at a pre-set time – for instance during working hours in an overseas country.
* Programmed send: Load the machine with a series of documents each to be sent automatically to particular addresses at the same or different times. The necessary instructions can be stored ready to be used again and executed by pressing a single key.
* Card programming: similar functions may be carried out on some machines by inserting an Optical Mark Reader (OMR) card into a slot.

FACSIMILE – HISTORY

A form of electro-mechanical facsimile was used over telegraph circuits by a Scotsman, Alexander Bain, in the 1940s, but the pioneer of modern facsimile was Arthur Korn, an American. Early in this century Korn used a system very similar in principle to modern machines for transmitting photographs. Later, machines made by RCA were in use by the US newspaper industry and for disseminating weather maps, but the wider application of facsimile did not start until the 1970s.

In the early 70s there was a small specialized demand for facsimile equipment. The market leader in the United States was Xerox. In Britain, Muirhead had been producing machines for some years for specialized requirements, particularly for the Press. After the recession of the mid 70s the use of facsimile equipment in offices increased in the US and two companies came to the fore – Qwip and Rapifax.

In Japan a different kind of need was forcing developments. Facsimile transmission was an obvious way of by-passing the problems associated with the coding of kanji characters bit by bit for transmission. Impetus was also given to facsimile in other spheres – notably in the US space programme, in weather forecasting, and in the transmission of specialized data for the oil industry. The Alden Company in the United States and Muirhead in Britain were the market leaders for special equipment.

In the late 70s talk about "electronic offices" started. The cost of transmitting a business facsimile letter in about six minutes (a speed which had been used for some years) over the public switched telephone network (PSTN) was too great and this speed was too slow for general office use. New incompatible machines started to appear prompted by cost reductions on two fronts – rapid developments in cheap semiconductor technology, and faster, cheaper, transmission made possible by coding and compression.

For a time it looked as if leading manufacturers would attempt to establish de facto standards, but eventually there was some agreement that the common interest would best be served by collaboration in developing new standards in line with current technology. Consequently standards for group 2 and group 3 machines were born; draft standards for group 4 machines arrived later.

There was controversy during the introduction of these standards by the protagonists of new machines and new data reduction codes. The Japanese, emerging as a major force, had already developed codes which were different from those developed in Europe and America.

The wide adoption of CCITT recommendations was an important factor in the expansion of the industry although the efforts of pressure groups on standardization committees resulted in several compromises, notably the inclusion of "options". Quite a number of manufacturers now include with the CCITT recommended facilities and options, a number of non-CCITT options.

The potential problems that this might introduce have to some extent been overcome by the adoption of CCITT recommended "handshaking" procedures which establish, at the time of the first interconnection of two machines, which of the available facilities and options will be used for the current "conversation". Some manufacturers, doubtless in the belief that they can tie in a sufficiently large number of users to their own equipment, offer sophisticated machines without making any claims to CCITT compatibility.

Ancient telephone networks generate noise which affects fax images according to the amount of detail which is destroyed. This will lessen as networks are modernized. Meanwhile some of the more expensive machines include a relatively new, very welcome, addition – automatic error detection.

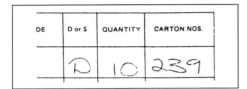

Large "noise resistant" characters

Information in information-rich areas of images without redundancy is most likely to be destroyed by noise. The vulnerability of text is inversely proportional to its size. Graphics are usually less vulnerable than text unless parts or all of a graphics image are information-rich. For example all parts of a survey image of the earth's surface produced by the Landsat satellite could contain important fine detail with zero redundancy.

The Figures show firstly (above), large characters which could still be readable in spite of some noise, and in the second figure (below), the originals and enlargements of the effect on small text of certain kinds of noise.

See also NOISE.

FACSIMILE – STORAGE-BASED FUNCTIONS

The inclusion of larger storage facilities (memory) in facsimile machines – now much more common because memory costs continue to fall – enables the contents of a document which has been scanned to be stored as a data file. Some machines include enough storage for 120 data files/pages or more.

Functions which become possible when storage is available within the machine include Group Dialling, Broadcasting, Relay Broadcasting, and Secure Mailboxes. To conduct these operations the communicating fax machines must usually be of the same make because the methods used by different manufacturers (there are no CCITT recommendations for these functions) may not be the same.

Storage-based new functions include:-

* Group Dialling

When it is required to send a series of telephone numbers to another machine, part of the memory in machines with suf-

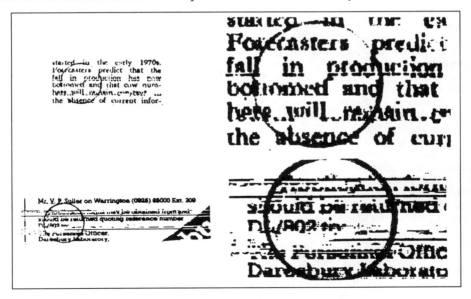

Original and magnified portions of text affected by noise.

ficient storage may be used to store numbers which may be sent by pressing one key.

* Broadcasting

A fax machine with sufficient storage can dial a number of remote machines automatically and send the same stored pages to each, or different stored pages to each.

* Relay Broadcasting

A fax machine with sufficient storage can automatically dial another machine designated for broadcasting, issue a series of stored telephone numbers to it, and instruct it to broadcast to those numbers.

* Secure mailboxes

A part of the memory in machines with memory may be allocated to a specific user as a "secure mailbox" into which his or her received messages are directed. Only the mailbox "owner" can obtain access to these messages by using either a password or inserting a coded card.

* RS232 Interface

An input/output arrangement enabling a fax machine to communicate with a computer. The fax can be used as a computer graphics printer, or (with the right software) as a scanner to input non-editable text or graphics to a computer.

* Mobile fax

The widespread use of radio-telephones in cars has prompted the use of in-car portable facsimile machines. The basic requirements are a small easily operated machine, a power supply so the machine can operate from the car's 12 volt supply, an "interface" – that is a connection between the fax and the mobile radio – and full error correction.

In CELLULAR RADIO, communications with mobiles in a small zone of the country are established through a local low-power fixed radio station. Before getting out of range a car leaving one zone is automatically passed on to the station in the next.

Special error correction is needed to cope with interference, signal fluctuations, and the station changeover instant. Muirhead, for example, offer a "Cellfax" equipment specially for the purpose.

Fax is also being used for non-cellular radio communication. A company called Globecom offer their "Shuttleboy" portable fax machine

with an acoustic coupler for use with those mobile radios embodying a Motorola power supply, for about £1400.

Other features include:-

* Colour fax

Colour copiers are gaining ground and, colour fax, or a combined fax/copier may become more generally used.

* Fax switching

A fax switch connects an incoming call from a single line to either a fax machine or to the telephone so that the subscriber's telephone number is also his fax number. The switch listens for the fax tone from the sending machine and connects the line to the recipient's machine if it hears it, otherwise it rings the telephone.

* Plain paper printing

The special paper used in thermal printers will retain the image for a long period unless subjected to excessive heat, and unless the paper is stored against a surface, as in some types of plastic folder, which will cause the image to fade because of chemical interaction. The alternatives are thermal transfer printers which use a ribbon between the head and special paper, or machines which print on ordinary paper. Either method increases the price of the fax machine and increases paper costs, but the extra cost is diminishing as economies of scale take effect.

FAIRTHORNE, ROBERT A,

Robert Fairthorne joined the Royal Aircraft Establishment at Farnborough in 1927. Later he became a Senior Principal Scientific Officer at that Establishment. In the 60s he worked at Herner & Co., Washington, and from 1967 onwards was a visiting professor at the School of Library Science, University of New York at Albany.

Fairthorne is a mathematician who studied information science in the early days. He was particularly interested in Shannon's work and clarified its relationship to information systems.

His various papers, particularly *The Mathematics of Classification* were models of clarity at a time when many new devices were being tried out for information storage and retrieval and clear thinking was badly needed. Fairthorne considered and discussed the possibilities and limitations of new technology.

FARADAY, MICHAEL
Faraday was a chemist and electrical engineer, born in 1791, died 1867. He became scientific assistant to Sir Humphrey Davy at the Royal Institution in 1812 and subsequently invented the electrical generator, and discovered electro-magnetic induction introducing the idea of magnetic lines of force.

Faraday also discovered the polarization of light by a magnetic field, invented methods for liquifying gases, and carried out numerous experiments earning him the title of "the greatest experimentalist of all time". He set the tradition at the Royal Institution for the popularization of science, himself being famous for popular lectures.

FAX
FACSIMILE.

FCC
Federal Communications Commission.

FDDI
FIBRE DISTRIBUTED DATA INTERFACE.

A standard recently agreed for high speed LANs using optical fibre cables. See under STANDARDS.

FDM
Frequency Division Multiplexing.

FEP
Front End Processor.

FET
FIELD EFFECT TRANSISTOR.

FFT
Fast Fourier Transform.

FIBRE DISTRIBUTED DATA INTERFACE (FDDI)
See under STANDARDS.

FIBREOPTICS
Fibreoptic communication is achieved by modulating a light source such as a Light Emitting Diode (LED), or for greater energy a laser, with digital electrical signals. The modulated light is propagated along a thin glass fibre and detected the other end by a photodiode which generates electrical signals when light falls on it.

The basic principle of propagation was demonstrated by John Tyndall at the Royal Institution in 1870. He showed that light could be transmitted within and along a curved glass rod by total internal reflection. However it was not until 1966 that two engineers, Kao and Hockam, working at Standard Telephones & Cables, predicted that low loss fibres "with an important potential as a new form of communications medium", could be made (Kao 1966). It was this work which prompted the research which led to the introduction of the first practical fibres made at Corning Glass in 1970.

Optical fibre and its accessories are a relatively expensive type of cabling. It has a very wide bandwidth enabling high transmission speeds. Fibre provides a high degree of security along with immunity from environmental factors such as an electrical noise. Users need equipment to convert electrical signals to light pulses and back again.

See also COAXIAL CABLE and TWISTED PAIR.

The bandwidth of fibreoptic cable can be up to 100 GHz per Km of cable, meaning that data transmission can take place at enormous bit rates over long distances. For newly created private networks such as LANs or Cable-TV networks the choice between coax and fibre is a matter of function and economics.

The cable is made by depositing compounds in vapour form (which will become the core) on to the inside of a silica tube (which will become the cladding). The tube is then collapsed and drawn out into a thin fibre. When the core diameter is about 1.4 microns, light introduced at a particular angle is propagated (monomode) with little energy loss along the fibre providing a data transmission medium capable of at least 1000 Mbps per Km without repeaters.

Fibreoptic cable is thin, light, and flexible. The bandwidth can be up to 100 GHz per Km and light losses can be as low as 5% per Km so very long lengths can be used – for example in undersea cable – without the need for regenerative repeaters, needed in other types of cable.

Fibreoptic cables are not susceptible to induced noise or interference, and the impending Fiber Distributed Data Interface

(FDDI) standard is likely to increase the popularity of fibre in Local Area Networks (LANs).

Fibreoptic cables inspire a certain amount of controversy. It has been said that fibre often becomes over-expensive overkill. 95% of all network connections fall within 100 metres of the wiring closet. Users only need 100 metres of cabling between closet and house, and twisted pair can provide this capability in the most cost-efficient way possible. Connection between closet and exchange is another matter.

When the public telephone system is required to handle data at speeds for which it was not designed, parts of the network must be replaced. Those parts carrying heavy traffic – for instance in the trunk network – do not need replacement; fibre has been economically viable and the preferred cable for PTT heavy traffic for some years.

But at present all cables radiating out from local exchanges to subscribers – representing a large part of the whole system – are copper pairs cable of bit rates up to about 150 Kbps on average. For "end-to-end" broadband telecommunications to be available, broadband cables must run all the way between individual subscribers.

Different authorities have different ideas about when to make this very large investment, probably in fibreoptics. For some years fibre has been about to become competitive for the "local loop" but this never quite seems to happen. It has been recently claimed that fibre would not be commercially viable to the home for at least ten years.

Although British Telecom anticipated running fibreoptic cable into some homes to replace "local loop" copper pairs when necessary for the ISDN, nothing has happened yet. C.Quinlan of the UK Cable Authority said at a recent RACE workshop in Brussels that "fibre would not be commercially viable to the home for at least ten years, and B.L.Egan of Columbia University said that it would cost $3000 to reach a subscriber.

Fibre has been economically viable and the preferred cable for PTT heavy traffic for some years. However if the hopes for a "Broadband ISDN" first to businesses and then to homes are to be realized, fibreoptic cable with its enormous bandwidth will become essential.

FID
Federation Internationale de Documentation.

FIELD
1. The transmission of an image in a television or video system by scanning it, line by line, from beginning to end. In an INTERLACED system a complete FRAME consists of two fields. The first field consists of every other line in the frame, the second the intervening lines.

2. A part of a record designated for a particular kind of data. For example each record in a car-part file might contain a field for the name of the part, a field for the manufacturer's name, a field for the part number, etc.

FIFO
A storage circuit operating on the principle of First in – First Out.

FILE
A named collection of computer records, usually with common attributes – for example descriptions of car parts. A file may be stored and recalled as one unit by name.

The major types of computer file are program files, which are executable – that is they may be run, often for control purposes – and data files which store information to be used under the control of a program.

FILES – INVERTED
Until quite recently serial searching of full text online has been unacceptably slow, and searching of suitably arranged surrogate records has usually been used. The inverted file and the multilist or threaded-list file are the most widely used out of several schemes for directory searching which have been developed for medium to large databases.

The inverted file seems to have gained widest acceptance. It is a directory to the keys used in records. A key is simply a search term such as a word, an author's name, a chemical formula etc. This idea has been mentioned before – peek-a-boo cards are an inverted file system.

For example a database might comprise a series of records describing company reports. Each record might be a surrogate with report titles and added keywords, author, data, and a shelf number indicating where the print-on-paper report itself is kept.

In an inverted file system it is the relatively small key directory which is searched by the computer, not the relatively large totality of surrogate text in records (or the full text in systems where each record contains the complete document). Inverted files are often searched using Boolean expressions – for instance in "Find records containing ELECTRONIC MAIL and MICROCOMPUTER" the machine has to identify the addresses of records containing both keys in a list in order to locate hit records.

The keys will be selected according to certain rules – for example there may be a "stop list" of trivial words ("the", "of" etc.,) which are not used as keys.

The number of hits resulting from this directory search can be displayed without the need for the records themselves being retrieved so that the user can quickly reformulate his question if necessary. The records can, of course, be retrieved as needed because their disc addresses remain stored in computer memory as a result of the search.

Penalties are paid for the convenience and operational speed of an inverted file system in the form of software complexity and storage space. When a new record is added to the record file, information must also be added to the separate key/record address directory (the inverted file).

Even if the keys are already in the directory, the address of each new record must be included with the other records containing those keys. If the record contains new unlisted keys, those keys as well as the record's address must be added to the directory.

The key directories occupy considerable storage space. Depending on the diversity of the file this space can approach that needed for the records themselves. In a batch system, a collection of new records are added periodically and the necessary re-organization process for that collection is carried out at some convenient time. Until that time, use of the new records is denied to users.

In a sequential search, the computer searches through the full text of the surrogate records which also serve as the index, not through a separate directory of indexing terms.

For sequentially ordered files no elaborate "loading" software is required since there is no key directory to be created when new records are added. Nor is there any need, in an online system, to arrange for searching operations to proceed simultaneously with updating operations.

In sequential file searching the problem avoided in the inverted file system remains – how can the computer find records containing, say, the strings ELECTRONIC MAIL and MICROCOMPUTER with an acceptable response time after the question is posed when it has to search the whole of each record?

FILES – RAPID SEARCHING OF A SEQUENTIAL FILE

If special methods for searching a sequential file are not introduced, the machine will simply search serially through the records until it finds a hit. Assuming that the records are stored on disk, the machine will transfer a block of records to the CPU and match them, character by character, against the query string. It will continue to do this until all records have been tried.

The response time will probably be long on most mainframe computers and will take several minutes on most microcomputers even if only a few thousand records of, say, 300 characters each, are stored on disk.

Various methods of overcoming this problem are available, and all require some additional software. The principle is usually to represent the contents of records by encoding them, to use the same code to encode the search query, and then to carry out the search by matching the encoded query against the encoded records. If the system is for online interactive use it must be possible to enter a new record into the system and then carry out a search in which the new record is immediately available as a potential hit.

FILES – TRANSFERRING DATA BETWEEN

For inter-computer communications some kind of interface – usually a plug-in card – is needed between the computer and the single telecoms channel or LAN, together with either separate software which handles inter-computer transactions on a "peer-to-peer" basis. Networked communications software may be needed, or most of it may have been included in the operating system.

The software may incorporate any of the file

transfer adjuncts such as Kermit, X,Y,Z, modem, and X on/X off.

File transfer software is available to allow any two computers on which it has been implemented, regardless of vendor, to communicate through RS232 serial ports, using either a hard-wire or telephone-line link with asynchronous modems. It can transmit and receive binary or text files and console commands. It provides easy to use menu screens auto-dial/auto logon and unattended operation. See MODEMS.

Mac-DOS-Mac file transfers are relatively easy when software such as WordPerfect, Pagemaker, etc., exists (as it does) in both Mac and DOS versions because both versions use the same file formats. Otherwise file conversion is necessary.

Additional software is needed for Mac/DOS printers – useful if a DOS user wants to use, say, a MAC laser printer. A package called TOPS will deal with it.

FILENAME EXTENSION
Between 1 and 3 letters placed after the name of a file to indicate its purpose. These letter are normally separated from the filename by a dot (period).

FILM
See MOVIES.

FINTEL
Financial Times Electronic Publishing.

FIRMWARE
A program which is permanently stored in a computer hardware device, often as a circuit which always performs the same functions when triggered.

FLA
Fellow of the Library Association.

FLASH MEMORY
See SEMICONDUCTORS – MEMORY CHIPS.

FLATBED SCANNING
A scanning procedure in which an illuminated document is moved on rollers driven by a stepping motor past a photo-sensor strip so that it is flat when opposite the strip. See SCANNERS.

FLIP-FLOP
A bistable multivibrator.

FLOATING POINT NUMBER
The representation of a number by integer(s) multiplied by the radix raised to a power e.g. 105 becomes 1.05×10^2. This form or representation is more convenient for computer handling; it allows for a large dynamic range and high relative precision.

FM
Frequency Modulation.

FOI
Freedom of Information Act.

FOLDER
The computer analogy of a paper or cardboard folder. A "container" of objects or documents.

FONT
A collection of printed characters of the same size e.g. 10 point Goudy Heavyface Condensed, or 8 point Times Bold Italic.

A font is printed with a particular pitch – for example a setting of 6, might provide a character repetition of 6 per inch for fixed width characters (mono-spaced font) where each character occupies the same amount of horizontal space. With a proportionally spaced font each character occupies a different amount of width.

FOOTPRINT
Of a Direct Broadcasting Satellite. Geographical area over which a satellite signal can be received.

FOREGROUND PROCESSING
Processing operations controlled by user intervention (as opposed to BACKGROUND PROCESSING).

FORTRAN
FORmula TRANslation, a high-level computer programming language developed by IBM.
See COMPUTERS – LANGUAGES.

FOURTH GENERATION
See COMPUTERS – FOURTH GENERATION.

FRACTAL

A fractal is a curve constructed from a mathematical formula such that any small part of it, when enlarged, has the same statistical character as the original. In many objects, small portions resemble larger portions as in ferns, snowflakes, coastlines, etc. Accordingly codes can be devised to eliminate redundant geometric information by scaling-up or scaling-down images, thereby providing very high compression ratios.

Fractal geometry is about "scale invariance", a property of natural objects first observed by Renoit Mandelbrot of IBM around 1961. Mandelbrot noticed that the coastline of Britain looked much the same when viewed from different distances. Coastal indentations viewed from 1 Km look similar to inlets and peninsulars visible at 5 Km which look similar to a larger collection visible at 30 Km etc., of which the smaller collections have become a part. See also under COMPRESSION.

FRAME

1. An element of a coded message ending with a unique bit pattern used in telecommununications systems. The detection of the pattern by the receiving terminal indicates that another frame is about to start thereby maintaining synchronization between transmitter and receiver.
2. A self-contained message element, for example a PACKET, to be handled in a specified manner. "Framing", or element handling, may occur at fixed time intervals, or may be controlled by data contained within each element.
3. One complete picture on a television or a computer screen. See also FIELD.

FRAME GRABBER

A device for capturing a video frame and storing it on a computer.

In a microcomputer fitted with a frame grabber board, the user observes a television programme and selects a single frame, which is then stored and displayed for processing, by pressing a single key. A frame could come from a number of different sources with different characteristics so the frame grabber must ideally be able to cope with whatever range of sources the user has in mind.

It must also provide visible frames which are compatible with the micro's display or an external monitor, and it should also be able to output to a video tape recorder.

The important matters which the board must cope with are modifying the characteristics of the grabbed frame so that it may viewed as a stable image on the screen and on an external monitor if one is used, and to provide facilities for editing it. The most generally required edit function is to overlay captions created on the computer for viewing by the user, for viewing as a future presentation if the composite picture is to be recorded on tape, or for viewing as print on paper.

A board such as Raster Op's 364 (Santa Clara, CA), used in a Mac II computer, enables 30 frames/second in 24 bit colour video to run in a window on the screen. The live video continues and more frames may be captured provided storage is made available. Any frame can be captured with a single keystroke, saved either in RAM storage on the board or in disc, and displayed at full screen size.

Processing facilities provided with the associated software include operations on single or groups of pixels, convolutions (operations for noise removal, edge enhancement etc), producing and controlling overlaid graphics or text, and many others. To make processing easier RGB may be converted to HSI (Hue-Saturation-Intensity) data. Processing then usually only requires the examination of one component instead of three.

FRAME RELAY

A fast variation of packet switching developed from the X25 LAP-B PROTOCOL. A frame relay packet can be handled several times faster than X25 because it dispenses with the ISO layer involving error correction and acknowledgement signals.

In consequence there is a much smoother flow of packet frames. It is assumed that error control will be taken care of by a layer three protocol operating in some other part of the system. Frame relay will be of particular advantage when traffic speeds in LANs are increased.

FREE TEXT RETRIEVAL

Free text retrieval software includes indexing arrangements for handling the searching of very large text blocks for the occurrence of particular strings. Searching is likely to include proximity matching – that is the search terms must be located within an indicated distance of each other.

Free text search systems usually include the optional use of a thesaurus. In a free text search the text to be searched may be arranged in the form document, section, paragraph, sentence and word so that the retrieved wanted part of it may be as broad or as narrow as may be needed. The major general purpose free-text search multi-user software is provided in Assassin, Basis, BRS, Cairs, Infotext, Mimer and Status.

Applications include searching law reports, corporate reports. organization minutes etc.

See also DATABASES – FULL TEXT SEARCHING.

FREQUENCY-DIVISION MULTIPLEXING
A technique that divides the available bandwidth of the transmission medium into a number of narrower bands or sub-channels separated by guard bands. Often used for multiplexing analogue signals.

FREQUENCY MODULATION (FM)
A method of varying the frequency of a carrier of fixed amplitude above and below the normal carrier frequency at a rate corresponding to changes in a modulating signal.

FREQUENCY SHIFT
A method of modulation in which 0's and 1's are signalled by shifting abruptly between two tones of different frequencies.

FREQUENCY-SHIFT KEYING (FSK)
A data modulation mode that transmits digital data by assigning a different frequency value for a zero or a one in each data bit. Normally used in 1200 bps MODEMs or lower.

FRONT END PROCESSING
Processing which is carried out in a special unit ahead of the main body of a computer, before it is sent to the computer for further processing.

FSK
FREQUENCY SHIFT KEYING.

FTAM
File Transfer Access and Management.

FULL TEXT DATABASE SEARCHING
See DATABASES – FULL TEXT SEARCHING.

FUZZY LOGIC
A method of representing smoothly variable (analogue) functions on digital computers. A person must write the rules for the execution of statements such as "if the temperature of the brakes is low and the speed is rather slow then slightly decrease the brake pressure". Fuzzy logic provides a smoother and wider range of control that would be provided by the alternative method of expressing the variables in terms such as "greater than 200°".

FUZZY SYSTEMS
It is usually difficult to attribute a single software discovery to one man, but there are at least two cases of original work – Codd's relational database (Codd 1970) and Zadeh's fuzzy logic (Zadeh, 1965). Although dating from 1965, Zadeh's work was not applied until processing power made it feasible. Fuzzy logic enables decisions to be made from data approximations. For example the suction power of a vacuum cleaner may be automatically adjusted according to signals from a sensor measuring the surface drag from the material being cleaned.

G

GaAs
GALLIUM ARSENIDE.

GALLIUM ARSENIDE (GaAs)
See SEMICONDUCTORS – GALLIUM ARSE-
NIDE.

GARFIELD, EUGENE
Born in 1926, Garfield is President of the Insti-
tute for Scientific Information, Philadelphia.
He published some experimental editions of
Current Contents in the early nineteen fifties.
The first major edition was *Current Contents
Life Sciences*, published weekly from 1958; it
provides timely information about the current
literature and is very widely used.

Garfield is best known for inventing the *Science Citation Index* (SCI) which was first produced as a commercial product during the
early sixties. It provides an entirely new way
of accessing the scientific literature based on
the idea that there is likely to be a connection
between the subject matter of a cited article
and later articles which cite it. The *SCI* is currently used not only as an information retrieval tool, but also as a means of studying the
behaviour and achievements of scientists and
scientific institutions, a relatively new field
called SCIENTOMETRICS.

GATE
A gate is a circuit which produces a binary
digit at its output (that is one of two possible
voltages) when two or more binary digits are
applied to its input. Gates are used for binary
logic functions and are rightly called the
building bricks of computers. For example a
gate with two input terminals which produces a 1 only when a 1 is applied to both
inputs is called an AND gate. Several other arrangements are possible and combinations of
gates can provide a whole range of calculating
and control functions.

Current trends are to manufacture arrays of
inter-connected gates of the smallest possible
size with the fastest possible switching speeds
on a chip using the materials and techniques
described under SEMI-CONDUCTORS.

Several integrated circuit gate arrangements known as Transistor Transistor Logic
(TTL), Emitter Coupled Logic (ECL), Diode
Transistor Logic (DTL) and Integrated Injection Logic (I²L) are manufactured using bipolar transistors. Multi-electrode transistors
with an input connected to each electrode are
sometimes used.

In another arrangement Schottky diodes
are associated with the transistor to clamp or
limit the level of each input voltage. A
Schottky diode is characterized by a low voltage drop across its electrodes. High input
impedance amplifiers may be included in a
gate circuit to reduce the load on preceding
circuits with low impedance "emitter followers" at the output to reduce the effect of
loading capacitance.

GATES, WILLIAM
Bill Gates was born in 1956 and grew into an
infant prodigy. At school he learned a three
page monologue for a play in one reading and
was able to recall it perfectly after two minutes.

Gates and Paul Allen started to work on a
computer language after having read about
the newly introduced Altair computer in 1974.
They wrote a language called BASIC (See
COMPUTERS – LANGUAGES) on a
larger machine and it worked on the Altair. Later
Allen and Gates moved to Seattle and bought
a piece of software called the Disc Operating
System (DOS) for $50,000 and agreed with
IBM that their company, Microsoft, would
write the operating system for the forthcoming IBM/PC, charging a royalty for every
copy used on each PC machine.

IBM also agreed that Microsoft could licence the same software to other manufacturers. The net result is that MS-DOS is
currently used on at least 60 million microcomputers and earns Microsoft over $200 Mil-
lion a year.

Later Microsoft extended their range of
software products and eventually introduced
Windows 3.0, another extremely successful
idea. Gates is now believed to be the richest
man in America with a fortune in excess of $6
billion.

GATEWAY

1. A communicating processor connected to at least two networks which enables messages to pass between them and therefore between stations connected to different networks. A gateway can interconnect two networks employing different architectures ideally using all seven layers of the OSI model in the process. For example it would be used to interconnect a network using a proprietary architecture to an OSI network. The term gateway is currently applied (although it may have been previously used in a more general sense) to a network inter-connection device in the progression: BRIDGE, ROUTER, GATEWAY.

2. An interconnection between two or more host computers established so that an online user can easily access databases available at different hosts.

Gbit
Gigabit (One thousand million bits).

Gbps
Gigabits per second.

GCR
Graphics Code Recording.

GEISCO
General Electric Information Services Company.

GENLOCK
The means by which two video sources are synchronized so that, for instance, an image from one source and text from another may be viewed as a stationary superimposed single picture.

GEOSYNCHRONOUS ORBIT
A satellite orbits the earth at a fixed distance from it when its velocity, which tends to carry it away from the earth, is exactly balanced by gravitational pull. When positioned over the equator at a height of 35,860 Kms moving in the same direction as the earth, it completes one orbit in the same time as the earth takes to complete one rotation; it then appears to be stationary over a point on the earth's surface and is said to be in geosynchronous orbit. See also SATELLITES.

GHz
Gigahertz (thousand million Hz).

Giga-
Thousand million.

GIGABIT
1000 million bits.

GIGAFLOP
One thousand million (1 billion) floating point operations per second.

GKS
Graphics Kernel System.

GKS STANDARD
The Graphics Kernel System Standard, now an ISO standard, defines the "primitive" elements from which an image may be constructed – lines, arcs, polygons, etc. The elements may be described by a standard code called CGM (Computer Graphics Metafile).

GLYPH
A member of a FONT – a more specific term than the generalities "character" or "letter".

GNP
Gross National Product.

GOSIP
Government Open Systems Interconnection Profile.

GOURAUD SHADING
A means of altering individual pixels to produce smooth changes in appearance. See also PHONG SHADING.

GRAPHICS SIGNAL PROCESSOR
In the period 1985-1988 an extraordinary effort was made by the chip manufacturers to provide the means for rapid information transfer and the display of information in colour on Cathode Ray Tubes. The Hitachi HD63484 graphics co-processor chip was announced in 1984 but the main contenders now seem to be the Texas 34010 or later versions, and the Intel 82786.

The graphics co-processors or Graphics

System Processors (GSPs) developed to deal with this problem may be regarded as separate computers. A GSP consists of two separate processors – the Graphics Processor, which receives CPU commands from a special instruction set, and the Display Processor. Both have access to an important new component – a display Video Random Access Memory (VRAM), a special form of buffer memory.

A GSP, given the appropriate command, can execute complex operations on large blocks of pixels and can address (typically) 128 Mbits of memory – adequate to hold high resolution representations of pages to be displayed or printed in colour.

The Texas 34010 32-bit GSP contains over 30 32-bit registers and can be programmed in high-level languages – for instance to control animation in real time. Pixel colour control is handled by the 34070 Colour Palette chip – capable of displaying colours selected from a palette.

The manufacturers have coined appropriate new hype words to convey the explosive urgency of these chips. A "Barrel-Shifter" – for use in specialized graphics applications – enables a pixel field to be rotated. "Bitblitting" (BitBlt) describes the function of moving pixel arrays (whose size is programmable) en block and "Pixblitting" (PixBlt) is the moving of multiple-bit pixels containing extra bits specifying halftones or colour.

Blocks of pixels may be moved from a source area and fitted into a destination area of different size – as, for instance, when transferring pixels between windows. Moreover the software, anticipating that some "window clipping" may be required, will inhibit time-consuming operations on pixels overlapping the edges of the new window.

Pixels from a source and destination array may be combined thereby producing a different colour, or a pattern of designated pixels in the destination array may be made "transparent" so that when the source pixels are moved, some appear in the "holes", producing various special effects. Small pixel arrays representing characters in special fonts can be fitted into new positions. Operations of these kinds require logical mathematical operations to be carried out at high speed.

With a GSP, delays in the execution of these effects are hardly noticeable. Without a GSP, delays would probably be intolerable, even with elaborate programs and additional supporting chips.

GSPs for displays could not work at the required high speeds if the associated memory was a conventional display RAM where the picture up-date and continual CRT refreshing operations operate in turn through a single port. A VRAM memory is a "two port" device – up-dating and refresh proceed in parallel. The VRAM contains a "shift register" which is filled with a row of bits during the brief interval between CRT scanning lines. When a new line commences the bits are clocked out to form a line of displayed pixels for refresh purposes.

The effect on performance is remarkable – there is a 40 times reduction in "overhead" refresh time-wasting. The latest VRAMs come as 1 Mbit chips with an access time of 80 ns. As an example of operations, a board called the "Intelligent Graphics Controller 20" from Hewlett Packard appeared in January 1990, incorporating a TMS 34020. Operating at 30 MHz, it will speed up graphics operations even when displaying 1280 x 1024 pixel images. The display of windows or CAD drawings appear about six times faster when the board is used on a VGA machine.

GRAPHICS USER INTERFACE (GUI)
The part of a computer which gives rise to the "look and feel" of the machine – namely the screen and the method of controlling it. The GUI was invented by Apple with its WIMP arrangements – windows, icons, mouse and pop up menu. For the first time a computer could be controlled by pointing and selecting instead of typing a code exactly correctly.

See also MAN-MACHINE INTERFACE.

GREEN PAPER
A term used to describe a Paper setting out a policy or other new governmental proposal. It may be followed by a WHITE PAPER which amounts to a declaration that a policy will be executed.

GREMAS
Genealogische Recherche mit Magnetband-Speicherung. An organization concerned with the representation and analysis of chemical structures using computers.

GREYSCALE

The representation of a tonal scale from black to white. For a digital representation of 256 shades, for example, the scale could be represented as an 8-bit number.

See HALFTONES.

GROUPE SPECIALE MOBILE (GSM)

A system established in 1982 under the aegis of the CEPT for a mobile telephone network throughout Western Europe in the nineteen nineties to replace five first generation incompatible services.

A speech-coding method was agreed for GSM in 1987 which also uses a standard signalling system for network control.

Vodaphone announced that it expected to launch a GSM network in the UK covering 90% of the country in May 1993. Cellnet is expected to follow.

See also NETWORKS – PERSONAL COMMUNICATION.

GROUPWARE

Groupware, sometimes called Computer Supported Cooperative work, is a term used to describe software which enables a group of people with some common interest to coordinate their work. It includes features such as electronic mail, an appointments calendar, address lists, and in more elaborate systems such as BT's Cosmos system, facilities for structured working, report writing, transfer of information between machines and so on.

GSM

GROUPE SPECIALE MOBILE.

GSP

GRAPHICS SIGNAL PROCESSOR.

GUI

Graphics User Interface.

H

HACKER

A person who gains entry, usually illegally, to another person's computer software.

Hackers have been viewed as "folk-heroes" – for example the teenager in the film "War Games" – but when a person interferes with someone else's data or programs, however clever the method, such an act is irresponsible and probably criminal.

The distinction between Hacking and "Computer Crime" is blurred. In 1989 and 1990 a number of raids were carried out in the United States by the secret service and hardware and software was seized. It was considered that in some cases the First and Fourth amendments to the Constitution were being disregarded. To ensure that they were not, the Electronic Frontier Foundation was formed by a group of computer experts.

In the UK, one reaction to hackers was a private member's anti-hacking Computer Misuse Bill which started on its passage through the House of Commons in 1989. It became law in September 1990. The act makes it an offence to attempt to gain unauthorized access to a computer, punishable by six months imprisonment, or a maximum fine of £12,000. Damaging a computer's memory is punishable by up to five years in prison.

Curious forms of "co-operation" between hackers and hacked, with the hacker sometimes acting semi-benignly, have hitherto deterred the labelling of hackers as criminals. When Schifreen and Gold broke in to British Telecom's system, Schifreen reported this failure in security to British Telecom. BT's response was to prosecute, but both were acquitted on a point of law.

Three West German hackers were arrested for espionage and given suspended sentences for hacking into military networks. One of the "Chaos Computer Club", as they were called, was trapped by bait set by Clifford Stoll of Berkeley Labs who had noted that someone was using a computer, but had no address to which bills should be sent. He allowed the hacker, Markus Hass, to roam networks and find a package containing fictitious data about Star Wars. Hass was so interested that he stayed on the line long enough for his terminal location to be backward-tracked through the networks.

Hackers are said to be typically young somewhat immature individuals who are looking for adulation so as to carry out their intrusions silently and without record. It has been suggested that this is like asking a good fisherman not to tell you about the really big one he just caught.

A hacker usually dials up a remote machine via a non-confidential telephone number, and then attempts to enter the system by a supposedly confidential password. In March 1993, in spite of the existence of the UK 1990 Computer Misuse Act, the prosecution of an admitted hacker failed on the grounds that there was no conspiracy in the offence with which he was charged.

The case was brought in this manner to ensure maximum publicity, which it would probably not have received had it been brought in a magistrates court with a maximum penalty for unauthorized access of six months imprisonment or a £2000 fine, or probably much less for a first offence.

See also CODES, ENCRYPTION, PRIVACY & FREEDOM, TRANSBORDER DATA FLOW, VIRUSES & WORMS.

HALF DUPLEX TRANSMISSION

Transmission possible in both directions alternately, not simultaneously. Compare DUPLEX, FULL DUPLEX (simultaneous 2-way) and SIMPLEX (one direction only).

HALFTONES

Halftones are displayed or printed with the aid of software to provide simulated tonal effects by variable dot clustering, enabling laser printers to print acceptable halftones. Very small areas are filled with zero to many dots by "dithering" (filling with a dot pattern) in order to produce white through grey shades to black when the area is full.

The illustration of the "boats at San Francisco" shows a dithered picture printed on a Lasermaster RX300 300 dots per inch printer having been input with a 300 dots per inch

"Boats at San Francisco" dithered laser print

scanner. It represents typical results from relatively inexpensive equipment.

The second illustration shows that reasonably good input resolution can be made to look very good given a high resolution printer (IBM 4250) and image enhancement.

200 dpi enhanced, with high resolution printing (By courtesy of IBM).

The contents of the small area is determined by the average brightness of a corresponding small area of input pixels. An area accommodates a matrix of 4 x 4, 8 x 8, or 16 x 16 dots as determined by the software.

A larger area produces better halftones at the expense of a loss of detail since the small dots which would otherwise resolve fine detail are replaced by small clusters – a new minimum-size display element.

When 600 dots per inch laser printers became available the areas of clustered dots could be made smaller to restore detail otherwise lost.

The dithering software may be adjusted for best tonal or best detail reproduction. The first "snow scene" picture (see over) is set at 8 x 8 clusters for good halftones.

For fine detail, the setting in the second picture is 2 x 2 producing only 5 tonal gradations (0 to 4).

The illustration on p. 114 is an enlargement of a laser printed halftone picture scanned and printed at 600 dpi to show the dot structure. It also shows that dithering is capable of providing good tonal gradations.

See also SCREENS.

HAMMING CODE

A code in which extra bits are automatically inserted into a code group by a transmitting device so that a receiving device capable of carrying out the necessary checking procedures can detect and correct single bit errors.

HANDSHAKE
An exchange of information between inter-communicating devices to establish compatible operating conditions and procedures.

HARD COPY
A "print-out" of data on paper. A printed copy of data (text, image, etc.,) output from a machine in human-readable form.

HARDWARE
A general term used to describe the electronic or mechanical components of a communications systems: e.g. satellite, computer terminal, TV set, etc.

HARVARD ARCHITECTURE
A microprocessor design differing from von Neumann architecture due to its separate program and data buses. The separate buses provide parallelism in instruction fetch and execution. The goal is to achieve very fast processing.

HASHING
A technique used for rapidly looking up an item which has been added to a table, when every new item has been added in a random or unpredictable manner.

Before placing a new item in the table, a hashing function is used to map the key for the item on to a number (address) which ranges over the table. The hashing function is

Halftone reproduction: adjusted for best tonal gradations (top); adjusted for best detail (bottom)

Laser-printed halftone reproduced at 600dpi

chosen to distribute the keys evenly over the table so more than one key may be mapped on to one address. If the table is not more than about 60% full an item can be on average located by examining not more than two positions in the table. A position in a table is sometimes called a BUCKET.

HBLC
Host Based Library Catalogue.

HDLC
High-level data link control. An international standard communications protocol developed by ISO in response to IBM's SDLC.

HDTV
See TELEVISION – HIGH DEFINITION.

HEALTH
In IT, "health" usually covers hazards arising due to the use of a VDU. The strain affects the eyes or limbs. The possible effects of radiation has received much attention in the last few years.

In late 1989 a New York City bill was vetoed by the departing Mayor Koch, and the Supreme Court struck down a law introduced in Suffolk County, NY. This law included mandatory 15 minute work-breaks every 3 hours, and company payments of 80% of the costs of annual eye checks. In 1989 a bill was proposed in California, which among other things, would set up a committee to establish guidelines for pregnant computer operators.

W.H. Cushmann, using a Visual Fatigue Graphic Rating Scale in a series of subjective tests, found that "reading continuous text with dark characters on a light background was more fatiguing than reading the same copy printed on paper, but reading light characters on a dark background was not".

V.M. Reading in a letter to the Lancet considered that "there was no significant difference in respect of eye strain or pain between full-time typists and VDU users".

In a letter to *Byte*, W.G. Nabor said "I have yet to measure any ionizing radiation from any CRT, old, new, colour, or monochrome... claims to the contrary are misleading to the point of fraud".

In a review of the subject, N. MacMorrow rebutted claims "that VDU's are connected with adverse pregnancy outcomes" and said "none of the reliable studies shows any link", nor do "VDUs cause epilepsy". "Attention to the ergonomics of the workplace" should avoid the development of such complaints as "Kangaroo paw, tenosynovitis, writer's cramp, and carpal tunnel syndrome".

MacMorrow says that it was the Swedish Board of Occupational Safety and Health (no reference), and the UK Health and Safety at Work Magazine (no reference) who reported that VDUs engender discomfort in various parts of the body.

However it would seem that if you spend a lot of time sitting and staring at a VDU (or in front of anything else), you need a decent chair and frequent breaks. Torque and loading forces affect the system of levers comprising the legs, arms, and spine. To reduce those forces, arrange your body to reduce the leverage.

In 1988 The Daily Telegraph said that VDU workers "talk about their eyes swelling or being out on stalks, seeing pink spots, or their actual eyesight changing". An organization called "The VDU Worker's Rights Campaign" in London accused the UK Health and Safety Executive of "extreme complacency" in the matter.

Also in 1988 the World Health Organization produced a report called "VDU's and Worker's Health", saying that "the visual discomfort experienced by many VDU users must be recognised as a health problem". The UK Central Computer and Telecommunications Agency (CCTA) is reported as saying "After hula hoops and skateboards, VDU health reports are the latest growth industry in the UK".

Perhaps CCTA might have added "in the US as well". According to the Sunday Times on August 7th 1988, "researchers at the Kaiser-Permanente Medical Care Programme (Oakland, CA.) noted that pregnant women working with VDUs for more than 20 hours a week suffered twice as many miscarriages as women doing other office work".

In 1989 the Financial Times reported that "several UK trade unions are pursuing a number of claims for Repetitive Strain Injury (RSI) on behalf of their members... NALGO (a UK union) found that among keyboard workers in Newham, London, more than 80% reported visual problems and a high degree of depression and irritability". In 1989 this had become "operators of keyboards face high risk of limb disorders" – a finding of the Institute of Occupational Medicine in Edinburgh.

By 1992 evidence had been accumulating that working with a VDU for long periods could cause eyestrain and backache and a European Directive 90/270 was published about the subject.

Effects on pregnancy have again been dismissed by a UK Health and Safety Executive study of effects on 450 women, but the subject of the effects of CRT radiation is still controversial.

An article in the September 1992 issue of *Computer* concludes that "Any frequency magnetic field exposure near VDUs is biologically insignificant. The increased cancer risk associated with ELF electromagnetic fields is about the same as the risk of solar radiation burns from engaging in nude moon bathing".

A common sense view comes from Nigel Heaton, University of Loughborough "If an employee's work is well designed, the job description is well defined, and you've still got problems, then, and only then, would you have to conclude that VDUs affect user's health.

HEAVISIDE, OLIVER

Heaviside was born in 1850 and gave his name to the "Heaviside Layer" – a layer of ionized gas in the ionosphere capable of reflecting radio waves. Heaviside predicted its existence – it was not actually discovered for another 20 years.

He is not so well-known for his work on telecommunication transmission lines. He wrote some equations predicting the necessary conditions for achieving distortionless transmission in telephone lines. Later the appropriate loading coils were designed and produced the effect which he predicted.

Heaviside was not well-recognized by his contemporaries because he had no formal academic credentials and lived like a hermit. His published work was hard to understand.

HEMT

When somebody said "you know, Mr. Heaviside, that your papers are very difficult indeed to read", Heaviside responded "that may well be, but they were much more difficult to write".

He was involved in an acrimonious exchange with W.H. Preece, Chief Engineer of the Post Office. It was Preece who said, when it was suggested that the Post Office might start installing telephones, that they were "not needed in Britain, because of the abundance of messenger boys". Commenting on one of Preece's papers, Heaviside said "Mr. Preece is wrong, not merely in some points of detail, but radically wrong, generally speaking, in methods, reasoning, results and conclusions". Such frankness did not endear him to his contemporaries.

HEMT
High Electron Mobility Transistor.

HERTZ (Hz)
The unit of frequency equal to one cycle per second. Cycles are now referred to as Hertz in honour of the experimenter Heinrich Hertz.

HERTZ, HEINRICH RUDOLF
Hertz was born in Hamburg in 1857 and died in 1894. He observed electromagnetic waves in 1886, demonstrating that they obeyed the same laws as those of light. He is sometimes considered to be one of the inventors of "wireless".

HEX
HEXADECIMAL.

HEXADECIMAL (HEX)
A numbering system to the base 16. The length of, say, the number 256 in binary, while being no problem to a computer, is already becoming inconveniently long for human handling, and numbers – for example to specify addresses in a large store – have to be keyed and used by programmers.

A numbering system to the base 16 – the Hexadecimal ("Hex") system – is often used instead of binary for convenience, and most machines are able automatically to translate a Hex number into Binary which is the system that the machine can work with. Hex uses the numbers 0 to 9 as in the decimal system, but then A to F for the numbers 10 to 16. 135 in

Hex is 87 which is much more convenient to handle. It is composed as follows:-

$7 \times 16^0 = 7 \times 1 = 7$ decimal = 7 Hex
$8 \times 16^1 = 8 \times 16 = \underline{128}$ decimal = $\underline{8}$
$135 87$

The decimal number 65536, which is 2^{16}, was once a popular byte-storage capacity for microcomputer memories. It is a number in the series of rounded off numbers corresponding to 2^{14}, 2^{15}, 2^{16} etc., usually referred to as "14K", "32K", "64K", etc. 65536 is 2^{16}, so the Hex symbols for it corresponding to 1×16^4 and 0×16^3, 0×16^2, 0×16^1, and 0×16^0, is 10000. This is much more convenient than the binary 10000000000000000.

To make the system clearer, here is the composition of the Hex number E60B for decimal number 62987:-

$E(15) \times 16^3 = 15 \times 4096 = 61440$ decimal
$6(6) \times 16^2 = 6 \times 256 = 1536 ..$
$0(0) \times 16^1 = 0 \times 16 = 0 ..$
$B(11) \times 16^0 = 11 \times 1 = \underline{11} ..$
$ 62987$

HIGH DEFINITION TELEVISION (HDTV)
See TELEVISION, HIGH DEFINITION.

HIGH LEVEL LANGUAGE
A language enabling programs to be written relatively quickly in which each instruction embodies two or more instructions of a lower level language – e.g. assembly or machine language. A programmer writing source programmes will usually use a high level language, but parts, and occasionally all of a program will be written in assembly language for special purposes. Instructions in a higher level language take longer to execute than in assembly language.

HIGH MEMORY
See MEMORY.

HI-OVIS
See VIDEOTEX.

HIGH-PASS FILTER
A filter used to block out low frequency components of a signal, thus allowing only the high frequency components to pass.

HISTORY
See associated subject, for example TELECOMMUNICATIONS.

HIT
A retrieved item which matches a query submitted during a computer database search.

HMOS
High Speed Metal Oxide Semiconductor.

HOBBIT
The name given to a low power high performance processor made by AT&T, formerly called the "ATT92010". Its architecture was originally designed for the optimization of programs written and compiled in C. The Hobbit is unique in that it uses memory-to-memory architecture so that there are no registers accessible to a programmer. The Hobbit is intended to be used in small personal computers.

HOLLERITH, HERMAN
1860-1929. American inventor. Hollerith invented the punched card tabulating machine while working in the United States patent office in 1886. The machine proved its worth during the census of 1890. He founded the Tabulating Machine Company which later merged with others to become IBM.
See also COMPUTERS – HISTORY.

HOME BANKING
A term used to describe a service for calling up a bank for information about a bank account, transferring money from one account to another, paying bills, etc., from a home terminal, using an interactive videotex or cable system connected to a bank.

In 1981 a bank in Knoxville, Illinois, concluded an agreement with Compuserve, an "electronic" information service operator, for software and other operations, and with Radio Shack for the supply of modified home computers (TRS 80s). The objective was to provide a banking service for viewing statements, paying bills etc., for local customers.

The computer included a modem into which the customer plugged an encryption card to provide secure telephone line communications with the bank. A service company would rent a TRS80 and special modem for $25 a month. 300 customers were using the service in 1981.

The Nottinghamshire Building Society announced its Homelink service in 1982, believed to be the first in the UK of its type. It used Prestel for bill payments and home shopping. By 1984 it was said to have several thousand users.

In February 1985 the Bank of Scotland took a whole page in the *Sunday Times* to announce its Prestel-based home banking service:- "turning science fiction into fact". Clearly it did not think much of its existing services since with its new service there would be "no more queues, no more delays, no more confusion". You would be able to:- "monitor the ebb and flow of your current account... pay bills by lifting a finger... and move your money where the interest is".

An interesting aspect of home banking systems came to light in 1988 by which time several organizations were offering services. A person paid a Barclaycard bill via the Nationwide Anglia system on August 10th. It was debited to his account the next day but not credited by Barclaycard until August 18th which came into the next period so he had to pay an extra month's interest on the amount. Nationwide require 6 working days for clearance, TSB 4 days, Bank of Scotland 2 days.

In February 1991 the Bank of Scotland offered a lightweight portable terminal to users of its Home and Office Banking Service free if a minimum of £500 was kept in their account. Alternatively the terminal could be purchased for £95. It plugs into a telephone socket. The Bank advertised the system quite widely. "HOBS is already revolutionizing the way in which many businesses and households throughout the UK manage their bank accounts, saving time, postage, and travelling", they said.

But the novelty of home banking seems to have worn off.

HOME BUSSES – CEBUS
The inter-connecting "Bus" – a major, more realistic, concept for the control of domestic equipment – arrived in the early eighties. Philips was a pioneer with its 1980 D^2B bus, a simple interconnect and control scheme enabling a control device to manage other devices connected to a two-wire bus. Since that time work on developing busses has continued.

By 1985 the matter had become important enough to warrant a whole issue of the Institute of Electrical and Electronics Engineers magazine *Spectrum*. In one article there is an illustration of a lady in her Biotherm Hydromassage Bath Attachment, tastefully sur-rounded by "heated air bubbles", drinking a glass of champagne. Even the IEEE could not resist the dry (my pun is of course not in-tended), slightly humorous, caption – "cham-pagne not included".

For the most part the articles are dead serious, if somewhat disappointing. In one piece three TV sets, four speakers, and some laserdisk/tape/CD players/recorders/am-plifiers, are shown. There are also 10 IBM PCs containing special control boards, linked by a LAN, to deal with the telephone system, se-curity, heating, ventilation, air conditioning, and audio and video.

However the house control system hints at, although does not spell out, the need for an inter-connecting bus. In the reference section of the *Spectrum* issue, mention is made of the "Consumer Electronics Bus Committee" run by the Electronic Industries Association.

By 1985, engineers were starting to think about Standards as they affected home elec-tronics, because the cable and television industries "have developed their products with little regard for each other... and have complicated the interface to the degree that both are faced with customer dissatisfaction and confusion".

By 1986 telecommunications for high-tech homes were becoming more widely dis-cussed. It was thought that in Germany broadband telecoms would start to be used in homes in between 1990 and 1995. Restrictions on all types of service will largely disappear when the broadband ISDN arrives. Video communication will be the major home application.

Home services envisaged include:- "Video communication which supports a given com-munication situation and makes it more lively... video really counts in problem-solv-ing situations or personal contacts with some emotional touch... gestures and display of material items make a difference... a variety of broadband signals from all conceivable sources distributed for entertainment can be enlarged remarkably".

Transmission systems would consist of a "broadband star network for videotelephony and a bus network for TV and radio... and multiservice home terminals". Predicted applications controlled from outside the home include "remote meter reading, heating

control, security and messages, and comfort, (lighting, loudspeakers, heating), data collec-tion (temperature, oil reserve), and timing (heating, alarm clock, dates)".

But another author remained sceptical. He examines the development of the video-cas-sette recorder, predicted in 1968 to penetrate 20% of house-holds by 1970, but which flopped, and concludes:- "Forecasters easily envision end-state scenarios in which the technology is used in a myriad of applica-tions. This is symptomatic of technological determinism – the technology's capabilities suggest utility for a multitude of potential uses".

In 1987 it was announced that Thorn-EMI, Philips, Tompson, Siemens, GEC and Electro-lux would get together to agree Standards on how signals would be exchanged between ap-pliances connected to a home network, antici-pating an "intelligent-home" market. These companies, accounting for up to 80% of dom-estic appliances manufactured in Europe, planned to spend at least £12 million on the exercise during 1987/1988.

In 1987 in the US a home consumer bus was under consideration because "a wider mar-ketplace is sure to emerge". But an extra bus may turn out to be unnecessary; NEC announced the use of the electricity mains as the bus – the method currently used by cheap baby-crying remote listening systems.

An ebullient industry showed its wares at the Chicago 1987 International Summer Con-sumer Electronics Show. Mitsubishi demon-strated a home systems console controlled from touch-tone telephones either plugged into a jack in any room and connected to it by wiring, or by radio, or from any PSTN tele-phone. Costing $1200 the console controls air conditioning, TV cameras and receivers, se-curity system, etc. The System inter-con-nected and ready to use would cost $10,000 or more.

Apple founder Steve Wozniak's new com-pany, CL9, showed "CORE" (Controller of Remote Electronics), selling for $195, at the same show. CORE is a "programmable mas-ter controller that interacts with most infrared controllable equipment such as stereo, tape recorders, TVs and satellite receivers".

But this ebullience may have been mis-placed. "So far, despite continuing efforts by home-automation start-ups, US consumers have shown little penchant for elaborate home-control systems" says a 1988 report.

By this time the CEBUS Standard was being developed under Electronic Industries Association sponsorship, with active participation by some 50 manufacturers in a variety of home products.

The Standard spells out a common home networking protocol for two-way communication over multiple media including existing in-house power lines, twisted-pair wiring, coaxial and fiber cable, RF, and infrared devices etc. The software protocol is based on the 7-layer OSI model.

Dedicated CEBUS chips, depending on the application, will cost between $5 and $30 each. But they must "ideally reach prices as low as 50 cents each", said one report. Having pioneered busses since 1980, by 1988 Philips had several teams working on interactive home systems. Their Homebus (HBS) system for consumer appliance inter-working seems to be proceeding independently of American and Japanese work. European standardization is being pursued under the aegis of the EEC Eureka, Esprit, and Race programs.

The Eureka effort was described in 1988. It is a "two year project to define a European Standard by which domestic appliances may be interconnected by a common bus network". This Standard is being prepared by the European companies mentioned earlier.

The figure shows a system embodying some of the ideas. Telecoms is by radio or infrared, or via the electricity mains wiring, twisted pair cable, or coaxial cable. Alternative speeds are available of between 1200 and 9600 bauds, 64 Kbps multiplexed, or 2 Mbps, according to the type of service required.

The Gateways in the figure inter-connect the parts of the system operating at different speeds. One gateway to external telecoms (the PSTN) is shown. There could be more – for instance to the ISDN, or to a higher speed line.

The "Home Bus System" is in line with a Standard prepared by the Electronic Industries of Japan. It is not clear whether this means that this Standard will be compatible with the Standards already mentioned.

In October 1989 details of the Consumer Electronic Bus Standard for CEBUS were still being hammered out by a committee of the Electronic Industries Association working groups. The Standard will count as successful only if people buy home-control networks and products.

"All that remains is to add the interface device that connects the appliance to the media and converts the incoming home-automation message into a code the appliance's microprocessor understands. It should cost $10 or less" claims an enthusiast.

It is said that account is being taken by the EIA of other work in Japan and in the European Eureka project, GEC's (US) Home-net, and the offerings of another company, Smarthouse. "CBSC must coordinate its work with other efforts" says a report, but it does not say whether it is, or is not, being co-ordinated.

The term "ROUTER" (from the world of LANs) is now being used for a linking device. Data will be transmitted in packets using CSMA/CD protocols. The packet embodies in its preamble the "wait and try again" concept of that protocol, followed by routing/address data, an instruction of some kind to a domestic device, and an 8-bit checksum.

In 1989 a company called AISI Research were marketing a $5 chip for controlling information transmission to devices connected to CEBUS. The chip was used at the 1989 Consumer Electronics Show in Las Vegas in a demonstration of the control of several domestic appliances.

By 1990 work had advanced sufficiently on CEBUS for an evaluation of bus performance to be carried out and development tools "to provide a complete development environment which allows an engineer to design, debug, and test devices communicating over a CEBUS network" to be made available, according to a report.

In the US CEBUS has a competitor – the "smart house" proposal by the National Association of Home Builders which intends to license its use.

European manufacturers realize that with giant hard-to-beat Japanese companies well established in Europe, it would be better to co-operate with them in advance. Bus interchange "D2B" codes have been agreed between Philips, Matsushita, Thomson, and Sony. A Philips TV set with a D2B socket is already on sale.

A range of appliances from the likes of these companies, all working off the same bus, would be rather convincing. Numerous announcements of the imminent replacement

HOME COMPUTERS

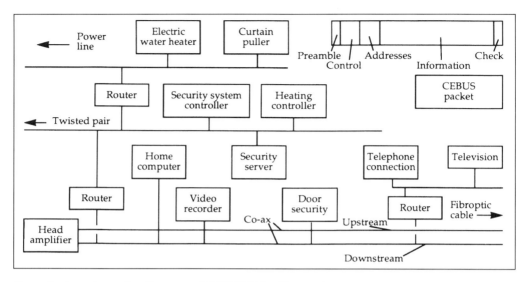

Example of a system using the proposed CEBUS (After Hanover)

of twisted pair copper wires by fibreoptic cables in the local loop have been made but nothing happens. It still costs about three times as much to run fibre into the home as it does to run copper. And that's only for phone service. High-capacity broadband cable costs five to ten times more than copper" says a report referring to the position in the United States. If that is still true it's a very good reason for the inactivity.

By 1992 the EIA CEBUS Committee completed its work to provide a home network for providing a standard method for controlling and monitoring home appliances.

HOME COMPUTERS
In the nineteen eighties there were some differences of opinion about the applications of home computers.

In a 1980 home-computer survey of a university community's applications, 20% of the 1313 responses received were for game-playing, 15% for text creation, 10% for record-keeping of various kinds, and 5% for budgets. Among smaller usages were 2% for keeping recipes and 1.5% for other household applications.

Moving on to the UK in 1984, it was estimated that about 3.5 million microcomputers were in use of which about 90% were used solely for games. "We believe that not one in

fifty is going to make the transition to program writing. Many of the so-called domestic application packages... are better carried out on the back of an envelope... it is hard to think of a single domestic application which can be cost justified".

It seems that even if home users were going to be mainly playing games they would need to communicate with each other – hence "Homenet", a network for within-city use. A small version was built for feasibility studies, presumably meaning technical feasibility studies. No information is provided about what kind of information would be exchanged over it.

However quite a different story is told in a 1985 report. Micro-computer-based home educational systems had arrived according to this report which says:- "Educational software has performed solidly to the extent of accounting for half of all software sales into the home". One reason for this is:- "appeals to fear and guilt... the ads have as good as warned that you should get on to the micro-in-education bandwaggon or your kids will grow up to be bums".

But "serious questions are arising regarding this market segment's staying power". Since nobody else found at that time that educational software had reached anything like this percentage of the home serious questions must also be asked about the report's accuracy.

Comments from the University of California at Irvine are similar to most others – home computer applications in order of popularity are Entertainment/Games, Finance, Word Processing, Business Use, Hobbies/Education. In their survey of members of computer clubs they found (predictably) that since the home computer arrived:- "time spent with family and friends decreased and time spent alone increased".

Following the rapid demise of the "home-recipe", "electronic games", "children's education" and "office technology transfer" (i.e. people who do office-work at home) syndromes, home computer marketing strategies have been tried but have been found wanting".

Since then there have been at least two marketing ploys.

The first is the "consumer electronics interchange" strategy. The idea is to force coalescence between a home computer (as the "control centre") and such devices as TV, video recorders, stereo reproducers, telephone, microwave oven, CATV, etc.

The industry seems to believe that if cannot think of any new applications why not put more processing power into what we have got, include some fuzzy logic, and provide improved functions in one box previously provided by two or more boxes. This will also reduce size and costs per function.

See also HOME INFORMATION TECHNOLOGY.

AT&T and Sharp are given as examples of companies providing plug-in frame capture boards for grabbing and presenting video pictures, and Panasonic for providing the means of connection between the computer and the video tape recorder. However this seems bound to reduce the market to that fraction of home computer users who have the necessary technical knowledge to handle the far from trivial problems likely to be encountered.

"A large number of consumers must have a basic level of computer literacy to make computing in the home viable", says a report, and "Standards are absolutely necessary for success in the home computer marketplace".

The second ploy is the "Home Information Systems" strategy. It is claimed that "a cluster of related technologies have already become available to the American household in the last 3 or 4 years.

They include: cellular mobile phones, videotex, home banking, electronic shopping, electronic bulletin boards, home security networks, and database reference systems... whose collective pressure makes them a considerable force... once we accept the perspective of the household as an information centre... with sufficient computing power to acquire information internal and external to the house-hold and engage in a wide variety of computer-based activities".

But there are some caveats:- "... there are any number of examples of technologies that appeared to be unaffordable at the time of their introduction but gained acceptance as soon as the consumers began to appreciate the benefits". It is pointed out that the interval between introduction and popular acceptance was 15 years for the car (assuming that 1910 was the "popular acceptance" year, which seems remarkably early), and 30 years for the telephone.

In the nineties perhaps genuine popular acceptance has grown, partly because computers are used at schools, partly because some business computing is done at home often with a portable, and partly because a range of new applications with some domestic appeal have arrived – for instance multimedia.

According to an August 1992 forecast, although the multimedia "consumer/ entertainment" sector shared 18% of a $626 million market in 1991, the same sector is forecast to share 55% of a $12.4 billion market by 1996 – an increase of over 6000 times.

In a mid-1992 article it is claimed that "for the consumer, information must be personalized and casually accessible. By considering end-to-end services we have identified a set of core technical issues that must be addressed". Having decided that window-based interfaces are entirely inappropriate, it is suggested that simple interaction via a simple device with simple choices are required delivered at a bit rate of 1.5 Mbps.

The data would be supplied against a profile modified by user feedback.

Another idea was to offer video-game systems with telecommunication facilities – a kind of Memex-TV system.

All these ideas depend on the incentive of

the home-user to seek information from a source competing with existing sources such as newspapers and television. There is not much evidence to suggest that there will be a large demand from home users who have become sufficiently information-thirsty and are prepared to pay for it – however this is an encyclopaedic dictionary and not a book by Nostradamus.

See also TELECOMMUTING and HOME INFORMATION TECHNOLOGY.

HOME CONSUMER'S ELECTRONIC BUS STANDARD (CEBUS)
See under HOME BUSSES.

HOME INFORMATION TECHNOLOGY
In a 1980 forecast people at home were visualized programming for garden planning layouts, sowing and planting, flipping through the pages of an electronically displayed book and so forth.

It was suggested that at some unknown future date computer power is "clearly going to be used for the controlling of devices in the home. The only reasonable assumption we can make regarding the linking of home machines is that a universal high-bandwidth digital network will be available, enabling the joining of any two systems that wish to communicate".

It is remarkably easy to describe scenarios of this kind if no mention whatsoever is made about the time of their arrival. You can dream up what you like but if it's not going to happen until, say, 2080, when almost nobody now alive will see it, it is not really of much interest or value except to the readers of a science fiction magazine.

In 1981 Warner-Amex Qube Cable inaugurated some special services for the home. The sensors in a home security system could be connected to the local police station, smoke detectors to the local fire station, and an emergency button to the local ambulance service. Furthermore Qube ran a "push-button voting system" to enable subscribers to provide yes-no answers to questions posed on TV followed by a display of the totalled results.

This set off further expectations – for instance the Yankee Group organized a "Home of the Future" technology up-date in London on January 11th 1982 following several similar meetings held earlier in the United States. The blurb said:- "The home of the future market is very important in Europe – home information and entertainment delivery systems will represent a significant market for computer and communications technology. The Yankee Group has proved it in the USA – we will now demonstrate it in Europe".

In 1989 it was said that the excitement (about two-way home services) has finally died. Neither the technology, the consumer, the industry, nor the mass market was ready. "Will it too be soon forgotten as an example of yet another over-fascination with technology for its own sake?", said one observer.

"Although a rented videotape must be collected and returned, the cost, at about $0.50 an hour of usage, compares favourably with local telephone service at about $2 per hour. Could the progress of technology become so rapid as to provide 4.5 MHz of video bandwidth for $0.50 an hour, when 4 KHz of telephone bandwidth presently costs $2 per hour" says a commentator. He seems to have a point.

In February 1982 a feature article about the subject appeared in "The Futurist" . Earth-sheltered energy-efficient homes would be built, buried into hillsides. Another type of home was due to be demonstrated at Orlando, Florida, constructed from "interlocking domes formed by spraying a quick-hardening plastic foam on to removable molds". It would require one quarter of the energy needed to heat or cool a conventional house.

The authors became quite lyrical about their proposals. The central family room in these dwellings would be transformed into the "media room" by the addition of telecomputing and other home entertainment devices with a computer "tying all the separate systems together to provide the central focus or "electronic hearth" around which the family will gather for work, play, and fellowship".

"The ultimate house may be a structure whose computer brain, equipped with sensors and linked through telecommunications networks to computer banks and the brains of other houses, has developed an awareness of its own existence and an intimate knowledge of its inhabitants".

Household needs are classified in terms of different services as follows:-
* Commercial in-home.
  Database, Financial, Shopping, Security.

Entertainment, Work- at-home.
* Public in-home.
Network infrastructure, Electronic mail, News, Local schedules and emergency information, Home security network.
* Government in-home.
Government information, Emergency services, Polling, Automated billing. Local government bulletin boards.

In a 1991 article about "Intelligent Buildings", it is claimed that the various groups involved in constructing a building seem not to talk to each other very much. "Buildings" do not include homes so that the groups don't talk to the "Intelligent Homes" people, if any, at all.

It is said that ISDN, BISDN (See NETWORKS), and optical fibres with better reach all paint a very confusing picture to the building constructor who wishes to outfit his building properly with a powerful communications system, the core of the building's "intelligence".

It may be concluded that it will not make sense for any potential user to start building up his "intelligent home" until he is convinced that a particular technology is stable enough for him or her to see that he will have a choice of add-on devices over the next few years which will actually work. These considerations will be offset by powerful marketing efforts to persuade potential customers that Hyper House-o-Matic has already reached that status.

The videotelephone is now a service thrown in for good measure when home systems are discussed. What seems to be forgotten is that AT&T spent hundreds of millions of dollars a few decades ago in discovering that there was little or no consumer need for seeing the face of another person while talking by telephone.

Several fibre experiments are being conducted in different countries. For example in March 1989 British Telecom announced that about 500 businesses and homes would be wired to demonstrate the feasibility of "stereo television, high fidelity stereo radio, information technology, telephone, and other interactive services".

BT provided further details in 1990. In one system a switch located in a street cabinet routes telephone, radio, and two out of a choice of 18 TV channels into each home. A director of a participating company, Fulcrum Communications, said the trials "would allow BT to secure the maximum return on the massive investment needed to replace its existing copper-pair local loop networks with fibre". Other similar experiments are taking place in Amsterdam and in several German cities. A Philips estimate costs a fibre network at around 15% more than copper by the mid-nineties if by then components are in mass production.

British Telecom recently demonstrated a hand-held machine consisting of a cordless telephone and an LCD image display – in other words a mobile videophone. Another home-gadget example is NEC's "PC-VCR" fitted with a multi-pin interface socket, designed for applications requiring videotape storage and retrieval.

Every frame on a videotape is numbered so that it may be retrieved by controlling the VCR's tape-winding mechanism. At present the time taken to find a required frame is rather slow – about two seconds of searching time per minute of playing time at the normal speed.

Another example of converged functions is the Video-CD, expected to be on sale in 1996. To enable this combination to become feasible it MUST include higher recording density, a smaller laser spot and an improved compression system.

HOME SHOPPING

A method of viewing, ordering, and paying for goods at home, usually implying some form of interactive viewing system.

The Japanese started the Hi-Ovis scheme in 1976 in which 71 of the participants in experiments over a fibreoptic network used the "home shopping" service which ran for a year in the Tokyo area. Still-picture transmission of goods was used as a substitute for a sales catalogue. Subscribers, using a TV display, could select, order, and pay without leaving home. The service was "well accepted", although "ways of improving the quality of TV broadcasting are needed".

The service was supplied free and the total cost of Hi-Ovis was 25 billion Yen – about $150 million. It is not known how much of this cost could be attributed to the home shopping experiment.

One of the earliest attempts was implemented by Telaction, a J.C. Penney company. Experiments in Chicago using 125,000 "test households" gave "positive" results. Shoppers could browse or shop by product category and could get close-ups of certain features and a detailed voice-over description".

Special technical arrangements, no doubt necessary to provide adequate bandwidth/ resolution, were made on a "shared facilities" basis. They included a local FRAME GRABBER relaying pictures (presumably a succession of frames at a rate of about one per second per household) to up to 40 households connected to a cable-TV video channel on a cable network.

Customers issued their commands on a separate narrow-band telecoms channel – the PSTN. They dialled a special phone number using a standard "touch-tone" telephone as a key pad.

In 1985 Littlewoods and Great Universal Stores started teleshopping services and Comp-U-Card set up a networked service for Commodore microcomputer users to access a database of 22,000 items, order, and pay by credit card. Several pioneering examples using Prestel were described in the following year.

In 1987 ex-Acorn founder Chris Curry planned to give away 500,000 simplified Prestel-like machines for home shopping, shops on the system being charged a 5% commission on goods ordered. In this case the system was said to be able to accept every-day language commands.

In 1988 a company called Trintex, jointly owned by IBM and Sears Roebuck (CBS, a co-founder pulled out) started to test their "Prodigy" home shopping system in which customers use their own home computers. The system provided for the necessarily slow transmission of images (limited by the bandwidth of a telephone line) with, like the text information, attached advertisements necessary to generate the revenue.

The UK Keyline home shopping system planned is still being planned but more so. It is claimed that it will be responsible for a home shopping boom.

Development costs of £500,000 are still being spent and 500,000 terminals are to be distributed free. The membership fee will be £50 and over 17 companies committed to the system. Phase one, will provide terminals to

thousands of customers as a test activity. The terminal, to be plugged in to a telephone socket, includes a 1200 bps full duplex modem. It is said that it has enough spare capacity for managing electronic mail or holding a personal diary or phone directory.

Keyline has reached an agreement with Mercury for communications over its X25 packet switched network and all calls will be charged at the local rate. It will be competing with a number of less ambitious home shopping services running on Prestel.

Little is said these days about the need for the realistic presentation in colour of the goods for sale with a resolution at least as good as current 625 line TV – a feature of the Hi-Ovis system. Prestel, of course, is unable to provide anything but the most simple graphics. Home shopping providers seem to have resigned themselves for the time being to the bandwidth-imposed limitations allowing lists, descriptions, easy payments etc., (however see Teleaction below), but no pictures.

CD-ROM or CD/V might become an attractive method of distributing high quality "catalogues" if their capacity is to be increased by sophisticated compression systems, as seems likely. Lists, ordering, payments etc., would be provided via an interactive on-line terminal, with CD pictures triggered automatically for TV presentation.

Some comprehensive information about teleshopping comes from Jonathan Reynolds. Reynolds was supported by retailers, notably Tesco Ltd., to enable him to do some thorough research.

"In the United States, J.C. Penney closed its Teleaction service in April 1989 with the company announcing write-off costs of $20 million on top of the $106 million already invested" says Reynolds. One interesting aspect of this system was an attempt to overcome the barrier, even on a relatively wideband cable system, of presenting satisfactory images. An image could be requested on a first come/first served basis via a frame-grabber by the 15 customers who shared it.

The IBM/Sears Prodigy system which started with 10,000 subscribers in 1988 is claimed now to have nearly a million. By 1990 $600 million had been invested in it including 1000 man years of work. The subscription to it is $9.95 a month; it uses a videotex system.

Reynolds provides a list of Prodigy's problems headed "Technology rather than customer led?: Limitations of display technology: Appropriate equipment?: Is Prodigy 15 years too early?".

Reynolds also includes a discussion of its advantages, namely:- "Large capital investment... willingness to commit to long term payback... well thought out and executed". He also says that "the respectability and track record of the main players in Prodigy may mean that these players can achieve success where others have failed... brand strength has been a critical factor".

Prodigy continues to trade but in 1993 it is still losing money.

Under the heading "Hard lesson in the UK", Reynolds lists a number of benefits/ requirements for home shopping systems:- "Speed of home delivery: Quality of service: Up-to-dateness: Prompt handling of returns: Ease of use: Reliability: Customer cost. He discusses several UK systems which have failed because of the unsatisfactory nature of one or more of these items.

Of the French Minitel "Supers à domicile" service (See also VIDEOTEX) he says that the suppliers, given the critical mass of home tele-service users required to understand the characteristics of the marketplace, have targeted a customer base consisting of people open to the use of technology and belonging to households with children within socio-economic groups which would permit them effectively to buy additional leisure time through the use of the teleshopping distribution channel". He supplies a table of users and their reasons for using Minitel. Home deliveries and speed are the prime reasons.

Like Prodigy, Minitel, when properly costed, is also steadily losing money.

US home shopping networks achieved a turnover of more than $3.5 billion in 1989, but home shopping in the United States should not be used for forecasting progress in Europe because it occupies a very particular niche. People have a high propensity to consume through mail order. The home shopper is a very different animal from those traditionally thought of as target markets for teleshopping.

Reynolds says that many consumers see teleshopping as an inevitable development but are not ready to welcome it with open arms. Fundamental social changes arising out of the incremental adoption of teleshopping are unlikely to take place in the 1990s. He identifies four key opportunities in the UK over the longer term:-

* The opportunity to make shopping for essential goods easier.
* The opportunity to improve the quality of the non-essential shopping trip by providing additional choice within the home.
* The opportunity to ease the transfer of time from essential to non-essential shopping activity.
* The opportunity to inform the buying decision better.

HOME – WORKING AT,
See under TELECOMMUTING

HOPPER, REAR ADMIRAL GRACE
Hopper was born in 1906 and obtained a Ph.D in maths at Yale. After joining the US Naval Reserve in December 1943 she was posted to the computer laboratory at Harvard where she used one of the first digital computers to be built. After the war she worked on the Univac design and had a hand in designing Cobol programming.

Retiring in 1966 she was recalled and asked to impose a standard on naval computer languages. In 1975 an Act of Congress was passed enabling the Navy to promote her to Captain, and in 1983 she received a Presidential appointment to the rank of Rear Admiral. Subsequently she worked for 20 years at the Pentagon. She was the only woman and the first American to be elected a distinguished Fellow of the British Computer Society.

HOST COMPUTER
A computer which provides services and facilities that may be used via other computers and/or terminals on the network.

HP
Hewlett Packard.

HSI
Hue-Saturation-Intensity. See COLOUR.

HUE
A colour named from its subjective appearance and determined by the frequency of its radiated energy. See also COLOUR.

HUFFMAN CODE
See CODE, HUFFMAN

HUMAN ENCODING
A typical human subject can only remember 9 binary digits after reading them once but can remember 8 decimal digits (25 bits), 7 English-letters (33 bits) or 5 monosyllabic words (50 bits).

Gilbert discusses a whole series of experiments such as sight reading at the piano, typing, tapping targets, marking squares, reading word lists etc., in attempts to obtain high "signalling rates" to realize the "full capacity of the human channel". "The best rates obtained were about 40 to 50 bits per second. These results are hard to interpret but they do make one wonder what possible use a television viewer makes of the millions of bits of information he receives each second". Indeed it does, particularly as the viewer now gets all those millions of additional bits from Sky TV and BSB as well.

This subject is reviewed at length by Herbert Simon (1974). In introducing the work of G.A. Miller (1950) and later in 1956 in the Psychological Review, Simon quotes "The contrasts of the terms *bit* and *chunk* serves to highlight the fact that we are not very definite about what constitutes a chunk of information... we are dealing here with a process of organizing or grouping the input into familiar units or chunks, and a great deal of learning has gone into the information of these familiar units".

The answer appears to be that humans are extremely good at *recoding* information. Experiments with grand-masters of chess and ordinary players showed that after a ten second inspection of 24 randomly arranged pieces both were able to place only about 6 pieces correctly. From these and reviews of numerous other experiments, Simon concludes that "A chunk of any kind of stimulus material is the quantity that short-term memory will hold five of".

HUMAN-MACHINE INTERFACE
One aspect of the information itself which has received considerable study is its transfer at the human-computer interface. Sutcliffe and Wang (1991) cite 36 other articles describing work in this field. The "Jackson" system uses structure diagrams to study the sequence, selection, and iteration activities in human-computer interaction as an aid to the design of programs.

Important human factor studies are included in this type of work such as how much information to display, how much can be held in the user's memory, when to include guidance, how to provide informative error messages, etc.

Smura, a member of the Xerox PARC team said "Our objective is not to define an architecture but to further consider the problems that have to be solved in attaining an eventual structure. While designed arrangements may be said to have structure, only the ones that have weathered the tests of the market place gain the status of architecture. Our objective is the status of market needs – a structure for processing and communicating all kinds of information".

"An information system may be defined as an input/output structure which acquires, stores, communicates, processes, re-arranges, and/or distributes intellectual information in an organised manner. To achieve the status of architecture, it must serve objectives needed by mankind, it must over time settle into a stable pattern, and it must please its users".

Considerations such as these gave rise to the design of a man-machine interface for computer-based information systems which was the first real advance in making machines easier to use since the computer was invented. Until then (and still in many systems today,) machines can only be made to work by typing a string of meaningless symbols bearing little resemblance to natural language.

One of the earliest attempts to incorporate graphics and text in an easily understandable screen presentation controllable by a user who is not required to type coded commands was a system called Sketchpad developed at MIT by Ivan Sutherland in the early 60s. In those days user tools included light pens and joy sticks and these were used to good effect later in the 60s by Douglas Englebart. Englebart also experimented with a device later to become known as a "mouse".

Later the idea of "touch input" devices were introduced – the most successful seems to be a "point and select" action using one finger on the surface of the CRT screen".

In the early 70s these beginnings were taken much further by the PARC team. They built a prototype machine called Alto and then a further 1200 of them which were destined to be developed into the Star, introduced in 1981. This was the first machine embodying windows, icons, a mouse, and pointer – the "WIMP" concept together with a high resolution screen and laser printer marketed as "WYSIWYG" – What You See Is What You Get. This was the first machine of its type to be offered for sale to the public.

Subsequently these principles were adopted in the Apple Lisa machine and then in the Macintosh which came out in 1984. In 1990 the design of this "man-machine interface", was the subject of a battle in the courts between Xerox and Apple to decide who has contravened various patents and design rights.

The interfaces just described are usually "object-oriented" – for example an object such as a small picture of a folder appears on the screen to represent a data file in the computer. A more elaborate object might be a series of inter-connected boxes with names in them. An object is an abstraction replacing lines of descriptive text, or coded commands, which can normally be easily used without reference to instruction books, or without having to memorize a series of commands peculiar to a particular system.

Object-oriented user interfaces with sufficient detail shown on the screen to make it quite clear what is intended, and with one screen following another at a rate which does not delay the work of the user, have become possible because of the power and storage capacity available in current hardware.

Even if successive screens of information may be considerably different, the information will follow without delay because the bandwidth of the system is wide enough to enable the huge number of bits required to form a new image to be replaced at very high speed. This problem becomes acute if the information on the screen is presented in a large number of colours. For a black and white presentation one bit per pixel suffices, if, however a pixel is to be represented as, for example, one out of 16 million different colours then each pixel may require up to 32 bits to describe it.

Developments in this area have proceeded at a very rapid rate and a number of different kinds of interfaces, window presentations, and complex pictorial displays with representation in a huge number of colours have become available.

The objective of the design and arrangement of the content of a screenful of information in any of the above systems must be firstly to enable the user to communicate his information requirements easily to the machine and secondly that the machine must be able to supply information to the user in a way which is easily assimilated. Two major uses of machines in the areas under discussion include information retrieval and communication with other machines.

In information retrieval applications an important aspect, which must affect the screen design and content, is the behaviour of a user under different circumstances. The basic question in information retrieval applications, which the machine might ask the user, if it were able to speak is, "what information do you need to perform your job".

The question supposes that the user can pose the necessary questions in such a way that the machine will give him the right answers. In fact this is usually not the case. One of the purposes of the intermediary, who is often placed between the user and the system, is to force him or her to describe what he wants. The other purpose is to translate the description into the optimum manner for querying the machine. Thus, even if the man-machine interface was so good that the questioner would have no difficulty in posing his requirements to the machine, the session may fail because the user has not properly expressed his needs.

Back in the 70s some ideas about the required characteristics of an interface were already being developed, although graphic systems were relatively crude.

Miller makes a number of comments about system requirements. These include the response time – meaning the time a user is prevented from continuing his work until the machine has dealt with the previous command – system command languages, command organisation, prompting and default values, character string searching, file manipulation and so on.

Miller continues with such items as the design of key-boards, the desirable physical characteristics of the display, and the use of input devices for graphics, such as Englebart's mouse, which had recently been introduced. He identifies three requirements for the man-machine communication:-

1. In the case of a dialogue, whether the information exchange is guided by the user or the system, or whether the user has to make a choice of his input from the set of presented alternatives or is able to provide a free response.
2. Whether the machine can be controlled by the user's speech – at a very early stage at that time.
3. The need to construct graphics such as specifying the co-ordinates of points in order to form connected lines, sizing (scaling), and so on.

So far as communication is concerned human requirements are well exemplified by the situation in business. Kulnan suggests that communication is needed for one or more of the following four reasons –

1. For the acquisition of factual or technical data.
2. Communication between people relating to duties and responsibilities for control purposes.
3. Communication between people to realize objectives, to elicit co-operation etc.
4. Communication between people for emotional reasons for instance to establish credibility or to express feelings.

These considerations are rather different from interfaces previously discussed since they result from the introduction of new modes of communication such as electronic mail and messaging, computer conferencing etc. In this case the content of the screen will be rather different. For example in response to the question "what messages are there for me?", earlier events in conjunction with the machines' software will display a list of peoples' names and times relating to messages. In response to a command from the user, a selected individual message may be displayed.

HUMPTY-DUMPTY SYNDROME

An allusion to Lewis Carroll's *Through the Looking Glass* conversation between Alice and Humpty Dumpty where the latter categorically defines the meaning of meaning (See Figure). It also defines the problem that everybody else has with meaning – hence the diffi-

culty of devising an effective indexing system. See also INDEXING.

Humpty-Dumpty says it all

HYBRID
A telecommunications term for a 2-wire to 4-wire converter (or vice-versa).

HYPERCARD
See HYPERTEXT.

HYPERTEXT
Hypertext is a class of software for exploring information by alternative paths as opposed to the fixed path or structure available in conventional printed systems. The best known example is Apple's Hypercard designed to be used by non-programmers. Hypercard's Fields, Cards, (a Mac "screen-full" with a border looking like a card) and Stacks, roughly correspond to Fields, Records, and Files in a database.

Hypercard was preceded by and co-exists with a number of older systems which are broadly similar but not generally available. Some similar new systems are available competing with Hypercard – the huge customer base for IBM PCs and others running on the

MS/DOS operating system made competition inevitable.

The contents of the cards using the indexing terms must be classified manually, a considerable chore, so it is difficult to use hypertext effectively. This and other problems in the field seem to have restricted Hypercard to academe. However Hypercard, or one of its more recent alternatives such as Supercard or Hyperdoc, is a convenient form of multimedia program to control a presentation comprising text, sound, music, voice, graphics, pictures, animation or motion video.

A statement called a Script in the Hypercard Hypertalk language (with words in English) is associated with each Object on a Card. When the cursor is placed over a Button, normally captioned, the mouse is clicked, and a Message is sent to a Script for it to be executed to perform some kind of action.

For instance the action might be to activate a link to another card in the same, or a different, stack to retrieve that card. It is relatively easy to create a simple Hypercard system using the wide range of ready-made facilities provided. Writing Hypertalk Scripts, which consist of standardized English phrases or words in order to create more elaborate schemes, requires a longer learning commitment but is still relatively easy.

A Card is Hypercard's smallest unit of information – the minimum amount of displayable information is one Card. Hypercard Fields of information are displayed on a 342 x 512 pixel size numbered Card – in other words a Mac screen-full. The Field for editable text is displayed in a window which can occupy most of the screen. It can contain up to 30,000 characters and graphics in scrollable lines; the text is all in the same font selectable from a number of alternatives.

A "Find" command will search through all Cards in a Stack for a character string in a named Field. A Card actually overlays a Background which may be invisible if the Card completely overlays it. Usually a Background is visible and contains information common to a number of Cards, or to all the Cards in the Stack. As a simple example, consider a Stack consisting of three Cards – an article, a glossary, and references.

The three Cards might have the same Background consisting of a small rectangle at the top containing the author's name, a larger rectangle containing the title, and a considerably larger rectangle acting as a window for the text of the glossary, article, or index. The same operational facilities are available for a Background as for a Card, Backgrounds are numbered – in this example Background number 1 is being used with Cards 1, 2 and 3.

A Background resembles a form in some respects. In the case above, the form consists of rectangular spaces for the author's name and title, and a large rectangular space for the text. An author is provided with facilities for "form" design – thus the size and location of the rectangles on the Background may be designed into a fixed position.

A Hypercard system may contain many or no "Information" Stacks, but it must contain a special Stack called the Home Stack used for "housekeeping" purposes. The First Card in the Home Stack is shown on the next page.

A Card typically contains up to about 100 Kbytes of data plus its associated Script. Stack size may be up to 512 Mbytes. A whole Card is brought into memory and 2 Mbytes of RAM is recommended for the Mac, plus a hard disk of, say, 20 Mbytes.

Hypercard activities are initiated by Messages which may be commands such as "find", or within-system descriptive messages such as "mouse is within button area" or "mouse up" when the mouse is clicked. A user can send a message which must include a Keyword, to the current Card, or to an Object by typing it into a special area called a Message Box.

Messages are sent to Objects such as Buttons, Fields, Background, Stack, Home stack, and Hypercard in that order. Each object has an ID number. A stack must have a name, and other objects may be given names at the author's option.

Each of these six Objects has a Handler attached to it. A Handler comprises statements in the Hypertalk language collectively called a Script. The Keyword of a message in transit is matched against the Keyword of a Button's script – the first Object it meets. If there is no match it goes on to try a Field, then Background for a Keyword match, and so on through the hierarchy. When a match is found with an Object a Script is executed.

One of the most interesting features in Hypercard is a Button. A Button is a small labelled rectangular area. When the cursor is

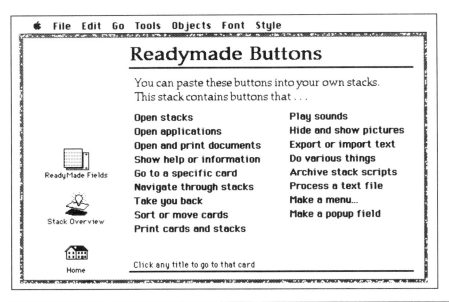

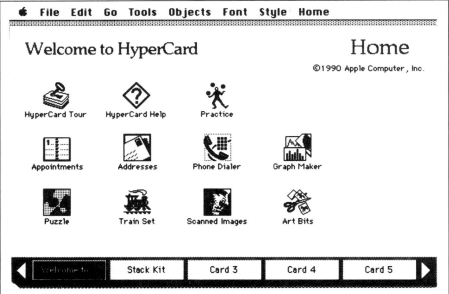

Hypercard: The home card and ready-made buttons

directed over it with the mouse and the mouse is clicked, a Script is executed to perform some kind of action. A Button may be on the Background, in which case its action is the same whatever the overlaid Card, or it may be on a Card, in which case its action applies to that Card only.

Perhaps the most important Hypercard "extra" not present on a conventional database, is the Button action which links to another Card in the same or in another Stack, causing it to be displayed.

"Integral buttons" are shown here in the Hyperties (a Hypercard-like system) Figure

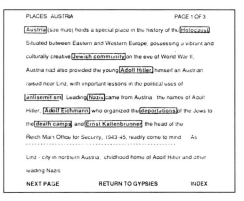

```
PLACES  AUSTRIA                               PAGE 1 OF 3

 Austria (see map) holds a special place in the  Holocaust
Situated between Eastern and Western Europe, possessing a vibrant and
culturally creative  Jewish community  on the eve of World War II,
Austria had also provided the young  Adolf Hitler  himself an Austrian
raised near Linz, with important lessons in the political uses of
 antisemitism   Leading  Nazis  came from Austria  the names of Adolf
Hitler,  Adolf Eichmann  who organized the  deportations  of the Jews to
the  death camps  and  Ernst Kaltenbrunner  the head of the
Reich Main Office for Security, 1943-45, readily come to mind     As
...................................................
Linz - city in northern Austria, childhood home of Adolf Hitler and other
leading Nazis

NEXT PAGE            RETURN TO GYPSIES          INDEX
```

The Hyperties "Browser" system

where a bounded item in the text may be "clicked" for switching to the subject indicated.

Hypercard version 1.2, introduced in late 1988, included some improvements taking it into the Multimedia area – for instance to use data from a CD-ROM drive connected to the Mac, included text, sound, and music data.

Cards are arranged in a tree structure – a "hierarchical data structure" – so there must be a vocabulary to classify each card by at least one term, and there should be a relatively uniform distribution of classification terms among all Hypertext cards. Both criteria are difficult to achieve.

See also MULTIMEDIA – HYPERCARD CONTROL.

Hz
Hertz (replaces "cycle")

I, J

I/O
INPUT/OUTPUT.

I₂L
Integrated Injection Logic.

IBM
INTERNATIONAL BUSINESS MACHINES.

IC
Integrated Circuit.

ICI
Imperial Chemical Industries.

ICL
INTERNATIONAL COMPUTERS LTD.

ICON
A pictorial representation of an object, or the miniature representation of a complete picture.

IDA
Integrated Digital Access. A term used by BT to describe part of an experimental ISDN system.
See also NETWORKS – ISDN.

IEE
Institute of Electrical Engineers.

IEEE
Institute of Electrical & Electronics Engineers.

IFIP
International Federation for Information Processing.

IIS
Institute of Information Scientists.

IKS
Image Kernel System. A variation of PIK devised by Lowell University, Massachusetts, intended as a "portable image standard" – that is a "device independent" framework enabling images to be transferred between different types of machine.

ILLUSTRATOR
Proprietary name of software originated by ADOBE who also designed POSTSCRIPT and which is used in conjunction with it. It provides for enhanced typographic and artistic effects in DTP systems. To provide two examples;-

The cursor may be moved to any point on a curve displayed on the screen and a tangential "handle" may be pulled out from it; by dragging the handle using the Mouse the curve may be changed into a different form – for example into a sinusoidal waveform.

An image may be moved bodily to any location on the screen by dragging it with two crosshairs intersecting at its bottom left. That part of it lying above and to the right of the crosshairs will appear in the new position on the printed page.

Illustrator may be used as an aid for the professional artist. For example it will provide a faint displayed image, of, say, a scanned-in sketch so that the user can trace over it in bolder lines, modify it to produce a radically different sketch, augment it, in-fill it, or change details. Alternatively Illustrator may be used to ease the creation of an own-drawing.

IMAGE STUDIO
A software package introduced by Letraset, London, in 1988 for image (particularly) halftone images imported from scanners) editing on Macintosh machines. The software normally expects images to be stored as TIFF files with 256 halftone levels. It provides facilities for pixel editing, airbrushing, retouching, changing contrast and brightness levels, etc.

The quality of halftone reproduction using Image Studio is excellent.

IMAGES
There are four main branches of electronic imaging:-
* Picture Management
* Document Image Processing (DIP)
* Multimedia
* Image processing
"Picture Management" means concept indexing, inputting, storage, transmission,

and reproduction of fine art, museum arte-facts, photographic archives, and general commercial and industrial artwork. This branch is characterized by its large data vol-ume. A picture in colour which closely re-sembles an A4 size original may require a resolution of 200 pixels per inch with colour at 24 bits per pixel – a total of about 96 Mbits or 12 Mbytes of data. The major operations in this branch include indexing, database oper-ations, massive storage, and fast data transmission.

Document Image Processing refers mainly to office operations where large numbers of documents are digitized to ease storage, handling, and rapid retrieval. It is said that about 5% of the data in an average business is computer-managed and that the other 95% occupies 200 times as much storage space.

Much of the data is text but diagrams, forms, graphics, signatures etc., are included. A dig-itized document typically occupies about 400 KBits or 50 Kbytes of storage. Document flow management operations include fast image capture and non-concept indexing, network-ing and workstation organization, storage ar-rangements and rapid retrieval and printing.

Multimedia involves all types of pictures and images stored, retrieved, and presented with the aid of various media including cam-eras, television, tape, magnetic discs of various types, and motion pictures.

Presentations include sound but not smells – at least not yet.

The phrase "Image Processing" is used here to describe operations which modify a picture or an image in some way such as by "electronic cleaning", enhancement, contrast or colour modification, and by a range of operations concerned with object segregation, detection, recognition, etc.

In all branches the type of equipment and software used varies according to the applica-tion. Certain aspects may be mentioned at this point.

Picture Management covers operations with relatively small numbers of very large records, while DIP covers operations with large numbers of relatively small records. Requirements, or imagined requirements, are ahead of the technology and the means of rap-idly delivering required material following a request requires special consideration of stor-age and transmission.

Image sources may be:-
* Broadcast television frames consisting of several hundred scanning lines.
* Television frames directly received from TV cameras or recorders.
* More recently developed recording dev-ices such as laservision players, CD-ROMs, and possibly later CD derivatives.
* An electronic stills camera (e.g. the Can-non Ion with PC board and software) which sends images to disc.
* A scanner which converts printed page data into electrical form.
* Drawn or "painted" images synthesized with the aid of computer software.

Electronic images are reproduced by means of Cathode Ray Tubes or other forms of dis-play capable of changing electrical into visual representations, or printers able to change digitized or analogue data into a print-on-paper representation.

Images may be in "bi-level" form (com-posed of black-and-white elements), in half-tones (commonly known as "grey-scale" – that is in degrees of greyness from white to black) – or in colour. They are stored and reproduced on a CRT usually as a "bit-map" formed from pixels (picture elements), dis-tributed in a series of closely-spaced scanning lines, invisible on the screen, called a "raster". Printed images are reproduced as dot-struc-tures formed by making marks on paper.

An image is captured by a scanner for dig-itization, or a TV camera, or a CCD camera. These devices are designed to accommodate the properties of an image – resolution, brightness, colour etc; if the device does not inherently digitize (for example a TV camera), an analogue to digital convertor must be included.

A good example of imaging database hard-ware and software is provided by Mintzer and McFall's IBM-devised art catalogue sys-tem designed to accommodate up to 10,000 pictures – in particular a large number of "pieces of art" by the artist John Wyeth. It includes provision for recording 200 x 200 pixel by 8 bit (320 Kbit) colour pictures in a "picture index database" associated with a relational database containing the artist's and the curator's notes for record and retrieval purposes.

The archival database contains the 1024 x 1024 x 16 bit (16.8 Mbit) images used for appreciating the same pictures. Thus when 10,000 pictures are in place, 16.8 x 10,000 = 168 Gbits (21 Gbytes) of storage is used. 32 bit colour pictures may well emerge for general use in due course; 10,000 pictures of that kind would then occupy 335.5 Gbits (42 Gbytes).

Some of the implications of advertised software are exemplified in a January 1991 review of a motion video board with software where the following statement appeared:-

"SuperMac products allow video to be stored on the computer like any other data file... the Screenplay software that comes with the Video Spigot board allows you to preview (motion) video in a small window. By using a frame rate of 10 frames per second, the digitisation of a 160 x 120 pixels clip lasting 10 seconds required between 2 Mb and 2.5 Mb".

This is a board with software for enabling you to string together bits of motion video with the objective of producing, say, a multimedia presentation. The operation just described is an example of one of many kinds of operation which may be carried out using Premiere with another software package called ScreenPlay together with Supermac's VideoSpigot video capture board for Apple Macs. Premiere is Adobe's name for a software editor called Realtime for use with Apple's QuickTime software, re-named after Supermac sold it to Adobe.

If you want results from Screenplay you must possess an appropriate Apple microcomputer with Quicktime, Supermac's VideoSpigot board with Screenplay, a hard disc large enough for storing video clips, and a suitable monitor. The motion video, once it has been "assembled" for presentation purposes, will probably be stored on videotape.

Apple's operating system, System 7.0, was first announced in 1989 supposedly to become generally available in 1990. It arrived in June 1991. The "extended operating system", Quicktime, was expected at the same time. But evidently System 7.0 was only made available for review purposes and Quicktime was "unavailable" in January 1991 so there was not much point in buying Premiere/Screenplay/VideoSpigot. Moral; the best time for becoming interested in a product is after seeing it being used by someone who has actually bought it.

Premiere provides clip-editing functions

reproduced with just adequate picture quality for that purpose, but edited output on motion-video media, probably video tape, is needed. Premiere, like the longer established Macromind Director, is simply supplying "editor/drivers" for delivering multi-media material to the additional equipment needed to assemble the End product ("Ends"). The packages do not include the necessary "consumer" or "professional" options for this purpose.

Consequently the user must get involved with these options costing at least another £5000. In general they are to do with arranging that such items as sound, graphics, animation, motion video, etc., end up as Ends on tape in the manner required by the user who has dealt with editing, timing, organizing etc.

"Processing" – the last of the branches of imaging listed above – is rather a vague word which may mean handling and/or modifying images prior to reproduction as print on paper or for "electronic" delivery. "Processing" also refers to special applications in fields such as pathology, radiography, dentistry etc., and to the automatic reduction of degradation caused by blurring and noise using restoration algorithms.

Imaging activities fall into the categories "Means" – the tools of imaging, "Ends" – the processed images, and "Management" – the organization of the Means to produce the Ends.

People concerned with the Means include those who supply imaging hardware and the software packages to use it. The people interested in the Ends have to put together, Manage, and use the Means, or they may be presented with the Means all ready to present the Ends in the desired form – for example in order to pose questions to a picture database and display pictures retrieved from it.

People primarily interested in producing images for a particular purpose will first have to assemble the Means – that is a hardware and housekeeping software system – in order to pursue their Ends. They need a tool consisting of the necessary inter-connected compatible equipment and software ready to use with the minimum amount of time-wasting making-to-work and learning-to-use time.

An ebullient highly competitive computer industry in the throes of a depression needs to talk up and sell image equipment and software. Descriptions of vapourware must be scrutinized and the right questions asked, before purchase, about the essential information that is left unsaid.

The factors which make a significant difference when a microcomputer is required for imaging applications are:-
* Disc access speed
* Cache memory
* Frequency and type of main processor
* Maths Co-processor
* Graphics/digital signal processor (DSP) card
* Bus structure
* Special imaging software
* Display screen and electronics

"Imaging" varies from a requirement to input, digitize, store, and display small simple black and white stationary diagrams of low but adequate resolution, to a requirement to modify, edit, overlay, compress/de-compress, and show in 3-D, still or motion pictures with superb colour and very high resolution.

As might be expected, these requirements will require a microcomputer which some would call a workstation.

However there is still a considerable difference between what are usually understood to be "workstations ", and "microcomputers". The boundary is blurred but the performance of both keeps on improving. It appears that it is still not possible to make an IBM PC or compatible behave like a Sun workstation whatever you do to it.

At the present time the cost of microcomputers has reached an all-time low. Some of them come with quite comprehensive imaging facilities with the added advantage that if the micro also uses the widely adopted MS-DOS operating system, applications will probably be transportable on to many other machines.

See also ABINGDON CROSS BENCH-MARK, COLOUR, and HALFTONES.

IMAGES – DOCUMENT IMAGE PROCESSING (DIP)

There is one area in which indexed images are the basis of the application – "Document Image Processing" (DIP) used in large offices. But it is the *textual content of the document* which is being indexed. The purpose of DIP systems is to replace paper documents by digitized documents to ease handling and processing problems. These documents may contain some graphics which will be digitized with the text. DIP describes a specific area of image processing. It is a technology used in usually large offices for storing retrieving and displaying digitized document images as an aid to workflow management.

As in other areas the development and convergence of affordable technologies has encouraged DIP development. Scanners, optical storage, and high resolution screens backed by the required processing power are the main ingredients.

DIP systems include stand-alone PC-based systems, LAN-based client/server systems using workstations and shared scanning, indexing, printing services, and host-based minicomputer or mainframe systems.

For document capture, cameras or rotary cameras, optical raster scanners, or facsimile machine scanners are used. High speed cameras can record up to 600 A4 pages per minute – provided the pages are in a form which makes high speed paper handling feasible. With rotary cameras, as used for microfilming, index information is collected automatically from data inserted by the operator within a rectangular blip placed above or below each frame for automatic retrieval.

With optical scanners, capture speeds range from 3 pages a minute to 30 pages a minute for high speed both-sides-of-the-paper scanners. The bottleneck is the need to prepare the documents for scanning and the physical state of the documents.

Optical scanners output an array of pixels representing bilevel, continuous tone, or colour images which are "cleaned up" to reduce the amount of data held. The documents are then indexed, assigned a storage address and transferred to permanent storage on optical discs. The main advantages of the media are high capacity and longevity – said to be 30 to 40 years. Disadvantages are relatively slow access and data transfer rates, and lack of standardization.

Quite a lot of information is published about graphics in connection with the usually large systems used for DIP, in organizations like the US Patent Office, Prudential, and TSB.

The Figure shows the equipment units in a large commercial installation using microfilm storage.

The space-accommodation arithmetic pro-

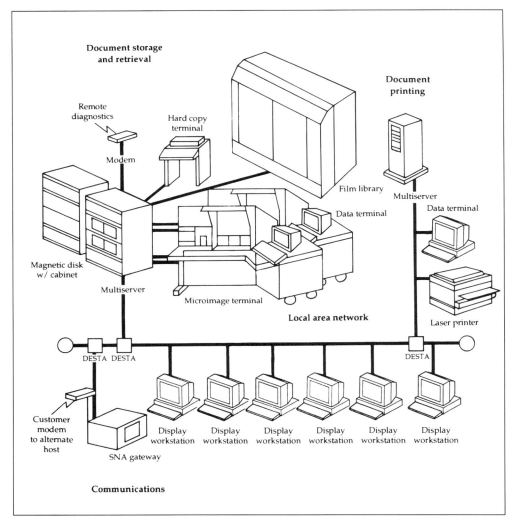

Example of units of equipment in a DIP installation

viding the incentive for DIP is suggested by Helms, as mentioned in a previous entry:- "Today only 5 out of 100 items are stored in a computer. Each of the remaining 95 pieces takes about 10 times as much space per piece because of its non-coded nature. Thus it takes about 200 times as much space to store that 95% as the original 5%".

The indexing method used for DIP systems is discussed by Hales and Jeffcoate:- "Index information usually consists of the document identifier, a description of its content, and a number of keywords. Such information is held in a database... and is entered by the operator after the document has been captured and before it can be moved into permanent storage... a well designed index database is crucial to the success of the operation".

The bottom Figure opposite represents a number of storage units arranged so that archival least-used files are stored in the bottom row of stores with relatively slow access.

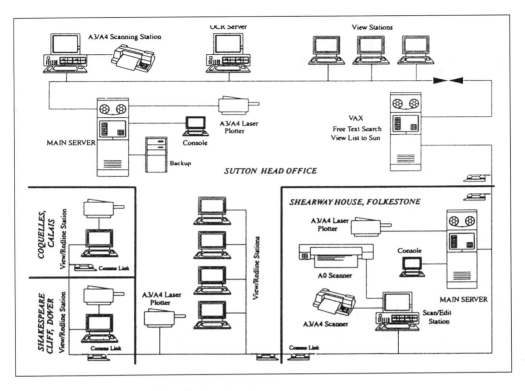

Trimco's DIP pilot scheme for distributing drawings

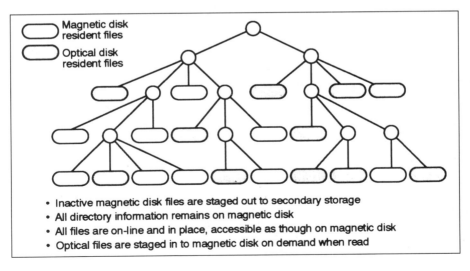

Staged storage (by courtesy of Epoch Systems Ltd)

Files are moved upwards in stages to the local disc at the top, in a user's workstation. All files are logically on line. Staging is arranged so that storage units never fill up. A user's activities are monitored and his or her most active files are moved into local storage.

An example of a typical installation is shown in the top Figure on the previous page. The purpose of this installation (Figure by courtesy of Trimco, Ealing, UK.) is to manage large quantities of A0 size drawings required on a number of sites for a large project on a daily basis. The complete installation is much larger than the pilot scheme shown, although the figure gives a good idea of its main features.

However, as already mentioned, in such systems the items to be indexed usually consist of images of text in "office documents", digitized for easier storage and processing. Graphics may be included in a document but provision for indexing the content of graphics is not usually provided.

For large picture or DIP systems, the general principle is to store data hierarchically in an attempt to locate the stored data most likely to be needed close to the user in order to minimize the time taken to retrieve and deliver it.

IMAGES – FUTURES

Further advances in Graphic User Interfaces (GUI) will include Gesture recognition for character and command input, real-time 3-dimensional animation, and sound and speech including visual and acoustic cues to improve comprehension and retention.

According to Alan Kay and Raj Reddy, leaders in the art, workstations will execute 1 Giga-instructions per second, have 1 Gigabyte of memory and a Gigabyte Bus, and will cost less than $10,000. They will support real-time dimensional graphics with transformation and smooth shaded rendering at about 1 million triangles per second.

A gesture translation, for example, will change 2 dimensional mouse movements into 3-dimensions. For instance if a user adds a propeller to a computer model of an aircraft, the object will be projected into screen space and the axes compared to the vector formed by the cursor's start and end positions. Translations will automatically display a 2 dimensional shadow in 3 perpendicular plains on to a "stage" setting, including the newly added propeller, in order to aid spatial perception.

The problem of authoring for multiple media, continue Kay and Reddy, is far greater than the sum of the authoring problems in the individual media because it is necessary to coordinate and synchronize the media into a coherent presentation. Video and sound materials are especially demanding, since few users have experience in video editing. Skilled interdisciplinary teams of cognitive psychologists, user-interface designers, graphic designers, and content-area specialists will be required to produce user interfaces that help users do useful work and produce material of lasting value.

It will become possible to direct a design assistant, for instance, to "alter the shape of the corners on the dinner plates designed last week so that they fit production methods for Rosenthal china and meet hotel restaurant durability requirements".

Note that some parts of this directive can be expressed by natural language, some by pointing, some by sketching, and that feedback in the form of a realistic pictorial display is essential. Some of these technologies are within our grasp but fully general natural-language understanding will take considerably more time.

IMAGES – INDEXING

Databases for storing and retrieving images and/or information contained within images, must be indexed. The need to test the effectiveness of image retrieval systems will arise. Test methods might be based on the work carried out by Cyril Cleverdon and others who pioneered indexing systems when it became feasible to handle large volumes of text back in the early sixties.

The major method used for image indexing is to label (index) the image with terms (words) considered to be appropriate by an indexer. The image is retrieved from the database when the terms, chosen by a user, match the indexer's terms associated with the image.

Alternatively the image is described, preferably automatically, in terms of its elements or constituent parts, and retrieved when a user's choice of descriptive picture elements matches those associated with an image in the database.

The technical feasibility of storing and manipulating graphics became evident during the development of the Xerox Star. The need for indexing was expressed, although not discussed in detail, by Smura. Records would contain:- "an information classification element for captured graphic and lexical data... in a personal medium it may be a symbolic representation for the image or a simple text statement. It can also be a mosaic or a low resolution picture".

To start with, virtually all graphics indexing development was of the "label allocation" type – that is using words. The notion that the automatic recognition of image elements might be feasible had to await the arrival of recognition software. This, in turn, had to await the arrival of hardware of appropriate processing power and cost.

Pettersson describes a very simple system using words in a dictionary stored on an Apple II to retrieve associated graphics from a Laservision player controlled by the Apple. One Swedish indexing word appears to have been allocated to the content of each page.

The two major methods by which images might be indexed are by words, and by content. However replies are needed to several questions. Is there a range of image and picture collections which should be indexed and placed in a database for the greater benefit of users? What proportion would form a small database of simple images amenable to indexing, and what proportion would form a large database of hard-to-index complex images? Are numerous collections awaiting attention in such places as libraries, museums, art galleries, private houses etc?

Would a latent demand be revealed if relatively inexpensive technology and effective methods of indexing were brought together? What kinds of collections of images, particularly electronic representations of *objets d'art* (mainly pictures), require to be indexed?

IMAGES – INDEXING, CASE EXAMPLES

A publication from the Museum Documentation Association lists a large number of software and database software packages with the names and addresses of suppliers and a list of the two or three hundred museums, colleges, universities, trusts, and other organizations using them. *MODES* for cataloguing is the most widely used package by far, followed by *MIS* for inventory and *Recorder* for biological locality recording. *DBase* is easily the most widely used database.

From this data, and that provided earlier for the US, we can extrapolate to perhaps 5,000 museums and like organizations world-wide, of which perhaps 1000 are running computerized systems. Some hundreds of these are probably using or contemplating using images with many more thinking about their introduction.

Some examples showing how indexing has been carried out in particular circumstances follow.

The Library of Congress videodisc project

In 1982 the Library of Congress embarked on a programme to provide access to a portion of its collection of 12 million graphic items – original photographs, historical prints, posters, architectural drawings, and so on. In a pilot project about 49,000 graphics were photographed and recorded on videodisc, with the videodisc player controlled by a microcomputer for searching.

The system designer comments "The dilemma for custodians and researchers of graphic collections is that words cannot entirely represent an image, but the image cannot be comprehended entirely without some words of identity. Researchers must verbalize what they are looking for, however vague".

The LC decided to index the collection using a modified shortened MARC format. At the time, a MARC format for visual materials was under discussion but had not been finalized. A "Thesaurus for Graphic Materials" was due to be published in 1986. "The videodisc captions consist of fields from the MARC format with a concentration on the controlled vocabulary access point fields most useful for picture searching".

The time taken to index an item varies greatly, but the average is believed to be about 5 minutes. No information is available about retrieval performance or about the effect of changes in indexing policy on performance.

The historic textile database at the University of Maryland

The database consists of images of coverlets (decorative loom woven bed-coverings) and carpets. "Design motifs found in coverlet centerfields, borders, corner blocks, cartouches, and logos are coded on the back of the infor-

```
⌐⌐L
NOTE  Ac....p....u by a photograph and 4 pages.      ..entary ..aterial.
NOTE  Contents:
         Cover sheet. With sketch map by Jay T. Liddle (b. 1906), Daniel A. Finlayson, Harry
         E. Weir (b. 1907) and Charles Dabbs Krouse (1A-39522)
         Sheet 1. Floor plan by Weir, Harry W. Phillips, A. Hays Town (b. 1903) and Liddle
         (1A-39523)
         Sheet 2. East and west elevations by Weir, Finlayson and Town (1A-39524)
         Sheet 3. North elevation by Krouse, Weir, Town and Liddle (1A-39525)
         Sheet 4. South elevation by Weir, Liddle and Town (1A-39526)
         Sheet 5. Detail sheet of cornice, corbel and baptismal font by Weir and Town
         (1A-39527)
         Sheet 6. Iron work details by Liddle and Town (1A-39528); LC-USZA1-784 (b&w
         neg.)
NOTE  HABS/HAER Database Control No. MS0058.
NOTE  B&w reference copies available in Prints & Photographs Reading Room; full size repro-
         ducible drawings also available.
NOTE  Transfer, Historic American Buildings Survey, Department of the Interior.
COLL  HABS-18
DESC  CHAPEL OF THE CROSS (MANNSDALE, MISS.)
DECT  ANGLICAN CP    ``ES
F       `'CC`  `DI
```

The Index for an LC special item using Marc records

mation sheet and then entered into the motif database. This makes it possible to search for specific design motifs".

Nothing more is said about the coding scheme except that "untrained students would be hired to enter the data... so it must be easy to update records and learn the basic tasks of entering, appending, and editing the data". Presumably an efficient coding scheme for all possible patterns has been devised and is easy to use.

The problems which arose in this case were not in the indexing area but in the imaging equipment. They sound predictable because "the lack of funds forced many difficult compromises". *PicturePower* software enables images to be imported from a video camera into a database running on a PS/2 via an image capture board, and integrated with text. Formats are compatible with *DBASE III*, chosen for the database. However modifications were required because of the inconvenience of searching with this database.

Inadequate picture quality was improved by two methods. A standard camera was replaced by a professional camera and lense. System resolution was improved and colour was replaced by a 4-bit greyscale. It seems that 16 levels of grey were preferred to poor colour. The impression conveyed by the designer is that the system does the job in spite of the cost constraints.

History information stations at the Oakland museum

A number of "History Information Stations" for the use of visitors have been installed at this museum. Each consists of a microcomputer, 19" monitor with touch screen, disc drive, videodisc player, and stereo amplifier and loudspeakers. The primary goal of the scheme is to "provide, identify, and interpret, information about each of the 6000 artefacts on exhibition".

However "A clear favourite" is the interactive map. The map includes "landmark icons to help visitors select the area in which they found the item in question". A montage of display cases is shown, and the visitor selects the case and then the artefact. "The map allows the visitor to filter out most of the gallery from the decision making process with one touch of the finger".

The information is contained on videodisc (i.e. motion video to the NTSC standard) with large-size text stored on the hard disc. The authors say that "we chose to use a 286 class of computer because it has just enough speed to load full pages of test at an acceptable rate".

The CMC (Delhi) Art Records prototype

Chaudhry and Roy describe a government

of India scheme called the *Arts Record Treasury System* operated by CMC. A prototype art object imaging system is now in use at the Indian Centre for Cultural Relations.

The objective of the scheme is to enhance an existing online Art Object Catalogue with images. The online catalogue is organized as an SQL/DS relational database running on an IBM 4361 in Bombay. It is accessed over the Indonet SNA network which has nodes at a number of centres in India with a connection to CMC's London office via a gateway to an international packet switch network. The catalogue covers a collection of Indian paintings, sketches, etchings, statues, sculptures, lithographs etc., exhibited at various locations in India and abroad.

The image capture system consists of an Eikonix CCD type 850 camera for producing 4000 x 4000 pixel images in colour from standard size 22.5 x 15 cm photographs, a PC/AT microcomputer, and Philips optical disc storage. Compression is not used for fear of degrading the images. Each image is accompanied by a textual description of image attributes managed using Oracle RDBMS SQL software with interactive menu-control for user searching.

Hits are picture identification numbers each associated with an image displayable on a 500 x 500 pixel Mitsubishi colour monitor. Details of how the contents of pictures are described or indexed are unfortunately not provided.

Significantly, and in common with image collections elsewhere, a problem "prevalent in the Indian scenario is the lack of uniformity in categorizing various schools of thought, styles, etc., leading to an ad hoc classification scheme".

Unlike books in libraries the objects in a museum's collection are physically diverse and they have to be named before they can be added to the catalogue. A nomenclature for naming these objects has yet to evolve in India.

The Globe project

The system seeks to provide access to rich interactive kiosks in museums so that visitors may move from a glancing experience to a deeper involvement with an underlying idea.

The potential now exists to "extend at least part of the public experience with all its drama and senses into the private world of the home... A visitor produced multimedia presentation which can be recorded at a public space site on to videotape can be taken home for viewing". The development of the Globe theatre project is an example of these ideas.

This system is to be used in the International Shakespeare Globe Centre which includes the re-built Globe theatre. The original Globe, built in 1598, was closed by the Puritans in 1642 and demolished to make way for tenements in 1644. Sam Wanamaker decided to rebuild it. A plaque on a brewery wall on the south bank of the Thames commemorates the original Globe. Rebuilding started in 1988 and Phase II is in progress.

The museum and research centre will be built on the site as well as the theatre. Some preliminary work on a multimedia system for use by visitors was done by IBM. Several modules were considered including one to provide general information for visitors, a second to assist students, and a third to provide for several research options.

An ambitious scheme described by Friedlander received Apple encouragement and is gradually being developed. Historical advice has been supplied by Andrew Gurr, Professor of English at Reading University. Part of the design provides for the production of animations using *Macromind Director*. Another part will enable Shakespearian plays to be made available as multimedia presentations. The plays could, for example, may be "edited" into various stage settings.

IMAGES – INDEXING LANGUAGES

Special languages may be developed for the purposes of reducing the indexing effort, or making it more amenable to computer operations. They include various kinds of machine-processable shorthand with which to describe the structure of an image.

Leung has described experiments using a Picture Description Language for the coordination of terms, object descriptions, object attributes, relationships and events. Boolean searching and thesaurus assistance will be incorporated. Picture data are stored in an SQL relational database.

Leung claims that "In the context of still pictures... the main semantic concepts of entity, attribute, and relationship... closely correspond to the noun, adjective, and verb which are the essential components of a simple description of a picture". The allocation of these components to SQL relationship tables will enable more efficient searching to be carried out.

An addition to the system called "adaptive tuning" is due to be tested. When a picture is retrieved, its description could be augmented or adjusted by that user to provide improved access for the next user.

S.K.Chang describes a method of picture indexing and moves on to providing a description of a more fully worked out scheme. The idea is that spatial relationships between objects may be represented by strings of characters enabling questions like "What objects are situated between a lake and a forest in the picture". Objects appear to be named icons *representing* objects, not objects themselves which have been automatically recognized and named – a far more difficult operation.

The idea is expanded to where the segmentation of objects is carried out by measurements expressed as character strings generated when traversing vertical and horizontal cutting lines intersect edges, but the objects are not recognized and named.

Chang also suggests that a combination of image keywords, pattern recognition, image processing, and image understanding might be used for retrieval. The user must inform the system in advance what methods are required and it will prepare indexes for the particular case. The more it is used for that application, the more it acquires knowledge to optimize its retrieval strategy.

IMAGES – INDEXING PROBLEMS

Sustik and Brooks discuss problems of indexing graphics stored on interactive videodiscs:-

"Merely storing data on a videodisc does nothing to facilitate recall and precision – effective indexing does... Many people think that text is easier to index... but the difficulty of indexing stems from the problem of identification and naming".

"Objects consist of an infinite number of embedded qualities. Very few are at any one time considered useful, interesting, or worth noting... Idiosyncratic nomenclature and cross-classifications will proliferate unless working agreements are made about categories... people categorize objects because they belong together and follow a rule". Sustik and Brooks provide the categories shown in the figure.

If, as Sustik and Brooks' say, "many people believe that text is easier to index", then people who start indexing graphics for the first time are in for a shock. Text is not just

CATEGORY	EXAMPLE
Descriptive: Possess same physical attribute	All six-legged crawling animals
Inclusive: One includes the other	All people who were US presidents
Exclusive: One excludes the other	All wallpapers not pre-pasted
Identity: They are really the same thing	All pictures of John Kennedy
Ordinal: In a particular order	Stages of embryo development
Causal: Some things make others happen	Hiroshima after the bomb dropped
Probabilistic: Connected under certain conditions	Results of vitamin deficiency
Temporal: Connected in time	Impressionistic painting 1879–1880
Spatial: Connected in space	Buildings in the Federal Triangle

Sustik and Brooks' categories for graphics

easier, but far easier, unless the graphics collection to be indexed consist of a small, narrowly defined collection of simple objects.

The number of alternative terms that an indexer could choose to index a graphic is likely to be large, perhaps very large. This reflects a searcher's requirement who may want to conceptualize a picture using his own, probably numerous, words.

The choice of terms to describe the concept "graphics indexing" itself is not that small. One publication chooses the phrase "scene interpretation" to index an article about "visual-scene understanding". Another phrase used when discussing graphics is "visual materials".

As technology and falling prices enable more and more people to use picture processing equipment, indexing is often ignored. There are several reasons – the library-based approaches are making difficulties by looking for perfection in a grant-aided situation without the cost-effective test of the marketplace, or there are areas where the indexing of the content of the image is of no great importance.

Drawing attention to indexing difficulties negates sales prospects for the positive technical people who sell image handling hardware, and so they simply do not mention it. Effective inexpensive methods for indexing images have not yet reached the market place.

Menella and Muller believe that the major consideration in assessing tasks during the capture of compound documents for inclusion in an online database is the cost of "equipment used, and user expectations... since our users indicated that figure captions were useful for queries and for locating the page containing the graphic mentioned in the text, our decision was to preserve graphic captions".

A "compound document" is one containing graphics, but in this case the graphics are not converted into transmissible data presumably for reasons of cost. Presumably users would not pay for graphics conversion, transmission, or storage costs, so author's captions as a low-cost means of "indexing", or merely to signify the existence of a graphic, were better than nothing. You get the graphic by ordering the hard copy.

IMAGES – INDEXING, RETRIEVAL BY CONTENT

The eye-brain can recognize objects with such ease that by comparison, machine vision systems seem to be, and indeed are, in a very early stage of development.

The many attempts being made to recognize images are nearly all still at the stage of segmentation – the division of an image into its constituent parts for further processing. The major processing activities involved in segmentation are "edge detection" using the continuous boundaries formed by adjacent black and white pixels or abrupt changes in grey levels, and "pattern recognition".

The ideal way of retrieving a graphic would be to describe it in your own words, or provide a sketch, and the machine would translate that description into a graphic representation which it would match against all graphics in the database and retrieve the ones most closely resembling your description.

It will be many years before Expert Systems, Pattern Recognition or Neural Networks have advanced to the point where this becomes possible in operational systems, but the potential for something of the kind was recognized some years ago. Igor Aleksander, to become well-known for pattern-matching between human face graphics for retrieving the "mug shot" most similar to a reference face, recognized it in the early eighties.

Weems suggests that 23 million instructions per second are needed for a typical video requirement, but "Many researchers believe that one hundred thousand times that amount is required". He considers that "pattern recognition techniques by themselves are inadequate... it is clear that vision involves both sensory and knowledge-based processing".

To retrieve an image automatically by its content some method of formulating a query must be devised. It is hard to visualize a system which automatically generates words or structural descriptions for search purposes when a search question is posed. Alternatively an actual structure resembling that of the required image must be input for matching purposes.

S.K.Chang's work, which is an attempt to describe areas with coded strings – a cross between word indexing and recognition, was mentioned in the last section. C.C.Chang has taken the work further in order to use the data in S.K.Chang's "2-D strings" as a similarity measure for retrieving those images containing features similar to a known image.

Bordogna describes a method of identifying images by parts having a characteristic shape. The images chosen to demonstrate the technique are Galaxies exhibiting various features such as "arms" etc. Again this scheme could equally well be called a "descriptive word" scheme because each item is retrieved by using "picture data" which has previously been used to describe objects.

For example in Bordogna's galaxies, the silhouette of the structure would be described in terms of the co-ordinates of its width, body length, arms, end-points etc.

There must be some doubt about whether the various schemes of this kind, only a few of which have been described here, will function for more complex objects. At present only the simplest kinds of objects are chosen for description/recognition. The ultimate effectiveness will depend on the extent to which more power (which is undoubtedly on the way) is all that is needed, and whether the time taken for human descriptive indexing, which is likely to become prohibitively large, can be automated in some way.

Another measure of similarity has been proposed by Lee for classifying irregular areas of similar shape and size by pattern matching involving strings of pixels. This kind of operation is computer intensive; a 256 x 256 pixel image took more than two hours on a Mac II.

In a few cases that structure may already exist and a representation of its patterns may be input to a machine and matched against the patterns in known images in the database. One such case is the recognition of human faces.

One of the most advanced systems is based on Alexsander's work on human face recognition done in the early 80s, now being further developed by Rickman and Stonham at Brunel University, UK. It is one of the few content recognition systems which has reached a demonstratable stage. Since it works by pattern matching a collection of images in a database against an input image, a suitable image for inputting must be available in the first place.

The Brunel system can be tested on a facial image database consisting of 500 black and white images, each of 32 x 59 pixels. Each node in a neural network locks on to a particular feature of an image by a consolidation or rejection learning process during successive presentations of the test image. Each interconnected node learns by being encouraged to collect more data about a group of elements which it has already amassed.

This identification of the "Principal Components" of an image is achieved by the adjustment of a weighting function associated with eachnode, each having "locked on" to a feature.

After learning, each node will generate output data whenever presented with that feature. Several such nodes will output when several features representing the complete image are presented to them. The objective is to maximize discrimination of the Principal Components across the data set so that features of the image are identified with minimal overlap. Any other image in the collection sufficiently similar to the learnt image will produce similar outputs enabling image selection by matching to be performed.

Issue 12, volume 22 (1989) of *Computer* carries on its cover a picture of an open photograph album showing period photos, with the legend "Image database management". There are five lengthy articles about the topic inside the issue.

In an introduction it is said that "In the computer vision community, interest has focused specifically on the design of image databases and efficient retrieval of iconic information".

The paper by Brolio et al on this issue may be representative of state of the art research and goes some way towards the realization of methods which will enable the content of a graphic to be analysed and matched with a user's query with little or no indexing effort needed.

Brolio et al explain:- "Our fundamental object is the token... which can represent an image event such as a line or a homogeneous region in an image, or an aggregate of events such as a group of parallel lines, a geometric structure or the regions hypothesised to belong to some object... we have written functions for storing tokens in the appropriate cells and for retrieval based on eight types of spatial regions – point-to-point, line-to-line,

 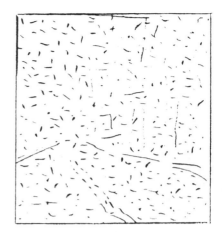

Brolio: auto-analysis (right) of photo (left)

region-to-region, etc."

The figure (sketched from photographs in the Brolio article) shows, on the left, a halftone photograph of a road in a forest, and on the right, a machine automatic analysis of it using the processing software. Analysis takes about 30 minutes using a Sun work-station. The system is currently being up-graded to work up to 10,000 times faster.

The converse operation is to submit a rough outline drawing to the system for matching against a collection of photographs and the system will select the most similar photo. Fuzzy matching is used – an exact match is not required for a "hit".

Rorvig (1993) describes a method for "Automatically abstracting visual documents". The work represents a change of method compared with Seloff's "Visual Thesaurus" described in the entry IMAGES – INDEXING, WORD SYSTEMS. Frames from film sequences of space shuttle launch operations are digitized and a range of features such as grey levels, edge slopes, line lengths, angles, etc., are extracted using some of the methods described in the entry IMAGES – PROCESSING.

Data from these features are summed into a single value representing the structure of each frame and the values for a sequence of frames are compared. A proportion of the numbers from the tails of the curves showing the distribution of the numbers are selected in order to provide a set of images with appreci-able differences. A reduction, typically in the ratio of 700:1, from a mass of images, many of which are similar, to a set showing significant changes, is obtained.

IMAGES – INDEXING, UNIMPORTANCE OF

It should be here mentioned that image indexing is not universally considered to be a difficult operation.

Pamela Danziger, Director of information research services at Franklin Mint, is surprisingly dismissive of graphics indexing. "Designing an indexing scheme for a picture database is basically no different from any other indexing scheme... the special requirements for indexing images on optical disks are little different than designing any other database... To determine the descriptive criteria needed, identify only those elements that will be used to select pictures for the database".

It is hard to reconcile this statement with the effort demanded by other schemes in order to provide an indexing language needed to control the presumably large number of terms that indexers need to use properly to describe some types of image. Comprehensive indexing is necessary to accommodate a wide range of possible search questions.

From 1989 onwards, a number of articles were published about "image processing systems" usually excluding any mention about finding a graphic, and never mentioning retrieval using automatic content-analysis systems.

For example in a section entitled "Subject Access", within a 1990 review of the topic by Lunin containing over 150 references, the author could find only two articles, 1983 vintage. They express the hope that research will commence. The title of a second article by McGregor in 1989, sounds as if it might be about automatic recognition. It turns out to be about a scheme for the human-indexer coding of visual features occurring or not occurring in a collection of paintings.

Issue 3 of the 1990 volume 29 of the *IBM Systems Journal* contains 13 articles about image technology and management. The cover depicts various art objects with the caption:- "One aspect (of ImagePlus) involves cataloguing... the other... locating pieces for loan. The combination of visual and textual information is beneficial for this application".

As is usual in this journal, which covers systems available now, not items still in the R&D department, most of the articles are of a high standard. But graphic indexing considerations are virtually invisible in its nearly 200 pages. The title "The image object content architecture" looks promising. An "object" is an area of a document containing "text, image, graphics, and fonts".

"To perform the indexing, the customer is identified through a standard data terminal. Then an "Index" transaction is executed to collect data about the document". The meaning of this phrase is obscure.

And elsewhere:- "Each object directory is an indexed table in the database that is part of each object storage group. The relational characteristics and multiple index capability of the database allow objects to be selected and updated in different ways for different types of storage management with the expectation of reasonable performance. Efficient selection of objects that require processing is the key to automatic object storage management".

In an otherwise comprehensive article by Ryman, among various functions such as "File", "Scan", "Print", "View" etc., indexing does not appear. "Find" is not discussed. So much or indexing concepts.

In Lunin's review just mentioned there were only two references to indexing. Lunin concludes:- "One of the main areas of concern is how to represent structural information in a database mode. This calls for thinking in terms of spatial continuous grey-scale information. The designs and techniques for image databases still have a long way to go before users can retrieve by "language of the image" and browse among these databases easily and efficiently".

Eight years ago Nagy (1985) conducted a survey of the image database literature and concluded that "the development of image database systems represents a huge amount of thought and effort, yet few, if any, are approaching the critical size necessary for operational application. Seldom can the developers devote sufficient resources to the user interface, to maintainability and reliability to data integrity, to device independence..." and so forth.

This is not surprising because the nature and support of academic research (most imaging research is academic) makes it unnecessary for researchers to become involved in the mundane activities listed by Nagy. They are interested in research and somebody else is expected to be sufficiently motivated to take it further. The long term R&D needed and the risks associated with developing a successful product in this field discourage commercial organizations from entering it.

The Docmix report (Anon, 1988) of 366 pages compiled by a team of nine says nothing about indexing. The report says that "The attraction of electronic image banks lies in the availability of large numbers of high quality images including colour, moving images, digital imagery, stills, cartoons etc., combined within a structured database which gives rapid and user friendly access to the required item". However unless substantial progress is made with methods of indexing, "structured databases", will be singularly unattractive.

Applications are said to include those "in which the image plays a vital role of communication: advertising, publishing, broadcasting, tourism, education... the availability of catalogues or collections of images are vital for information ... and for educational-training purposes".

The growth prospects for imaging as at 1987 (Frost & Sullivan estimate) mentioned in the report, are said to be from a $580.4 million market in 1986 to a $1576.4 million market in 1990. They include "artificial vision, graphic art, printing & publishing, medical, remote sensing, and geophysical". Yencharis Consulting estimate the market to be nearly $1000 million.

In an article about PACS medical imaging indexing was virtually ignored. It was also virtually ignored in a recent special issue of *JASIS* about imaging.

In Maurer's (1991) article about museum and "viewseum" systems it is concluded that "As the automatic integration of material depends on keywords, pictures alone are useless for the purposes of the viewseum... first discussions with organisations in other countries make it likely that integration problems are solvable". As up to 100,000 images are currently being digitized for the "viewseum" Maurer must be expecting a great deal from these "first discussions".

IMAGES – INDEXING, WORD SYSTEMS

The following factors require consideration before an indexing project is started:-

1. Performance needs to be expressed in an appropriate manner. It may be unrealistic to consider Cranfield-type tests, but some method is required for comparing the effectiveness of alternative methods of image indexing.

2. The more elaborate the indexing method, the longer indexing will take. The longer it takes the less likely is that the necessary time/effort will be devoted to doing it.

3. If it is difficult for a user to learn how to use the system a skilled intermediary may be needed – perhaps requiring much more skill than intermediaries who assist with most existing online text retrieval systems.

4. Can methods be developed which are appropriate for collections of images with an arbitrarily simple content and of arbitrarily small size, and also for collections above those levels of content and size?

A frequently used method is based on a specially compiled thesaurus of hierarchically arranged descriptive terms chosen to cover the contents of the images in the collection. Both indexers and users are forced to convert the descriptive words they might otherwise choose into the nearest thesaurus terms.

Iconclass

A thesaurus called ICONCLASS is used at a number of centres – namely at the University of Leiden (for illustrated books, a collection of 10,000 Italian prints, and another collection of 65,000 engravings), at Marburg for a huge microfiched collection, for the Provenance Index to several collections at Santa Monica, at Utrecht for describing valuable objects in churches in the Netherlands, and for the Courtauld collection of paintings of the American school in the Witt Computer Index.

ICONCLASS was published in the period 1973 to 1985. It consists of 17 volumes of hierarchically arranged codes associated with a textual description in English, designed for classifying the content and subject matter of fine art material.

The thesaurus is organized in a number of levels commencing with nine primary codes "1. Religion and Magic", "2 Nature", "3. Human Being, Man", "4. Society, Civilization, Culture" etc. The first two characters of the code are digits and the third is always a capital letter permitting 25 sub-divisions (J is excluded) at the third level.

A part of the section classified by code numbers is shown on the next page.

When a new word or phrase is added to the thesaurus in its correct alphabetical position, its notation is composed as a primary symbol and a succession of symbols representing successive levels of sub-divisions of the primary code. Notations at the same level may be combined, as indicated by a "+" sign.

Newly compiled codes are also entered into the associated "Key Number Index" which lists all codes allocated from the third level downwards, together with their associated lower-level codes thus:-

Key to 25F and sub-divisions:-
25F1 Animals used symbolically
5F11 Bestiaries "physiologus"
25F332 Antlers; horn

To code the well known Van Gogh "bandaged ear" painting, for instance, different sections of the thesaurus would be consulted. The indexer would find the notation for each wanted term (e.g. "ear", "easel" etc.,) by looking it up in the alphabetical index.

During thesaurus composition the words "easel" and "ear" would have been allocated codes determined from the level they occupy under the appropriate primary headings. Thus "easel 48C5151" is a sub-division of "Tools of the painter 48C515", descended from "4. Civilization and Culture".

To the uninitiated it seems curious that lower level codes are so specific – for example

+32	trunk
+32 1	sexual organs
+32 11	male sexual organs
+32 12	female sexual organs
+32 2	buttocks
+32 3	entrails, internal organs excreting +45 9
+33	head
+33 1	skull
+33 2	antlers; horn
+33 3	ears
+33 4	fang, tusk
+33 5	snout, jaw, beak, nib
+33 6	tongue
+34	limbs
+34 1	claws, paws
+34 2	wings
+34 3	tail
+34 9	track, trail
+35	external appearance
+35 1	skin, fleece, hide, fur, leather
+35 2	feathers
+35 3	scales
+36	shell, snail-shell, etc.
+4	animal behaviour
+41	birth
+41 1	from an egg
+41 2	brooding; hatching egg +91
+41 3	'larva', grub
+41 4	'pupa', chrysalis
+42	feeding and care of young
+42 1	nest, den, burrow bird's nest 25 F 3 (+42 1)
+42 2	'educating the young', playing with young
+42 9	killing own breed
+43	courting and mating

ICONCLASS: directory of keys (by courtesy of Dr. Catherine Gordon, the Witt Collection, Courtauld Institute of Art)

a very specific code is allocated to an object in a rather complex picture by Teipolo.

Presumably if anyone wanted to pose the question "is there a picture showing Hercules Galicas captivating his audience with a golden chain going from his mouth to their ears" – allocated a special code – they would know the painting and so would ask for it by name – but perhaps this apparently highly specific representation may be used elsewhere.

Henri van den Waal (University of Leiden), the originator of ICONCLASS, said "the material offered for consultation should always be visual. Any other reference – either verbal or by means of codes – can never be more than the first stepping stone".

Dr. Catherine Gordon, project director at the Courtauld Institute of Art, London, is using the system to index a collection of about 1.5 million paintings, drawings, and engravings, by some 75,000 artists. The project was started with the support of the J.Paul Getty Trust to compile the Witt computer index of the American section in the Witt library.

At first site it might appear that ICONCLASS is simply a duplication of the effort put into the AAT (See below). But a comment by Gordon (1990) emphasizes the order of difficulty of classifying graphics; even within the same general area, account must be taken of the need to accommodate nuances of human perception.

Gordon says:- ".. ICONCLASS allows classification where we lack knowledge... where a specific narrative or topic is not recognised, it is still possible to classify what is seen. In more traditional systems what cannot be identified may not be able to be filed".

This need is exemplified by one of the component classification structures of ICONCLASS called "Key Numbers" as shown in the figure. These codes function as qualifying adjectives or phrases. With this order of detail, presumably searches of "high precision" become possible. Presumably the risks of missing a relevant object associated with the consequential low recall are also present.

This comment would not necessarily apply if the system is being used for Information Recovery rather than Information Discovery – in other words to handle queries like "what is the location of the picture in the library showing the collapse of the Brighton chain pier" rather than "show me any paintings which contain tigers".

The art & architecture thesaurus (AAT)

This system was developed along the lines of the National Library of Medicine's MeSH system.

AAS originated at a meeting called by Professor Dora Crouch, a historian at the Rensselaer Polytechnic in 1979. Crouch was motivated by her need to select slides from a large collection for lectures.

The result was an on-going project involving a number of people and eventually the publication in 1990 by Oxford University Press of the *Art and Architecture Thesaurus* (AAT) in three volumes and a floppy disc edition.

The AAT contains about 40,000 terms "Hierarchically arranged according to a rigorously constructed, internally consistent structure", using standard thesaurus conventions, modelled on the National Library of Medicine's MESH (Medical Subject Headings).

During its development, terms were drawn from the Library of Congress Subject Headings (LCSH), but as time went on it became clear that there was a need for an arrangement more in line with MESH. The Thesaurus is compiled and managed by art historians, architects, and information scientists.

Keefe describes how the AAT is used in the Marc-like records of the publicly searchable INFOTRAX database covering a Rensselaer slide collection. Keefe says indexers needed "An initial training period of at least three months". After that training it takes about 47 minutes to complete a slide worksheet and enter the details into the database.

At the time the Keefe article was written 1300 slides had been indexed. One full time indexer would take 3.5 years to complete 10,000 slides. Unfortunately Keefe does not provide any information about retrieval performance. The figure shows a displayed record from the database. In this case the indexing for a number of slides has been con-solidated in one record – a policy generally adopted during compilation which results in a substantial reduction in the number of records needed.

Lunin describes the AAT applied to fiber art graphic databases. Lunin considers that "There appears to be almost universal agreement that the image is desired in the database record together with textual information... even with a mass of information available to apply to a work, it is difficult to describe the concept and other important aspects with just a few index terms or a classification".

The AAT is used at Rensselaer Polytechnic for indexing a collection of 65,000 slides. In a report, by Jeanne Keefe, the magnitude of the undertaking is revealed. Keefe's estimate for the time taken to deal with 50,000 slides is seventeen man years.

Evidently labelling an image for retrieval purposes is a time-consuming process to be carried out by subject experts. In the AAT work described by Keefe, refinements took several years. In addition to the investment made in compiling a thesaurus, there may be an on-going investment to up-date it.

One might expect that this kind of effort would be needed to deal with only a very diverse collection. However the AAT is designed only to handle Western art and architecture out of the totality of art and architecture. ICONCLASS covers a similar area with a difference in emphasis. Objects within the totality of art and architecture represent only a minute fraction of all possible objects – for instance the range of objects that might be encountered in a newspaper's library of photographs.

```
TITLE    : Sydney Opera House; post-1945, aerial view
   BY    : Utzon, Jörn
SUBJECT  : Opera houses, auditoria, auditoriums, ceremic tiles, performing arts
           buildings, concrete halls, music halls, music auditoria, symphony
           halls, movie theaters, theatres, cinemas, restaurant, ribbed vaults,
           ribbed arches
           concrete beams, concrete paint, podium, roof trusses, roofing, roofing
           tile, ribs, vaulted roofs, shell roofs, reinforced concrete, lattice
           roofs, shell structures, shell vaults, towers, steel trusses,
           ceremonial ways
           workspaces, workshops, wood walls, wood ceiling, wooden ceilings,
           concrete vaults, concrete structures, concrete pilings, concrete
           joints, glass, glass walls, laminated materials, cables, cable roofs,
           cable-stayed structures, ridge boards, precast concrete, granite,
           granite powder cement, bronze window mullions, ridge beams
   SITE  : Australia, Sydney, New South Wales, Benelong Point
  DATES  : 1957 - 1973
   SIZE  : 2x2 in. color
HOLDINGS : 3 plans, 11 sections/drawings, 2 aerial views, 29 exterior views,
           3 interior views, 3 details
```

Record from Rensselaer's Infotrax database (by courtesy of the Rensselaer Polytechnic)

Johnson Space Centre (JSC) collection

Seloff describes a system devised to manage a collection of more than one million transparencies and films and about 10,000 motion video and audio reels in the Johnson Space Centre (JSC) collection in Houston, growing at the rate of up to 65,000 new images per year.

Seloff mentions the indexing syndrome which everyone involved in indexing knows so well "The viewpoint of the cataloger invariably changes from one week to the next and is always different from the perspective of the engineer or the scientist... the wider the disparity in the points of view, the less likely the appropriate item will be retrieved".

The JSC thesaurus was compiled by automatically processing a number of existing catalogues but it was felt that a visual thesaurus was also necessary. Accordingly a Hypercard system was developed enabling "a descriptive term from the thesaurus to retrieve its associated image as well as broader, narrower, and related terms along with their associated images". The "data retrieval engine", Personal Librarian, used in this work, ranks hits in order of relevance. This is obviously a very large project and future plans for its further development are described.

Telclass

Telclass is yet another variation of the thesaurus principle.

It was developed by Evans at the BBC's Film and Videotape Library. Evans says that the scheme "differentiates Words from Concepts... paying due regard to the relationships between categories and objects". Methods of applying this principle are shown in Evans's examples of the way subject terms are used to label media material.

IMAGES – INDEXING, VISUAL THESAURI

The Berkeley prototype

Besser describes the IMAGEQUERY software implemented at the University of California at Berkeley. It will run on workstations including SUNs, PS/2s with AIX, or MACs with AU\X.

Besser talks about the often inadequate availability of rich information sources such as collections of photographs:-

"A set of photographs of a busy street scene a century ago might be useful to historians wanting a "snapshot" of the times, to architects looking at buildings, to urban planners looking at traffic patterns or building shadows, to cultural historians looking at changes in fashions, to medical researchers looking at female smoking habits, to sociologists looking at class distinctions, or to students looking at the use of certain photographic processes or techniques".

UC Berkeley already run campus-wide online library services so it is proposed that IMAGEQUERY be made available as a kind of enhanced Online Public Catalogue (OPAC) over the existing network and workstations. This would allow the user "to browse visually through the group of small surrogate images associated with an initial hit list". These images would be taken from the Architectural Slide Library, the Geography Department's Map Library, and later, the Lowie Museum's Anthropology collection of photographs of their objects.

A form based on a spreadsheet is first displayed which forces the user to make the appropriate entries by selecting options from pull-down menus.

Thus the "fields" menu for the architectural database offers the option "place". If "Venice" is chosen, that word appears in the upper part of the spreadsheet. If the "Authority List" is then chosen, classes of existing images are displayed for selection by the user e.g. "piazzas". At this point a more complex Boolean logic query may be added or the "do query" button pressed and a hit list displayed in the bottom part of the screen. For example "Venice...San Marco" might be selected from the list.

Upon selection of "browse", slide-size images are displayed on the right hand side of the screen. The display area may be expanded to include the whole screen if necessary, allowing up to 30 images to be displayed together. Finally, any of these images may be replaced on command by a high resolution colour enlargement.

Hogan's suggestions

Hogan et al (1991) say "Many current information systems used to access images simply transfer the text-based methods of information storage and retrieval to computerized systems. Because the multiple aspects of visual access to images has long been neglected its development is still woefully in-

150

adequate... The inter-relationships between text and graphics need to be thoroughly explored as does the creative possibilities in visual-based retrieval systems... Visual thesauri and their applications to the museum community incorporate a complex mix of political, economic, and design issues".

Hogan reminds us that picture thesauri have been around since John Amos's *Visible World*, published in London in 1672. I remember being given a book called *The English Duden* many years ago. I believe it was originally published in German. Every other page represented a scene showing many numbered objects. These pages were entitled "The Car", "The Farm", "The Bank", "The Railway Station", etc. The opposite pages contained the names of the numbered objects.

This was the basic arrangement but there was also some kind of logical ordering of pages and the number of objects in each picture was very large. I don't remember whether there was any cross referencing or duplication of objects in different scenes.

Hogan says "It is relatively quick and easy to browse the page of a visual dictionary even though the book may have a large number of pages... This type of browsing is difficult in a visual environment... rapid traversal of displays is difficult... what is lost to the user is the ease of determining the underlying structure which becomes quickly apparent with the use of a print dictionary", and so on.

However there are some on-going attempts to extend this principle into computer-based system and Hogan briefly discusses Besser's Ximagequery, the NASA visual thesaurus, and the event display system used by physicists at CERN.

Advances in this area would, of course, be of great interest not just for museum collections but for all kinds of collections. Hogan et al review research and then describe a prototype visual thesaurus being developed at Syracuse University.

They make the point "...visual images make it possible simultaneously to compare all the features of two patterns. Therefore information is matched in parallel... in contrast to features described verbally which are not all accessible at the same time and must be compared serially". They also suggest that a computer can rotate images for pattern matching much faster then the brain can.

This is not a good comparison to bring into the part of the paper headed "Human Information Processing" which contains some otherwise interesting reflections. Brain-computer object-rotation comparisons are not very helpful. Computer pattern matching as a method of retrieval by similarity, which is implied here, has some severe limitations.

A computer is unable to recognize the similarity between two quite simple objects when one of them is viewed from a different angle. The ease and speed with which a human accomplishes this task and can deduce the appearance of a complete object from a single viewing is unlikely to be matched by a computer in the foreseeable future.

It is not usually feasible to pose a question in the form required by a pattern matching system, namely "here is the kind of image I am seeking – which image in the collection most nearly matches it?".

The authors propose a way out of this difficulty, eliminating text entirely by, in effect, providing a user with the tools of the kind which are already used now – e.g. rotation, scaling, mouse dragging, curve construction, etc., for modifying a simple image drawn from, say, a "clip art" collection. The type of question now becomes "is there an object in the database resembling this one?"

The user's simulation has become the formulated query which he or she asks when it is felt that the artistic attempts have produced a reasonable simulation for presenting to the database for matching. The machine signals the number of hits which may then be visually browsed by the user. Prompted by the resemblance, or lack of it, between his or her sketch and hit images, the sketch is adjusted and the query repeated.

This is a bold start to attempt to break out of a strait-jacket. The course of the research is likely to be long and difficult, but it could be ultimately successful.

Hogan et al follow these ideas with the comments "When considering information retrieval in general we are looking for alternative ways of image retrieval, ways that are less dependent on familiarity with existing taxonomies and their assigned authorities. Accomplishing this end is less clear-cut."

From the foregoing description of existing systems described in the literature, and discussions about projects at the research stage, it must be concluded that nothing is yet available that will replace current methods of image retrieval – that is by searching text terms inserted by an indexer which are associated with the image.

However some form of system based on automatic recognition of content should appear in a few years time in order to retrieve simple graphic objects from a small collection. Improvements will follow such as methods of inputting search data, increased complexity of objects, and increased collection sizes of increasing diversity. We might see commercially available image-content retrieval systems at a price and with a performance adequate for some applications within five years.

IMAGES – MEDICAL

Picture Archiving and Communication Systems or PACS embody new developments which are of interest to anyone involved in multimedia. The objectives of PACS are to digitize, display, and if necessary enhance, images capture by computed tomography, magnetic resonance, computed radiography and other techniques, and bring order and accessibility via wideband networks to the files of film in which they are stored.

PACS include databases, communications and application activities. One aspect is how to deal with the immense amount of data required to represent high quality pictures – a major issue in PACS systems. A computed radiography image contains 2000 x 2000 x 10-bit = 40 Mbits of data. Wide bandwidths are needed for the networks which transport this data.

The Ultranet network with Sun Sparcservers type 490 connected to it is used to satisfy the general PACS yardstick of 4 Megabytes/32 Mbits per second data rates. The total data rate in an Ultranet hub required to manage five client-server exchanges of data is nearly 14 Megabytes/112 Megabits second. At these speeds optical fibre with the FDDI standard is appropriate.

IMAGES – PROCESSING

A block diagram of a frame-grabber and image processing board – Data Translation's DT2867, a relatively simple board – is shown on the following page.

It plugs into a PC/AT bus and accepts frames from up to four monochrome NTSC or PAL television sources with sync. and trigger inputs indicated by the arrows on the left. It outputs RGB and composite sync indicated by the arrows on the right. It is supported by appropriate software, performs on-board 16 bit processing at 25 MHz, digitizes signals for processing purposes and then restores them to analogue for display.

It contains two frame stores so that data from one frame may be added, subtracted, or overlaid on the other. It contains a triple ALU and multiplier so that convolution operations are speeded up by a factor of three. It will also perform histogram contrast-changing operations. Convolution, Hough Transform and other transforms, and Thinning operations are processing operations included in some general processing software.

A transformation process usually means that data is extracted from an image, is processed in some way, and is represented in a form more amenable to analysis. Frequently used techniques include the extraction of data from blocks of pixels as part of a compression operation, or the extraction of edge and line data.

Convolution is a basic type of group pixel processing for calculating the weighted average of the intensity of a group of pixels around each and every individual pixel over an area of a given size.

The several figures which follow are reproduced by courtesy of Data Translation Inc.

Hough Transform processing software consists of line-finding algorithms for finding straight line segments in images preceded by edge-detection and line thinning operations. Thinning is an operation aimed at constructing a skeleton by the removal of contours which do not contribute to a basic shape

Enhancing an image or extracting information or features from an image is one form of processing, however image processing is often concerned more with the manipulation of graphic elements of an image than with visual interpretation of the scene. "Processing" in this context usually refers to operations on an image such as edge detection, image enhancement, and feature extraction for pattern recognition.

Applications of image processing in the medical industry include the analysis of X-ray

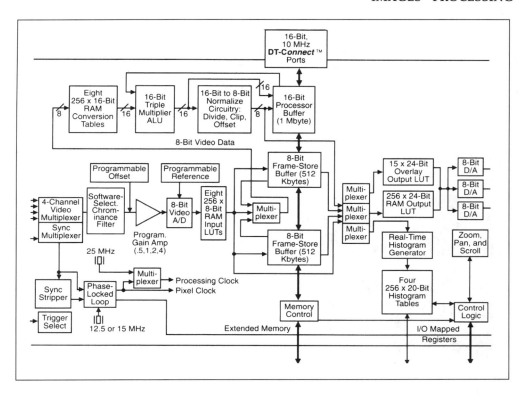

Block diagram of Data Translation's DT2867 frame-grabber board

images and photographs of diseased cells or cultures. Images are enhanced and areas are colour-coded for easier interpretation by medical staff if a problem is suspected.

Imaging arithmetic includes such operations as the addition of images (to improve signal to noise ratios in a sequence by taking account of inter-frame coherence) or subtraction (to see if an object has moved between video frames).

Other common functions include multiplication, inversion, square-rooting, norm- alising, logical manipulation (AND, OR, XOR, etc) and converting between magnitude/phase and real/imaginary data – as required when working with two-dimensional Fourier transforms of images.

Image analysis generally represents operations that extract non-statistical information without changing the image. Simple examples are the counting and labelling of the number of discrete objects in an image (see

Figure below), finding centroids, and calculating the moments of inertia of parts of images.

The figure on the next page shows an original digitized picture (above) and below it the same after having been passed through a filter

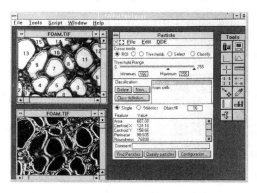

Object counting with Data Translation's Global software

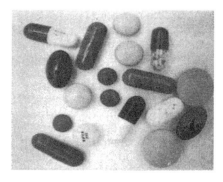

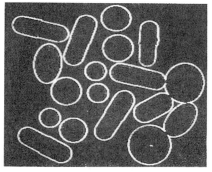

Data Translation Global software original and filtered objects

which allows edge elements to be enhanced.

Neighbourhood transforms are operations that give an output value for a pixel according to the intensities of pixels in its proximity. The best known functions are edge detection and convolution masks.

Fourier transforms may be used to perform pattern recognition, edge enhancement, noise removal and image compression, as well as basic frequency analysis within individual images and over a sequence. Other transforms (such as the Radon) may be used to highlight particular patterns within an image. Wiener filtering and least-squares restoration, as well as operations performed only in the vertical or horizontal planes are also used. Blurred images may be made recognizable.

The main reason for performing a transform is to display the signal in an alternative form or representation, to accentuate features of it not easily recognized in their original time domain form, or to facilitate more efficient digital encoding of the signal informa-tion.

In image coding which involves intensity or grey scale data, the discrete co-sine transform is more appropriate than the Fourier transform for blocks of image pixel data. It can result in compression of information in the image only if significant spatial frequency components are retained; constant intensity sections of the image possess only a single transform coefficient value.

A simple procedure is used to measure the length of the perimeter of an object. Convolu-tion/edge detection is used, and the resulting image is automatically thresholded with an intensity histogram. The binary result repre-sents an edge contour, the pixels of which can be counted to determine the perimeter. The final shape may be recognized by a Fourier description process.

The display shown in the second figure on the preceding page illustrates another kind of imaging operation. The image is being pro-cessed to ease the examination of objects in a particle analysis application.

See also under IMAGES – INDEXING, RETRIEVAL BY CONTENT.

INDEXES – CITATION
See SCIENCE CITATION INDEX.

INDEXING
An index is an ordered list of descriptive terms.

When computers were expensive and mys-terious in the early seventies instead of cheap and mysterious, edge-notched cards were quite widely used for indexing personal col-lections. Experiments for the machine sorting of cards in larger collections were being car-ried out in the same period.

Information about an article, including, say, its number in a file of printed articles, is writ-ten on to an edge-notched card, and the aspects of interest are coded by converting numbered holes round the edge of the card into notches with a clipping tool.

To find a paper of interest, needles are inserted into the holes of the edge of a pack of cards, corresponding to the codes symboliz-ing the topics of interest. The cards describing articles containing those topics will fall out since appropriate holes will have previously been turned into notches. The corresponding articles are then found in the article file.

This method was a significant advance on indexing cards filed in order of a single attribute – say major subject. Articles embodying a particular combination of required attributes could be found, and articles containing a combination of items not anticipated as being a requirement at the time of indexing could also be found. Unlike conventional indexing cards, edge-notched cards do not have to be maintained in any particular order.

The system is an example of *post-coordinate* indexing where the searcher may go directly to the classes of interest listed in one place. A *pre-coordinate* index, such as a conventional catalogue-card index, requires that the searcher must look in several places for all the cards listing the different classes of interest.

In systems where a number of different people share an information system and each is free to insert his or her own indexing terms the indexing problem becomes acute. User A might consider that the word "Production" unambiguously specifies his information requirement, being unaware that user B indexed articles about that topic but used "manufacture" for his indexing term. One way is to accept the additional cost of a controlled indexing system – a "thesaurus" which forces usage of preferred words.

Indexing problems have not been decreased much with the advent of computers. A wanted item in a computer file may be missed because the searcher's choice of words to describe it differ from those used by the indexer. A browse through Roget's Thesaurus shows the richness of the English language in synonyms and shades of meaning.

A thesaurus contains lists of synonyms and other words, referring the indexer and the user to the preferred words which both must use. In medicine, synonyms are a major problem. A thesaurus covering drugs would need to take account of the equivalence of chemical, generic, and trade names.

The Figure on the next page shows a thesaurus (by courtesy of IEA Coal Research) for the Coal research database running on ASSASSIN. In a thesaurus a time overhead is transferred from users to the human compiler. The compiler has to add new words to the thesaurus when they appear. Alternatively a "new word list", automatically created when adding information to a database in a computer-based system with the appropriate software, will have to be examined and edited. This may require a considerable effort with a complex nomenclature – as, for instance in medicine. If it is not done quickly a user will not find items about newly named subjects entering the literature.

The indexing of scientific and technical articles containing a number of concepts has received much attention. Indexing in non-personal collections is usually done by people who are doing the job on behalf of, if not the whole world, at least for a body of users who are mostly unknown to them. Consequently the indexers have to say to themselves "bearing in mind meaning ambiguities, what words are users likely to choose if they wish to find the subjects discussed in this article?".

The purpose, subject matter, and indexing requirements of articles, reports etc., are rather different from memoranda, correspondence, etc.

Indexing may be done either by the user, or by someone on behalf of the user – for instance a member of a group using the same database – or by someone unknown to the user – for instance a staff member of the supplier of the database being used. However if the system is to retain the advantages of being personal, its staffing should preferably be no more than the user and one assistant.

Robert Fairthorne, an information science pioneer, recalls an anecdote, said to come from Germany towards the end of the last war, which illustrates with black humour a traditional method of classification.

"A German with a starving wife and family sought help from the Winter Aid Fund. Entering an imposing building he found himself facing two doors, one marked "Party members", the other "Non-party members". Going through the second door he was faced with two more doors, one marked "Subscribers to the fund", the other "Non-subscribers to the fund". Going through the latter he found two more doors, and so on.

After an hour or two he reached two more doors marked "Family men", the other "Non-family men". Opening the last he found himself out in the street where he had started. A friend asked him if he had received any help. "Oh no", he replied, "but what a marvellous system!".

PRESTEL indexing, using a succession of 10

GYROSCOPES		HAFNIUM ALLOYS	
RT	MEASURING INSTRUMENTS	BT	ALLOYS
RT	PRECESSION	NT	HAFNIUM ADDITIONS
RT	ROTATION		

GYROSCOPES
- RT MEASURING INSTRUMENTS
- RT PRECESSION
- RT ROTATION

H CODES
- BT COMPUTER CODES

H-COAL PROCESS
- BT COAL LIQUEFACTION

HABITAT
- RT ENVIRONMENT

HAEMATITE
- USE *HEMATITE*

HAFNIUM
- BT REFRACTORY METALS

HAFNIUM ALLOYS
- BT ALLOYS
- NT HAFNIUM ADDITIONS

HALIDES
- BT HALOGEN COMPOUNDS
- NT CHLORIDES
- NT COPPER HALIDES
- NT FLUORIDES
- NT IODIDES
- NT ZINC HALIDES

HALL EFFECT
- RT ELECTRIC CONDUCTORS

HALL GENERATORS
- USE *MHD GENERATORS*

UF	Used for (indicates the non-preferred term from which reference is made).
UFC	Used for (indicates the non-preferred term for which the main term is one of the substitute descriptors).
SF	Seen for (indicates the non-preferred for which the main term is a more specific substitute).
BT	Broader term (indicates a more general term, one level higher in the hierarchy, which defines and limits the use of the narrower terms).
NT	Narrower term (indicates a more specific term, one level lower in the hierarchy, which helps to define the broader term but which does not limit its use).
RT	Related term (indicates an associative relationship between terms not related hierarchically).

Entries in the Coal Database Research thesaurus

broad choices per menu, gradually narrowing the choice to a specific subject, is an extension of the two-choice (binary) German door system.

The "German doors" story is an example of an apparently fool-proof system but an indexing system based on the same idea may not necessarily be fool-proof.

For instance in the Universal Decimal Classification (UDC), indexing terms are hierarchically arranged. Thus "Apparatus with Wheel Mechanisms" includes the subset "Calculating and Adding Apparatus" which in turn includes "Slide Rules" – but the latter are certainly not a sub-set of "Apparatus with Wheel Mechanisms".

A more flexible system, illustrating simple indexing principles book, is shown in the figure.

Mercury	125
Microcomputer -s	
CPUs	177
files, moving	187
growth forecasts	144,169
hardware	
ACT	167
Apple Lisa	167
Hewlett Packard	168
SEE ALSO Discs, floppy	
Modem -s	
SEE Telecommunications	

Example of an index

The index is alphabetized and subjects such as Microcomputer are sub-divided and set out in up to three levels as shown in the Figure.

To keep down the index size and to lead a user to related subjects, SEE entries are included. Thus "Discs", perhaps with several sub-divisions, are set out under "D" but there is a SEE reference to "Discs" under "Microcomputers".

This arrangement anticipates that a user might want to find related topics – e.g. "Discs, floppy".

Such an arrangement has to do with the specificity of an indexing term and the number of postings beneath each term. For example Telecommunications" has many facets: "Satellite Telecoms" is more specific, and "Transponders used in Satellite Telecomms" is yet more specific.

The generality of the term "Telecommunications" is such that a user would have to refer to many pages before an article about, say, "Satellite Transponders" is found on, say, page 91. The arrangement shown in Figure below would be unhelpful.

Telecommunications 1, 2, 57, 58, 69, 70, 84, 91, 103, 104-108

Unspecific indexing

In the previous example the frequency of postings per term is more limited and so is the number of lookups needs to check each item.

The alphabetization of an index is open to various options. The London telephone directory uses the arrangement shown in the next Figure. However the alphabetization rules would arguably be more helpful, if they were altered to provide the arrangement shown in the second Figure.

S.W.Trading
Sacre K.J.
Sacred Heart Convent
Saint G.V.
St. Agnes Youth Centre
Society for Underwater Science
Society of Aviation Artists

Sacred Heart Convent
Sacre K.J.
Saint Agnes Youth Centre
Saint G.V.
Society (of) Aviation Artists
Society (for) Underwater Science
S.W.Trading

Alphabetization alternatives

The great advantage of doing your own indexing is that since you are the only user you can take liberties which the impersonal indexer cannot. For instance you will habitually use the same synonyms which do not, therefore, need so much attention.

A personally indexed system is likely to be used at least as often for *information recovery* as for *information discovery*. The user put the material into the system in the first place, partly, at least, as an "information insurance policy" – that is to avoid time-wasting by having to search in the outside world later. This situation appears to reduce the need for comprehensive indexing. If the user knows the item is in the system, he or she will usually be able to answer the question "what terms would I have used for indexing that item?" with the right answer.

When the collection becomes larger and older, older items tend to play more of an "information recovery" role. A personal system is an "overhead". However valuable, that overhead is likely to receive limited attention.

Typically an office contains hard-copy in the form of box-files of cuttings, reprints, etc., books, catalogues, reports etc. They will probably be located according to their *physical attributes* not their *information content*. This practice generates questions like "did I read that in a book, or a report, or did I put it in that pink folder"?

In a typical personal own-indexed computerized system, the PC database consists of records which contain descriptions, indexing terms, and location codes for the associated hard-copy items housed in the office or nearby. You can include any kind of hard-copy item in a personal system including tapes, discs, whole journals, newspaper cuttings or whatever.

See also IMAGES – INDEXING, DATABASES, and HUMPTY-DUMPTY SYNDROME.

INDEXING – AUTOMATIC

Serious work on Automatic Indexing probably started in the 1950s prompted by the arrival of the necessary computer power and funds from the US Government. H.P. Luhn was working in this area at IBM in the late fifties. In 1961 he described some of the earliest results reported in this new field. Luhn is best known for his "Keyword in Context" (KWIC) invention.

Since then work has been continued until the present time notably at Cambridge by Sparck Jones and others on automatic keyword classification, and in Gerard Salton's SMART term-weighting experiments at Cornell. In a 1986 review, Salton compares manual searching of the Medlars medical database with a semi-automatic session. The machine generates a ranked list of documents from weighted term searching, and the user then improves his query formulation and conducts another search. Salton concludes that semi-automatic systems can be as good or better than manually indexed systems.

A current experiment based on this kind of work in which Boolean and weighted searching are compared has been described by Robertson. Another aspect which is receiving attention is the expert system approach for developing a "natural language interface". The objective is to enable people to ask an information retrieval system a question in plain English rather than in an artificial query language as has been required until now.

Status/IQ, a system enabling queries in natural language, with retrieval using relevance feedback, has been described by Pearsall. Status/IQ extracts search terms from literals, word patterns, capitalized phrases, phrases isolated by stop-word breaks, and phrases linked by "and", "or", or commas, from a search statement. It then calculates search term weights by considerations of word frequencies and clustering, word appearance in particular fields of a document, and word occurrence in contiguous paragraphs etc., and then searches and generates a ranked list of documents.

For example, on posing the question to a database running on a machine using Status/IQ software:- "Can drunkenness or intoxication provide a defence to a charge of murder or manslaughter under the Crimes Act of 1900"?, the machine responds with a list of 246 documents with 1 document scoring 75%, 3 scoring 50-65%, a further 15 in the range 25-60%, and the remainder less than 25%.

The Tome Searcher is another system, developed for more general applications, which acts as an interface between a user and any of a number of database systems in order to translate a search statement in English into search terms understood by the system.

As a simple example it would translate the question "I would like to know about optical disks used with PCs excluding Apples" into ("Optical Disc OR Optical Disk OR Optical Storage) AND (PC OR Personal Computer) AND NOT Apple". Tome Searcher is based on work carried out by Vickery et al, who have described their development work.

The systems just described are breaking new ground and are not to be confused with numerous POSH (Plain Ordinary Software Hype) packages embodying the fashionable words "Expert System" in their titles.

Quite a different approach to automatic indexing is used by the Institute for Scientific Information (ISI) in their "Related Records" concept in the CD-ROM versions of the Citation Index (SCI) or Social Science Citation Index (SSCI) databases. It uses a technique called BIBLIOMETRIC COUPLING.

Each "hit" in a search carried out in a conventional manner is followed by a number indicating the number of "related records", ranked in order of similarity, which are available for display on demand. Articles without references cannot be included because the similarity of articles is measured by the number of references they have in common. If another current article exists with all ten of its

The human factors of computer graphics interaction techniques. James D. Foley et al. IEEE Computer Graphics & Applications, November 1984 13-48	Behavioral issues in the use of interactive systems. Lance A. Miller et al. Int. J. Man-Machine Studies 9, 509-536, 1977

Bennett J.L.
* Chapanis A.
Conrad R.
Engle S.E.
* Englebart D.
Flanagan J.L.
Foley J.D.
Gould J.
* Kennedy T.C.S.A.
* Miller L.A. (1977)
Miller R.B.
Thampson D.A.
Van Cott H.P.

ten references identical to the ten references in the retrieval article, then it would almost certainly be the first related record displayed.

In the Figure the two articles shown both contain references to the authors listed beneath, either to identical articles by those authors (not starred) or to different articles by the same author about the same subject (starred). The level of bibliographic coupling in these two articles is exceptionally high.

INDEXING – COORDINATE INDEXING

One of the earliest attempts to apply multi-aspect co-ordinate indexing methods was with "Batten cards". The idea is to get immediate answers to questions like "how many red 1989 Jaguar XJS cars offered for less than £30,000 and fitted with anti-pollution exhaust systems have I got in stock?"

A glimpse of what might be forthcoming when mechanization got under way was provided by the card systems developed during 1948 to 1960. These included "Batten card", "Uniterm", "Peek-a-Boo", and "Edge-notched card" systems.

The significance of these devices can be understood by considering a car dealer's stock reference system. Say he wants to classify cars in terms of their brand name, model, year, engine size, and type.

If one stock card listing these attributes is made out for each car, he could file the cards alphabetically by brand name, then alphabetically by model within each brand, then in year order by models, etc. Thus the cards would be ordered as in the Figure below.

To find a Blue Jaguar XJ6 a dealer would go to Jaguar and flick through the cards observing the second attribute, model, until he came to the XJ6's and then check through those cards for a blue car. But suppose he wanted to know how many red 1990 1600cc saloon cars he has in stock. He has got to sort through a large number of cards to find those containing the three required attribute values – a time consuming process.

Ford 1992 Sierra GLS Red Saloon 2000cc
Jaguar 1991 XJS Blue Saloon 4200cc
Jaguar 1992 XJ6 Blue Saloon 3500cc
Rover 1990 215S Green Saloon 1600cc
Rover 1991 215SX Red Saloon 1600cc
...and many others

Indexed stock cards

This is called a Pre-coordinate indexing system because the "attribute" (e.g. colour) and the attribute "values" (e.g. red) have been indexed and filed in a fixed order before use and the cards must be accessed by reference to that order.

The card systems named at the beginning of this entry embody a facility for post-coordinate indexing. For example in a "peek-a-boo" car stock system, the dealer would arrange for master cards to contain all the details of each car, and would file these cards in numerical order.

He would also possess a set of peek-a-boo cards capable of having holes punched in specific positions. If he knows he will have up to 1000 cars in stock he would have a set of cards with 1000 positions for holes, with each position numbered. Each card represents the value of an attribute. Thus there would be a card for "Jaguar", another for "XJS", another for "1991" etc. These cards are kept separately in alpha-numeric order.

When a car arrives – say a Ford Fiesta 1990 1200cc red saloon – the dealer makes out the next master card – say number 427 – and enters the details of the car on it. He then gets out the Ford peek-a-boo card, and punches a hole in position 427. He also gets the Fiesta card and punches that at 427 and so on.

Suppose now he poses the same question as before: "how many 1990 1600cc saloon cars have I in stock?". He pulls out the peek-a-boo cards marked "1990", "1600cc" and "saloon" and aligns them. The numbers of any holes in the same position on each card – visible because light can pass through the cards at that point – will indicate the numbers of the master cards listing 1990 1200c saloon cars to which he can then refer.

This is called "post-coordination" because the coordination of terms is performed not at the time of indexing but at the time of selection. When this principle is applied to conceptual information, a degree of pre-coordination is often performed in order to avoid "false drops" (co-ordinations which are spuriously generated and do not match the query) or to reduce the need to use a large number of indexing terms.

For example a person interested in "The production of uranium in Canada", using the terms "production", "Canada", and "uranium" to retrieve documents about this topic would also retrieve an article about "The effect of uranium radiation during the production of fuel rods in Canada".

One way of dealing with this is to pre-coordinate word pairs or triples which occur frequently, as done in the Permuterm Subject Index published by the Institute for Scientific Information (See the Figure below). For example under the frequently occurring triple term NUCLEAR-SPIN-LATTICE will be found the other terms which have co-occurred in titles. For example if the word pair "MAG-NETIC-FIELD" is looked up in the word list beneath the triple, all articles with the triple and "MAGNETIC-FIELD" will be found including for example "Crystal field and magnetic field effects on nuclear spin lattice relaxations in solids.

NUCLEAR-SPIN-LATTICE
    CRYSTALS   Prager GH
    MAGNETIC-FIELD   Myles CW
    RELAXATION   Clark LG
                        Edwards J

Permuterm subject index

INDEXING – ONLINE SYSTEMS

When browsing the index in a typical online system, article titles or abstracts containing the wanted word and variants will be shown. The hit frequency – that is the number of articles containing the word – provides a clue about the next step to take. Should an alternative or additional words be used? Is the chosen word insufficiently specific?

For instance, in the Figure, Enkephalin on its own is too broad and in a computer system this entry would encourage the searcher to consider what aspect of the subject is of interest. He might try "Enkephalin/ AND Naloxone" so that items containing Enkephalin are retrieved only if Naloxone appears in the item as well.

WORD	NUMBER OF HITS
Enkephela	1
Enkephalin	1188
Enkephalinamide	61
Enkephalinamides	4
Enkephalinase	42
Enkephalinases	3
Enkephaline	2
Enkephalinergic	23
Enkephalinol	1

Enkephalins	250
etc.	

Table of title word occurrences

But the indexing of Enkephalin by a system indexer might be as shown in the next figure. In this case a user is led to an aspect of interest in a one-step process because intellectual indexing has been carried out. The user does not now need to proceed step by step to decide how to put the question.

Enkephalin -s
  behavioural effects of-
  Naloxone, interaction with-
  secretion stimulation in:
    dogs
    man
    rats
  structure of-

Index of titles

Another great advantage of a computerized index is that it can be up-dated automatically each time new "documents" are added to the database without intellectual intervention, in a way which is no more and no less satisfactory than the rules, usually rather crude, put by a human into the controlling software to determine the words to be selected for indexing terms. In other words it would certainly not be as good as the arrangement shown in the last figure.

See also DATABASES – FULL TEXT SEARCHING.

INDEXING IMAGES
See IMAGES – INDEXING.

INDEXING PERSONAL SYSTEMS
See PERSONAL INFORMATION SYSTEMS.

INDEXING – SYSTEM PERFORMANCE, EXHAUSTIVITY AND SPECIFICITY
These two indexing parameters are the main factors controlling the RECALL and PRECISION of an information system. Exhaustivity is the depth of indexing accorded to the topics in a document. For example, the terms "leukocyte", "interferon", "hepatitis" and "virus infection" plus terms describing diagnostic and analytical methods – say "Lowry's

method" – might be used exhaustively to index a document. The potential for high Recall now exists because if a user wants high Recall, and he is interested in articles indexed by the above four terms, he can find them. Unfortunately high Exhaustivity reduces Precision because there is no means of knowing the treatment of the subject in the article. There may be 50 articles mentioning Lowry's method, but a complete description of the method is given in only one.

If low Exhaustivity indexing is used, "Lowry's method" will be used as a term only when the article is substantially about that topic. For instance its use could hardly be avoided for an article entitled "Lowry's method for protein determination". In this case a searcher using that term would be led only to such articles and not to articles in which Lowry is merely mentioned. Specificity is the degree of precision of indexing terms. Thus the terms "hepatitis A" and "hepatitis B" are more precise then "hepatitis", just as "Telecoms", "Telecoms: satellites", and "Telecoms: satellite transponders" represent increasing degrees of precision. As might be expected, indexes containing many specific terms provide the potential for high Precision, while indexes with fewer, more general, terms do not.

The number of articles described by each specific term will be relatively small, so if the specific term "CRT resolution" is used, aspects of that subject contained in articles about "Image processing", had this less specific term been used instead, will be missed unless it occurs to the searcher to check all articles indexed by "Image Processing" in the hope that some may contain something about "CRT resolution".

Over-specificity – the use of a large number of different terms for indexing – will reduce Recall, although the average number of terms used to index each document does not much effect performance according to Cleverdon.

Another of Cleverdon's findings came from experiments using an average of from 7 up to 60 terms per document. It seems that if you want good Recall, the allocation of a few well-chosen indexing terms (making the indexing chore less onerous) for each document provides much the same results as using a much larger number of terms. Presumably this must have something to do with the limited number of topics above some arbitrary level of im-

portance that are discussed in most articles. Review articles may be an exception.

INDEXING – SYSTEM PERFORMANCE, RECALL AND PRECISION

The nature of the items retrieved from of an indexed collection of documents depends on the indexing language and method, and the objectives of the searcher who frames the search questions.

Other matters of importance are the subject area covered by the collection, the time and convenience of searching, the retrieval performance and the response time – that is how long it takes to search the collection once the questions are posed.

An investigation was carried out some years ago which shed a new light on indexing principles and performance. In 1954 Cyril Cleverdon, Librarian at the Royal Aircraft Establishment, Farnborough, reported on some experiments using the then new "Uniterm" systems developed by Mortimer Tauble in the United States. Having moved to the Cranfield Institute of Technology he obtained a grant from the National Science Foundation to compare the effectiveness of several different indexing methods.

Tests were carried out on a collection of 1400 aeronautical research papers indexed in different ways by searching with 221 different search questions and subjectively judging the relevance of the retrieved articles. Subject experts participated in the work and about 300,000 test results were examined. It was mainly from this work that the following conclusions were reached.

The degree of success achieved when a searcher retrieves some relevant documents is called the *Recall Ratio*. It is defined as the percentage of relevant documents retrieved out of the total number of relevant documents in the collection. For instance 10 documents retrieved out of the 20 known to be relevant is a Recall Ratio of 50%.

The *Precision Ratio* is the percentage of relevant documents retrieved out of the total number retrieved – a measure of whether unwanted documents were retained within the collection. If 50 documents are retrieved of which 10 are relevant, the Precision Ratio is 20%.

Recall and Precision are related by a curve of similar shape for any collection reflecting their relationship.

If a searcher asks a broad question in an attempt to ensure that he retrieves all relevant documents, he will also retrieve an increased number of unwanted documents – Precision will decrease. If however a narrow question is asked in an attempt to retrieve only relevant documents, some will be missed – Higher Precision is accompanied by lower Recall.

100% Precision with 100% Recall means that every relevant document is found unaccompanied by any unwanted documents – a possible result for a collection of documents indexed factually. For example if details of employees are kept on cards (or in a set of records in a database) a question like "what are the names of employees who speak French?" might be asked. Errors excepted, the names of all relevant employees will appear unaccompanied by details about those who do not speak French.

However when a question is addressed to a collection of documents in which different concepts are discussed, the retrieval performance is a matter of probability, not certainty. It will depend, for example, whether the indexer has anticipated all possible questions that might be asked in an attempt to find the document he or she is indexing, and whether the searcher can compose a question describing all the attributes, as indexed, of the concepts in which he is interested.

A story is told about the economist who, using data stored on a CD-ROM, wished to find statistics about the yearly import of rubber boots to Manitoba. Searching proceeded for twenty minutes prompted by helpful shouts from the economist's colleagues like *"try imports, boots, shoes, latex, stockings, feet, socks, clothing, leather goods, waterproofing, stream fishing gear...etc"*. At last the data was discovered under the keywords *"Footwear, manufactured, prairies, trade"*.

This is a relatively simple example compared with the problems of indexing and retrieving an article entitled "Effects of human leukocyte interferon on hepatitis B virus infection in patients with chronic active hepatitis". The topic of interest, contained in this article, is "procedures adopted in double-blind patient tests".

INDEXING – THESAURI

Indexing problems have not been decreased much with the advent of computers. A wanted item in a computer file may be missed because the searcher's choice of words to describe it differ from those used by the indexer. You have only to look in Roget's Thesaurus to appreciate the richness of the English language in synonyms and shades of meaning.

A thesaurus contains lists of synonyms and other words, referring the indexer and the user to the preferred words which he must use. In medicine, synonyms are a major problem. A thesaurus covering drugs would need to take account of the equivalence of chemical, generic, and trade names.

In a thesaurus a time overhead is transferred from users to the human compiler. The compiler has to add new words to the thesaurus when they appear. Alternatively a "new word list", automatically created when adding information to a database in a computer-based system with the appropriate software, will have to be examined and edited. This may require a considerable effort with a complex nomenclature – as, for instance in medicine. If it is not done quickly a user will not find items about newly named subjects entering the literature.

INFERENCE ENGINE

Expert system software embodying a set of rules for solving problems using data from a knowledge base.

See also ARTIFICIAL INTELLIGENCE.

INFORMATION

1. The reduction of uncertainty.

2. A collection of meaningful data usually assembled with the objective of increasing the knowledge of a human who assimilates it.

INFORMATION MANAGEMENT

The subject has been discussed under several headings:-

* The variety of successful systems.
* Value/productivity gains; competitive advantage; strategic potential.
* IT management (not Information Management). IT managers & overlords.
* Managers lack of understanding of IT.

In the seventies it was intended to devise computer systems which would handle office processes – that is they would perform a particular job by controlling a sequence of tools. Zisman suggested that "knowledge-based systems" would be developed – an early use of a phrase which has since become commonplace. The main problems would be human; there would probably be a period of employee resistance and alienation, but "Systems might become available in five to ten years".

Some undramatic truths emerged when a programme for testing office installations under working conditions was put in hand by the UK Department of Trade and Industry (DTI) in 1981. Twenty test sites in the offices of Central Government, Nationalized Industries, and Local Authorities were equipped. Site annual costs varied between £6000 and £10,000 per terminal. The programme concluded in 1985 having cost about £5.5 million.

This was a bold move – it provided working demonstrations of what could be done and gave users and equipment suppliers much needed experience. Implementation and evaluation was conducted by a consultancy group, and a report for the DTI was published in 1986.

"Case Handling" work – that is the handling of multiple records for single cases such as an insurance policy or an employee – was done at six sites. Half of the sites concentrated on Text Production processes. Management Support applications were run at three primary sites, and eight other sites ran them as secondary applications.

The Case Handling sites were a disappointment "reflecting largely on the state of the Office Automation Industry in 1982". Text production included text preparation, telecommunication, and storage and retrieval. Although equipment and supplier's support ranged from very good to very bad and telecom software and equipment compatibility was a problem, the trial was considered valuable and all groups wanted to continue working with the support of Information Technology.

The main impact in office systems has come not from steady progress towards informa-tion flow in the Electronic General Office but from Specific Service Applications. See also EXECUTIVE INFORMATION SYSTEMS, and WORD PROCESSING.

INFORMATION MANAGEMENT – DEGREE OF INTEREST

Once the system requirements have been sorted out, the selection, design, and effectiveness of the services running on it will require at least as much attention as the system.

Why is it, then, that the information tools receive so much attention, and the end results so little?

There are several reasons why the technology rather than the information has received so much attention. One is the great difficulty of evaluating added information. Grace Hopper, computer pioneer, said "We have totally failed to consider the criteria for the value of information". She could have said "in spite of numerous attempts, nobody has proposed a satisfactory general method for evaluating information, nor does it seem likely that they ever will".

A need to control rapidly rising costs – guaranteed to receive attention in businesses – arose when the expenditure on small computers and software started to get out of hand.

Information technology enables information to be acquired, arranged and presented in ways which were not formerly possible. The processing of particular kinds of information, sometimes transactional, sometimes not, may be far more conveniently handled by computer than by shuffling around paper. Information services of an entirely different kind may become possible.

Some examples are given in the 89/90 Price Waterhouse Information Technology Review where four objectives/examples are provided:-

One of these applications – ELECTRONIC DOCUMENT INTERCHANGE (EDI) – is one of a number of information-handling/pro-

Increased market	Customer capture	Supplier capture	Product improvement
Airline displays flights on screen in prime position in booking hall	Supplier places stock list and prices on terminal on customer's desks	Retailer uses EDI to implement preferential payments and discount scheme	Publisher classifies and stores words in database for producing various types of dictionaries

Information management objectives

cessing activities such as ELECTRONIC FUNDS TRANSFER AT POINT OF SALE (EFTPOS), ELECTRONIC MAIL, etc., where the information itself calls for no special comment – it's the systems, standards (or lack of them), processing and communication which command attention.

Price Waterhouse publish an annual review of trends in Information Technology.

According to their 89/90 Information Technology Review, the top cause for concern in that period was "Integrating IT with corporate strategy... for the first time a technical concern with making the computer work had been ousted by a management concern with making it work for the company. Having seen how American Airlines and a hospital supplies company invigorated the bottom line, everybody started asking the same question – how can we use IT to gain competitive advantage?"

Competitive advantage received a good deal of attention and some more examples were given:- "an elevator company who created a control database for maintenance, greatly reducing costs; a cookie chain who reduced overheads by transferring data for decision making to PCs at branch level; a petrol supplier who introduced automated filling stations without staff; the Finnish paper industry which introduced a computerized system for order placements reducing delays from weeks to hours".

In the Price Waterhouse 1990 report another topic singled out for special mention was "how to migrate gracefully towards open systems while maintaining systems that support the company's operations", and in the PW 1990/1991 review:- "Integrating IT with corporate objectives has gradually revealed itself as a rich source of intriguing side effects... and has steadily increased its lead being now voted the main concern by forty seven percent of computer bosses".

With regard to technology:- "A rationale for what should be decentralized can now be put into practice. Although the mainframe is technologically dead, its equivalent is now being revived under the more democratic name of server which... maintains a database of all information used in common by the various applications.

This, together perhaps with a basic, high volume transaction process which underlies the whole business operation, is known as the core system".

On the subject of control the report says:- "In 1989 the boards of the world despaired of holding down their computer spend. The last year of the decade saw an unparalleled rush to appoint IT directors to the board to sort it all out... 41% of recently surveyed companies employing over 500 staff now have an IT director and 68% of Chief Executives intend to appoint one within three years".

In the 1991/92 report the major issue is how to contain costs – almost approaching in importance the issue of the integration of IT with Corporate Strategy in which interest remains high but has fallen slightly.

By 1992/93 cost containment has become the major issue with a fall in interest in integration; one company says that the number of PCs on networks has risen from 10 to 350 in 12 months. The top solution by far in the opinion of respondents for advancing IT is to have a "board level champion" for the cause.

The 1992/93 report says that "there is little profit in simply distributing computers. Last year IBM cut the price of its high performance workstations from $130,000 to $52,000. The average price of personal computers has been falling by between 25 and 40 per cent a year causing carnage in the distribution channels".

There seem to be quite a few examples where IT is claimed to be the prime ingredient for worthwhile progress. According to Burch:- "Top management at McKesson made a strong policy commitment to establish a strategic information systems plan which would provide management with sufficient information, increase the productivity of employees, and provide customers with unmatched service".

"Today, McKesson is the world's largest drug distributor... most of the credit is given to its information system". For example using hand held scanners, druggists scan the inventory items they want to re-order, key in the quantity, and the system does the rest.

Ordering data go to a distribution centre where picking, packing, and loading instructions are prepared automatically and druggists get delivery the next day. The best the competition can do is a three or four day turn around".

Professor Wilson, head of the department of information studies at the University of Sheffield, well known for his activities in the information science information-per-se field, does not discuss the Management of Information. His 1989 article is about IT and "information system strategy (ISS)".

Wilson's list of ISS features, rank ordered by importance, are:-

* Development of business transaction applications.
* Development of management information systems.
* Planning the introduction of telecommunications and computers.
* Creation of system standards and architecture.
* Development of business planning systems.
* Improving productivity in information systems and computing.
* Developing appropriate staff resources.
* Development of internal support systems such as payroll, personnel, etc.

Wilson concludes that "At the very least it can be said that the idea of information systems strategies is recognized by a good proportion in the Times 500 group and has really taken hold in the financial services sector".

INFORMATION MANAGEMENT – DEGREE OF SUCCESS

Commenting on the appointment of so many IT directors, Harvey quotes the author of the Price Waterhouse report as saying "It is premature to conclude that the battle has been won. Some boards are saying we've failed to get to the bottom of this chronic problem so let's give the whole lot to one person to sort out".

In the United States, Chief Information Officers have enjoyed a meteoric rise to fame, only to be sacked when they did not produce results. "I hear that nearly one third of the top IT men were demoted or fired last year. I can believe it. It's certainly the toughest job in the executive suite right now", said an American observer.

John Griffith of the National Computing Centre (NCC) UK is quoted as saying that a few cases of the good use of IT by users like Thomson Holidays and American Airlines "led people to the false conclusion that information technology creates competitive advantage". Consequently some IT professionals have wasted their time "searching for the Holy Grail".

In a study of the use of IT by 800 European managers by Tomlin Associates, Nicolle reports that "Information technology does not sit comfortably in many UK boardrooms and attitudes towards it remain an enigma... the best climate exists in Germany, the worst in France" but "the UK shows the weakest ratings for positive attitudes to IT".

The problem of providing adequate IT arrangements in UK local government have lead Cane to suggest that nothing less than a government chief information officer or possibly an IT minister at cabinet level may be necessary. Account would then be taken about what had to be done to cope with impending changes in legislation.

Changes in transactional information when the poll tax was introduced required one local authority to nearly double its staff. The total cost of raising the tax (Audit Commission figures) was £411 million compared to the cost of £200 million for the rates tax which it replaced. There is no sign that the IT implications of the changes in the health service designed to improve cost control have been considered. They will be dependent on adequate IT backing.

Harvey reports on a survey which found that two thirds of the sample admitted that their efforts in measuring the contributions of the systems to overall performance have been inadequate. Only 12% claimed to have had above average success in tackling the problem.

Although most systems are not amenable to traditional methods of analysis, most companies use return on investment and cost-reduction for assessment. "It is the increasing difficulty of unravelling the impact of systems from other parallel changes in organization, management procedures and related factors which is seen as the problem".

Harvey says that most organizations are flying blind because without meaningful measures organizations cannot assign priorities to systems. Unless there is a shared world view, systems development becomes arbitrary. Making it user-driven begs the question as to who determines priorities. IT could suffer a backlash because of past evaluation problems.

Tracking the results of a range of companies over the past 10 ten years has shown conclusively that there is no correlation between investment in IT and corporate performance.

Paul Strassman, a well known consultant, concludes that what accounts for "superior and inferior performance is not capital investment but management. That is the active ingredient to be analysed".

KPMG Management Consulting, in a survey reviewed by Whyte say that 64% of chief executives of a variety of small and medium size companies feel that IT in their company gives good value for money. Only 8% considered that it gave very poor value. This contrasts with the information provided in other surveys of larger companies where the opposite opinions have been expressed.

Price and Spurr from KPMG, say that there are three reasons for buying a PC, being connected at an estimated 25,000 a day at the time – improving productivity, access to corporate information, and improving internal communication. Most are still at the first stage – automating existing tasks where tangible benefits can be seen.

A few have progressed to trying out new ideas, but none "have reached the third stage where IT opens the door to new ways of doing business and information is used in ways which break new ground for the company... making whole layers of organizations superfluous."

INFORMATION MANAGEMENT – FACILITIES MANAGEMENT

"Facilities Management (FM)" – the idea of getting a specialist company to provide your IT – is gaining ground. It is an extension of "Outsourcing" – where you get programming, disaster recovery, etc., done by outside contractors. With FM, IT operations, support, systems, and technology are undertaken by the FM company. The host company no longer needs IT expertise. It controls the services, not the IT resource.

But what happens if things go wrong? "You would have to rebuy your kit and renegotiate to get back your staff who may have been sent off by the facilities management company on other projects so you have lost the good people you hired originally" says Vowler. No one is left "to cast a technically competent eye over the invoices or monitor performance levels". In practice you would have to keep sufficient expertise in-house for these reasons and also to develop the company's IT strategy.

However with facilities management there

is "no more nerve-racking gambling on the residual value of the kit, and no more worries about losing staff or whether it's time to chuck out old systems or invest in more capacity. The company can get on with its own business rather than running IT systems".

Gongla et al describe a knowledge-based system called SPARK designed to help managers identify competitive applications of information and information technology.

The most important part of the system is the "examples database" containing summary diagrams and stories about schemes adopted by a number of companies. The examples database was being expanded to about 300 examples at the time that the article was written.

They included an online computer system used by Pacific Intermountain Express for tracking truck shipments, Otis Elevator's system for tracking bids and contract awards in order to gather intelligence about its competitors, Citibank's marketing reports compiled from processing of their credit cards, and many others.

All the schemes are claimed to be successful and are designed to improve the competitive position of the companies using them. The SPARK system provides the user with a choice of analyzing business and IT issues choosing an issue and viewing related examples, or working with a consultant to establish business issues and to provide ideas for tackling them.

In one case, following a user-machine question and answer session, the "browser" module selected six examples and the "facilitator" module decided which example to select "using knowledge of the situation and of the selected conceptual frameworks. ... once the examples are presented SPARK offers assistance in analysing them and in applying them to the user's situation.

INFORMATION MANAGEMENT – IMPLEMENTATION

Sir John Harvey Jones was a strong believer in IT when he was chairman of ICI – it was he who instigated it at head office. In an interview in 1990, Harvey Jones said he would be the first to admit that there are no magic routes, but the implications of IT are just beginning to dawn on senior management.

The trouble is that company boards have to spend a long time discussing it because it has become so expensive. Harvey Jones advises the minimization of risks by taking small steps at a time. "Either apply a leading edge machine to a job you know or use a tried and trusted machine for a leading edge concept". A continuous re-appraisal of strategy is essential – you must keep your IT competitive.

The approach advocated by John Framel, sometime executive director of information resources at Gulf Oil, is to treat information resources as assets, not expenses.

"What to manage" varies from organization to organization but six key areas are identified as "being vital to the successful establishment of an effective Information Asset Management process" – Management Direction, Integrated planning, Matching Needs and Technology, Expenditure Priorities, Linking Information Users and Information Organizations, and Cost Effectiveness. Information activities embraced by Information Asset Management is much wider than is traditionally imagined. They include:-

Data Processing	Systems Development
Data Communications	Graphics
User Co-ordination	Education and Training
Data Architecture	Security
Forms and Forms Control	Office Systems
Voice Communications	Reproduction
Libraries	Records
Decision Support Systems	Planning
Methods and Procedures	Policies and Guidelines
Publishing, DTP	Electronic Mail

Framel says "What is the payoff for initiating an IAM process in an organization? Quite simply, the major payoff is competitive survival."

David Dantzig, consultant at Booz-Allen & Hamilton, provides a story to back-up his comments about "the great promise of Information Systems which makes managers feel compelled *to do something*".

The VP Operations of a $30 billion bank company initiated a project to bring processing for 95,000 MasterCard customers in house "acting reactively and moving ahead too quickly". $4 million funding was approved and most of the information systems staff were committed to the project. However after 18 months effort and an expenditure of over $1 million, it was realized that these objectives conflicted with long-term policy which focused on non-consumer product areas. The project was "put on hold".

Dantzig advises five steps in planning

Information Systems Methodology:-
* There must be a useable model of the enterprise's business and competitive plans to provide a framework for not only identifying gaps in information system support, but the relative importance of filling these gaps.
* The business contribution and the technical quality of current applications and proposed systems must be evaluated.
* A discretionary funds pool should be established so that IS activities can be funded without budgetary increases.
* Candidate projects should be analysed for their expected impact on business and the risks of delays or outright failures.
* The ability of the organization to meet the plan should be determined.

It should be quick. The analysis should be completed in four to six months or its value may rapidly diminish.

Harvey summarizes major points made in *Excellence and the IT Factor*, a 1990 report from MSA in the United States. You cannot have an IT strategy unless you have first written up your business strategy. In leading companies, top management is invariably involved in focusing systems strategies on business priorities. Successful exploiters of systems are rarely, if ever, technological innovators. They are early followers and not pioneers.

Citibank spends $1.5 billion a year ($19,000 per staff member) on IT, United Bank of Switzerland $240 million ($12,000 per staff member), and a large anonymous British clearing bank $520 million ($4600 per staff member). While banks are leaders large companies are also spending heavily, very few believe they are getting value for money. But most of those in a Kobler (Imperial College UK) Unit survey are planning to increase their investment.

To regain control the Unit advises that there must be a corporation strategy based on management goals "derived from the company's sense of its business mission, feedback from its customers, and information about its competitors".

INFORMATION MANAGEMENT – INFOMAPS

Horton summarized his "InfoMap" ideas for co-ordinating information sources in 1991. He suggests that present sources be identified and assessed, that gaps and required new sources be identified, and that "automation and interconnection opportunities also be identified".

"Most work activities within an enterprise are, at best, only supported by computer and telecommunications in efficiency contexts... what is even more important is how the information can enhance effectiveness goals. Information mapping gives the corporate information organization a practical tool to help it integrate the information resources (not just the information technologies) that are isolated, splintered, and compartmentalized all over the corporate landscape."

Horton has developed a software package called "InfoMapper" as a dBASE IV application to assist in "a step-by-step process to discover, map, use, and evaluate the gold mines of the information age – information resources".

INFORMATION MANAGEMENT – INFORMATION TECHNOLOGY

Broadbent and Koenig introduced Diebold's 1989 description of Information Resources Management (IRM) as "a new way of thinking about information by managing it as a resource in much the same way that other corporate resources are managed. Developments in information technology were necessitating the development of corporate information policy".

"As the various information technologies converge, so do the managerial implications and requirements... different islands in the archipelago are typically spread across the organization with data processing reporting to the chief financial office, telecommunications to the vice president for administration, the libraries to the vice president for R&D, and so forth. This dispersion means that a real convergence or co-ordination is a major managerial task".

The more closely an organization can allocate its costs to its outputs the better will be its decision making and performance:-

"As the proportion of an organization's resources that are being devoted to information functions increase, the organization can less readily afford to treat those functions as unallocated costs", say Broadbent and Koenig.

They continue by pointing out that there has been an over-emphasis on the technology at the expense of the value of the information being served. In the IRM field, however, there has been "a concern for the management of document resources as well as information systems. This partly explains the separate literature and research that have differentiated it from the work on automated information systems".

Lewis and Martin, in trying to clarify the information management concept, say "information resource management is broadly understood to refer to the management of information per se, whereas information resources management entails management of all the information resources of an organization – sources, stores, technologies and people".

"IRM was an explicit attempt to recognize information technology as a resource that required management. Its main purpose was to free management to look beyond technology to the management of information itself. This in turn gave way to the competitive analysis stage which involved the analysis and use of information and its associated technologies for competitive advantage".

"Although many organizations have scarcely reached this level of development, others have now reached the fifth stage which is that of strategic information management. In essence, this involves integrating information management into the overall management structures and strategies of the organization, making it a key corporate level activity rather than a support function".

In the UK a "fair amount of activity can be reported. Some of this is librarianship... while a much greater proportion involves various forms of data management... those who would claim to be involved in the management of information for strategic or competitive purposes are in a minority... but growing. The future would seem to lie with developments at this strategic level and for all practical purposes information management now means strategic information management".

"Critical also is the need for its recognition and sponsorship by a "critical mass" of top decision-makers... it is hard to see the concept advancing much beyond its current and comparatively low level "without such top management patronage" (referring to the UK).

INFORMATION PROVIDER

An organization that supplies the information stored on the computer of a public videotex or private "value-added" data service e.g. banks, news agencies, mail order firms, travel agencies, and databank hosts.

INFORMATION SCIENCE

The science of information classification, retrieval, and evaluation.

The phrase is said to have first appeared in the United States in 1959. The above definition is controversial. In the first chapter of the first edition of the *Annual Review of Information Science and Technology* (1966) the definition is discussed at length and the discussion terminates with "Which of these points of view is correct? No one can say".

A 1972 comment has it that "The picture that emerges is one of utter diversity and lack of agreement on even a single basic concept underlying the discipline of Information Science, except of course the concept of information itself, which, however, is highly ambiguous and mostly ill-defined".

INFORMATION TECHNOLOGY

Processing or communicating information with the aid of electronic machines.

INFORMATION TECHNOLOGY – MARKETING, IN

A great deal is published about marketing – so much so that it has its own journals such as *Marketing Science* and the *Journal of Marketing*. Articles with erudite titles like "An integrated model-based approach for sales force structuring" and "The perceived veracity of PIMS strategy principles in Japan" appear in them.

"At one extreme there is a perception of marketing people within some organizations as "flower arrangers"... at the other extreme there is what may be described as "macho marketing".

Marketing has been described more politely as:- "A social and managerial process by which individuals and groups obtain what they want through creating and exchanging products with others". Kotler & Armstrong define a marketing information system as consisting of "people, equipment, and procedures to gather, sort, analyse, evaluate, and distribute needed, timely, and accurate information to marketing decision makers".

The various kinds of benefits to be expected by using IT for marketing have been recognized for some years. Back in 1983 it was said that "Doctors get the ICI message through their surgery microcomputers and farmers receive it through their Prestel television sets".

In 1984 the management at Foremost McKesson, a US distributor with a mediocre performance, "examined each step in their value added chain to find ways of executing the steps as efficiently and as effectively as possible". One of the steps was in the marketing area where they provided terminals for their drug-store customers. This allowed the stores to enter orders direct. Foremost McKesson, in return, offered delivery within a guaranteed time.

"The customer was now performing the order-entry job for the distributor thereby reducing his costs. However the customer could cut his inventory levels because of the guaranteed delivery and was therefore quite willing to add the very low – if any – marginal cost of ordering his own supplies.

Larger payoffs came from several additional moves. In one particular move McKesson discovered, via their computer links, that drug-store customers often went to insurance companies to get payment for medicines and supplies. "The company then volunteered to collect funds from the third party which saved the drug-store the cost of doing the job... This not only provided a link to the insurance firm, but provided the company with a new product – claims processing and collection... information technology created a new strategic opportunity for the business".

Marketing departments require:-
* Complex analysis of volumes of data from within and outside the organization.
* Provision of networks to manage marketing information flow.
* Provision of modelling tools and graphical presentation tools accessible with minimum training.
* An open-ended design to cater for new data and new models ultimately including knowledge-based technology.

However marketing information systems suffer from the usual "system problems" including "poor quality and inconsistent data, defining a manager's information needs, educating users in the potential of the system, and technical computer-related problems".

As one author drily comments "Our problem is not one of data, rather it is one of information. We have too much of the former and too little of the latter". "No amount of investment in hardware or software can outweigh the non-technological aspects of systems development, including relationships. Of particular concern here is the key relationship between the marketing and information systems professionals".

Professor Beaumont (School of Management, University of Bath) differentiates between three kinds of Geographic Information Systems (GIS):-

* Electronic Data Processing Systems.
  EDPS are traditional transactions systems... including point of sales systems, financial accounts management (including the use of ATMs) order processing, and distribution".
* Management Information Systems.
  MISs provide regular (and exception) structured reports on different activities such as branch and/or product sales performance and inventory management. Summary customer profiles derived from geo-demographic analyses can also be useful management information.
* Decision Support Systems.
  DSS have received a lot of attention over the last twenty years from academics, managers, and IT vendors... DSS involve structured and/or unstructured, simple and/or complex problems that can be explored in an interactive or recursive manner by decision makers.

"At present, the majority of uses of GIS in market analysis, marketed frequently as Decision Support Systems, are of the Management Information Systems type – historical data status reporting of sales and market share.

There is a requirement for a more analytic impact reporting on, say, price elasticity, advertising effectiveness, and site location and merchandise mix, which should be extended from their traditional market size/share format to incorporate financial investment appraisal".

In responding to the question "What is the GIS pay-off"? Beaumont says "At present it remains largely unknown". A real difficulty exists however, because the value of the information for the decision-making process has to be anticipated when databases are purchased... the information really only possesses latent value".

"Should we wait to make the investment? No! If you can justify the decision as a business investment now, my recommendation would be do it! However, how many organizations unfortunately still view GIS as an administrative cost, rather than as a business investment?"

Robert Shaw (Shaw Consulting Ltd) has something to say about three kinds of databases – for Direct Mailing, for Direct Response Tracking, and for Telemarketing, predicting a "dramatic growth in direct marketing systems. With a Database Management System (DBMS) you can "attach data together in relational or hierarchical structures allowing fast and efficient access to various fields without having to process the entire file".

But "The first time a sales or marketing manager hears about DBMSs and their advantages is when a proposal from the computer department lands on his desk. Just as he is beginning to learn about computers (marketing managers are assumed to computer-illiterate) he is plunged into a new and baffling area of jargon".

Shaw gives some advice about the performance of relational, hierarchical, and flat files, and lists a number of software packages for direct mail, mainly supplied by bureaux (which have excited negative comments) and for telemarketing, mostly originating in the US.

He thinks that the benefits of using IT in marketing have been "improved customer service, meeting customer needs, and selling more products". He also says that "It appears that technology has not succeeded in reducing marketing campaign failures and problems, or in helping to promote cross selling of products... nor has it apparently had a very positive effect on cost reduction or on the control of marketing budgets".

Miles Faulkner of the OASIS company provides some tips when selecting an integrated system:-

* Look at package software to collect ideas about typical applications.
* Develop requirements using own staff, or

consultants not in the software sales business.

* Insist on a fully documented plan for every phase of the project and make the time scales demanding.
* Focus on the benefits to justify an investment and charge only the recoverable, quantifiable, benefits to the business for budgeting purposes – a very difficult evaluation problem.
* Develop paper-based analysis and use example software to create prototypes right away.
* Check that the latest technologies are represented and that advantage is taken of all the available options.

The Henley Organization offers the Household Marketing System (HMS) for market analysis and targeting which performs operations on the National Consumer Database (NCD) containing information about 42 million consumers living in 21 million UK homes. It supplies information about lifestyle data obtained from questionnaires, investor data from share registers, and household data from public sources of household and demographic information. Big Brother knows about you even if he is not watching you.

"At the core of HMS are three important determinants of user behaviour – House price, Household income, and Net wealth (assets minus debts). Several potential examples are given of applications using this data in conjunction with Henley's Database Management System (DBMS).

For instance:- "A car manufacturer, by matching a sample of current owners to the NCD, could model statistically the likelihood to buy and thus identify key prospects from the NCD or client's own database, identify key target localities for specific dealer marketing activity, and map local market potential to compare dealer sales performance to it."

Information Resources describe several actual application cases of their PcEXPRESS system:- "Over 900 copies of PcEXPRESS are used throughout Glaxo Pharmaceuticals UK for a wide variety of financial, sales, and marketing applications. Helping the company to monitor around 70-75% of the total UK pharmaceutical market, EXPRESS combines information from around 28 data sources and provides their marketing team with rapid

systems development and fast, flexible, reporting, analysis and modelling capabilities".

"Field intelligence has significantly improved as their several hundred strong sales force can now electronically access data the day after it arrives – it used to take four weeks and was only available on paper. EXPRESS multi-dimensional data architecture easily accommodates reporting changes across sales forces and territory structures as they occur".

"The simplicity of their distributed system is such that sales representatives can easily report, analyse, and model sales data on their own laptop PCs, looking at individual subsets of the mainframe database which contains over 2500 products across 1700 geographic areas over time, without any need for programming knowledge".

"PcEXPRESS gives brand management the ability to track sales and profit from the time the brand is produced and shipped via distributors and wholesalers to the time it appears on the shelf of the retail outlet. The project ("ISIS") helps management to monitor performance, look at measures such as price elasticity and market share, track advertising expenditure and competitor performance, and produce brand models and forecasts using field intelligence and historical data". According to SPSS their package the "industry standard SPSS/PC+" goes beyond the capabilities of spreadsheets, databases, and other statistical software" and can be used for "gleaning insights from customer surveys, allowing you to target your products and services more precisely. See Figure on next page.

INFORMATION THEORY

Information Theory has become divided into two subjects – the communication and correct reception of meaningless symbols and the communication of meaningful information. It was probably SHANNON himself who instigated the confusion. Although he said in his classic paper that "semantic aspects of communication are irrelevant to the engineering problem", a little later he could not avoid the temptation of talking about the English language "to give a visual idea how this series of stochastic processes approaches a language".

Shannon was concerned with "amounts of

A Corporate Pricing Decision					
Step	Action	Elapsed Time Days	Hours Used	'Phone Calls	Xerox Copies
1	Staff meeting – review proposal by finance	4	32	60	200
2	Agreement to draft change. Create working group	7	8	6	30
3	Actual work on policy revision	4	22	25	60
4	Distribute draft for review	2	40	10	400
5	Redistribute draft within functional organizations	13	220	130	540
6	Coordinate, reconcile, clarify staff views/comments	2	25	20	40
7	Meeting to review consolidated staff comments	7	18	60	360
8	Release summary recommendation for management approval	2	11	4	100
9	Management approval	1	5	2	25
10	Commence implementation of system changes	30	65	110	680
11	Policy distributed	42	1020	270	7600
12	System implementation, field briefing, revisions to control system	15	600	122	620
		129	2066	819	10655

Bureaucratic decision making processes

information" ($\log_2 n$, bits where n is the number of symbols in a message selected from a list of meaningless symbols). This led to the thrust of his paper in the *Bell System Technical Journal*, July and August 1948 – the capacity of a noisy telecommunication channel and the codes required for transmission. However Shannon's preliminaries were seized upon by academics as offering a way to tangibilize the intangible. Hundreds of papers were published about "amounts of meaningful information". Later, disillusionment set in and that's how many information scientists see it today.

Shannon's theoretical channel capacity – the criteria at which all telecommunication design engineers aim – has been accompanied by the most intense activity in the development of efficient codes since such codes are the means of approaching that criteria. HUFFMAN'S code was one of the earliest and most effective.

The scheme adopted in CCITT V42bis recommendation is an ingenious adaptation by British Telecom of an idea by Ziv based on Shannon's reasoning. It enables MODEMS to intercommunicate at around 20 Kbps over the Public Switched Telephone Network – a speed approaching the Shannon limit which would have seemed to be impossible two or three years ago. An encoder observes strings coming from the transmission source for a period and accumulates high-frequency relatively long strings in its store. Upon the next occurrence of a stored string it outputs a short codeword in substitution.

In 1928 R.V.L. Hartley suggested a way of specifying the "quantity of information (H)" transmitted. If you send a message of n symbols chosen from a list S, assuming that each symbol has an equal possibility of being chosen, $H = n \log_2 S$ *bits*. For instance if the list contained only 8 symbols, the amount of information in a 10-symbol message would be $10 \times \log_2 8 = 30$ bits. $(\log_2 8 = 3)$. A 10-symbol message chosen from a list of 64 symbols would contain 60 bits.

The notion of a *bit* can be observed in the process of identifying a symbol from a list by asking a series of questions to successively halve the list, the answer to which is either yes or no – 1 or 0. Thus for a list of 8 numbers from 0 to 7, the questions/answers to "is it in the top half of the list 0-7?" – "yes"; "is it in the top half of the list 4-7?" – "yes"; "is it in the top half of the list 6-7" – "no" identifies the number 6 by three "yes-noes" written as 3 bits -110, $\log_2 8 = 3$.

Generalizing, $H = \log_2 n$ bits per symbol... (1)

Note that *meaning* is not considered. All that is being claimed is that "more information" is being sent if the possibilities of choice are larger; put another way, if the sender always chooses from a list of 1, the receiver has no *uncertainty* what is intended when a symbol is received.

When the list is increased to 2 there is some uncertainty until a symbol is received, and more still if increased to 4. The larger the list the greater the uncertainty, the greater the reduction of uncertainty, the greater the increase of "information". The use of the word "information" for something without meaning has been the cause of a great deal of confusion in the interpretation of Information Theory.

In the opening remarks of his 1948 paper Shannon said that the basis for his theory was contained in the important papers of NYQUIST and Hartley. The first part of the paper is devoted to defining the "amount of information" contained in *ergodic* messages containing symbols, independently chosen from a list, which are not equally likely to occur. (Ergodic simply means that the frequency of occurrence of any symbol observed in a long section of a very long message is the same as its frequency of occurrence in any other long section).

The average information content, $\bar{H}$, per symbol is :-

$$- \Sigma_i \, p_i \log_2 p_i \text{ bits per symbol.} \dots \dots (2)$$

In other words the average "information content" of any symbol, i, is the sum of the probabilities of the log of the probabilities of the symbols in the message. Note that the minus sign is needed to make H a positive number because the logs of p_i are fractions. This is easier to appreciate if a very simple example is considered; the principles apply equally well to much larger collections of symbols. Say a message is composed from four symbols w, x, y, and z, and say every other symbol is a w on the average – i.e the probability of occurrence of w is 0.5, while x, y, and z occur with probabilities 0.25, 0.125, and 0.125 respectively. The average amount of information per symbol in a long message is :-

$$\bar{H} = - (.5 \log_2 .5 + .25 \log_2 .25 + .125 \log_2 .125 + .125 \log_2 .125)$$
$$= .5 + .5 + .375 + .375$$
$$= 1.75 \text{ bits per symbol.}$$

We can see that the code:-

$$w = 0$$
$$x = 10$$
$$y = 110$$
$$z = 111$$

will actually achieve this value, since the average number of bits in a long message of n symbols using it will be :-

$$n (.5 \times 1 + .25 \times 2 + .125 \times 3 + .125 \times 3)$$
$$= n \times 1.75 \text{ bits.}$$

Information Theory became tarnished mainly because equation (2) was applied to information with meaning for which it was inapplicable. As Shannon states (1948, page 379):- "Semantic aspects of communication are irrelevant to the engineering problem. The significant aspect is that the actual message in one *selected from a set* of possible messages" (his italics).

Ironically it was probably Shannon himself who fuelled speculation that equation (2), and aspects of the discussion which led up to it, might be applied to "meaningful information". A few pages later he cannot escape the temptation of discussing language (i.e. meaningful language) and probability "to give a visual idea how this series of (stochastic) processes approaches a language". Stochastic means "controlled by the laws of probability". He gave further encouragement to "speculators" in his 1951 article (Shannon 1951).

The denouement of the 1948 article is the equation for channel capacity – the part which has so far been discussed is the preamble. The two parts have become separated by applicators. Broadly speaking the first part was taken up by theorists and is none the worse for that, except when taken up by bad theorists. The importance to technologists of the part to be now discussed can hardly be over estimated.

NYQUIST (1924) showed that the maximum signalling rate obtainable in a communication channel with a bandwidth of W Hz is 2W distinguishable symbols per second. 1 symbol is one bit, or one impulse, or one signalling element, commonly called 1 *baud*. We can imagine someone pressing a key to connect an 8 volt battery to the line to signify the symbol "1", waiting a little while, pressing the key twice to signify "2" and so on – a very crude arrangement.

A much more efficient idea would be to send one signalling element by selecting one of 8 batteries to signal a voltage between 1 and 8. These 8 different voltages could be a prearranged code for providing information to the remote receiver about, say, 8 different prevailing weather conditions, but using only *one signalling element* in the process.

Combining this idea with equation (1) we have :-

Information rate in a band-limited channel,
$$H_r = 2W \log_2 n \text{ bits/second} \ldots (3)$$
In the above example, 2W, the maximum rate possible with the "single battery", has been increased three times to $2W \log_2 n = 2W \times 3 = 6W$ bits per second. It would be nice to imagine that we can extend this principle further by signalling 16, or 32, or more "levels", for each signalling element, in order to increase the bit rate by 4 or 5 or more times respectively. Unfortunately this is prevented by *noise* – fluctuations present in all communication channels.

The small difference between levels, when there are a lot of them, becomes comparable with a noise impulse; the receiver can't tell the difference. Noise introduces *errors*.

The capacity C, of the communication channel – the maximum rate at which "information" can be sent – is equation (3) modified by the effects of noise:-
$$C = 2W \log_2 n (S + N) - 2W \log_2 n N$$
$$= W \log_2 (1 + S/N) \text{ bits per second} \ldots (4)$$
where C = channel "Information" capacity
S = average signal power
N = average gaussian noise power

Equation (4) may be regarded as the major outcome of the Shannon paper. It is the maximum theoretical rate for data transmission through any channel – a target rate which may be approached by a highly efficient system but never reached. Since speeds and costs are the most important factors in today's telecommunication networks such a yardstick is extremely valuable.

It is necessary to remind ourselves about what was said in the first section to appreciate the importance of Information Theory – not on meaning and measurements of "quantities of information", but on coding and compression, currently the subject of a tremendous R&D effort.

Equation (4) embodies the findings of equation (2) about average amounts of information per symbol based on *symbol probabilities in long messages*. The implication is that "ideal or nearly ideal encoding requires a long delay in the receiver and the transmitter... it is possible to send information at the rate C through the channel with as small a frequency of errors as desired by proper encoding".

A second requirement is that for maximum transmission rate a message source must deliver data to a transmitter at a speed to match that rate ("statistical matching"). "A teletype channel will not always be transmitting information at the maximum rate – whether or not the actual rate reaches this maximum depends on the source of information which feeds the channel". (The quotations in the last two paragraphs are from the 1948 paper).

As will be observed from equation (4), once noise has been reduced to a minimum and the signal power raised to a maximum, the potential for improvements resides in $\log_2 n$ by designing codes for dealing with probabilities and statistical matching. Progress in this area has been remarkable.

Little has been said about "meaningful" information theory" – an area which excited enormous, mostly ill-judged, interest in the nineteen fifties and sixties. Some interest endures in this area but its value pales into insignificance compared with its usefulness in fields such as human and electrical communication, coding, data compression systems and the man-machine interface.

It appears that many people in the library and information science fields define "information systems" rather narrowly. They stay within the "documentation/computer based systems" area. That may be a wise decision in view of the size of the whole "information" field. It depends whether you wish to become an expert who knows more and more about less and less.

It could equally well be argued that "documentation people" who do not show much interest in allied areas may be missing aspects which have a direct bearing on their everyday activities.

See also CODING, HUMAN.

INITIALIZED

1. The process of preparing storage media in readiness to receive data.

2. The procedure for setting up a computer device prior to using it.

INKJET PRINTER

A printer in which a jet of ink is broken up into charged fine particles which are steered on to paper by an electrostatic field.

INMOS

A company founded in the UK in 1978 primarily to manufacture TRANSPUTERS. The company was mainly financed by the government and was eventually sold to Thorn-EMI, who in turn sold it to the French company SGS-Thomson in 1989.

INPUT

The data to be input. The transfer of data from a peripheral device into a computer.

INPUT/OUTPUT

1. A general term for the peripheral equipment used to communicate with a computer, commonly called I/O.

2. The data associated with such operations.

INRIA

Institut National de Recherche en Informatique et Automatique.

INTEGRATED CIRCUIT (Chip)

A sub-strate of semiconductor material carrying a number of interconnected circuit elements. The whole is packaged in a very small container with metallic projections for external electrical connections.

See also MICROCOMPUTERS, and SEMICONDUCTORS – INTEGRATED CIRCUITS, CHIPS MARKETS.

INTEL

An American semiconductor company who manufactured the first 8 bit processor in 1974, immediately followed by an improved version the 8080. The 8080 was combined with other components to produce the first commercially available personal computer developed by MITS – the Altair 8800. The 8080 was followed by a much improved processor – the 8086 which included a number of additional facilities and an expanded version of the 8080 instruction set.

The 80286 introduced in 1982, included virtual memory, on chip memory management, and a protection hierarchy. It was followed by successive improvements, the 80386 and 80486. The 80486, which operates at 50 MHz requires a complex motherboard. In 1992 the company introduced the 486DX II which works at 25 MHz, but whose internal clock speed is still 50 MHz.

Its floating point unit, internal registers, cache etc., work at 50 MHz, while the sections accessing other chips on the motherboard, such as main memory, run at 25MHz. In 1990 Intel ranked 8th amongst the world's semiconductor manufacturers by revenue, earning $2.4 billion. The only larger western manufacturer was Texas Instruments, all the others being Japanese.

Intel specializes in microprocessor chips where it has 58% of the market. Intel's next processor will be the P5 or Pentium expected to contain 3 million transistors. It will process instructions about 2.5 times faster than the 486. Its clock speed will probably be 100 MHz.

Intel has been involved in a long running

copyright lawsuit with Advanced Micro Devices (AMD). After a court ruling that AMD was not in breach of copyright, a United States court later ruled that AMD was in breach of copyright.
See also SEMICONDUCTORS.

INTELLIGENT NETWORKS
See under NETWORKS – INTELLIGENT.

INTERACTIVE MODE
Computer processing which proceeds in steps with human intervention to observe, modify, or input new data according to results or requirements.

INTERFACE
1. The boundary between computer or telecom hardware devices or functions. The word may be used to cover details from plug and socket pin connections to quite complex control software.
2. The boundary between the device presenting information and the human observing it.
See also MAN-MACHINE INTERFACE.

INTERLACING
A method of scanning used in television systems in which two FIELDS of alternate lines are transmitted to form a complete FRAME. The reason for adopting such a system is to achieve economies by transmitting a complete frame at half the rate which would otherwise be required to reduce flicker.

INTERNATIONAL BUSINESS MACHINES (IBM)
IBM is easily the world's largest computer company. It was founded as the Computing Tabulating Recording Company in 1911 as a result of the merger of three companies, including Hollerith's Tabulating Machine Company which was started in 1896.

IBM earliest major achievements were the Selective Sequence Electronic Calculator built in 1948 which used valves (vacuum tubes) making the "Mark 1" machine completed in 1944 which used relays, completely obsolete. IBM built the Sage Air Defence System jointly with the Lincoln Laboratory at MIT in 1952 and developed many of its capabilities at that time.

In 1954 it came out with the 704 computer. It invented disc storage in 1956. Its major computer family, System 360, was launched in 1964 to be followed by an improved version the 370 in 1970. The Winchester disc was an IBM invention and the company introduced its personal computer in the United States during 1981.

Notable amongst its current range are the Enterprise System 9000 series, an extension of the system replacing the 370 – System 390 – the PS/2 range of personal computers, and the AS/400 middle range. IBM grew steadily until 1984 when it made a profit of nearly $12 billion. It predicted further expansion expecting that its revenues would reach $100 billion by 1990.

By 1990 the company employed nearly 400,000 people and was earning nearly $70 billion, but in the year 1991 it lost nearly $3 billion following a large restructuring and retirement programme. It reduced its work force by nearly 30,000 people. It expected some improvement in the following year and may form an autonomous group of companies, eliminating layers of management. IBM's proprietary Standards no longer exert the power that they use to have; the company has been subjected to heavy competition by smaller faster-moving companies.

INTERNATIONAL COMPUTERS LTD (ICL)
British computer company formed by a number of mergers. In 1959 Powers-Samas and The British Tabulating Machine Co. merged to form International Computers and Tabulators Ltd (ICT). Subsequently ICT absorbed GEC computer activities in 1961, EMI computer activities in 1962 and Ferranti computer activities in 1963.

Meanwhile English Electric absorbed Leo Computers in 1963, Marconi computer interests in 1964 and Elliot Automation in 1967. The company was then known as English Electric Computers (EEC). Finally ICT and EEC merged in 1968 to form ICL.

In 1984 it was not making good progress and was acquired by STC (Standard Telephones and Cables) with ICL accounting for 62% of the group's total turnover. During this re-organization the company became much more successful, focusing particularly on the retail market with point of sale equipment. It acquired Datachecker – a US point of sale specialist.

By mid-1990 ICL had a turn over approaching £2 billion, with a number of manufacturing sites in different parts of the world, and about 22,000 employees. Its main hardware products were the series 39 range, the DRS Unix range, and a number of smaller systems and workstations.

At the end of 1990 control of ICL was acquired by Fujitsu, which owns 80% of it, 20% being owned by Northern Telecom – a remnant of the deal when Fujitsu bought ICL from STC. In 1991 ICL acquired Nokia Data, a Finnish company, for £230 million.

Fujitsu appears to be controlling the company at arm's length and ICL continues to be successful, having retained much of its identity and independence.

INTERNATIONAL STANDARDS ORGANIZATION

An organization established to promote the development of standards for the international exchange of goods and services, also to develop mutual cooperation in areas of intellectual scientific, technological and economic activity.

INTERNATIONAL TELECOMMUNICATIONS UNION (ITU)

See also separate entry CCITT.

INTERNET

A large computer network formed out of some thousands of interconnected networks initially in the United States and latterly in countries throughout the world. It supports a whole range of services such as electronic mail, file transfer, database access etc. Two UK companies UKnet and Pipex will provide a connection to Internet enabling a subscriber to use any of its services.

Transmission speeds go up to 1.5Mbps or more and costs can be from $20 to several thousands of dollars per month. Internet can be used simply to provide access to a host computer or to a service with which the user runs an account.

The electronic mail system on Internet was improved by the addition of multimedia and cryptographic facilities during 1992, and a range of additional information-searching services were added. Internet also now carries a wireless broadcasting service to mobiles where the receivers can be of almost any kind,

providing they are capable of receiving data from a satellite down-link.

INTERPRETER

A program which fetches and executes an instruction in a high level language before proceeding to the next instruction.

See also COMPUTERS – LANGUAGES.

INTERRUPT

A signal generated in a computer system to indicate a requirement to the CPU with some previously assigned priority rating. For example a signal may be received from a printer port to indicate that the printer is ready to receive data. The CPU may then interrupt the program currently running if the interrupt has a higher priority, supply the data, and then return to the program.

The most common type of interrupt comes from a peripheral device which presents an interrupt request to the Interrupt Controller. Interrupt requests include signals indicating that a key has been pressed, a mouse has been moved, etc.

INTREX

Information Transfer Experiment.

INVERTED FILE

An ordered index file derived from documents in an associated collection. The file contains all the indexing terms used for the documents with pointers to the associated items in the document file. It is searched by matching the search question against it and retrieving the documents so found, from the document file.

The inverted file must be up-dated each time a new document is added and it may become very large.

IPS

Instructions Per Second.

IPSS

International Packet Switched Services. A service offered by British Telecom for connecting data from the UK to the North American Telenet and Tymnet and other networks.

IR

Information Retrieval.

IRIDIUM

IRIDIUM
A system designed by Motorola for providing a worldwide mobile service by the use of 66 satellites orbiting at 8 kilometres. It is estimated that the project will cost over $3 billion.

ISBN
International Standard Book Number.

ISDN
INTEGRATED SERVICES DIGITAL NETWORK.

ISDN-2
A British Telecom (BT) service offering basic rate ISDN conforming to international standards specifications.

ISI
Institute for Scientific Information.

ISO
International Standards Organization.

ISOTROPIC RADIATION
Radiation with equal intensity in all directions. A radio transmitting aerial (antenna) designed to provide a service to the area surrounding it would radiate isotropically. A satellite dish serial beamed at some area of the earth is an example of anisotropic radiation.

ISPN
International Standard Program Number.

ISTEL
Information System for Telecommunications.

IT
Information Technology.

ITA
Independent Television Authority.

ITDM
Intelligent Time Division Multiplexing.

ITT
International Telephone and Telegraph Co.

ITU
INTERNATIONAL TELECOMMUNICATIONS UNION.

ITV
Independent Television.

JPEG
Joint Photographic Experts Group.
See also COMPRESSION.

K

K
Thousand.

Kbit
Kilobit. One thousand bits.

Kbps
Kilobits per second.

KBS
Knowledge Based System

Kbyte
One thousand bytes.

KELVIN, LORD
Born in Belfast in 1824 as William Thomson, Kelvin did important work in many branches of physics and was also a prolific inventor. He played a major role in the conception of the first trans-atlantic telegraph cable. In addition to theoretical work on temperature measurement and energy radiation, he invented the mirror galvanometer, the Kelvin Standard Balance, an improved form of compass, a tide prediction device and numerous other machines. He died in 1907.

KERMIT
Kermit was devised at Columbia University in the early eighties. It is a comprehensive attempt to set a de facto standard for file transfers since and has become quite widely used. As one of its designers says :- "Kermit accommodates itself to many systems by conforming to a common subset of their features". The resulting simplicity and generality allow Kermit on any machine to communicate with Kermit on any other machine – microcomputer-to-mainframe, microcomputer-to-microcomputer, mainframe-to-mainframe.

The back and forth exchange of packets keeps the two sides synchronized; the protocol can be called asynchronous only because the communication hardware itself operates asynchronously.

KERNING
A kern is the projecting part extending beyond the body of any character. Kerning is a term used in printing meaning closing up characters so that the projecting part of one character overlaps a part of another without touching it.

KEYFAX
A teletext service introduced by Field Electronic Publishing, Chicago. It is transmitted via satellite to cable TV companies for distribution to their subscribers.

KEYPAD
A small device resembling a pocket calculator containing miniature keys. For example a keypad is used for controlling a television receiver. A videotex receiver keypad embodies keys numbered 0 to 9 and three or four control keys.

KHz
Kilohertz.

KNOWLEDGE BASE
The database in an expert system, input by a human subject expert.
See ARTIFICIAL INELLIGENCE.

KU BAND
The microwave frequency band 12-18 GHz, used by both line-of-sight radio links and communication satellites.

KWIC
Key Word in Context.

KWOC
Key Word Out of Context.

L

LAN
LOCAL AREA NETWORK. See under NET-
WORKS.

LAN STANDARDS
The US Institute of Electrical and Electronic
Engineers (IEEE) assumed responsibility for
LAN Standards based on the OSI model as
follows:-
   IEEE 802.3 CSMA/CD (Ethernet) standard.
   IEEE 802.4 Token Passing (Arcnet)
   standard.
   IEEE 802.5 Token Ring (IBM Micronet)
   standard.
   See also STANDARDS.

LANGUAGES
See COMPUTERS – LANGUAGES.

LAP [followed by a letter]
Link Asynchronous Protocol. The letter indicates version used (currently M). LAP is an
inter-modem communication procedure
whereby one modem forces another to respond in order to prompt error correction by
an added "polling" bit.

LASER
(Light Amplification by Stimulated Emission
of Radiation). A laser consists of a cavity (The
Fabry-Perot cavity) with partially reflecting
mirrors at either end. In a semiconductor laser
a layer of semiconducting material inserted
into a p-n sandwich forms the waveguide cavity. Radiation occurs and the dimensions of
the cavity reinforce radiation at a particular
wavelength by resonant reflections between
the mirrors.
   The development of lasers was reinforced
by the incentive to provide a light source for
fibreoptic undersea cables. In the late 1970s,
quite a time after the original fibreoptic proposals were made by Kao and Hockham at
STC in 1966, lasers were developed to produce a narrow beam of intense monochro-
matic light from a chip 0.3 mms long made
from layers of InP and GaInAsP with minute
mirrors at either end. The light, corresponding to several milliwatts of power was pro-

jected from one end.
   Subsequent developments included the
double injection-locked laser which produced
a light beam less than 0.003 nanometres wide
which would not spread much in a fibreoptic
cable 100 Kms long.
   By 1990 CO_2 and helium gas lasers for industrial and medical purposes with powers
above 500 watts had been developed, and
"diode pumping" had been introduced.
   The extraordinary benefits of a laser light
beam for communication, industrial, or control purpose is that the light is radiated at a
virtually single frequency very short wavelength with the power concentrated into an
extremely narrow beam. The beam may be
easily controlled from its electrical source and
optically by using collimating optics, and
directed by mirrors.
   The Japanese soon appreciated the laser's
unique properties and they developed a
family of very small controllable read or write
lasers to be used in printers, CDs, videodiscs,
etc. Intense R&D followed by mass production resulted in low cost rugged reliable
laser systems.

LASER VIDEO
Philips Laservision and the Sony laser videodisc recording system are the major laser-
based videodisc systems. The Sony system,
for example, will record about 36,000 still pictures or 24 minutes of motion video with associated sound on a 12 inch disc. When a laser
beam is turned on by a frequency modulated
signal a phase change is produced in the four-
element Antimony-Bismuth alloy layer which
increases its reflectivity. To receive, reflected
light from a low-power illuminating laser is
sensed.
   The random access time of the Sony system
where the disc rotates at 1500 rpm with Constant Angular Velocity (CAV), is 0.5 secs
(average). The system will record either NTSC
or PAL analogue television signals.
   A number of commercial recordings were
produced in the nineteen eighties including
the Pergamon Patsearch system for displaying patent drawings which was discontinued

in 1984. The Domesday discs covering UK nationwide people and places were one its greatest successes where remarkable results were achieved with, by today's standards, low performance computer equipment.

A large number of training discs have been produced covering Finance, Electronics, Science. Gardening, etc. Although laser video recording is quite widely used it seems to have been overtaken by digital recording systems, notably the CD family, for most purposes including IT applications and entertainment.

LATCH
A term describing the logic level holding action in a computer FLIP-FLOP circuit at its current level until re-set.

LC
LIBRARY OF CONGRESS.

Lc
Lower case.

LC/H
Lines of code per hour.

LCD
LIQUID CRYSTAL DISPLAY. See under DISPLAYS.

LCLV
Liquid Crystal Light Valve. See under DISPLAYS.

LEASED LINE
A line reserved for the exclusive use of a leasing customer without the necessity for exchange switching.

LED
Light Emitting Diode.

LEMPEL-ZIV ALGORITHM.
A method of error correction on which British Telecom based its BTLZ algorithm adopted by the CCITT for compression in the V42bis standard. A fixed length code word is automatically generated (by lookup from a stored table) from a variable length string of characters whose length, on average, is considerably longer then the code word.
See also MODEMS.

LEO
The first computer to be used by any organization in the world for commercial data processing. It was used by J Lyons and Co. in 1951, its design being based on the EDSAC machine built at Cambridge University. It was used to work out the night's cooking requirements for supplying food to Lyons 200 tea shops from information telephoned in to headquarters. The machine used a Mercury filled delay line as a memory.
See also COMPUTERS – HISTORY

LIBRARIES – COMPUTERS IN
Computers are used in library general business administration as in other offices. Activities specific to libraries will be discussed here.

The most important are to do with the acquisition of books, creating and using library catalogues including Online Public Access Catalogues (OPACs), the control of circulation, the purchase and control of serials, the organization of library networks, and finally integrated library systems sometimes called library management systems, in which these activities are combined. Many types of computer have been pressed into service from mainframes to microcomputers depending on service complexity and the size of the library.

Other uses of computers in libraries outside "mainline library management" are the online searching of remote databases containing bibliographic or full text records.

Interest in all these aspects, including SDI – online searching's predecessor – started during the sixties when data processing equipment started to become available at lower prices. Although one of the earliest publications surveying computer applications in libraries came from Cox et al (1966) in a US/UK team at the Newcastle University library, the UK library community took perverse pleasure in claiming a much slower rate of progress than anybody else.

At the 1966 Brasenose conference one speaker said "If Oxford has gone less far then the British Museum, Cambridge has gone less far than Oxford". The speaker described the catalogue in his library as an "archaeological deposit". In spite of that, UK library computer activities were on a par with those in the US by 1969.

The history of computers in libraries is characterized by the piecemeal computerization of services, often starting with catalogues, sharing time on a machine not belonging to the library. Later, there was steady progress towards turnkey systems embodying all major management requirements using a dedicated library computer.

Bibliographic descriptions

Some early work was done by Kilgour using computer generated catalogue cards at Yale, and Buckland produced a machine readable catalogue from a perforated tape typewriter at the Library of Congress, Washington.

In 1963 G.W. King et al reported on the possibilities of automating bibliographic records at the LC and concluded that it should be possible but might take ten years. Ideas in this report were taken up in the Machine Readable Cataloguing (MARC) project at the LC which started in 1966, and was destined to become probably the most important library computer project ever undertaken.

The growing catalogue was sent weekly on tape in a number of participating libraries. The improved MARC IT format appeared in 1967. MARC was developed to cater not only for a standardized bibliographic representation for books, but also for serials, and eventually for reports and almost anything else that might need to be exchanged between libraries.

MARC continued to be developed in the late sixties and in 1969 an attempt to develop an Anglo-American code by modifying MARC II was made by the British National Bibliography (BNB).

A standard format for bibliographic information exchange on magnetic tape was proposed. By 1970 agreement was reached to make MARC records used by the BNB and Library of Congress almost identical, leaving minor differences in sub-field codes.

Many other countries in Europe and elsewhere started to adopt MARC type formats. By 1973 18 major libraries in the UK were using BNB/MARC tapes on IBM 360 or ICL 1900 series computers.

An international MARC format was proposed in 1975, later called UNIMARC, by the US and major European countries. In 1976 a European group called INTERMARC became the European Library Automation Group (ELAG) which held seminars through the eighties covering developments in library automation. In 1980 a second edition of an internationally agreed format was published called The Anglo American Cataloguing Rules 2nd edition (AACR2).

"Pre-MARC" data is available from a US company called Carollton Press who can provide about 5 million records about material at the Library of Congress. In the UK the British Museum's library catalogue of printed books is being converted into a machine readable form of over four million records.

These cooperative efforts failed to prevent other formats for describing published material coming into widespread use, either because MARC was simply ignored or because other formats were considered more suitable for specific purposes.

Most machine readable databases do not use a MARC format. An attempt to standardize database formats was made by UNISIST with the publication of a Reference Manual in 1974. They persisted with the idea in a 1981 second edition. An attempt was also made under the aegis of UNESCO in 1978 to develop yet another format which could be used for all purposes. These efforts do not seem to have made much progress.

In the UK the Office for Scientific and Technical Information (OSTI) supported two cooperative ventures. One became BLCMP Ltd., specializing in cataloguing but later introducing a circulation control system called Circo running on Data General Eclipse machines. The second became SLS Ltd., which started with a circulation control system and then moved on to cataloguing systems. In 1986 SLS offered an integrated library management system called Libertas.

Online public access catalogues (OPACs)

By 1986, interest in OPACs justified a special issue of the journal *Program* about the topic. OPACs are in use in the US, UK, Australia, and other countries.

The OPAC interface and functions provided in the DOBIS/LIBIS integrated library system are described at length by Brophy who points out that "if users cannot understand the online instructions which help them move through the screens, an OPAC program is failing in its purpose". They criticize the system in this respect. (It would be interesting to find out if good instructions have ever been written for any computer system of any kind for any purpose in any country).

According to Mazur-Rzesos "most OPACs are user-friendly". "User-friendly" is the computer enthusiast's synonym for "fiendishly difficult to use". No disrespect is meant to Elizabeth Mazur-Rzesos – perhaps some OPACs really are the first ever user-friendly systems. Mazur-Rzesos describes some additional navigational features built into NEW-WAVE, a system used at the Biblioteque Royale in Brussels, so that retrieval of related records via inter-record links becomes possible.

Acquisition control

Acquisition control became quite widely introduced and ordering, catalogue card production, label product etc., were computerised on an ad hoc basis. With the increasing adoption of microcomputers in libraries some attempts were made to use database management software such as Dbase II for this purpose. The control of serials was handled online by the compilers of commercial databases and some large libraries operated online acquisition systems.

Adams describes an inter-library loan control system called AIM demonstrated at Leicester Polytechnic in the UK either for borrowing from British Library Lending Division (BLLD), now British Library Document Supply Centre (BLDSC), for lending to, or borrowing from other libraries. A system called DMS produced by Compsoft using CP/M or MD-DOS operating systems on micros was selected by Leicester; Commodore and later Cifer 2684 micros were used. BLLD loans could be ordered by telex after protocol problems had been overcome.

Circulation control

The data processing equipment which became available in the early sixties was not quickly adopted for circulation control purposes mainly because it was thought to be too costly. A real time system was working at Illinois State University library in 1967 using an IBM 1710 with a disc file for circulation transactions.

By 1979 several systems were running in the UK. An online system for library-desk transactions was in operation at Queen's University, Belfast. A control system for serials should be able to deal with budget, renewals, check-in, routing, and listing holdings.

In recent years circulation control seems to have become merged with multi-functional library systems.

Integrated library systems

The first attempt at an integrated library was an ambitious scheme implemented at the Massachusetts Institute of Technology (MIT) called The Information Transfer Experiment (INTREX), planned to start in 1965. It was to be nothing less than a project to provide computer-controlled access to the University's total information resources, including the library, departmental files, reports etc., using touch-tone telephones, keyboards, displays, copying facilities, etc., with a communications network connecting to outside sources and users.

INTREX continued until 1973. A whole range of ideas were tried out but the experiments centred on an online catalogue to information stored full text on microfiche with computer-controlled fast access to the fiche. The project ended with some curious results. It was reported that microfiche was preferred to hard copy whether the latter was charged or supplied free.

However in the final report it was stated that no economical method was found to provide rapid access to the full text of documents electronically – a situation which prevails to this day although there have been numerous experiments since.

At about the same time as INTREX started, another more modest project called project SHARP was in use on an IBM 7090/1401 computer at a US naval establishment. Catalogue cards, report and serial accession lists, and periodical subscriptions were handled by the machine.

Commercially available packages became available in the eighties and were reviewed by Powell et al who listed nine systems. Powell proposed that a searching examination of several aspects of a system should be carried out before choosing one – software and operating system, size and type of computer, disc storage capacity, interconnections and telecommunications, proposed terminal and printers, installation details, training, growth plan, and hardware and software maintenance.

Another review of integrated systems in the UK market was provided by Manson, highlighting the difference in the number of references that it was considered necessary to provide in such reviews. Lucy Tedd provided 102, Manson 3 (without any reference to

183

Tedd's article), and Blunden-Ellis's article (1987) market study, rich in factual information, with one reference.

Several of the systems were described in detail in these reviews. The "Bookshelf" system from Logical Choice, for instance, originated at the Cairns Library, John Radcliffe Hospital, Oxford. It is an integrated system for libraries with budgets in the range £25,000 to £250,000 and has been described in detail by its designer, Leggate.

DOBIS/LIBRIS is fully described by Brophy et al in a special book. This system was developed from software written at the universities of Dortmund and Leuven. By 1988 it was being used on 100 different sites. It ran on IBM 370 and System/38 machines. "All functions of the system work with one set of data (records)...which depend on pointers to a series of indexes".

CLSI Libs 100 has been discussed by Batt, in charge of Croydon, UK, library, where it is installed. McDonnell Douglas URICA, running at the University of Limerick, is described by Reddan and by Dickmann at Surrey County Library. Dynix at Glasgow College is described by Crawford, Sydney on a VAX at ICI headquarters where it co-exists with DEC All-in-one, by Russell, and at Coopers and Lybrand Deloitte running on a Microvax, by Bryan.

LIBRARIES, OSI in
see under STANDARDS – OSI.

LIBRARY OF CONGRESS (LC)
Founded in 1800, the LC lost most of its books during the British Bombardment of the Capitol in 1814. These losses were made good by the purchase of Thomas Jefferson's Library shortly afterwards. It continued as the congressional library for many years and later became the National Library of the United States. The Library of Congress Catalogue Service was begun by Herbert Putnam, Librarian until 1939.

See also LIBRARIES – COMPUTERS IN, and SCANNERS.

LIGATURE
A term used in printing when two or more letters are cast on one piece of metal type. A ligature is considered to produce a more pleasing result – it is a composite glyph designed from normally separate glyphs usually "f's", "l's" or "i's" such as the glyph formed by "ffi" in the word "efficient". Proportional spacing means that glyphs are allocated spaces according to their size.

See also DESKTOP PUBLISHING.

LIGHT PEN
A pen-like device connected to a computer which may be pointed at the screen for selecting a displayed item, or used to draw with. A light pen comes with the associated software to enable it to be used for controlling a microcomputer. Also used at some point-of-sales terminals for "reading" bar codes.

LIM MEMORY
An EXPANDED MEMORY system named after its originators Lotus, Intel, and Microsoft.

LINE, MAURICE
Maurice Line, born in 1928, was appointed to succeed D. J. Urquhart as Director General of the British Library's Lending Division in July 1974. He retired in 1988 to be succeeded by David Russon. He came to BLLD (now BLDSC) via several university libraries, and the National Central Library when it became part of the British Library in 1973.

Line has been a prolific contributor to library and information science literature.

LINEAR PREDICTIVE CODING (LPC)
A speech coding method that analyses a speech wave form to produce a time varying filter as a model of the human vocal tract.

LINK ASYNCHRONOUS PROTOCOL (LAP)
The letter after "LAP" indicates the version used (currently M). An inter-modem communication procedure whereby one modem forces another to respond in order to prompt error correction by an added "polling" bit.

LIQUID CRYSTAL DISPLAY
See DISPLAYS – LIQUID CRYSTAL.

LIQUID CRYSTAL LIGHT VALVE (LCLV)
See DISPLAYS.

LISP
See ARTIFICIAL INTELLIGENCE – EXPERT SYSTEMS.

LOCAL AREA NETWORK (LAN)
A data communications network used to interconnect data terminal equipment distributed over a limited area, typically up to 10 square kilometres. See NETWORKS

LOCAL LOOP
A term (of American origin) used to describe the telephone lines between a subscriber and the telephone exchange.

LOVELACE, LADY ADA
Daughter of Lord Byron, Lady Ada was born in 1815. She became a skilled mathematician. In 1833 when aged 17, she met Charles Babbage, starting a life-long friendship. Having translated a French paper about Babbage's machine she added some notes to it including some examples of programs and also discovered that some of Babbage's own calculations were erroneous.

Ada died of cancer in 1852 having previously lost most of her money because of her addiction to gambling on horses. It has been suggested that she used some kind of mathematical system to help her to back putative winners. See also COMPUTERS – HISTORY.

LOW-PASS FILTER
A filter used to block out high frequency components of a signal, thus allowing only the low frequency components to pass.

LPC
LINEAR PREDICTIVE CODING.

Lpi
Lines per inch.

LQ
Letter Quality.

LSI
Large Scale Integration.

LU 6.2
IBM software for communication between programs in distributed processing. It replaces the idea of intelligent mainframes with dumb terminals by distributing intelligence around the network and providing secure communications within IBM's SNA scheme.

LUHN H. P.
IBM employee who devised the Key Word In Context (KWIC) system.

Born in 1896, Luhn joined IBM in 1941, and in 1947 became involved in the design of an "electronic searching selector". In the 1950s he became manager of information retrieval, developing SDI system, automatic coding and abstracting etc. His name is particularly associated with "Keyword in Context" (KWIC) indexing. Luhn wrote numerous papers and took out many patents. He died in 1964.

LUMINOSITY, LUMINANCE
Synonyms for Brightness. See also COLOUR.

M

M
Million.

MAC
Multiple Analogue Component. A method of television transmission by satellite.

MACHINE LANGUAGE
A set of binary-coded instructions for execution by a particular computer. Machine language instructions are directly executed by the computer so machine code may often be the object or target code which is produced by a higher level language. These days it is unlikely that machine code will also be the source code – that is the code used by the programmer to write the program.

MACHINE TRANSLATION
See TRANSLATION BY MACHINE.

MACHLUP, FRITZ
Machlup, an American economist, wrote an influential book *The Product and Distribution of Knowledge* in 1962. At that time his analysis credited 29% of the US GNP to the "knowledge industry". It prompted work by Bell, Porat, Parker and others in creating the notion of an Information Society.

Machlup considered that "Information science, at the present stage of its development, is not a fully integrated assemblage of systematic studies of the processes regarded as information.

MACRO
A named series of source program lines which are inserted en bloc by an assembler program when named. A macro is a programmer's time-saving aid since a frequently used series of instructions can be added without the need to write out the full code.

MAINFRAME
A relatively large self-contained computer with a variety of peripheral devices connected to it.

MAN
Metropolitan Area Network.

MAN-MACHINE INTERFACE
See under HUMAN-MACHINE INTERFACE.

MANAGED DATA NETWORK SERVICES (MDNS)
Network connections provided and managed by the supplier on behalf of their customers. See also NETWORKS.

MANTISSA
The significant integers of a number raised to a power. In the floating point number 6.8×10^3, the mantissa is 6.8.

MAP
Manufacturing Automation Protocol. A detailed paper specification of communications protocols for integrating computerized machines.

MARC
Machine Readable Catalogue.
See also LIBRARIES – COMPUTERS IN.

MARCONI, GUGLIEMO WILLIAM
Marconi was born in 1874 at Bologna, Italy, studied at Oxford, and subsequently worked mainly in Britain. He successfully tested his wireless telegraph apparatus, encouraged by the Postal Telegraph Service in the UK, capturing attention by sending messages from Queen Victoria to the Prince of Wales on his yacht. He founded Marconi Wireless Telegraph Ltd., in London in 1897 and established wireless communication across the Atlantic in 1902. Marconi won the Nobel prize for physics in 1909.

MARKETING, INFORMATION TECHNOLOGY FOR,
See under INFORMATION TECHNOLOGY.

MATTHEW EFFECT
A social phenomenon describing the progressive accumulation of possessions, recognition, fame or other attributes once a certain

"critical mass" has been reached. The phrase was originated by R. K. Merton with particular reference to scientific reputation. Its origin is the New Testament quotation in Matthew, Chapter 13, Verse 12, "for whosoever hath, to him shall be given, and he shall have more in abundance".

MAUCHLY, JOHN WILLIAM
Mauchly was an American physicist born in 1907, who jointly with J. P. Eckert is credited with the invention of the first (probably erroneously) electronic digital computer called Eniac in 1946. Later he became Director of System Studies at Remington, being responsible for the development of Univac machines. Mauchly died in 1980.

MAXWELL, JAMES CLERK
Maxwell was born in Edinburgh in 1831 and died at Cambridge in 1879. He formulated two pairs of equations which expressed the continuous nature of an electric and magnetic field, thereby laying the theoretical foundations of electricity and magnetism and their relationship to light and radio waves. Hertz later demonstrated the existence of radio waves, and Marconi developed their application.

Colour photography was another of Maxwell's interests. He showed that three photographs of an image, taken through red green and violet filters would reproduce a complete colour photograph of the original when superimposed. This method of additive colour photography was the basis for all subsequent later processes.

Mbit
Megabit. One million bits.

Mbps
Megabits per second. May mean Megabytes per second if so indicated by the context.

Mbyte
Million bytes.

MCA
Microchannel Architecture.

MCGA
Multi-Colour Graphics Adaptor.
See DISPLAYING COLOUR AND GRAPHICS.

McLUHAN, MARSHALL H.
McLuhan, a Canadian, was born in Edmonton in 1911 and died in 1980. He studied at Cambridge and became a Professor at St. Michael's College, Toronto. He is well-known for his literature on communication in the media. He is particularly remembered for his comment that media are messages in the sense that they determine and embody what is considered to be the appropriate social organization. A new media provides human beings with new psychological-structural equipment.

McLuhan thought that technology would have a de-centralizing effect, breaking up concentrations of power in the state and in industry. His best known books are *The Gutenberg Galaxy* (1962), the *Making of Typographic Man* (1962) and *The Medium is the Message* (1967).

MDA
Monochrome Display Adaptor.

MDNS
Managed Data Network Services.

MEDLARS
MEDical Literature Analysis and Retrieval System.

MEDLINE
MEDLARS Online System.

Mega-
Million.

MEM
Modified Frequency Modulation.

MEMORY
A memory is a device for storing data from which it can be later retrieved. The word may refer to a computer's main RAM memory controlled by operating instructions and composed of semiconductor elements, to DISC memory, or to other types of semiconductor memory.

Microsoft Disc Operating System (MS-DOS or "DOS"), the most popular OPERATING SYSTEM, was designed to address a memory with a capacity of 640 Kbytes which seemed enormous at the time, but has since been found to be inadequate for many of today's software packages.

EXPANDED MEMORY (DOS). A refinement of EXTENDED MEMORY devised by Lotus Intel and Microsoft in which additional memory, as available within the machine, is selected in 16 Kbyte blocks. Such memory is added to the machine on a card containing the necessary chips designed to the EXPANDED MEMORY specification.

EXTENDED MEMORY (DOS) above 1 Mbyte may be fitted in a DOS machine and may be addressed by a scheme developed by Lotus Intel and Microsoft called Extended Memory Specification.

HIGH MEMORY (DOS). The first 64 Kbytes of Extended Memory commencing at 1 Mbyte. It is addressable by 286, 386 and 486 processors.

UPPER MEMORY (DOS). In machines embodying 1 Mbyte of memory, the region between 640Kbytes and 1Mbyte, used by auxiliary software for items like video adaptors, network adaptors, and so on. If a machine contains only 640 Kbytes of memory, part of it will be occupied by this auxiliary software reducing the amount available for user data.

VIRTUAL MEMORY. A method of extending the capacity of RAM memory by swopping data with Disc memory. Operations depending on RAM-disc data swopping will proceed much more slowly than they would if sufficient RAM memory made disc swopping to be unnecessary.

MEMORY – RANDOM ACCESS (RAM)
A form of electronic memory that allows data to be both written to or read from any location independently of other locations.

A major use for RAMs is as the main fast memory in a computer. A RAM multi-celled chip, containing thousands of elements, comes in a very small plastic container with numerous connecting tags. The capacities available range from "1K byte" to "4Mbyte" and above. Much larger RAMs are contemplated (1 byte = 8bits and often represents one character). Prices dropped so rapidly that by 1986 a 250K RAM chip was available at less than $3.

A Dynamic Random Access Memory (DRAM) requires to be periodically "refreshed" to preserve its state. A Static Random Access Memory (SRAM) retains its state without refreshment as long as its operating potentials remain.

It is expected that memory chips in 5 years time will have a capacity of 1 Gigabyte with access times of 20 nanoseconds.

MEMORY – TYPES
The general requirements for a semiconductor memory are fast access time and high capacity in the smallest possible space to handle the longest possible word lengths, together with any special characteristics that may be necessary for the application.

In July 1989 IBM set up a production line for 4 Mbit 80 ns dynamic RAM (DRAM) memory chips in Germany. Most other major manufacturers such as Hitachi, Toshiba, Motorola, and others followed. DRAMs are very widely used and US manufacturers abandoned the market in the mid-eighties when the Japanese jumped to 256 Kbit and then to 1 Mbit DRAM mass production with substantial price cutting. One company, Toshiba, makes one third of the world's consumption. In July 1989 Toshiba allocated over £300 million for 4 Mbit DRAM manufacture.

In January 1991 Bellcore (Livingstone, N.J.) announced a laser semi-conductor array holographic memory which does not require a scanning beam to retrieve 100K pages of information in 1 ns. The total capacity of the 1 cm square device is 10 million pages or 1 billion (= 1 terabit = 1 billion = 1 million million) bits (not bytes). Ways of dealing with and storing the bitstream have still to be worked out.

Memories operating today which have reached the market and are fitted within equipment fall far short of the performance just discussed. There are several types for different applications. A RAM usually consists of a large number of transistors each charging or discharging an associated capacitor to store one bit.

Dynamic RAMs, (DRAMs) widely used for main memory, are cheap but "volatile" – the capacitor charge leaks away so they require periodic "refreshment". Static RAMs (SRAMs) require less power, are non-volatile, but are more expensive.

The other types in major use include Erasable Programmable Read Only Memories (EPROM), erasable by exposure to ultraviolet light for some 20 minutes, and Electrically Erasable PROMs (EEPROM). These memories are used to retain data programmed into them ready for use when the equipment is switched on again – for instance for "Booting", that is to load sufficient software to make a computer ready for use.

in 1989 a new kind of memory resembling an EPROM called a Flash Memory appeared. It is a high capacity memory often arranged with associated software to look like and behave like a very fast disc. One application is as a "solid state disk" on portable computers – as in the Psion MC400 machine.

Flash memories offer storage which does not need an applied voltage (as do SRAMs) to retain data, and may be partially or completely re-programmed within the host machine (EPROMs must be removed to be erased by 20 minutes UV exposure). Flash memories cost much less and are smaller than EEPROMs (although they cannot be re-programmed at the individual byte level). They may displace EPROMs, EEPROMs, or SRAMS in some applications.

In 1991 NEC announced that they were experimenting with small memory elements which do not need to be refreshed, using 0.2 micron multi-layered niobium and aluminium oxide Josephson junctions. Switching speeds of about 1.5 ns have been announced with very low power dissipation.

A major problem is to eliminate the need to immerse the device in liquid helium and work needs to be done to find out whether the principle can be made to work at higher temperatures.

MENU
A computer-displayed page offering a number of choices. Typically each choice is numbered and a particular choice is executed by depressing a numbered key.

MERTON, ROBERT K.
An American academic noted for his work on the sociology of science. Merton's major work was carried out when he was at Columbia University.

MESFET
MEtal Semiconductor Field Effect Transistor.

MESSAGE
A series of symbols of any length which con-

vey information. The symbols in a message may signify text, graphics, illustrations etc. "Message" as used in telecoms does not mean "a brief communication".

MESSAGE SWITCHING
A method for transmitting messages over a network, often implying a "store and forward" technique. For example a series of telex messages could be input to a message switching terminal which is already sending messages, to be stored and queued for transmission to addressees listed in headers.

METAL OXIDE SILICON (MOS) TRANSISTOR
A transistor in which the conductivity of the silicon between two p-type regions is controlled by an aluminium Gate electrode.

In the MOS an aluminium "Gate" electrode controls the conductivity of the silicon between two p-type regions. The basic MOS is often called The MOS "field effect transistor" (FET) because it is the field created near the gate which changes the conductivity of the silicon locally between the "source" and "drain" regions. MOS devices may be called PMOS or NMOS according to the type of silicon used near the gate.

The first microprocessor used P-MOS; the pioneering Intel 8080, still in widespread use, uses N-MOS; N-MOS is widely used in today's microprocessors such as the Intel 8086 and 80286.

Integrated circuits used in computers are now predominantly MOS devices because they are easier to manufacture and consume less power.

MFLOPS
Millions of Floating Point Operations Per Second.

MHz
Megahertz (million Hz).

MICROCHANNEL ARCHITECTURE (MCA)
A relatively new 16/32 bit bus used in most IBM PS/2 micro- computers.

MICROCOMPUTER
The transistor is the most important micro-computer circuit element – see also TRANSIS-

MICROCOMPUTER

TOR and SEMICONDUCTORS. Nearly all the circuits in a microcomputer contain transistors.

There were two early leaders who manufactured processors for microcomputers – Intel and Motorola. In the late seventies, Intel received a contract for the IBM PC which was launched in 1981. This established the 8088 16 bit processor as the leading CPU.

In 1949 the EDSAC computer contained 3000 valves, consumed 15 Kilowatts of power, and occupied a special room. In 1989 a chip containing over one million transistors appeared (the 80860). It is infinitely more powerful than EDSAC and occupies a few square centimetres.

The major parts of a microcomputer are the microprocessor Central Processing Unit (CPU), Main Memory (and associated Cache Memory), Input/Output Controllers interconnected by multiple-line Busses, and Peripheral Devices such as keyboard, discs, display, and printer.

To relieve the CPU processor of certain subtasks which have become more complex, subsidiary semi-autonomous processors controlled by the CPU have been developed. Many current machines include at least one of them.

A microprocessor executes a series of logical arithmetical steps when controlled by input signals. Advances in CPUs have been mainly responsible for microcomputer performance improvements. Matching improvements in other parts have been necessary and the performance of complete microcomputers have steadily improved.

Sometimes expected or actual advances in the technology of these other parts have been advances in their own right – for example advances in display technology and Graphics Signal Processor (GSP) chips.

The perception by users of the benefits of advances in microcomputer performance is reflected in their purchasing policy.

The 486 was considered to be overkill for many users day to day personal computing requirements (as reflected in the survey described below) until new software came along for which better performance was almost essential.

In 1990 a survey was carried out in Northern Ireland of users in government, financial services, health, industry, and commerce. The

Amstrad 386 laptop microcomputer

main objective was to find out what proportion of respondents were going to, or had plans to, invest in microcomputers using 80486 microprocessors. 67% knew about the new micros but most said they had no plans to introduce them, although they might consider it in 3 to 4 years time.

6% said they definitely would introduce them soon, and a further 8% said they had no intention of ever introducing them. "A massive 90% of all respondents said that their future strategies for altering future computer-systems would be largely software based. 16% of all respondents and 17% and 28% of those in central government and industry and commerce respectively said that they had plans to replace existing minicomputers with multi-user microcomputers.

Although about 2/3rds of organizations in Northern Ireland were expected to have LANs by 1992, in many cases companies may not actually need a LAN at all. Possibly all that is needed is to connect terminals to a central machine running a multi-user operating system. It is also clear that customer acceptance of the 80486 is by no means assured. There is a case for marketing its potential as say, an alternative to a small LAN.

These rather interesting findings may be less interesting in 1993 because new software packages to which new features are always

190

being added and whose performance may depend on the speed of the machine in which they are installed, may be ahead of hardware performance. The two fields drive each other along. The widespread adoption of WINDOWS is a case in point. Furthermore LANs are becoming widely used.

Further changes are of course on the way. IBM points out that "Customers in 1981 were impressed by the original PC's 4.77 MHz 8088 processor, its 16 Kbytes of memory and 160 Kbytes of floppy diskette storage".

Referring to their PS/2s, The IBM note continues "Systems configured with the new 50 MHz card benchmark at over 57 times the performance of the original PC, offer over 1000 times the memory capacity (64 Mbytes) and 10 thousand times the storage (1.6 Gbytes)".

"In the next few years... using verbal commands as though entered from the keyboard, PCs will be able to "type" documents by dictating into the microphone and the words will appear on the screen". Other fore-casts include pen-based computers and video conferencing on the desktop, both of which have had mixed success.

According to International Data Corporation (1992) there were about 86 million business microcomputers installed worldwide in 1990 predicted to rise to 118 million in 1993. Of the 1993 total, it is estimated that 37% were connected to LANs. A higher percentage were connected to LANs in the United States than were in Europe. Of the 1993 total 43 million business machines were installed in the United States of which 59% were connected to LANs. Of the 26 million machines in Europe 48% were LAN connected.

See also WORKSTATIONS, IBM, and APPLE.

MICROCOMPUTER – MULTIMEDIA PC

A multimedia PC is a fast PC with a high resolution colour display, CD-ROM drive, a plug-in board for sound, and an above average amount of RAM and hard disc memory. The most popular sound card is probably Sound Blaster. This enables music, sound effects, digitized voice, and text to speech to be managed. Windows 3.1 is likely to be the most suitable software.

The Apricot XEN-LS II includes a security system, networking facilities, audio, a CD-ROM drive, stereo speakers, a software mix-ing desk, a large memory and disc storage. It costs almost twice as much as other 486DX2 66-MHz systems. It will accept input from a microphone, a MIDI interface, audio signals from PCs, and from its own CD player and FM synthesizer. An Intel 596 Ethernet co-processor is used for networking.

The IBM Multimedia machine includes XGA-2 graphics, a 600 Mbyte CD-ROM II drive with Extended Architecture (XA), CDx loaded with program tools and samplers, 16-bit sound quality and a built-in loudspeaker. A 212 Mbyte hard drive with 12ms average access time and an 8 Mbyte RAM are fitted. IBM have recently announced a new series of "Ultimedia" machines.

See also MULTIMEDIA.

MICROCOMPUTERS – PERFORMANCE

A number of factors which affect performance, particularly speed of operation, are discussed below.

The frequency at which the clock in a microprocessor operates dictates the speed at which a microcomputer will execute instructions but this is far from being the only factor which affects speed.

RISC Architecture reduces the number of cycles per instruction and reduces the need for memory accesses since some instructions can be executed by register to register communication only. IBM introduced a machine in January 1986 called the RT PC incorporating its own RISC processor. In 1987 Acorn announced the Archimedes machine using its own 32 bit chip with RISC. Acorn claims that the machine outperformed the Compaq 386 in benchmark tests.

Wait-States – necessitated, for example, by the processor having to wait for a slower memory – are non-operational clock periods. Thus the IBM PS/2 Model 50 which uses an 80286 processor operating at 10 MHz – a 100ns clock – adds one wait-state to both memory access and Input/Output (I/O) operations. A memory access in the Model 50 takes two clock periods plus one wait-state, or 300 ns.

Cache Memories are controlled by software designed to access whatever data is most likely to be needed next, fetched from main memory into cache. The objective is to obtain a high "hit ratio" – i.e. to make as many accesses to cache and as few to main memory as possible. Small caches have access times as fast as 20 ns.

Pipelining is the overlapping of operations normally taking place at different times, or even the simultaneous occurrence of operations otherwise occurring in successive clock cycles.

Static Random Access Memories (SRAMs), unlike dynamic RAMs which are widely used for memories, do not require refreshing periodically – the stored data endures. They are expensive but the latest static RAMs have access times below 10 ns.

Co-Processors, which may be equal in power to the main processor (CPU), are effectively small computers in their own right.

Memory Size. Continually falling prices encourage the trend to provide large memories providing more space for large files such as image files with consequently fewer disk accesses.

Disc Drive Interface. There is a degree of standardization in drive interfaces, type ST506 being the slowest, then SCSI, ESDI, and SMD which is the fastest.

Data Transfer Method. Disc controllers may work 1 byte at a time, a method used with the IBM PC, or much faster Direct Memory Access (DMA) may be used. Differences between the way memory is handled by the processor will affect large files particularly. For example the 8088 and 80286 processors deal with memory in 64K segments which makes graphics handling awkward but the 68000 series of processors treat memory as a large linear address space.

The speed of the slowest part of a microcomputer must be a prime consideration if the machine's overall response time is to be reduced.

To speed up the processing rate of the offending part either a re-design may be necessary – for instance some form of parallel processing might be used, something clever must be done with software, or some new development in technology must be awaited before the performance of the whole machine can be improved.

Speed starts at the CPU but there is no point in having a given speed unless the remainder of the system can exploit it. A processor may be capable of 45 MIPS – the kind of power which may be soon become common-place in "high end" RISC microcomputers.

Fast cache memories may operate at up to 1860 Mbps but main memories fall far short of this. Assuming 149 Mbps to be comfortably manageable by main memory, it will be working at up to 149/1860 = 8% of the speed of the cache. A fast cache memory with a hit rate of 92% inserted between CPU and main memory would be a satisfactory combination.

A "92% hit rate" means that the design of the cache is such that on average only for 8% of the time must it fetch data from main memory because it does not contain that data within itself. (In practice there may be peaks of demand where the cache cannot do as well as this so main memory will then have to do better than 149 Mbps).

Extremely fast bit rates are needed when high resolution rapidly changing colour pictures are to be displayed without delays. At a 480 Mbps rate, a screen pixel capacity of 480/60 = about 8 Mpixels is implied, since the screen must be refreshed 60 times a second (US). If the pixels are 8-bit 256-colour pixels, the actual number of on-screen pixels is then one million – about the number present on a 14″ (diagonal) CRT at 100 x 100 dots per inch.

This performance may be achieved if special BUSSES are used.

Improved CRTs are becoming available. For example a 14″ (diagonal) screen displaying 300 x 300 dots per inch contains about 8.7 Mpixels on its surface. For 8-bit colour pixels (256 colours) the total becomes about 70 Mpixels – a fill-rate of 4200 Mbps if the refresh rate is included. To operate in this manner, advanced compression, bit-plane parallel processing, and other special measures will be needed to reduce the bandwidth.

MICROCOMPUTERS – PROCESSOR DEVELOPMENTS

In the 1950s methods were developed for the mass productionof units consisting of interconnected transistors and other circuit elements on silicon wafers. Each wafer yielded a number of "Integrated Circuits". Very small leads were welded to IC connection points, and the IC mounted in a small container containing an array of lugs or pins to which the other end of the internal connecting leads were attached. External connections to other parts of the micro were made via the lugs, producing a packaged "chip".

Later the number of circuits were increased and other circuits, formerly on self contained chips, were added into a single chip, giving rise to the idea of Very large Scale Integration (VLSI).

VLSI is not material-specific – it is a phrase used to cover methods of producing large numbers of circuit elements on one chip – say 250,000 gates with features (circuit elements) spaced at less than one micrometre.

A project called the Very High Speed Integrated Circuit (VHSIC) program to try and achieve ambitious goals was put in hand in the US for military equipment.

The main effort is directed towards "scaling" – that is size reduction in order to increased the number of circuit elements per chip, and to reduce inter-connection lengths and capacitances in order to obtain speed increases. It is considerably easier to scale down MOS devices. Scaled down bipolars are prone to breakdown at low voltage.

The reduction of the current required by each of the thousands of active circuit elements in an IC, as is achieved by using CMOS, is also important because of the much lower drain on the battery in portables and because of a substantial reduction in the power dissipated in the form of heat. More elements can be packed into a smaller space without overheating.

The Intel 80286 processor embodies 130,000 semiconductor elements on a square chip with sides of little more than 0.25 inches. The microprocessor used by Hewlett-Packard as a CPU in their 32 bit microcomputer uses nearly half a million elements on an even smaller chip. An electron beam is used to make the masks required for its manufacture to enable conductors to be spaced 1 micrometre apart with 0.25 micrometre tolerance.

In 1986 it was suggested that later in the 1980s the target would probably be raised to one million transistors per chip and that an advance of this kind would require three major ingredients – hierarchy, regularity, and design tool automation.

Design hierarchy means splitting up the design into manageable portions which are then joined together in a complete design. Regularity refers to the need to use the same kind of circuit element with the same interface as often as possible. Design tool automation means the computer generation of layouts for standard functions as used in memories, gates, etc.

One trick used to improve economies of scale is to use a standard multiple-circuit-element design with standard fabrication sequences up to the last operation which is the only "special" part of the manufacturing process – the addition of the metallic layer which interconnects the myriad basic circuits. These circuits may be interconnected to form various basic logic arrangements, to be in turn connected to form units such as blocks of RAM cells, Counters, Registers, etc.

The manufacturing data needed to complete the final computer-controlled interconnecting process is a matter for the designer of the complete chip. The designer supplies the data as an on-disc program which controls the final process.

Although Intel contracted for the IBM PC's processor, Motorola continued to develop its 68000 series and in 1987 the 32 bit Motorola 68020 and Intel 80386 microprocessors were announced. There was a good deal of controversy about the speeds of these chips when used in microcomputers. The 386 was believed to be faster on average although the different characteristics of the machines in which they became available made chip comparisons difficult.

In September 1989 Intel announced the 80960 specifically to handle input/out intensive operations such as Local Area Network (LAN) control. A version of the 386, the 80386SL, was also produced for use in "notebook-size" computers. The chip includes the processor, cache memory controller and mapping logic together with power conservation logic to reduce current consumption when the machine is relatively inactive.

In April 1989 Motorola announced 1.2 million transistors on a single chip – the 32 bit 68040 (sometimes called Complex Instruction Set computer or CISC), beating Intel's announcement of the 80486 by a few weeks. A chip containing over one million transistors had arrived on time as predicted. It offers about four times the performance of the 68030, and is compatible with it and with earlier chips in the series.

The 68040 is claimed to work at 20 Mips, compared with Sparc's, (another competitor) 18 Mips, and 80486's 15 Mips, or in other terms, at 3.5 Mflops compared with Sparc's 2.6 Mflops, and 80486's 1 Mflop. The 68040 has a built-in co-processor, large cache memories, and highly parallel architecture.

The Intel 80486 – compatible with the earlier 286 and 386, and able to work with software designed for those processors – includes a maths co-processor, cache memory, and memory management on the same chip. It is designed to be clocked at 25 MHz, and to process 20 million instructions per second (Mips). By 1992 a version of this chip is expected to process at 120 Mips. Note that these figures do not tie up with those in the preceding paragraph.

The actual speeds realizable in applications remain to be seen and will vary considerably from one to another.

The Intel series will run in "8086" mode so that they may be used with earlier single-user software, or they may be used in multitasking "protected mode" where arrangements are made for access to more memory with secure isolation for each user.

For example IBM's OS/2 software in conjunction with certain PS/2 computers provides for addressing 16 Mbytes direct, and a theoretical gigabyte or more of virtual memory (by swapping data in and out of disc memory).

The 16 bit 80286 may be easily switched from 8086 to protected mode, but a special procedure is needed to switch back. Protected memory is allocated to processes in 64K segments. The 32 bit 80386 can be switched easily from 8086 to protected mode or vice versa equally easily and a very large segment of memory without the need for segment allocation can be used.

If the 386 is used with software specially written for it, it will run applications up to four times faster than the 286. The 486 is essentially a fast 386 with co-processor and cache memory. One application where the increase would be evident would be in faster number-crunching – as needed, for example with large spreadsheets, an application where a 486 micro should work about twice as fast as a 386.

Intel faces competition from a chip function-analysed and reverse-engineered from a 386 microprocessor chip – the AMD AM386DXL from Advanced Micro Devices. Copyright infringements cloud its usage. Not only is the chip an exact replacement for the 80386, its normal power consumption is much lower and it will also "sleep", consuming only 1 ma of current while maintaining intact all its data. It is claimed that Intel's attempt to block the production of legal clones prevents healthy competition. Users everywhere will benefit from it.

There is always somebody round the corner with something faster for the chip market. 1990 dawned with an announcement by Motorola that they can provide a chip – the CPUAX – containing four million transistors, capable of operating at 200 Million Floating Point Operations per Second (MFLOPS). There are a number of redundant cells in the chip's cellular design. If any cell fails the chip repairs itself by connecting a replacement cell.

In February 1991, Mips Computer (Sunnyvale, CA) announced a 64 bit microprocessor – the R4000. It is a RISC chip and runs at 50 MHz.

It would be reasonable to conclude that there is still a lot of mileage for advances in microcomputers before it becomes necessary to break into a radically new technology. This thought was reinforced by Mudge et al in 1991:-

"The next time someone says "I'm just off to use my GaAs Mesfet E/D DCFL" you will know that the ideas of Mudge et al from the University of Michigan and Vitesse (Camarillo, CA) have come out right. They believe they can build a 170 Mips microcomputer running at 250 Mhz.

You will of course have recognized GALLIUM ARSENIDE Metal Semiconductor Field Effect Transistor Enhancement/Depletion technology – which is what Mudge proposes to use in his processor.

The single-chip 32 bit processor and floating point accelerator will be associated with a 3 ns SRAM with cache, controller, and bus on a single small module. Circuit simulations indicate that it should be possible to clock at 250 MHz.

During the last few years, many microprocessors and microcomputers have embodied what are collectively referred to as RISC (Reduced Instruction Set Computer) chips originated at the University of California at Berkeley in the seventies. RISC represents a fairly considerable change from the "pre-RISC" CPU.

There is more to RISC than simply discarding a range of instructions that are rarely used. The idea has been extended to include "streamlining", involving caches, pipelining, and channel bandwidth, with a trend towards the ideal of completing an instruction in one machine cycle instead of the many cycles usually required.

Formerly, instruction sets included a comprehensive set of instructions; each instruction word triggered a small ROM stored microcode program which could take many machine cycles to execute – hence the title of this type of system – Complex Instruction Set Computer (CISC). At least 20 cycles could be taken just to load a register and 100 or more to do simple arithmetic. When memories were slow there was not much incentive for speed improvements.

IBM did some experimental work in the early eighties and used a RISC chip in a workstation introduced in 1986. Hewlett-Packard also took up this technology in 1986 in its 3000 series in which the instruction set was reduced from the normal 300 or more instructions, to 140 shorter instructions. Inmos was an early adopter of RISC with only 70 instructions for its transputer processor.

RISC techniques using small instructions sets, imply more, faster, register-to-register operations, and fewer register-to-memory operations, consequently it makes sense to separate and optimize the transmission paths for these two kinds of transaction. For example the average number of machine cycles needed to complete an instruction for the Motorola 68010 is 12. With RISC ideas as implemented on the 68030, referred to as "streamlining", an average of only 5.5 cycles are needed.

Considerable research interest in Neural Networks has prompted the supply of experimental chips. Intel are developing an Electronically Trainable Analogue Neural Network (ETANN). The device consists of 64 analogue neurons and 10,000 synapses with trainable weights. The chip will work at a interconnect rate of 2 GHz. The major applications are expected in pattern recognition areas.

MICROCOMPUTERS – SPEED

The "required speed" is hard to specify. It would hardly be acceptable if the hardware and software took an hour to reproduce each new image. When you are working with a microcomputer the delay between a user action and the presentation of each result on the screen should be negligible. This is particularly important when the final image is the result of a series of interactions between display and user.

Most microcomputer systems do not display a high quality colour image instantly when demanded from storage. The larger the screen, the higher the resolution and the better the colour, the larger will be the number of bits needed to represent the image. But a high quality picture may not be backed up by the necessary power to fill the screen with bits in an acceptable time – say, two seconds. You may not have to wait for an hour, but you may have to wait several minutes or more which may be quite unacceptable.

Speeds with Windows 3.0 software result in such long waiting times that a number of "Windows 3.0 accelerator boards" are available from competing suppliers. The best can reduce an operation which takes 1.5 minutes before the result is displayed, to 30 seconds. It will cost about £1000.

Several inter-related items affect speed. The faster the main processor the faster any process will be, but not pro rata. 12 MHz is about the minimum speed for imaging and 24 MHz is better but most operations will not then be done in half the time.

Disc-accessing time is important and depends mainly on the drive and the disc/machine interface. One of the fastest is the Small Computer System Interface (SCSI). The actual time it takes to get data includes the average access time, the rate at which data flows once accessed, and the bandwidth of the bus system.

To improve disc data delivery rates per se on an existing machine is very expensive. However there is another method which does not increase the data rate but uses data more effectively.

For operations which are mainly disc-based – and that will often include imaging activities – a *cache* should speed up the apparent retrieval from disc substantially. A cache is a semiconductor memory containing data controlled by software which anticipates what data from disc you are most likely to want next. That data is available for use almost immediately.

Cache semiconductor memory is robbed from main memory thereby reducing the use of the latter for other purposes. Because of the amount needed for the cache to be effective it will almost certainly be necessary to add to the 640K memory often supplied with DOS micros although the "standard" amount of supplied memory is becoming larger. Speed is also covered under other MICROCOMPU-TER headings.

MICROFICHE
See MICROFORMS.

MICROFILM
See MICROFORMS.

MICROFORMS
Micrographic Systems provide for the creation, processing, retrieval, and reproduction of small images for viewing. Microforms are photographs of images, often from printed pages, which have been reduced in size for easier storage. Special machines are available for page photography which usually operate on a step and repeat basis using either a flat bed or rotary method.

The development of microform systems seemed to have reached a plateau by the nineteen-eighties. They seem to have found their niche where there is a requirement for the distribution of high volume reference data which needs to be periodically up-dated at intervals of greater than a day or two.

The up-dating costs are low; massive quantities of information on cheap fiche cards are replaced by massive quantities of information on new cards sent by post. People will put up with reading a few lines of references or component data on a viewer, knowing that it is up to date.

For page by page reading, microforms are sometimes used in libraries to provide access to a very large collection of documents or books. It may not be possible to justify the storage cost of print on paper for massive volumes in city centres for public usage when the demand is relatively small.

A cabinet of fiche and a viewer may be a cost-effective substitute if the once only filming and indexing cost can be justified. The filming job may, of course, already have been done elsewhere. Library clients, confronted by a situation where they can have access to a collection – for example of UK House of Commons proceedings (Hansard) – which otherwise could not be on site, have to use the microform viewers (unwillingly – see below).

A 1987 review pointed to many major microform projects in the library field. But almost without exception these projects were initiated before 1980; there was little discussion about present or future projects.

Nevertheless microforms continue to be important because they bring benefits to the users of academic libraries especially in the humanities and the social sciences. The use of microcopying to preserve the contents of books subject to acidic decay also continues to be important. But because they are in a completely different format from books, microforms have presented special problems in acquisition, cataloguing, and use.

Microphotography has not radically altered the nature of libraries and has not been generally used to save space. It is passing through a transitional phase because of the development of computers and other new equipment. Microform systems are still to be found in libraries, banks, and spare-part stores.

In 1988 a spokesman for the UK company Microfilm Reprographic was reported as saying "this is a market with an enormous growth potential". The comment was made on the occasion of an offer of $18.6 million for a US company, Computer Microfilm Corporation, engaged in microfilming activities.

Microforms were not even considered for archival storage in the 1988 "Knowledge Warehouse" project. In a discussion comparing the merits of different media for archival purposes, only tape, magnetic discs, and optical discs were mentioned.

While storage on CD-ROMs and WORMS must be making big dents in the microform market, hybrid systems are still being offered. For example in a Business Newsbank service in which articles from 600 publications are indexed on CD-ROMs, published every month, it is said that limitations in CD-ROMs storage space are overcome by supplying about 6,500 full-text articles on ten fiche with each CD-ROM.

However a comprehensive report about Document Image Processing systems for business purposes published in 1990 said that micrographic systems are likely to remain preferable for many small or medium-sized document systems on economic grounds. There is a substantial installed base. It has been estimated that there are between four and five million microfilm readers world-wide and about 200,000 Computer Assisted Retrieval (CAR) systems, mostly in the USA.

There are many major document capture projects already under way, involving substantial investments, which will not be able to change storage media. In a table of nine hardware suppliers provided in the report, three include microform storage. However microforms are used in only one of the ten "case history" large-organization applications described.

Advantages

A fiche cabinet surrounded by microform viewing machines would result not only in space economy, but also in many fringe benefits such as ease of handling, low cost of storage space, easier administrative control etc. The fact is that such a scenario is not commonplace.

Disadvantages

Some reasons for the unpopularity of microforms include:-

1. Some microform originals or some viewers produce fuzzy images. Some are hard to use or cannot be viewed off-axis.
2. The wanted image may also take time to find. Special attention must be paid to the overall speed of microform retrieval because unlike print on paper, images are not immediately visible. Perhaps the special need for good indexing does not receive the attention it deserves in some systems.
3. You cannot annotate or make marks on microforms.
4. Microforms are not portable. You cannot read them in the train or the loo (UK/US translation = john).
5. Cross referencing, scanning, browsing etc., is not so convenient. This indicates an even greater need for good indexing. The unpopularity of microforms for users have prompted many articles. At a conference of the National Micrographics Association, the audience was asked to indicate personal possession of a microform viewer. Disastrously, only two hands went up. Gwyneth Pawsey, a librarian at the Rolls Royce research centre, published a report which gave the reasons for the limited use of US government reports supplied on fiche. It included some of the items in the above list. In 1993 the same comments still apply.

MICROFORMS – HISTORY

The first patent for microfilm was granted in 1859. Microfilm was used during the Franco-Prussian war to send carrier pigeon messages from besieged Paris in 1871. Little use of the technique was made until microfilming was carried out in libraries during the first world war to ensure the preservation of important material. Wider use came with the Kodak Recordak continuous microfilm recording camera developed in 1927. This camera was used in 1928 to photograph cheques. Microform images were viewed in a US court to identify endorsements in a fraud case in the following year.

In the 1930s an American, Eugene Power, realised that microfilming could be used to bring copies of documents in European libraries to US libraries. He founded University Microfilms, still thriving today, to do the job.

Atherton Seidell used film strips called Filmstats in a microform system in 1935 and in 1939 he microfilmed periodicals at the US Army Medical Library, later to become the National Library of Medicine. During World War II war, microfilming of air-letters was extensively carried out for weight-reduction purposes, but microforms did not become generally used until well after the war.

In 1976 it was claimed that microform had almost disappeared. The most important trend had been and would continue to be the integration of microforms into larger information systems – growth would come from the disappearance of microforms by integration into systems where they were appropriate.

In 1980 Bernard Williams, a leading microform authority, wrote a defensive article in the face of what he called "microchip jitters". He claimed that a steady growth of about 20% per annum continued and that microforms had come into widespread use for the storage of business documents, providing several examples, and citing situations where microforms score:-

1. For storage and retrieval of engineering drawings, maps, plans, and similar documents.
2. As a third mode of computer output complimenting paper and online access.
3. For publications where demand in printed format would make production

uneconomic.
4. For utility publishing of parts lists, patents, theses, etc.

Williams admitted that although viewing devices had improved they needed to be better but considered that neither print nor microfilm would be easily displaced. He anticipated inroads from videotex and videodisc.

MICROFORMS – RETRIEVAL SYSTEMS

In the late 60s and 70s, the microform world received the impact of convergence, integrated circuits, compact reliable electronics etc., and this led to the production of a number of automated viewing systems. Typically they consist of an electrically operated magazine, "carousel" style, for holding a number of fiche cards, and a computer based indexing and retrieval system for selecting a fiche by means of a code associated with it. The fiche is then rapidly selected and projected from the computer-controlled carousel.

A carousel manufactured by Image Systems (IS) became quite widely used in a number of automated systems. For example the Daily Mirror newspaper group used ten IS carousels controlled by a Univac computer for a morgue file. About 15 "Telefiche" systems, made by Planning Research Corp., were in use in the US in 1979.

In this case characters from a fiche were digitized, the fiche having been selected from a remote terminal. Data was sent along a telephone line to be displayed near the remote terminal.

Various combinations of microform image systems, computers, telecommunications systems etc., have since come into use in which the microform element has become one component in several converging IT systems.

MICROFORMS – TYPES
Film

Microforms may be produced as image frames on 35mm roll film typically 30 metres long, contained in a cassette or cartridge. The film can be run through a motorized viewing machine which may have facilities for frame selection using a code, such as a bar code, signifying indexing terms which were filmed with the image.

The machine stops at those frames containing terms selected from a keyboard and a frame is reproduced at a convenient size for viewing by means of a light source, optical system and viewing screen. Some machines provide for the printing of a copy of the image.

Fiche

Alternatively microforms may be produce in flat film format. With Microfiche, the most common, a number of images are stored on a piece of photographic film, typically as a 6 x 4 inch film card. A popular reduction size is x 42 with 208 frames per card. Size reductions have been used down to about x 140 providing 3200 frames per card.

In a manually operated fiche-viewing machine the wanted fiche is roughly identified visually and the card, mounted on a movable carriage, is moved around beneath a magnifier until the required frame is positioned The magnified image is usually viewed on an integral screen.

Colour fiche

Colour fiche and colour fiche viewing equipment are available although not widely used. A x 24 reduction fiche at a processing cost of about 2 cents per frame is probably the most popular.

Computer Output Microfilm (COM)

The rate of production of microfiche can be increased by the Computer Output Microfilm (COM) technique in which images on a Cathode Ray Tube are successively microfilmed by a step and repeat camera at 250 frames per minute or more. The CRT is driven by a computer with software to control the generation of the images at high speed from date on tape.

Alternatively a film image may be created by a computer controlled laser beam writing on to thermally dry-processed film. COM fiche cards usually contain 270 images at x 48 reduction, or 208 at x 42. An eye-legible title is provided at the top of each card.

Computer Input Microfilm (CIM)

CIM is a term usually used to describe equipment which scans microfilm and converts the images to analogue or digital data to be telecommunicated for reproduction remotely or stored for further processing. Compuscan, Digiscan, IBM and others manufacture equipment for this purpose.

MICROFORMS – VIEWING EQUIPMENT

Modern manual fiche viewers are compact and many produce clear images, provided the filmed images are properly recorded, but it is not easy to produce a really portable high quality viewer.

In 1972 an ingenious attempt was made to overcome the portability problem by Izon. The Izon book-size viewing machine used 500 tiny lenses spaced about one inch from an image on film reduced 25 times. The screen was 7" x 9" and the lense system eliminated the need for the usual long optical path which determines the minimum size of conventional viewers.

It was thought possible to mass produce the viewer and sell it for around $5. By 1978 $6 million had been spent on R&D, and the selling price was expected to be $250 when mass produced. The machine has not been heard of since.

An elaborate machine called Mnemos said to have cost over £5 million to develop, appeared in 1982. It used a flexible transparent disc with a radial slot for access. Moire fringes recorded round its periphery were used for accurate positioning. A set of concentric rings of transparent microfilmed images at x 88 reduction were recorded upon it. An image positioned under a recording head was projected on to a viewing screen. It did not get into production.

Reader-printed 35mm roll film machines have been available for many years. The film is motor driven and is rapidly passed through the machine, stopping as instructed at a selected frame. Bar codes, sensed by the selection mechanism, are recorded along the edge of the film. The selected frame is magnified and projected for viewing and can be printed.

MICROPROCESSOR

The integrated circuit elements on one or more chips which form the Central Processing Unit of a computer. A microprocessor performs arithmetical functions and includes a control unit which will respond to a set of commands called an Instruction Set. The microprocessor industry is dominated by Intel with 58% of the market who sold over 20 million units in 1991.

At the beginning of 1992 a typical microprocessor chip contained 1 million transistors with spacings at 1 micrometer and an operating frequency of 33 MHz. In 5 years time it is expected that a typical microprocessor will contain 40 million transistors with 0.25 micrometer spacings operating at 250 MHz and including 4 Mbytes of cache memory and 64 bit instruction word lengths. It will operate at 1 billion instructions per second. See also MICROCOMPUTERS.

MICROSECOND
One millionth of a second. Abbreviation us.

MICROSOFT
An American software company who prospered following the acceptance by IBM of their MSDOS software, and who later developed another widely used software package called WINDOWS.

See also GATES, WILLIAM.

MICROSOFT DISC OPERATING SYSTEM (MS-DOS)
See OPERATING SYSTEMS.

MICROSOFT WINDOWS
See under WINDOWS.

MICROWAVE
Very short wavelength radio waves which are used for high capacity terrestrial point-to-point and satellite links.

MIDI
MUSICAL INSTRUMENTS DIGITAL INTERFACE.

See MULTIMEDIA – VOICE AND MUSIC.

Mil
One Thousandth of an inch.

Milli-
Thousandth.

MINITEL
See VIDEOTEX.

MIPS
Millions of Instructions Per Second.

MIS
Management Information System.

MIT
Massachusetts Institute for Technology.

MITI
Ministry for International Trade and Industry (Japan).

mm
Millimetres.

MNP [followed by a figure].
Microcom Network Protocol. The figure indicates the version (currently up to 9). A method of error correction introduced by Microcom is incorporated where bits are added to a transmitted message so that the receiver can detect errors. When detected, a repeat of the erroneous block is automatically demanded.

MMU
Memory Management Unit.

MODEM
Telecommunications signalling at either end of an analogue PSTN or leased line telecoms channel is performed by modems (MODulator DEModulators) which exchange data in a form suitable for transmission in the channel. Modems are driven by machines at either end – data terminals, computers, workstations, fax machines, videotex terminals, etc. These machines usually generate and receive signals in machine format and the modem converts machine signals to channel signals or channel signals to machine signals.

The cost of a PSTN "data call" is the same as the cost of a voice telephone call – in the UK according to the duration, distance, and time of day.

The connection to a "node", or inter-connection point, on a data network such as PSS, will normally be made via the PSTN or a special analogue line, so a modem will be required which will work satisfactorily with the modem at the node.

For special services, such as fast computer-to-computer communications, all-digital communications may be used. Conversion to analogue signalling is then unnecessary so either a "Baseband Modem" or "Line Driver" is required for short/medium distances. Short or long distance communications of this kind will probably be handled by proprietary equipment, networks, and protocols.

At one time modems were contained in grey boxes wrapped in a mystique fostered by the PTTs never to be revealed to subscribers. The closest the subscriber came to them was the bill showing the take it or leave it rental price. The arrangement had the virtue of simplicity with the disadvantage of high prices and out of date design.

The advent of liberalization or privatization brought with it the removal of the PTTs modem monopoly in many countries. The processing power and low cost of semiconductor chips enabled improved design at lower cost. The market became highly competitive. In consequence there is now a very large choice of modems, some at very low prices. New modems keep appearing with better performance at a lower price. The once simple arrangement has become a matter of difficult choices.

Modems are available for a wide range of speeds, but perhaps the most interesting development has been the introduction of improved modems for the PSTN. At one time it was thought that the PSTN could be used at up to 2400 bps, so modems were available up to that speed. Faster modems are available for better, more expensive, analogue leased lines. These work over a range of speeds corresponding to the maximum speed at which the grade of line for which they were designed can operate, in order to get the best cost advantage.

The theoretical "Shannon" maximum of the PSTN is 25 to 30 Kbps (assuming a signal to random noise ratio of 30 db) – a yardstick which will never be reached. However the size of the market has prompted some ingenious ways of getting every penny of value out of the PSTN by modem designs with speeds approaching 20 Kbps – thought to be impossible a few years ago.

Higher speeds are mainly achieved by data compression and working at more bits per baud; susceptibility to noise increases accordingly so error correction is included to reduce the effect of noise.

In the BTLZ method of compression, a "dictionary" of short fixed length codewords is compiled from high frequency strings of characters which are accumulated in a store as transmission proceeds. When a listed string re-occurs a short codeword is substituted.

MNP and LAP-M are different methods of dealing with errors. With MNP a repeat of erroneous blocks is automatically demanded. In LAP-M the quality of the line is monitored and the better it is the longer the blocks of characters which are checked and re-transmitted if erroneous. Predictive compression based on string occurrences is included.

In the Dowty/Case Trailblazer modem – one of the fastest – the frequency spectrum of the channel is divided into 500 bands. Having optimized the modulation method, message bits are distributed between bands according to each band's capacity, with a panoramic display showing the current bit rate for each band. Typically the modem works over an average PSTN link at between 15,000 bps and 17,000 bps.

A standard for modems which exceeds the speed standardized under CCITT V.32bis (14.4Kbps) is under discussion with the appropriate name "V.FAST". This is in anticipation of a more widespread introduction of modems of faster speeds. A new scheme called V.32 terbo specifies modems with speeds from 14,400 bps up to 19,200 bps using quadrature amplitude modulation. This recommendation will fill the gap up to the CCITT V.Fast standard which will specify a rate of 28,800 bps maximum.

MODEM – CHOICE AND CONNECTION

There are four major considerations when choosing a modem for PSTN use – price/performance, universality, low risk with average performance, and higher risk with high performance.

For price/performance the important considerations are cost per bit taking into account the modem and the telecoms cost, and whether the nature, traffic volume, availability of services from remote modems, and user's time saved justify a higher speed modem.

"Universality" means whether or not the modem is going to be used between points where it is known that other identical modems are situated. If that be the case modems using proprietary methods of compression, correction etc., may be a good choice. If all inter-communicating modems are the same model made by the same manufacturer it is quite likely that the claimed performance will be achieved.

If the modem is going to be used for general purposes, then something up to the V26 level seems to be indicated, on the assumption that most other modems will be compatible with yours.

In general, the lower the V number the more certain is it that the modem will work reliably and predictably, with a known performance. At the upper end, on the other hand, the market is in a state of flux. Proposed standards may not be confirmed, the large number of "features" on modems must prompt the question as to when and if their benefits can be realized, and more complex, just in production, equipment – whether it be cars or modems – tends to be less reliable. Is the claimed performance achieved under optimum or average conditions?

Bell Telephone and the CCITT set up standards independently in the early days, but latterly international standards have been set by the CCITT.

For many years a "standard" called RS232 (adopted by the CCITT as V42) sufficed to describe the interconnections between terminal and modem. It may still be encountered by users when they first get to grips with a modem.

There are three "classes" of modem user – those who become interested in telecoms after they have purchased their computer equipment and purchase a modem later, those who buy a modem incorporated with the computer at the outset, and those who are taken care of by technical expertise on tap so they don't have to be concerned with details like modems anyway.

A person who is not a computer buff should probably not buy a modem which is "bound to work" because the purchaser is assured that it "conforms to RS232C, the current version" and will "plug straight in to his machine which has a "RS232C socket at the back".

The chances are that it won't work and the user will fiddle about for hours trying to find out why, not knowing whether the "fault" really is in the connections, the modem, the telecoms software, the computer, or the call-up or logging-on procedure.

The reason is that the manufacturer may not have followed the connections specified in the standard so the modem may not match the machine to which it is connected. The best course of action is to get hold of an engineer with know-how and a "break-in" box. When the box is interposed between connections, lights come on indicating which lines are "high" and "low" (in voltage). This immediately tells the engineer about the state and correctness of the connections.

Some kind of emerging pattern of commercial adoption of new developments has to precede the setting up and ratification of a standard, consequently standards always lag behind the marketplace. Modem manufacturers are competing against the latest designs of other modem manufacturers, not modems made to the out of date performance specified in the standard. Consequently a manufacturer with a comprehensive range of modems attempts to offer modems both to the standards and to the "state-of-the-art".

MODEM – TYPES

The simplest type of modem – an Acoustic Coupler – is a small box which is connected electrically to a terminal, and to the telephone line via the telephone handset which is inserted into a shaped receptacle on the Coupler. The receptacle contains a microphone to pick up telephone line tones from the earphone fitted within the handset.

The tones are converted into digital signals. Digital signals from the terminal are converted into tones fed into a small loudspeaker to be picked up by the microphone in the handset.

Acoustic Couplers usually operate at up to a few hundred bps. Once popular because of low cost without the need for a special connection to the telephone line, their use has declined because of their susceptibility to acoustic noise, the now widespread use of plug-and-socket telephone connections, and the arrival of cheap direct-connect modems.

Modems on a plug-in board to be used in a PC slot are convenient and popular. Standard modem circuits are available on chips and a modem board usually contains two or three chips with a few separate components also mounted on the board. Alternatively, modems are supplied in free standing boxes with cable/plug-and-socket connections.

During the last year or two CCITT activities have speeded up to the extent that potential new standards get allocated a number in the V series sooner than they used to as a kind of indicator as to what is likely to happen. The V series of numbers is not devoted exclusively to modems. For instance V24 contains a list of definitions for data exchange lines between a terminal and a modem equivalent to the US RS232C standard; V42 is a recommendation for error correction, and so on.

The most notable advances include higher speeds (over the PSTN in particular), compression, error correction, and lower prices.

The technical advances should be considered together because they are interdependent. Higher speeds are mainly achieved by data compression and working at more bits per baud; susceptibility to noise increases accordingly. Error correction reduces the effects of noise. Compression enables more data per bit to be transported.

Compression starts with the adoption of the principle first introduced by Samuel Morse who noted the size of the stocks of letters and hence their frequency of occurrence, when visiting a local printing house. He designed the Morse code accordingly with E as ".", and Q as "- - . -". Today's codes follow suit.

Added improvements and complexity, are, as usual, enabled by cheap storage and processing power. In the BTLZ method, a "dictionary" of short fixed length codewords is compiled from high frequency strings of characters which are accumulated in a store as transmission proceeds. When a listed string re-occurs a short codeword is substituted.

Most error detecting/correcting systems are based on the automatic addition of extra bits to a block of a given number of data bits at the transmitter to enable a checking procedure to be carried out at the receiver. Effectiveness depends on the frequency of occurrence of the check bits in the transmitted sequence and on the arithmetical ingenuity employed in the "checksum". When an error has been detected, the offending sequence of data bits will be automatically corrected at the receiver, or (in simpler systems), the receiver will demand a re-transmission of the offending sequence.

The European market for modems was estimated at well over $2.5 billion in 1989, of which the UK's share was about $400 million. Growth is at about 20% per annum. British Telecom holds nearly half the UK market, followed by Dowty/Case with 24%, and Racal-Milgo with 10%. Prices have fallen at about 20% per year for the last five years in real terms. The impact of the Japanese is yet to be felt but there is as yet no indication when or if it will be felt.

MODFET

MODULATION DOPED FIELD EFFECT TRANSISTOR.

MODULAR
A method of assembly in which units of hardware, software, or devices are connected to form a complete machine.

MODULATION
A method of converting data from the form in which it is generated into a different form which enables it to be transmitted through a channel unable to convey the data in its original form. For example data pulses may be changed into audible tones which can be conveyed by the telephone network.

MODULATION DOPED FIELD EFFECT TRANSISTOR (MODFET)
A MODFET is characterized by an excess of free electrons in layers of GaInAs without doping with impurities. An applied external field modulates the mobile electrons.

It is claimed that various improvements in the device, invented in 1978, have made it the fastest existing semiconductor device. A problem due to parasitic charge modulation was removed when MODFETs were made using GaInAs thin films.

MONITOR
See DISPLAYS.

MONOCHROME DISPLAY ADAPTOR (MDA)
See DISPLAYING COLOUR AND GRAPHICS.

MONOPOLIES
See DEREGULATION.

MONTE CARLO ANALYSIS
A mathematical technique that (in the IT context) predicts the effect of statistical variations on circuit performance by randomly changing component values.

MOORE, GORDON
Gordon Moore originally worked with William Shockley who invented the transistor. Later he became one of the eight founder members of Fairchild who produced the first commercially available integrated circuit in 1959. In 1969 he and Robert Noyce established a company called Intel who produced the first microprocessor in 1971. Intel processors were guaranteed success by their adoption in the

IBM PC.
See also INTEL.

MORPHING
An automatic method of transforming one image into another as used in certain animation systems. The first and last objects are chosen, and the intervening sequence of images required to effect a smooth transformation are constructed by the system.

MORPHOLOGY
The study of form and structure.

MOS
METAL OXIDE SILICON.

MOSFET
Metal Oxide Semiconductor Field Effect Transistor.

MOTION VIDEO
See MOVIES, MULTIMEDIA and TELEVISION.

MOVIES
Film is, of course, a major information and educational media as well as being the media for "The Movies" – whether in cinemas or via television. Directly viewed pictures from 35mm film are of high quality; that quality is unlikely to get through when film is used on TV.

The problems of showing film on television include the aspect-ratio of film (bits get cut off the sides on narrower TV screens), dealing with the problem before it gets on to television by having to transfer from film to videotape centralising the action during the process, or having to use poor quality 16mm film, used for distributing copies, of about the right aspect ratio for TV.

If and when the public gets accustomed to the high quality of non-film HDTV, with digital wideband (wideband audio, that is) sound, and eventually with fully digitized picture transmission, the lower quality of material broadcast from film and shown on HDTV will become glaringly obvious.

The costs of making a film on 35mm stock, and considerations about making a profit from the showing of the film at the movies and from showing it on TV with acceptable quality, may bring about the radical change of making it on HDTV videotape in the first place. In the late 1990s perhaps cinemas will enjoy a short lived resurgence by showing Features from HDTV tape. It will be short-lived because the incentive of "getting out to see a big-screen movie" will diminish (but will not disappear because of the attractions of "going out") once you've got a high quality big screen at home.

Will "film entertainment" of the future be reduced to viewing videotape recordings on TV at home, 35mm film having become obsolete? Exactly how will the elaborate chain of creation and distribution in the existing film industry be affected? Will 35mm film still be used, but specifically re-designed for HDTV use or will it simply disappear?

See also MULTIMEDIA – MOTION VIDEO and VIDEO.

MPC STANDARD
MULTIMEDIA PC STANDARD.

See also MUSICAL INSTRUMENTS DIGITAL INTERFACE and MULTIMEDIA.

MPEG
Motion Picture Expert Group.

MP/M
Multiprogramming Control Program for Microprocessors. A multi-user operating system for microcomputers, derived from CP/M.

Ms
Millisecond. One thousandth of a second.

MS-DOS
MICROSOFT DISK OPERATING SYSTEM. See under OPERATING SYSTEMS.

MS-DOS MEMORY
See under MEMORY.

MTA
Message Transport Agent.

MTBF
Mean Time Between Failures.

mu
Microsecond.

MULTI-ACCESS
The ability for several users to communicate with the computer at the same time, each working independently on their own job.

MULTICOLOUR GRAPHICS ARRAY
See under DISPLAYING COLOUR AND GRAPHICS.

MULTIDROP LINE
A communication system configuration using a single channel on-line to serve multiple terminals. Use of this type of line normally requires some kind of polling mechanism, addressing each terminal with a unique ID. Also called multipoint line.

MULTIMEDIA
The word "multimedia" is used to embrace all manner of things. Successful multimedia applications include videodiscs and interactive video for training and education, video-conferencing, interactive videodiscs for marketing, and CD-ROMs in libraries.

If the meaning of a word may be discovered from its usage, then "Multimedia" means "The processing of information derived from or presented in several different media". "Hypermedia" appears to be a synonym for "Multimedia".

But "Multimedia" is a portmanteau word that "means what I choose it to mean" in the immortal words of HUMPTY DUMPTY. It gets tacked on to undeserving software packages to enhance their sales appeal. Following Humpty's precedent, I choose it to mean "the presentation of text and graphics with added "special effects" – sound, animation, and motion video with colour, but not (so far) smell".

The Multimedia "end-product" at the present time is usually a "multimedia presentation". Multimedia enhancements seem to add real value in educational and training, and it is in these areas where applications are appearing. The presentation of text with graphics, derived from several different "media" such as WORMS, CD-ROMs, scanners etc., may be labelled "multimedia", but multimedia now includes the presentation of information with sound, animation, and motion video as well as text and graphics.

In multimedia, extra dimensions of information are added to OBJECT – orientation so that the user employs all his or her senses in the exchange of information with the machine.

A multimedia system enables a television-type programme to be created. A system consists of a microcomputer, external "peripheral units" connected to it for storing and delivering data, software for running the system, and "application software" for controlling the sequence of data which constitutes the presentation. The professional appearance of the presentation depends on system facilities and the ability and experience of the creator.

A good route into multimedia is to use an Apple Mac micro-computer with a decent separate large-screen colour monitor. Software, plug-in boards of electronics for controlling peripherals such as a CD-ROM drive, a sound digitizer, a videodisc player, a video tape recorder, and possibly a page-scanner for inputting illustrations, may be appropriate as well.

Something simpler is available at a much lower cost – a Commodore CDTV, which includes a CD-ROM drive. A number of CD-ROMs, for instance children's stories providing for "user interaction", are available for it.

"HYPERCARD" software, supplied free with APPLE Macintoshes, is the system software on which many multimedia applications are based. A screen-full of information consisting of text or graphics is displayed as if on a card. The card is one of a "stack" of such cards. Any other chunk of information on any other card may be called on to the screen by selecting a labelled "button" with the mouse. Cards may include commands to operate peripherals when needed.

But the most expensive item, if properly costed, is likely to be user's time – including learning and creative time, both dependent on computer background knowledge. It would not be realistic to entrust a novice with the task. "Authoring" is a skilled task.

The easiest and quickest way to create a multimedia presentation is to buy a "data library" of text, music, pictures etc., to be stored on the peripherals, together with application software enabling you to select items from the library, string them together, and store them on, say, videotape, ready to provide a complete presentation.

The software will include a "stack of cards", including cards of information with already-labelled buttons for calling up other cards and for controlling and selecting data stored in peripherals.

See also MICROCOMPUTERS – MULTIMEDIA PC.

MULTIMEDIA APPLICATIONS – GENERAL

The potential exists to extend at least part of the public experience with all its drama and senses into the private world of the home. A visitor produced multimedia presentation which can be recorded at a public space site on to videotape can be taken home for viewing.

A multimedia system is proposed for the International Shakespeare Globe Centre which includes the re-built Globe theatre. The original Globe, built in 1598, was closed by the Puritans in 1642 and demolished to make way for tenements in 1644. Sam Wanamaker decided to rebuild it. A plaque on a brewery wall on the south bank of the Thames commemorates it. Rebuilding started in 1988 and Phase II is in progress.

The museum and research centre will be built on the site as well as the theatre. Some preliminary work on a multimedia system for use by visitors was done by IBM. Several modules were considered including one to provide general information for visitors, a second to assist students, and a third to provide for several research options.

This ambitious scheme received Apple encouragement and is gradually being developed. Historical advice has been supplied by Andrew Gurr, Professor of English at Reading University. Part of the design provides for the production of animations using *Macromind Director*. Another part will enable Shakespearian plays to be made available as multimedia presentations. The plays could, for example, be "edited" into various stage settings.

The recently announced "Multimedia Encyclopedia of Mammalian Biology" published by McGraw Hill, Maidenhead, UK, on CD-ROM, uses three TELCLASS-type thesauri under the primary terms "Taxonomic", "Biogeographic", and "Thematic", and embodies DVI. Sound and motion-video are available if you possess Windows 3.0 with multimedia extensions software and a DVI board. 300 clips of motion video with a total

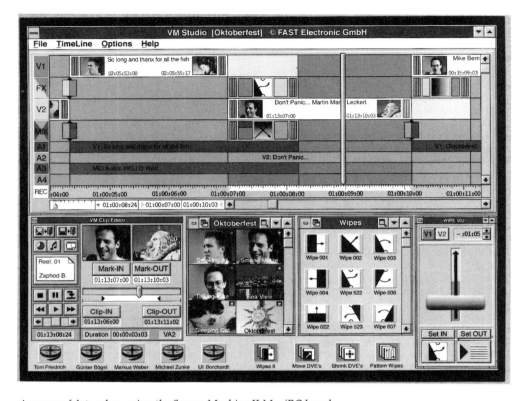

A screen of data when using the Screen Machine II Mac/PC board

duration of 20 minutes are included.

The Figure shows a screen from one of the latest boards – Screen Machine II, by courtesy of Fast Electronic, showing at the top electronic mail messages sent during the times marked along the scale. In the bottom half of the screen pictures with clipping facilities are shown and a choice of "wipe" operations with a "slider" to control the rate of the wipeaction.

According to a report produced by Ovum in 1992 there were only two significant multimedia business applications in 1991 – interactive training systems, and point-of-information/sale kiosks. By 1994 the applications will include multimedia enhancements for spreadsheets and WP packages, business presentation packages, and information packages which will include publications, databases and tools. By 1997 there will be two more applications – electronic mail packages, and groupware including videoconferencing.

Ovum's definition of a multimedia system is "a computer platform with software tools that support the interactive use of at least one of the following types of information. Audio, still image and motion video and all non-computer generated media that have to be converted from analogue format".

See also QUICKTIME and VIDEO.

MULTIMEDIA APPLICATIONS – MUSEUMS

There are over 10,000 museums and Visitor Centres in the US and Science Centres are visited by more than fifty million people every year. Multimedia offers to people working in public space a set of new tools to augment their 3D displays and a way to extend the experience of visitors to greater depth and other environments. Through access to interactive kiosks in museums, for example, it is possible for visitors to move from a glancing experience to a deeper involvement with an underlying idea.

The Smithsonian's "Information Age" multimedia exhibition is shown at the National Museum of American History on Constitution Avenue, Washington. It is appropriately housed because this part of the Smithsonian contains such relics as Morse's original telegraph, examples of Bell's first telephones, and the ENIAC computer.

The system has been running since May 1990. The visitor's inter-active PCs are linked by an IBM token-ring LAN. A number of the PCs embody touch-screen windows with choice provided by touching the image of a frame from a video clip.

Evidently the most popular program in the exhibition relates to code breaking. It runs on two stations. Visitors played it 314,564 times in the first year so it had approximately 471,846 viewings. With this program, visitors can encipher their name using a simulation of the German ENIGMA cyphering machine. They then decode it by remembering the machine rotor settings they used to encode it. Finally they can see actual German messages that were intercepted and decrypted during World War II.

The monitoring equipment, linked by an Ethernet LAN, handles the bar-coded guide used by visitors for logging-in to terminals, and is also used for checking operational status and collecting statistics about visitor's behaviour.

"Treasures" was designed in 1987/1988 from the data then available about CDIs. CDI players became available in the US at the end of 1991. Motion video has since become feasible.

From the description of CD-Is given elsewhere it will be noted that interactivity and motion is achieved by shifting relatively small amounts of new data on to the screen against a background of larger amounts of "old" data which changes infrequently.

This mechanism is not particularly useful for the "Treasures" presentation. The CD-I facilities for combining commentary, music, and text as used here, will enable users to change a limited number of full-screen images but this is still a considerable advance on standard CD-ROM.

About 150 "treasures" are covered in the form of audio-visual presentations with the best available pictures, a narration, and a soundtrack with music and sound effects which reinforce the interpretation of the object being presented.

A visitor may select a treasure by date, by museum, by category, or by associated person. A "tour" of several different sets of treasures connected by some common theme may also be selected. A CD-I was published for commercial sale in October 1991.

MULTIMEDIA – FUTURES

OASiS, a marketing company, visualizes a marketing role for multimedia – "Just think – you could store 20 5-minute videos of case studies, calling up the right one depending on the customer interest. It would run with explanatory text highlighting the product features involved in the video. It could then drill down into a full technical description, going to any level of detail, with additional video clips explaining any particular feature. A compact disc will store 72 minutes of compressed video".

The applications market is considered to be in Education, Training, Simulation, Internal and External Business Communications, Retail Product Information, Museums, and Domestic (Home). In education the "£2000 barrier" is important.

It has been concluded that growth of the multimedia "User-model" growth will be slow – 5 to 10 years for it to become pervasive, but for the "traditional-model" it could become an overnight success, like the Nintendo phenomenon, or alternatively it might remain a niche capability".

It has been forecast that by 1994, 18 multimedia applications, 22 "market segments", and 14 "end user platforms" will be in place. The major markets in 1994 (in current millions of dollars) will be Consumer 4337, Heavy Manufacturing 2211, Government 2055, Motion PIctures 1239, Education & Libraries 850, Computer and Information Services 450, and Retail Trades 352, Other 2103. Total $13,597 million.

The bones of the multimedia idea can be seen in the OBJECT-ORIENTED scheme incorporated in the Star machine devised by the people at Xerox's Palo Alto research labs in the late seventies. If a user is able to invoke the behaviour of an object on the screen which embodies certain properties of data, then the system may legitimately be called "object-oriented". The system interacts in a familiar, real world manner with the user, instead of imposing the mechanics of its hardware and software upon him.

In multimedia, extra dimensions of information are added to object-orientation so that the user employs his or her senses in the exchange of information with the machine. The situation is made to seem quite like the familiar real world environment, extended further by a multimedia application called VIRTUAL REALITY.

We may speculate about where this new phenomenon may lead. Perhaps MCLU-HAN'S vision is on the way to fulfilment. In one of his books, *Gutenberg Galaxy* (1962), McLuhan suggested that communications media determine the nature of social organisation. New media provide humans with new psychological-structural equipment.

Lewis Mumford thought that:- "by centring attention on the printed word, people lost that balance between the sensuous and intellectual, between the concrete and the abstract... to exist was to exist in print: the rest of the world became more shadowy". Mumford also thought that McLuhan was pressing forward in the interests of the military and commerce to a scenario where the "sole vestige of the world of concrete forms and ordered experience will be the sounds and images on the constantly present television screen or such abstract derivative information as can be transferred to the computer".

The boundaries between Information, Entertainment, Education and Commerce are becoming even fuzzier. It is already being claimed that Multimedia databases will radically change the way you look at and work with information". A database containing Binary Large Objects (BLOBs) may present you with any combination of data fields, images, and text objects and may contain spreadsheets, graphs, fax, object-code modules, satellite data, voice patterns, or any digitized data... it could be very large – up to 2 gigabytes".

The presentation of information about, say, houses for sale, could be accompanied by the sights and smells of the neighbourhood. Shareholders could receive clips on videotape showing the products of their company in use, with the annual report. A multimedia system could be a computerised entertainment centre combining the functions of today's audio and video systems, television set, games machine, and home computer.

MULTIMEDIA – HARDWARE

In 1990 Apple introduced the Mac IIfx with a 40 Mhz 68030 processor and 68882 co-processor, cache memory, and 3 auxiliary processors. This made the machine up to four times faster than the improved Mac II (the Mac IIx). Apple also introduced the 20 Million Instructions Per Second (MIPS) 8/24 GC display card, with a 30MHz RISC processor on board, providing 8 bit colour at 640 x 480 pixels, or 8 bit (256 level) grey scale at 1152 x 870 pixels.

The Mac II became the multimedia leader as the board slots opened it up to third party suppliers and a huge range of add-on hardware and software became available. As someone said, in multimedia applications the "Mac is doing what it does best – providing a consistent user interface, seamless data exchange, and gorgeous 24-bit colour graphics". In 1993 Apple announced new models, such as the Quadro, with greater power.

The Commodore Amiga microcomputer was noted for its colour before the Mac. It could also display video images from an external source synchronized to on-screen effects produced by its user ("Genlocking"). However for several years it has been eclipsed by Apple. But in 1990 Commodore made a strong bid to catch up with a new machine – the Amiga 3000 – having a performance nearly matching the Mac II at half the price.

The 3000 is a 32 bit machine with the same processors as the Mac IIfx – 68030 and 68881 co-processor – running at up to 25 MHz. The machine includes an enhancement of the Amiga special set of three controller chips which provide much of its multimedia capabilities. The "Agnus" chip is a graphics processor providing functions like fast drawing, filling, and moving blocks of pixels; "Denise" deals with computer and video resolution and scanning; "Paula" handles sound.

Memory is from 1 to 16 Mbytes, with internal hard disc up to 100 Mbytes. The screen displays 4 bit per pixel colour out of 4096 colours at 640 x 400 pixels. Four expansion card sockets are provided. A 200 pin socket is also fitted ready to accept a next generation 68040 processor. Ports are similar to the Apple II. In addition to its new Amiga version 2.0 operating system, the 3000 will also run Unix.

In August 1990 Commodore introduced the CDTV interactive graphics CD-ROM player/ microcomputer. CDTV disc preparation is much less expensive than preparing CD-I discs.

The CDTV is a CD-ROM player and integral Amiga computer with a 68000 processor and a set of ports including RS232 serial and parallel, external drive, stereo out, video out, composite video out, MIDI interface for music, and the usual ports for desktop peripherals.

There are several CD-ROM points of interest in the CDTV. First, a proprietary compression system – the importance of effective compression can hardly be over estimated. The capacity of CD-ROMs for the CDTV will be increased by using the six spare 8-bit control channels for graphics. CD-ROM sound technology is the same as CD sound technology.

CDTV "user authoring" will be developed, and professional authoring is well under way with suppliers of ready to use entertainment discs, using conventional mastering processes, coming to the market. The machine includes a 64 Kbyte card memory slot, but no floppy disc drive.

In 1993 Commodore launched the Amiga 3000T with a 68040 25 MHz processor, 200 Mbyte disc drive, 5 Mbyte RAM and 32 bit bus. It has numerous slots for external peripherals and sells for less than $3000.

At present the equipment needed to provide a fully fledged multimedia show is untidy and may be expensive. It may require a Mac ll with additional boards, CD-ROM player, videodisc player, videotape player, external sound amplifier, and loudspeakers, with assorted software, interconnecting cables, and the space to accommodate it all. This is the penalty for using a cobbled-together rather than a purpose-designed solution.

Most of the units are mass-produced for a competitive market. Only if the multimedia market becomes large enough are we likely to see a purpose-designed "one-box" machine. This approach has already been started with machines from Apricot and others. The design will have to be very ingenious to compete with the flexibility of choice provided by the present multiple-boxes multiple-software arrangements.

The separate units of a typical multimedia outfit are shown at the top of the Figure on the next page. At the bottom an IBM analogue multimedia system is shown. "5159" is a set of communications distribution ports while "FTM" represents a field TV network. An "F-coupler" merges TV analogue signals and digital signals from a LAN on the same cable. (These figures are reproduced by the courtesy of IBM).

The figure on p. 211 shows a PS/2 IBM Ultimedia machine incorporating XGA graphics, CD-ROM player, and multimedia presentation manager software and a SCSI controller for up to five external peripheral devices.

Another service which comes under the heading of multimedia is teleconferencing.

Digital Television rates for high quality colour pictures are normally over 200 Mbps, but British Telecom say that at the 2 Mbps rate used for teleconferencing using a CODEC, "it requires a keen eye to spot the difference between a compressed and a broadcast picture". This kind of compression must soon become more widely available for multimedia purposes and its effects will be considerable.

A colour frame as currently used is typically represented by about 1 Mbyte (8 Mbits) of data. At 30 frames per second, a run time of one second requires 30 Mbytes of storage. Compressed to 2 Mbps the run time would be about 2 minutes for the same amount of storage.

MULTIMEDIA – HYPERCARD CONTROL OF

Facilities for controlling peripheral equipment on which images are stored makes HYPERCARD, or one of the competitive HYPERTEXT products which are also available, a convenient and frequently chosen way of retrieving and controlling them.

Cards contain "buttons" which, among other things, may be mouse-selected and "clicked/pushed" to execute an external command or XCMD, routed through the appropriate "driver" (software compatible with particular external peripherals such as a videodisc player, CD-ROM etc.).

Hypercard was developed primarily for the manipulation of cards containing text, with

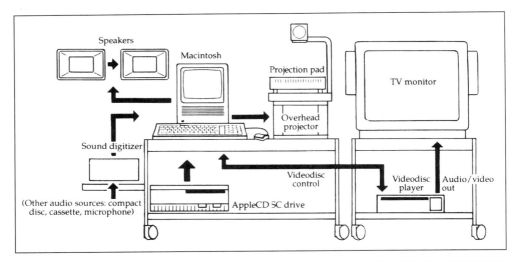

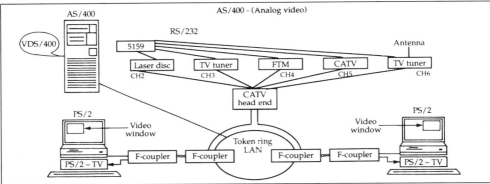

A set of multi-media devices (top) and an IBM Ultimedia system (bottom)

image-control as a bonus. The principle has been developed further for systems designed specifically to manage images and component parts of images.

For example with the *Macromind Director* multimedia software, the system is frame-based rather than card-based, with the means for controlling both external equipment and objects within a frame on the screen. The role of Director's "XObjects" is to a frame similar to the role played by Hypercard's XCMDs to a card.

MULTIMEDIA – MOTION VIDEO AND IMAGES

The major sources of still graphics or full col-our illustrations are scanned items, computer-generated graphics, and art of various kinds, either user-created or imported from other software. Video frames and motion video may be captured from television receivers or video cameras.

A Hypercard can contain graphics and illustrations in colour up to a size of 18" x 18", 1280 x 1280 pixels. If parts cannot be seen because the screen is too small, those off-screen parts may be scrolled on to the screen.

Animation – meaning usually relatively unsophisticated motion – may be created without excessive cost or effort. Greater re-alism requires more expense and pro-fessionalism. One way of making animation

IBM PS/2 Ultimedia machine

sequences is to create a picture, copy it on to second card, alter it slightly using Apple paint, copy the altered picture on to a third card, and so on.

Studio One from Electronic Arts consists of software for animation control from Hypercard stacks with XCMD driver control for loading and playing sequences. It includes the automatic creation of intermediate stages of smooth animation between two different scenes – which will save an enormous amount of time.

Video data in a given colour (the "key" colour) may be replaced with a different set of video data for adding special effects. To capture and digitize video frame-by-frame, a "frame-grabber" is used, and output frames with animation are added frame-by-frame under Hypercard control.

Presentations may be prepared using, for instance, the Overview window in Macromind Director – a program enabling most of the functions described above to be implemented. Event sequences including text, graphics, sound, transition effects, and animation are controlled with the aid of selection icons and a display of the complete sequence.

A separate good quality monitor is desirable for these operations and essential for some of them. Monitors, or more particularly

the CRT's inside them, continue to improve. The most popular currently are probably the 14" and 17" (screen diagonal) 640 x 480 pixel (IBM VGA resolution) monitors.

The line scanning speed of Mac II's normal 640 x 480 display is fixed but third party video adaptors offer alternatives, such as 800 x 560 for the 37" Mitsubishi monitor, with up to 1365 x 1024 pixels. Scanning speeds and frame rates are likely to be different for different monitors.

An auto-tracking monitor where the scanning rate automatically synchronizes is the best choice. Typical ranges are 30-57 KHz horizontal and 40-75 Hz vertical.

Capturing, processing, and outputting motion video on a microcomputer requires care. Motion video, usually in either NTSC or European PAL analogue form, may be imported from TV receivers, cameras, videotape or videodiscs.

Data is displayed on a TV CRT by smooth pixel-to-pixel changes of brightness and colour in direct proportion to the light reflected from the original objects. The NTSC system uses 525 scanning lines per frame repeating 30 (60 half interlaced frames) times per second. PAL uses 625 lines repeating 25 (50 half interlaced frames) times per second. Both systems use interlaced scanning in which the frame is divided into a field of odd-numbered lines followed by a field of even-numbered lines, providing 60 and 50 fields per second respectively, reducing the flicker which would otherwise be noticeable.

In computer systems, images are usually composed as an array of picture elements (pixels) represented by bit codes until they are translated for display on the CRT. The resulting colour differences between systems are the consequence of differences between TV and computer representations of pictures.

Incoming data must be digitized if it is to be processed by the computer user. If not digitized and not processed, it must be synchronized so that when combined with any internally generated data, the result may be viewed as a stable display.

Considerable processing power must be available to move very large numbers of bits if image changes produced by the user's processing and editing commands are to be viewed without delay and a monitor with appropriate resolution, scanning rate, and colour capabilities must be used for viewing the work. The presentation may be edited and recorded for repeat performances.

The main motion video function which can be handled using a Mac II with 4-8 Mbytes of RAM, at least 80 Mbytes of disc, a colour monitor, and a variety of third party plug-in boards and software, is the import of TV-standard NTSC or PAL motion video from a Hypercard-controlled video-videodisc player or a camera, to be displayed in real time in a window on the Mac's screen or on a separate monitor. The system is not fast enough to allow full-screen colour at TV resolution.

For a direct full-screen colour TV-resolution display of motion video, the monitor must be connected directly to a video source, such as a videodisc player, with the videodisc controlled from Hypercards, while associated material is viewed on the Mac's screen.

Mac text and graphics non-interlaced picture data are overlaid and synchronized ("Genlock"), with the imported interlaced composite TV signals (which contain all the synchronizing and picture data within the signal) and then the composite pictures in NTSC or PAL format, may be recorded on VHS, or S-VHS videotape for presentations elsewhere.

The tape may be used for mastering videodiscs for interactive presentations. The random access seek time for Level 3 Laservision-type Constant Angular Velocity (CAV) videodisc players with Hypercard control via an RS232 connector, ranges from 3 seconds, to 0.5 seconds for more expensive models.

A desirable feature in monitors for motion video is to get one capable of running from NTSC or PAL composite video signals, RGB analog, or RGB TTL. With these alternatives the monitor should cope with almost any requirement.

Motion video can be operated in Microsoft Windows with a software algorithm which runs on any PC containing an Intel 486 microprocessor and Microsoft Windows 3.1 operating system. Video files can be run at up to 25 frames per second in a small window. Compression is included in the software and the faster the CPU or accelerator the better the quality and the bigger can be the window.

The most recent (1993) plug-in boards claim to be fast enough to extend the power of their host machine to provide full-screen video at high resolution and at TV frame repetition rates. The suppliers of Screen Machine II for example, claim that the board will digitize PAL colour TV signals to YUV 4:2:2 and display TV frames at 640 x 480 pixels at TV repetition rates.

See also COLOUR, DISPLAYING COLOUR, MOVIES, TELEVISION.

MULTIMEDIA – PC STANDARD

A data and hardware Standard produced by the Multimedia Marketing Council for multimedia systems including sound interfaces. Several manufacturers adopted in late 1992.

MULTIMEDIA – PRESENTATIONS

A large amount of multimedia software is available of two kinds – that which comes with "ready to play" media, and that which is available for loading into a machine to assist in low-cost "authoring", that is for the creation of multimedia presentations.

Apple multimedia is often controlled by HYPERCARD.

Hypercard, or one of its more recent alternatives such as Supercard or Hyperdoc, is a convenient multi-media program to control a presentation comprising text, sound, music, voice, graphics, pictures, animation or motion video.

Multimedia interest in Hypercard centres on access to third party software. A Command is a Message containing a keyword which will cause the script for an object containing that keyword to be executed. A Function is some kind of instruction. External Commands (XCMD) cause a "resource", or code module, written in Pascal or Assembly language, to be executed by a command message. An XCMD can be used to control Driver software associated with an external device such as a videodisc player.

A resource has to be written by a programmer but when Hypercard-compatible devices, and software or special purpose software is used this is not necessary because the software includes ready-made resource code and driver and the XCMD can be installed in a Hypercard stack. The user may then create a button, labelled appropriately, to execute a script containing the XCMD.

See under HYPERCARD for more details.

To create a purpose-designed presentation using "own data", a more experienced operator able to assemble the data, and able to write the "scripts" (instructions for linking cards) may be required. As scripts consist of statements in English the operator will not need programming experience. Presentation-specific data created with the computer, such as text, captions, graphics, or scanned-in pictures may be enhanced with music, motion video, and other effects drawn from the library. Software is available to select, view, and combine the data.

A suitable outfit would comprise an Apple Mac with multimedia card, a CD-ROM drive, a Sony Video-8 tape recorder for data and motion-video storage respectively, and a conventional videotape machine for recording complete presentations. Hypercard with MacroMind Director or Mac- Mind Mediamaker software is recommended.

The Figure on the next page shows an "overview window" viewed during the preparation of a presentation using Macromind Director.

With another Macromind multimedia software package – Mediamaker – as the operator selects each data item to be used in the first part of the presentation, a "picon", or pictorial representation of it, appears in a small "window" on the screen. A screenful of picons acts as an index. An "assembly track", calibrated in minutes, is provided along the bottom of the screen.

An operator points at a picon with the mouse-controlled cursor and drags it into position on the track. The length of the picon on the track automatically changes to indicate data duration. The operator continues to "point and drag" creating a track composed of a succession of picons representing the content and duration of the presentation. To view the presentation, the picons on the completed track automatically pull the data which they represent from storage and display it in seamless continuity on a monitor. It may then be edited and replayed into a videotape recorder for future use.

According to a UK national newspaper "Organizations buying computer systems generally ignore the largest costs. . . the cost of disruption and training is commonly up to double the cost of developing and testing the software which is itself double the cost of the hardware".

To cover the cost of the technical effort and

expertise needed to acquire and use appropriate multimedia hardware and software, together with the time, and the artistic and creative effort of providing a presentation, the number should probably be doubled again. Multimedia processing, particularly motion video processing, is severely constrained by processing power. Sufficient power could become available quite soon. Graphics processing, which requires a dedicated computer within a computer, and compression hardware and software will also help.

In a recent review of *Macromind Director*, the writer says "The Overview Module allows business people to create excellent presentations easily", but in the same publication, the potential user of a multimedia board advertised as being for "reasonably knowledgeable people who aren't computer experts" found that "there was not one single sentence in the instruction manual that she understood".

Graphics processing, which requires a dedicated computer within a computer, is advancing rapidly. IBM claims that its PS/2 90 and 95 machines include "dazzling XGA (Extended Graphics Array) which provides a new standard in high resolution quality, conjured up in the blink of any eye".

However multimedia processing, particularly motion video processing, is still constrained by processing power. Real time graphics processing requires about 20 Mips, and rendering to produce photographic realism requires 300 Mips. Sophisticated compression must soon become available for multimedia purposes. A colour frame as currently used is represented by about 1 Mbyte (8 Mbits) of data. At 30 frames per second, a run time of one second requires 30 Mbytes of storage. Compressed to 2 Mbps the run time would be about 2 minutes for the same amount of storage.

MULTIMEDIA – SOUND DIGITIZATION

If sound is digitized, sound passages of any length may be represented on the screen as if the sound waveform was frozen, and all kinds of control and editing functions become possible. However the real, playable, sound, behind the screen representation of it, eats up computer storage space.

To digitize, the value (level) of the amplitude of the sound waveform is periodically

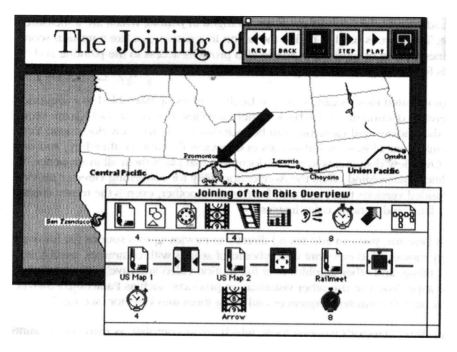

Overview window using Macromind Director

sampled. A 4 bit sample, providing 16 different values, would provide poor quality since there is insufficient data to properly reconstruct the wave-form; 16 bits are needed to provide high quality. If the sampling rate is too low, data between samples which should be digitized will be lost and the high frequency response will suffer. Sampling 22,000 times per second with 8 bit (256 levels) per sample produces digitized sound of quite good quality.

The figure shows the duration of a sound track and the storage space it occupies for several different values of the number of sound samples taken per second. The greater the number of samples the better the quality up to about 40K samples per second above which there will be little audible improvement.

If the sound amplifier and speakers are of high quality, and it is important to reproduce a piece of music with the highest quality, an increase of the rate to 44K 8-bit samples per second may be needed, requiring 1 Mbyte of storage for a 22.7 second recording.

The uninterrupted duration of a passage of sound stored in memory is proportional to memory size. If the memory is too small and must be re-filled from disc during the passage, there will be a break in the sound unless special measures are taken.

The Farallon Mac Recorder Sound System 2.0 outfit is a small electronic digitizing box which plugs into the serial port of a Mac for voice, sound effects, or music input.

Farallon's Hypersound software creates a stack with XCMD Commands to record or play sound. Sound Edit is an associated software package which provides a range of facilities including compression options, cut and paste sounds represented as waveforms on the screen, mix sound channels, alter quality, and so on.

MULTIMEDIA – VOICE AND MUSIC

The Mac II contains a small loudspeaker and also includes a stereo output socket for connection to an external amplifier and loudspeakers. Sound quality and cost considerations are the same as those applying to domestic hi-fi equipment.

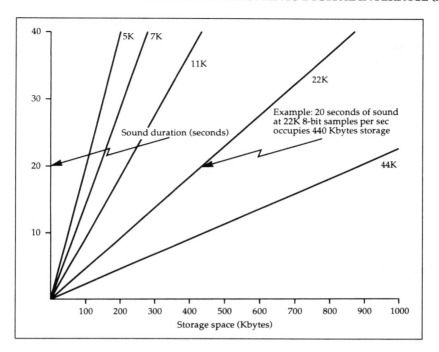

Sound duration, sampling rate, and storage

One way of adding sound to visual material is to use an Apple CD-SC drive, which plays CDs or the audio tracks from CD-ROMs, in conjunction with Apple Hypercard CD Audio Toolkit. The toolkit provides XCMDs for a stack to control the player by accurately selecting passages of speech or music from the disc. The CD-Audio Stack from Voyager., for example, will select tracks and automatically generate the selection buttons.

Musical instruments and synthesizers are another source of music; connection to computers has been standardized in the Musical Instrument Digital Interface (MIDI). Apple make a MIDI connector interface which plugs into a Mac serial port and also provide the driver and software to manage incoming sound. See also MULTIMEDIA – SOUND DIGITIZATION, MULTIMEDIA – PC STANDARD, MIDI.

MULTIPLEXER
1. A device which organizes the data from two or more circuits to be transported in a single telecommunications channel.

2. An electronic switch used in computers successively to connect a number of sources or destinations to a single bus. The switch may be multi-pole – for example it may connect data from any of several 8-line sources to an 8-line bus.

MULTITASKING
An operating system for undertaking several tasks at once.

MULTIVIBRATOR
An electronic circuit consisting basically of two transistors with the output of each coupled to the input of the other producing positive feedback. The on-off states of the two transistors depend on the coupling method.

MUSE
Multiple Sub-Nyquist Sampling Encoding.

MUSICAL INSTRUMENTS DIGITAL INTERFACE (MIDI)
A specification published by the MIDI Manufacturers Association in 1983 for sound

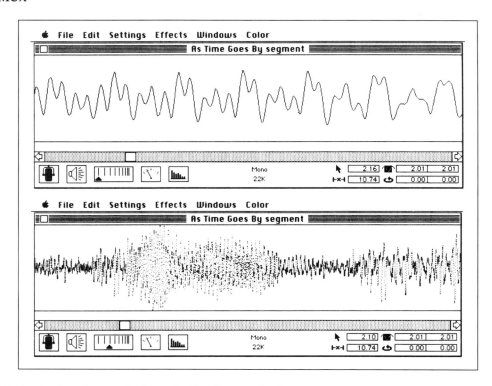

Display for changing sound when using Farallon sound-edit program

derived from synthesizers. It is a code which defines notes, their duration and synthesizer source details as a kind of music description language. A MIDI interface is needed at the input to a microcomputer.

See also MULTIMEDIA and MPC standard.

MUX
Multiplexer.

MVS
Multiple Virtual Storage.

N

NAPLPS
NORTH AMERICAN PRESENTATION LEVEL PROTOCOL SYNTAX. See under VIDEOTEX.

MNP [FIGURE].
Microcom Network Protocol. The figure indicates the version (currently up to 9). A method of error correction introduced by Microcom whereby bits are added to a transmitted message in such a way that the receiver can detect errors. When detected, a repeat of the erroneous block is automatically demanded.

NANO-
Thousand Millionth.

NARROWCASTING
Term used to refer to the aiming of programmes at specialised interest groups. It involves a step beyond "broadcasting", where programmes have to contain a mass appeal, and is technically feasible in broadband cable systems.

NATIONAL TELEVISION SYSTEM COMMITTEE (NTSC)
The committee which gave its name to the standard used in the United States based on 525 horizontal lines per frame at 30 frames per second. The US specification for a colour television frame is similar to RS-170, but includes colour data which is contained in a narrow segment of the frequency band occupied by the complete TV signal.

NBS
National Bureau of Standards.

NCC
National Computer Council.

NCR
National Cash Register.

NETBIOS
Network Basic Input Output System. A telecom protocol/interface for connecting IBM PCs, PS/2s, and compatibles to each other via a LOCAL AREA NETWORK. The protocol works by establishing a communication session between named stations. The sessions begin after Call and Listen commands are exchanged with a session number.

A 1Kbyte block of data is sent, and is received until the End of File block signal is transmitted. This procedure continues until the session is ended by a Hang Up command.

Netbios facilities include the provision for naming the LAN adaptor cards in machines connected to the network (in addition to the unique name provided by IBM for all adaptor cards) and a set of commands providing for the transmission of information to any other machine.

Netbios commands are hardware independent – they can be used with various networks e.g. Ethernet, Token Ring, Arcnet, etc., – and are also independent of LAN software such as Banyan Vines, Novell Netware, 3Com, etc., which include a Netbios interface.

NETWORKS
1. Library. Co-operative arrangement between several libraries, for example for borrowing or loaning books, or an electronic network within a library or interconnecting different libraries.
2. Telecommunications. General term used to describe the interconnection of devices (telephones, data terminals, exchanges) by telecommunications channels, e.g. public switched telephone network (PSTN), packet switched data network (PSDN), local area network (LAN), or wide area network (WAN).

A Telecommunications Network is a system consisting of communicating devices, such as terminals, an inter-connecting media, such as cable, and a means of establishing communicating paths through the media between the communicating devices.

Networks represent attempts to cater for the needs of people with information-intensive occupations, mainly in the business area. A *Managed Network* is a network organized and maintained by a telecoms organization on behalf of a client. A *Metropolitan Area Network*

(MAN) is a "Super LAN" fibreoptic ring operating at 150 Mbps or more over an area of about 50 Kms. More efficient within-site short-distance private networks designed for data exchange between terminals and computers called Local Area Networks (LANs) are now widely used.

LANs set up in different parts of the same site may be inter-connected, so a station on one site may exchange messages with a station on another. A LAN group on one site may be connected to a LAN group on a distant site by a suitable link able to convey messages satisfactorily over long distances. The arrangement is then called a Wide Area Network (WAN) – a label also applied to almost any type of long distance network.

MANs and LANs do not usually use switches to make fixed connections between stations for the duration of a message; instead, messages passing along the network contain address headers which are recognized by the addressed station which then captures the message.

Specialized types of network have been developed in the last 15 years (with the exception of WANs which came into use earlier), and new ideas are emerging almost daily. The main driving forces have been the arrival of compact, powerful, cheap technology and the need for business compunications which the PTTs have been unable to fulfil quickly enough.

The telegraph was displaced by the telephone network which uses dialling impulses to control an elaborate switching hierarchy in order to establish a connection between telephones. The system is usually run by a public authority. Private telephone networks consist of an internal exchange for inter-connecting telephones within one site, and lines leased from the authority to inter-connect exchanges on different sites. Later this system has become used for data transmission perhaps based on a Private Automatic Branch Exchange (PABX).

More recently still, Metropolitan Area Networks (MANs) have been developed to convey messages over intermediate distances – for example between LANs linked to other LANs in the same city.

A major objective in these various types of network is firstly, to make the network system transparent to the user. This means that a user sends a message to another, unaware of the complexity of the intervening media and of the routing procedure.

A second objective, particularly important when one user communicates with another in a different organization, say overseas, using equipment and networks supplied by a different manufacturer, is that in spite of these differences, messages may be satisfactorily exchanged. The objective of the international OSI effort is an attempt to make this possible.

A new phrase "Enterprise Network" has been introduced to describe a network providing access to all kinds of information via an organization's all-pervading network. For large organizations this means the provision of LANs on different sites in the same or in different countries inter-connected by a Wide Area Network. According to Laws, who quotes a KPMG Peat Marwick report:- "although 50% of IT investment goes on the desktop, less than 5% of the top 1000 UK companies have achieved complete integration of their computing environments".

The British Library internal telecoms system is a good example of inter-connection methods. It consists of a Case 6000 46 node LAN complying with GOSIP Standards at the R&D department at Sheraton St., London, linked by an IBM SNA gateway to the Blaise database in Harlow and a gateway to a 64 Kbps leased line to a UK publications database on a VAX at BLDSC, Boston Spa.

It includes other LANs and connections to mainframe computers. A Case 6000 series LAN at the Science Reference Service, Holborn with 50 nodes is gatewayed to the Sheraton St LAN via a 64Kbps leased line.

The whole system cost about £280,000 excluding PCs.

LANs are being taken seriously by library telecoms people. There will be a LAN in the British Library's new building at St. Pancras, London, for about 1300 users costing about £1.5 million including the cost of the fibreoptic backbone. It will include twisted pair spurs for Ethernet LANs, and Novell's netware will be used.

To implement the changes described above nationally and internationally, a tremendous effort is needed to introduce standards so that users operating a variety of different machines supplied by different manufacturers can communicate over a route comprising copper, fibreoptic, or satellite channels, with users at the remote ends possessing a motley collection of machines.

NETWORKS – ADAPTERS
A cable spur from a network connects to a card called an adapter card plugged into a microcomputer. The card contains the necessary intermediate components which work with "driver" software – that is software designed to work with the network being used – often to IEEE standards in order to satisfactorily connect the machine to the network. For example 3Com offers an adapter for IBM PC and PS/2 machines to connect to Ethernet, and a different adaptor for Apple Mac to Ethernet connection.

NETWORKS – APPLETALK
A telecommunications protocol designed to enable Apple machines to inter-communicate over a LOCAL AREA NETWORK.

Each machine on an Appletalk network is allocated a network number. Appletalk consists of three elements – the link access protocol which controls the mechanics of the CSMA/CD network, the Datagram Delivery Protocol which manages the communications between stations, and the Appletalk Transaction Protocol which controls the dialogue – for instance a file transfer request – between Appletalk stations.

Appletalk runs on an Ethernet CSMA/CD network or on Token Ring. Novell and 3 Com provide compatible networking systems so that Macs can be used as workstations and share data with PCs, Unix, DEC and IBM minis/mainframes.

NETWORKS – ASYNCHRONOUS TRANSFER MODE (ATM)
A protocol defined by the CCITT and ANSI for fast switching over wideband/broadband networks.

ATM uses a PACKET SWITCHING technology which can handle streams of data both at CONSTANT BIT RATES (CBR), such as audio and video data, and at VARIABLE BIT RATES (VBR). The technique is called CELL RELAY. ATM may be favourably compared with SYNCHRONOUS TRANSFER MODE (STM) which is likely to introduce delays into transmissions caused by error correcting or other procedures.

ATM FRAMES can accommodate a stream of data from STH sources. ATM processing works in two stages. The adaptation layer reformats incoming data into fixed length 48 byte chunks, adding a 5 byte header. The physical layer strings the cells into envelopes, adds additional framing data, and despatches it.

USER NETWORK INTERFACES (UNI) are likely to be provided for data communications running at 155 Mbps or 622 Mbps (approx.) or faster, over SONET fibreoptic channels. ATM transmission speed depends on the method of transport – for instance a system called FibreChannel will run at several rates in the range 100 Mbps to 1600 Mbps. The short length of ATM cells means that real time video and voice will be transmitted without problems.

With ATM no bandwidth is consumed unless the source is actually generating data so it can carry data in bursts or continuously equally well – it should efficiently handle text, facsimile, video etc.,

Eventually SDH/SONET will become available on the B-ISDN public network using the ATM protocol. During 1991/1992, 60 companies joined the "ATM Forum" in an attempt to speed up ATM developments and organise interoperability. See also TERANET.

NETWORKS – ATM
See under NETWORKS – ASYNCHRONOUS TRANSFER MODE.

NETWORKS – B-ISDN
BROADBAND INTEGRATED SERVICES DIGITAL NETWORK.

NETWORKS – BRIDGES
Bridges operate at OSI layer 2, the data-link layer, and connect networks with dissimilar protocols. Bridge functions have been substantially increased to connect LANs to WANs and manage traffic patterns.

NETWORKS – BROADBAND ISDN (B-ISDN)
The B-ISDN, a more ambitious concept than the ISDN, is a public network which will work at speeds of around 155 Mbps – adequate for digitized television signals. Further advances are planned with the introduction of the Syn-

chronous Optical Network (SONET) with a foreseeable maximum speed of 2.4 Gbps.

The outcome of these developments is expected to provide integration of multiple electronic media which will allow for the full range of communication capabilities ranging from telemetry and voice at the low end to HDTV at the upper end, stimulating the extensive use of high resolution image communications and high speed data exchange between computers.

The B-ISDN will require a much larger investment than the ISDN in different lines and techniques. The most likely method of transmission (protocol) will be ASYNCHRONOUS TRANSFER MODE (ATM) which will be its major protocol, to be carried by the SONET transport system, both as described elsewhere.

It is assumed that the B-ISDN will require interconnection via an Network Node Interface (NNI) to a SONET-type monomode fibreoptic network with special switching, and that subscriber rates will start at 155 Mbits per second. This immediately raises questions about the time it will take for the existing narrow-band copper subscriber loops to be replaced by fibreoptic or other fast loops to convey data at this rate and the enormous investment required to install it.

NETWORKS – GATEWAYS
A network interconnecting device. A Gateway can work at any of several OSI layer levels. The most sophisticated works at OSI layer 7, the application layer, and so (for incoming messages) can handle data which has passed through all the OSI layers. A Gateway may handle several different kinds of protocol. It can, for example, interconnect a network running on an IBM protocol, and another running on a non-IBM protocol.

NETWORKS – INTEGRATED SERVICES DIGITAL NETWORK (ISDN)
The CCITT's definition of ISDN is "a network evolved from the telephony network that provides end to end digital connectivity to support a wide range of services, including voice and non-voice, to which users have access via a limited set of standard multi-purpose interfaces". Preliminary world standards were set in 1984. It has taken until 1992 for its slow development to lead to many applications,

controlled as it is by the policy of the PTTs, not by market demand. Meanwhile it soon will be facing competitive alternatives.

The ISDN is a concerted PTT attempt to provide a switched communication system from an Integrated Digital Access (IDA) point, to a Network Terminating Equipment (NTE) point, via an Integrated Digital Network (IDN) which will use digital local exchanges.

It is a CCITT-Standards project for telecommunication networks employing digital transmission and able to handle digitized voice and data on an "end-to-end" (subscriber to subscriber) basis.

In the UK, "System X" exchanges with the appropriate facilities are gradually being installed and the system is being "overlaid" – that is gradually being substituted for – the existing PSTN. The objective is to enable subscribers to use all-digital voice and data services. Subscribers can opt for an NTE providing IDA channels for two 64 Kbps voice/data, usually arranged as one for digitized voice and the other for data, and an 8 Kbps signalling for control purposes. The relaying of cables from subscribers to local exchanges is not necessary since existing lines have the necessary bandwidth.

Heavy voice/data users can opt for a multiline NTE providing 2 Mbps of total capacity made up of 30 64 Kbps separate channels, typically for the connection of Private Automatic Branch Exchanges (PABX) to the IDA.

There is a severe "critical mass" problem which inhibits the widespread adoption by business users, the information-conscious section of the public, or the public at large, of a new "information network" which somehow has to get itself into a "take-off" situation long since surpassed by the telephone system.

The number of telephone subscribers far exceeds the critical mass needed to encourage new subscribers to join. Potential subscribers know that they will be able to talk to a significant fraction of the world's population should they install a telephone.

The ISDN is ultimately supposed to become a National and International Network. The general opinion of non-PTT commentators seems to be that it has been developed too slowly, that little attempt has been made to market it, and that its supposed virtues are inadequate and may be overtaken by other schemes able to work at the higher speeds called for today.

The present network provides two subscriber options :-

* Basic Rate Access: 2 64Kbps "B" channels for data or voice, and a "D" signalling channel. Typically one B channel would be used for digitized voice and the other for data.
* Primary Rate Access: 30 B + 1 D channel (Europe), 23 B + 1 D channel (US).

The Broadband ISDN is a future concept providing two data speeds of 155 and 620 Mbps.

The public ISDN network represents a transformation stage of the telephone system into a wideband data network, where the data may be speech, text, graphics, halftone or colour images, or motion video.

Several of the world's major PTTs are in the process of converting the telephone system into a subscriber-to-subscriber ISDN data system without interrupting existing facilities.

Data circuits in multiples of 64 Kbps will be offered – 2 circuits and a signalling circuit to subscribers currently served by their twisted-pair telephone wires to the local exchange at a speed which most lines will handle (2 x 64 + 16 = 144 Kbps), and 30 circuits plus signalling (about 2 Mbps) using blocks of lines or special cable for subscribers with heavier traffic.

A 64 Kbps circuit will be used either for digitized speech or data. A typical domestic terminal will consist of a PC with special plug-in card or a purpose designed terminal which will use one circuit, and a digital telephone which will use the other. Consequently, for instance, two subscribers could talk to each other and at the same time exchange diagrams, illustrations, etc., between terminals, the necessary control signals being exchanged over the signalling circuit.

Later the intention is to introduce the broadband or "B-ISDN" with speeds of around 155 Mbps – adequate for digitized television signals. Further advances are planned with the introduction of the Synchronous Optical Network (SONET) with a foreseeable maximum speed of 2.4 Gbps.

Although the ISDN has still made little impact in the US, the next stage is being confidently forecast. "I expect broadband ISDN to be economic on a parity basis probably around late 1993" says a Bell South spokes-man. In spite of that a more reasonable forecast seems to be that the ISDN may arrive in the late nineties if it is not overtaken by something better, and the Broadband ISDN early in the two thousands. However it would not be impossible for the ISDN, or something like it, to arrive sooner over an embryo existing wideband network – the Cable-TV network.

At one time it seemed that the ISDN presented the best prospect for the creation of a critical mass of data and information service users, but it has proceeded extremely slowly. In the UK, British Telecom has not made an appropriate marketing effort. The Department of Trade and Industry (DTI) sponsored an ISDN Business Application Forum, but then decided that ISDN applications were not a national priority and shut it down.

However a CEC sponsored European ISDN users forum, which first met in September 1990 in Brussels, appears to have got off the ground. The ISDN cannot live without users. "Until the equipment suppliers and public network operators that have driven ISDN developments for the last two decades realise this and ensure an adequate role for users in standards, applications, and tariff definition, the market uncertainty that has dogged ISDN will not end" says a commentator. Moreover the ISDN has limitations in respect of the volume of data needed to be transmitted, particularly images, because it will be too slow.

In the UK (and probably in the most other countries), for higher speeds it will be necessary for the foreseeable future to make special arrangements with BT (e.g. for Kilostream/ Megastream service) or with Mercury for private channels, since a publicly accessible network working at speeds exceeding 64 Kbps will not be available until the "BROAD-BAND" or "B-ISDN" arrives much later.

Between service points a number of 64 Kbps Primary Rate Interface (PRI) channels may be MULTIPLEXED within a single channel in accordance with the CCITT G732 FRAMING standard. Signalling on channel D is carried in a time slot on the G732 frame. 30 channels multiplexed together provide a signalling rate of 2.048 Mbps. Further multiplexing is carried outon trunk networks at up to 1920 channels for a total bit rate of about 139 Mbps per second. Multiplexing employs the principle of SYNCHRONOUS TRANSFER MODE (STM) and the SYNCHRONOUS DIGITAL HIE-

RARCHY (SDH) described elsewhere.

The ISDN with STM multiplexers based on accurate timing were considered to be a reasonable way of extending and modifying facilities on existing telephone networks to provide for faster signalling rates without any basic reconstruction work.

The "Internationalization" of the ISDN requires system standardization and then implementation by stages. The connection between AT&T in the United States and France Telecom was first made in 1988, to be followed by a connection between France Telecom and Deutsche Bundespost Telekom. Interconnection between a number of other European countries, including the UK, followed during 1991.

By March 1992 most of the applications were voice, but about one third were to do with data communications – for instance for bridging between LANs at 64Kbps. The third most popular application was video conferencing following progress in standardisation and compression.

A number of different devices are available for ISDN ranging in cost in the UK between about £500 and £1500. Some come as cards enabling a PC to be used for ISDN work, others are in self-contained boxes.

NETWORKS – INTELLIGENT

A term, coined by the Bell Organization, indicating that a range of easily selectable services will be available over a network. It may include the provision of a Private Virtual Network, that is a switched network of the type normally only available in a private line system, but whose costs are closer to the costs of a public network. Such a network would include the facilities of an ISDN network, with enhancements.

The phrase has come into use to describe the facilities which are expected to evolve with these networks. The network will embody the necessary circuits and software needed to control and deliver the kinds of services permitted by the much wider bandwidth.

Central databases will control a wide range of network services such as billing and credit card services. When a customer initiates a toll free or credit card call, it will be intercepted and managed by the signalling network which directs it to a centralized database. The database handles the call and returns it through the network to the appropriate switch for completion. The network provides "intelligence" centralized in databases and its features are no longer solely dependent on resident network hardware and software.

NETWORKS – INTERNET

Internet consists of over 500 wide-area networks interconnecting local area networks. The backbone WAN is ARPANET and the network protocol is TCP/IP.

Internet is claimed to be the largest network in the world providing connectivity among up to half a million computers and over a million people. It is devoted to supplying information for research, but was not intended for the general public or commercial use although it is now becoming more generally available.

In 1990 a Bill passed a Senate committee directing the National Science Foundation to promote development of information services over the National Research and Education Network. The proposal includes the provision of about $400 million to develop a network operating at a data rate of 3 giga-bits/second or say about 600,000 pages of A4 text per second.

NETWORKS – ISDN

See under NETWORKS – INTEGRATED DIGITAL SERVICES NETWORK.

NETWORKS – LIBRARY

A "Library Network" often means a library resource-sharing cooperative, not necessarily a number of libraries connected to a computer network. Library networks in the general sense have been functioning for many years simply because few libraries can supply the needs of clients from their own stocks and it makes sense for smaller libraries to make their combined stocks available to all their clients.

Computers were adopted by library networks to make their task easier and in due course enabled other resources to be shared as well as book or serial stocks. A small network, NELINET, was operating between five New England University libraries in 1968. Requests to computers in a central office were made from terminals in outlying libraries for catalogue card production, book labels etc.

The Library of Congress has been a library-system leader in the US, but its activities were matched by the Ohio College Library Center, which became the Online Computer Library Center (OCLC Inc.) and aggressively introduced several innovations. Another leader in the US was Research Libraries Information Network (RLIN). Both these organizations have been active in developing library systems and networks.

But Hildreth in two comprehensive articles reviewing the "dreams of bibliographic utilities" says that they never materialized because of the trend towards decentralization. Local integrated systems, local resource sharing, and the knowledge about computers acquired by librarians provided very strong competition. The utility's response has been to develop new networked services and license their software to others.

The arrival of computer-based integrated library systems encouraged the use of within-site LANs for sharing various resources, and the use of LANs in a small number of libraries in the UK and US was reported by Levert. Other applications included the support by a large public library of its services at its branches, the provision of special software access for clients, and arrangements for access to a catalogue from networked micro- computers.

NETWORKS – LOCAL AREA (LAN)

The selection of a LAN includes the choice of the type of network, the plug-in card to enable a PC to connect to it, and the operating system software which controls network operations. Widely separated LANs may be interconnected by leased lines which in many cases need be capable of speeds no higher than 64 Kbps. Various offerings are available in this country from BT, Mercury, and Cable companies at this and higher speeds. in the US a T11.544 Mbps link is widely used.

The major types of LAN protocols are Contention and Token Ring. The first contention LAN, called ALOHA, was developed at the University of Hawaii around 1972. Ethernet, developed by Robert Metcalfe at the Xerox Palo Alto laboratories in the mid seventies, became a commercial leader. It interconnected Alto computers – precursors of the Xerox Star from which was descended the Apple Macintosh.

Ethernet uses Carrier Sense Multiple Ac-

cess with Collision Detection (CSMA/CD) transmission. Message data travels in packets at up to 10 Mbps round a single cable and are received only by the station to which they are addressed. All stations listen and only transmit when the cable is clear. In the event of two stations transmitting at once, one or other jams the network, waits for a period of time of random length, and then tries again.

Early Token Ring or "Token Passing" systems were developed at the University of California at Irvine and at Cambridge University. Empty data packets circulate and a station wanting to transmit detects empty packets, enters an address and data, and empties the packet after reception when it next comes round. All stations examine all packets, accepting only those addressed to them. IBM and Microsoft support ring LANs; Arcnet, another major supplier and LAN pioneer, sell ring LANs operating on a slightly different principle.

A token is a 24 bit "invitation to transmit". Once captured, a station attaches a "frame" to it. A frame consists of a header followed by the message of up to 4500 bytes. Long messages consist of several tokens/frames. After the frames have been received by the station to whom they are addressed and have circulated back to the sending station the frames are eliminated leaving empty tokens available for re-use. A number of non-message frames to do with management and control also continuously circulate round the ring.

Low and medium speed *wireless* LANs get rid of the cabling problem and enable workstations to be easily sited in the most convenient positions. *Radio* LANs may require a licence and are liable to interference, but are better for the higher speeds. *Infrared* LANs are less expensive, but are obstructed by line-of-sight obstacles.

There used to be considerable controversy about the merits and capacity of competitive LANs and they were classified according to topology or protocol. Now that data rates have become faster they tend to be divided according to speed – Low/medium: 10-20 Mbps, High: 50-150 Mbps, Supercomputer: 800 Mbps (proposed), and Ultragigabit (proposed): 1000-10,000 Mbps.

NETWORKS – LOCAL AREA (LAN) – FIBRE DISTRIBUTED DATA INTERFACE (FDDI)

Characteristics of typical LANs
(Abstracted from Farena, 1990)

LAN Name	Supplier	Type	Protocols	Speed (bits\sec.)	Max. Users
3+Open Manager Advanced	3 Com	Ethernet, Token Ring	XNS, Netbios TCP/IP	10M	Unlimited
Vines	Banyan	Ethernet, Token Ring, Arcnet	X25 Netbios TCP/IP SNA	10M	Unlimited
IBM Token Ring	IBM	Token Ring	Netbios Netware TCP/IP	4-16M	Unlimited
Zlan 10E	3 Net	Ethernet	Novell Netware, DECnet 3Com 3+	10M	1024

NETWORKS – LOCAL AREA (LAN) – FIBRE DISTRIBUTED DATA INTERFACE (FDDI)

As speeds have increased there has been a strong trend towards the use of fibreoptic inter-connecting cable in spite of remarks about over-kill. An "inter-operability" centre set up to test different LANs at the University of New Hampshire, USA, had already acquired 28 FDDI vendor members by the end of 1990.

FDDI, the Fibre Distributed Data Interface – an American Standard (ANSI) X3T9.5 – was agreed in 1990 for operations at up to 100 Mbps. A particular requirement is the connection of LANs, which may be working at relatively slow bit rates, to an inter-connecting tively slow bit rates, to an inter-connecting fibre main "backbone" cable for fast transmission over relatively long distances.

FDDI stations use cheap Light Emitting Diodes (LEDs) for the transmitting element and PIN Field Effect Transistors (PINFETs) for reception. An FDDI network consists of two contra-rotating rings for increased reliability.

The Standard is comprehensive. For example it specifies minimum signal levels for receiving units and the permitted attenuation of signals in the network in order that errors shall be kept to a minimum. It also covers reliability – for instance "self-healing" by automatically by-passing any faulty station. It includes a requirement for built-in network management.

Characteristics of fast LANs
(Abstracted from Gerla, 1991)

Name & supplier	Data rate Mbps	Media	Max no. stations	Max. cable length, Kms	Protocol
Concentrator 5000 DEC	100	Fibre	500	200	FDDI
Fibretalk 3000 Integrated Networks	100	Fibre	500	100	Token
Altair Motorola	15	Radio	32 per cell	–	Random access
PS32-132 Network systems	800 & 1600	Fibre	64	10	New (Framing)

FDDI is having severe birth pains mainly to do with agreement over compatibility between systems. Systems have been installed but network management Standards await ratification. This is delaying the growth of FDDI networks.

NETWORKS – LOCAL AREA (LAN) OPERATING SYSTEMS

IBM's NETBIOS was the first network operating system and was designed primarily to enable DOS-based PCs connected to a relatively small LAN to access print or file servers.

A number of software products with limited operating systems, mostly running LANs at up to 2 Mbps have been described by Udell who says "if you are looking for ways to build small to medium-size work groups, read on".

More comprehensive systems usually run on a server and arrange for users to access network resources in such a way that the access mechanism is "transparent". It appears to the user, working on his own application with his own computer operating system such as MS-DOS, OS/2, etc., that he or she is accessing files, databases, etc., in his or her own machine.

The operating system should ideally be able to run on servers using well known databases such as SQL relational systems, be able to connect to equipment on the network made by various manufacturers using various protocols as it is added to the network, and be able to support the major transmission standards such as Ethernet and Token Ring – in other words to cope with an environment which is becoming more and more OSI-like and which will ultimately be OSI compatible.

Two types of operating system dominate the market – Novell, who recently bought in to Digital Research for £72 million, are alleged to have 75% of it with its Netware operating system, and Microsoft's Lan Manager 2.0 has most of the remainder. Suppliers/systems include Netware 386, Banyan Vines 4.0, 3Com 3+Open, etc.

3Coms's 3+OPen LAN Manager network operating system, for example, based on Microsoft's LAN Manager, will work in conjunction with DOS, OS/2 operating systems and applications, and Macintosh applications. It will also run network services such as electronic mail and network management.

By including an operating system in inter-computer communications a user will be able to do much more than simply exchange files. In effect a remote machine on a network appears to the user almost as if it is his own machine. Traditional 3270 terminal emulation and basic file transfer is replaced by arrangements where the mainframe looks after the corporate database, and networked workstations provide user-friendly information presentation.

It was said that 60% of PCs will be connected to a LAN by 1992. LAN networking, or any kind of networking for that matter, introduces several new considerations. A fairly heavy memory overhead is added to participating micros and unless they are sufficiently powerful, operations are likely to be slow.

For accessing databases outside the networks a shared gateway is required with enough ports to provide adequate service per user assuming that some maximum fraction of users will require simultaneous service.

Once two or more users are able to access the same file, all users except the user making changes must be locked-out until they are completed. In the case of shared access to a database, special arrangements need to be made if lockouts are not to seriously slow-up access. Methods include locking out on an individual record basis, read locks for queries and write locks when the database is being up-dated, or better still, lockouts on a row by row basis.

Such arrangements require database reorganization – for instance the database and the database management software reside in a server, while each PC contains a database user interface.

NETWORKS – MANAGEMENT

Network Management usually means the inclusion of the necessary monitoring facilities to enable faults to be diagnosed and reliability maintained. But it can also mean controlling other machines or facilities on the network from a "host" machine for "one-to-many" (or vice versa) sessions such as teacher control of machines in a class of pupils.

The most well known system is the Simple Network Management Protocol (SNMP) developed for the real world of TCP/IP networks. OSI people are beavering away at the OSI compatible equivalent CMIP (Common Management Information Protocol) but it will be a long time a-coming.

At least 30 different SNMP software packages are available. Each arranges for a dedicated machine, which must include a good GUI (Graphics User Interface), nominated the "Network Management Platform", to be used by the manager for monitoring the state of the network. The software arranges for data like network topography, traffic levels, errors, faults, etc to be displayed. The human Manager can customize display modules to include, for instance, a building plan showing wiring and stations.

The latest standard – FDDI – specifies that certain facilities be built-in to the FDDI adaptor cards used on communicating stations. A form of automatic network management is used in FDDI networks; if a fault or discontinuity occurs, the ends of the contra-rotating rings are automatically connected together in a few milliseconds on either side of the fault.

FDDI is being held up over certain other aspects of network management, as explained under NETWORKS – LOCAL AREA – FDDI

NETWORKS – METROPOLITAN AREA (MAN)

A Metropolitan Area Network is for distances not exceeding about 50Km. Token-ring is used at lower speeds. Fibreoptic cables with FDDI are usually used for those MANs which operate at up to about 100 Mbps.

The US standard IEEE 802.6 covers Switched Multi-Megabit Data Services (SMDS) for MANs working at 100 Mbps and upwards. As their title implies, MANs are intended for medium-distance across-city use.

NETWORKS – PEER-TO-PEER.

Peer-to-peer means communication between similar devices on anetwork. IBM Netbios for DOS PCs on a LAN, for instance, enables one PC to access a disc or printer belonging to any other PC.

NETWORKS – PERSONAL COMMUNICATION (PCN)

A new generation of cordless telephones called CT2 was developed in the UK and later the idea spread to the United States where there were a large number of applications to the FCC for licences. A user would be connected to the public network via his portable telephone and antenna (aerials) along major highways, thus providing wireless access to the PSTN. Later, Ericsson introduced a third generation system called CT3 which included two way calling.

In 1991 a UK licensee called Unitel supplied a test group with handsets and a simulated service. They estimated that there were nearly 8 million households as potential users. The trials indicated that there could be 1.8 million households who would actually use the system.

In 1993 the FCC is likely to allocate frequencies of 900 MHz and 2 GHz for personal communications.

PCN is intended to provide communications over a wide area. Accordingly the access network of fixed radio stations are placed in cells in a similar manner to existing cellular radio. CT2 was planned as a low cost digital system for speech in localized areas.

The Digital European Cordless Telecommunications (DECT) system is a development of CT2 able to run on the ISDN and working in the 1880-1900 MHz band. The DECT standard was finalized by ETSI in July 1992. Each European country which is a member of the EC must make the frequency band 1880 to 1900 MHz available for DECT system. These could include business or resident applications, mobile radio or personal communication services.

GSM 900 is a complete network system for Pan European Digital Cellular network operating on a 890-915 MHz band uplink, and 935-960 MHz downlink. The appropriate standards for GSM were approved by ETSI in 1990 and incorporated in the DCS 1800 standard. The standard provides various options and design alternatives.

See also GROUPE SPECIALE MOBILE.

Personal Communication Networks will fit in somewhere between Mobile Cellular Radio and Telepoint. Telepoint's success will be badly affected unless it is well established before PCN arrives.

In fact PCN appears to be a much improved Telepoint. The system will be quite similar to Mobile Cellular – radio handsets, base stations in cells, and network accessing and interconnecting services. The range of the pocket-size radio handsets will be shorter so there will be more cells – perhaps including individual short-range cells covering a household or a farm.

Personal Communication Networks progressed from idea to development work to service licensing in a remarkably short time. In January 1990, the UK Department of Trade and Industry (DTI) awarded PCN licences to Mercury/Motorola/Telefonica, British Aerospace/Matra/Millicom/Pacific Telesis/Sony, and Unitel formed by STC/US West/Thorn EMI/DBP Telekon.

PCN users will carry cheap portable radio telephones communicating via the PCN basestations. The companies just mentioned are re-thinking their positions because of slow take-off. The technology has not yet been fully worked out – but that does not deter the forecasters.

It has been estimated that the European market will be worth £635 million by 1995, with the UK taking 43%, France 11%, Germany 8%, and others 38%.

NETWORKS – PUBLIC TELEPHONE (PSTN)
In the public telephone network any station is connected to any other by a *switch*. large organizations may own a network of lines leased from the telephone authority, for example to carry heavy traffic between sites.

NETWORKS – REPEATER
A device operating at OSI level 1 to extend the range of a LAN.

NETWORKS – ROUTER
A device which interconnects LANs using identical protocols conforming to OSI layers 1-3. It usually embodies software capable of determining the best route for interconnections (OSI layer 3) from information contained in a packet.

It can handle several connection paths and determine least cost paths. A "Brouter" includes some of the functions performed by a bridge.

NETWORKS – SATELLITE
The Inmarsat-C network operates via 8 Inmarsat satellites and special ground stations where incoming data is stored and converted from Inmarsat-C format into a format suitable for the ground sender or vice versa. This is a store-and-forward-process which may take a few minutes for completing message delivery. Each subscribing user's terminal

is allocated its own number and only messages addressed to that number will be received. New terminals must be commissioned into the system and appropriately tested.

NETWORKS – SERVERS
A dedicated file-server or client-server is usually a fast micro-computer or larger machine with large memory and disc capacity connected to a network with sufficient power to "host" a database for the use of network clients using their own machines, or to provide storage of sufficient capacity for the files of network clients.

The idea is that a shared resource of this kind should be a considerably less costly solution compared with the possession of comparable facilities by individual users. A non-dedicated file-server is a lower cost alternative where a workstation acts as a server as well as functioning as a user's workstation.

If a powerful PC is used, a number of users can access it at the same time with some degradation of performance. For example in throughput tests of a Storage Dimensions Filemaster II machine, the speed degradation when there were 4 users instead of 1 was 41%. The Filemaster II contains a 33 MHz processor and 4 Mbytes of memory with cache and two 150 Mbyte discs.

NETWORKS – SMDS
Switched Multimedia Data Service. A service proposed for use on MANs.

NETWORKS – SNMP
Simple Network Management Protocol. A multi-vendor protocol originally for TCP/IP systems management, now being extended.

NETWORKS – SONET
NETWORKS – SYNCHRONOUS OPTICAL NETWORK.

NETWORKS – STM
NETWORKS – SYNCHRONOUS TRANSFER MODE (STM).

NETWORKS – SYNCHRONOUS DIGITAL HIERARCHY (SDH)
The synchronous digital hierarchy is based on multiples of 155.52Mbits as the standard bit rate. SDH is expected in due course to grad-

ually replace STM bit rates. SDH leads to the standardization of an NNI.

Since SDH is not based on element timing, it does away with a considerable disadvantage inherent in the STM system where supposedly synchronous bit rate multiples are not in fact exactly synchronous and have to be brought into synchronism by bit stuffing, or "plesiochronous" methods. Dummy bits have to be added in order to make up elements of the right length to ensure synchronization. With SDH no re-synchronization of this kind is necessary.

NETWORKS – SYNCHRONOUS OPTICAL NETWORK (SONET)

Sonet is an ANSI interface standard for synchronous data transmission at a hierarchy of speeds commencing at 51.84 Mbps and going up to 2488.32 Mbps. Sonet will probably be used as the transport layer (see under OSI) in the B-ISDN with ATM protocol.

Sonet uses SDH channels to carry ATM-based data, embodying ATM's various advantages. In other words the new SDH digital hierarchy devised for Sonet will be able to carry data based on the old STM hierarchies.

A Sonet FRAME carrying ATM-based structures consists of an "overhead" section, and a data load section within which the ATM-based data is carried.

The new synchronous digital hierarchy based on 155 instead of 154 (approx.) Mbps, calls for a new standardized unique Network Node Inter-face (NNI) for subscriber connections.

NETWORKS – SYNCHRONOUS TRANSFER HIERARCHY (STH)

A family of digital synchronous transfer channels recommended by the CCITT. Channel capacities are 2.048Mbps (30 channels), 8.448Mbps (120 channels), 34.368Mbps (480 channels), and 139.264Mbps (1920 channels).

NETWORKS – SYNCHRONOUS TRANSFER MODE (STM)

A method of transmission controlled by accurately synchronized timing impulses. Each signalling element is FRAMED by a sequence of timing impulses from which terminals can also derive their synchronization.

STM is associated with MULTIPLEXED channels because in the commonly used Syn-chronous Time Division Multiplexer (STDM) signalling elements from multiple sources are accommodated by allocating specific time slots in the multiplexed stream to each data source. STDM is inefficient for sources which send data intermittently because time slots will then be unoccupied. This inefficiency in the STM fixed rate transfer method may be improved by buffering, or matching to the characteristics of the source channels.

STM and STH may be gradually replaced by SDH if and when SONET becomes widely used.

NETWORKS – TCP/IP

Transmission Control Protocol/Internet Protocol. Introduced by the US Department of Defense anticipating, and for the same purpose, as OSI – to try and standardize methods.

NETWORKS – TOKEN RING

A network architecture configured on the basis that each station (node) on the ring awaits arrival of a unique short sequence of bits (a token) from the adjacent upstream node, indicating that it is allowed to send information toward the downstream node. The network is configured in a manner that ensures that only a single token is present on the ring at one time.

This method of transmission is used in LANs where a station wishing to transmit awaits the arrival of an empty packet. Packets circulate round a ring channel in one direction. A station receiving a packet addressed to it copies the data, and the packet circulates to its transmitting station. The station checks it for errors, removes it if correct, and re-tries if not.

There are several variations of the method, notably the "slotted-ring" and the "permission token ring".

NETWORKS – VIRTUAL CIRCUIT

An arrangement for user end-to-end exchange of data over a network without a switched connection.

NETWORKS – VIRTUAL PRIVATE

A *Virtual Private Network* appears to be the brain child of the US Sprint Communications company who run a long distance fibreoptic network in the USA. They have teamed up with Cable & Wireless, owners of the North

Pacific and PTAT Atlantic cables, to offer a 64 Kbps ISDN-like service, aimed at multinationals. One stop billing and integration with private networks will be included, and users will appear to be using their own international network.

Many businesses already have extensive private networks. The requirement of a Virtual Private Network (VPN) is to get at least the facilities currently obtained by using leased lines but at a lower cost. A VPN includes dynamic bandwidth allocation purchased on a "pay as you use" basis as an alternative to paying for dedicated lines which are only occasionally used at full capacity.

NETWORKS – WIDE AREA (WANs)
A *WAN* is any network covering a wide area – for instance a private leased line network.

In the commonest type of telecommunication network – such as the telephone network – any station is connected to any other by a *switch*. A network does not have to be switched. Large organizations may own a network of leased lines to carry heavy traffic between sites, for instance carrying LAN-originated traffic.

Two examples of WANs are shown on the next two pages. The first shows the British Library Network, reproduced here with their permission, as it is now before consolidation within their new centre. It consists of a number of LANs in London and Yorkshire, each with numerous PCs connected to it, with the LANs interconnected with bridges and 64Kbps private lines.

The second Figure, by courtesy of Spider Systems, illustrates the use of Spider equipment for interconnecting several types of network.

NEURAL NETWORKS
See COMPUTERS – NEURAL NETWORKS.

NLM
National Library of Medicine.

NLQ
Near Letter Quality.

NMOS
n-type Metal Oxide Semiconductor.

NNI
Network Node Interface. See under SONET.

NODE
A computer or switching device situated at connection points on a communication network to monitor, switch, or attach communication channels.

NOISE
Unwanted signal. Interference caused by random electron motion, or by the intrusion of signals from external electrical equipment.

Electrical noise is manifested as a hiss in audio equipment. It produces errors in data transmission where noise signals may be mistaken for data signals. Electrical noise is of four kinds – thermal noise, flicker noise, shot noise and popcorn noise. Thermal noise is generated by the random motion of electrons in resistors; flicker noise is associated with emission from a hot surface such as a heated cathode; shot noise is generated by charges moving within semiconductors, and popcorn noise is a popping noise which is probably due to impurities within semiconductors.

Noise value is usually expressed as the sum of the RMS values of the different noise sources in volts. Much noise is of the "white noise" type which means that it is generated over the entire frequency range of the equipment; accordingly the wider the bandwidth the greater the noise level.

"Thermal", "Gaussian", or "White" noise is a fundamental property of all electrical circuits. This type of noise manifests itself in audio-frequency circuits as a steady background hiss which may be almost inaud-ible, but often becomes obvious on long distance circuits. The noise voltages generated are normally small compared with "signal" voltages – that is those conveying information – and do not cause trouble.

The telephone network is a complex of cables, switching devices and other equipment some old, some new. Bad contacts at switching points cause noise, so do the impulses caused by dialling which can break through by inductive coupling from one line to another.

Non-telephone electrical equipment and electrical storms can also cause impulsive noise. It is this kind of noise, heard as clicks and crashes which may go on intermittently

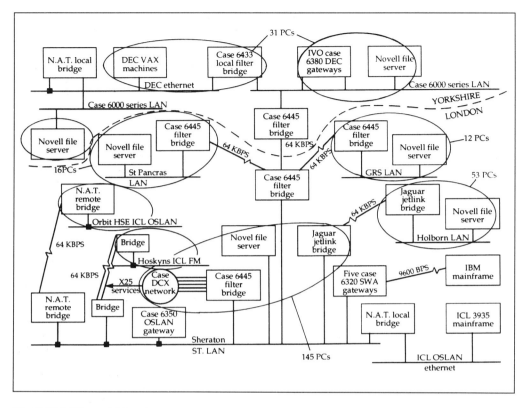

The British Library Network

in the background, or may make conversation unintelligible, which causes problems when telephone lines are used for data transmission.

One remedy is to "dial again", in which case you may get rid of the fortuitous string of "noise generators" present along the first chain of connections. The newer the equipment along the way the less the impulsive noise. One reason is that the metal-to-metal sliding contacts which have been used for many years are being replaced by better devices or "contactless" switches – e.g. semiconductors.

The PSTN was designed for voice and not much useful information about the level or nature of impulsive noise on it is available. Speech may be acceptable in the presence of noise because of redundancy in the language, or you can ask for a phrase to be repeated. That same noise level could well result in an

unreadable word, line, lines of print, or portions of an image.

On private lines leased from the PTT noise levels are lower. The number of inter-connections is smaller and in the case of UK Tariff T (Schedule D), the impulsive noise limit is specified at a lower level. But it is not as simple as that because in the UK BT specifies impulsive noise as "not more than 18 impulse noise counts to exceed the threshold limit in any period of 15 minutes" for its private lines. Presumably any or all of those impulses could cause trouble. No information is provided about impulses on the UK PSTN where noise is likely to be much worse.

NORTH AMERICAN PRESENTATION LEVEL PROTOCOL SYNTAX (NAPLPS)
See VIDEOTEX.

NOYCE, ROBERT N.

Noyce was born in 1927 and with others founded the Fairchild Semiconductor Co., and later Intel. He developed integrated circuits and the planar process for transistor manufacture.

NRZ

Non-Return to Zero.

Ns

Nanosecond. One thousand millionth of a second.

NTSC

NATIONAL TELEVISION SYSTEM COMMITTEE.

NUI

Network User Identifier.
  See SONET.

NYQUIST RATE

Harry Nyquist was born in 1889 and died in 1976. He did some pioneering work on communications and holds numerous patents for transmission systems. He published a seminal telecommunications article specifying the maximum signalling rate achievable over a communication channel – 2W bauds is the maximum element signalling rate for certain reception through a channel of bandwidth W Hz (the "Nyquist Limit"). 1/2W is known as the Nyquist Interval.

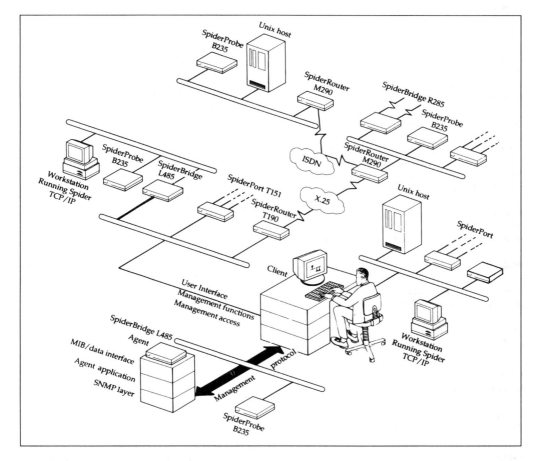

A network interconnected by Spider equipment

O

OBJECT CODE
The machine code used for running programs on a computer. Programs are not now written in the object code. They are automatically translated from a higher level language which is converted into the object code when a program is run. See also COMPILER.

OBJECT ORIENTATION
Object-oriented ideas were incorporated in the Star machine devised by the people at Xerox's Palo Alto research labs in the late seventies. If a user is able to invoke the behaviour of an object on the screen which embodies certain properties of data, then the system may legitimately be called "object-oriented". The system interacts in a familiar, real world manner with the user, instead of imposing the mechanics of its hardware and software upon him.

In an ideal object/orientation system objects would not be related to other objects so that they can be easily changed into a different part of the program. An object consists of data, and a set of operations which can be performed on the data. By passing a message to the object one of its resident operations can be performed upon it. A property called Inheritance is associated with classes of objects. Thus once a car object has been placed in the system, all other cars will inherit certain functions of a car such as engine size, rate of acceleration, etc.

OBJECT ORIENTED DATABASES
See under DATABASES.

OCC
Other Communications Company.

OCLC
Ohio Computer Library Centre.

OCR
OPTICAL CHARACTER RECOGNITION.

ODA
OFFICE DOCUMENT ARCHITECTURE.

ODBS
Optical Disk Based System.

ODETTE
Organization for Data Exchange through TeleTransmission in Europe. It controls automative industry EDI message standards and file transfer protocols. Now being adopted in allied industries. See also EDI.

OEM
Original Equipment Manufacturer.

OFFICE DOCUMENT ARCHITECTURE (ODA)
The ISO ODA recommendation is related to X400 and is compatible with it. ODA caters for the efficiently coded representation of multimedia documents – that is a mixture of text and raster or bit map images such as graphics or illustrations. ODA software is used to format documents for transmission at the time they are created. To format a document already in page form, pages will have to be first presented in electronic form for format tagging.
ODA defines:-
* Characters representing written text.
* Geometric shapes, lines, curves etc., for drawings.
* Raster graphics for facsimile or other images.
The ODA standard defines graphic element and control functions, how elements are to be positioned, and provides the means for transforming content into the correct layout structure by reference to a set of attributes.

OFFICE SYSTEMS
See INFORMATION – MANAGEMENT entries.

OFTEL
Office of Telecommunications.

OLE
Object Linking and Embedding. A way of individually designating different parts of a document as objects so that they may be

treated in different ways.

ONA
Open Network Architecture.

ONLINE
Connected to a computer.

ONLINE SYSTEMS – INDEXING
See INDEXING – ONLINE SYSTEMS.

ONLINE SYSTEMS – SEARCHING
See DATABASES and FILES.

OPAC
Online Public Access Catalogue.

OPCODE
An instruction for an operation to be carried out in a computer program.

OPEN SYSTEMS INTERCONNECTION (OSI)
See STANDARDS.

OPERAND
The quantity or function upon which an operation is performed in a computer program.

OPERATING SYSTEMS
An operating system consists of a suite of utility programs which perform computer management functions and organize and allocate the resources of the machine to deal with Jobs. A Job is simply a sequence of processes several of which may be in progress concurrently – for example an overlapping of computational and input/output processes. The operating system handles peripherals and interrupts and deals with errors.

It controls the computer system, manages the memory, and the various processes for file operations and file maintenance. Other important functions include management functions in a microcomputer development system and in machines on which several programmers can work simultaneously ("multiuser" machines).

See also NETWORKS – OPERATING SYSTEMS and WORD LENGTHS.

OPERATING SYSTEMS – APPLE SYSTEM 7.0
Apple recently introduced its answer to OS/2 – System 7.0. It includes Inter-application Communications Architecture enabling another Mac anywhere on a network to extract a file from a particular host computer and send it in a specified format. Macs can work simultaneously as servers and clients on all-Mac networks. The System 7.0 communications toolbox handles hardware, e.g. drivers to emulate different terminals, and also alternative protocols. User selection is made very easy – you simple choose the Apple "folder" icon labelled with the required terminal or protocol.

System 7.0 includes an interesting "publishers update system". A named document can be broadcast to "subscribers" on the network from a Mac, and subsequently that document can be automatically up-dated by broadcast from the originating Mac to the subscribers.

Mac-DOS-Mac file transfers are relatively easy when software such as WordPerfect, Pagemaker, etc., exists (as it does) in both Mac and DOS versions because both versions use the same file formats. Otherwise file conversion is necessary. Additional software is needed for Mac/DOS printers. This combination can be useful if a DOS user wants to use, say, a MAC laser printer.

OPERATING SYSTEMS – DOS
In 1980 Bill Gates bought the rights to a Disc Operating System from a local company and in 1981 made a deal with IBM that so that his company, Microsoft, would develop the operating system for the new IBM personal computer. At that time CP/M-80 was the dominant operating system for 8 bit computers and MS-DOS maintained the appearance and main functions of CPM-80, but was written for the new 16-bit processors.

Several functions made the system far more flexible – in particular the directory structure allows the user to group files containing similar information in separate directories, and to move from directory to directory when the user specifies a path across the filing system's tree structure.

Another feature of MS-DOS is the facility for creating a set of commands which run automatically each time a system is started up in order to put all parts of the operating system into required modes of operation. Another major feature of is the BIOS section of

MOS-DOS which is described under that heading.

Later, a number of changes and additions were introduced – version 1.25 added support for double sided discs, 2.0 provided for a hierarchical file structure and hard discs, 3.0 supported 1.2 megabyte floppy discs, 3.1 higher capacity hard discs, 3.2 Microsoft networks and 3.5" floppy discs.

Version 3.3 was issued with some improvement to support IBM PS/2 machines, version 4.0 supports hard disc partitions greater than 32 Mbytes and version 4.01 is a debugged version of 4.0.

In mid-1991 DOS version 5.0 was issued. DOS 5 can be installed over the top of earlier versions and has been tested far more extensively to minimize complaints about bugs. A major advantage is that for machines using an 80286 processor or above most of DOS 5.0 will run in the HIGH MEMORY area of EXTENDED MEMORY providing more room for running application programs, so that an extra 45 Kbyte of RAM is available for applications (See under MEMORY).

The DOS 5.0 shell includes a presentation of files and directories as icons in a tree structure and applications can be implemented by pointing and clicking. A sophisticated new help system has been added and there are a number of other improvements.

DOS 6.0 arrived early in 1993 with two major improvements – compression and memory management. Compression will nearly double the amount of data which may be stored on disc. The memory management makes better use of High Memory.

It is said that there are now about 100 million installed copies of DOS worldwide, with about 4 million in the UK.

The major difference that ex-CP/M users will find between CP/M and DOS are the file organizations – DOS is hierarchical (a "tree" structure) CP/M is not. This allows for files to be grouped together in several directories. The "root" directory for WordPerfect 5.0 is called "WP50".

If the system was being used by two people where "WP50" is the name of a Word Processing software package, each with their own sub-directories and files, the "tree" would look like this:-

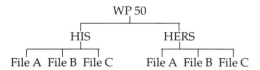

A file is located by its disc and by its "path" through the tree described in a specific manner. Thus the path for "HIS" file B on drive C would be "C:\wp50\HIS\file B". This is how the file must be identified from the DOS prompt. If you are working with a sub-directory already, say "HERS", and you want "file C" the path is simply "file C".

OPERATING SYSTEM 2 (OS/2)

Operating System 2 was developed for XT-286 and PS/2 computers with up to 16 Mbytes of memory based on 80286 or 80386 processors.

OS/2 is a complete 32 bit operating system with a graphical user interface for which there have so far been 5 versions – 1.0, 1.1, 1.2, 1.3 and 2.0. OS/2 requires a machine using a 32 bit cpu – that is an 80386 or better. The memory requirement is 4 Mbyte with a 60 Mbyte hard disc. OS/2 2.0 is a multi-tasking operating system with concurrent task processing, all applications running in protected modes.

DOS and windows applications are supported as are OS/2 and windows multi-media extensions. OS/2 2.0 uses an object oriented graphical interface resembling the Macintosh interface. It can manage far larger memories than DOS; its physical memory can be up to 4 Gbytes in size and it will manage 512 Mbytes in a virtual OS/2 session.

OS/2 was introduced by IBM in 1987 with the emphasis on communications. The meaning of multi-tasking is self evident; a processor schedule may be set up by the user – for example with high priority for interactive use and low priority for a lengthy routine programme. Spreadsheet re-calculations can be proceeding in the background while new data is being entered.

As another, perhaps more important example, at least one application can be running with communications in progress as well. In "protected mode", applications are kept separate from each other and from the operating system.

The extended edition of OS/2 followed some months after the main launching date. It includes a database manager and a communications manager. For the moment it is one of the most complex existing operating systems for small computers, occupying 20 Mbytes of disk storage in total.

The database manager includes an SQL (Structured Query Language) relational database engine and a front-end application Query Manager.

The goal of the communications manager is to allow an OS/2 workstation to interact simultaneously with several other systems. With such a workstation you could check a number of things at once – for example, parts inventory on a mainframe database via a 3270 link, a customer database on another OS/2 system on a local network, and stock prices on a COM link to Dow Jones News Retrieval, says one observer.

OPERATING SYSTEMS – UNIX

A multi-task multi-user operating system designed at the Bell Laboratories. Unix, with its Microsoft version Xenix for the IBM/AT is gradually becoming more widely used. It features special access and security.

Unix is a 80286/386/486, 68000, or RISC 16/32-bit multi-tasking multi-user operating system. Developed at AT&T, it is claimed to be outstanding for software development with many built-in tools, and very good for advanced text preparation and choice of terminal types by "virtual terminal" selection.

Other virtues include its ease of transfer of applications ("portability") across machines with different architectures, the fact that it is ready for LAN and WAN communications, and, of course, its multi-user facility. Its disadvantages are its lack of operational messages and its complexity.

A Unix-to-Unix communication subsystem for automatic file servers, E-mail, remote printing etc., are part of the system and the only extra needed is a modem. File sharing among users takes place in such a way that different machines can combine their file systems and users can work with any files in any machine regardless of its location.

Unix seems to evoke strong comments. One user says "Unix is a pain to work with..., has never made the slightest concession to the user..., was developed by programmers for programmers. It offers no significant applications", but another says it "displays models on a computer with as much detail and flexibility as in the mind... most impressive graphics performance can't be measured by benchmarks.. will emulate DOS but even the most complex DOS program would seem wimpy by comparison".

However Unix is steadily becoming more successful. The Unix Systems Laboratories supplied the technology to China in 1992, and in that year Unix became more widely used in IBM and Hewlett-Packard computers.

OPERATIONAL AMPLIFIER

A direct coupled amplifier whose performance is a function of the amount and method of application of negative feedback.

OPTICAL CHARACTER RECOGNITION (OCR)

A process where a device scans printed or typed characters and converts the optical images into machine readable data, usually ASCII code.

A patent for an OCR machine was granted in 1809, but the first useful machine was invented in 1983. The machine was able to read single font typewritten documents and produced punched-card output. Today OCR software often comes with SCANNER software which otherwise provides a bit-mapped image of characters.

The recognition method may be by matrix matching, in which each character location is considered a matrix of elements within which lie the pixels representing the unknown character. The software matches each incoming unknown character with a set of stored reference characters and generates the appropriate ASCII code if there is a correct or nearly correct match.

An alternative method of recognition, called feature analysis, is to specify a character as a set of component features formed of loops, diagonals, vertical and horizontal elements etc. The unknown incoming character is matched against each specification and the best match is selected as being that of a particular character.

For example Omnipage software costs about £500 and rapidly recognizes a wide range of fonts. More specialized OCR machines and/or software such as Kurzweil

OPTICAL COMPUTERS

Discover include expert system software for separating text from graphics, for splitting ligatured characters, and for resolving ambiguities by matching doubtful words against word dictionaries.

OPTICAL COMPUTERS
See COMPUTERS – OPTICAL.

OPTICAL DISCS
Optical discs offer large storage capacities and the increasing demands of software and data storage have made them increasingly popular. CD-ROMs (preceded by CDs), WORMS, Magneto-optical, Floptical discs started to receive attention in the late nineteen eighties. Analogue laser videodiscs, led by Philips Laservision, will provide about 30 minutes of TV standard playing time per side.

However the introduction of the mass produced CD musical entertainment player has been the basis for a family of players using the same or a very similar technology. The most widely used optical drive and disc in IT is the CD-ROM.

A CD-ROM basically consists of holes punched by a laser in an aluminium layer and is read by a low-power laser. A floptical depends both upon initial heating by a laser and on the polarization of light being changed by magnetic effects on light reflected from an aluminium layer.

A WORM (Write Once Read Many) offers gigabyte storage capacity in sizes up to 14" in diameter.

Re-writable optical drives carry discs of either 3.5 or 5.25 inches in diameter. Their capacities run from about 100 Mbytes up to about 1 Gbyte. Many are based on magneto-optics. A laser heats up a spot on the disc enabling the magnetic polarity to be altered. A magnet on the opposite side determines whether a 0 or a 1 shall be recorded. When the disc is cool, and the laser set to low power, it reads the magnetized spots without heating them.

See also DISC and COMPACT DISC.

OPTICAL FIBRE CABLE
See FIBRE.

ORACLE
A teletext system offered by Independent Television (ITV) companies in the UK via their television channels. Data is broadcast during an interval within each frame unoccupied by "conventional" TV signal data.

OROM
Optical Read Only Memory.

ORPHAN
An Orphan is the first line of a paragraph really belonging on the next page appearing at the bottom of the preceding page.

OS
Operating System.

OS/2
See OPERATING SYSTEM 2.

OSC
Operating System Command.

OSI
OPEN SYSTEM INTERCONNECTION. See STANDARDS.

OTS
Orbital Test Satellite.

OUTSOURCING
The handing over of an operation, normally done in house, to a third party for a fee.

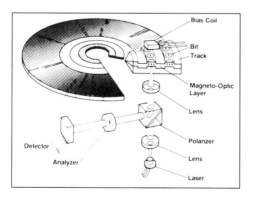

Kodak drive for re-writable disc (By courtesy of Kodak Ltd)

P

P
Pica (million millionth).

PABX
PRIVATE AUTOMATIC BRANCH EXCHANGE.

PACKET
A group of bits of defined size conforming to a sequence protocol, being a part of a message usually comprising address, controlling data, and the sender's data, which has been sub-divided for transmission purposes.

PACKET ASSEMBLY/DISASSEMBLY DEVICE (PAD)
A device which enables terminals without a suitable interface to connect to a PACKET SWITCHED Network.

PACKET SWITCHING
A method of transmitting data through a net-work via computer-controlled store and for-ward nodes to ensure efficient error-free transmission. Nodes are usually intercon-nected by at least two telecom channels. A message is split into a number of PACKETS. Packets are stored and despatched indepen-dently through any network path that may become available. Upon arrival at the node to which the addressee is connected the packets are assembled into the original sequence and the part of each packet containing the sender's data is assembled so as to be presented to the addressee as a complete message.

PACS
Picture Archiving and Communication Sys-tems. See IMAGES – MEDICAL.

PAD
PACKET ASSEMBLY/DISASSEMBLY DEV-ICE.

PAGE FORMATTING SOFTWARE
See DESKTOP PUBLISHING.

PAL
Phase Alternate Line. European specification for a monochrome television frame formed from two fields of interlaced lines of video and synchronising data, each displayed 50 times per second. A complete frame contains 625 lines and is displayed 25 times per second.
See also TELEVISION.

PARALLEL PROCESSING
Execution of tasks in parallel. Accomplished in single processors by switching between tasks and in multi-processor arrangements by delegating different parts of a problem to each of the several processors. See also COM-PUTERS – SUPER COMPUTERS.

PARALLEL TRANSMISSION
The simultaneous transmission of data along parallel conductors. It is faster but more ex-pensive than serial transmission.

PARC
Palo Alto Research Centre.

PARITY BIT CHECK
A form of error checking where a bit is added to a bit-group in order to make the group bit total always an odd or always an even num-ber (as agreed between sender and recipient). If such a total is not produced when the bits are added at the receiver, an error is present. 7 bit bytes nearly always include an 8th parity bit.

PARSER
Software used in natural language expert sys-tems for breaking down a sentence into its component parts with reference to stored grammatical rules.

PASCAL
A high level language developed by Nicholas Wirth at the University of California (San Diego) in 1970. It became used after 1978 when compilers became available.. It is grad-ually displacing Basic since it has a well defined standard and is designed specifically for programmers. See also COMPUTERS – LANGUAGES.

PASCAL, BLAISE
See COMPUTERS – HISTORY.

PATENTS
A patent or "letters patent" grants a monopoly in an invention for a limited period. The procedures vary in different countries although there was unification in Europe, to which Britain contributed, with the 1977 Patent Act. A major change was the requirement that a patent should exhibit "absolute novelty" involving the furtherance of knowledge by an "inventive step".

There is a delay between the filing of a patent and its publication – usually about 18 months in the UK, and a further delay until the actual granting of the patent. In the USA a patent covers an invention or process for 17 years during which the patentee has a monopoly. In the UK the maximum period is twenty years.

There is no such thing as "world patents pending" – a phrase often applied to new products. The European Patent Convention, established in 1978, grants a patent covering 14 countries, if the application is successful, from the European Patent Office (EPO) in Munich. The more states included, the higher the cost. Under the proposed 1993 Community Patent Treaty a single application will cover all EC states automatically.

It should be remembered that in the US the "first to invent" establishes invention priority and an application may be filed up to one year after commercialization, remaining secret while pending.

In nearly all other countries priority is established by "first to file". There is a "period of grace" between filing data and commercialisation, with a routine delay between filing and publication.

If a competitor uses the invention between publication and granting, the owner of the patent cannot do anything until the patent is granted. He can then sue the infringer with regard to the infringer's activities back-dated to the publication date.

Current interest in IT patents seems to be mainly centred on attempts to get computer software defined in such a way that existing definitions about what is patentable may also apply to it as well.

In the UK, software patentability seems unlikely in view of the dismissal, on appeal, of Merrill Lynch's 1989 application to patent a novel computer-based shares trading system. The judge ruled that the system was "a way of doing business". In 1991, Norman Gale applied for a patent for software in a ROM chip which was initially accepted, but then rejected by the Patents Office Court. Gale wanted to appeal to the House of Lords but decided he could not afford to. See also figure on opposite page.

PBX
PRIVATE BRANCH EXCHANGE.

PC
1. Printed Circuit
2. PERSONAL COMPUTER. See under MICROCOMPUTER
3. PERSONAL COMPUTER INFORMATION SYSTEM. See under PERSONAL INFORMATION SYSTEM.

PCI
Peripheral Component Interface. A bus proposed by Intel for 486DX and Pentium 64 bit processors capable of transferring data at 128 Mbps.

PCM
PULSE CODE MODULATION.

PCNET
Personal Computer NETwork.

PDI
Picture Description Instructions.

PDN
Public Data Network.

PEL
Picture element.

PEN COMPUTERS
See COMPUTERS – PEN.

PERIPHERAL DEVICE
An auxiliary device such as a printer or scanner external to the main body of the computer.

PERSONAL COMPUTERS
See HOME COMPUTERS.

PERSONAL INFORMATION SYSTEMS – ACCESS TO FILED PAPERWORK

Microcomputer software for the organization of indexes to paper files or folders in cabinets or on shelves is widely available for retrieving information covering occupational needs. The "system" may consist of a series of records numbered 1,2,3...n, describing the contents of the associated ordered shelved documents numbered 1,2,3...n.

To up-date the document collection, the user calls up the next blank record, numbered say 5003, types in a description of the new document, labels it "5003", and shelves it in order.

To retrieve information, the user keys in terms describing wanted information and the numbered records containing matching terms

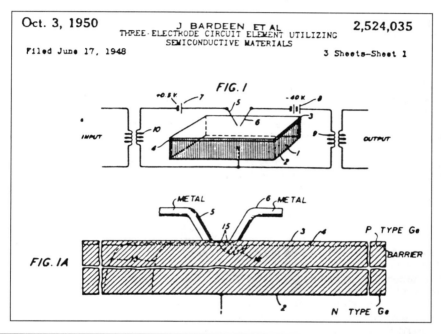

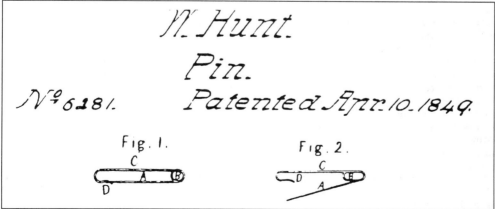

Two famous patents

are retrieved and displayed. The user goes to a shelf and pulls out the correspondingly numbered documents.

Various additions to the basic arrangement are available such as telecoms software for use with a modem for auto-dialling and logging on to a line for downloading information from a remote database. The system I use is ISI's Scimate which is no longer available. ISI now market Procite – a rather similar software package.

A major benefit of this type of system is the convenience of having information at your elbow. The importance that people attach to having information to hand is well known. People working on research who usually have an excellent central library often maintain their own local collection of publications because they value convenience.

When personal system software first arrived, Gerald Lundeen of the School of Library Studies, University of Hawaii was loud in his praise:- "A number of studies have shown that researchers rank their information sources primarily in order of convenience". In one study "59% of the references cited in researcher's publications were found to be in their personal collections".

PERSONAL INFORMATION SYSTEMS – BROWSING

When documents are sequentially numbered to correspond with record numbers and are shelved in sequence, they will normally also be in chronological order. If the documents are processed as they arrive, the latest documents will be about whatever range of subjects happen to be covered in that batch. The latest information can be browsed by taking the last few documents off the shelf.

This process is much improved if the major subject areas are sub-divided and the associated hard copy is filed in alphabetically ordered containers, with the documents in numerical order inside them. Thus instead of the documents being filed in numerical order along the shelf, they are filed in discontinuous numerical sequence within each broad subject area.

If a shelf be divided into twelve subjects A to L, the order of documents in, say, container E, might be 86, 87, 89, 91, 92, 93, 98, 99, the intermediate numbers having gone into other sections. Thus all the documents in each section are in chronological order, allowing the n most recent documents in the chosen subject area to be browsed – the collection is subdivided into subject areas, in turn sub-divided into records/chunks, in turn sub-divided into documents/terms.

Records may be searched on the machine by browsing the "hit records" produced by the query, say, "Subject area B" AND 1988", but provided the number of chunks is not too large, direct access, and the satisfaction of directly browsing hard-copy is to be preferred. Moreover you do not have to get the machine going, select the software, and go through the menu processes.

PERSONAL INFORMATION SYSTEMS – DATA INPUT AND CHUNKING

In 1961 H.P.Luhn published what must have been the earliest paper about computer-based information retrieval using punched-cards. The figure on p. 83 shows an edge-notched card of the type which was in use at that time. Wanted cards fell out of the pack when needles were inserted through the holes selected corresponding to those cards which had been notched according to a subject code describing their contents. The idea worked but the effort of maintaining the system was too great.

A personal systems is, among other things, a form of insurance – "I may not need it now but I probably will need it later". The information goes into the system for later "information recovery". It may turn up again when the system is being used for "information discovery".

Christiansen, Editor of the IEEE journal *Spectrum*, writes "The engineer (or the architect, or the physician) wants to pinpoint a sometimes elusive answer that is embedded in a burgeoning volume of arcane information – papers, conference records, reports, and the like".

"One of the responses to the current situation is that engineers tend to save what the think they may need to retrieve in the future. One told *Spectrum* that the engineer in the office above her, as she glanced up warily at her ceiling, is concerned that his cache of journals and other reports is exceeding the building code's floor-loading limits."

"The scan-and-save" process is deemed an unnecessary burden by many engineers.

Hard copy, they say, will always have its place, but they would like to be able to use the fruits of their own technologies to ease the search and retrieval process". Evidently this does not mean that they would like to use a computer-based personal information system. They prefer that their *potential information* should reside in a heap, hoping that they can recall the details later.

An obstacle in the way of computer-based information is the problem of data entry. The prospect of keying in hundreds or thousands of records may discourage potential users. Indeed it does.

The input effort depends on the number of documents you are prepared to process, the width of your interests, and your definition of a document. If your interests are wide and the definition includes journal articles, press cuttings, reports, catalogues, reprints, and even books, then the input effort may be considerable. The effort of running an effective system must be taken into account. The inevitable consequence if the effort becomes excessive is that enthusiasm wears off and the system falls into disuse.

What you need to retrieve from the system is a record containing a *chunk* of information, but how big is a chunk? It's quite helpful to vary the size of the chunk; it could be information about one article if that article relates to your "main line" interest and needs to be indexed in some detail, or it could be several items if the subject is of marginal interest. For example for a chunk comprising several catalogues the information on the record could consist of simply "Scanners resolving at 300 dots/inch or more. Catalogues. May 1, 1993".

The payoff for time spent in pre-sorting items into chunks is a reduction in the number of records in the system, a reduction in the number of separate items on the shelves, and a reduction in indexing time.

Chunking also helps to maintain the "amount of information per record" at a roughly constant level; as just mentioned, one record may contain a description of one item regarded as being important, perhaps containing several topics of interest, requiring exhaustive indexing. Alternatively several items may be chunked together and covered by a description which covers all of them.

PERSONAL INFORMATION SYSTEMS – FILOFAXES

In the early eighties micros kept dropping in price, software became commercially available and the literature about personal information systems took off.

But the enormous sales of personal computers for at-home use has evidently *not* been accompanied by the sales of software for home information systems. One of the standard examples which used to be trotted out was the "recipe book" application – an idea which sounds reasonable until the organization, inputting, and maintenance effort is compared with the alternatives.

One of the most successful personal information system is a system which is entirely manual – the Filofax. It does not purport to be able to handle a mass of occupational information. According to one author "the main users are rural clergymen and military officers... Filofax plc still has sheets for Church Family Records and Commander's Personnel Records".

The system must meet much wider needs because 1978 sales of £47,000 had become £12.9 million by 1987. "the sustained demand must also substantially derive from its functionality as a personal portable retrieval system. As such it may represent one milestone of an information society in which information work is a general, rather then a specialized activity".

"If cheaper more-widely distributed computer workstations and networking can be regarded as a top-down realization of information society, then perhaps Filofax usage represents a bottom-up effect".

"Filofax has certainly caused a significant increase in the population of people filing and retrieving information methodically; introducing users to methods, dilemmas, and nuances of alphabetization and amending, deleting, and inserting in indexed files – previously the province of professional filers like archivists, librarians, information scientists and other "hapless clerks". Since they are no longer a new phenomenon little has been heard about them recently but presumably they are still used and presumably "hapless clerks" still include Information Scientists.

Filofaxes do not seem to have any special indexing arrangements although they include varieties of index pages with category headings, printed stick-on page thumb-tabs, A to Z tabs etc.

Perhaps the amount of information normally stored in a Filofax permits sub-divisions with adequate resolving power.

PERSONAL INFORMATION SYSTEMS – HISTORY

In Sauvain's 1978 annotated bibliography, only three items listed in it were microcomputer-based systems. One used a North Star machine, the second was for Z80 64K CP/M disc-drive machines which were just becoming available. The third also used a Z80 64K machine with discs called "PRIMATE... a microcomputer-based system to help manage, among other things, files of reprints".

In the Sauvain bibliography of 56 articles about personal information systems, nearly all the applications were to managing research document collections. Machines used included IBM 360, PDP 11/20, PDP-1 and Texas 980, all with specially written software. Microcomputers were just reaching the stage where the convenience of an own self-contained desktop system looked as if it might be feasible.

As microcomputer power increased further and prices continued to drop, vendors provided personal system software adding more and more "features". Every new system needs more bells and whistles – for the salesman's benefit and sometimes for the customer. PRIMATE was one such system – basic, fast, and simple. Out of it came SCI-MATE with numerous added features. This in turn gave way to PROCITE. These three systems stem from the original systems aimed at meeting the needs of researchers.

Database software became available for much larger microcomputer-based databases with the arrival of the IBM PC-AT; Ashton Tate with its dBase series, was a leader. Database organization may still be based on the earlier personal information systems but the word "personal" has been dropped and new structures have been introduced. (See under DATABASES). The software is directed particularly at the business market. To this end, features such as data-entry form design and processing and control of the data in the forms are usually included.

More recently database versatility has been enhanced with the development of SQL (Structured Query Language) by IBM during the 70s for Relational Database Management. This became available for microcomputers around 1987. The strength of a relational database lies in its tree-like hierarchy with "across the tree" links and pointers between record tables enabling enhanced spreadsheet-like operations such as "join tables together to form a new table" to be performed.

Furthermore, SQL-based operations with the database stored in a "server" computer with networked "user client" applications being run in conjunction with the server by users from their own micros, are now being used.

More recently still, a number of systems called "Personal Information Managers" (PIMs) have appeared, designed to formalize and inter-connect assorted items of information. These appear to be aimed at nobody in particular and seem to be up-market "Organizers". They come from software vendors who know that even if only a small fraction of microcomputer owners buy them they could be profitable. Lotus's PIM is :-

"Designed to handle the random, freeform entry of short pieces of text (words, phrases, sentences, or lists); they are all purpose tools flexible enough to manage anything from lists of sales contracts to brainstorming sessions with aplomb, and they can link the unstructured bits of information you enter, enabling you to establish working relationships between otherwise separate items".

MDI Systems (East Linton, UK) market an expensive system called the Tips system. They offer a PC, optical disc drive, hard disc, scanner, laser printer and software.

It handles your jottings and miscellaneous paperwork by turning them into images and is said to "replace at least four filing cabinets, a photocopier, and an in-tray, as well as manage your PC files no matter what application software you are using".

Another adjunct to a personal information system is offered by Desktop Data (Waltham MA). An FM receiver connected to a computer picks up five business news services. The software causes items containing terms which match your profile of terms stored in the machine, to be retained in storage. The system is offered on a one year lease which includes the use of two of the services and connect time at $7500.

"Personal Information" can, with the accent on the "personal", refer to the kind of information which helps you to "get organized" in the way that a diary and address book helps. In may also mean "occupational-need information" – the mass of paper-based information about your occupation or profession and global information about the environment within which you practice it.

Harold Geneen – formerly head of ITT, described his systems in a 1984 Fortune article:- "If you are in the firing line you are going to have 89 things on your desk, ten others on the floor besides you, and eight more on the credenza behind you. Your own filing system is right there on your desk – acquisitions at the far right, budget figures on the near left, compensation and personal recommendations on the right of the budget figures, and so on".

"There are, arbitrarily speaking, two kinds of business executives: one has a clean desk, the other a cluttered one. It's been my impression through the years that when I come upon a man who has a gleaming, empty, desktop, that I am dealing with a fellow who is so far removed from the realities of his business that someone else is running it for him".

Piles of papers as a method of indexing has a lot going for it, but with a bit more effort, better results can be obtained with the aid of a microcomputer.

Returning to Personal Information Systems/Databases we may note that many of them have been subjected to the bells-and-whistles treatment and have now called "Text Retrieval Systems" (TRS). A small TRS – that is a TRS with its "non main-line features discarded" – appears to be very similar to a "Personal Information System" as here discussed.

What was unusual about PRIMATE was that the almost universally used inverted file indexing system was not adopted – storage and speed considerations did not permit it. Instead, searches were conducted by searching serially through the database. Highly compressed versions of each record were matched against search questions compressed using the same scheme. Records could be searched at a rate of about 100 per second – quite adequate for most people's personal collections.

PERSONAL INFORMATION SYSTEMS – INDEXING HAZARDS

Unfortunately the examples which follow show that even indexing performed by indexing experts does not necessarily produce the results that might be expected. This simply confirms that for the non-expert doing his own indexing, the compromise between time spent in indexing and the need to keep down the cost of non-productive time needs the most careful attention.

Thorngate comments that the success of keyword schemes – a commonly used method – "depends greatly on... the extent to which keywords faithfully encode information... distinguish the information they encode... and are the ones we use to retrieve it".

He provides the story of the economist who wished to find statistics about the yearly import of rubber boots to Manitoba. "The CD-ROM did its thing for twenty minutes prompted by helpful shouts from colleagues like *"imports, boots, shoes, latex, stockings, feet, socks, clothing, leather goods, waterproofing, and stream fishing gear.* At last it was discovered with the keywords *"footwear, manufactured, Prairies, trade"*.

Thorngate was prompted to find out more about "the cognitive aspects of information retrieval in keyword search tasks" in a series of experiments. He compared the keywords chosen by professional indexers when compiling the PsychLIT version of *Psychological Abstracts* on CD-ROM, with those chosen by a PsychLIT retrieval-testing team including seven professors who were subject experts.

His extraordinary findings were that "Fewer than 10% of the descriptors used by professors and graduate students were those used by PsychLit to code the articles they read... If we were to assume that the three or four descriptors generated for each article would be used in a PsychLIT search for it, we would expect fewer than a 35% chance of retrieval. In other words a PsychLIT user is at least twice a likely not to retrieve a given article than to retrieve it".

Professionally organized information services also been found wanting by others. Following some discussions with engineers about the topic, Christiansen says:- "Yet while almost all had personally tried to use existing search and retrieval systems, and many had high hopes for the future success, most were disappointed in their current experience".

"Many saw the problem as a superabundance of literature but deficient programming that cannot converge on the few sources they needed for a particular project". A number of engineers found the systems "not user-friendly. One computer designer said he would not spend the hours required to learn to use a particular system".

There are some software packages available which claim to assist indexing processes. The DTP software Ventura includes a module for creating and sorting words with page numbers. A package called Micro-OCP goes a good deal further. It is a PC version of the Oxford Concordance Program, used on a mainframe to help to compile the OED, and can be obtained from Oxford University Press at Walton St., Oxford. A user has to write his own programmes for it but this is alleged to be simple.

A major feature is the provision for including coded annotations/references in the text to identify words or sections for indexing purposes. Various operations may be performed with these codes. The reviewer calls it "a very clever syntax-smart template editor for creating command files... which makes programs very easy for beginners... it is an immensely flexible indexing tool".

PERSONAL INFORMATION SYSTEMS – INDEXING PRINCIPLES AND REFINEMENTS

Personal information systems have to be used in a world where we try to predict how much system-time will be required according to past experience, and base the design and the time to be made available to maintain the system on that experience. If the system is going to work it must provide you with timely information, conveniently available.

In practice incoming print-on-paper piles up, and what should be accessible remains in an inaccessible pile. The stuff tends to be handled in batches on a time available basis. Since there never is any time available, the latest information which ought to be in the system languishes in the heap.

In the system being here discussed, a record contains a description of the information in a document or chunk. The descriptive record is searched during the retrieval process for terms matching the query terms so it is *also the index*. Consequently the description must include appropriate terms – if necessary in the form of added keywords.

There are two aspects of indexing strongly affecting retrieval performance which were discussed by Cleverdon and Fairthorne (1968), some years ago.

Exhaustivity is the depth of indexing – the more the number of terms, the more exhaustive the indexing, and the greater the number of documents retrieved, including irrelevant ones ("high recall").

Specificity is the degree of exactness provided by a term – in other words the extent to which the term retrieves every relevant document. The greater the specificity the higher the chance that some relevant documents will not be retrieved ("high precision"). Fairthorne comments on a somewhat different aspect:- "Provided that the position of a document is known, one need not look at every individual document, but can approach the position quickly and roughly and then examine documents in the neighbourhood in detail".

Fairthorne explains that finding a particular item on a book page quickly depends on the "resolving power" of a page and of the "thumb indexes" (as used, for instance, on directories) which should have an appropriately lower resolving power:- "One does not have thumb indexes on every page... the finest sub-divisions must be coarser than the ultimate units of search to an extent depending on the penultimate resolving power".

"Chunking", discussed earlier, is a variation of this principle.

A record will be retrieved from the database when the terms assigned to it match the terms in the retrieval question, but only if the assignment of terms has been carefully considered will that record be likely to contain the desired information.

In non-personal systems "Indexing uncertainty and search uncertainty are the primary cause of information retrieval difficulties. Indexing uncertainty arises because different expert indexers can assign different index terms for a given document. Search uncertainty arises because searchers have latitude in choosing terms to express a query and the search strategies they employ in acquiring information.

Most self-appointed indexer/searchers *are*

not expert indexers or people who are interested in information systems per se. He or she simply wants to get at locally-stored information with the minimum effort. To him or her the system is an overhead. Any time needlessly expended in system operations is wasted time. Its design must be in accord with the dictum "time spent on system operations must be no more than that which is needed to obtain a just acceptable retrieval performance". This may be the most important criteria for personal information system design.

Sauvain suggested that "An important part of personal retrieval systems is that the end user generally does not want to rely upon anybody else's indexing terms. The motivation for building a personal database is usually that personal indexing or organization must be performed to make the stored information truly useful".

In other words, a large part of the usefulness of a personal database is that the information has been evaluated by the collector relative to a personal conceptual framework. This is in contrast to large "public" retrieval systems where the diverse nature of the audience make it necessary to rely on "general purpose" indexing.

The fact that the user must suffer the time-wasting costly chore of indexing is not mentioned.

The reason why it is rarely mentioned is that most articles and sales leaflets describing information systems are written by system designers, system salesmen, or librarians/information scientists. These people have a professional interest in information systems and find it hard to visualize that most other people are more concerned about avoiding increased costs and avoiding chores associated with the system; to them it is just a tool.

Others sing the praises of self-indexing without mentioning the cost/time penalty. Since the user defines the subjects, each is indexed in the user's words; there is no need to wonder how a distant librarian may have indexed a particular area of interest. For an area of special interest the user can establish categories that are more detailed than would seem appropriate to a librarian who must consider the needs of the entire scientific community.

Peta-
Thousand Million Million.

PHASE-SHIFT KEYING (PSK)
A data modulation mode that holds the frequency constant and transmits information by means of a phase change.

PHIGS
Programmers Hierarchical Graphics System. An extension of GKS for describing 3D graphics by means of data arranged in a tree structure.

PHONEME
A speech sound forming a complete word or part of a word, or a sound which distinguishes between two words. Thus the "s" in "set" and the "g" in "get" are phonemes because they distinguish between these two words.

PHONG SHADING
An improved version of GOURAUD shading.

PHOTO CD
A recently introduced scheme by Kodak to enable CD images to be reproduced from domestic 35mm film for domestic use.

The idea is to supply special equipment to processing centres for making the compact discs. Customers take their 35 mm exposed colour films to the centre and their film strips are transferred to the disc as digitized images. To view the results the customer either runs the disc on a CD-ROM XA player, microcomputer, and display (or TV-set display), or looks at the prints which are also supplied. The player will cost about £300. One disadvantage is that current widely-used players will not do.

However Photo-CD is CD-I compatible so the two systems may assist each other to catch on. The Performer 600, for example, can be purchased with a fast CD drive, the Apple CD300i. This drive will support the Kodak-CD operating system. Ordinary colour film from an estimated 250 million 35 mm cameras world-wide will thus become available for display on TV receivers, home computers, or for publication in magazines at a price and quality appropriate for the application. It has not been feasible until now to use 35mm film as the starting point for full-page magazine quality pictures.

CONFIGURATION OF IMAGE LIBRARY SYSTEM

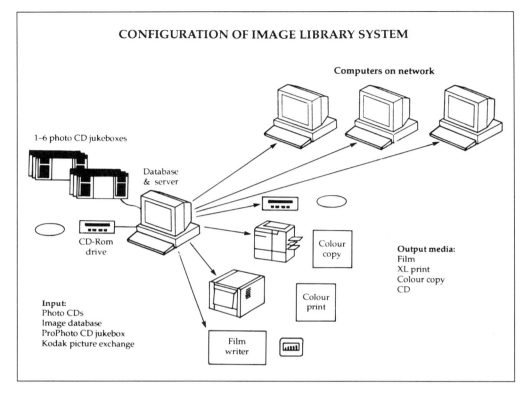

Kodak Photo-CD system. A picture distribution system (reproduced by courtesy of Kodak Ltd)

Specific applications for using images transferred from the disc include desktop publishing, multimedia, advertising – for example by Estate Agents, and so on. Kodak estimate that the market for desktop colour imaging will reach $5 billion by 1995.

A disc will be able to store about 100 6 Mbyte photographs. A photograph will be digitized at 2000 x 3000 pixels with 24 bit colour – a total of 144 Mbits or 18 Mbytes, and compressed to 6 Mbytes. The cost of supplying a disc with 24 photos on board and also supplying colour prints from the customer's film strip will be in the range £12 – £16. The disc is returnable for adding new photos.

The processing equipment will include a Sun workstation to receive images from a film scanner with three parallel CCDs each handling one primary colour, and output them to a printer which will provide a printed set of disc pictures on a small card to act as an index, and also to a CD disc-writer developed by Philips which will create the CD. For supplying colour prints the CD will be run on a separate system which applies the data to a thermal printer.

The software supplied will provide for all the processing, and will include colour management and control to the Kodak PhotoYCC specification in order to provide consistent colour. The system will run on MS-DOS (Windows 3.0), Macintosh, Unix, and OS/2 machines.

Consistent colour reproduction has been a problem for years. PhotoYCC might be adopted as a de facto standard. As a good start, Adobe will support it when they introduce level 2 Postscript.

The entire system processes images at 2000 x 3000 pixels with 24 bit colour. Customer's prints are produced on a Kodak XL 7700 digital continuous tone machine which receives

CD-ROM data and prints pictures by overlaying combinations of CMY (Cyan-Magenta-Yellow) colours from a three-colour ribbon. An A4 size colour print received from Kodak looks like a high grade conventional colour print. The quality is quite remarkable for a printer of this kind.

The complete processing/reproduction kit will cost around £75,000.

Provision is made for utilizing only as much data as may be needed from the 6 Mbyte per picture input being received by the microcomputer from the CD-ROM player, according to the requirements of the application. For example a 720 x 480 VGA display with 16 bit colour can only accommodate about 5.5 Mbits (less than 700 Kbytes). Thus in this case the storage, speeds, bit-rates etc., in a microcomputer appropriate for a VGA display will not be attempting to cope with excessive data.

On the other hand if the images are being output to, say, a Linotron printer capable of utilizing, say, 20 Mbytes (uncompressed) per image to produce photographic-quality pictures, then all the picture data will be supplied to it.

Similarly the cost of transmitting images to a remote point will be no more than is needed for images of the required quality.

Obviously the arrival of this system will provide colour pictures, with storage problems greatly eased, of a quality way above anything currently in use in the "low-end" market. With appropriate printing a picture will look like a professional colour print.

The quality of amateur photography captured on 35mm 36-exposure film available from High Street shops for about £4 and processed as just described should be adequate for almost any application. When Kodak follow up, as presumably they will, by providing software for producing colour separations for making printing plates, excellent quality will appear in quantity-produced pictures derived from an "amateur photography" source.

PHOTODIODE
A type of photosensor used in image scanners in a similar manner to a CCD element. A photodiode is a semiconductor device in which the reverse current varies according to the incident light.

PHOTOELECTRIC SCANNING
The original form of image scanning in which light reflected from the image is picked up by a photoelectric cell.

PHOTON
A packet of electromagnetic light energy.

PHOTONICS
The study of computers using PHOTONS instead of electrons. See also COMPUTERS – OPTICAL COMPUTERS.

PHOTOSENSOR
A device which converts light energy into electrical energy.

PICTURE PRESTEL
See VIDEOTEX.

PIK
Programmers Image Standard. Under consideration by ANSI as an image specification for use in medical, machine vision, satellite imaging and other areas

PIN
1. Personal Identification Number
2. P-i-n photodiode

PIPE
A one-way communication mechanism for passing a character stream from one task to another in multitasking software such as OS/2. Named Pipes are a variation for communicating large blocks of data in both directions across a network. One useful application is the use of a pipe to feed a long output from one application directly to the input of another.

PIPELINING
A method of speeding up the execution of a computer program by fetching and executing instructions in the same machine cycle.

PIRA
Printing & Packaging Research Association.

PIXEL
Picture element, the smallest discrete element making up a visual display image. In the CRT of a digital computer system, data bits converted to analogue voltages are supplied to beam

modulating electrode(s) in order to present a pixel on the screen. The data may be one bit for black and white, or multi-bit to present a half-tone or colour pixel.

PKA
Public Key Algorithm.
 See also ENCRYPTION.

PLASMA PANEL
A panel divided into small glass cells containing a gas which glows when a voltage is applied. Plasma panels are a potential replacement for the cathode ray tube, being thin, flat, and strong, but they are still relatively expensive.

 The cells in the plasma are switched by the control system acting through a grid within which the cells are located. In 1992 the manufacture of large colour plasma screens improved, and very large displays have been manufactured. Large plasma screens may compete with LCDs within the next few years.

PLESIOCHRONOUS
See SDH.

PLPT
Presentation Level Protocol.

PMOS
P-type Metal Oxide Semiconductor.

POINT
See TYPE FACE.

POINT TO POINT
A limited network configuration with communication between two terminal points only, as opposed to multi-point and multi-drop.

POLLING
A method of interrogating a number of transmitting devices with the intention of triggering data transmission if they have data to send. In facsimile, polling means one facsimile machine calling another and receiving a facsimile transmission from it having initiated the transmission with a password.

PORT
The place provided on a computer for the connection of some peripheral device such as a printer, modem etc.

POSTSCRIPT
A programming language devised by Adobe Systems which controls the beam of a laser printer to print almost any kind of symbol or illustration. Image dot structures are changed into vectors (quantities having magnitude and direction).

 The benefits are economies in data, versatility, and resolution limited only by the printer in use.

 Postscript takes a file, typically a file describing a Pagemaker or Ventura page, and changes the dot-structure description of text, graphics, and illustrations into a vector description.

 A vector is a quantity which has magnitude and direction. A rectangle in Postscript would be described by a co-ordinate representing a starting point on a page, the co-ordinates of its corners, the thickness of a line, and the instruction "move to". The printer then draws the rectangle. The instructions are coded in ASCII code. Postscript describes every item on a page in terms of its constituent lines, curves, polygons, etc.

 In bit-map form, for example, a ruled line 20 bits wide and 1500 bits long requires 30,000 bits to describe it. In Postscript the description would be in the form "Start in position X and perform a 20 point line from A to B". This instruction would require perhaps 200 bits of code.

 To execute this operation two main processes are required. First, the DTP bit-map has to be converted into ASCII-coded vector form. The ASCII code is then sent to the printer's Raster Image Processor (RIP). The RIP changes it back into the line by line form required by a laser printer.

 The benefits of this apparently cumbersome process are:-
1. The printed resolution is limited only by the printer, not by the file format. For instance if an instruction to draw a sharply curved line is issued, it may be reproduced as a series of small zig-zags on a relatively low resolution printer.

 However if a high resolution printer is used the same instruction would produce a smooth outline. The practical value of this is that while a "coarse" version of a DTP page may be good enough for checking purposes, a disc containing DTP output may be sent to, say, a bureau with a 1200 dpi Linotype page-setter for quantity printing. The result will be 1200 dpi quality.

2. Almost any shape can be designed by the user if he knows the language. Alternatively a library of ready-made designs may be purchased on disc ready to be called onto pages. The value of this depends on the application. "Stunt-images", receive considerable attention in Postscript publicity. A user may or may not require the numerous fonts and shapes suggested by Adobe.

3. The amount of data required to represent an image in Postscript is usually far less than in a bit-map.

4. It is only necessary to store the description of a font in a single size. To call up the font in a different size, only a simple Postscript scaling instruction needs to be applied. The disadvantage is that the time taken to print a Postscript page is longer, and may be much longer, than the time taken using other methods.

Plug-in boards and software are available to convert a non-Postscript printer into a Postscript printer, and Postscript "go-faster" boards are also available.

POTS
Plain Old Telephone System.

PRAGMATICS
The study of the usage of a language.

PRECISION
See INDEXING SYSTEM PERFORMANCE – RECALL AND PRECISION.

PRESTEL
See under VIDEOTEX.

PRI
PRIMARY RATE INTERFACE.

PRICE, D. J. DE SOLLA
Derek Price was born in London in the 1920s and died there in 1983. He spent much of his working life in the United States at Yale University. He was the first to appreciate the significance of the exponential growth of science and the scientific literature. His book *Little Science Big Science*, published in 1963, is a classic. It was followed in 1965 by a paper which is almost as well known, *Networks of Scientific Papers*, published in *Science*. Price's other major interest was in ancient scientific instruments.

PRIMARY RATE INTERFACE (PRI)
An ISDN interface consisting of 30 B channels and one D channel each running at 64 Kbps and multiplexed in order to form an appropriate interface for a large PABX or a computer processor. See also NETWORKS – ISDN.

PRINTERS – COLOUR
There is a considerable gap between printing colour directly on to paper from a DTP system using one of the several kinds of relatively inexpensive colour printer now available, and printing by overlaying from colour separation transparencies.

With a direct colour printer all that the user sees is the print in full colour emerging from the printer, the process of constructing the image from its component colours being taken care of by the machine. The results are moderate, but getting cheaper and better. The machine may take some minutes to produce the first print and then produces each subsequent copy rather more quickly. The method is suitable for short printing runs.

Colour separation printing involves the preparation of four transparencies – black and white films carrying data about those parts of an image containing the colours cyan, magenta, yellow and key (black) (CMYK) respectively. A colour print is produced by firstly, making four printing plates from the transparencies, and secondly performing four printing passes using inks of these colours from each accurately aligned plate. After that copies are produced at high speed.

Tektronix produce a range of printers which exemplify the possibilities of direct colour printing. The Phaser thermal-wax Postscript printer is suitable as a nodal resource on a network and costs £17,000. Heated needles transfer ink by impact through a moving roll carrying three colours and black inks on to high quality paper.

The perceived colour depends on the relative proportions of inks used in each pass. Postscript is the printer control language widely used with laser printers which changes bit-mapped images into plotted descriptions which are independent of printer resolution; high resolution printers produce high resolution images.

The Tektronix 4693DX digital colour printer comes with a plug-in card for a PC with 8 Mbytes of storage and costs around £8000. Their 4696 inkjet colour printer sells for £1576. In late 1989 Tektronix introduced their Color-Quick inkjet printer for Macintosh machines at $2495, printing at 216 dots per inch. It builds an image in bands as four ink jets spray cyan, magenta, yellow, and black as the head passes in front of plain paper.

Hewlett Packard also manufacture an inkjet colour printer which is less expensive ($1395), but has a lower resolution (180 dots/inch). Incidentally printer suppliers prefer to talk about "dots", "pixels" being reserved for CRTs and other electronic display devices.

Tektronix have recently introduced a software package with its inkjet printer, costing $50 on its own, called TekColor. It provides adjustments for colour while the user observes both CRT RGB colours and transformed CMYK values from the printer on the screen, so that the printer may be adjusted to generate colours which most nearly match the RGB results. Colour selection and numerical readings given during the adjustment process conform to the CIE model mentioned earlier.

The Toshiba "3-in-one" dot matrix colour printer must be one of the least expensive available, selling at $949 in the US. It prints at 180 x 360 dots/inch from a 24 pin head, the same type of printing head still being used probably more than any other. It prints up to seven colours from combinations available on a cyan/magenta ribbon and is said to produce remarkable results.

In 1990 a new technique appeared called dye diffusion whereby colour dyes on a ribbon diffuse into special photographic paper producing what may well be the best colour yet from direct printers. Mitsubishi recently introduced their S340 printer, which costs £8250 in the UK, using this technique. In due course it will be possible to colour correct stored images from a control panel on the printer. The method has its disadvantages. It is very slow, taking 3 to 5 minutes to produce a print at a cost of about £3 each.

See also COLOUR – PRINTING.

PRINTERS – DOT MATRIX AND LASER

Dot matrix printers have been improved in the last few years by the incorporation of more resident storage capacity and by the inclusion of more pins. A 24 pin printer running at Letter Quality speed produces type without a visible dot structure. The top price of a dot matrix is still considerably less than the bottom price of a Laser.

If an inexpensive dot matrix printer is connected to a microcomputer using Word Perfect 5.0 WP software, fonts may be changed in the course of composing a document by pressing control keys, consulting a font menu, selecting a font, and returning to the text. The selected font continues until further notice. Some examples are shown below.

Note that if a compressed font is inserted within a line that the software takes care of the line length automatically.

The styles/fonts shown are Superscript, Outline, Shadow, Redline, Strikeout, Roman 5 characters per inch (cpi), Roman 12 point condensed proportionally spaced, Roman italic

---

Work is the curse of the drinking classes

Work is the curse of the drinking classes

Work is the curse of the drinking classes

Work is the curse of the drinking classes

~~Work is the curse of the drinking classes~~

W o r k   i s   t h e   c u r s e   o f   t h e

Work is the curse of the drinking classes

Work is the curse of the drinking classes

Work is the curse of the drinking classes

Work is the curse of the drinking classes

WORK IS THE CURSE OF THE

20 cpi, Sans Serif 12 pt condensed prop. spaced, Sans Serif italic 12 pt double underlined, and Roman 12 pt caps proportionally spaced double-wide bold, respectively.

If a dot-matrix printer is controlled to print "draft" it will print acceptable characters but with a visible dot structure, much faster than when it is in the "letter quality" (LQ) mode. The dot structure in the LQ mode is virtually invisible.

Laser printers cost at least twice and usually three or four times as much as 24-pin dot matrix (DM) printers but provide better quality print and much better graphics.

With WP software, the fonts available depend on the resident software and its relationship with the resident software installed in the printer's memory.

A "driver" of the right kind must be included with the microcomputer software. A driver is a software module specific to the printer. If the type of printer is changed, the micro has to be re-loaded with the correct driver. Usually the WP software will include drivers for many popular printers so this is just a matter of designation from a menu.

Laser and multiple-pin dot matrix printers enable characters to be constructed as they print – a whole range of designs may be produced by software control of the dot pattern ("soft fonts") which controls the printer to lay down a pattern of dots to form characters in the chosen font. A "Low power" microcomputer with a dot-matrix printer is likely to be very slow when this method is used.

Many extra fonts can be added if required, either by purchasing special font software which is compatible with the WP software, by buying fonts stored within a cartridge which is plugged into a socket provide for it on the printer, or by buying "soft fonts".

During the last few years improved dot-matrix printers have led to the gradual demise of the daisy-wheel printer – one of the least expensive ways of printing solid type. Such printers are inflexible because although they produce good quality characters, most only allow one font in normal or "bold".

To change fonts you have to switch off and change to another wheel so a change of font or style is not really practicable.

See also DISPLAYING HALFTONES and SCREENS.

PRINTERS – THERMAL

A printer embodying a strip of transistor/resistor elements which are heated and make marks on heat sensitive paper. It provides better quality than electro-etch recording. Improvements made by replacing the elements with thin film print heads enable a page to be printed with a 200 elements/inch dot structure in 15 seconds.

Thermal transfer printing was introduced later, using a ribbon between heads and paper so that plain paper could be used. The ink melts on to the paper, but the cost of the ribbon offsets the cost of the cheaper paper. Colour printing becomes possible by using ribbon with colour bands.

PRIVACY AND FREEDOM

"The liberty of the people lies in their private lives: do not disturb it. Let the government... be a force only to protect the state of simplicity against force itself". So said Saint-Just in the nineteenth century.

Similar sentiments are to be found in Judge Brandeis' remarks, made during the Olmstead v United States case, about the intent of the makers of the Constitution. "They conferred, as against the government, the right to be let alone – the most comprehensive of rights and the right most valued by civilized men".

The same rights are declared in article 8 of the European Convention on Human Rights "Everyone has the right of respect for his private and family life, his home and his correspondence".

Information technology has added the dimensions of computer-based information storage and retrieval of information about people, and access to it via communication networks.

Privacy in the United Kingdom

"Persons who carry high responsibility in Britain tend to assume that they cannot be expected to explain their actions fully to ordinary people, who would be unable to understand even if they wished to. This is the residue of old-fashioned aristocratic principle which remains firmly embedded in British democracy." (Andrew Schonfield, English economist).

In some countries in Europe, and particularly in Britain, secrecy is pervasive. The UK climate is set by the Official Secrets Act, passed hastily in 1911 during a spy scare, and changed only slightly since.

Conveniently for the government of the day the Press was fully occupied at the time with the Kaiser and the Agadir crisis. Governments take refuge behind this blanket measure, although before every election pledges are given to reform the Act.

The Act has become a symbol of government inertia – extreme reluctance in getting to grips with data protection is one of many examples the Act has been used by successive governments for their greater general convenience. To acknowledge a public "right to know" as opposed to a governmental "right to secrecy" requires a complete change in attitude.

An attempt was made in 1989 to introduce a privacy bill in the UK parliament. It was prompted by widespread indignation about press intrusion and the inadequacy of the Press Council in dealing with it. It failed to become law because the UK parliament, once again, showed its lack of interest. The vote was 98-1 in favour, but a private member's bill required 100 votes in favour to make further progress.

The Official Secrets Act became discredited following several failures of application. In 1990 a new Act became law replacing part 2. Previously a private members bill attempting to allow unauthorized information disclosure in the public interest – that is where a crime or abuse of authority had occurred – had been defeated.

The new Act is a slight improvement in that it replaces generalized catch-all powers by specifically defined areas of protected information – defence, security and intelligence services, international relations, and confidential information entrusted to other states or international organizations. Servants of the Crown have to preserve confidential information for life.

The absence of a written constitution in the UK in which freedom of expression is afforded a degree of constitutional protection is very clear. The basic assumption is that Parliament may make any laws it chooses – very different from the wording of the first Amendment – and that the courts are obliged to give effect to these laws.

The absence of a yardstick, such as that provided by the first Amendment, has meant that our judges have little to go on and instead have adopted the relatively easy course of simply following, literally wherever possible, the words of parliament, seldom enquiring into their spirit.

The British public do not seem to be concerned about the new-technology Big Brother Syndrome. In a 1982 Mori poll, two thirds of those asked disagreed with the statement:- "I'm suspicious about the possible effects of new technology", and only 4% disagreed with the statement:- "On balance new technology is a good thing". So far as I am aware privacy questions, with the exception of reform in the Official Secrets Act, have never been an issue at election time, so there is no political mileage in the subject.

A *Right to Know Bill* received its second reading in the UK Parliament on the 19th February 1993. It incorporates the earlier *Freedom of Information Bill* together with provisions for reforming the *Official Secrets Act*.

The Bill relates to the *Companies Act* in respect of the requirements in it relating to the disclosure of certain company information. The new Bill includes the provision for the right of access to official records held by public authorities and requires that companies should publish more complete information in their annual reports.

The Bill ought to go through its final stages later on in 1993, and if it becomes an Act it will go some way towards ameliorating obsessive government secrecy.

The UK data protection act

The new version of the Data Protection Bill was published in November 1983.

The purpose of the bill was to implement the 1982 White Paper on Data Protection (Cmnd 8538) and to enable the UK to ratify the European Convention. Some would say it was grudgingly introduced for that purpose and for no other. It was enacted in July 1984.

It established eight data protection principles – fair and lawful processing; specific purposes; confidentiality; sufficient but not excessive data; accuracy and timeliness; keep no longer than is necessary; individual right of access and correction if necessary; proper security.

The Act set up a Registrar of data users and bureaux who hold or provide services involving personal data. Provision is made for enforcement and appeal and a tribunal was set up.

Of 2500 UK complaints received by the registrar, 45% are about direct mail marketing, 17% consumer credit, and 8% about refusal to grant access. In the year ending May 1990 there were nine enforcement notices and 14 registration application refusals. The registrar took legal action against 30 users winning all those cases heard so far.

Privacy in the United States

"The liberties of the people never were, nor ever will be, secure, when the transactions of their rulers may be concealed from them" (Patrick Henry, American revolutionary).

The ubiquity of computer facilities introduces a tendency to obtain information by consulting records instead of asking. In the United States the Privacy Protection Commission observed:- "most record-keeping organizations consult the records of other organizations to verify information they obtain from an individual and thus pay as much or more attention to what other organizations report about him than they pay to what he reports about himself".

According to Gandy:- "... new technologies make the pursuit of information through surveillance more extensive, more efficient, and less obtrusive than former methods, because advanced electronics allows innovations not originally designed for surveillance to be integrated into the pool of surveillance resources".

For example improved technology provides the potential for automating telephone tapping – a once labour intensive activity. Speech can be automatically logged using a voice actuated recorder and many lines can be monitored by scanning (similar to "polling" where one line is used for transmitting data from many intermittently generating sources connected in turn to the line). The recording can be networked from a central interception point to "subscribing" agencies.

In the United States freedom of speech and the press are referred to in the first amendment to the constitution, proposed by James Madison during the first Congress in 1789. It says:-

"Congress shall make no law... abridging the freedom of speech, or the press; or the right of the people peaceably to assemble, and to petition the government for redress of grievance".

These rights have been argued and extended into other media – for example in NBC v United States (1943) ensuring the expression of diverse views and in Winters v New York (1948) dealing with entertainment and doctrine.

The climate in the US is further exemplified by the Privacy, Freedom of Information and other Acts. Problems associated with the FOI Act include the many cases in which one or more of the nine exemption clauses have been invoked. Administrative problems resulting from the 1974 amendments have been much discussed. The two major "Sunshine" Acts illustrate some of the conflicting requirements in privacy legislation.

The FOI Act provides for an individual or "legal person" (e.g. a corporation) to request and be supplied with any non-exempt government record but not "private" records in certain defined categories. The Privacy Act permits an individual to inspect government records about him or herself, but about another only with another's written authorization. Neither Act provides for information disclosure by private organizations. Inspection of credit ratings, etc., held in private files, is covered by other Acts.

See also CODES, ENCRYPTION, HACKERS, TRANSBORDER DATA FLOW, VIRUSES & WORMS.

PRIVATE AUTOMATIC BRANCH EXCHANGE (PBX)

A PABX is an automatic private exchange with a number of exchange lines and a large number of subscriber lines providing for the transmission of calls to and from the public telephone network, often with each subscriber having his own diallable telephone number.

A PABX, now usually called simply a PBX because non-automatic systems have almost disappeared, is an in-house telephone exchange. It enables users to dial each other or to dial "outsiders" via a line to the local automatic public exchange. Many PBXs also enable users to have their own telephone numbers directly diallable by outsiders. A PBX looks like and is a special purpose software-controlled computer with an attendant operator who can intervene and assist users.

A PBX may have from about 12 up to thousands of lines to its internal users. It also has an appropriate number of permanent lines, or a multi-channel coaxial cable, connecting it to the local public exchange.

Modern digital PBXs handle digitized voice or data and provide all manner of services ranging from a printed log of calls made, to "voice message" facilities where digitized messages from callers are stored until the caller wants to hear them by, for instance, calling in with his own code from outside.

PBXs are a typical example of incompatibility in a competitive area of IT where the need to "keep ahead of the competition" by incorporating "advanced features" is considered by manufacturers to be more important than the ability to communicate with a competitive product.

Current interest is centred on resolving the problem by:-

* Standardization of incompatible signalling systems used by competitive PABXs, notably for inter-working between two major systems called DPNSS and IPNS.
* Standardization of Computer Supported Telephony (CST) protocols which enable a PBX user to access a computer database and obtain an immediate information display.
* Standardization of Digital European Cordless Technology (DECT) to cover "third generation" cordless PBX systems (CT3). A cordless PBX enables users carrying portable telephones which communicate with the PBX by radio to use their phones within some area – for example within the town in which the PBX is situated.
* Deciding which of the various PTT or standards authorities is going to deal with the problems. When the situation becomes sufficiently chaotic and the idea of a standard is broached it needs to be current, mutually acceptable, and able to be easily and quickly implemented. Since standards rarely fulfil these conditions its helpfulness in resolving the chaos may be less than expected.

A term sometimes used in connection with PBXs is "data under voice", meaning the use of a single telephone extension line to carry both voice and data, anticipating a function of the ISDN.

There are nearly half a million PABXs and "key systems" (small manually operated on-each-desk PBX-like instruments) in use in the UK with GPT (GEC/Plessey) comfortably the leading supplier.

PRIVATE VIRTUAL NETWORK (PVN)
A private switched network similar in effect to a public switched network, but provided by a telecoms authority at a price much lower than a network using leased lines. See also NETWORKS.

PROCESSORS
The word processor is often used as a synonym for CPU although all processors are not CPUs.

Processors started as 4-bit devices in the early nineteen seventies. Since then their word lengths and speeds have steadily increased to 8, 16, and then 32 bits.

In 1992 the first commercial 64-bit processors arrived – the Mips R4000 and the Dec Alpha. Software and language support will follow in due course and will eventually result in considerable improvement in performance.

See also MICROCOMPUTERS and SEMICONDUCTORS.

PRODIGY
Prodigy is a computer-based shopping scheme organized by Sears Roebuck and IBM. By 1992 it had attracted over one million subscribers. The software for getting into the system costs $50; thereafter there is a $13 monthly subscription.

PROGRAM
A sequence of instructions to perform a computational process.

PROM
Programmable Read Only Memory.

PROOF
Primary Rate ISDN OSI Office Facilities. An Esprit project, due to be completed in 1992, for investigating ISDN-linked LANs.

PROSODIC
Patterns of stress and intonation in a language.

PROTOCOL
A set of rules governing the exchange of data in a telecommunications system. Some proto-

cols require complex software in order to perform operations on codes contained in messages.

PSI
Permuterm Subject Index.

PSK
PHASE SHIFT KEYING.

PSS (PACKET SWITCH STREAM)
The public packet network of the UK's PTT, British Telecom; it offers a national packet switched data service and has been available since 1981. It uses the X.25 interface protocol, providing full duplex working at a range of speeds up to and including 48,000 bps. It can also provide inter-communication between data terminal equipment operating at different speeds. Connections to other public

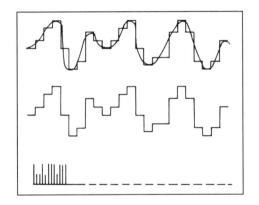

Pulse Code Modulation. Quantized levels are transmitted as code groups

packet networks can be made.

PSTN
Public Switched Telephone Network.

PTT
Post Telegraph & Telephone administration.

PULSE CODE MODULATION (PCM)
PCM is used to convert analogue speech to digital speech and vice-versa. For good quality speech it is considered that 8-bit sampling 8000 times per second should be used. This produces a bit-rate of 64 kbps, requiring a transmission channel of a relatively wide bandwidth.

The variations and improvements on PCM include Adaptive Differential PCM (ADPCM) using 4 bits per sample.

Continuously Variable Slope Delta Modulation (CVSDM) with only 1 bit per sample 32,000 times per second, and a relatively new method dependent on chip processing power called Codebook Excited Linear Predictive coding (CELP) have been introduced recently.

CELP analyses the speech pattern during a short interval of time and consults a "speech pattern reference table", compiled from speech pattern statistics, which shows what kind of pattern is most likely to follow a given pattern. It then applies the difference data between the two patterns to the first pattern and sends it as the second pattern. The result is a very low bit rate of under 5 Kbps. See also REEVES, A.H.

PVN
PRIVATE VIRTUAL NETWORK.

Q

QAM
QUADRATURE AMPLITUDE MODU-
LATION (QAM).

QUADRATURE AMPLITUDE MODULATION (QAM)
A form of data modulation that adds multiple amplitude levels to PSK modulation in order to increase the number of bit encoded in each baud.

For example four 90 degree phase shifts and two amplitude variations provide a choice of eight signalling states thereby providing 3 bits per baud.

In a 16 state QAM system almost four symbols can be transmitted in a single element. The method has possibilities for band-width reduction in delivering wideband services via the LOCAL LOOP.

QUANTIZATION
A process in which the amplitude range of a signal is divided into a finite number of smaller subranges, usually in digitizable steps.

QUANTIZING ERROR/NOISE
Error or noise caused by a change from one finite value to another in a digital analogue (or vice-versa) conversion process, as opposed to an ideally smooth change between levels.

QUANTUM EFFECT CHIPS
Electrons can be made to behave in a manner which is somewhat similar to their wave-like behaviour in microwave waveguides, although the physical mechanism is quite different. The behaviour is initiated by constructing a layered semiconductor in which the layers are composed of materials in which electrons exist at different energy levels.

By an appropriate selection of materials and by specially arranging the electrodes for applying external voltages, electrons may be constrained to follow narrow paths about 0.04 microns wide. This indirect method of attaining small dimensions avoids the problems associated with direct small-dimension fabrication.

AT&T are experimenting with a quantum effect transistor which consumes very little power. It uses Gallium Indium Arsenide layers 25 atoms thick and is said to run at 24 GHz.

QUEUED PACKET SYNCHRONOUS EXCHANGE (QPSX)
A packet switching system devised by the University of Western Australia, likely to be adopted in SONET.

QUICK RING
A bus system proposed by Apple for multimedia computers capable of transmitting data at 350 Mbps.

QUICKTIME
A software package introduced by Apple for its Mac and other machines.

Multimedia has advanced with the arrival of Apple's Quicktime, for any Mac with a 68020 or later processor. This "multimedia control architecture" was announced at Apple's 1989 Boston gala; it makes the problem of cobbling together a multimedia outfit that much easier. Apple's new operating system 7.0 suffered a series of delays, delaying Quicktime which is an extension of it.

The main ingredients of Quicktime are an inexpensive video capture board and software (including high-ratio compression), probably to be supplied free with each Mac computer. One consequence of the compression is that 24-bit motion video can be displayed in a window at up to 30 frames per second. "24-bit video" means "3 x 8-bit Red, Blue, and Green colour – a displayed colour may be produced from any combination of one out of 256 Red levels with one out of 256 Blue levels with one out of 256 Green levels. Very few people will require a higher colour quality than this.

The standard type of file in this system – called "Movie" – may contain text, colour graphics and illustrations, sound, animation, and motion video. The next version of a number of well known multimedia packages such as Macromind Director, Mediamaker, and Authorware will support Quicktime.

Quicktime has four parts – system software, file formats, compressors/decompressors, and interface standards and utilities. The system software comprises the Movie Toolbox, the Image Compression Manager, and the component manager. A movie includes presentation slides, animation, image and sound montages etc.

Compression/decompression works for images, animation and video, and the most recent version Quicktime 1.5 supports the Kodak Photo CD Standards. The Image Com-pression Manager applies to all Quicktime software. The Component Manager enables classes of software objects to be found and used.

When a Quicktime device is installed with a Frame Grabber or Digital Signal Processor the Quicktime driver is included in the component manager folder and the new device works correctly with the rest of the system. The sound manager enables applications to create and play sounds from a Mac loud-speaker, and a 16 bit stereo sound manager is planned.

See also MULTIMEDIA.

R

R/W
Read/Write.

R&D
Research & Development.

RACE
Research in Advanced Communications for Europe.

RAID
REDUNDANT ARRAY OF INEXPENSIVE DISCS.
　See DISC ARRAYS.

RAM
RANDOM ACCESS MEMORY. See also SEMICONDUCTORS – MEMORY CHIPS.

RANDOM ACCESS MEMORY (RAM)
See MEMORY.

RANDOM SUPERIMPOSED CODING
Random superimposed coding was used on edged-notched cards when there was an insufficient number of notches to accommodate the codes which would be used to indicate the subjects covered on the card. The idea was taken up by Calvin Mooers with his Zatocode system.

If the dictionary of codes for the index requires that a code using P holes must be used and the average number of subjects per card is Q, the total number of holes available for punching had to be sufficient to limit those cards which dropped out, because of a code being synthesized incorrectly, to an acceptably small number.
　See also ZATOCODING.

RANGANATHAN, S. F.
Ranganathan was born in 1892 and died in 1972. Trained in London during the 20s, he considered that most classification systems were inadequate and in 1933 devised a new system called *The Colon Classification*. He published a full description of it in 1937. Although not widely used, the principle has had considerable influence in classification the-

ory. Ranganathan was instrumental in establishing libraries and library schools in India and was very well known for his work in international organizations such as the FID and UNESCO.

RASTER
The pattern of scanning lines on a CRT screen produced by a spot which traces out a line and then rapidly flies back to trace another adjacent line until the whole screen is traced.

RAY-TRACING
A semi-automatic process provided with certain kinds of imaging software which calculate the effect of imaginary rays of light on surfaces and then alters an image to improve realism and to provide a photographic quality.
　See RENDERING.

REACTION INDEXING
This subject with its difficult classification problems, was pioneered by Weyl in his massive work *Die Methoden der Organische Chemie*, published in the first decade of this century. Its successor, Houben-Weyl's 32 volume *Methoden der Organische Chemie*, an encyclopedia, was started in 1952 and is still incomplete. The problem is simply the effort needed to keep it up to date.

An alternative method, introduced by Weygand, is probably better known, since it was adopted in a modified form by Theilheimer in the widely used *Synthetic Methods of Organic Chemistry*. Since 1980 this book has become a part of the *Journal of Synthetic Methods*, published monthly in machine readable form by Derwent. It includes coverage of patents.

The difficulties of classification in this field arise because relevant aspects to a chemist who wants to synthesize an end product as easily as possible and with a high yield, include starting materials, reaction products, reacting and formed bonds, reagents, conditions, and so on. Computerized systems are able to handle these various concepts together and help the chemist devise suitable strategies.

Users may be divided into end users, information professionals, and patent searchers. End users want a few good leads and often ask questions based on a small substructure. Information professionals know how to ask detailed questions and refine large answer sets; they tend to be concerned about inclusiveness. Patent searchers want all reactions from a given patent to be included in the database – as provided, for instance, in the IDC GREMAS database.

READ CODE
Relative Element Address Designate code – a two dimensional code of Japanese origin used in some facsimile machines.

READING (from the screen)
See ELECTRONIC BOOKS.

REAL TIME
A computer operation, such as an airline reservation, or a Prestel page display, which is executed in the immediate present.

RECALL
See INDEXING SYSTEM PERFORMANCE – RECALL AND PRECISION.

RECORD
A collection of items containing data with common attributes – for example descriptions of car components – together forming a file.

REDUNDANCY
See COMPRESSION – REDUNDANCY.

REEVES, A. H.
Reeves invented a method for converting analogue sound into digital code. He took out British Patent 535860 in 1939 covering the method. Circuits for economically using the invention were unavailable at the time, but the technique subsequently became Pulse Code Modulation (PCM).

PCM came into widespread use following the introduction of complex digital circuits which could be cheaply manufactured. Reeves is also credited with a substantial contribution, if not the invention, of the Type 9000 target location system, usually known as OBOE, widely used during World War II, particularly on D Day.

See PULSE CODE MODULATION.

REGISTER
A computer storage circuit usually used in a CPU for storing the bits in one word.

REGULATION
See DEREGULATION.

RELATIONAL DATABASES
See DATABASES.

RENDERING
A method of improving the realistic appearance of an image by adding light, shade and shadows to appropriate surfaces using a RAY-TRACING technique.

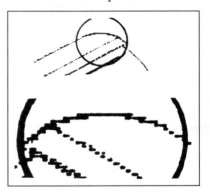

Inadequate resolution makes lines jagged

REPEATER
A device used to regenerate (increase and restore) signals in a communication link.

RESOLUTION
The capability of an electronic display to reproduce data of a given minimum size so that it may be seen. If the resolution is inadequate one effect is to portray curved or diagonal straight lines as jagged lines (See Figure showing original and magnified lines); the dot structure should be finer to reduce such effects.

In the two diagrams on the next page the top map is displayed at a resolution of 200 dots per inch and the bottom map at 300 per inch. The type size is about 5 point.

Note that the words "Constitution Ave" are illegible in the top map but just about legible in the bottom.

See also BIT RATES and DISPLAYS.

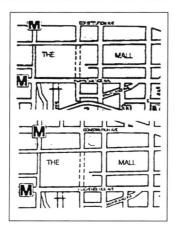

Resolution
Top: map 200 lines/inch
Bottom: 300 lines/inch

RESPONSE TIME
The time a system takes to react to an input, particularly with regard to a change in a computer display after some command input by the operator.

REUTERS
English news and financial information company, founded in 1850 by Paul Julius Reuter, but acquired in 1953 by the Press Association with a later guarantee of independence under the Reuter Trust Agreement.

Reuter ran a carrier pigeon service between Brussels and Aachen but in 1851 decided that London should be his base for a cross channel news service following the laying of the Dover-Calais submarine cable. Reuters is now a world wide company employing over 5000 people and owns a United States subsidiary Rich Inc., which supplies completely equipped financial trading rooms.

Reuter's services included the Monitor range covering news, money, rates, bonds, commodities, oil prices options and reports, shipping cargo data etc.

RGB
Red Green Blue. See COLOUR.

RISC
Reduced Instruction Set Computer.
See SEMICONDUCTORS.

RJE
Remote Job Entry.

RLIN
Research Libraries Information Network.

ROM
Read Only Memory.

ROUTER
See NETWORKS.

RS-170
US specification for a monochrome television frame formed from two fields of interlaced lines of video and synchronizing data, each displayed 60 times per second. A complete frame contains 525 lines and is displayed 30 times per second.

RS232
A standard introduced by the Electronic Industries Association (EIA) for the interface between data terminal and data communication equipment. The original standard RS232 was introduced in 1962, version C was published in 1969 and the current version is EIA 232D introduced in 1986; it corresponds to CCITT V24 and V28, and also to ISO 2110.

The standard defines the electrical and mechanical characteristics of the interface although it does not specify any particular telecommunications message format. It was intended for signalling rates of up to 20 Kbps although it can be used at considerably higher speeds.

RS232-C
EIA standard for terminal-modem serial data transmission interface, equivalent to CCITT V24. Although the current revision is RS232D, the C version is still widely used.

RS-330
A US specification closely resembling RS-170 except for certain differences in sync. arrangements. Used in a few TV cameras.

RS422
An improved version of the RS232 standard to

allow for faster speeds, nominally up to 10 Mbps. RS422 was introduced in 1975 for use with balanced transmission lines.

RS485
An improved version of RS422 providing for multiple driving circuits and multiple receivers.

RUN LENGTH CODING
See under COMPRESSION.

S

S-VHS
SUPER VIDEO HOME SYSTEM.

SAA
SYSTEM APPLICATIONS ARCHITECTURE.

SAMPLING
The process used for converting a continuous time (or analogue signal) into a digital signal. Sampling provides a train of impulses whose amplitudes correspond to the value of the continuous time signal at the instant of sampling. If sampling is carried out at a frequency of at least twice the frequency of the maximum frequency of the signal being sampled, all the information about the signal is extracted. The duration of the sample must be much smaller than the frequency of the signal being sampled.
See also PULSE CODE MODULATION.

SATELLITES
In 1945 A.C.Clarke drew attention to the balance of velocity and gravitational forces for geostationary earth satellites:- "One orbit with a radius of 42,000 Km has a period of exactly 24 hours.

A body in such an orbit, if its plane coincided with that of the equator, would revolve with the earth and would thus be stationary above the same spot on the planet... for a world service three stations would be required".

Clarke provided the sketch shown in the figure below to illustrate the concept and was sufficiently confident about his extraordinary prediction, which he considered to be "a logical extension of developments in the last ten years", to suggest that "a transmitter output of only 50 watts" might be required; this turned out to be a remarkably accurate estimate. Twenty years later, following the launch of several other orbiting satellites, the first geostationary satellite, Syncom, was launched.

A series of satellites followed designed primarily as telephone service relays; INTELSAT 1 (Early Bird) provided 240 voice channels; the 4 tonne INTELSAT VI, launched by an Ariane rocket in October 1989, provides 120,000 channels at less than one hundredth of the cost per channel. INTELSAT VII, launched in 1992 has a still higher capacity and a series of narrow spot beams.

Satellites soon became used as television network relay stations – transmissions from a central point are relayed to ground stations from which cable TV services are provided to local residents. A US NTSC 525 line TV relay channel is equivalent in capacity to about 340 digital telephone channels, a PAL 625 line channel to about 400.

A transponder (receiver/transmitter) on a geostationary satellite is able to communicate with any ground station within its terrestrial "footprint" without the need for a network of switched wiring – a compelling advantage. In practice, footprints do not usually represent one third of the world's surface but are restricted by directional aerials (antennae) to smaller areas to obtain a greater concentration of transmitted power and to cover designated

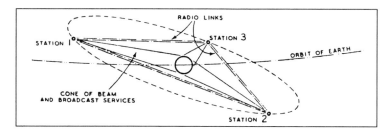

How it all started.

territory.

Satellites used to be glamorous remote gadgets which were occasionally co-opted by information providers to add a touch of class. Access was restricted to special agency research – a CEC (Luxembourg) experiment was proposed in the late seventies and in 1983 became APOLLO – the Article Procurement with Online Local Ordering system. Page data was to be sent via a transponder on the Eutelsat satellite.

The nicely contrived acronym was not enough to provide success, but APOLLO had in mind a second major advantage of satellite transmission – wide bandwidth; large volumes of data may be transmitted at very high speeds. With the arrival of new technology, deregulation, and Direct Broadcast Satellites (DBS), cost-effective information services are spreading.

See also DEREGULATION – SATELLITES.

SATELLITES – TECHNICAL

The power output of a satellite transmitter is usually provided by a special travelling-wave tube (TWT) amplifier capable of operating at very high frequencies and delivering typically up to 60 watts, although the TWT in the Olympus 1 satellite delivers 230 watts. The power actually radiated in dBW (power above 1 Watt) by a satellite is measured as the Equivalent Isotropically Radiated Power (EIRP) to take account of the power gain produced by the aerial's concentration of energy into a beam. "Isotropically Radiated" means radiated in all directions.

Spot beams with frequency re-use, frequently discussed from 1979 onwards, have been a long time acoming. They are fitted on INTELSAT VI which has one "half-global" beam, two continental beams, and four zone beams radiating 31 dBW to concentrate the energy where it is wanted and enabling smaller aerials to be used on ground stations.

Spot beams can be arranged to cover specific small or very small areas of the earth's surface. Frequency re-use means independent circuit sharing of a single channel by signal interleaving and high speed switching whereby signals arriving on one beam may leave by any other beam. INTELSAT VI uses 560 MHz of the frequency spectrum, but by frequency re-use provides the equivalent of over 2600 MHz of bandwidth.

The most recent generation of satellites include INTELSAT VI for global communi-

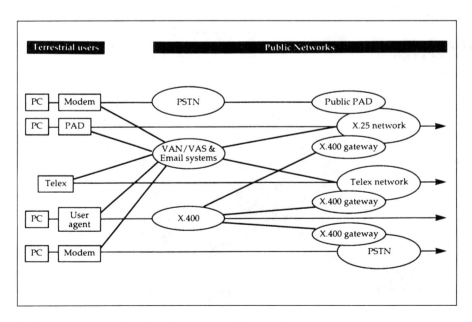

Linking to Inmarsat-C services (by courtesy of Inmarsat)

cations owned by the International Telecommunications Satellite Organization consortium of countries, launched in October 1989. INTELSAT VII launched in 1992, includes narrower spot beams radiating 45 dBW permitting yet smaller ground aerials.

Ways by which the several interfaces for a service called Inmarsat-C may be used to communicate with a mobile station via a satellite are shown in the figure on the previous page.

Astra, the Luxembourg owned satellite for West European DBS services with an EIRP of 50 dbw, was launched in November 1988. TDF-1 for TV owned by France and West Germany is already orbiting. Tele-X a nordic countries satellite is being made ready. These last two have an EIRP exceeding 60 dBW, enabling ground aerials of less than 30cm diameter to be used.

Direct communications between satellites and Very Small Aperture Terminals (VSATs) – that is ground stations with small dishes – have recently been developed.

PTTs who retail capacity on satellite links customarily make nearly 100% profit so transmission prices are high compared with the US. Eutelsat links cost three to five times as much as equivalent links in the US.

See also DEREGULATION – SATELLITES

SATELLITES – VERY SMALL APERTURE TERMINAL (VSATs)

A VSAT system consists of a hub station which transmits data to a transponder on a satellite for relaying to a number of small ground stations, each of which can usually transmit back to the hub via a satellite. The arrangement calls for ground station to hub traffic control typically using an RA/TDMA (Random Access/Time Division Multiple Access) system. The ground stations complete for burst-transmission time-slots on the same communication channel. Readers who are familiar with LANs (Local Area Networks) will recognize this technique.

TATs (Tiny Aperture Terminals) have been introduced in the US using dishes not exceeding 8" in diameter, implying a powerful relay satellite. The price for a complete two-way system is said to be $4000. Sales were forecast at $100 million in 1990 rising to $6 billion in 1994. Mobile satellite terminals in the U.S. estimated at 20,000 in 1989, are expected to increase to 2 million by 1995, a compound growth rate of 150% per year. It is not clear whether the capability of such systems enables them to compete directly with conventional VSATs.

In the US a number of VSAT networks are operating and are presumably competitive with other telecom systems. Farmers Insurance operates a network of 2400 stations, Walmart 1400 stations in its stores network, Holiday Inns 2000 stations at hotels, and Chrysler a system which will grow to 6000 stations interconnecting headquarters and dealers. PanAm-Sat in conjunction with Hughes

Hughes Ku Band "Personal earth station"

Network Systems is offering a shared VSAT hub service for people with VSAT terminals in South America, and a similar service in the US via a link from its Florida teleport.

Regulatory problems discourage potential users from using VSAT facilities. They use terrestrial links instead. A number of European countries who are signatories to EC directives are afraid of foreign entry into their monopolies and are reluctant to allow VSATs to be used, but sweeping deregulatory changes are in progress.

About 6000 VSATs were ordered in 1991, following orders for 30,000 in the previous year, making it very hard to forecast future demand.

By November 1992 there were estimated to be about 100 VSAT networks in Europe compared to about 100,000 in the United States, the latter figure probably being a gross exaggeration.

SATURATION

The amount of white light in a colour (contributing to the vividness of the HUE. High saturation means a small amount of white. See also COLOUR.

SBS

Satellite Business Systems.

SCANN -ER -ING

Many types of desktop scanners became available following the development of DESKTOP PUBLISHING systems in 1985. Hand held scanners can be manually swept across a part of a page and an on-paper copy of the scanned strip emerges as the sweep progresses from integral electronics and printing arrangements, or from the computer to which the scanner is connected.

"Flatbed" scanners embody a glass plate upon which a page, or the open pages of a book, are laid. A sensor strip beneath the glass observes a strip of the image, moves up the page to scan the adjacent strip, and so on until the whole page is scanned. In a "roller fed" scanner the page to be scanned is fed into the machine through rollers and line scanning is carried out by stepping the paper across a fixed sensor strip.

The method originally used is shown in the top diagram on the following page. The paper was wrapped round a drum which rotated beneath a sensor which moved axially. A helical scanning path was followed which appeared as almost horizontal scanning lines on the unwrapped paper.

The arrangement of a modern roller-fed scanner is shown in the bottom diagram.

In two-level scanning, each sensor generates an impulse when the incident reflected light exceeds a fixed value, representing a "white" pixel, and no impulse when the light is below that value, representing a "black" pixel.

In half-tone scanners, the continuous voltage level generated by each sensor in proportion to the intensity of the incident light is quantized into a series of fixed values representing a "greyscale". Typically 256 values are provided (8 bits).

For generating scanned pages in colour, the CCD array makes three passes, letting in light through three different filters. Alternatively a triple 3-filter/CCD is used requiring only one pass.

In electronic dot-generation scanners, such as the Crosfield Magnascan Scanner, "scanning" refers to operations at the output end of the machine by a laser dot generator device which produces colour separations for printing purposes.

Following some preliminary work which started in 1978, The Library of Congress awarded a contract to Integrated Automation to provide scanners, Winchester disc temporary storage, Thomson jukebox 100 Gbyte optical disc WORM storage, laser printers, work stations and monitors. System control is provided by a minicomputer connected to an IBM mainframe.

The pages from a 3 year run of 74 prime scientific journals and other document collections were digitized and indexed to provide a test database. Within-LC users searched the database from their terminals and pages retrieved from the optical discs were passed to terminals for viewing. Monitor resolution was 300 x 150 pixels/inch, printers 300 x 300. The objectives of the experiment were to preserve digitized copies of important documents, test alternative technologies, and assess user reactions.

The mainframe receives commands from terminals, searches LC databases, and passes retrieval commands to the minicomputer which sends page images to requesting

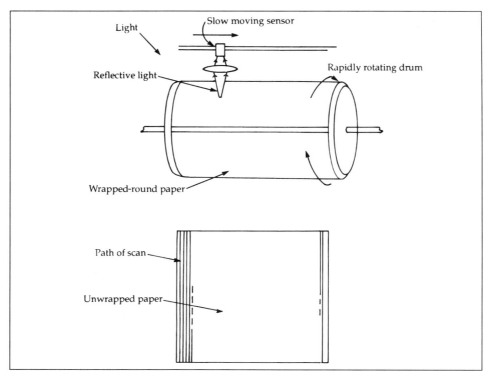

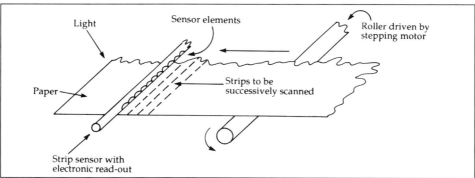

Original helical scanning method and (below) roller fed CCD scanning

terminals.

The objectives and equipment at the National Library of Medicine are broadly similar but particular attention has been paid to throughput rates of material of variable quality. For example a special scanning jig has been constructed for easily scanning and turning over book pages.

The material may consist of reasonably good quality bilevel pages, poor contrast faded bilevel on yellowing paper, variable contrast with stains and bleed-through, pages containing halftone (greyscale) material, or compound pages with mixed text and halftones.

At input stations image enhancement is

applied; compound pages are split up for enhancement appropriate to different parts and then re-combined into a single page. Indexing is unnecessary because the pages will have already been indexed under the NLM Medline system and records are available within that database.

Page storage is on local 20 Mbyte (160 Mbit) BERNOULLI discs. The average compression ratio per page achieved for this particular collection is 14, enabling about 600 pages scanned at 200 dots/inch each containing about 3.7 Mbits of uncompressed data to be stored per disc. The stored pages are periodically transferred to the main, optical disc, storage.

The average throughput time per page input from bound volumes with this system is 50 seconds, inclusive of preparation, capture, quality control, and archiving to optical disc.

In a project at the Centre de Documentation Scientifique et Technologique (CDST), Paris, a division of CNRS, all aspects of an "electronic document delivery service" were tested by delivering pages taken from current issues of 100 prime biomedical journals to users requesting them. Integrated Automation scanners digitizing at 200 pixels/inch, CIT/Alcatel laser printers, and a Thomson optical disc were used.

The objectives were not particularly to test throughput times and indifferent documents, but to study the behaviour of scientists in a real fee-paying situation which involved details like copyright payments to journal publishers, effective telecommunication links etc.

Page conversion cost is very sensitive to conversion time. It can vary from 3 pages per minute for desktop scanners designed for PC-based systems to 30 ppm for high speed scanners such as TDC's Docuscan DS-2400 in which both sides of the documents are captured at one pass. Page sizes and paper thickness/quality will be different with non-uniform content and contrast. Page edges may not be flat. Other kinds of incoming paperwork such as delivery notes, invoices, orders, etc., may be worse.

At the other extreme pages to be scanned could come straight from a Printing house as a pristine ream of A4 80 gramme paper carrying contrasty text, already containing terms required for indexing printed in a fixed position on each sheet. Such sheets could be fed into a scanning machine at high speed by the kind of paper handling system used on fast copying machines.

The recently introduced Microtek Scanmaker machine can scan black and white, negative or colour 35mm slides at 1850 dots per inch with an 8 bit grey scale or 24 bit colour.

3D scanning may be carried out using a technique called "laser stripe triangulation". A laser beam scans over the surface capturing several hundred points. Multiple images from different viewpoints are needed and images may be captured either by using several sensors or by moving the sensor around the object.

A new scanner by Sharp provides 1200 dots per inch resolution with 36 bit colour and laser printer output resolution equivalent to 800 x 800 pixels.

See also TIFF and CCD.

SCHIKARD, W.
See COMPUTERS – HISTORY.

SCI
SCIENCE CITATION INDEX.

SCIENCE CITATION INDEX
This index is published by the Institute for Scientific Information (ISI), Philadelphia. Each edition of the *Citation Index* lists earlier works which were cited by articles published in scientific journals in a particular year. The associated *Source Index* for the year describes each article in more detail. The *Citation Index* is ordered by *cited* author, the *Source Index* by *citing* author.

"By using author references to index documents, the limited ability of a subject indexer to make connections between ideas, concepts, and subjects, was replaced by the far superior ability of the entire scientific community to do the same thing. This meant that a citation index would interpret each of the documents it covered from as many of the viewpoints as existed in the scientific community", says Eugene Garfield, its inventor.

In other words the subject matter of all or part of a cited article is related to the subject matter of the later articles which cite it.

The arrangement of the *SCI* provides for unique kinds of Information Retrieval. A researcher interested in, say, "The development of Surface Physics in the 20th century" would find it hard to unearth information about this topic using conventional methods. However a look-up in a succession of annual SCI's of "FRANKLIN B. 1752 Phil.Trans. Roy. Soc.", describing his observation of effects at a surface, would produce a collection of articles, each having cited Franklin's article, because partially or entirely they are about the same subject.

A citation index uses article citations as subject symbols. The Figure shows part of the Science Citation Index.

SUTTGEN G					
77 Havtarzt26	277				
Reimer G	Arch Derm R	270	313	81	
SUTTIE JW					
72 J Dairy Sci	55 790				
Ekstrand J	Act Pham T	488	433	81	
77 Physiol Rev 57	1				
Gottschalk KE	Theochem	1	197	81	
Walsh PN	Fed Proc	40	2086	81	
SUTTKUS RD					
etc. etc.					

Entries in the 1981 Science Citation Index (By courtesy of the Institute for Scientific Information)

A citation index enables the user to find published scientific articles. Descriptions of earlier articles are followed by later articles which cite them. A searcher enters the index at a known article of interest and is led to later citing articles.

In the Figure, the 1977 article by Suttie in the Physiological Review, vol. 57, page 1 is cited by the Gottschalk and Walsh articles. Its subject "The biochemistry of vitamin K" is unambiguously symbolized by "SUTTIE JW 77 Physiol Rev 57 1". It is an article of repute about that topic. It is assumed that the searcher knows it already and uses it as an entry point to the index. Entering, in this example, the 1981 index at those symbols he is led to the two 1981 citing articles. The Walsh article is entitled "Platelets and coagulation proteins" – information which can be obtained from a different section of the index, the Source Index, which provides details about all the 1981 citing articles.

Note that neither the Suttie nor the Walsh articles include "vitamin K" in the title. Vitamin K plays an important role is blood clotting.

Citation Index information is arranged in such a way that questions like "Has any further investigation of Einstein's unified field theory been pursued in the last few years?" may be answered with fairly high RECALL and PRECISION. Authors researching this subject can reasonably be expected to cite the foundation paper.

SCIENTOMETRICS
The study of science based on bibliometrics, that is by the analysis of the bibliographies contained in scientific articles and books.

SCRATCHPAD
A type of memory that usually has small capacity but very fast access.

SCREENS AND PRINTING
The photograph ("bromide") of a continuous tone illustration, used by printers to make a printing plate, is taken through a piece of glass with closely spaced lines ruled on it. This "screen" produces lines of variable width corresponding to grey levels on the photograph which take up ink on the plate and produce a halftone reproduction. The screen is usually rotated through an angle – often 45 degrees – to avoid interference effects associated with vertical or horizontal lines in the original.

A screen of 150 lines or dots per inch is adequate for very good quality reproduction of printer illustrations. Detail scanned in at a higher resolution will not then appear. Since the quality of reproduction of the tones in an illustration is usually of greater importance than the fine detail, attention is shifted to good reproduction of a wide range of tones, ideally at least 256, sensed during scanning.

The number of halftones that can be printed depends on the number of printed dots per inch (since the size of the smallest dot effectively dictates the tonal range) and the screen pitch, as calculated from :-

Number of halftones = printed dots/inch^2/ screen pitch^2) + 1.

If the printer can provide 300 dots/inch and the screen pitch is 150, the number of halftones (nH) can be nH $= (300^2/150^2 + 1 = 5$. The "+1" is for the non-printed halftone "white". If a "high resolution" printer – such as a Linotron 300 running at its maximum 2540 dots/ inch is used, and the screen is 150, nH $= 2540^2/$

$150^2 + 1 = 287$ (approx), assuming of course that this amount of halftone data was input.
See also HALFTONES.

SCRIPT FILE

1. A file containing Hypertext data.
See HYPERCARD and HYPERTEX.
2. A small file for setting up the operational telecommunication requirements of a computer.

A script file can range in comprehensivity from setting basic requirements like bit rates, modem designation etc., to controlling quite elaborate tasks, as in the Hayes Smartcom III modem system such as automatically logging on to and polling a remote database periodically, querying the database, and downloading data, all in "background mode" – that is while the computer is being used for some other task.

A script file may consist of a form in which the user is prompted to enter the various parameters required, which then automatically becomes a telecoms control file, or it may be written as a program in a script programming language to control specific requirements.

A script file may also include passwords, telephone numbers, etc., which are used automatically as needed.

SCROLL

Moving an image virtually or horizontally to view data which is outside the normal confines of the screen.

SCSI

SMALL COMPUTER SYSTEMS INTERFACE.

SCVF

Single Channel Voice Frequency.

SDH

SYNCHRONOUS DIGITAL HIERARCHY.

SDI

Selective Dissemination of Information.

SDLC

Synchronous Data Link Control. A data link control protocol developed by IBM, superseding BSC.

SECAM

Sequential Couleur a Memoire.

SECRECY

See PRIVACY.

SECURITY

The security of computers and computer files are subject to normal kinds of physical security, including a need to "backup" files periodically on duplicate storage which remains intact if the computer crashes.

In recent years files have been accessed by unauthorized local or remote users (HACKERS) or have been corrupted by the immediate or delayed action of VIRUSES or WORMS, calling for special forms of security

Data ENCRYPTION is an additional form of security and one way of doing it is shown in the illustration on the next page (by courtesy of Port Knox) in which all hard disk data is encrypted. A "touch key" (the white disc attached to the key ring) touched against a receptacle on the keyboard activates a chip controlling the key code with one of 281 trillion combinations, allowing the data to be read after a password has been typed.

SEMANTICS

The principles which govern meaning in a language.

SEMICONDUCTOR

A material, such as silicon or germanium, whose conductivity increases with temperature, and may be made more conductive permanently by the introduction of other chemicals.

SEMICONDUCTORS – ASICs and EPLDs

An Application Specific Integrated Circuit (ASIC) means a chip designed for a specific application, sometimes available as a standard take-it-or-leave-it product, but usually made specifically in small "custom built" quantities for people who cannot get a standard chip for the job in hand and cannot justify the costs, nor require the quantities, associated with tooling up for mass production.

The "custom built" kind may be "wholly customized" that is designed and made from the ground up, or may be "customized from an existing chip" – for example the ASIC might be a chip consisting of a number of logic

The Port Knox touch-key encrypting device

gates whose interconnections may be altered by burning fuses on the device. It is possible to buy a PC based system for a few thousand dollars for performing this operation enabling a user to produce his own prototype chip.

An alternative approach is for the chip supplier to mass-produce partially finished chips arranged in such a way that a whole range of chips for different applications may be produced by a relatively small amount of "finishing touches".

The advantage of this approach is low cost and rapid delivery of special purpose chips usually in relatively small quantities from about 1000 upwards. In the US a semi-standard ASIC gate array would cost about $15,000 to modify for a specific purpose, and somewhat less than that to produce the first 1000 items. The total time for the job would be a few months. A chip completely purpose made from scratch might cost up to $250,000 to develop, would take more than a year, and would require a production run of an least 75,000 to be worth doing.

In the later eighties ASICs became available "off the shelf" for a variety of small-demand analogue applications of which there are still many in spite of the general trend towards digitization. Typically a chip consists of a number of inter-connectible "tiles", number-

ing up to about 50, ready to be arranged for a specific application. Circuits include operational amplifiers, switched filter sections, photo-diode arrays, and controllers.

A slower variation of the ASIC called an Electrically Programmable Logic Device (EPLD) appeared in 1989. Typically it consists of a number of logic circuits having many possible input and output combinations which can be changed by a program which alters an elaborate pattern of fused links. If a mistake is made the connections can be erased and the program re-started. EPLD's tend to be relatively slow because of the propagation delays introduced by the lengthy interconnection lattices.

SEMICONDUCTORS – FUTURES

During the last few years questions have frequently been asked about the extraordinary rate of progress of semiconductor technology. At whatever factor you look it seems as if performance and speed will continue to increase more or less indefinitely – "feature size" (meaning the size of circuit elements, or their spacing) has been halved every six years, and prices continue to fall.

It was said that at some point it would not be possible to fabricate smaller devices – and smaller size is essential for higher performance. The limit was said to be somewhere between 0.5 and 0.1 micron spacing between circuit elements, at which point further developments in optical lithography (the basis for design layouts) would not be possible.

The situation was reviewed in 1990 by Myers. Myers quotes Gordon Moore, Intel Chairman, who expected at that time that the Intel i860 microprocessor, containing over 1 million transistors on a single chip, would be replaced in due course by chips with up to 50 million transistors on a chip.

"The number of transistors produced doubles every year. Each successive number of this series was equal to more than the sum of all the previous numbers. This means that the industry had to find additional markets each year as large as the sum of all the previous markets. To do that, of course, means the price had to fall. It did – by a millionfold".

"To keep the industry on this curve, each man, woman and child in the developed countries having consumed a million transistors last year, would have to account for two million this year and four million next. He himself acquired about 16 million last year – on his boat, in his home PC, and in his office PC. Did each of you consume your four million transistors last year?" he asked.

However there is one aspect of all this where costs are increasing rapidly. The unit price for manufacturing equipment such as a lithography machine or an evaporator used to be about $12,000. Unit prices are now about $55 million.

A similar extrapolatory argument was put forward in greater detail by Andrew Rappaport quoted by Myers. Using current 1 micron technology, theoretical memory density is 9 Megabytes per square inch and logic density 4 million transistors per square inch. In 1999 using 0.3 micron technology the figures could be 150 megabytes per square inch and 70 million transistors per square inch.

The relative cost could be about 833 microcents and 330 micro-cents per unit element in 1990, expected to become 29 microcents and 14 microcents in 1999. Rappaport said that "he was just doing order of magnitude calculations on assumptions that he believed to be possible". It looks as if we are heading for a glut.

However Myers also quotes Edward Davis, President of Raynet whose thesis is that the telecommunications industry could easily consume a high proportion of these cheap devices.

"I am about to describe the industry that is going to keep the silicon factories very, very, busy. The local loop (subscriber to exchange telephone connections) market is very big; rebuilding copper plant runs to about $10 billion a year in the US alone. My belief is that within two years the cost to install a fiber system will drop to that of copper. ... once fiber has been installed its inexpensive and unused bandwidth will permit services never before delivered or previously considered".

To the best of my recollection fiber has been expected to break even with copper next year, every year during the last 10 years. Davis said that he expected that very little copper would be installed in the telephone network anywhere in the second half of the nineties. It seems to me most unlikely that the rate of bringing fiber into homes will proceed at anything like this rate.

A more likely future possibility is the pro-duction of the equivalent of an IBM PC AT on a chip. The size of such a computer is likely to be dictated by the fact that it must have human interfaces such as a keyboard, disc drive, and display. Such a chip has been proposed. It is called the AMD 286LX. It contains a 286 processor, clock, and controllers for peripherals, memory, input/output and display (the basic support functions) and a power-economy system. Add a memory chip, the necessary busses and some minor bits and pieces and you have a power-economy PC AT.

SEMICONDUCTORS – GALLIUM ARSENIDE

Electrons move faster through a GaAs crystal lattice than they do through silicon and GaAs transistors will operate at up to four times faster than the fastest silicon devices. Cray have built a supercomputer using GaAs technology and several manufacturers can now supply relatively expensive GaAs gate arrays for use when very high speed outweighs price considerations. GaAs electrons have low mass and high mobility. Theoretically there are several advantages. GaAs devices operate at lower voltages and lower powers than silicon – up to five times less power. They will switch at much higher speeds, and will work over a wider range of temperatures. A GaAs gate switches in about 10 picoseconds with the theoretical potential of being clocked at about eight thousand million times per second (8 GHz) compared to a maximum of about 200 MHz for silicon circuits.

So far most devices have been MEtal Semiconductor Field Effect Transistors (MESFETs) or MODulation Doped Field Effect Transistors (MODFETs) with a source and gate about 4 micrometres apart and a deposited metal gate one micrometre (0.001 mm) wide between them. The acronyms describe different methods of manufacture, superiority being claimed for MODFETs.

Gallium Arsenide devices were demonstrated in the United States in 1978 based on the earlier work of Esaki and Tsu. A number of manufacturers produced experimental circuits in 1984; considerable manufacturing problems are being overcome and GaAs has gradually become more widely used.

To realize anything like GaAs potential, stray capacitance has to be reduced by using the shortest thinnest connections. With dimensions down to the micrometre region the state of the manufacturing art is being stretched to its limits.

The 1984/85 optimism about GAAs was short lived. Billion dollar forecasts were hastily revised. GaAs transistors were known to be able to switch very quickly but it was not until 1986 that it became possible to make reliable devices with repeatable performance.

However GaAs chips are now being used to fulfil certain premium requirements. The Cray 3 computer uses small 400-gate GaAs chips, and circuits with up to 4000 gates supplied by GigaBit Logic are being used in the Cray 4. 4Kbit SRAMs with an access time of 3 ns have been made by GigaBit. NTT claim to have made GaAs 4K ROMs with 1.2 ns access times.

100,000 gate arrays were made in 1991. Texas Instruments have developed a 32-bit 150 MHz pipelined RISC processor. GaAs circuits were expected to enable microprocessors to work at clock frequencies of around 250 MHz by about 1992. In practice a company called Tarquint offered a component running at 500 MHz in that year but applications of the material still seem to be mainly limited to small devices because large wafers of GaAs cannot be fabricated – the substance is brittle.

In 1992 MODFETs made from thin layers of GaInAs films were described increasing the current gain cut-off frequency from 50 to 250 GHz.

(See also MODFET). The 1992 market was between $290 million and over $600 million. Speed at any price was seen to be a false dogma.

In April 1993 it was discovered that a gallium-sulphur compound can be used to add a layer to GaAs devices which increases their performance by at least six times. The process can be accomplished with little increase in production costs.

SEMICONDUCTORS – GRAPHICS, IMAGING CHIPS AND VRAMS
See GRAPHIC SIGNAL PROCESSORS.

SEMICONDUCTORS – INTEGRATED CIRCUITS
From the 1950s onward, methods have been introduced for the mass production of interconnected transistors with other circuit ele-ment on a small slice of silicon in order to provide more uniform and more reliable performance, with more components packed into a smaller space and faster switching speeds with less power and less heat dissipation.

Semiconductor mass production and uniformity have been achieved by improvements in the design of photo-mask techniques, and in the chemical vapour deposition of thin films, ion implantation, and diffusion on silicon wafers (the "planar" technique). Patterns of different materials are built up on the oxidised silicon surface by deposition through stencil-like masks in a series of separate photo-etching processes.

Impurities which change the properties of existing materials are diffused into areas not protected by masks to a pre-determined depth by heat treatment. The properties of materials can also be changed by ion implantation; this involves the ionization of an impurity material and the application of a high voltage to accelerate its ions so that they penetrate the surface of the host material to some required depth.

Many complete chip circuits are fabricated on a single wafer of silicon. Each is cut from the wafer and sealed into a small plastic container. Fine wire connections are made between the IC and pins protruding from the container. The pins match mating sockets suitable for mounting on a printed circuit board.

Integrated circuits have enabled more and more information to be processed faster at lower cost. Information is presented not by the information-rich words of human communication but by apparently inefficient strings of "bits" – 0's and 1's. The word "information" requires at least 77 bits to be represented by these symbols. Processing speed depends on the rate at which bit-processing circuits can be switched on and off.

See also CHIP MARKETS.

SEMICONDUCTORS – INTEGRATED CIRCUIT PERFORMANCE
Apart from the need to keep down the size, weight, and cost of packages containing thousands of transistors, unwanted electrical capacitance – which absorbs energy and reduces speeds – is proportional to the size and nearness of circuit elements. Capacitance can be reduced by using very small elements

connected by very short wires.

We are used to assuming that electricity is conveyed "instantaneously" at about the same speed as light. In terms of today's circuit performance ns (1 ns = one thousand millionth of a second) delays are important. The voltage required to switch a circuit must be generated by a flow of current from the switching source. An electrical current travels about 30 cms along an ideal conductor in 1 nanosecond (ns) but in practice delays are introduced by unwanted capacitance and possibly some inductance, increasing the delay to about 2 ns.

A good analogy of electronic switching is a water tank which must be filled with water before you can take a shower from the sprinkler connected to an outlet at the top of the tank. The way to get a shower quickly when the tank is empty is to fill the tank up from a hose whose diameter is so large that it offers little resistance to water from the supply which comes rushing through it at a great rate.

In electronic terms the voltage required to switch the circuit has to be raised to the required level (the change in water level) as quickly as possible by a flow of current (the water through the hose) into the circuit's capacitance (the volume of the tank) until the capacitance is filled.

The major factor limiting the switching speed is the rise time of the voltage to the switching value. An approximate figure for the rise time can be calculated from $Tr = EC/I$, where Tr is the rise time in nanoseconds (ns) E is the voltage in volts, C is the capacitance in picofarads (pf) and I the current in milliamps.

Values in a microcomputer circuit could be 2 volts for the switching voltage, 100 pf for the circuit input capacitance (which will include the capacitance of interconnecting wiring), and 1 ma for the current. From the above equation the rise time then works out a "rather slow" 200 ns.

To repeatedly switch a circuit – for example to move a stream of data from computer storage on to a Cathode Ray Tube (CRT), sufficient time must elapse for the control voltage to switch the circuit, for it to remain switched for a short period, and for it to recover in readiness for the next switching voltage.

If these events took, say, 400ns, at least that time interval must elapse between clocking (synchronized switching) impulses. The clocking rate to accommodate successive switching could be no greater than 1 sec/400 ns = 2.5 million times per second or 2.5 Megahertz (MHz). This is slow by today's standards.

SEMICONDUCTORS – MEMORY CHIPS

The general requirements for a semiconductor memory are fast access time and high capacity in the smallest possible space to handle the longest possible word lengths, together with any special characteristics that may be necessary for particular applications.

Expected performance in the near future is exemplified by the targets set by Sematech, a consortium of US manufacturers, who put up $1 billion with the major objective of developing manufacturing techniques and production equipment to reduce the dimensions between chip circuit elements. The objectives, which have probably already been overtaken by events, included single chip 4Mbyte Random Access Memories (RAMs) in 1990, leading to 16 Mbytes by 1993 or earlier.

In 1988 IBM announced that it had manufactured circuits with 0.5 micron spacing using X-ray lithography. In February 1989 IBM claimed that it had made 128 Kbyte Static RAM memories using 5 micron CMOS technology working at 5 ns speeds. Size reduction and well understood CMOS has been the choice, rather than a change to more exotic material.

In February 1990 IBM said it had made 16 Mbit CMOS DRAMs on its production line. Toshiba claimed to have made prototype 16 Mbit 45 ms DRAMs in late 89.

The technology likely to be used is a combination of bipolar and CMOS to capitalize on bipolar's ability rapidly to deliver current, and CMOS's low power requirements. Perhaps Sematech will jump to GaAs technology. The Japanese are currently well ahead in the memory field in production, price, and performance. In November 1989, Toshiba claimed to have made one Mbyte SRAMs with an access time of only 8 nanoseconds.

In July 1989 IBM set up a production line for 4 Mbit 80 ns dynamic RAM (DRAM) memory chips in Germany. Most other major manufacturers such as Mitachi, Toshiba, Motorola, and others followed. DRAMs are very widely used and US manufacturers abandoned the market in the mid-eighties when the Japanese jumped to 256 Kbit and then to 1 Mbit DRAM mass production with substantial price cutting. One company, Toshiba, makes one third of the world's consumption. In July 1989 Toshiba allocated over £300 million for 4 Mbit DRAM manufacture.

In 1989 there was not a proportional drop in costs per bit as the large capacity chips arrived. At around $17, 1 Mbit chips cost much less than 4 times the cost of 250 Kbit chips, but 4 Mbit chips were expected to cost about $100 each in quantity, much more than 4 times the cost of a 1 Mbit chip.

By 1993 the Sematech objectives mentioned above appeared too modest by far. The resources for developing chips with very large memories have become available by intercompany alliances. IBM, Toshiba, and Siemens Nixdorf expect to jointly develop 256 Mbyte memory chips. While the Pentium will contain over 3 million transistors, an AMD – Hewlett Packard alliance is aiming to reduce spacings to 0.35 microns and put 10 million transistors on a chip. The investment is about one billion dollars and first results are expected in 1994.

Memories operating today which have reached the market fitted within equipment fall far short of the performance discussed above; there are several types for different applications. A RAM usually consists of a large number of transistors each charging or discharging an associated capacitor to store one bit. Dynamic RAMs, (DRAMs) widely used for main memory, are cheap but "volatile" – the capacitor charge leaks away so they remain periodic "refreshment". Static RAMs (SRAMs) require less power, are non-volatile, but are more expensive.

The other types in major use include Erasable Programmable Read Only Memories (EPROM), erasable by exposure to ultraviolet light for 20 minutes, and Electrically Erasable PROMs (EEPROM). These memories are used to retain data programmed into them ready for use when the equipment is switched on – for instance for "Booting", that is to load sufficient software from disc to make a computer ready to use.

A new type of RAM appeared in 1989 using a polarizable capacitor made of a ferroelectric material. A polarized capacitor stores an applied voltage, without requiring to be refreshed, until a depolarizing potential is applied – a process which takes as little as 1 ns. Such a capacitor can store a large charge since its dielectric constant is hundreds of times larger than that of the capacitors in other RAMs. Production and applications of this device are in progress.

Also in 1989 a new kind of memory resembling an EPROM called a Flash Memory appeared. A flash memory may displace EPROMs, EEPROMs, or SRAMs. Flash memories offer storage which does not need an applied voltage (as do SRAMs) to retain data, they may be partially or completely re-programmed within the host machine (EPROMs must be removed to be erased by 20 minutes UV exposure), and they cost much less and are smaller than EEPROMs (although they cannot be re-programmed at the individual byte level). One application is as a "solid state disk" on portable computers – as in the Psion Mc400 machine.

Most microcomputers available today embody RAMs with access times in the range 400 to 100 ns associated with clock frequencies of up to about 10 MHz, and more recently up to 50 MHz with no wait states. Microcomputer manufacturers push components to their limits to obtain a competitive edge. In April 1989 a Taiwanese manufacturer, Acer, introduced a microcomputer, the 1100/33, with its 80386 microprocessor running at 33 MHz. This machine overcomes the speed limitations of the best available RAMs by using a dedicated chip for controlling a RAM cache – the 82385 – which will work at 20 ns. Other new machines working at this speed soon followed.

SEMICONDUCTORS – MICROPROCESSOR AND VLSI DEVELOPMENTS

Very Large Scale Integration (VLSI) is not material-specific – originally it was a phrase used to cover methods of producing even greater numbers of circuit elements on one chip – say 25,000 gates with dimensional control down to 0.5 micrometres. In the US a project called the Very High Speed Integrated Circuit (VHSIC) program to try and achieve these goals is in hand for military equipment, no doubt with Japanese-competitive spin-offs also in mind. The program seems to be based on an extension of mature silicon technology rather than on riskier GaAs.

The main effort is directed towards "scaling" – that is size reduction in order to increase the number of circuit elements per chip, and to reduce inter-connection lengths and capacitances in order to obtain speed increases. It is considerably easier to scale down MOS devices. Scaled down bipolars are prone to breakdown at low voltages.

The reduction of the current required by each of the thousands of active circuit elements in an IC, as is achieved by using CMOS, is also important not only because of much lower drain on the battery in portables, but also because of a substantial reduction in the power dissipated in the form of heat. More elements can be packed into a smaller space without overheating.

The Intel 80286 commercially available microprocessor embodies 130,000 semiconductor elements on a square chip with sides of little more than 0.25 inches. The microprocessor used by Hewlett-Packard as a CPU in their 32 bit microcomputer uses nearly half a million elements on an even smaller chip. An electron beam is used to make the masks required for its manufacture to enable conductors to be spaced 1 micrometre apart with 1/4 micrometre tolerance.

In 1986 it was suggested that later in the 1980s the target would probably be raised to one million transistors per chip and that an advance of this kind would required three major ingredients – hierarchy, regularity, and design tool automation.

Design hierarchy means splitting up the design into manageable portions which are then joined together in a complete design. Regularity refers to the need to use the same kind of circuit element with the same interface as often as possible. Design tool automation means the computer generation of layouts for standard functions as used in memories, gates, etc.

One trick used to improve economies of scale is to use a standard multiple-circuit-element design with standard fabrication sequences up to the last operation which is the only "special" part of the manufacturing process – the addition of the metallic layer which interconnects the myriad basic circuits.

These circuits may be interconnected to form various basic logic arrangements, to be in turn connected to form units such as blocks of RAM cells, Counters, Registers. The manufacturing data needed to complete the final computer-controlled interconnecting process is a matter for the designer of the complete chip. The designer supplies the data as an on-disc program which controls the final process.

In 1987 the 32 bit Intel 80386 and Motorola's 68020 microprocessor were announced. There was a good deal of controversy about the speeds of these chips when used in microcomputers. The 386 was believed to be faster on average although the different characteristics of the machines in which they became available made chip comparisons difficult.

In April 1989 Motorola announced 1.2 million transistors on a single chip – the 32 bit 68040 (sometimes called Complex Instruction Set computer or CISC, competing with RISC described below) beating Intel's announcement of the 80486 by a few weeks. A chip containing over one million transistors had arrived on time as predicted. It offers four times the performance of the 68030, and is compatible with it and with earlier chips in the series.

The Intel 80486 – compatible with the earlier 286 and 386, and able to work with software designed for those processors – includes a maths co-processor, cache memory, and memory management on the same chip. It is designed to be clocked at 25 MHz, and to process 20 million instructions per second (Mips).

In 1990 TRW/Motorola announced that they could provide a chip – the CPUAX – containing four million transistors, capable of operating at 200 Million Floating Point Operations per Second (MFLOPS). There are a number of redundant cells in the chip's cellular design. If any cell fails the chip repairs itself by connecting a replacement cell. In September 1989 Intel announced the 80960 specifically to handle input/output intensive operations such as Local Area Network (LAN) control.

The Intel P5 or Pentium chip is expected to arrive during 1993 enabling manufacturers who have invested in 80486 chips to recoup some of their investment.

In 1992 Fujitsu claimed that it had developed an HEMT transistor capable of operating at 9.6 Gbps. IBM announced that it had manufactured a MOSFET device 20 times smaller than anything previously manufactured which could be used as a memory element in 4 Gbit DRAMs.

The size of the market for chips is now so large that it has been feasible to progress from the processor, through the processor plus co-processor stage, to the "embedded" processor. A sufficient number of machines are required for special applications as to justify a purpose-designed but mass-produced chip "embedded" to handle just that application.

SEMICONDUCTORS – QUANTUM EFFECT
See QUANTUM EFFECT CHIPS.

SEMICONDUCTORS – REDUCED INSTRUCTION SET COMPUTERS (RISC)
There is more to RISC than simply discarding a range of instructions that are rarely used. The idea has been extended to include caches, pipelining, and wider channel bandwidth, with a view to completing an instruction in one machine cycle instead of the many cycles usually required.

There has been some confusion about exactly what is covered by the term RISC. It has been suggested that the definition should include:-
* Single cycle execution of all instructions
* Single-word standard length instructions
* A total of 128 or fewer instructions
* Four, or fewer, addressing modes and instruction formats
* All operations by within-CPU register to register, except Memory access which should be by load/store instructions only
* Hardwire controlled
* A relatively large CPU register file (at least 32 registers).

In terms of semiconductor development RISC first appeared in a series of chips or chip sets all using CMOS technology led by Inmos with the T800 and Novix with a specialized chip for image processing. The idea was taken up by IBM, using its own or Intel chips, and gathered pace when the Sun company, leading workstation supplier, introduced its Fujitsu-manufactured SPARC chip in 1987.

Sun was taken over by AT&T and Xerox endorsed the use of SPARC, followed by Unisys. RISC had obviously arrived in workstations, but its potential was soon realized by the big guns of the industry.

Motorola announced a RISC chip set in 1988

consisting of the 165,000 transistors 88100 processor with two 88200, 750,000 transistor, cache and memory management chips, a total of nearly 1.7 million transistors. It was quickly adopted by a leading manufacturer of workstations – Tektronix. in September 1989 Advance Computers introduced a machine using 500 88000 series processors.

What Motorola did not expect was the arrival of another Intel chip, much more remarkable than its 80486 CISC, the up-market 64 bit 1 micron static CMOS i860/80860. Intel sometimes uses its "i" trademark e.g. the 80860 becomes the "i860". To add to the confusion the 80860/i860 was formerly known as the N10. The 80860 runs at 50 MHz. It is said to operate at 85,000 Dhrystones per second – twice as fast as the SPARC chip.

RISC chips like the 80860 are not compatible with the 286/386/486 series because they are primarily designed for use in workstations with the UNIX operating system. CAD is a major workstation application and to this end 7% of the 860's die is for handling graphics, and 15% is for vector processing – a special requirement for CAD graphics. Intel states that the development costs of the 860 were $176 million, and the manufacturing plant cost $338 million.

The development of the 80860 has been described in considerable detail. Intel leap-frogged to 64 bits against the 32 bits of their competitors. Leslie Kohn, project leader, formed a small team with Sai-Wai Fu, design manager, to speed up the project of minimizing bureaucracy. A major breakthrough was the achievement of parallelism to enable three operations to be completed in one clock cycle.

IBM will adopt the 80860 to be used on some of the IBM PS/2 series of PCs to boost their performance to near-Cray levels.

SEMICONDUCTORS – SMART CARDS AND SMART TAGS
See SMART CARDS.

SEMICONDUCTORS – SWITCHES
Brian Josephson earned a Nobel Prize for his discovery in 1962 that electron tunnelling at the junction of two metals could be controlled by a magnetic field provided the junction is immersed in liquid helium. The arrangement could be used as an extremely fast switch. IBM considered developing a computer using

Josephson junctions in 1963 but decided that it would be too costly.

SEMICONDUCTORS – TRANSISTOR
A semi-conducting device invented by Bardeen, Brattain, and Shockley in 1947, following experiments with semi-conductive rectifiers similar to those used on the earliest "crystal radio" receivers. They duly received a Nobel Prize.

After the invention of the transistor, semiconductor versions of the valve wartime circuits developed by Alan Blumlein, F.C.Williams, and others appeared, but the transistor versions worked much faster, occupied far less space, and dissipated very little heat.

A number of people joined Shockley's group but in the sixties Noyce, Moore, and others left it and tried to obtain some finance for further work. They were unable to get support from any of the thirty companies which they approached. Eventually they got started in 1968, backed by Seymour Fairchild, a camera inventor, who provided them with $1.3 million of venture capital. It was the people from this company who were later mainly responsible for founding the "Silicon Valley" industry around San Jose.

Two microprocessor leaders emerged – Intel and Motorola. In the late seventies Intel received a contract for the IBM PC which was launched in 1981. This established the 8088 16 bit processor as the standard.

In 1949 the EDSAC computer contained 3000 valves, consumed 15 Kilowatts of power, and occupied a special room. In 1989 a chip containing over one million transistors appeared (the 80860). It is infinitely more powerful than EDSAC and occupies a few square centimetres.

A transistor functions in many respects like a radio valve (US "tube"). It amplifies a signal applied to a control electrode, or if a larger signal is applied, the current through it may be cut off, so the transistor acts like a switch.

But a transistor generates almost no heat, is very reliable, and is very small. Improvements in technology have enabled its size to be further reduced and its other properties to be improved so that when acting as a switch it will operate very rapidly. Increases in switching speed have resulted in major advances in logic gates, the basic circuit elements in a microprocessor.

We usually assume that light or an electric current travel between two points almost instantaneously. An electric current takes about 1 nanosecond (1 ns = 1 thousand millionth of a second) to travel along a wire 30 cms long. During March 1990 IBM succeeded in running an experimental transistor at 75,000 million Hz; each cycle then lasts for about 13 picoseconds (1 ps = 1 million millionth of a second). The semi-conducting layers in this transistor are two millionths of an inch thick. in the world of transistor switches, the speed of an electric current requires consideration.

A transistor is formed from two types of semi-conducting materials – "p-type" and "n-type". The atomic structure is such that the p-type material will accept electrons from n-type material. When such materials are deposited in layers, and the appropriate potentials are applied between them, the transistor may be used as an amplifier, or switch.

The microscopic size of a transistor enables thousands, or hundreds of thousands of them, to be formed by chemical deposition methods in an extremely small space. The transistors may be inter-connected to provide electronic circuits of extraordinary complexity and performance, the arrangement being manufactured as a "chip" – a very small container with numerous metallic connections to the circuits contained within it.

SEMICONDUCTORS – TRANSPUTERS
A Transputer is a semiconductor device manufactured by an English (or more correctly ex-English) company called INMOS, founded in 1978 mainly on government money. The funds required to back R&D and production were under-estimated and the company was hawked round the market until being purchased by Thorn-EMI. The total investment from its inception until the company was sold to the French company SGS-Thomson in 1989 was probably about £800 million.

Inmos's first products appeared in 1984. The company moved into profit in 1988 having sold at least 100,000 Transputers in that year compared with a few thousand in 1987.

A present generation Transputer is a chip containing a CPU, some memory, a scheduler for changing on-chip links, and four serial communication channels. The arrangement is designed for the implementation of Communication Sequential Processes (CSP) in which one or more Transputers run a number of sequential programs concurrently, exchanging messages over the communication channels, thereby providing parallel computing. A Transputer is a RISC inasmuch as the instruction set is simple – there is a stack of only three registers plus three control registers.

The T414 Transputer is a 32 bit device replaced by an improved version, the T800. In late 1989 the price of a T800 was reduced to $20 and the H1 was announced with 8 channels using 1 micrometre spacing on the chip. It will process at over one hundred million instructions per second.

The Transputer was designed for multiple-Transputer parallel processing and in this form provides the cheapest fastest form of ready-made parallel processing available. One factor which has inhibited its adoption is unfamiliarity with the special programming language OCCAM which goes with it. OCCAM, designed by Professor Hoare at Oxford and David May at Inmos, Bristol, organizes the handshaking between Transputer links, among other things, freeing a program designer from this chore.

A small company called Meiko is at the top of the world league for supplying "highly-parallel" inexpensive very fast computers. It uses a Transputer array. Another Transputer machine called Supernode was developed under a CEC ESPRIT project and is produced by Thorn-EMI, who retain a foothold in this field through its company Parsys. 20 machines working at 400 Mflops were sold in late 1988, and sales of over 200 were forecast for 1989. In another ESPRIT project called Genesis, Supernode II is being developed for UNIX applications.

In October 1989 a company called U-Microcomputers announced a board for the IBM PCs or PS/2s incorporating one T800. In reported tests, when this board was used in a 68000 processor microcomputer, the time taken to carry out complex molecular design work was reduced from minutes to seconds.

A special effort was made in the UK to publicize Transputer applications by setting up SERC/DTI funded regional support centres, since extended to the US and Europe. This has fostered a good deal of work at universities.

SEMICONDUCTORS – TYPES
Until comparatively recently there were two major planar (layer by layer fabrication) technology products – Bipolar and MOS (Metal Oxide Silicon). The elements of Bipolar transistors in ICs function rather like the original junction transistor. In the MOS an aluminium "gate" electrode controls the conductivity of the silicon between two p-type regions.

The basic MOS is often called The MOS "field effect transistor" (FET) because it is the field created near the gate which changes the conductivity of the silicon locally between the "source" and "drain" regions. There are several variations of both types – for instance MOS devices may be called PMOS or NMOS according to the type of silicon used near the gate.

The fastest working devices at present are bipolar Emitter Coupled Logic (ECL). ECL is a two-transistor circuit specifically arranged to reduce delays in current switching to the absolute minimum. In spite of that, integrated circuits as used in computers are now predominantly MOS devices because they are easier to manufacture and consume less power.

The first microprocessors used PMOS; the pioneering Intel 8080, still in widespread use and to be described later, uses NMOS. NMOS is widely used in today's microprocessors such as the Intel 8086 and 80286.

In 1974 RCA manufactured the Complimentary Metal Oxide Silicon (CMOS) 1802 microprocessor and this technology was introduced by others as improved manufacturing techniques enabled CMOS to be reconsidered. Until then this technology, invented in 1962, was thought to be too complex and expensive to make. One driving force was the need for low power in small portable applications like digital watches.

In CMOS a current of less than 0.1 microampere (ua) is drawn when one of two complimentary MOS transistors is "on". No current is needed periodically to maintain this condition. Appreciable current flows only for the brief period when the transistors are switched from "on-off" to "off-on".

The voltages in a memory of CMOS transistors used to represent either 1's or 0's, do not gradually decay. Data remains stored so long as power is applied, unlike memories using earlier transistors which required "refreshing" every few milliseconds by a charging current. CMOS transistors consume little power when used in portable battery-operated equipment. The equipment can be switched off leaving only the memory connected to the battery without losing stored data.

See also SEMICONDUCTORS – GALLIUM ARSENIDE and BIPOLAR.

SENSOR
A device for detecting change in light intensity heat, pressure, sound etc., and converting it into an electrical signals.

SERIAL TRANSMISSION
The transmission of data, one bit at a time, down a single communications wire. See also PARALLEL TRANSMISSION.

SERVER
A station (node) on a network that provides a service by managing a communal resource such as storage, printing, etc.

SGML
STANDARD GENERALIZED MARKUP LANGUAGE.

SHANNON, CLAUDE E.
Claude Shannon, born in 1916, was a student of Vannevar Bush at MIT. His thesis, written in 1938, showed how symbolic logic could be applied to relay circuits, particularly those used in telephone exchanges. This idea transformed the trial and error methods then used for switching design into precise mathematically defined functions.

In 1948 his *Mathematical Theory of Communication* was published. It gave rise to "Information Theory" which for some years was applied to a range of problems for which it was ill-suited. Currently it is being used as was originally intended – in particular for dealing with various problems in coding, required in order to improve telecommunication transmission rates and reduce errors.

Claude Shannon's first job was at MIT, obtained by responding to an advertisement for a research assistant to run the Differential Analyser, a machine invented by Vannevar Bush. After four years he moved in 1941 to the Bell Research Laboratories and worked in a university-like atmosphere with the mathe-

matics research group. He said later:- "Had I been in another company aimed at a more particular goal, I wouldn't have had the freedom to work that way".

While working at the Bell Labs during World War II, Shannon did some research enabling the scrambling apparatus used for long range telephone calls between Churchill and Roosevelt to be designed. The coding system which was used remains secure to this day. Shannon, who is now 75,lives appropriately at "Entropy House" near Boston. It is full of various gadgets.

In 1985 Shannon turned up at an information symposium in Brighton UK incognito. Having been persuaded to make a speech following the banquet, but thinking his audience might be bored, he pulled some balls out of his pockets and started juggling, to the cheers of the delegates. Juggling was one of his hobbies – he has built several juggling machines.

SHELL
1. INFERENCE ENGINE software in an expert system which is domain independent. A general purpose set of rules which should be able to solve problems and derive conclusions from different kinds of knowledge data.
2. A structured way of containing data.
See also ARTIFICIAL INTELLIGENCE.

SHIFT DOWN
See AUTOMATIC FALLBACK.

SHIFT REGISTER
A string of inter-connected FLIP-FLOPS each of which may be either on or off, constituting a store. The circuit arrangement lends itself to particular kinds of operation – for instance digits may be shifted along the device from input to output by control signals.

Each F-F can be accessed by an input and output terminal in addition to its connection to the next one. All F-F's can be connected to control lines. There are several ways the circuit can be used. For example the F-F's input terminal can receive a succession of digits for storage, and subsequently these digits may be shifted along the device.

The shift register has been used as a parallel to serial convertor. Alternatively data can be shifted into the first F-F in the chain and along the register, and when the sequence is stored all digits can be read out simultaneously from the output terminal of each F-F. It is then being used as a series to parallel convertor. Modern shift registers will clock at nanosecond speeds.

SHOCKLEY, WILLIAM B.
Shockley was born in London in 1910 but later went to the US and joined the Bell Telephone Laboratories. He was awarded the Nobel prize for Physics in 1956 for inventing the point contact transistor jointly with Bardeen and Brattain, and is credited with the invention of the junction transistor in 1952.

SIDEBAND
A band of frequencies resulting from a modulation process, displaced from the carrier frequency.

SIEMENS, SIR CHARLES W.
Charles Siemens was born in Germany in 1823 and became a naturalized British subject in 1859. He managed Siemens Bros., – active in telecommunications engineering and designers of the steamship *Faraday* for cable laying. He was also an inventor, designing a steel furnace which became widely used, a pyrometer, and other devices. His brother established telecommunication factories in Germany. Siemens is now one of the largest telecommunication companies in Europe.

SIGNALLING SYSTEM NO. 7
See COMMON CHANNEL SIGNALLING SYSTEM NO. 7.

SILICON CHIP
A wafer-fragment of pure silicon, only a few millimetres square, upon which an integrated circuit is printed. See also SEMICONDUCTORS.

SIMPLEX
Transmission in one direction only.

SINK
Synonym for Destination.

SLIC
Subscriber Line Interface Circuit.

SMALL COMPUTERS SYSTEMS INTERFACE (SCSI)
An ANSI standard, originally introduced in 1986, derived from IBM360 computer practice. The SCSI interface is used to interconnect computers and disc drives, printers, scanners, optical storage systems etc. The standard specifies the requirements for busses and peripheral devices. Later there was some confusion between an interface introduced by Shugart known as SASI the details of which were incorporated into the SCSI.

The SCSI consists of a 50 way bus to carry bits, correction bits, ground lines, and power and control lines. The SCSI can support up to 8 peripheral units and a large number of "logical sub units". Its advantages are twofold. For users, equipment with an SCSI interface provides a choice of compatible peripheral items. For vendors the same interface may be used on a number of their products.

Because some recently introduced hard discs stream out data faster than the SCSI interface can handle it, SCSI-2 was introduced in August 1992. It includes a doubling of the transfer rate and also provides for 16 and 32 bit data paths. Appropriate changes must be made at both the drive end and host computer end for the improvements to be realized in practice.

SMART CARDS
A smart card resembles a credit card in appearance. A credit card may include magnetic stripe storage, but a smart card contains a thin microprocessor with (in the latest version) an HCMOS RAM main-memory chip. HCMOS requires less power and works at higher speeds than the older HMOS or CMOS types.

A smart card may be filled or emptied of data by magnetic induction or via metal contacts which match with contacts within the terminal into which the card is inserted. Other contacts supply power. A card usually also contains ROM and EPROM memory and can contain up to 256 Kbytes of RAM.

The RAM is used for storing data associated with transactions when the card is within the terminal. This data disappears when it is removed. The microprocessors's operating and security system is held in ROM. Data to be exchanged between the host computer and the card is encrypted before transmission to maintain security at the terminal and in telecom channels. Details of on-going transactions are held in EPROM.

The simplest application is to use the cards

for payments until its authorized stored credit is exhausted and must be renewed. An experiment is in progress within the UK where a smart card is used as a medical record and data collection card. However the main market is in France where a big future is expected for smart cards for paying retailers, following a large scale experiment with 20 million cards.

Philips have developed a telephone which will accept smart cards capable of operating a flight reservation system. Ticketing data will be imprinted on the smart card at the time of reservation and when the card is put into another machine at the airport a boarding pass will be obtained.

Smart tags are variation of smart cards. A smart tag usually consists of a microprocessor and ROM or EPROM memory with inductive or sometimes battery-powered communication facilities.

Applications include personnel identification, identity of containers, and as an automatic "log" of production line processes or for issuing special instructions – for example as a car proceeds along a production line.

SMDS
SWITCHED MULTI-MEGABIT DATA SERVICE.

SMPTE
Society of Motion Picture and Television Engineers.

SNA
SYSTEMS NETWORK ARCHITECTURE.
IBM's layered communications architecture which has been closely, but not exactly, followed in the OSI model.

SNOOPING
a term used to describe the action of a CACHE when checking how peripheral units in a computer are accessing memory.

SOFTWARE
The collection of programs used on a computer including accompanying paperwork such as instruction manuals and documentation for recording design, coding etc.

SOLITON
A wave which can travel enormous distances. The phenomena seems to have been discovered in canals. There is a critical speed at which the displacement wave caused by a barge assumes a circular motion, rolls along the canal's bottom, and returns to the underside of the vessel where it is travelling in the same direction of the vessel.

Specifically it is said that a horse working on the Glasgow-Paisley canal in 1831 took fright pulling a boat. When a speed of 9 miles per hour was reached the horse was able to pull the barge without effort. Later an express service was introduced using light weight boats drawn by galloping horses. The important modern equivalent is the discovery of a light wave travelling along a single mode fibre for enormous distances. The effect is due to an interaction between dispersion and the fibre's non-linear properties. In 1991 it was discovered that a soliton can be amplified to make it travel almost limitless distances.

SONET
SYNCHRONOUS OPTICAL NETWORK. See NETWORKS.

SOURCE CODE
The code of the high level language in which a program is written. It is translated by a compiler program into the object code – the machine code in which the program is actually run.

SPECIFICITY
See INDEXING SYSTEM PERFORMANCE – EXHAUSTIVITY AND SPECIFICITY.

SPEECH
If the continuous analogue speech waveform from a microphone is converted into a pulse code to represent speech fluctuations, the speech may then conveniently be stored, transmitted, or processed in digital equipment like any other data. The digitized speech is transmitted as a stream of pulses or signalling elements. Moreover pulses which become weak in long transmission channels may be boosted by noiseless regeneration, unlike analogue waveforms where amplifiers which introduce noise have to be used.

The digitization of a continuous waveform is carried out by sampling its level at intervals. NYQUIST showed that there must be at least 2W samples of a continuous waveform per second for it to be properly reconstructed later, where W is the highest frequency in that waveform. Thus for a waveform containing frequencies up to 4000 Hz, there must be 8000 samples per second.

Each time a sample is taken, data about the value of the sample must be sent. The quality of reconstructed speech will be affected by the amount of detail – e.g. from 0 to 10 levels, from 0 to 100 levels, etc. In practice 256 levels are usually used partly because a further increase in detail would not produce much improvement, and partly because 256 levels may be represented by an 8 bit code ($256 = 2^8$). Accordingly in this arrangement for digitizing speech the speech waveform is sampled 8000 times per second, and 8 pulses (bits) are sent per sample. The signalling rate is 64,000 bauds (signalling elements per second).

Digitization brings with it numerous benefits although digitized speech of good quality requires a bit rate of 64 Kbps. 64 Kbps implies that a channel of 32 KHz bandwidth will be required. The same speech in analogue form could be accommodated within a frequency band of 5 KHz so digitization requires much more bandwidth.

In an engineered digitized system, the extra bandwidth is needed to accommodate the transmission rate of the code groups describing the speech samples – a factor not covered by the theory. Fortunately the twisted pairs of wires often used to carry analogue speech – for example to connect telephone subscribers to the local exchange – have a much wider bandwidth than their purpose requires.

It turns out that they can convey data at up to about 140 Kbps. When a telecoms authority feels able to digitize the telephone system from end-to-end, they will have to replace the largest part of the system known as the "local loop" – the thousands of cables which radiate from each local telephone exchange to subscribers – if the data is required to flow at more than about 140 Kbps.

SPEECH RECOGNITION

Most speech recognizing systems now use either an acoustical event sequence analysing technique or a pattern recognition technique. It is hard to provide a jargon-free understandable description of the first method.

Briefly, speech recognition consists of extracting a sequence of events from the electrical signal generated from a microphone. These events correspond to characteristic changes in the sounds of a spoken word. Models of words in the form of changes in the state of events have been previously stored in the machine. The sequences of the modelled words are then matched against the sequences representing incoming words. The stored modelled word which most nearly matches the incoming word is signalled as the recognized word at the output of the machine.

The alternative method is to match one or more features extracted from words with stored representations of words in the same form. The features could be the amount of word-energy contained in different parts of the frequency spectrum, waveform zero-crossing rate, etc. Whichever stored pattern best matches the input pattern is signalled as the recognized word. Because the incoming pattern changes according to the rate of pronunciation, matching must include appropriate variations in the stored words by applying a process known as "dynamic time warping".

To cope with the differing characteristics of words uttered by different speakers, each word must be stored in up to about 15 variations. During a "training" session the nearest stored variation is earmarked as the model to be used for matching whenever the machine is subsequently used by that speaker.

Further processing is needed to cope with connected speech. For instance the words in the phrase "but a way must be found" pronounced in fluent speech may sound like "butterway must be found" which is quite different from the sounds of the words pronounced separately.

Speech recognizing machines may have to cope with background acoustic noise and electrical noise in the telecommunication channel – particularly if a telephone line is being used.

A simple but useful machine need only recognize a few words such as "pass" or "reject". For complex tasks a machine would need to recognize more words and would also have to understand their meaning. This requirement moves us into the realms of natural language processing which is a branch of ARTIFICIAL INTELLIGENCE beyond the scope of this entry.

Consider, for instance, the complexity of a voice-controlled terminal to be used for online database searching, which is capable of recognizing, understanding and executing the com-

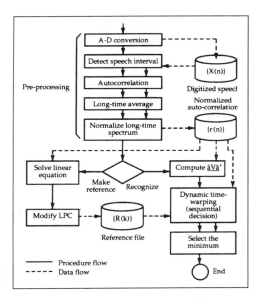

| A-D conversion |
| Detect speech interval |
| {X(n)} Digitized speech |
| Autocorrelation |
| Long-time average | Normalized auto-correlation |
| Normalize long-time spectrum | {r(n)} |

Pre-processing

Solve linear equation		Compute āV̄ā'
Make reference Recognize		
Modify LPC	{R(k)}	Dynamic time-warping (sequential decision)
Reference file		Select the minimum

—— Procedure flow
----- Data flow

End

Bell Telephone speech recognition and time warping system for telephoned speech.

mand "find me a review article about natural language processing".

SPEECH SYNTHESIS
Intelligible speech may be conveyed electrically as an analogue waveform in a channel with a frequency bandwidth of 4000 Hz, but there are many advantages in digitizing speech. Digitization involves converting values of the changing analogue waveform into a sufficient number of coded impulses to describe them. A 4000 Hz speech spectrum needs to be sampled 8000 times per second with 8 bits per sample – a rate of 64,000 bits or pulses per second (64 Kbps) for good reproduction. The penalty of requiring a channel of wider bandwidth for these pulses is easily outweighed by the benefits.

See PULSE CODE MODULATION.

For speech synthesizing purposes, slower waveform changes need processing at bit rates between about 1 and 3 Kbps. Expensive storage (at 64 Kbps 200 words taking about 80 seconds to speak would require over 5 Mbits of storage) is avoided.

Synthesizers may either produce speech from typed text, or they may speak messages under software control. Most synthesizing systems consist of an analyser which extracts the electrical equivalent of acoustic features from words or phrases, and a synthesizer to which the features are applied which modifies them electrically in a manner rather similar to the way in which the human voice tract modifies voiced sounds.

One method used in text-to-speech analysers is to read the text into a look-up dictionary which provides about 300 pronunciation rules for splitting words up into PHONEMES (basic sounds) and for determining which variation of the phoneme is being used. Since the rules cover a large number of words there is no restriction on the speech vocabulary.

Phoneme variations, called allophones, are formed by the co-articulation effects of the phonemes which precede and follow a particular phoneme – for example consider the "k" sounds in "allocate" and "evoke". The stress, pitch, and duration characteristics of the allophone may be expressed as data for application to the synthesizer.

In less ambitious systems a limited vocabulary – perhaps adequate for a narrowly defined subject – is stored in a read-only memory and words are addressed and called up under software control. A simpler form of analyser suffices for deriving synthesizer data.

The human voice consists of voiced airpulses from the vocal chords whose frequency determines the voice pitch; other sounds, produced when speaking the letters s or f, are heard as hissing noises. An alternative method is to dispense with the analyser and simulate voice with an oscillator generating impulses with a "white noise" oscillator for generating unvoiced sounds. The synthesizer then modifies these sounds to produce words.

There appear to be two main types of synthesizer. the Formant Synthesizer (FS) otherwise known as the Formant Vocoder is widely used. An FS is an electrical filter with variable bandpass frequency characteristics; this restricts the spectrum of data passing through it to a band of frequencies whose width may be varied, and whose position in the spectrum may be altered.

This electrical modification is analogous to the acoustic modification produced by the human vocal tract.

When the output electrical signal is reproduced through a loudspeaker, speech of a fairly natural quality is heard. Satisfactory performance is achieved if the filter characteristics are periodically re-set to accommodate speech "frames" of duration 10 to 30 milliseconds.

In the human vocal tract, sounds are modified by resonant cavities and by acoustic adjustments produced by movements of the tongue and lips. The alternative major type of synthesizer – the Linear Predictive Coding (LPC) synthesizer – sets out to simulate the vocal tract more directly with an electrical analogy of the human acoustic "circuit". Codes which control the electrical characteristics are compiled and stored for the words or phrases to be used. For the desired word to be reproduced the approp-riate code is called up and applied to the synthesizer.

Typically, when excited by an artificial voice, each LPC code for such a synthesizer will control pitch, adjust sound energy, and set ten different filter characteristics.

SPL
Sound Pressure Level.

SPOOLING
Queueing. A Spooler is a scheduling program for resources such as disk or printer, whereby processes are queued and take their turn.

SPREADSHEETS
A Spreadsheet consists of a grid of cells displayed on the screen of a CRT. Data entered in any cell may be related to data in other cells according to a chosen Formula. One of the simplest and most frequently used relationships is "Z1 = A1 + B1 + C1... + Y1", where the software arranges that data in a bottom cell, Z1, is the sum of the data in the column cells A1...Y1 above it. If the data in, say, cell K1 is changed, Z1 immediately shows a new figure for the summed data.

Much more complex mathematical relationships may be incorporated and spreadsheets are particularly useful for posing "what if" questions to accounting data ("financial modelling"). Typically a screen cursor controlled by a mouse (the cursor's movement corresponds to the movement of a hand-held carriage – the mouse is moved over a flat surface) is moved to a space reserved for an appropriate formula, clicked, and the formula is entered.

After entering data, usually on a prepared form rather than simply in columns and rows, an alteration in one cell, made by a cursor "point and enter" action, will generate appropriate figures in other cells. If, say, salary increases were made in March on the financial model in the figure, consequential changes would be made in all other appropriate places – for instance to net income in March and later months.

Assets	Jan	Feb	Mar	Apr	May	June
Acct.s Receivable	1000.00	1050.00	1102.50	1157.63	1215.51	1276.28
Inventory	300.00	500.00	525.00	551.25	578.81	607.75
Other Assets	250.00	262.50	275.63	289.41	303.88	319.07
Total Assets	1550.00	1812.50	1903.13	1998.28	2098.20	2203.11
Liabilities						
Acct.s Payable	1000.00	916.67	840.28	770.25	706.07	647.23
Accrued Storage Cost	50.00	50.00	50.00	50.00	50.00	50.00
Accrued Salary	100.00	105.00	110.25	115.76	121.55	127.63
Accrued Other	50.00	52.50	55.13	57.88	60.78	63.81
Total Liabilities	1200.00	1124.17	1055.65	993.90	938.39	888.67
Earnings before tax	350.00	688.33	847.47	1004.38	1159.80	1314.43
Dept. Allowance	100.00	100.00	100.00	100.00	100.00	100.00
Taxable Income	250.00	588.33	747.47	904.38	1059.80	1214.43
Taxes	75.00	176.50	224.24	271.31	317.94	364.33
Net Income	175.00	411.83	523.23	633.07	741.86	850.10

Spreadsheet example

A spreadsheet calculator called Visicalc, developed by Dan Bricklin of Software Arts Inc., appeared in 1978 for the Apple II. Each boosted the sale of the other. Visicalc remained the leader until 1983 when the IBM PC appeared and so did Lotus 1-2-3 (Spreadsheet-Database-Management-Business Graphics).

The Lotus package fully utilized the instruction set of the 8088 CPU used in the IBM; it ran a much larger spreadsheet (2048 rows x 256 columns) faster, using 500 Kbytes of memory instead of 64K as previously used. Lotus expected their first year's sales to be about $3 million. In the event it turned out to be $53 million and, like Visicalc before it, this boosted sales of the hardware – the IBM PC.

1-2-3 did not use software translation based on the earlier CP/M operating system as did many of the early PC packages. It was written directly for the PC's 16 bit operating system. Many other spreadsheet packages are available.

SQL
Structured Query Language.

SRAM
STATIC RANDOM ACCESS MEMORY. See

also SEMICONDUCTORS – MEMORY CHIPS.

S-SEED
See COMPUTERS – OPTICAL COMPUTERS.

SSSO
Special Service Satellite Operator.

STANDARD GENERALIZED MARKUP LANGUAGE (SGML)
An "Open System" (ISO 8879) tagging system for marking up a document to indicate its elements, attributes, and structure in order to standardize electronic document interchange.

If an author is asked to use special codes so that his text on disc may be read by a typesetting machine – for example using SGML codes – he will have to spend a good deal of extra time doing it. SGML codes are attached to "document elements" e.g. Author's name, Address, appendices, abbreviations, headings, paragraphs, sections, and many more, enabling the document to be abridged, rearranged, published in different forms, etc., simply by issuing a set of instructions to the typesetting machine.

A number of benefits should accrue to both authors and publishers from this procedure. The publisher will be able to go directly from author's text to print at a much lower cost than previously and the printed result should look much better. He will also be able to rearrange or republish the text in different ways – for example a set of journal articles by the same, or by a number of different authors, could easily be republished in book form, abridged as necessary.

The author will presumably share in these benefits, since he or she will be paid more for the extra work involved. If and when he relinquishes his copyright to the publisher, he should be party to a re-use agreement enabling him to approve the manner of the re-use and to receive a royalty payment for each re-use.

Document interchange between author and publisher still usually takes place via any one of four main data transportation paths – via disk/OCR/disk, telecoms/protocol converter/disk, disk/disk converter/disk, and disk direct. Equipment called "media convertors" and "protocol converters" are required.

All of the routes require the use of expensive in-house equipment or bureau services, but may be worth adopting if justified by frequency of use. A route will take time and trouble to set up but if an author regularly submits data to the same publisher it may be worth it.

In the case of the free-lance author who submits articles to a number of different publishers the chances of any kind of standard procedure other than the use of camera-ready copy are slim, although methods are changing slowly. At present, if the author uses one of the popular microcomputers with a popular word processing package, the situation is at its best because the publisher should be able to read the author's disks. If the publisher uses the disk as is, the layout will be as good as is permitted by utilization of the WP codes.

In the case of a publisher who employs his own authors in-house – for example a newspaper publisher – the publisher has the whole process under his control and can arrange for total compatibility, imposing on authors whatever procedure he likes in order to make the text from their WP machines immediately useable.

SONET
Synchronous Optical Network. A SONET standard has been agreed internationally for the transport of data along optical paths. Sonet takes account of the fact that optical communication channels will need special interfaces for the inter-conversion of electrical data at very high rates and that special synchronising and multiplexing arrangements will be needed. Signalling rates are expected to be from about 50 Mbps upwards, using a packet-switched system called QPSX.

See also NETWORKS.

STANDARDS
An IT Standard is an agreement to make equipment or software to a particular specification. Accordingly an item conforming to Standard XYZ should work properly when forming part of a system if the system participants decide to adopt that Standard.

The International Telegraph Union was formed in 1865. The International Telegraph and Telephone Consultative Committee (CCITT) is a major section of it. The CCITT issues telecommunication recommendations which amount to standards.

In complete contrast to the CCITT's methodical, painstaking, highly detailed work, followed by PTT methodical, rather leisurely implementation, telecommunication equipment for computer services, which may often be inter-connected via a public network, has often developed according to a supplier's interpretation of the needs of the marketplace. As one or other supplier gains dominance, the operating characteristics of his equipment become the the de facto "Standard".

If potential customers were likely already to possess that manufacturer's equipment, it behoves other manufacturers to make their own equipment connectable to it if they want to advance their sales. The dominant manufacturer has an incentive to maintain his customers captive in this manner, and has little incentive to adopt any "International Standard" until that standard becomes really pervasive.

The next move is made by a competitor. Perceiving the complacency of the king supplier he introduces something newer, faster, better, and with more features. Its superiority outweighs the need to stick to the de facto standard and he makes some sales. He may become a threat to the king who, in due course, reacts accordingly.

In short, we have the two worlds of the gradually changing public services with huge slowly depreciating assets, and the dynamic rapidly changing private equipment supplier bringing out new models to compete with those available from his aggressive competitors.

Inter-human and inter-machine communication have a common need for a mutually understandable language. Denied the power of a brain able to deal with the subtleties of human communication, inter-communicating machines require to have every alternative in a "conversation" anticipated and controlled by a *protocol* (set of rules).

Certain developments in electronics were needed before inexpensive facsimile machines could be built, but just as essential was an international agreement about protocols. Nothing happened until that was achieved in the late seventies and we know what has happened since.

Agreement on FACSIMILE protocols took a long time – and they covered only one type of machine and a use over a single type of unified network – the PSTN. International agreement about protocols covering any kind of machine over any kind of network is a different matter.

If hardware and software – that is input and output devices, computers and telecomms – are purchased from one supplier (and there are not many who can supply the whole lot on any scale) then assurances would probably be obtainable that they should all work together. In official computerese they would be "compatible".

But all items might not be state-of-the-art, some might be unduly expensive, and should you wish to replace or extend your network you are locked-in to the same supplier. An item purchased from another supplier may not work with the existing equipment.

A supplier, if dominant, could dictate prices and stifle the competition. Competitive forces in a field as fast-moving as IT are felt to be a necessary benefit.

The rate of introduction of Standards, which it is hoped will resolve these problems, is such that a Standard may be out of date by the time it is adopted. A manufacturer's standardized item may be uncompetitive because it is out-performed by a competitor's less expensive more up to date item which has not waited for the Standard to arrive. A dominant supplier may not feel the need for adopting a Standard because he enjoys de facto standardization by reason of the widespread use of his systems.

An IT Standard typically gets taken up for general discussion about 3 years after the first suggestion of a need for one. It becomes feasible for manufacturers to consider its adoption in about the 5th year by which time a draft agreement has been reached. Publication of the Standard occurs from about the 6th year onwards. A concept such as OSI takes much longer before it gets widely adopted.

Businesses are run on realities and system buyers are not going to change to a standardized but untried system until problems arise with what they already have, and a tested and tried alternative becomes available. However a problem may arise eventually anyway – for example the increasing difficulty in expanding a telecoms network based on obsolescing Standards.

STANDARDS – FIBREOPTIC DISTRIBUTED DATA INTERFACE (FDDI)

The requirements for a Fibre Distributed Data Interface (FDDI) standard arose from a demand in the US in 1982 for a 100 Mbps dual-ring (one main, one backup) Token Ring Network. Another likely application arises from the need to interconnect "copper" LANs with long links; the arrangement would be copper LAN to FDDI bridge, FDDI link, FDDI bridge to copper LAN.

A number of major suppliers have announced their support for the standard which is under consideration by ANSI. FDDI is compatible with OSI at the Datalink and Physical layer levels. FDDI will work at 100 Mbps over shielded twisted pair cabling. A variation permitting operation at up to 200 Mbps is expected.

STANDARDS – ISO QUALITY

Several standards numbered ISO 9000-9004 were introduced in 1992 aimed at improving the quality of software and engineered components. Unfortunately they are alleged to be 10 years out of date. Even so many products in Europe must be certified as being to the ISO quality Standard.

STANDARDS – OPEN SYSTEMS INTERCONNECTION (OSI) – ASSOCIATED STANDARDS

The functions which must be dealt with in an end-to-end OSI-based standardized telecoms complex are divided into groups – Physical layer through to Application layer. That part of the equipment which performs the functions of each layer will need to conform to the relevant standard for those functions.

The OSI model fleshes out and identifies as discrete functions items which are mostly already present, are perhaps not easily identifiable, and which may be proprietary.

For example a file-transfer service conforming to ECMA 101 (ECMA is a European Computer Manufacturers Standard) – a recognized standard residing at level 7 – might operate over a LAN in which it would be hard to identify the "functions" and "levels" as defined by OSI because they are a continuum in a proprietary system.

A number of OSI-based standards exist and some are in widespread use – the most im-

portant being X.400 covering Electronic Mail (Applications layer), and X.25 covering packet-switch protocols (Network layer). See the table which follows for a selection. They will be linked to other parts of telecom systems which may or may not be OSI-based.

In June 1989, an organization with about 70 members, including AT&T, BT, France Telecom, Televerket, Tandem Computers, Ungerman-Bass, and NTT called the OSI/Network Forum, met in London. The objective was to develop products which will work with one another. OSI received another boost in 1989 when American Airlines ordered 50,000 workstations for its SABRE reservation network from AT&T, IBM, and Tandy. X.400 and X.25 standards will be used. X.25 is specified in the OSI Network and Datalink layers and is also used for the ISDN. Other parts of the ISDN will incorporate OSI standards.

US government policy is to purchase OSI-based products, where possible, from August 1990. A similar policy exists in the UK where government departments are guided by Government OSI Procurement (GOSIP).

It is suggested by ICL that there are five steps to success for organizations who want to get to grips with OSI:-
1. Commit to Open Systems.
2. Survey and know the standards.
3. Survey supplier's products.
4. Define your needs, driving forces, and constraints.
5. Define a clear migration strategy.

At present the survey suggested in 3. is likely to be brief. There are few totally OSI products, although there are many which embody one or more of the Standards mentioned above.

The EC is another driving force for OSI. "In IT, unlike many other sectors, the need is not so much to harmonize existing regulations and standards, but to get standards accepted for the first time and to ensure that from the beginning, those standards are accepted throughout Europe" said an EC official. The EEC Council Decision 87/95/EEC requires reference to IT standards in public procurement.

There are a number of telecom/computer standards-making bodies in Europe who are presumably giving Directive 83/189/EEC some attention. This directive obliges member states to notify the Commission in advance of

STANDARDS – OPEN SYSTEMS INTERCONNECTION (OSI)

Application layer. The interface with the user. Includes such services as File Transfer And Management (FTAM), Office Document Architecture (ODA) Messaging, and terminal support

ISO 8649, 9545, 9804.	Service definitions.
ISO 8650.	Protocol specifications.
CCITT X.400-X.430	Message handling systems ("Electronic Mail"). A widely used standard with many facilities to be extended to include Electronic Document Interchange (EDI) and ultimately Office Document Architecture (ODA) – a means of exchanging documents between WP systems having different formatting codes.
CCITT X.500	Directory services (a worldwide directory of people to be made possible by the interconnection of directory systems, still undergoing revisions.

Presentation layer. Correct representation of data.

ISO DIS 8822	Service definition.
ISO DIS 8823	Protocol specifications.

Session Layer. Establishment, maintenance, and management of user to user dialogue.

CCITT X.215/ISO 8326	Service definition.
CCITT X.225/ISO 8327	Protocol specifications.

Transport Layer. Control of quality of service (e.g. errors, sequence, etc).

CCITT X.214/ISO 8072	Service definition.
CCITT X.224/ISO 8073	Protocol specifications.

Network Layer. "Transparent" transmission of data between systems.

CCITT X.213	Service definition.
ISO 8473	Protocol for connectionless mode service.
X.21	Terminal to network interface for circuit switched synchronous operation on data networks.
X.25	Widely used terminal to network interface for packet switched dedicated circuit on data networks. X25 plug-in cards are available for PCs to communicate over packet-switched networks. This part of X.25 controls routing of data via nodes and virtual circuits in packet-switched networks.

Data Link Layer. Control of connections and data flow.

CCITT X.212/ISO DIS 8886	Service definition. ISO data control procedures (several) Example: IBM/3COM Heterogeneous LAN Management (HLM) based on the ISO Common Management Information Protocol (CMIP). X.25Terminal to network interface for packet switched dedicated circuit on data networks. This part of X.25 controls data reliability.

Physical Layer. Mechanical and electrical connection characteristics.

CCITT V24, V28, EIA RS-232-C	Terminal to data coms equipment interface for serial binary
X.25	data Terminal to network interface for packet switched dedicated circuit on data networks.

all draft regulations and standards concerning technical specifications that they intend to introduce into their own territory.

To set their seal on the matter, the EC have devised yet another list of standards with their own numbering system called "European pre-standards (ENVs)" issued "before the time is right for a European standard

(EN)".

The major outstanding problem with standards within the OSI framework, and therefore the realization of painless universal end-to-end networking, will be the actual realization of the standards in equipment. At the "upper levels" of OSI a major problem exists because of the variety of computer operating systems in use. Even Unix, controlled and administered by AT&T, exists in several partially compatible versions, and has required an OSI-like operation to sort it out – the IEEE has defined a system-to-application interface called POSIX for the purpose.

STANDARDS – OPEN SYSTEMS INTERCONNECTION (OSI): CURRENT PROGRESS

For on-going progress a publication called *SPAG* keeps you up to date. *SPAG* (Standards Publications and Applications Group) is published in Brussels at Avenue Louise 149, Box 7, 1050 Brussels, Belgium. *SPAG* is an association of product suppliers and users, from which comes a publication of the same name.

SPAG makes valiant attempts to break "the chicken and egg" problem, often quoted in the press and by users, where vendors are portrayed as being reluctant to sell OSI products as there is not sufficient market demand for OSI, and users are unable to purchase OSI products due to their non-availability".

In the Summer 1991 issue of *SPAG* their Service Implementation Statement (SIS) is introduced. It also introduces a new tongue-twister "interoperability". That word means just what it says and what users want to know about. If I buy a turboencabulator from the Dynamic Orthodontics Company and connect it to my Ethernet Local Area Network will I be able to send output to a four-barrelled rumbler at Silent Printers Ltd., via IPSS and Silent's Arcnet system?

This question is less frivolous than it sounds. The number of rules which would need to be available to cover each type of system in the question, and to which each would have to conform, is so enormous that the inherent complexity of OSI protocol machines makes them practically and economically impossible to test exhaustively.

As one commentator says there is a "combinational explosion in the number of allowable situations which should be theoretically explored in order to carry out a complete conformance assessment. Clearly, conformance testing has to stop where testing costs become prohibitive. Consequently there is a broad requirement for a scheme which makes "one-stop testing" possible and acceptable to all parties".

SPAG is quite frank about OSI. It points out that the only OSI products on the market are for message handling and file access, and it quotes those relevant Standards covering them which can be accommodated within the OSI model. It also points out that many options available in that theoretical model are irrelevant or even incompatible. "Functional standards, or profiles, were developed to address this problem by providing practical combinations of OSI standards for practical real-life situations".

SPAG proposes to alleviate this problem with something called "Process to Support Interoperability" (PSI) plus a "Service Implementation Statement" (PSI). PSI is a multivendor code of conduct for interoperability by design. SIS is a "blueprint for a workable conciliation process" between an equipment vendor and a buyer.

PSI says that it should work, SIS says this is the testing procedure and how the vendor will sort it out if it doesn't. A vendor who enters a product for the PSI trademark has to sign a legal agreement to participate in conciliation.

It seems likely that attention will be focused in the near future on the "OSIfication" of particular widely-used cases of inter-operability, particularly in government departments where the use of OSI equipment is becoming mandatory. Having been made to work, and being seen to work, this will lend strength to the extension of OSI.

Large commercial users of information systems are no doubt thinking about OSI with a view to getting their feet wet. Implementation will be very slow. It is hard to say when the average user will notice much difference.

STANDARDS – OPEN SYSTEMS INTERCONNECTION (OSI): DESCRIPTION

Descriptions of OSI nearly always include the diagram in the figure on the next page or something very like it. Recognizing that a series of operations or functions must be implemented when equipment users exchange messages via a network, the OSI model separates and defines them.

Ignoring the thick solid line and the dotted lines for the moment, the model on the left shows service functions in seven idealized layers. There is a Standard specifying each function and a Standard describing the rules (protocols) to be used for communications between layers.

These functions are already usually performed in the numerous hardware/software systems already available. Some conform to one or more of the Standards accommodated in the OSI model, but many do not. Two or more functions may be performed within a single part of a system, but even then the individual functions will usually be recognizable.

Any hardware/software system manufacturer may claim OSI compatibility so long as the system performs the service described in the standard, and so long as the protocols for communicating with adjacent layers are as described in the protocol Standard.

The top three layers of the model are concerned with processing or application functions and should be present within the user's equipment. The bottom three layers are concerned with telecommunications and should be present in nodes (inter-connection points) in the network. The Transport layer, which is within the user's equipment, is a telecom services intermediary. For instance it might be appropriate for a number of individual connections to be made to the network in parallel to increase traffic throughput.

The thick solid line in the diagram indicates a message route down from a machine of some kind through the layers, along a telecoms channel, and up to a receiving machine. Alternatively the message may be going in the opposite direction. An OSI "layer" is a process through which a message passes at the sending end which is decoded and acted upon during its passage to the addressee. The action taken by an OSI layer depends on the "header" at the beginning of every message.

A header is a section containing control data which may be added by any layer through which it passes. The header includes the address of the corresponding layer at the receiving end. Accordingly a message may contain up to 7 header sections when it enters the telecom channel.

As a message progresses towards a receiving machine, the first layer through which it

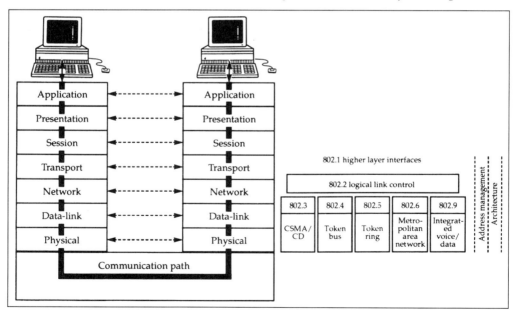

The OSI model

passes, observing its own address, acts on the control data, and strips off its part of the header. Each subsequent layer does likewise. Eventually, all of the header having been stripped off, only the message arrives at the destination machine for the attention of the user.

A header inserted by, say, the presentation layer at the sending end, and addressed to the presentation layer at the receiving end, will be acted upon by that layer. This logical communication between sending and receiving layers of the same kind is called "peer-to-peer" communication. The effect is indicated by the horizontal dotted lines the diagram; it appears to a user as if information is being directly exchanged between corresponding layers.

The disadvantages of OSI, apart from the complexity needed to deal with a complex problem, are not often spelled out. They include up to 400 Kbytes of memory needed to handle the layer-by-layer processing software, and the in-transit time of information. Little seems to be known about the latter because of the lack of implementation of complete OSI-model systems. System response times for many kinds of information processing with humans waiting for answers are very important.

OSI is European oriented although it works closely with ISO within which the United States is active. The United States considered it unnecessary to conform, but something like a warning appeared in 1991 (Edelstein, 1991):-"Given the immensity of the European market – larger than that of the US – vendors outside Western Europe will have little choice but to conform to EEC-sanctioned Standards. Enforcement will include requirements for product certification and warranty and purchasers may require certified compliance as a contractual element".

"Many countries and major computer vendors have adopted – or intend to adopt – some form of the OSI model... yet a great many de facto standards based on existing technologies remain, despite rapidly growing interest in OSI, among consumers who have been captive to vendor-proprietary architectures and standards... proprietary systems are not likely to disappear but the open systems concept is the wave of the future bringing vastly broader opportunities for competition in the development of software-based systems".

When the US Institute of Electrical and Electronics Engineers (IEEE) formed its 802 committee to consider for Local Area Networks (LANs),it also considered how their standards should relate to the OSI model; the relationship is shown at the right in the diagram.

Five IEEE Standards define the protocols for the three major LAN types, for Metropolitan Area Networks (MANs), and for integrated voice and data communications. They reside at the physical layer. Information about FDDI optical LANs and the FDDI standard is provided in the entries under NETWORKS.

There is one anomaly. 802.3 specifies a version of CSMA/CD transmission. In fact most people use the Ethernet de facto version which is slightly different and incompatible with 802.3.

802.2, at the OSI data link level, defines the functions of Logical Link Control for two types of service provided by the "lower" systems – first, "Connectionless", without provision for a receipt-acknowledgement procedure, and second, "Connected" with a procedure for the establishment of a "connection". A "connection" in this context means the temporary establishment of a message exchange procedure between two users, not a switched connection as in the telephone system.

802.1 specifies how other IEEE 802 Standards relate to each other and to the OSI model. The reason for this special IEEE effort was the urgent need to get LANs under control before they followed the usual path of comp-eting proprietary systems each attempting to become the de facto standard. By then, separate developments had gone too far for any single system to become the Standard.

There are certain kinds of telecom system which will not benefit that much from OSI, namely those in which the individual components were designed at the outset to work together. The public telecom systems come into this category including those relatively unadventurous items in the "terminal service" list which have been gradually introduced by the public authority. Private computer/telecom systems such as all-IBM SNA, and all-DECNET offerings will not intrinsically benefit much from OSI.

Private systems created by assembling parts selected from different vendors as being the best for the job currently require a budget which includes generous provision for resident purchasing, fitting-together, and maintenance expertise. Small organizations unable to marshall such resources and who do not adopt a single vendor purchasing policy will almost inevitably run into horrendous making-to-work time wasting. Both of these scenarios will benefit from OSI.

When two people communicate face to face, their brains size up a huge number of variables almost instantaneously. Circumstances, surroundings, other person's background knowledge and appearance, required language, conversational gambits etc., are all processed in the wink of an eye and compared against a colossal fund of stored knowledge.

For instance, if the first person, versed in a particular art, perceives that the other is not understanding a conversation using the art's jargon or "coded short-cuts" of inter-communication, he or she will instantly (we hope) and effortlessly harness immense processing power and knowledge known as "common sense" to adjust transmitted messages so that they *are* received and understood.

Machines don't know about French, English, or German, have no general knowledge background, cannot make appropriate adjustments, and have no common sense. Everything must be spelled out in fine detail. If a simple black and white sketch with a caption is produced on a terminal's screen and must be produced on a different type of remote screen in a different terminal made by a different manufacturer via international telecom links, an enormous amount of information must be conveyed.

To consider but one set of functions – it's no good passing data via a Local Area Network, packet switched public network, satellite link, and then through various links at the other end unless all the en route effects such as different transmission techniques, error creation, delays, code changes, machine variations, etc., have been taken care of.

In OSI, user's source data must be accompanied by control data, which must be put there (preferably automatically) in the first place, in the expectation of encountering a number of "managing" devices along the way, each reading the segment of data addressed to it. Each takes the appropriate action to onwardly route the unchanged

message. Finally, the terminating device must be able to interpret the instructions addressed to it so that the message is correctly reproduced.

STANDARDS – OPEN SYSTEMS INTERCONNECTION (OSI): DEVELOPMENT

Open Systems Interconnection (OSI) originated as a model from the International Standards Organization (ISO) described in ISO 7498 as "Information processing systems: Open Systems Interconnection". The OSI "seven layer model" is described in the June 1979 ISO report ISO/TC97/SC16/N277. The parts of the model are described in numerous associated standards.

These few words conceal an immense ongoing undertaking and a great deal of political wrangling. The idea originated in 1973 by when it had become evident that "information processing systems", particularly the telecommunication aspects, were in a chaotic state.

A factor which is slowing down the development of OSI is the existence of several quite widely used de facto standards. TCP/IP (Transmission Control Protocol/Internet Protocol) is one such. TCP/IP was introduced in the 1970s by the US Department of Defense for the very reason that OSI is now being introduced internationally – and it is expanding, not dying.

Delays in OSI, the availability of ready-to-use TCP/IP systems, the adoption of TCP/IP by the BBC and others, and the size of the TCP/IP CIX (Commercial Internet Exchange) in the US prompted the foundation in 1991 of a UK TCP/IP network called UKIC (UK Internet Consortium). It will be linked to the CIX network.

IBM's SNA (Systems Network Architecture), with an estimated 16,000 users – among them being the largest users in the world – is a well tested system for which many products are available. Most of these users will not want to move to OSI but may experiment using an OSI-SNA BRIDGE or ROUTER to try out alternative OSI systems. However under SAA (see next section) there will be other possibilities.

OSI was not born easily; proposals for it were adopted by one vote at the 1977 ISO meeting in Sydney. Since then its eventual adoption has become inevitable. OSI received its biggest boost when General Motors announced in 1984 that their manufacturing control system MAP (Manufacturing Automation Protocol) would be based on OSI. Around 1987 Boeing announced that its TOP (Technical Office Protocol) would also be OSI based.

In view of the value of future procurements made by these two companies this was a message that suppliers could not ignore. Later it was announced that MAP and TOP would be linked and co-ordinated, re-inforcing the message.

But the problem with OSI is that it is still being developed and is incomplete. For example in 1988 an attempt to link several different types of library networks was abandoned because it became apparent that attempting to hit a moving target (the evolving OSI Standards) and compatibility with the continuing development of the existing Linked Systems Project would be very costly.

But even this problem can be overcome if those systems which already confirm to OSI are adopted. Preparing for the future by piecemeal adoption of those systems which are OSI-ready as a way of encouraging further adoption of OSI is the policy now pursued by the UK and other governments.

OSI embodies a collection of completed, developing, and to be developed Standards, so piecemeal adoption of equipment conforming to those Standards is possible. In 1990 the Central Computer and Telecommunications Agency (CCTA) defined its GOSIP (Government OSI Profile) procurement policy as is being done in other countries, defining the OSI protocols to be used now. GOSIP has already been applied to procurements for the Inland Revenue's office automation project.

OSI is an international attempt to harmonize connectivity and functions for the transmission of messages (e.g. Speech, a page of text, a half-tone illustration, an "electronic mail" message, etc). The OSI Reference Model provides a framework into which individual standards may be fitted. Provided a set of OSI-based standards and rules (protocols) are observed at all stages during the creation, transmission, and delivery of a message, then the format, presentation, and content of the recipient's message should be virtually identical to the sender's.

The EEC clashed with IBM who were secretive about their SNA system for networks and had showed little interest in OSI. In 1984, following a deal with the EEC, IBM agreed to publish details of their SNA protocols. Since then IBM has introduced a new network strategy "Systems Applications Architecture" (SAA) taking in SNA but also including an "OSI communications sub-system".

An IBM press announcement dated September 1988 listed several of its systems for which OSI and/or TCP/IP support would be provided.

In its "Announcements Overview" publication of the same date, IBM announced their support for OSI, extending and complimenting its commitment to open architectures and international Standards. This was a remarkable change from the company's earlier attitude, which was more overbearing, to a new policy:- "if you can't beat 'em, join 'em".

As part of a negotiated agreement IBM agreed to publish details of its well established OSI-like telecommunications protocol, Systems Network Architecture (SNA). In 1987 IBM saw fit to publish an article about OSI-SNA interconnections in its Systems Journal which showed the similarity between the so-called layered structures of SNA and OSI, and discussed design considerations for an OSI-SNA gateway based on IBM LU 6.2 inter-session logic.

In relation to its AS/400 mid-range computer system, IBM said that a "type 8209 LAN bridge" is available for SNA/OSI protocol conversion providing a customer with "a mixed vendor communication capability". A few years ago such a phrase coming from IBM would have been greeted with incredulity.

IBM has also included OSI protocols within its Systems Applications Architecture (SAA).

STANDARDS – OPEN SYSTEMS INTERCONNECTION (OSI): LIBRARY APPLICATIONS

Opportunities for using OSI standardized systems in libraries arise as follows:-

* Transfer records from a bibliographic utility to an integrated local library system or between a simple local library system.
* Link libraries for inter-library loan and reciprocal borrowing.
* Link local library system with a book

STAR NETWORK

serials jobber.
* Financial and name/address data transfer between a local library system and a non-library system to avoid re-keying.
* Search local-library system from non-library systems.
* Search remote databases from any local library system terminal.

STAR NETWORK
A network in which each terminal and computer is linked to a central computer. Because of this structure, all communication between various computers and terminals take place through the central computer.

STATDM
Statistical Time Division Multiplexing.

STATIC RANDOM ACCESS MEMORY (SRAM)
A memory system usually composed of transistors in which a particular state will be maintained, so long as power is applied, without "refreshment". See also DRAM.

STATISTICAL MULTIPLEXER
A statistical multiplexer divides a data channel into a number of independent circuits in such a way that the total capacity of the circuits is greater than the total capacity of the undivided channel. The data is distributed so that all circuits always work at near-maximum capacity.

STD
Subscriber Trunk Dialling.

STDM
SYNCHRONOUS TIME DIVISION MULTI-PLEXER (STDM). See under TELECOMMUNICATIONS.

STH
SYNCHRONOUS TRANSFER HIERARCHY.

STI
Scientific & Technical Information.

STM
SYNCHRONOUS TRANSFER MODE.

STORE AND FORWARD
Any electronic device for storing data and transmitting it later – a technique used in many different kinds of system.

For example there is a facility available on some facsimile machines for transmitting one or more documents to one or more addresses automatically at a pre-chosen time. The transmitting and receiving machines need not be attended during transmission and reception.

STREAMER
A streamer is a high-speed magnetic tape designed to be used as a back-up store for magnetic disc units. A streamer can have a capacity of over 2 Gbytes.

STRING
A sequence of characters. The word is often used to collectively define a word or words, a phrase, or a longer sequence of characters.

SUBROUTINE
A sequence of computer instructions in a program which can be used repeatedly as needed.

SUPER VIDEO HOME SYSTEM (S-VHS)
An improved version of VHS with higher resolution, claimed by some to provide results almost as good as professional systems.

SURROGATE
A Substitute. In IT the term is most commonly used to mean a concise description of a lengthier item. For example a bibliographic reference (which may be a searchable item in a database) is a concise description or surrogate of a journal article.

SWITCHED MULTI-MEGABIT DATA SERVICE (SMDS)
SMDS is a CELL-based service similar to SDH for providing a high speed public service over a wide area, if not internationally. SMDS will enable various kinds of data to be carried over a single service. The idea was initiated in Australia and SMDS services have been available in the United States operated by local carriers, their range being restricted by regulations. SMDS operations have been based on the IEEE 802.6 standards for metropolitan area networks.

SYNCHRON- IZE -OUS -ATION
See under DIGITAL.

SYNTAX
The rules governing the grammar of a language.

SYSTEM X
A family of digital telephone exchanges controlled by computer software manufactured by GEC/Plessey, or later GPT.

SYSTEMS NETWORK ARCHITECTURE (SNA)
IBM proprietary telecommunications standard. It defines the logical structure along with the formats, protocols and operational sequences used for transmitting data through a network. It consists of a set of products which conform to the structure and implement the rules. See also under NETWORKS.

T

T1

A type of telecommunication channel widely used in the USA. It is made up of twenty four 64Kbps lines capable of transmitting data at 1.544Mbps.

TANDY

An American microcomputer manufacturer which also owns the network of Radio Shack retail shops through which it sells its computers and related accessories. Tandy is best known for its TRS 80 machine, one of the early microcomputers which achieved substantial sales. It has remained a major manufacturer in spite of the failure of many of its contemporaries, by bringing out innovative new models and by the expansion of its captive sales outlets.

TAUBE, MORTIMER

A pioneer in the information field, Taube formed a company called Documentation Inc., in 1953 – one of the first commercial organisations to become involved in the post-war growth of information systems. Taube's company produced the ZADOCODE system using RANDOM SUPERIMPOSED CODING.

Tbit

Terabit. One million million bits.

Tbps

Terabits per second.

TCP/IP

TRANSMISSION CONTROL PROTOCOL/ INTERNET PROTOCOL.

TDM

TIME DIVISION MULTIPLEXING.

TEDIS

Trade Electronic Data Interchange System.

TELCOS

Telephone Companies.

TELECOMMUNICATIONS

Until about 1975 telecommunications was about telegraphy and voice communication. Subsequently most of the investment has been in data transmission, and today virtually all of it is. All "information", including voice is being digitized. If you tapped in to any digitized telecoms channel you would observe a stream of bits which might represent speech, fax, teleconferencing, television, etc.

The addition of a single voice subscriber to a communications system so that voice (digitized) appears to arrive at the other end almost simultaneously requires that the system has the capacity for a sufficient number of 64 Kbits per second channels. But the addition of a single subscriber who wants to send a coloured illustration which appears to arrive almost simultaneously at the other end requires a bit rate of around 50 Mbits per second – 780 times greater than voice capacity.

However it should be remembered that time is of the essence. If the person the other end can wait for, say, 30 seconds for the coloured illustration to be transmitted, then the extra capacity needed is 780/30 – only 26 times that of voice.

Even if people's requirements for moving data, as well as voice, increases quite modestly, their telecommunication requirements increase enormously. The data communications market in the United States was estimated to be \$90 billion in 1990, and by 1994 is expected to be \$94 billion. The growth of the image market, is expected to be much faster – from \$22 billion to \$74 billion in the same period.

Vertical Systems, a consulting and forecasting agency, says that the standard high-speed T1 (1.544 Mbps) lines in the US carried voice and data in the ratio 80%: 20% until 1985, 56%: 44% by 1990, and will be 39%: 61% by 1995.

According to the organizers of the EEC RACE research projects – noted for their ebullient optimism – who have allocated large sums for broadband network research, revenues of about 1 billion ECU's are expected from the one million businesses using fibreoptic networks by 1995.

TELECOMMUNICATIONS – HISTORY OF

William Watson, using a crude electrical generator, showed that electricity could be conducted along a wire 2 miles long. In 1837 the electric telegraph was adopted in England. It was first widely used on the Great Eastern and other railways.

In the United States, Samuel Morse installed a telegraph system for the Washington-Baltimore Railway in 1843. By the end of the Civil War Western Union controlled most of US telegraphs and started to extend the system into Siberia via Alaska to establish a connection to Europe. It abandoned the attempt when it became clear that the transatlantic cable would be able to offer regular services.

This cable was laid due to the initiative and finance of Sirus Field, a Massachusetts paper manufacturer, in 1858. When it was completed Queen Victoria sent a 90 word message to President Buchanan which took over an hour to be correctly received. The cost was 7 shillings a word – over £600 at today's prices. No doubt the slowness of the message was accounted for by the time it took for the current to cope with the electrical characteristics of the lengthy cable – a "system" of very narrow bandwidth.

In 1876 Alexander Graham Bell invented the telephone and described his results in some detail. Bell constructed a telephone from a diaphragm of gold-beaters skin which moved under control of a soft iron armature fixed to its centre, when current flowed through an adjacent electromagnet. The circuit was completed by a battery and another similar telephone. A friend was sent into an adjoining building and muffled, sometimes intelligible, speech was heard when "familiar quotations" were spoken such as "to be, or not to be, that is the question, a horse, a horse, my kingdom for a horse, etc" (See Figure).

In 1878 Bell delivered a lecture to the British Association in London. He encountered considerable opposition, notably from Sir William Preece, Chief Engineer of the Post Office, who made the famous remark "there are conditions in America which necessitate the use of such instruments more than here; we have a super abundance of messenger boys. The absence of servants has compelled Americans to adopt communication systems".

PROCEEDINGS

OF THE

AMERICAN ACADEMY

OF

ARTS AND SCIENCES.

VOL. XII.

PAPERS READ BEFORE THE ACADEMY.

I.

RESEARCHES IN TELEPHONY.

BY A. GRAHAM BELL.

Presented May 10, 1876, by the Corresponding Secretary.

1. It has long been known that an electro-magnet gives forth a decided sound when it is suddenly magnetized or demagnetized. When the circuit upon which it is placed is rapidly made and broken, a s˙   ˙n of ex⁻'⁻⁻˙   ⁻˙ ⁻procee⁻'˙ from the magnet. ⁻˙ ˙˙ ⁻aneously ˙⁻ ˙˙˙ ˙˙one in ˙˙˙ ˙ ˙˙ouse. A friend was sent into the adjoining building to note the effect produced by articulate speech. I placed the membrane of the telephone near my mouth, and uttered the sentence, " Do you understand what I say?" Presently an answer was returned through the instrument in my hand. Articulate words proceeded from the clock-spring attached to the membrane, and I heard the sentence : " Yes ; I understand you perfectly."

The articulation was somewhat muffled and indistinct, although in this case it was intelligible. Familiar quotations, such as, "To be, or not to be; that is the question." " A horse, a horse, my kingdom for a horse." " What hath God wrought," &c., were generally understood after a few repetitions. The effects were not sufficiently distinct to

Part of Bell's famous paper describing his invention of the telephone

In the United States Western Union realized eventually that their telegraph monopoly was in danger and they started to back infringers of the Bell patents. However development of the telephone in the US was controlled by the Bell System until 1894 when the patents expired. Bell continued to control long distance lines by setting up a separate company called The American Telephone and Telegraph Company. In 1907 J.P. Morgan and associates took over AT&T and under its President, Theodore Vail, the company started to buy out independents.

In London, the Telephone Company Limited installed some private telephone lines in 1879, and later set up a city telephone exchange in Coleman Street. By the end of 1881 there were three exchanges and 1100 subscribers. In 1884 various licence restrictions were lifted and the National Telephone Company was formed by amalgamation.

The Post Office started to take over trunk

lines and by 1914 had taken over the whole system except for services at Hull, Yorkshire. Developments in Europe followed at about the same pace. In 1868, after the Meiji restoration, foreign technology, including the telephone, was introduced into Japan.

Moving on to post second world war period, the monolithic organizations which have gradually been created during slow developments are up against controversy about the virtues of monopolies, regulated monopolies, liberalization, and finally privatization. A "natural monopoly" is said to exist when there is room in the market for only one organization to operate on a large enough scale to achieve substantial cost economies. It has been claimed that this is the situation for a telephone network and the argument has been used for the continuance of a monopoly regime.

A second concept, "welfare economics", has been associated with the need for a regulated monopoly. It is argued that the value of the telephone service to society is maximized if the charge levelled on each additional subscriber is simply the actual costs incurred in taking him on – that is that prices should be related to "marginal costs". There should be no cross-subsidization – one type of service should not be priced above its marginal costs so that another type may be priced below it.

In practice no organization has followed these ideal concepts, either because marginal pricing is very difficult to implement, or because other social priorities are considered to be more important – for instance that people who can afford to pay should be charged more for service than subscribers who need the telephone, but where the cost would be prohibitively large if they were required to pay all of it – as, for instance, for the connection of a small remote community.

PTTs are geared up to supply reliable unchanging telephone service which calls for a very large investment in lines, exchanges, and other equipment having a long life. Computer techniques such as "store and forward" electronic telephone exchanges have been steadily introduced in recent years. Attempts have been made to provide data services using a system ill-suited for the purpose. Demands have been made for faster and better data services.

The current upheaval in many countries in

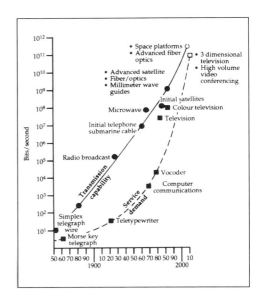

Telecommunications progress from 1850 onwards

the way telecoms is organized has arisen mainly for these reasons associated with degrees of political dogma, and the vested interests of power groups such as PTT administrations, large protected telecom equipment manufacturers, and large labour forces often with powerful trades unions.

See also DEREGULATION

TELECOMMUNICATIONS – MANUFACTURERS

According to Dataquest (1992) the worlds largest manufacturer in 1991 was Alcatel with a revenue of $15.5 billion. Alcatel was followed by AT&T with $10.3 billion, Siemens $10 billion, Northern Telecom with $8 billion, NEC with $6.7 billion and Ericsson also with $6.7 billion. GPT's (UK) revenue was $2.2 billion.

TELECOMMUNICATIONS – SPECTRUM, THE

The transport media and some of the present and expected services are shown along the top of the figure opposite with their approximate dates of actual or expected introduction. Growth has been associated with discoveries enabling wideband media – Coaxial cable, Satellites, Fibreoptic Cable – to be introduced to accommodate larger volumes of data

Copper wires Telegraphy	Telephony	Coaxial Cable Telex Television Press Fax	Satellites Colour TV Med. Speed Data Mobile Telecom	High speed & Pkt. data Videoconf Elec. Mail	Optical switching HDTV V. high speed data Colour fax Motion Multimedia
1850	1880	1930	1960	1990	?

Date

1	10	100	1K	10K	100K	1M	10M	100M	1G	10G

Bits per second

.5	5	50	500	5K	50K	5OOK	5M	50M	500M	5G

Bandwidth (Hz)

required because of greater usage and a demand for faster more data-intensive services – in other words for more "information".

The scales along the bottom show how data-rates and bandwidths have increased. Availability and economics dictate telecom applications, together with user's ability to conceptualise a need which, in the absence of the means of realization, they had simply not considered before.

Ultimately a wideband switched network will become generally available. Prices will be such that the transmission of a succession of pages containing high quality illustrations in colour will become feasible; the quality of local reproduction may be as good as the quality of the original.

TELECOMMUNICATIONS – TELEPHONES

There were 384 million telephones in the world in 1974 but by 1990 there were 820 million. In the same period the number of facsimile machines grew from 100,000 to 16 million. These figures are provided by Siemens, who says that it spent $2.4 billion developing their EWSD switch for the public telephone system.

A big effort is being made by the US Belcos, BT, and the European PTT's to overlay the existing telephone system with the ISDN network (See NETWORKS – INTEGRATED SERVICES DATA NETWORK) which may be used either for digitized speech or data. The general arrangement of the ISDN is shown in the Figure on the next page. Note the AT&T 5ESS switch, typical of the switches, including the EWSD switch just mentioned, at the heart of any public digital telephone exchange.

While telephone growth is now steady at about 4% per year, non-voice terminals increase by about 25% per year; it is estimated that by 1990 there were about 43 million data terminals world-wide. Telecommunication services generate annual revenues of about $350 billion.

The simmering question of competition and the charging for international calls – a good example of the problems associated with telecoms competition – came to the boil in April 1990.

According to the Financial Times of April 3rd, 1990:- "Telephone users around the world are being overcharged by more than $10 billion a year for making international phone calls as a result of cartel-like arrangements between the world's phone companies which keep prices at an artificially high level".

Iain Vallance, Chairman of British Telecom explains:- "Historically, the relatively high profitability of call charges – particularly international calls, has been used by national monopolies (normally state-owned) to subsidize local network costs, thus keeping down exchange line rental charges... This imbalance distorts the effect of competition across the board because national operators have to subsidize local networks by overcharging for calls".

And subsequently Vallance wrote "In the UK these decisions (subsidising local networks) have been taken by the government and the regulator. They are not in British Telecom's interest and we expect them to be properly addressed in the forthcoming policy review".

BT inherited the "connected remote village" social syndrome – affordable telephones should be available for all. Desirable as they may be, not many businesses are saddled with such concepts. However a govern-

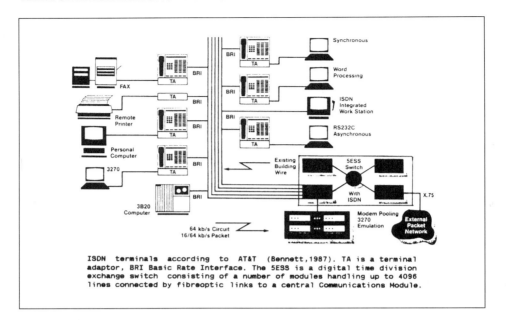

ISDN terminals according to AT&T (Bennett,1987). TA is a terminal adaptor, BRI Basic Rate Interface. The 5ESS is a digital time division exchange switch consisting of a number of modules handling up to 4096 lines connected by fibreoptic links to a central Communications Module.

ment decree removing the concept by allowing local call charges or line rentals to be increased so that international (mainly business) call charges may be reduced is unlikely to be a vote-catcher.

In July 1990, BT increased the cost of renting a line by 12%, but according to Michael Bett, BT's Managing Director, line rentals would have to be doubled for their costs to be recovered. More drastic increases were rejected by OFTEL on the grounds that "this was not part of the deal that OFTEL made with BT on prices two years ago. However, a thorough examination of the issues is needed as part of the November review".

In October 1990, Sir Bryan Carlsberg, OFTEL's director, discussed a number of the issues and concluded with the following remarks :- "...how should relative prices be determined? One relevant consideration is the effect of different pricing structures on use of the telecoms network in relation to the incremental cost of changes in use.

Lower call prices may encourage the use of the network in a desirable way, but higher exchange line rentals for everyone may discourage some people from having a telephone to the disadvantage of other users of the network as well as themselves."

"The pricing structures of other countries are also relevant. Some businesses use telecoms intensively today and if UK businesses are in competition with other countries internationally, they should have telecom costs that enable them to compete effectively".

See also DEREGULATION, and NETWORKS – TELEPHONE.

TELECOMMUNICATIONS – TRANSMISSION RATES

A "Channel" is the electrical link between data communicating devices. The near synonym "circuit" when used in this context is, perhaps, better reserved for individual data-communication paths within the channel. A channel may contain one or more circuits.

In 1928 H. NYQUIST showed that the maximum achievable signalling rate in a communication channel with a bandwidth of W Hz is 2w distinguishable impulses per second. Thus a channel with a bandwidth of 4000 Hz will transport data up to a rate of 8000 bauds, or signalling elements persecond. At faster speeds the pulse shapes become distorted and difficult to separate; errors will occur at the receiver.

These signalling elements or symbols could be produced simply by connecting an 8 volt battery to the channel and switching it on and off very rapidly. Say we could change the battery voltage to a value between 1 and 8 volts each time each time it was switched on.

Originally we had a system capable of sending two symbols per second, represented by 0 or 8 volts. Now we have one which can send 8 different symbols. We are still sending at one baud, but at a data rate of $\log_2 8 = 3$ bits per second.

This process cannot be continued indefinitely – the channel can only stand some maximum applied voltage, and if we arrange to select voltage steps which are too fine, the receiver will also accept small noise voltages resulting in errors; noise is present in all electrical systems. In 1948 C.E.SHANNON considered these factors and many others, including methods of coding. He then published a paper which was so extraordinary that it deserves a brief digression (See also INFORMATION THEORY).

The maximum rate of data transfer that is possible in a given channel is called the Channel Capacity. When the rate at which a message is sent approaches the limits of capacity the number of errors will increase. Channel Capacity refers to the amount of data that a telecommunications channel can carry at some arbitrarily defined Error Rate – but what is the maximum rate at which data can be transmitted over a particular channel?

Bandwidth, coding, and signal to noise ratio all contribute. These were the factors included in the celebrated channel capacity equation in the SHANNON paper of 1948.

One piece of earlier work already mentioned and cited by Shannon must be mentioned again. In a noise-free channel Nyquist showed that no frequencies would lie outside a channel with bandwidth w provided that the data rate did not exceed 2w signalling elements per second. For example the maximum signalling rate in a channel (e.g. a telephone line) with a bandwidth of 2500 Hz would be 5000 bauds. The remaining question is how many bits per signalling element can be included given typical signal to noise ratios?

This is quite a difficult question because it depends on what is typical, what method of coding is used and what error rate is acceptable. What we can do is to put some figures corresponding to the expected conditions into the Shannon equation and the answer will show what is theoretically possible – we will know that we should be able to get some-

where near that figure. For a 2500 Hz telephone line it turns out to be about 30,000 bps.

SHANNON'S 1948 paper – *A Mathematical Theory of Communication* – gave rise to Information Theory which would have been better called Communication Theory, since the word "Information" lent a nuance to the ideas contained in it which have since been frequently wrongly applied. The part of interest here is the equation:-

$C = W \log_2 (1 + S/N)$ bits per second

where C is the maximum number of bits per second receivable through a telecommunication channel with an arbitrarily small number of errors, W is the bandwidth in Hz, and S and N are the average signal and noise powers.

The realization of C depends on "ideal coding" to combat noise. This equation represents a performance yardstick for the design and maximum efficiency for all telecom channels. It also shows how one parameter may be traded for another.

For example if you cannot change the bandwidth or the signal and noise levels of a channel whose capacity enables you to send a given fax page in three minutes, then if you want to send more data to improve image resolution, you must decrease the bit rate in proportion.

When all-digital local telephone exchanges are installed, connected to other exchanges by high speed data links, and suitable equipment is installed at the exchange end and at the subscriber's end of the local loop, then the whole system may be used for end-to-end digital data transmission at a rate constrained by the part with the narrowest bandwidth.

This will normally be the actual wires in the local loop having a bandwidth permitting a data rate up to about 140 Kbps. End-to-end digitization is the condition necessary for the implementation of the Integrated Systems Digital Network (ISDN), to be discussed later.

Meanwhile the PSTN, designed for analogue speech in a frequency band of 300-3400Hz, and almost totally used for that purpose, is very widely available and so has been pressed into service for data transmission. Data now accounts for a few percent of its traffic.

Pending the conversion of the PSTN to a data network (including digitized voice) – a process which has hardly started – alternatives open to people who want to communicate at faster rates include an improved telephone line or, if justified by the volume of traffic, specially connected lines leased from the telecoms authority.

A second alternative is to use one of the purpose designed data networks which have been set up in many countries – for instance the Packet Switched Service (PSS) in the UK. Such networks are often available for international traffic and are supposedly much cheaper than an international telephone connection for data transmission.

TELECOMMUTING

A Telecommuter is someone who works from a home terminal connected to their employer's computer via a telecoms connection instead of physically commuting. Telecommuting makes a good "feature article" about the social and employment aspects of the practice and many have been published.

The credibility of effusive articles about telecommuting is tarnished by the regular appearance of two "pioneering" companies who employ telecommuters – Xerox and the FI Group. They have been trotted out as examples since 1980. Once the idea for another telecommuter story has been triggered, it appears from the inevitable appearance of these two that no others can be found. This raises suspicious about the claims about the "huge growth rate" of telecommuting.

The words "Telecommuting" and "Teleworking" seem to have been used first in the early eighties. There are many more stories than there is hard evidence for the progress of telecommuting.

Working at home using a computer terminal connected to a central computer via a telecommunication link was discussed in the late sixties. in 1971 the US Academy of National Engineering decided to work on a special project to be called "The New Rural Society" to examine "... the application of telecommunications toward upgrading life in rural communities to encourage a voluntary decentralisation of people, business and government".

The idea was taken up by an engineer, Peter Goldmark, a Hungarian who was in charge of television at Pye, Cambridge, in the thirties, emigrated to the US, and subsequently invented a method of colour TV transmission and long playing records while at CBS in Stamford. Goldmark later formed his own company, Goldmark Communications, and became involved with "Audio Teleconferencing" and in a kind of "remote education" cable TV system.

In a recent "review of the literature", only ten references were provided. Experiences with seven cases of software development from remote terminals using time-shared computers on ARPANET are described.

It has been claimed that remote expertise will become increasingly valuable and easy to obtain. Face-to-face contact will remain important and should be anticipated; it is necessary for ill-defined tasks, for group identity, and for general demonstration of judgement, ability and competence.

Telecommuting will become an ordinary, though augmentative component of work involving highly motivated knowledge workers with well-developed social skills. Such work will be loosely coupled and less hierarchical.

Numerous articles written in a lighter vein mainly cover the ground which has been explored to exhaustion during the last ten years. Some of them claim something new, or predict either growth or stagnation.

There is now an organization called "Telcommuting Powerhouse" in the UK. For a £12 membership fee "you get a regular newsletter and the opportunity to register on a central list which is used to match individual's aptitudes to the work available" Needless to say the inevitable stories about Xerox and F1 Group are included.

Evidently there is a move to promote telecommuting in the United States supported by a number of organizations who would profit from it. An organization "Telecommuting Solutions for America" hopes to implement ideas and technical standards for telecommuting. It is supported by several US government departments and MCI, Ameritech, Sprint, Novell, Hewlett-Packard and Northern Telecom.

However some cold water is also flowing. A report from Surrey University's Institute of Manpower Studies says that:- "The idea that a large proportion of the workforce will carry out all their work tasks at a computer terminal is no longer realistic". This implies that someone once had that notion. It was considered (by employers) to be incompatible with established management practices. Several companies (in a survey) adopted teleworking not as part of a long-term business plan but in response to a short-term crisis.

Perhaps Robert Kraut's appraisal (1989) is nearer the truth. He says "Why – despite the popular image of telecommuting and the Electronic Cottage – have we seen so little employer initiated workplace substitution?... The defining component of a conventional office is the co-presence of other workers for a substantial part of the day".

"Physical proximity is the technology that organizations use to support the informal communication that underlies much group work and the social relationships attendant upon this communication... it is frequently the basis of supervision, socialization, social support, on-the-job training, and the spread of corporate know-how and culture. Moreover the informal communication among co-workers helps provide the major satisfaction denied to home workers – socialising and friendly social interaction".

Kraut is manager of the Interpersonal Research Group at Bellcore, Morristown, New Jersey. The last of the 61 references in his article is appropriately to Zipf's book (Addison Wesley 1949) "Human behaviour and the principle of less effort".

1993 pronouncements still not only inform us that the idea – 20 years after its introduction in the seventies – is "new", but that the same two organizations – Xerox and F International (from the F1 Group) – are now, as then, "typical examples". Could this be because they still can't find any others?

Telecommuting and home-working are nearly always treated as synonyms. Undoubtedly much larger numbers of people are now working at home, but few of them are telecommuting – that is using a terminal in order to work for their employers over a telecommunications link instead of physically commuting.

If the point of interest is the growth of home telecoms it may not be necessary to distinguish between "home-workers" who use a telecoms link to send in their work, or home-workers who do not. At least some of the latter probably use telecoms for other purposes – e.g online access to databases or electronic mail, adding to the totality of home telecoms use for data exchange.

The editor of *Telecommuting Review* claims that we're seeing the same kind of growth curve with telecommuting as we did for personal computers. But despite the popular image of telecommuting and the "electronic cottage" there is little evidence of an employer-initiated workplace substitution.

It has been said that a major component of the conventional office is the co-presence of other workers for a substantial part of the work day.

In the absence of a cheap universal reliable telecommunication system, and because most humans are gregarious – a trait which will endure while technologies come and go – we may conclude that telecommuting is a slow-growth industry. There is as yet no evidence to suggest that the growth rate will speed up enough between now and 1995 for the figures in numerous ebullient forecasts to be realised.

TELECOMMUTING – HISTORY

The Association of Electronic Cottagers, based in California, was started in 1985 to assist in setting up work-at-home people, but this had been preceded by stories affording a much greater importance to telecommuting than was warranted at the time. Its importance continues to be exaggerated.

In a series of *Byte* (1986) articles both your own home-based computer-oriented business, and working for someone else (telecommuting) are discussed.

In the US the Unions asked the Department of Labour to rule against telecommuting because of problems like "assuring the payment of at least a minimum wage, protecting employee fringe benefits, and guaranteeing the right to organize in order to deal with unreasonable employer demands". The sequence of *Byte* articles which follow are mainly about the use of computers at home by people with various kinds of disability.

In 1987 a Canadian survey of 78 managers and 63 employees was described by three academics. The results showed that "Managers are not enthusiastic about remote work. While their attitudes are significantly more negative than those of employees, it should be noted that employees themselves are ambivalent (or neutral) towards telecommuting. Neither group perceives that the organization support the idea". The reasons given were concerns with issues like "social interaction, professional development, and promotability".

In spite of that "more and more Americans are joining the telecommuter class" according to a 1987 newspaper article. "The number of major companies with stay at home salaried workers has grown from 200 to 350 since 1984 says the Link Resources research firm".

Vague predictions about the growth of tele-commuting are provided in numerous articles. For instance although a 1988 work-at-home experiment "has proven very promising" there are "no immediate plans to expand our number of home workers" but "many other companies have telecommuting trials under way".

An interesting aspect of home banking systems came to light in 1988 by which time several organizations were offering services. A person paid a Barclaycard bill via the Nationwide Anglia system on August 10th. It was debited to his account the next day but not credited by Barclaycard until August 18th which came into the next period so he had to pay an extra month's interest on the amount. Nationwide require 6 working days for clearance, TSB 4 days, Bank of Scotland 2 days.

In Forester's opinion (1988)- "While home informatics may be of interest for various reasons, developments on this front are unlikely to lead to a substantial increase in economic activity in the home or an increase in the consumption of IT-based services in the home of a sufficient volume to amount to the revolutionary change in lifestyles depicted in the electronic cottage scenario... things have not changed very much... it must be concluded that the electronic cottage is largely a myth".

Miles (1988), responding to these comments, said:- "Tom Forester's critique of the electronic cottage pours much-needed cold water on some of the more hot-headed predictions about a shift of employment and services back to the home". But he continues:- "... he fails to give due weight to the role of new consumer technologies, which, we can be fairly sure, will be accompanied by social innovation".

The technologies which he has in mind and discusses "will allow users to specify (and change their minds about) the outputs of domestic equipment, and to have outputs more or less routinely tailored to known personal requirements". Additionally the technology can be applied interactively to the provision of hitherto labour-intensive public services such as "large components of health, education, and even welfare activities".

Predictions and counter-predictions about teleworking continued in the nineties. According to a 1991 report by Link Resources, telecommuting workers represent "the fastest growing segment of the work at home trend". The "trend" is a substantial increase of home-workers in general in the US to 5.5 million in 1991.

US findings were backed up by in a 1991 London conference where it was claimed that "A move to home-working will accelerate telecoms markets over the next 20 years". At a meeting of the British Computer Society in the same year it was said that "working from home using information technology is becoming viable because of increased reliability and falling costs of computers and communications".

TELECONFERENCING/ VIDEOCONFERENCING

A conference between people at either end of a telecommunication line using computers or television equipment to simulate a face-to-face meeting. See also COMPUTER CONFERENCING.

TELEMATICS

An extension of services beyond voice, to data and video communications. It signifies the totality of techniques involving the marriage of telecommunications and computing.

TELEPHONE

See under TELECOMMUNICATIONS – TELEPHONE.

TELEPOINT

Telepoint – a new voice communication idea which made a big splash – seems to have run out of steam already. The idea is that a network of small base-stations (radio transmitter/receivers) in public places, connected to the main telephone network, will enable subscribers with small pocket radio-telephones to make, but not receive, telephone calls, provided they are within about 100 metres of a base station.

The growth rate has been far slower than expected. There are about 6000 base stations and about 10,000 subscribers to the several participating companies, following an investment totalling perhaps £80 million.

See also NETWORKS – PERSONAL COMMUNICATION.

TELESHOPPING
See HOME SHOPPING.

TELESOFTWARE
A system for storing programs on pages in a teletext database so they can be captured by any user with the right equipment and fed into (downloaded) microcomputer storage via a communications channel for execution.

TELETEL
The national videotex service in France.

TELETEX
The name is ill-chosen; teletex has nothing to do with teletext. The system, comprising machines and protocols, was being supported by PTTs to provide a faster and generally improved form of Telex. It has not proved to be a success.

TELETEXT
See under VIDEOTEX.

TELEVISION
The first, and all later public electronic television systems, have been analogue systems.

Television camera tubes contain a plate upon which are mounted rows of very small photoelectric elements capable of generating a voltage proportional to the incident light. Light from the image is focused on to the plate which is scanned, row by row, by an electron beam. The element voltages are read off in a continuous stream forming a complete "field" representing a "snapshot" of the image. The process keeps repeating so that the camera tube outputs an analogue (continuously variable) voltage, field after field.

A video "frame" is formed from two fields, each of several hundred lines "interlaced" – lines from the second field fall between lines from the first – a way of reducing both flicker and transmission channel bandwidth. Synchronizing pulses are added.

At the receiver, the scanning electron beam of a cathode ray tube, running at approximately the same rate as the beam in a camera, is pulled into exact line, field, and frame synchronism by the received synchronizing impulses. The video data (line modulation) is applied to the CRT beam to vary the brightness.

These "all analogue" principles were used in the EMI system adopted when the BBC inaugurated the first electronic public TV service in the thirties, having rejected Baird's alternative. ALAN BLUMLEIN worked in Schoenberg's team at EMI to develop the TV system for the BBC.

The TV "picture plus sync" video waveform was his invention as was stereophonic sound, the AI radar system, and the H_2S airborne radar as well as dozens of circuits basic to wartime electronics. Blumlein was killed in an air crash in 1942 while testing an H_2S fitted with one of the first magnetrons.

NTSC colour television was developed from RS170 analogue TV – a format basically as just described – in the US. A colour TV camera amounts to three cameras viewing the image through Red, Green, and Blue (RGB) filters and outputting colour difference signals and a luminance (average brightness) signal called the "Y" signal.

In order not to make existing black and white receivers obsolete when colour TV was introduced, it had to be possible for a B&W receiver to provide B&W pictures from received colour transmissions.

The RGB signals are combined in a special way as "chrominance" signals which represent the HUE and SATURATION values of each minute area of the image as these areas are successively scanned. Chrominance data is sandwiched between "luminance" (brightness) data elements so the colour transmissions occupy a transmitted frequency band no wider than before.

This data, with a colour-burst reference signal added for decoding at the receiver, together with Y signals, comprises a spectrum of broadcast television signals occupying, in the NTSC case, a band 4.25 MHz wide.

These arrangements were implemented so that existing black and white TV sets, by ignoring the chrominance and colour burst signals, could reproduce black and white pictures.

A colour receiver decodes the composite chrominance/lumminance data into the RGB components which are applied to the three electron beams of a colour CRT. The beams produce a pixel by illuminating a three-element dot on the screen. The dot is formed from three chemicals which glow red, green, or blue with an intensity in proportion to beam currents when struck by the scanning RGB beams.

The combined glow produces a perceived single colour pixel. Signal data is blanked out for short periods after each line and each frame so that line and frame synchronization impulses to hold the time-base in receivers in step with the transmitter may be handled. Synchronizing signals are transmitted during these periods.

See also COLOUR and DISPLAYS.

World television, pioneered in the UK with a 405 line system in 1936, did not get under way until well after the war. Three incompatible systems NTSC, PAL, and SECAM were developed mainly for political reasons and have become entrenched since 1953 – NTSC in North America, Japan, and parts of South America; SECAM in France, parts of South America and the communist bloc except China; PAL in the rest of the world.

These schemes provide inadequate performance in a number of respects because of the design economies resulting from the need to transmit a lot of data through systems in which inexpensive mass-produced receivers are the most important component.

Un-natural effects are produced in existing TV from colour artefacts such as "dot-crawl", from patterning of various kinds, from scanning artefacts such as flicker and low frequency patterns, and from bandwidth limitations which limit picture detail and produce a break-up of motion.

Domestic videotape recorders provide pictures which are somewhat inferior. In VHS videotape recorders, 250 lines and a luminance signal bandwidth of 1 MHz is provided. Super VHS (S-VHS) provides 400 lines and 1.6 MHz. Tapes are interchangeable.

TELEVISION – COMPUTERS, FOR
Television systems provide a widely available source of electronic images. In order to buy and use equipment for capturing TV images an understanding of TV is needed.

Television sets and computers both use CRTs and raster (line by line scanning) displays and produce similar looking pictures.

However they are technically very different. Any device for TV/computer image handling must reconcile these differences which are mainly to do with frame formats, digitization, and field, and frame and line timing (synchronization).

NTSC interlaced fields contain analogue signals and repeat at 60 Hz. The 525 lines per frame are typically digitized by the computer at 640 x 480 pixels. PAL interlaced fields containing analogue signals, repeat at 50 Hz and the 625 lines per frame are typically digitized at 768 x 512 pixels. Consequently the line frequencies are also different.

The non-interlaced displays of digital computers have tended to be "standardized" as "EGA", "VGA" etc., containing different numbers of pixels, running at different line frequencies so an even greater range and a larger number of variables must be considered when adding boards or external monitors.

Given a particular computer, in order to acquire TV images via a "frame-grabber" board a suitable plug-in board suitable for computer and monitor must be used.

See also COLOUR, DISPLAYING COLOUR, MOVIES, MULTIMEDIA – MOTION VIDEO.

TELEVISION – DIGITAL
Analogue TV broadcast schemes provide inadequate performance in a number of respects because of the design economies resulting from the need to transmit a lot of data through systems in which inexpensive mass-produced receivers are the most important component. Un-natural effects are produced in existing TV from colour artefacts such as "dot-crawl", from patterning of various kinds, from scanning artefacts such as flicker and low frequency patterns, and from bandwidth limitations which limit picture detail and produce a break-up of motion.

At present the quality of television suffers because of the passage of the TV signals through the chain of mainly analogue paths and continuing use of the basically analogue systems. One major reason for retaining this technique for sometime is that the enormous installed investment, much of it made by consumers, can only be replaced slowly.

The benefits of digitization in overcoming problems associated with noise and amplification, and the comparative ease with which processing may be carried out on digital systems are well known.

If analogue UK standard broadcast television pictures are to be converted into digital format, the equivalent bit rate will be about 216 Mbps. When this data is transmitted through an existing 8 MHz channel (the available bandwidth for existing UK PAL analogue television) it must be appropriately compressed so that it runs at a bit rate of about 16 Mbits per second.

Compression rates of over 18:1 have been achieved by National Telecommunications Ltd., (the engineering division of commercial television). If implemented as a service, viewers will be able to receive the new transmissions via their existing TV aerial (antenna) and a conversion box.

At various stages within the telephone and television networks today's version of PCM (digital signalling) is widely used. The huge investment in the analogue "local loop" – the local distribution part of the Public Switched Telephone Network – and in television receivers, has been too great to encourage total digitization. The INTEGRATED SERVICES DIGITAL NETWORK (ISDN) all-digital service is arriving very slowly, and digital television for consumers even more slowly.

Eventually all television will become totally digital including the receivers. The development of semiconductor memories provided a significant impetus. Special effects – for instance showing successive positions of billiards balls after a cue stroke – became possible. A digitized frame sequence is stored and the frames are superimposed into a single composite still picture. The picture is then converted to analogue for transmission.

The present state-of-the art is demonstrated every day on public television with special effects, particularly in advertisements, usually produced on equipment supplied by Quantel of Newbury, UK – masters of the art of TV effects creation.

HDTV will provide the opportunity for a clean sweep to true all-digital television, but whether it will be seized on, or missed by implementing a hotch-potch of compromises for political reasons, remains to be seen. A television service could be provided by straightforward PCM encoding at a bit rate of 100 Mbps using the PAL system.

For HDTV the bit rate would be over 2 Gbps – i.e 20 time greater and requiring a far greater channel bandwidth than the current UK PAL service. Special coding techniques could reduce these rates substantially – perhaps down to 70 Mbps for HDTV.

TELEVISION – HIGH DEFINITION (HDTV)

HDTV has applications in high quality text and image display for information systems, as well as for entertainment TV. It impacts semiconductors, display devices, and general consumer electronics.

HDTV is a major service planned to be accommodated in the Integrated Broadband Communications Network (IBC) being developed under the CEC RACE programme. Commercial and competitive incentives could bring a universal network into existence sooner than would otherwise be the case. Information services could ride upon entertainment services.

High Definition Television provides improved viewing approaching that of a cinema theatre. The number of lines are increased so that more detail becomes visible and the screen is made considerably wider.

A TV colour signal of over 1000 lines requires a bandwidth of 25 MHz or more, compared with 6 MHz for conventional TV. To digitize HDTV – the way all signals will eventually be transported – a bit rate of around 2 Gbps may be required. To overcome difficulties in handling data at this rate there have been two lines of technical attack – firstly, compress the signals, and secondly devise a system which is compatible with existing systems.

Satellite transmission has been assumed, but Cable is a feasible alternative. The transmission of HDTV digital signals over fibreoptic cable is being carried out in Japan. The data rate is 400 Megabits per second (Mbps) for a digitized HDTV signal which occupies a bandwidth of 20 MHz when in analogue form. Various bit rates have been proposed in Germany and Japan at up to 2.24 Gigabits per second (Gbps) over main distribution cables and at up to 400 Mbps over subscriber lines. High-speed chips for switching are being developed.

Cable networks – that is wideband cable passing along a street to which households may be connected – have penetrated a large number of US households. Cable systems, many provided by small local operators, are often "networked" by satellite – that is programmes are distributed from a central provider by satellite up-down link to the local cable service who distribute to households.

Cable is used almost entirely to provide multi-channel TV entertainment. It is even more widely used in some European countries, particularly, Switzerland, Holland and Belgium, and it is growing in the UK.

TELEVISION – HIGH DEFINITION, in EUROPE

The Single European Act, signed in 1985 by the 12 member states, includes a requirement to strengthen the scientific and technological basis of European industry. Accordingly the Community has done some work on the adoption of a new broadcasting standard for satellite TV and the development of European HDTV technology. For TV transmitted via satellite, the new broadcasting standard will mean the end of the division of Europe into PAL and SECAM.

They will be replaced by MAC standards which were supposed to be introduced in late 1989/1990 in the TDF1, TVSAT2, BSB, and Olympus satellites. Signals from these satellites will be receivable on new MAC receivers and also on existing PAL and SECAM sets with the addition of a low cost converter.

The European reaction was organised jointly by the European Commission and 30 electronics companies led by Robert Bosch, West Germany; Philips, Netherlands; Thomson, France, and Thorn EMI, UK. The EC provided additional funds under the Eureka programme.

The objective was to develop an HDTV system to be proposed as a European, if not a world standard, at a CCIR meeting. In March 1989 the EC decided to increase their support of the UK and West German HDTV effort in the Eureka programme, providing up to 36% of the UK's expenditure of about $20 million in the years 1988 – 1990 and up to 50% of West Germany's spending of about $48 million in the period 1984-1990.

In November 1989 the EEC states, under the aegis of the Commission, discussed the idea of a strategic alliance between HDTV equipment manufacturers, TV stations, and programme producers for television and the cinema – reminiscent of Japanese MITI strategies. In December the Commission convened a meeting to launch the European Economic Interest Group for HDTV – a meeting attended by representatives of consumers, manufacturers, programme producers, broadcasters, and transmission authorities.

Dates around 1995 have been suggested for a start-up of HDTV broadcasting in Europe. The course which HDTV will follow during the next few years is uncertain. The political incentives to get on with it and the potential commercial gains are so high that it will certainly come, perhaps having a substantial impact on the telecommunication scene round about the year 2000.

In a mid-1992 paper by engineers in Germany and the UK it was said that "A range of sets with full HDTV quality will be launched in a large scale market introduction during 1994 more than a year ahead of schedule" and that the HDTV signal will be broadcast by satellites and cable networks using the analogue HD-MAC transmission standard".

Several RACE projects for HDTV over the B-ISDN are mentioned including multimedia programmes and telepublishing – for instance for catalogues and "electronic newspapers".

TELEVISION – HIGH DEFINITION, in JAPAN

The Japanese, who have been working on HDTV since the early seventies, consider that the width: height ratio should be 5:3 and that under the viewing conditions already discussed, increasing resolution above 1125 lines would not produce any appreciable improvement. At a meeting of the International Radio Consultative Committee at Geneva in November 1985, they proposed a world standard based on an 1125 line picture repeated at a 60 Hz rate.

In view of the huge investment in existing TV systems this was too much for the Europeans and Americans who reacted sharply. A year after a postponement, evidently introduced to provide time for reflection, the Japanese again proposed that the system which they had invented for High Definition Television (HDTV) should become a world standard. At this meeting – of the International Committee of Radiodiffusion (CCIR) at Dubrovnik held in May 1986 – resistance to the proposal hardened further.

The Japanese approach is to introduce an entirely new system which will displace existing TV, using a method for compressing the signals called Multiple Sub-Nyquist Sampling Encoding (MUSE). It was developed by a team under Takashi Fujio, Director General of the research laboratories of NHK, the Japan Broadcasting Corporation.

In mid-1989 the Japanese introduced a simple alternative to HDTV called Clear Vision (they call HDTV Hi Vision). In Clear Vision the TV camera records on 1125 lines which studio equipment converts to 525 lines for transmission. A Clear Vision receiver contains a frame store which records each frame and displays it twice.

Apparently this produces a remarkable improvement. New television sets with Clear Vision already sell for only #1600. Moreover a special reference pulse is broadcast with Clear Vision which is compared with a pulse generated in the receiver, enabling ghost images to be cancelled.

Yet another system is under development called Extended Definition Television (EDTV) – an improved but compatible version of the existing NTSC system, likely to be a contender for adoption in the US. HDTV data, including separated brightness and colour signals, ghost cancelling signals, and other processing data is broadcast in a separate 6 MHz channel. Existing receivers do not pick up this channel and reproduce a normal NTSC image. HDTV receivers pick up signals from the additional channel and reproduce a 16:9 picture shape.

MITI estimates the market for HDTV at $6 billion for hardware and $2 billion for programming. Appreciable market penetration to typical consumers is expected in 1995. There is no doubt that the Japanese are making the same single-minded effort and are using the same strategies to capture the market that they have used so successfully in other fields. They are already considering the programme-supply aspect of HDTV by buying US companies in the entertainment business.

TELEVISION – HIGH DEFINITION; TECHNICAL ASPECTS

In the Information Technology field, display resolution is usually specified in terms of so many "dots per inch". The best available monochrome cathode ray tube display has a resolution of about 300 dpi in the eleven inches available vertically on its "19 inch" (measured diagonally) screen. The actual display size is about 13.5" wide and 11" high.

In the television world, display performance is expressed in terms of the number of lines on the screen. On the CRT display just described, there would be slightly over 3000 lines, which is adequate for almost any viewing requirement. Standard 35mm film has a resolution equivalent to well over 2000 lines, but, for various reasons, the net effective viewing resolution in a motion picture theatre is about 800 lines.

To bring an added note of realism the width of the picture needs to be wider than it is on an ordinary television set. According to some research carried out by Philips at Eindhoven, HDTV "will have absolutely no effect in many living rooms if not combined with an increase in picture width.

For HDTV, Research in Japan indicates that a horizontal viewing angle of about 300 at a viewing distance of three times the screen height is required. For long viewing periods or for watching rapid motion, the distance should be increased to four times. The actual width used for HDTV depends on agreement about Standards.

TELEVISION – HIGH DEFINITION STANDARDS

The Europeans and the Japanese both have proposals for an international standard. There are a number of proposals in the United States – a representative system is Advanced Compatible TV (ACTV), similar to the Japanese EDTV, being tested at the Sarnoff Research Centre.

The main features dictating HDTV performance are the number of lines considered necessary for adequate resolution, the rate for repeating each complete picture or frame in order to provide the illusion of a steady flicker-free picture, the frame width, and the bandwidth needed for the telecommunications channel. The characteristics of three major systems are shown in the Figure on the next page.

The proposed European Standard is derived from the scheme devised by the Independent Broadcasting Authority (IBA) for TV DBS satellite transmission in the UK, called

System	Picture shape (W H)	No. lines.	Frames per sec.	Compression Bandwidth (MHz) Before After		Bit-rate if digit- used (Mbps)
NHK HDTV	5:3	1125	60	30	8 (Muse)	2000 (appr)
HD-MAC	16:9	1250	50	25	122	
ACTV	16.9	1050	60	-	6 (Sep.ch.)	

Proposed HDTV Standards

Multiplexed Analogue Component (MAC). A variation, called HD-MAC, doubles the number of lines from 625 to 1250 and increases the width of the picture.

Ordinary TV sets receiving the signals will reproduce a normal picture. To transmit the signals a channel bandwidth of 25 MHz is required so a compression system is used to reduce the required bandwidth to 12 MHz – feasible for available satellite channels.

TELEVISION – HIGH DEFINITION; TECHNO-POLITICS

The Japanese MUSE-E system specifies a 30 MHz bandwidth to accommodate a 1125 line picture with 5:3 display aspect ratio, and 60 Hz frame rate. The American reaction was the FCC notice 88-288 stating "Existing NTSC services will continue... at least during a transition period" and that any Advanced Television signals must be receivable on existing receivers.

The Japanese response was to devise "Advanced Definition TV" (ADTV) systems of various kinds – for instance "Narrow-MUSE" operating in a 6 MHz bandwidth compatible with NTSC when a low cost converter is added, providing improved quality.

Several US NTSC compatible proposals have been made but early in 1991 US engineers leap-frogged into 1575 line digital HDTV whereby NTSC compatible signals are transmitted in one 6 MHz channel and HDTV signals in a second. Present sets will receive only one channel, HDTV receivers will receive both. Digital methods bring with then a number of advantages.

Europe has had to cope with satellite politics – HDTV distribution by satellite will be almost essential. BSkyB, operating on the Astra satellite, classified as a "telecoms satellite" and using the PAL system, has presented the EEC with a fait accompli.

The EEC rules for a system called D2-MAC, capable of handling HDTV, only applies to "direct broadcast satellites". This is one of several problems requiring an EEC decision. Whatever the outcome it appears as if the European equivalent of HDTV – now being developed with Eureka support by a number of companies – will be different and probably inferior. For users it means lowering the chances of getting HDTV before the year 2000.

Vision 50, a European Economic Interest Group (EEIG), provided a series of High Definition Television demonstrations at Strasbourg on the 11th and 12th July 1990. A 30 square metre laser projection screen was demonstrated together with HDTV sets with the 16:9 screen-size ratio. The founding members of Vision 50 are BHD TV, Unitel, Nokla and BTS (Federal Republic of Germany), France Telecom, OFRT, SFP, and Thomson of France, RAI (Italy) and the BBC, Thames Television, Laser Creation, and British Satellite Broadcasting (UK).

Vision 50 is a CEC response to the Japanese who proposed a world standard at a Geneva meeting in 1985 which would have amounted to (quoting one comment made at the time) "the surrender of the lucrative television revolution of the 1990s by the rest of the world without firing a shot".

Since then Europe and the US, in the shape of the FCC, have adopted various delaying tactics until they can get their act on the road. They may have left it too late.

The boat was rocked again in 1992 when Reitmeier and others published a "The digital hierarchy – a blueprint for television in the 21st century" in the *SMPTE Journal*. They rightly said that with the advent of HDTV the opportunity is presented for " The US to set a technologically advanced video standard that will serve us well into the next century".

They outline proposals for a "digital hierarchy" involving re-coding when signals are used by differing domestic equipment and large compression ratios. Such methods would "satisfy all requirements" including defence and theatre applications.

TELEVISION – HIGH DEFINITION in the UNITED STATES

In September 1988 the US Federal Communications Commission (FCC) stipulated that NTSC receivers must not be replaced; HDTV signals should be transmitted in such a way that NTSC sets could receive the programmes or they should be transmitted on a separate channel. In both cases the programmes would be seen on NTSC sets, but special sets would be needed to display them in HDTV form.

Early in 1989 the Defence Advanced Research Projects Agency (DARPA) invited proposals for HDTV receiver displays and processors. It received 87 and selected 5 for funding out of its $30 million allocated for the purpose.

In 1989, The American Electronics Association, representing a group of US electronics companies, said that a minimum of $1.3 billion of Federal aid would be needed to organize a competitive HDTV system.

In February 1989 AT&T and Zenith announced a $24 million project to develop an HDTV receiver able to receive signals within the NTSC specified bandwidth of 6MHz. Additional information is sent during the short intervals between successive frames.

AT&T expects to develop Gallium Arsenide – a semiconductor technology capable of very fast switching, for signal processing. Philips plans to build a $100 million factory for making HDTV picture tubes in the US. They expect to produce tubes with screens of about 30″ size.

An HDTV bill was introduced in the House of Representatives in March 1989 to provide funding for an industry Consortium, probably to be defined by the American Electronics Association. Funding of $100 million a year for a 5 year period was proposed, and tax incentives for R & D were also suggested.

Current activity in the United States to select a new HDTV standard may include the consideration of compressing data into the currently available 6 MHz channels. This would require compressing HDTV data by about 5 times since the uncompressed data needs a bandwidth of at least 30 MHz. If this is to be accomplished digitally one way is to derive a set of motion vectors to be used for frame to frame prediction. Still portions of scenes can be encoded in a much simpler manner.

The possible social effects of HDTV have received some attention in a 1992 report from US Worcester Polytechnic Institute, following interviews with major figures in the TV field. "The sheer size of HDTV will make TV an even more important and potent medium".

The effects may include "making TV the main contact with the world... and an increase in the side effects of television culture".

TELEVISION – INTERACTIVE (ITV)

ITV is a system enabling a viewer to interact with a television programme in a simple manner. For example if a series of home shopping frames are shown further information can be requested by pressing a key on a "black box" attached to the TV set.

TELEX

The public switched telegraph data network.

TELIDON

See under VIDEOTEX.

TELSET

See under VIDEOTEX.

TERA

10^{12} (million million).

TERAFLOP

One million million floating point operations per second.

TERANET

A scheme called Teranet was demonstrated at Columbia University in 1992. It is capable of transmitting multimedia data at speeds up to 1Gbit (1000 Mbits) per second. It can carry telephone, facsimile, video conferencing and inter-computer communication in one network. Systems of this kind require fast packet switches for interconnecting signals arriving at any one of a number of input ports to any of a number of output ports. See also ATM.

TERM

A descriptive name, expression, or word. In information systems the label accorded to items in a record so that the record may be retrieved by using that label.

TERMINAL

A data input and output device.

A term used to describe equipment that displays data, usually on a screen, and enables data to be input, usually by a keyboard.

THERMAL PRINTER

See under PRINTER.

THESAURUS
See INDEXING – THESAURI.

THz
Terahertz (million million Hz).

TIFF
TIFF – an acronym for Tagged Image File Format – is a machine-independent standard proposed by Aldus with the support of other companies for the interchange of digital data between DTP input devices such as scanners, cameras, word processors, etc. It includes provision for compression of the kind standardised for Group 3 facsimile machines.

In the TIFF scheme each image contains a header – the Image File Directory – containing as few or as many tags as may be needed. The tags may point to individual lines, strips, or sections in line-art, grey scale, or colour with different resolutions.

The objective is not only to achieve editing functions and compatibility between DTP machines and paint/draw software but also to accommodate future additions or changes without the need to introduce a new standard or make earlier images incompatible with later ones.

TIGA
Texas Intruments Graphics Architecture.

TIME DIVISION MULTIPLEXING (TDM)
A method of sharing a transmission channel among multiple sources by allocating specific time slots to each source. Both synchronous and asynchronous TDM is used. Synchronous TDM wastes time slots if a device has no data to send. More refined methods require devices to reserve their time slots ahead of time or allow devices to use time slots of other devices that were unused on the previous cycle.

TITAN
French videotex system similar to viewdata requiring a degree of extra complexity, but using a different code and character repertoire accommodating accented and other special characters.

TOKEN RING
See under NETWORKS.

TOP
TECHNICAL OFFICE PROTOCOL. See under STANDARDS.

TOUCH SENSITIVE SCREEN
A screen in which the data displayed upon it may be controlled by positioning a finger over the required point on the screen. For example in a menu display, a finger can be used as a pointer to choose a particular item from it.

TPA
Transient Program Area.

TRANSBORDER DATA FLOW
The ease of access to a computer in another country via international communications and the country to country beaming of information via satellites bring with them many complex new issues.

At a 1978 colloquium, a Hughes engineer admitted that the Indonesian Palapa satellite, Hughes designed and NASA launched, could be turned off by Hughes or by the US Department of Defence. The title of an article by Jacobson (1979) about this topic – "Satellite business systems and the concept of the dispersed enterprise; an end to national sovereignty" – spells out the implications.

In 1979 the British Post Office was successfully demonstrating Prestel at an international exhibition in Paris, but the competing French Didon videotex system was not working. Shortly after a tour by the French telecommunications minister both of the Prestel connections to London were cut off. The exhibition organizers improvised another line but that too was cut off. The exhibition was held at the French PTT headquarters, but a French service engineer was unavailable. No other exhibitors had telephone line problems.

Transborder flow takes many forms. Television distribution by satellite in Europe is controversial. West German newspaper companies wanted to transmit to Germany via a Luxembourg transmitter outside the control of the German government. It was thought that this might enable publishers to gain excessive control over the media at the expense of the German public corporation monopoly, upsetting a carefully preserved media balance.

The United States has been particularly active sometimes successfully, sometimes not, in reducing foreign confidentiality regulations. It negotiated treaties giving it right of access to bank and business data held in the Bahamas and the Cayman Islands which over-ride the confidentiality of the regulations of those countries.

Other countries, including the UK, South Africa, and Australia, reacted sharply against attempts by the US Department of Justice to obtain access to confidential data. The UK passed the Protection of Trading Interest Act enabling the prohibition of the supply of certain data to foreign countries. Switzerland "was leant on" to reveal bank records if specially requested, while Liechtenstein refused such access.

See also CODES, ENCRYPTION, HACKERS, PRIVACY & FREEDOM, VIRUSES & WORMS.

TRANSCEIVER
A single device that is capable of both sending and receiving data.

TRANSDUCER
A device which accepts signals in one form and changes them into another – for example optical to electrical, electrical to acoustical etc.

TRANSFORM CODING
A method used in compressing an image by processing blocks of pixels to reduce redundancy. The new JPEG standard specifies transform coding. It works on the principle that a pattern of all-black or all-white pixels, for instance, contain very little new information and may be rapidly processed. However there is little redundancy in the rapid changes of detail in a chequer-board pattern which must be processed more slowly.

See also IMAGES – PROCESSING.

TRANSISTOR
See SEMICONDUCTORS – TRANSISTOR.

TRANSLATION BY MACHINE
Progress in machine translation was brought to a stop in 1966 by an American report from the Automated Language Processing Advisory Committee which concluded that automatic translation could not be attained at that time. However in 1989 a study supported by MITI concluded that the state of the art had advanced sufficiently for machine translation to be quite feasible.

There are three basic translation operations – the analysis of the source text, the transfer of items and structures, and the generation of the target text. The source material is usually text which might be input via an OCR system. Analysis consists of operations to yield a grammatic representation of a sentence to show the possible representations of its syntax.

The result is a series of records representing an "Interlingua Representation". The representation is transferred into the target language via a suitable algorithm. This complicated process has been much aided by recent increasing computing power. A typical mainframe translation system will be capable of processing at least 10,000 rules per second.

The best known system is Systran, which was developed at IBM and funded by the United States Airforce. It is currently commercially available from Systran Translation Systems. Siemens-Nixdorf can also provide a system with software and five workstations for about DM 250,000.

Other systems include Spanam and Engspan from the Pan American Health Organization, the Automatic Language Processing System (ALPNET) which will work on a microcomputer, and a system called Atlas G from Fujitsu in Japan. Rates of translation on a 386 computer vary from 10,000 up to 30,000 words per hour.

The country currently making the greatest effort in machine translation is probably Japan. In 1991 they were spending about $6 billion on document translation.

A big translation effort has been made by the EC with the result that before their AVIMA project was put in hand a staff of 85 was engaged in translating calls for tenders. By 1992 the results of using Machine Translation required the services of only two people. A more elaborate system for handling nine languages is expected to take another ten years before it becomes operational.

TRANSMISSION CONTROL PROTOCOL/INTERNET PROTOCOL (TCP/IP)
A protocol created by the US Department of Defence for the US ARPA network, and now

one of the most widely used computer communications protocols. It has been steadily up-dated – for example for connecting IBM PCs and PS/2s, using the NETBIOS interface, to otherwise incompatible networks.

Transmission Control Protocol/Internet Protocol (TCP/IP) anticipates OSI in that it enables different types of system to intercommunicate including Ethernet (IEEE 802.3), US public data networks, X.25, and token ring (IEEE 802.5). It is supported by numerous equipment suppliers including IBM, DEC, Apple, Sun, Tandem and Hewlett Packard.

At the end of 1988 IBM introduced software to enable users of its Multiple Virtual Storage (MVS) operating system to exchange files with TCP/IP systems. A group in the US is preparing software for gateway operations in hybrid ISO/TCP/IP networks enabling both protocols to be used during the period in which TCP/IP will probably be gradually phased out.

TRANSPONDER
A receiver/transmitter on a satellite which receives signals from a ground station and retransmits them to another ground station.

TRANSPUTER
A chip made by Inmos embodying communication links so that a number of inter-communicating transputers can provide parallel computing.

See also SEMICONDUCTORS.

TRE
Telecommunications Research Establishment.

TREE STRUCTURED INDEX
An index designed to enable a user easily to locate particular information in a series of steps progressing from the general to the particular, usually by a succession of multiple choice "menus".

TRELLIS.
A form of extended QAM providing a potential 32 signalling states, or 5 bits per baud, but using some of that potential for bits to enable automatic correction which reduces the effects of noise.

TTL
Transistor Transistor Logic.

TTY
TeleTYpewriter.

TURING, ALAN M.
Turing was born in 1912, and committed suicide in 1954. In 1935 he conceived a "Universal Machine", later known as the Turing Machine, and described it in a 1936 article. In the early 40s he designed and assisted in the construction of the BOMBE, an electro-mechanical machine for calculating permutations generated by the rotors of the German Enigma Enciphering Machine.

His work was further developed by others at Bletchley Park into the COLOSSUS Electronic Calculating Machine, first put into service in December 1943. In 1945 he joined the National Physical Laboratory and planned a machine to be named the Automatic Computing Engine (ACE), which used internal program storage.

Moving on to Manchester University he programmed the "MARK 1" machine in 1948. In 1950 he wrote a seminal article in *Mind* called "Computing Machinery and Intelligence" describing the "Turing Test" suggesting that if a machine responded to questions in a manner which was indistinguishable from a human response then it was exhibiting intelligent behaviour.

Turing also had a hand in dealing with messages enciphered by a more complicated machine called the *Geheimschreber*, German for "secret writer". Its transmissions were code-named Fish. Turing was unconventional and committed suicide one year after he was convicted for a homosexual offence.

TV
Television.

TVRO
TeleVision REceive Only.

TWAIN
TWAIN is an imaging standard which supplies a consistent mechanism for inquiring and setting attributes which have been quantified into fifty five distinct Source Capabilities. Through the Source manager, the available services and parameters of the selec-

ted image source are conveyed to the Application Layer.

Capabilities include transfer mechanisms (memory transfer, compression standards or file types) image depth and size, feeder status, available compression schemes, image data format, current image size etc.

TWAIN is a well thought out practical solution for hiding the device dependencies of image acquisition from the application and the user.

It represents a unique example of an ad hoc group rejecting self-serving polemics for a common industry benefit. With the adaptation of TWAIN by hardware manufacturers and software developers, integrating image acquisition into almost any application will become a reality, according to one enthusiast.

TWISTED PAIR CABLE.
Cheapest communication link available. The data rate without repeaters is about 16 Mbps per Km. Telephone lines between subscribers and the local exchange – the most common type of twisted pair connection – are usually able to transmit data far above the rate required for analogue speech for which they were designed. Consequently they will usually not need to be replaced when connection to the ISDN is made.

TWT
Travelling Wave Tube.

TYPE FACE
A collection of printed characters of the same style – for example Times, Roman, or Helvetica. The size of the type is measured in points. The point size is the distance between the top of the ascender in ''bdfhkl'' and the bottom of the descender in ''gpqy'' plus a very small allowance at top and bottom. One point is about 1/72 of an inch or 0.3515 mm.

See also EM, FONT, PICA, DESKTOP PUBLISHING.

U

u
(Greek) Micro (millionth).

UA
User Agent.

UART
Universal Asynchronous Receiver and Transmitter.

UDC
UNIVERSAL DECIMAL CLASSIFICATION SYSTEM.

UHF
ULTRA HIGH FREQUENCY.

UKIC
UK INTERNET Consortium.

ULTIMEDIA
The word chosen by IBM to describe their multimedia systems.

ULTRA HIGH FREQUENCY (UHF)
The range of frequencies extending from 300 to 3000 MHz.

UNESCO
United Nations Educational Scientific and Cultural Organization.

UNICODE
Unicode originated at Xerox PARC in the late seventies and was designed as a replacement for ASCII with its 7-bit, 128 character set. Unicode is the basis for a character set capable of including all known characters, ideographs, and symbols. It now forms part of ISO 10646 Standard and so far about 30,000 of its 16-bit codes have been allocated. It has received recognition from the industry by its adoption for WINDOWS NT.

UNINTERRUPTIBLE POWER SUPPLY (UPS)
A power unit containing batteries which provides the correct voltage/current supplies for an electrical device, such as a computer. The batteries are normally kept topped up by the mains supply. If the mains drops below a given value or is a completely cut off, the UPS takes over within a few milliseconds. When the mains is restored or when its voltage reaches its normal value, the UPS cuts out and recharges its battery.

A UPS supply will last for up to about 15 minutes according to its capacity and the load on it, and the battery recharges within 2 to 35 minutes.

UNISIST
United Nations International Scientific Information Systems.

UNIVERSAL DECIMAL CLASSIFICATION System (UDC)
See DEWEY, MELVIL.

UNIX
See OPERATING SYSTEMS.

UPPER MEMORY
See MEMORY.

URQUHART, DONALD J.
Having been at the Science Museum Library, Mr. Urquhart was appointed to head the National Lending Library of the British Library, which was set up in Boston Spa in 1962. As the first Director of the British Library's Lending Division Urquhart organized it to provide fast effective lending. As anyone who has visited it will know, it looks quite unlike an ordinary library. Urquhart retired in 1976, to be succeeded by Maurice Line.

us
Microsecond. One millionth of a second.

V

"V" SERIES (CCITT).

CCITT Standard	Speed (bps)	Mode	Modulation and tech.	Application
V21	300	Duplex	Frequency Shift (PS) Similar to Bell 103	PSTN
V22	1200	Duplex	Phase Shift (PS) Similar to Bell 212	PSTN
V22bis	2400	Duplex	Quadrature Amplitude Modulation (QAM)	PSTN
V23	1200/75	Asymmetrical Duplex (AD)	Frequency Modulation (FM)	PSTN Videotex
V26	2400	Duplex	PS	4-wire Leased Line (LL)
V27bis	4800	Duplex or Half Duplex (HD)	PS	4-wire LL
V29	9600	Duplex or HD	PS	LL
V32	9600	Duplex	QAM	PSTN
V32	9600	Duplex	Trellis Code Modulation (TCM). MNP-5 (See text)	PSTN
V32bis*	14,400	Duplex	?	PSTN
V33	14,400	Duplex	TCM	4-wire LL
V34*	19,200	AD/HD	For high speed fax	?
V42		Specification for LAP-M and MNP4 error correction.		

*under discussion

"V" series CCITT recommendations.

V21
The CCITT 300/300 bit/sec. full-duplex PSTN modem interface standard.

V22
The CCITT 1200/1200 bit/sec. full-duplex PSTN modem interface standard.

V22bis
The CCITT 2400/2400 bit/sec. full-duplex PSTN modem interface standard.

V23
The CCITT 600 or 1200 bit/sec. 2-wire half-duplex, 4 wire full duplex standard.

V24
The CCITT recommendation for the terminal-modem interface for serial data transmission. The only universally accepted and implemented CCITT recommendation.

V35
CCITT standard definition for higher-bit rate DTE-DCE interface circuits.

VADS
Value Added Data Services.

VALUE-ADDED NETWORK SERVICES (VANS)
A combination of communications and computers providing a wide variety of information and transaction services, e.g. electronic mail, videotex services and reservation and billing services.

VANS
VALUE ADDED NETWORK SERVICES.

VARIABLE BIT RATE (VBR)
Data which is generated at a variable bit rate and for which intermediate storage can be ac-

VBR

cepted in a data transmission system without incurring interpretation problems at the receiver.

VBR
Variable Bit Rate.

VCR
Video Casette Recorder.

VDU
VISUAL DISPLAY UNIT. See also HEALTH.

VECTOR
Many types of image may be broken down into component structures called vectors – lines, arcs, polygons, etc., described in terms of co-ordinates and dimensions. Such a representation is far more compact than a bit-map, and required much less storage. Its advantages were recognized by Xerox and later Apple who used it in Lisa and in Macintosh's Quickdraw software. Vector software, particularly that designed for cad/cam use, provides fast action and storage economies. A form of vector representation has been adopted for the Postscript language.

V.FAST MODEMS
See under MODEMS.

VERY HIGH FREQUENCY (VHF)
The range of frequencies between 30 and 300 MHz.

VERY SMALL APERTURE TERMINAL (VSATs)
See SATELLITES – VSATS.

VESA
Video Electronics Standards Association.

VGA
Video Graphics Adaptor. See DISPLAYING COLOUR AND GRAPHICS.

VHD
Video High Density.

VHS
Video Home System.

VHSIC
Very High Speed Integrated Circuit.

VIDEO
Video techniques appear in the entries DISPLAYS, IMAGES, MULTIMEDIA, and TELEVISION. Video plug-in boards, which have revolutionized the way microcomputers can process and display video signals were referred to in those sections.

Video boards are almost self-contained computers with their own processors capable of handle colour video either frame by frame or as motion video digitized sequences of frames. The Rapier XTV board from Videologic (See figure by courtesy of Videologic) for example, is for use with 386 or 486 PCs is one of a family from the range. The DVA-4000 board, for example, samples at 13.5 MHz and digitizes NTSC or PAL television frames "on the fly" and displays them in full screen 24-bit colour at TV frame repetition rates. RGB inputs for accepting computer graphics are also provided.

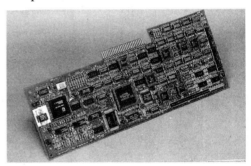

Videologic XTV full-motion video processor

The Figure on the next page showing the block diagram of a board from Sony displays some its features pictorially. This board will also manage video signals and superimpose computer graphics on motion video, although Videologic's remarkable digitizing capabilities are not included.

VIDEO CONFERENCING
See under COMPUTER CONFERENCING and TELECONFERENCING.

VIDEO GRAPHICS ADAPTOR (VGA)
A device introduced by IBM to control a CRT display. Its specification became the de facto standard for a CRT resolution of 640 x 480 pixels and 16 colours.

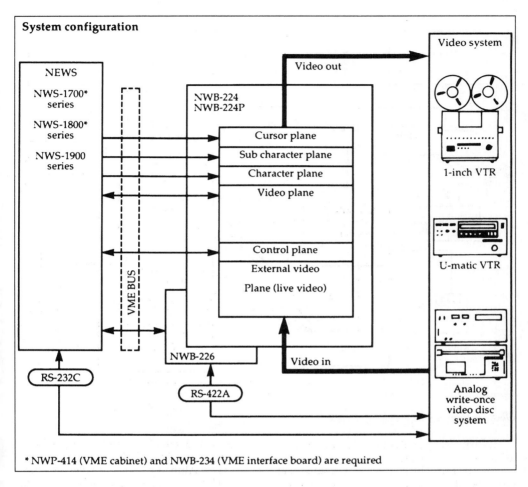

System configuration

NEWS

NWS-1700*
series

NWS-1800*
series

NWS-1900
series

VME BUS

RS-232C

NWB-224
NWB-224P

Cursor plane

Sub character plane

Character plane

Video plane

Control plane

External video

Plane (live video)

NWB-226

RS-422A

Video out

Video in

Video system

1-inch VTR

U-matic VTR

Analog
write-once
video disc
system

* NWP-414 (VME cabinet) and NWB-234 (VME interface board) are required

Sony videographics interface board

See under DISPLAYING COLOUR AND GRAPHICS.

VIDEO-CASSETTE RECORDER
A recorder which records and plays back video and audio signals.

VIDEODISC
See OPTICAL DISC.

VIDEOPHONE
An "audiovisual" (sound plus sight) communication system where subscribers can see and talk to each other.

VIDEOTEX
Videotex is a generic name covering systems for disseminating information electronically for display on terminals or modified TV receivers for viewers who are provided with easily understood control procedures. The original systems were called Teletext and Viewdata.

It describes systems for inputting, storing, transmitting and displaying information page by page using a simple indexing scheme.

See also VIDEOTEX followed by ANTIOPE, BILDSCHIRMTEXT, CAPTAINS, MINITEL, NALPS, PRESTEL, TELIDON, TELETEXT and VIEWDATA.

VIDEOTEX

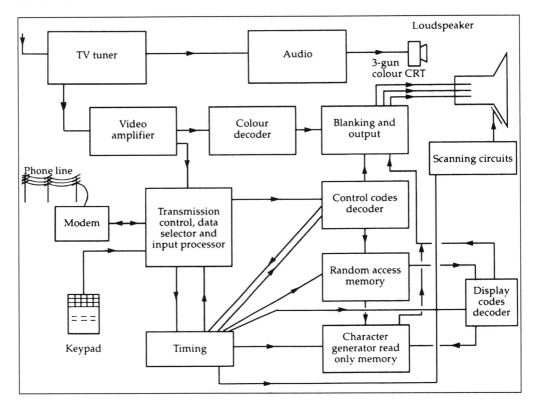

Block diagram of a basic videotex receiver

The British tried too soon to get international agreement quickly with a simple mass-produced Prestel-based circuit board that could be fitted cheaply to TVs. Eventually a compromise was reached, typical of standards politics, in which everybody was able to do their own thing. The CCITT 1980 recommendation S.100 proposed four different options "alphamosaic characters, geometric systems, Dynamically Redefinable Character Sets (DRCS), and photographic representation".

In 1985 a "World System Teletext Specification" called CEPT 5 was agreed listing five "presentation levels":-

Level 1: 1976 specification with some enhancements.

Level 2: 8 different character sets, 32 colours, no need for space before changing colour, extra characters, smoother mosaics, and other improvements.

Level 3: Method of implementing DRCS (anticipating POSTSCRIPT).

Level 4: Alpha-geometric display facilities.

Level 5: Alpha-photographic display facilities.

In 1989 it was suggested that "the jury is still out on public videotex while private videotex has been a modest success". At that time "public videotex" meant "systems supplying a wide range of information, normally run by the telecoms authority" and "private videotex" meant "services within an organisation".

Those definitions are now rather misleading because private organisations are running public videotex HOME SHOPPING services which have grown into probably the second largest videotex application. Although videotex is inadequate for the purpose, it has been adopted because nothing more suitable exists.

Anderla points out that searching a large database in the conventional online manner is three to four times more cost effective than on Minitel (where files like Medline and Kompass are available). However by 1989 Minitel use of such services had risen to 40% of all "electronic data transactions" while traditional online had dropped to 54%. The reason is probably because "Videotex is actually seen as user friendly, whereas conventional online searching is cumbersome and can be frustrating".

True to form, the videotex "Standards" adopted by the UK, France, the United States, and Germany are all different. This farce was preceded by a furious public controversy which prompted a comment from K.E.Clarke of BT research who said:- "The debate on Viewdata is the most bitter controversy about communications standards since the arguments about colour television 20 years ago". The result of those arguments had been the same – non-standard Standards.

In late 1989 the Bell company US West opened a videotex service using a gateway to residential customers supplied by the US offshoot of Minitel. Pacific Telesis, another Bell company, had postponed indefinitely a similar service scheduled for the San Francisco area. In March 1990, an intended connection between France and Italian videotex services was announced following a similar agreement between the French and othercountries. At that time there were already 100,000 users of Italian services.

But having had its ups, videotex has had its downs yet again. The Bell companies recent videotex efforts have been based on Teletel/Minitel, but following a report about Teletel's enormous losses in September 1991 a US telecoms analyst said it would be argued that "the Bells have no place in the information-content market".

The report continued "Many (European) companies interviewed said they can see no incentive to take part in a pan-European videotex system without some kind of policy for the mass distribution of terminals... and expressed frustration that no comprehensive database of existing services and terminal populations exits to assist businesses considering offering services internationally".

In September 1991 BT announced the closure of its Prestel Micronet service – a bulletin board/information service for computer users for which it charged £120 a quarter, with 7p a minute peak and free off-peak telecom charges. It attracted 12,000 users but needed 25,000 at current rates to break even.

Home-shopping videotex seems set for expansion and Minitel is likely to continue to be promoted as a success in spite of financial problems. In other areas videotex continues to tick over and will continue to do so until either it gets a new lease of life when wider bandwidth communications become available, or is rendered obsolete at that time by a different technology.

VIDEOTEX – ALPHA-GEOMETRIC CODING

A scheme for transmitting control codes and displaying videotex frames, providing for a wider range of colours, character sizes, and character sets than are provided in alpha-mosaic coding.

VIDEOTEX – ALPHA-MOSAIC CODING

A scheme for transmitting control codes and displaying videotex frames built up from a repertoire of symbols stored in the receiver. The selection and positioning of the symbols in small areas on the CRT screen are controlled by coded data.

The repertoire consists either of characters, occupying the whole of the small area, or smaller elements occupying all or part of the area, which can be combined together. A combination of small elements is used to construct graphics having a rather coarse structure. This method of coding, with variations, is used in most videotex systems, Telidon being a notable exception.

VIDEOTEX – ALPHA-PHOTOGRAPHIC CODING

A scheme used for controlling individual picture elements with as much within-receiver storage as may be necessary to display high resolution pictures on all or part of the screen. See Picture Prestel.

VIDEOTEX – ANTIOPE

A 16 bit system developed in France called Antiope was developed soon after PRESTEL was launched. The extra bits enable special characters and better graphics to be displayed at the expense or more storage at the receiver – at that time rather expensive.

VIDEOTEX – BILDSCHIRMTEXT
A VIDEOTEX system resembling PRESTEL introduced in Germany.

VIDEOTEX – CHARACTER AND PATTERN TELEPHONE ACCESS INFORMATION SYSTEM (CAPTAINS).
A videotex system developed by Nippon Telegraph & Telephone (NTT) in Japan capable of handling Kanji (Chinese) and Kana symbols which are reproduced by dot patterns in 8 x 12 blocks. Control signal and dot patterns are transmitted. In order to cope with the bandwidth/time problems a relatively high transmission rate is used with data reduction techniques. It requires quite a large store at the receiver.

VIDEOTEX – DYNAMICALLY REDEFINABLE CHARACTER SET (DRCS)
A scheme for transmitting control codes and displaying videotex frames built up from a range of patterns transmitted or stored at the receiver either to form characters, or to be combined to form graphics with good resolution. The graphics are formed from combinations of patterns such as Line, Arc, Polygon, etc., or by specifying a shape pixel by pixel.

VIDEOTEX – HI-OVIS
One of the most comprehensive VIDEOTEX tests was also one of the earliest – the Japanese Hi-Ovis experiment. The costs of this experimental scheme approached £100 million and the services provided were free. The home shopping experiment included the selection of a wide range of goods, ordering, and payment. Purchased goods were delivered. The system used fibreoptic telecoms and two way visual communication using normal TV screens.

Not much "demand information" can be gained from this experiment in view of its cost and charges. However, say the authors. "In order to exploit the potential fully... HDTV or some other ways to improve the quality are needed. It is necessary to provide services of the still picture type with photographic quality". If this be correct, videotex home shopping is in for a hard time given that TV quality, or better, is needed.

VIDEOTEX – MINITEL
In Europe, Teletel/Minitel dominates the "public videotex" scene. In one way, at least, it has something in common with teleshopping in the US. A huge investment with a long-term return had to be made to get going in both cases. In France "through a distribution policy of free or cheap terminals it had the largest installed base of 5.2 million terminals by February 1990 followed by FR Germany with 163,000 and UK with 155,500".

The French authorities did not provide any information about costs for the Minitel VIDEOTEX project. The public watchdog *Cour des Comptes* said that Teletel lost FF 530 million in 1988 and would still be losing FF 400 million in 1995.

However Teletel is thrusting ahead regardless. Having achieved a reported 5 million subscribers in France it arranged a joint venture in 1989 with Infonet which will provide an "information exchange" by enabling subscribers on the US Infonet network to access the Minitel directory. In late 1989 a company called Aldoda International announced that it would provide Minitel-emulating software for PCs and arrange a gateway to the Minitel network in France charging time at 7p per minute.

VIDEOTEX – PRESTEL
The viewdata/videotex service provided nationally in the UK by British Telecom. A network of interconnected geographically distributed computers are used so that local telephone call connection can be made by users. Page by page information is supplied by a number of information providers.

Samuel Fedida, head of the Post Office R18 research division, presented some ideas about a scheme called "Viewdata" (later re-named "Prestel") comparing it with TELETEXT as an information source. He also described an arrangement of networks for national or global coverage. Viewdata as first set-out is a scheme where a central computer is dialled up via the Public Switched Telephone Network (PSTN) from a terminal, and requested pages from the viewdata database are downloaded to it. The "terminal" is normally a TELETEXT/TV receiver. Viewdata embodies the same coding/store/display scheme as teletext so much of the receiving system is common to both.

For viewdata there is an additional modification comprising a "keypad" and a connection to the viewer's telephone line via a modem, so transmission technology is quite different to teletext's "line bursts". Although it is possible to send data much faster over the PSTN today, Prestel delivers data at the rather slow rate of 1200 bits per second. Thus once a page, comprising about 10 Kbits has been requested and found by the Prestel computer, it takes about 8 seconds to become fully displayed.

Data sent by a user goes at 75 bps which is adequate for most purposes.

Retrieval is eased by providing a tree-like index to the pages, of which there may be a very large number. The user is first presented with, say, a choice of 10 major subject areas. Upon choosing one, he is presented with a second display of ten sub-divisions of that subject and so on. If there are 100,000 pages in the database, 5 successive index-selection page displays would lead to a display of a record page containing the wanted information. Alternatively if the number of the wanted page is known at the outset, its number may be directly keyed.

This procedure is simple but cumbersome. Keyword access was introduced in 1987. A keyword provides access to broad "headings" – e.g. "trains". There is no boolean facility such as "trains AND Plymouth AND Sunday". Since all key-words are broad terms they provide an "index to an index" and take you to index pages at lower levels in the selection hierarchy, not to information pages. An attempt is made to deal with synonyms by Prestel staff who note word usage. Thus if "railway" was used frequently arrangements would be made for that word to trigger a display of the "railway selection" page.

Prestel is connected to other databases by a "gateway" – that is Prestel can route a caller to another system via a telecoms link where there may be additional search or processing facilities. If you are gatewayed to an associated service, you may be able to use these facilities. For instance if you access the Educational Service to find out, say, what turboencabulator courses are available, the system will process its current data and tell you what there is.

A number of other countries followed, mostly using the Prestel system, but there was an extraordinary row about the variety of new systems. The British had hoped to establish a Prestel-based standard, no doubt with an eye on the export market, and there was an acrimonious exchange in the 1981 technical press in which K.E.Clarke (UK) remarked "The debate on Viewdata is the most bitter controversy about communications standards since the arguments about colour television 20 years ago".

VIDEOTEX – PICTURE PRESTEL

A system developed by British Telecom for transmitting and receiving high resolution pictures. It exhibits various compromises in data transmission speeds, coding, receiver storage capacity, and percentage occupancy of the screen area by a high resolution picture.

VIDEOTEX – PREXTEND

A system developed by British Telecom to demonstrate the feasibility of using more complex coding compatible with Prestel software.

VIDEOTEX – STANDARDS

The international videotex standards situation is complex. At present there seem to be two pseudo-standards. The first, CEPT, adopted by virtually all European PTTs and under CCITT aegis, is a compromise solution to national differences in codes and character sets. It provides for a degree of standardization leading to the possibility of mass producing receivers and terminals. The US situation seems to be in the hands of AT&T who have introduced a de facto standard, NAPLPS – an adaptation of Telidon. See also under VIDEOTEX.

VIDEOTEX – TELETEXT

A class of videotex system in which a sequence of numbered information pages ("Magazine") is broadcast cyclically usually over a shared television channel. User interaction is limited to "frame grabbing" – the required page number is set on a dial and the page is captured the next time it is transmitted, typically 12 to 20 seconds later on average, and "frozen" for viewing.

Methods by which data and graphics could be transmitted and displayed by the page on modified domestic TV receivers were worked out by the BBC, the Independent Broadcasting Authority (IBA), and the British Radio Equipment Manufacturers Association. No representatives from the Post Office who would

323

VIDEOTEX – TELIDON

How Teletext started – introduction to the original specification

manage Viewdata, appear among the names of the "Combined Working Group" on their 1974 report. The cover of the report is shown in the figure. The idea and its implementation were considered to be a remarkable innovation. But state of the art technology, as it was at the time, was not enough. Teletext was a success, but for the major project, Viewdata, using the same technology, there was no market research, and the great hopes for it were not fulfilled.

The project would provide a broadcast information service by sending pages for display on a modified TV receiver consisting of 24 rows of 40 alpha-numeric characters (in ISO-7 ASCII code) or six-element graphic "characters", in 8 different colours, requiring 45 bytes per row including control data. This coded data would be transmitted at a speed of just under 7 Mbps in a time interval corresponding to two lines of each television field (spare lines unoccupied by TV picture

data). As fields are repeated 50 times a second this amounts to about 4 complete pages every second.

Modified TV receivers would contain a decoder and a store for one page of data. The stored data would be repeatedly scanned and displayed on the TV tube.

If a repeating "magazine" of 100 pages is broadcast, the net effect is of a database sweeping past every TV receiver every 25 seconds (approx). Each page is identified by a key enabling any viewer to capture and store it by setting his receiver to that key. The average waiting time for a selected page would be about 12.5 seconds.

In a PAL 625 line TV frame there are actually 16 spare lines unoccupied by television entertainment signals. Since 1980, some of these have been used to carry teletext signals enabling extra pages of information to be added without increasing the "page capture" waiting time.

For example the BBC now uses 7 of the spare lines and IBA 10. Other lines have been reserved to carry data for enhanced services as described in the "Standards" section above.

See also DATA BROADCASTING – TELETEXT.

VIDEOTEX – TELIDON
The Canadians decided that for their Telidon VIDEOTEX system, considerably better graphics were required than were used in Prestel. 8-bit codes were used to transmit picture description instruction co-ordinates to a microprocessor at the receiver which constructed graphics out of lines, polygons, arcs, etc.

VIDEOTEX – TELSET
A videotex service being tested in Finland using the viewdata system.

VIDEOTEX – VIEWDATA
The name chosen by the British Post Office (now British Telecom) for a videotex system which it developed, subsequently re-named PRESTEL. The components of viewdata are a central computer containing pages with a tree structured index, the PSTN, and modified television receiver "terminals". The TV receiver modifications include the means of connecting the receiver to a computer via a

dial telephone line and a keypad.

A menu command display and the tree structure of the index enable any page to be quickly and easily retrieved.

VIDEOTEX – VIEWTEL
A viewdata-type system developed and offered as a service by Online Computer Library Center, in Columbia, Ohio, USA. It started as a home library service and other services were added later. It is sometimes referred to as "Channel 2000" – the number of the channel to which a user's modified TV receiver is tuned.

VIDEOTEX – VIEWTRON
A viewdata-type system developed by AT&T and introduced by the Knight-Ridder publishing group for users in Coral Gables, Florida, USA.

VIRTUAL MEMORY
See under MEMORY.

VIRTUAL PRIVATE NETWORK (VPN)
A network operated by a telephone authority or a PTT on behalf of an organization requiring a large private network. The PTT uses its public network facilities to form a private network with its various network management facilities. The PTT provides the hub of the network which may be capable of sophisticated communications using whatever bandwidth which may be needed. VPNs are operated in the United States by AT&T, Sprint and MCI and in Europe by British Telecom, Mercury and other European PTTs.

VIRTUAL REALITY (VR)
"There can be no doubt that within the next few years Virtual Reality systems are going to have a tremendous impact on many aspects of our personal, professional, and business lives... When it comes to the buzzword of the year, Intelligence is out and Reality is in. In 1990 the forefront of our industry was multimedia, to day it is virtual reality".

So say the enthusiasts – the in-thing is Virtual Reality (VR). For fun, ingenuity, and maybe some applications, VR will take some beating as testified by 10 short papers delivered at a conference about the topic.

It is difficult to discern much significance among the 33 references appended to 6 of the papers.

Although the life of VR has been short, only two papers have a reference in common. In one paper Wittgenstein's *Tractatus logico-philosophicus* is cited but I can't make out why. But away with these carping comments; let us accentuate the positive.

There appear to be at least four technical constraints:-

The requirement that tracking should be natural, and there should be no time lag between user movement and system response.

The display must have sufficient resolution to cover the users frontal and peripheral vision; when the user moves his head he must be able to see what he would expect to see at the same resolution as the picture he saw before moving his head.

Realistic scenes must be displayed at an appropriate rate by advanced graphic methods to provide a natural looking scene. Existing graphics hardware cannot generate the graphics sufficiently randomly for this to look natural at present.

Software must be adequate to provide the necessary support for animation, modelling, and dynamic behaviour of the objects in a virtual reality scene.

Virtual reality is a computer-generated environment within which the human user appears to reside and with which he or she interacts.

Bricken (University of Washington) says that the "potential for VR... suggests an economic impact that rivals the Gross National Product". He mentions two applications with which he is engaged – the simulation of aircraft cockpits in design studies for Boeing, and "the implementation of multiple participant worlds for an application in telecommunications". After translation perhaps that means "teleconferencing".

Florian Brody (Austrian National Library, Vienna and The Voyager Company, Santa Monica) points out that different manifestations of VR have been around for many years. The designers of the gothic cathedral at Rheims, for instance, had "very clear concepts of how to achieve the desired effects of an "out of this world "virtual" reality... Drama has always been the very place of altered reality... trompe l'oeil architecture creates fake space", and so on.

You can buy the system described by Dr. J.D. Waldern (W. Industries, Leicester), inclusive of computer and software, visor embodying head tracking device and LCD stereo colour display, joystick control, feedback exoskeletal glove etc., for about £40,000. The system provides the necessary real-time graphics, sound for instructions and effects, motion and tracking data, and connection point to a LAN enabling users to "meet" each other.

Robert Stone (UK Advanced Robotics Research Centre) sounds some cautionary notes. As he discovered at NASA "VR is a compelling experience, there's no doubt about that. But VR is an illusion – currently a poorly implemented one at that. With today's levels of technology it's also a form of sensory deprivation... despite claims to the contrary it is glaringly obvious to most human factors or ergonomics practitioners that VR equipment... is not yet ready for ordinary people".

Stone says that VR will not be driven by sales to leisure arcades and he discusses several areas of possible applications. They include simulations in connection with undersea diving operations, spaceflight simulations, and in certain military operations. In particular he believes that "VR might broaden the horizons of mentally and physically disabled people". He is already engaged with a wheelchair system controlled by the tongue of a severely disabled supine person.

Bricken would probably take issue with Stone about human acceptability. He says "There is a tremendous compression ratio between digital information and human experience. Very approximately it takes a hundred million polygons to simulate what we see in one scene... computation will not come close to this bandwidth for a long time". However "Our cognitive plasticity permits even simple cartoon worlds of 500 polygons to be experientally satisfying".

Grimsdale (Division Ltd) describes a system for controlling VR devices which his company has developed. It embodies individual transputers each dedicated to controlling a VR device, together with an appropriate operating system. "Rapid sampling and interpretation of data and the generation of realistic displays" are needed for VR and Grimsdale says that VR systems are "dogged by inadequate update rates, poor synchronization, and high latency controls... the long term solution is massive parallelism". Division has developed a parallel architecture which starts to address some of these issues.

In a second paper Dr. Bricken discusses training for VR. "VR input is coupled to natural behaviour" he says. "The rule of thumb is that a child should be able to command the system. No command lines or mouse clicks, rather simple walking and pointing and speaking and grasping... the challenge in the design of training materials is to place learning in a natural (although virtual) context". If VR is that simple, it will be unique among computer systems and its progress will be greatly assisted.

In 1992 a car called the Racoon constructed at Renault was designed and developed using virtual reality. The car was "driven" under virtual conditions which are said to have speeded up the design process so that it was completed only 13 months after the project started.

Virtual reality seems to be at the stage where it is changing from a fascinating and expensive toy into a useful technique for specialized applications.

VIRUSES AND WORMS

A Virus is a stored program, a copy of which is transferred from one computer to another via a floppy disc or telecoms network, designed to create confusion or destruction in each new host. A Trojan horse is a variation fed into a program to do damage to that particular program. A Worm is rather different; it usually re-writes itself in memory and gets transferred to different parts of the system as a kind of challenge, generating a message on a screen.

One of the first viruses to receive publicity spread through the ARPA network in the United States on October 27th 1980, and brought it to a halt. It took three days to get rid of it. It worked by saturating network nodes on the network. Worms also appeared around 1980. The Cookie Monster Worm spread through a system at MIT and displayed messages such as "I'm a worm, kill me if you can".

Dozens of other viruses and trojan horses appeared such as the Bell Lab virus, and Israeli virus, the Lehigh virus, the MacIn virus, the Scores virus, and Xmas Card Trojan etc.

At the beginning of 1991 a destructive virus

326

appeared in the House of Commons Library computer system. It upsets the file allocation table. The virus affected only part of the network, but the extent of the damage is not known.

This virus is believed to be the work of the "Dark Avenger", a member of the Bulgarian virus factory which has produced 120 different viruses. It is similar to Evil, Phoenix, and V800, also written by the Dark Avenger.

Viruses can travel over networks but do not normally affect network operating systems, although they may affect executable DOS files. It has been suggested that each work station should have a signature scanner, a checksome scanner and a memory resident activity monitor. The signature scanner identifies codes known to be viruses, the check-some scanner checks the length of a file which could have been altered by the insertion of virus code, and memory resident monitors check viral-like machine behaviour.

Michelangelo is a virus that affected the personal computer industry quite widely. At least 25 computer companies in the United States are known to have been affected by it. Most of them detected the virus because it became known that it was due to become active on March 6th 1992, and anti-virus precautions were adopted in good time.

In March 1993 it was alleged that MS-DOS 6.0 may be susceptible to virus attack. It was launched at the end of March 1993 and includes anti-virus detection and repair facilities. It has been alleged that the anti-virus utilities do not provide complete protection. Viruses were introduced in about 1986 and by 1991 700 known different types were in circulation.

A rather good article was published in mid-1992 about "Managing The Personal Computer Virus Problem" by K. Bosworth (BT Technol J., 10(2) April 1992, pps 54-60).

A number of anti-viral software packages are available in the UK – for example Virex for Macs at £69, Virus-Pro for PCs at £49, and Disk Defender for PCs at $250. Most are designed to detect the presence of virus so the user can erase an infected file, replace it, or attempt to repair it using the detection software.

Sophos offer a package called Vaccine (£99.50) which will detect the presence of a virus by looking for changes in file contents and attributes, for new files or file disappearance, and changes in certain other items. Sophos's Sweep package contains code enabling it to detect any of 350 different viruses, and delete infected files. It is up-dated monthly (price £295 per annum).

Precautions to take against infection include buying software only from reputable sources, being suspicious of public domain and shareware packages, testing new software before use, and being meticulous about back-up to ensure that copies of all files are available.

See also CODES, ENCRYPTION, HACKERS, PRIVACY & FREEDOM, TRANSBORDER DATA FLOW.

VISTA
An experimental viewdata-like system developed by Bell Northern, Canada.

VISUAL DISPLAY UNIT
See DISPLAY, VISUAL.

VISUALIZATION
A technique used to change abstract or complex data into graphical, often three dimensional, form. Consequently the significance of very large amounts of difficult to assimilate numerical data become easier to understand.

The photograph on the next page (by courtesy of IBM) shows planes of atmospheric temperature associated with a particular part of the world. In the original NASA colour photo, pseudo-colour related to temperature data is added in order to clarify the data in a visual form.

VL BUS
A VESA specification for a 32-bit wide bus for supporting 32 bit 386DX and 486DX CPUs. It can transfer data at the rate of 67 Mbps.

VLSI
VERY LARGE SCALE INTEGRATED circuit. The Intel 80486 semiconductor chip, for example, contains 1.2 million transistors on a 0.4 x 0.6 inch die.

VME
Virtual Machine Environment.

VOCODER

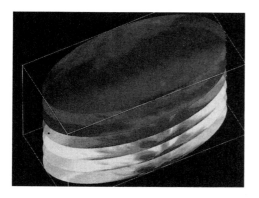

Visualization of global atmospheric temperature at different altitudes

VOCODER

In a vocoder speech is analysed in terms of the vocal tract parameters which created it and is reproduced by using a pulsed sound source modified by vocal tract parameter data. The information needed to provide very artificial but understandable speech created in this manner has been achieved with a transmission rate as low as 0.1 to 0.4 bits per sample.

VOICE MESSAGING

A system for the capture, storage, and retransmission of voice messages in digitized form. A means for recording telephone messages for later retrieval by the addressee.

Voice mail extends the technique of the telephone answering machine to a computer controlled system connected to an organization's PABX. Voice processing, started in the 1980s, compresses speech so that it can be stored on computer discs and released in real time as needed. A 1 Gbyte disc can store about 90 hours of voice messages and up to 6 drives may be linked.

On an average day each user will have about 3 minutes worth of data on disc. In late 1992 it was reported that voice messaging equipment was being supplied in the US to a market of about $60 million a year resulting in the creation of 1000 new mail boxes every day.

VOICE-GRADE CHANNEL

A telephone channel of sufficient bandwidth to permit the transmission of the human voice (typically 300Hz to 3400Hz).

VON NEUMANN ARCHITECTURE

A microprocessor design which shares one bus between data and program memory. Processing occurs in a serial fashion.

VON NEUMANN, JOHN

Born in Budapest in 1902, later a Professor of Physics at Princeton University, Von Neumann is considered to be one of the major pioneers of the electronic digital computer. He wrote a paper in 1946 describing architecture for a computer in which programs would be treated in the same way as data, instead of requiring separate circuits and storage. This idea was adopted and has been used on virtually all computers ever since. However Von Neumann Architecture, requiring sequential operations, has some limitations. Some machines now use parallel processing in order to achieve greater speeds.

VOXEL

Volume pixel. A pixel positioned in a 3D display according to defined X, Y, Z co-ordinates. The 3D effect is produced by the Z data which provides positional information about the location of a pixel on one of many "slices" through the object.

VPM

VIRTUAL PRIVATE NETWORK.

VR

VIRTUAL REALITY.

VRAM

Video Random Access Memory.

VSAM

Virtual Sequential Access Method.

VSAT

VERY SMALL APERTURE TERMINAL. See under SATELLITES – VERY SMALL APERTURE TERMINALS.

VTAM

Virtual Telecommunications Access Method.

W

WAN
WIDE AREA NETWORK.

WARC
World Administrative Radio Conference.

WATS
Wide Area Telephone Service.

WEIGHT
(Of a font). A collection of printed characters having the same bold, normal, or italic characteristics.

WFP
Wideband Flexibility Point.

WHEATSTONE, CHARLES
Born 1802, and the inventor of the electromagnetic telegraph. Wheatstone's Telegraph was first used between Paddington and Windsor on the Great Western Railway in the South-East of England. Subsequently it was widely used by newspapers for news reporting. Together with W. F. Cooke, he patented his system in June 1987 and demonstrated working systems some years before Samuel Morse invented his telegraph system in the United States.

Wheatstone is also credited with the invention of the Stereoscope, enabling a 3-dimensional image to be seen when viewing objects from photographs taken at slightly different angles mounted in a hand-held device. It was a considerable success in the Great Exhibition of 1851. Today his name is best remembered for a device which he did not, in fact, invent – the Wheatstone Bridge for accurately measuring electrical resistance.

WHITE PAPER
A term used for a document describing a policy or measure which the government intends to execute. See GREEN PAPER.

WHITE SPACE SKIP
A compression system fitted on many facsimile machines for substituting a short code for a succession of white elements as commonly encountered between lines of characters and elsewhere. The code signals to the receiving machine that it must re-insert a given number of white elements.

WIDE AREA NETWORK (WAN)
A communication network distinguished from a local area network (of which it may contain one or more) because of its longer-distance communications, which may or may not be provided by a common carrier or PTT. The term is sometimes used as another name for the public packet network of a particular country or region. See also NETWORK.

WIDOW
A Widow is the last line of a paragraph which belongs on the preceding page but which is printed at the top of the following page.

WIMP INTERFACE
A program interface that uses windows (W), icons (I), a mouse (M), and pull-down menus (P). Windows and the Macintosh interface are both WIMPs.

WINCHESTER DISC
See DISC.

WINDOW
A program controlled bounded space displayed on a CRT screen to contain information which may be manipulated independently or in association with information contained within other windows displayed at the same time. In order to provide sufficient flexibility, bit-mapping is usually used to construct windows within which text and graphics may be displayed.

WINDOWS
Microsoft Windows brings to the MS-DOS "command line" type of operating system, and therefore to the IBM PC, a graphics user interface akin to those available on the Mac – and it provides for multitasking.

A representation of Windows storage and presentation is shown in the Figure. Stored as a bit-mapped "virtual screen, windows may

WINDOWS

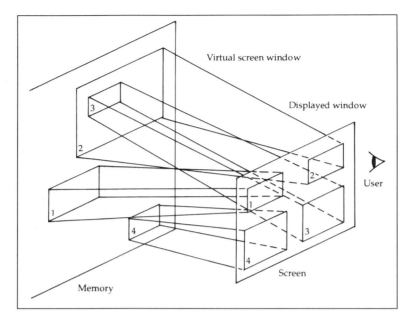

Virtual screen window

Displayed window

User

Screen

Memory

Windows storage and display

be selected and viewed as shown.

The first version, launched in 1983, was a failure. Its claims to multi-tasking were frustrated by the 640 Kbyte memory limit of MS-DOS, severely limiting the size of each task. When it was re-designed it incorporated "paging" – that is the provision of "virtual memory" by swapping pages of data between memory and disc.

Re-launched, "Windows 1.0" had its shortcomings; although it would run on 256 Kbytes of memory, paging made it very slow even when 640K of memory was used. Fortunately the Lotus-Intel Expanded MEMORY Specification (EMS) was introduced at about the same time. In Windows 1.0 tiled windows were used. A "zoom" button controlled expansion or reduction to alter the sizes of the non-overlapping windows.

When Windows 2.0 came out in 1987, overlapping windows were provided, control from the keyboard was improved, and Dynamic Data Exchange (DDE) – multitasking – was introduced, which was not available at that time from Apple. That was followed by Windows 286 which is Windows 2.0 for running on a micro with a 80286 processor and

LIM (See MEMORY).

The memory management provided with Windows 286 enables the "virtual 80286" mode to be used which allows several MS-DOS programs to run apparently simultaneously, each using 640K of RAM. The processor has sufficient power to run in this mode without much speed penalty.

A major feature of Windows 2.0 is that it connects with hardware via a "driver". A driver is a software package interposed between Windows 2.0 and hardware. To make Windows 2.0 run with a particular hardware item, the driver specific to that hardware is loaded. In other words Windows 2.0 is hardware independent. Many drivers are available for different printers, video boards, etc.

Microsoft stated that the Windows 2.0 user interface was very similar to "Presentation Manager", at that time under discussion for IBM's OS/2 software, to be integrated into it to provide the advantages of Apple's approach.

When Windows 2.0 was launched, there was not much you could do with it unless you were prepared to write applications programmes yourself because few such programmes were available.

At the time Windows 3.0 was announced in early 1990, a wide range of programmes became available on the same day for Desktop Publishing (including Page-maker 3.01), Telecoms, Graphics design, Word Processing, Databases, etc. – a total of 52 software packages.

The August 1990 issue of *Byte* contains a list of over 80 Windows 3.0 software packages in the fields of CAD, Communications, Databases, Spreadsheets, File Managers, Graphics, Multimedia, Networking, OCR, Personal information management, Programming, Project Management, Statistics, Text processing, and Others.

More memory is the major benefit. On 80286 machines it can be up to 16 Mbytes and yet more on 80386's. The memory management system provided with Windows 3.0 to use this memory evidently removes most of the restrictions in multitasking.

Differences of opinion about the benefits of the windows concept notwithstanding, Microsoft Windows 3.0, launched in May 1990, appears to be a great improvement over Windows 2.0. There is more memory, effective multitasking, protection between tasks, and support for a number of LANs.

Windows 3.0 came out with a whole range of applications ready to run. Some people think it is simply a scheme to extend the life of DOS, because Windows is a kind of shell including DOS. The fact is that Window enables multitasking to take place for which DOS itself was not designed.

The kind of application where the benefits should be felt are those involving large amounts of data such as multi-page documents with graphics. A review of Pagemaker with Windows 3.0 says it took over 90 seconds to flow about 10 Mbytes of data into 35 pages using Windows 286. It involves much swapping between memory and disc. However with Windows 3.0 on the same machine with 4 Mbytes of memory available, the job took 35 seconds.

The other area where more memory and faster operation is required is for colour applications. Windows 3.0 includes a palette manager enabling exact colours to be generated by combining known proportions of red, green, and blue, or by the adjustment of HUE, SATURATION, and LUMINOSITY.

Windows 3.1 is a 16 bit graphical operating shell that runs on top of the DOS operating system.

Windows, once set up, is useful as an interface for running DOS programs. A command line entry is replaced by pointing and clicking on icons. It is said that it does not function properly with some of the older DOS programs.

Some people find that software packages designed to run under Windows produce cluttered screens and rather slow operation. A large amount of space in RAM – at least 8 Mbytes – is now needed and about 30 Mbytes of hard disc. However Windows is a good interface for switching between DOS applications and several applications can be run from within it.

WINDOWS NT (NEW TECHNOLOGY)

A 32 bit multiprocessing system specifically designed for client/server applications to provide multiple operating system environments.

Windows NT was announced in 1992 and is due to be launched in the autumn of 1993. The Windows NT file system requires at least 30 Mbytes of hard disc space and the rest of the NT software may take up another 60 Mbytes so 90 Mbytes accounted is used without any applications software.

It may be necessary to have a total of 200 Mbytes available including the applications software. This compares with about 30 Mbytes for the OS/2 operating system. Up to 16 Mbytes of RAM is needed, reducing perhaps to 8 Mbytes when the system is finally launched; eventually hard disc requirements may be reduced as well.

However Windows NT and its applications are comprehensive. OS/2 2.0 comes on numerous floppy discs but Windows NT is available on CD-ROM. Windows NT includes Remote Procedure Calls conforming to the Distributed Computing Environment standard – an important feature of large networks where access to powerful machines is provided.

Windows NT is one of the first software packages to adopt UNICODE, whereas ANSI 163, a rather unsatisfactory ASCII replacement with more codes, is used in WINDOWS 3.1.

WIZARD ADAPTER CARD

The IBM PS/2 Wizard Adapter card, with OS/2 software developer tools and optional memory expansion incorporates the Intel i860 Reduced Instruction Set Computing (RISC) processor. Co-processor power has become a feature of present generation microcomputers. Computer-intensive tasks are taken over by a computer within a computer, freeing the main processor for a wider range of general tasks.

The Wizard card comes with 2 Mbytes of 85 nanosecond DRAM. The 64 bit processor runs at 33 MHz and the Wizard is capable of 64 Million Floating Point Operations Per Second (MFLOPS). It has been demonstrated creating fractal images at 33 MFLOPS, and performing seismic data processing operations at 55 MFLOPS.

WORD

The number of bits that a processor handles as a single block. Typically processors handle, 8, 16, 32, or 64 bit words.

WORD LENGTHS

A "word" in an 8 bit device is a sequence of 8 bits, in a 16 bit device, 16 bits etc. 8 bits = 2^8 and $16 = 2^{16}$ so 8 bits can represent 256 different numbers, and 16 bits 65536 (often called "64K") numbers.

Microcomputer word lengths started at 4 bits, then 8 bits became widely adopted to be followed by 16, 32, and very recently 64. This has become possible because improvements in technology, particularly in the packing density of semiconductor elements, have enabled the extra complexity needed to handle longer words to be introduced without proportional increases in cost, or decreases in reliability.

A major reason for longer words is to address each cell of larger memories. But it can also be done in a more cumbersome way; for example in 8 bit microcomputers the 16 bit address-word needed for the 65,536 locations of a "64K" memory is composed of one 8 bit word for the 8 "lower order" bits and a second 8 bit word for the 8 "higher order" bits. The 16 bits of the two words are transmitted simultaneously along 16 lines to memory as if they were one 16 bit address-word. Increasing the word to 32 bits enables over four thousand million memory locations to be addressed.

Single long address-words reduce the extra complexity and cost of organizing two or more words for the purpose. Larger memories can accommodate more sophisticated programs and more of the user's data which otherwise would have to be accommodated on disc which takes much longer to access than semiconductor memory.

The advantage of longer words for data is that more data can be moved about faster. If each 16 bit data-word is moved around at the same speed as an 8 bit data word, any task involving the movement of numbers of data words will be completed in a shorter time, and if 32 bit words are used, in a still shorter time.

For example, a row of 32 pixels (picture elements) representing black or white parts of an image could, in principle, be processed in four cycles by an 8 bit, 2 cycles by a 16 bit, and in one cycle by a 32 bit machine – i.e. four times faster by the latter.

For longer data-words to be moved about at the same rate as shorter data-words, extra bandwidth (or more bus lines) are needed with additional circuits and storage. However improvements in manufacturing techniques and rapid adoption on a big scale have enabled longer words to be used in microcomputers with the machine selling for less than the previous generation of short-word machines which it displaced.

The size of memory routinely fitted to most microcomputers is now at least 1.05 Mbytes, usually known as "1 Mbyte", and the operating systems cater for larger memories. MSDOS was originally able to access a memory of 1 Mbyte maximum size and could control up to 100 Mbytes of disc storage. Xenix could access 1 Mbyte of memory, and up to 230 Mbytes of disc.

Motorola's Versados could access 16 Mbytes and up to 192 Mbytes of disc. Versados and Xenix are multi-user multi-task operating systems, while MSDOS is a single user single task system. Later versions and newer operating systems comfortably exceed these figures.

When 16 bit systems were introduced there was nothing like the volume of software available for 16 bit machines as there was for 8 bits. Moreover the 16 bit software did not necessarily capitalize on all aspects of 16 bit potential – much of it was developed at minimum cost from 8 bits.

Many applications benefit when written for large memories and large amounts of data can reside in cheap Winchester discs; large memories mean that larger chunks of data can be brought into memory at each disc access. This enables faster processing to be carried out – for example more strings of text fetched from disc may be matched against query strings stored in memory during database searches.

When memory gets still more compact and yet cheaper, all data could reside in memory and this would result in yet faster processing.

WORD PROCESSING

The assumption in the nineteen seventies was that the nature of office work was going to be completely altered by computer-based office systems. The future for office workers was hypothesized in detail, not only in the tabloids but in the up-market technical journals as well.

Imagination was allowed to run riot even in the serious journal Telecommunications Policy. "By half past nine, Jim had handled virtually all his administrative tasks" – but not in his office. He has simply "moved out to his patio with the terminal". Being totally automated Jim accomplished some remarkable feats by 9.30 a.m., including "taking copies of his subordinates' status reports, editing them into summary form, combining pieces of related projects and adding his overview. He then takes one of his analyst's status reports, annotates it, provides further definition of the project, and returns it through the mails system".

But as an anti-climax a bland article appeared in the *Communications of the ACM* stating merely that "Automated office systems, especially text processing functions, can improve the quality of written documents".

The UK Central Computer & Telecommunications Agency came out with a report on a large scale trial about word processors. They paid up to £9000 for the machines – about £15,000 at today's prices. They concluded that "there were undoubted benefits to be derived from the selective use of WPs", but were careful not be too enthusiastic, perhaps in case they had to spend more money.

When using a word processing machine, an author specifies the format and layout of a document with a set of codes which determine margins, font, line and character spacing, and so on. The set of codes may be stored in a small file and retrieved into each new document. The layout of the new document, when printed on the author's printer, will then look like its predecessor – the coding job was only done once. Several such code sets, specifying different looking documents, may be stored and retrieved as needed.

When a document is typed, a series of ongoing codes are added to the text by the machine automatically specifying such items as indents and "tabs", new lines, etc. Both layout and text codes may be peculiar to the WP machine, so if the text is sent on disk (instead of as print on. paper, or as "camera ready" print on paper) it cannot be used by a publisher unless he has a machine which can read the codes.

The dividing line between WP and DESKTOP PUBLISHING has become blurred. Sophisticated WP software is available taking full advantage of the more powerful microcomputers with large memories now on the market.

For example Vuman specialize in WP software for multi-lingual and technical reports. Complex mathematical formulae may be produced. The latest version of Wordstar – the 2000 Plus package version 3.0 – will drive Postscript printers, provides a What You See Is What You Get (WYSIWYG) preview, will import art graphics, and handles line drawings. No less than 512K of memory is needed and the software is loaded from 21 5.25" floppy disks.

Sales of dedicated WP machines started to decline in 1985. In 1986 the UK market dropped by around 25% to about £70 million. By late 1987 the Amstrad PC selling at about £500 in the UK was being widely used for WP, among other things. World sales reached over 750,000 machines worth £375 million. By 1989 a degree of reaction had set in. "Is Bigger Better – recent upgrades raise the question: when do bells and whistles overwhelm a product and its users?" said a *Byte* article.

Word Perfect has been well reviewed and will be the representative of the genre discussed here. When Word Perfect 5.0 first came out it was awarded joint first place in a review and comparison with others and was considered "...hard to beat. Although it is rivalled in some respects by Wordstar, Total

Word, and Samna Word IV, I find it more impressive than any of these''.

When buying a WP system, demonstrations on the dealer's premises are likely to be inadequate. A good dealer should allow a buyer to acquire a system for 14 days on a sale or return basis. The microcomputer world is a highly competitive one and it is easy to be swayed by marketing hype emphasizing speed (above all), new features etc., most of which have little benefit for many applications,

''New generation'' WP systems show many advances over pre-1990 systems. For example Word Perfect 5.0, already replaced by 5.1, will run with the DOS 4.0 operating system on an IBM PS/2 model 30 machine. The processor is a 16-bit 8 MHz 8086. Memory is 640 Kbytes, with a 3.5" drive for shuttered diskettes and a 20 Mbyte hard disc. It may be compared with a previous generation WP package called Memorite running with the CP/M operating system on a Vector 4/30 8-bit Z80B 5MHz processor, with 128K memory, 5.25" floppy drive for open-slot discs and a 5 Mbyte hard disk.

The Vector/Memorite system was one of the best in its day. In the inexpensive IBM PS/2/30/Word Perfect combination, on the other hand, the computer is at the low end of the range. However the 16-bit 8 Mhz system has about 3.2 times more raw power than the old 8-bit 5 MHz system, a memory 5 times larger, and 4 times as much hard disc, but the PS/2 system complete, costs about one quarter the price of the Vectorgraphic in real terms.

The increase in speed reduces the response time and it takes a much shorter time for a page to be printed. Other functions such as disk copying and file retrieval are much faster than with the Vector/Memorite system.

A 24-pin dot-matrix printer is considerably less expensive than a laser, provides a choice of fonts, and offers a performance which is adequate for most purposes. The dot structure of the print is invisible. A PS/2 model 30/Word Perfect/24-pin dot matrix printer combination is entirely adequate for the average office. Its graphics capabilities are similar to more powerful up-range 80286 or 386 machines, although it is a good deal slower. The model 8503 MCGA 640 x 400 pixel monochrome monitor, which is included with the machine, provides an excellent display. If you want col-

our the MCGA "standard" display does not have quite as wide a range of colours as VGA, otherwise it is the same.

WORKSTATION

A computer equipped with comprehensive facilities for dealing with a specific complex task – for example Computer Aided Design. The term "Workstation" is often used inappropriately. One good definition is "a computer designed for a single user, built for network integration, and equipped with high resolution graphics and enough speed to handle demanding engineering and graphics tasks".

CAD and DTP are two common workstation applications both demanding graphics, floating point hardware, and CPU speed.

Because of the increasing facilities provided in microcomputers and a tendency in the industry to move terms originated for "high end" products downwards and apply them to "lower end" products for hyping-up purposes, there is a fuzzy boundary between micros and workstations.

Workstations came into use for electronics engineering work particularly for computer aided design and manufacturing (CAD/CAM). Over half of existing workstations are believed to be used for this kind of work. The remainder are used by scientists and, in smaller numbers, by others engaged in publishing, business etc.

Because the definition of a workstation is elastic so may be the ranking of the prime manufacturers. It is believed that IBM lead followed by Sun. The operating systems used are usually either DOS or Unix. A machine incorporating the MIT X WINDOW system is usually considered to be a form of workstation.

The Figure on the next page shows, by permission of Sun Microsystems, the SPARCstation 2 workstation with a 40MHz RISC processor and up to 64 MBytes of RAM on its motherboard with 414 Mbyte hard disc capacity on internal discs.

Another feature of workstations is the development of sophisticated plug-in boards which greatly enhance performance. For example a company called Computer system Architects provides a system containing up to 256 transputers which can be used together or partitioned for up to 16 users. Other trends to

Sun SPARCstation 2 28.5 Mips workstation

meet the demand for improved workstation graphics include a considerable increase in memory with 100 – 500 Mbytes being today's normal size, special image scanners and photo touch-up software, and between user networked applications on multiple machines.

With DTP systems using a Quadra 950, one reviewer says that FrameMaker proved to be well adapted to Mac user-interface conventions, as did. PageMaker. Data was easily exchanged between multiple text editors.

WORLD ADMINISTRATIVE RADIO CONFERENCE (WARC)

In the most recent of this periodical conference – WARC 92 – frequency allocations in the 1-3 Gigahertz waveband were revised. The conference took place in February and March in Torremolinos, Spain, andwas attended by 1,400 delegates from more than 120 countries, of which roughly half came from Europe, as well as 31 regional and international organizations such as the United Nations, Intelsat, the International Red Cross and the Commission of the European Communities.

It proved impossible to reach a worldwide agreement on a number of matters and the ensuing compromise foresees two allocations one for Europe, Africa, and Asia in the 21 GHz waveband, and another for the Americas in the 17 GHz waveband.

The aim was to reserve frequencies for future public mobile systems which will take the place of the second generation systems (such as GSM) in the area of mobile radiotelephony and DECT (for digital cordless telecommunications) at the beginning of the next century. WARC 92 allocated a 230 MHz band which should be sufficient for future mobile services which will be able to use either earth or space-based techniques.

WORM

Write Once Read Many.
 See OPTICAL DISCS.

WP

Word Processing.

WUI

Western Union International.

WYSIWYG

What You See Is What You Get.

X, Y, Z

X WINDOWS

X Windows was developed at MIT and consists of the server software with device-dependent code which controls the display, the user's application program, and the inter-process communication protocol which interconnects them. Any application will run on a particular machine once a server has been implemented for it.

X Windows is a graphical interface which has been implemented on almost all machines including Unix Workstations, PCs, Mac, Omegas, and Next. An X Window program should run on one machine and converse with another user on any other machine because it embodies a clear well defined publicly available standard. Its growth has been rather slow because it does not seem to have caught on in the general marketplace.

X Windows does not include a "look and feel design" – the intention is to enable a range of applications to run with a range of designs. However "tool-kits" are available, and so is ready to use X Windows software with an already designed graphic users interface.

X Windows seems to have found its particular niche in association with the TCP/IP protocol for interprocess communication and the Unix operating system. For instance a user with a micro requiring a workstation to connect to a Unix application on a host computer network can buy X Windows server software and TCP/IP to convert his micro to an "X terminal".

This is a special feature of X windows – the server and the "client" application can be on two different network-connected machines. Such an arrangement would make particularly good sense if the client application required expensive software running on a large machine, and a number of remote users need to access it via their X terminals. However the server, protocol, and application can all be on the same machine if required.

Note also that as if there were not enough confusion in the jargon already, the usually understood meanings of the terms "server" and "client" seem to have been reversed here.

A software package called X Vision is available in the UK from Visionware which converts a micro into a network-connected X terminal and allows it to run DOS and remote client X window applications at the same time so that mixed Microsoft Windows and X windows can be displayed on the same screen.

X, Y, and Z modem

X modem is the easily implemented de facto file transfer checking standard, introduced as long ago as 1977. Its simplicity is responsible for its longevity. It, or one of its descendants, is still often incorporated in today's elaborate telecom software packages.

It is a half-duplex method of checking whether a block of data is correct – the receiving station has to wait until a block of 128 bytes has been received. A block is checked by the "checksum" method; the simplest is to add bits at the sending end so that the addition of the bits in a byte or, in this case, block, always adds up to an even or odd number, as previously agreed. The receiver checks the total and replies after each block has been sent with either an ACK, or a NAK calling for re-transmission.

X modem was improved by using a more sophisticated block-checking method with longer blocks. Y modem is a further improvement – it uses 1 Kbyte blocks and files may be sent in batches, not just singly as in X modem. Also it takes account of error-correcting modems by including the option to omit ACK and NAK altogether. In Z-modem highly effective error correction was re-introduced.

X, Y, or Z protocols must be in place at both ends of the communication channel for the method to function, except in the case of Z modem, where if the transmitter finds that Z modem is not supported but X and Y are, it automatically selects Y.

X-OFF
Transmitter Off.

X-ON
Transmitter On.

X-SERIES

The CCITT standards for data transmission over digital data networks. See separate entries.

X12

See under EDI.

X25

CCITT recommendation for the interface between asynchronous Data Terminal Equipment (DTE) and the point of entry to a packet switched network (Data Circuit Terminating equipment (DCE). Although an X25 link can handle hundreds of simultaneous connections it can also be used for a single connection from a modem or PC with a Pad interface board.

The protocol is used in packet switched networks implemented in the lower three layers of the ISO seven layer model. An X25 packet consists of a flag, header, an area for data, a frame check, and a terminating flag. The protocol, known as the Link Access Procedure Balanced Protocol (LAP-B), controls data errors, and data flow rate.

The market for data networks was one of the first to be liberalized in Europe, and there were 16 operators of managed data network services (MDNS) with European revenues of more than ECU 3 million in 1992. X25 services are still dominant, according to a recent survey from Ovum. Telephone companies have an 80% share of the X25 market which is worth ECU 2.3 billion, and which will grow to ECU 7.3 billion by 1996.

X50

A CCITT recommendation for the format of streams of 64Kbps subscriber data in a multiplexed interconnection between synchronous data networks.

X75

CCITT recommendation for call control procedures and data transfer on international circuits between packed switched data networks.

X86

Industry jargon for any processor in the Intel series ending with the digits 86.

X400

A series of CCITT recommendations for message handling protocols to be used in computer-based message systems. They are particularly applicable to electronic mail systems, and are likely to become widely used.

Electronic mail started to be used in the 1980s, but subscribers to one service could not talk to subscribers of another. It was like the early days of the telephone when unconnected telephone exchanges were dotted about each with their own subscribers.

The X400 recommendation appeared in the CCITT 1984 "Red Book" and was the first OSI standard to be ratified. It provides the great potential benefit of "universal electronic mail". X400 resides in the OSI Applications Layer – the layer at the top which is of prime interest because that is the OSI "telematics services" level – the one closest to the user. Unfortunately X400 does not include anything about how users should be addressed – a rather important requirement.

X400 1984 version adopted a rather convoluted procedure to identify name and position functions designated "User Agent", "Message Transfer Agent" and so on. The technology moved on and the CCITT didn't get the system quite right so people adapted it to their needs with the result that Blogg's E-mail X400 was different to Mogg's E-mail X400, and they could not inter-communicate.

The CCITT people put their heads together and came out with an added "major feature" in 1988 primarily dealing with PC network functions – the most popular application. It is not clear whether "1984 X400" services are completely compatible with "1988 X400" services.

A message system, like a telephone system, needs a directory of subscribers in countries where there are systems, and it needs to be accessible in those countries. Agreement was awaited on another standard – X500 – covering online directories.

Effective directory services are still awaited. For instance both MCI Mail and Compuserve in the US conform to X400, but if you are running with one you cannot look up a number on the other. Another E-Mail problem is that while E-Mail providers will carry out a conformity test before allowing you to connect to their system (e.g. BT), that test is not necessarily the same one as is run by, say,

X500

MCI Mail, so a BT EM subscriber may not be able to connect to an MCI Mail subscriber. There does not seem to be any arrangement for international single billing either.

X500

A CCITT/ISO standard for an address specification and global directory. One of the major intentions of the standard is that it should be used in conjunction with X400.

XEROX STAR

The Xerox Star computer publishing system with its Smalltalk software was first demonstrated at the Palo Alto Centre (PARC) in 1978 with pages generated on a LASER PRINTER. The concept was ahead of its time and included WYSIWYG, IKONS, laser printing, and other innovations.

It was not a commercial success but the ideas of members of the PARC team had a wide influence on later machines, particularly on the Apple Lisa machine, first introduced for around $12,000 in January 1983, which after further work was followed by the successful range of APPLE computers.

XGA

Extended Graphics Adaptor.
See MULTIMEDIA – PRESENTATIONS.

XON, XOFF.

A simple method of bit flow control, used to control incoming bits during transmission according to the capacity of a buffer store. The receiver sends either XON or XOFF back to the transmitter as necessary.

XOR

Exclusive Or

YUV COLOUR

See COLOUR – DEFINITION OF,

ZATOCODE

Calvin Mooers devised a scheme called Zatocoding in 1960 for punching holes in edge-notched selector cards.

The Zatocode design answered the question "If the dictionary of subjects to be indexed requires that a code using p holes be used, and the average number of subjects per card is q, how large must be the field of holes available for punching to limit false drops to an acceptable number?".

The maximum number of holes was limited by the acceptable physical size for a card, and by the time spent in punching.

The scheme is an exercise in data compression because "random superimposed coding" is used – several overlapping codes may be punched in a field with a limited number of holes without excessive false drops if the design is right.

See also RANDOM SUPERIMPOSED CODING.

ZIPF, GEORGE K.

"Zipf's Law" is one of several empirical distributions which include "Bradford's Law" (see under BRADFORD), Pareto's law, and others. It was described in Zipf's book *Human Behaviour and the Principle of LeastEffort* published in 1972. Zipf describes the occurrence of words in the novel *Ulysses* to illustrate his Law; rank x frequency = a constant – a law resembling Bradford's Law.

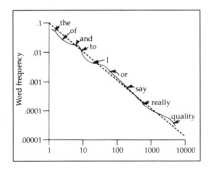

An example of Zipf's law. Shannon's word ranking

338

The tenth most frequently occurring word in Ulysses appeared 2653 times, while the 1000th most frequently occurring word appeared 26 times. The product of rank x frequency is about 26,000 in both cases. The 10,000th most frequently occurring word appeared only twice, the product again being around 20,000.

The figure shows SHANNON's ranking of words in the English language according to frequency of occurence – an example of Zipf's Law. In general, the more often a word is used the shorter and easier it is.

ZOOM

A means of providing an apparent propro-gressive enlargement of a selected area of a screen or window.

ZUSE, CONRAD

Computer pioneer who built a number of calculating machines starting in 1976. He has some claims to being the person who built the first electronic computer, in "competition" with COLOSSUS and ENIAC. He designed a general-purpose machine used at the Henschel aircraft factory during World War II.